Root & Branch

They have taken the root, but left the branches.
  Dying cry of a slave burned at the stake, Raritan,
  Somerset County, East Jersey, 1752, quoted in
  the *New-York Gazette and Weekly Post-Boy*,
  December 25, 1752

The

John Hope Franklin Series

in African American History and Culture

Waldo E. Martin Jr. & Patricia Sullivan, editors

Root & Branch

African Americans in New York & East Jersey

1613–1863

Graham Russell Hodges

The University of North Carolina Press   *Chapel Hill & London*

© 1999
The University of North Carolina Press
All rights reserved
Set in Monotype Scotch
by Tseng Information Systems
Manufactured in the United States of America
The paper in this book meets the guidelines for
permanence and durability of the Committee on
Production Guidelines for Book Longevity of
the Council on Library Resources.
Library of Congress
Cataloging-in-Publication Data
Hodges, Graham Russell, 1946–
Root and branch : African Americans in New York and
east Jersey, 1613–1863 / by Graham Russell Hodges.
  p.   cm. — (John Hope Franklin series in African
American history and culture)
Includes bibliographical references and index.
ISBN 0-8078-2492-5 (alk. paper). —
ISBN 0-8078-4778-X (pbk. : alk. paper)
1. Afro-Americans—New York Region—History.
2. Afro-Americans—New Jersey—History.   3. Afro-
Americans—History—To 1863.   4. New York
Region—Ethnic relations.   5. New Jersey—Ethnic
relations.   I. Title.   II. Series.
F128.9.N3H63   1999
974.7'100496073—dc21   98-48984
                              CIP
03 02 01 00 99   5 4 3 2 1

To my wife,

Margaret Washington,

for the years of love

and sorrow

Contents

Illustrations

Acknowledgments

Preparing a book of this size and scope took many years and placed me in debt to many people and institutions. The staff at innumerable libraries and archives graciously provided me with the manuscripts, books, and other materials that were used to complete this book. I thank the curators at the New York State Library, New-York Historical Society, Museum of the City of New York, Fales Library–New York University, Clements Library–University of Michigan at Ann Arbor, Monmouth County Historical Society, Alexander Library at Rutgers University, Bergen County Historical Society, Queensborough Public Library, Syracuse University Library, Rush Rhees Library at the University of Rochester, Public Record Office in London, Bodleian Library at Oxford University, University of Edinburgh Library, and Scottish Public Record Office for their patience with my incessant requests.

Working at a first-rate undergraduate college has many benefits, not the least of which are the wonderful students who assisted me in my research. Over the years they have included Peter Shaw, JoEllen Kelleher, Paul Townend, Scott Miltenberger, and Michael Galligan. Alan Brown, once of Colgate and now working at the University of Minnesota Press, was a constant helper in solving computer mysteries. He created the tables for this book, helped with rewrites, remained a steadfast believer in the project and became a very good friend. Colgate Faculty Development and Research funds underwrote much of the research for this book with many annual grants. Deans Charles Trout and Jane L. Pinchin provided support in many ways. In addition to those from Colgate, I received grants for research and writing from the American Council of Learned Societies, the National Endowment for the Humanities, the New Jersey Historical Commission, and the New York State Library.

My first draft of this book was almost a thousand pages long. Though I understood that cutting was imperative, I was reluctant to abandon the stories of the black people I had discovered. I am grateful therefore to the many editors who helped me publish excerpts in books and articles. They include Gregory M. Britton of Madison House Publishers, Gail Hunton of the Monmouth County Park System, Claudia

Hirsch, Rob MacKensie, Michael Galligan, and Kristi Long at Garland Publishing, and Peter Coveney at M. E. Sharpe. Other historians who used materials from that original draft include Ron Bayor, Martha Hodes, Bill Pencak, Paul Gilje, and Conrad Wright.

Over the years many other scholars have generously read this manuscript. Friends and colleagues who have read one draft or another include Mary Beth Norton, Sylvia Frey, Bill Pencak, Gary Nash, Ira Berlin, Shane White, Faye Dudden, Douglas Egerton, Alan Gallay, David Waldstreicher, Mary Lou Lustig, Dan Littlefield, Leo Herskovitz, and Amy Bushnell. I am especially grateful to Ira Berlin for allowing me to read his influential book *Many Thousands Gone* while it was in galleys. Carl Prince has remained a terrific mentor almost two decades after I completed my dissertation. Daniel Littlefield offered excellent commentary on a late draft. Doug Egerton deserves a special salute for his unstinting and insightful criticism. Others graciously offered bits of information. Henry B. Huff answered many genealogical questions. George Thompson Jr. supplied me with numerous newspaper citations for the early nineteenth century. Local historians Stephanie Stevens, Roxanne K. Carkhuff, Gail Hunton, and Arnold Brown helped me learn more about the intricacies of rural black life.

The staff at the University of North Carolina Press was highly supportive of this book. Lewis Bateman, the Press's executive editor, demonstrated great faith in it over the years. Ron Maner, Kathy Ketterman, and Kate Torrey backed the project with skill and enthusiasm. Trudie Calvert did a thorough but nonintrusive job of copyediting. I am very grateful to her for preventing many errors. Any mistakes that remain are entirely my responsibility.

My parents, the Reverend Graham R. and Elsie Hodges, helped me believe in myself and never failed to ask about the book. Thanks also to my stepdaughter, Celeste Creel, for her spirit and optimism. This volume is dedicated to my wife, Margaret Washington. A historian herself, she has been a deep intellectual companion. As she has worked on her biography of Sojourner Truth, Margaret and I have shared our knowledge of the myriad pathways of African American history in the North. Through these years as a loving partner, she and I have held many joys and, sadly, suffered many tragedies, the most painful of which is the loss of James, her son and my stepson. Through it all she remains a truly rare spirit and an inspiration to me.

Root & Branch

Introduction

According to the 1990 federal census, nearly 4 million black people, or about 13 percent of the nation's total, lived in the two mid-Atlantic states of New York and New Jersey. New York housed 2,860,590 African Americans, the highest single concentration in the United States, while another 1,035,386 lived in the Garden State. New York City was the home to 2.25 million African Americans, making it the most populous black city in America. The New York Standard Statistical Metropolitan Area, which includes surrounding counties in New York, New Jersey, and Connecticut, was the home to 3.45 million blacks, far and away the greatest concentration of African Americans in the United States.[1]

Much of the region's current black population stems from demographic trends resulting from long-term changes in the American political economy during the twentieth century. Blacks, however, have been a part of the region's society and culture from the very earliest days. During the mid-eighteenth century, for example, Kings County (Brooklyn) was over one-third black. Although the early history of African Americans in the southern colonies and states has received much attention, few historians have looked at the full sweep of black New York from the first settlements until the Civil War.

This book builds on the research and analysis of such historians as Edgar McManus, Shane White, and Roi Ottley to construct a history of blacks in New York and New Jersey over two and a half centuries from the arrival of the first African in 1613 to the Draft Riots of 1863, a method that allows me to consider important themes as they developed over time and space.[2] When one uses a broad compass over a long period of time, societies as complex as those in New York and East Jersey become more comprehensible. The geographic focus of this book includes New York City and County and nine surrounding counties: Kings, Queens, Richmond, and Westchester in New York and Bergen, Essex, Middlesex, Monmouth, and Somerset, known collectively during the colonial period as East Jersey. The city was the center of the regional society and economics while its hinterland supplied it with food, fuel, and raw materials for export. There was little separation between the rural and urban economies of the region, and political boundaries were often blurred. Within this geographic proximity, however, diversity characterized politics, economics and work, ethnicity, religion, and culture. For example, New York County and rural Monmouth included Dutch, English, Huguenot, German, Scots-Irish, Native American, and African, resulting in a multifaceted, biracial society. Numerically, blacks constituted nearly 20 percent of New York's colonial population and roughly 15 percent of East Jersey's. Later, these percentages declined, but African Americans remained a significant presence. Blacks were distributed widely throughout New York and East Jersey, living in dense concentrations in the city, in agricultural communities, and on a moving frontier. This plethora of experience requires a flexible, open-ended approach to the study of black life in the region.[3]

By using this method, I can discuss the connections between the free blacks of the seventeenth and nineteenth centuries (there were few free people of color in the eighteenth century before the American Revolution) and, in counterpoint, examine the tortured history of slavery from its beginnings to its conclusions. I have structured the book chronologically by major dates and events key to the region's black history. Accordingly, Chapter 1 covers the Dutch period of settlement from the arrival of Jan Rodrigues, a black sailor marooned on Manhattan Island by a Dutch explorer in 1613, to the conquest of New Netherland by the English in 1664. Chapter 2 incorporates the codification of slavery from 1664 until 1714, when local whites, reacting to the slave revolt two years earlier, enacted slave laws as severe as any in North America. Chapter 3 runs from 1714 until the massive, failed black conspiracy of 1741. Chapter 4 shows the effect of this stymied revolt on the prerevolutionary decades up to the British recapture of New York City and the creation of a neutral zone in rural New York and East Jersey in 1776. Chapter 5 encompasses the years of the American Revolution from 1776 to 1783 and is the linchpin of the book. Certainly, the period of negotiated gradual emancipation from 1783 to 1804, covered in Chapter 6, stemmed from the events and ideological transformations of the Revolution. Gradual emancipation took generations, and Chapter 7 discusses its effect on black society in New York and East Jersey from 1804 until 1827, the year New York abolished slavery. Chapter 8 runs from 1827 through the tumultuous antebellum days until the start of the Civil War in 1861. The epilogue accounts for the effect of the war on African Americans and the accomplishment of freedom in 1870.

Within this chronological construction, the book is organized by major topics, including the political economy and legal structure of freedom and servitude, demography, work, religion, secular culture, and resistance. A constant interplay compares the experiences of blacks in city and countryside. Examining these topics within particular time frames and paying attention to location allows me to portray the scope of the black experience in New York and East Jersey from initial settlement until the final demise of slavery and the construction of free black communities before the Civil War.

Several of these topics, including demography, the politics and economy of slavery and freedom, and work, are easy to grasp and can be explained within the contexts of time and place in each chapter. For others, brief introductory definitions are required. Freedom, for example, meant something very different for early Americans than it does today, when it is ours by birthright and guaranteed by the Constitution. Lacking such entitlements, white and black colonial Americans were subjects of a monarch and had to earn their freedom. Historians now agree that most early Americans spent at least some time as bondspeople. Freedom had to be earned by years of labor; for enslaved peoples, that could mean a lifetime of toil for another individual or family. The meaning of enslavement was contested. Africans coming to North America often had concepts of their bondage that conflicted with those of their new masters. Terms, treatment, and emancipation all were contentious terrains.

The principal means for understanding this conflict is religion. For whites, the Reformation of the sixteenth century split apart comprehension of pathways to baptism and salvation. Two types of Christians emerged in largely Protestant North America. The first were pietists who believed in a return to the original church, in Arminian or deeply personal concepts of religion. An outgrowth of the pietist denominations in New York and East Jersey was a patriarchal personality in which the head of the family decided how belief was conducted in the home, and, importantly, whether bondspeople were allowed to become Christians. Opposing this group were the paternalist creeds, in particular the state Church of England. In this denomination, and in associated sects such as the Society of Friends and, later, the Methodists, blacks could conceivably be saved in their lifetimes and members had a responsibility to God and the church to ensure Christian behavior among slaves. To do otherwise had sacred and political ramifications.[4]

For blacks in New York and East Jersey, Western religion possessed a "trickster" quality. Many blacks came to the region already converted to Catholicism, a faith unacceptable to both patriarchs and paternalists. Their enmity meant that many black Catholics had to hide their faith. For those willing or allowed to enter Protestant churches, that trickster quality was daunting. Becoming a Protestant Christian was always the best means of acculturating to local society and probably created the best chances for freedom, though that depended on the era. Blacks, however, continued to believe in the liberating properties of baptism. Defying such beliefs was the second message of Christianity: that enslaved peoples had a divine obligation to obey their masters and that submission to slavery was the only true path to salvation. Out of such conflicts came many battles between masters and slaves.[5]

Black religion changed after the American Revolution. Though dimly glimpsed during the colonial period, an African American theological leadership and congregation emerged after American independence. African American churches and ministers formed the bedrock for a nascent black nationalism in New York City and laid the seeds for communities in rural areas. They could do so only by separating from white churches, which, after a period of Revolutionary egalitarianism, succumbed to racism in the antebellum period. Ultimately, the history of black religion in and around New York is much of the story of black identity.

Not all enslaved peoples had the chance or the desire to become Christian. Although the sacred and the secular mixed within the African worldview, many activities of bondspeople in New York and East Jersey were plainly nonreligious, such as drinking, dancing, and gambling in taverns. Life in early New York and the surrounding countryside was resolutely material and sustained a slave culture. This culture included the daily, material actions and important rituals that existed outside of Christian or African belief systems. At times, the slave culture verged on the religious or used creeds for its own purposes.

Both slave religion and slave culture possessed qualities of resistance. New York and East Jersey saw day-to-day resistance ranging from theft to homicide. During major fractures of the social order, or when black grievances overflowed, conspiracy, rebellion, and, eventually, revolution broke out. Each of these characteristics had its history of time and place.

This is also the story of the melding of slavery and freedom between city and countryside. Barbara Jeanne Fields has carefully examined slavery in an urban environment. As Fields noted, however, a city cannot be abstracted from its context. The fate of slavery in a particular area depends, she argues, on its precise character and the nature of its integration into its surroundings.[6] In New York and its rural environs, slavery was sustained for almost two centuries because of the interdependence of city and hinterland. Where a black person lived made a great deal of difference in the qualities of his or her culture and experience. As this book shows, the boundaries between city and countryside were often permeable for any enslaved person. In the long run, however, slavery lasted later in rural areas because of cultural and religious reasons.

Religion, slave culture, and resistance were at the heart of the African American experience in New York and East Jersey. But their purpose was one. Faith and frolics were the flesh of black societies hemmed in by a slave system, churned by demographic trends, defined by work, and these activities energized the slaves' dynamic resistance to their plight and prepared them for freedom. That pilgrimage to liberty is ultimately the story of this book.

CHAPTER 1

Free People and Slaves

1613–1664

In June 1613, Captain Thijs Volchertz Mossel, an experienced Dutch explorer, and his crew of the vessel, the *Jonge Tobias,* journeyed from the West Indies up the coast of North America, into the harbor of the Hudson River and along the island of Montanges (Manhattan). When Mossell and his ship sailed away from Manhattan in May or June 1613, he left behind one crew member, Jan Rodrigues. Apparently their parting was caused by a dispute, although Rodrigues received wages of eighty hatchets, some knives, a musket, and a sword. While these commodities suggest that he had past experiences as a soldier, they may have been an advance on future services because it was common for sea captains to leave a man behind on new territories to sustain land claims. Mossel then returned to Amsterdam to claim monopoly rights to explore the Hudson River. A month or so later, in August 1613, a second vessel, the *Fortuyn,* captained by Hendrick Christiansen, landed on Manhattan Island. On shore he encountered Rodrigues, who informed Christiansen that he was "a free man." Rodrigues then entered Christiansen's service as an interpreter with local Rockaway Indians and facilitated a trade agreement between the Indians and Christiansen. In April, the *Jonge Tobias* returned. Angry with Rodrigues's disloyalty, Captain Mossel called him a "black rascal." A fight ensued in which Mossel's crew wounded Rodrigues, but Christiansen's crew was able to save him from further harm. After the two vessels departed, Rodrigues remained behind and fathered several children with Rockaway Indian women.[1]

Africans had traversed the Atlantic basin for centuries. Doubtless there were some among the fishermen, pirates, and anonymous explorers who visited the area before Rodrigues. The best known was Esteban Gomez, a black Portuguese pilot, who sailed up the Hudson River (and called it Deer River) in 1525. Gomez then departed with thirty-seven Indian slaves. Rodrigues was the first nonindigenous resident of Manhattan Island. As well the earliest known African American on the island, he is significant to this history for several reasons. First, his origins epitomize those of the cosmopolitan black seamen working in the Atlantic basin during the seventeenth century. Rodrigues's mixture of West Indian and African heritages was common in the man known as the Atlantic Creole. As Ira Berlin has emphasized about such people, Rodrigues's survival skills were impressive. He negotiated with avaricious ship captains and proved critically important for commercial relations with the local Indians by quickly learning local Native American languages and marrying into the Rockaway Indian tribe. Alone among these early explorers, he is known to have acculturated into both European and Native American life. Second, he declared himself a free man, though his employer regarded him as no more than a servant, a conflict that signaled the first of many such cultural collisions. Rodrigues was a prime example of the multiple talents displayed by the first generation of African immigrants to New Netherland.[2]

Building Freedom in New Netherland

Rodrigues was the sole nonindigenous resident on Manhattan Island for many years. Until 1621, any European settlement there remained an abstraction as competing investors vied for monopoly development rights in Amsterdam. That year the Dutch West India Company secured a contract to construct a settlement on the Hudson River. For the first few years, only fur traders, whalers, fishermen, and pirates visited the shoreline of New Netherland. In 1624, supported by the Dutch West India Company, which secured the patent on colonization, a group of Walloon pietist families arrived to undertake the task of colony-building.[3] The Walloons set up small farms just beyond the compound of Fort New Amsterdam, where they raised livestock and cultivated maize and wheat. Beyond these early facts of settlement, the Walloons are significant because they refused to learn Dutch or attend Reformed services, and they formed a separatist, pietist society that lived and worshiped under the shadow of the Dutch. By not assimilating into the larger culture, the Walloons established a pattern followed by other white and, eventually, black congregants.[4]

Company soldiers and officials arrived in 1625. The following year

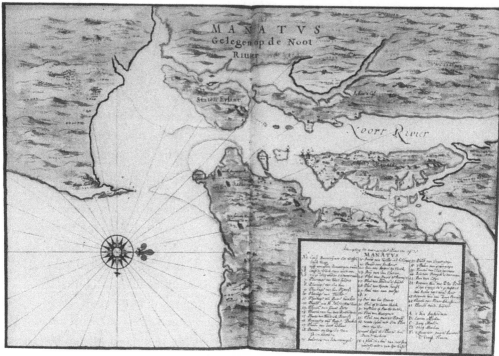

Manatus map of New Amsterdam. Drawn in 1639, this map was used as an advertisement to prospective settlers by showing the amount of land available on Manhattan Island. Shown on the map in the area around present-day Sixtieth Street and the East River is a site for the "company negroes," probably a work area. (Library of Congress)

pirates sold sixteen blacks who were captured from Spanish vessels to the West India Company in New Netherland. Two years later several black women arrived. These early African arrivals have attracted much scrutiny.[5] Initially enslaved, these first migrants were later emancipated and created a free black community in New Amsterdam. By the 1640s, however, they were joined by other Creole blacks and Africans brought to the tiny port to become lifetime slaves. How that initial generation gave way to a slave society is the terrible history of the period of Dutch control, which lasted until 1664. The second, and no less important, saga is how free and enslaved Africans in New Amsterdam laid the seedbeds for an African American culture in the region.[6]

The disparate origins of the first generation of blacks in New Amsterdam are evident in their personal names, which combined African, Portuguese, and Dutch influences. Among the first group of blacks, who arrived in New Amsterdam in 1626, were men with African names:

Paul D'Angola, Simon Congo; Portuguese names: Anthony Portuguese, John Francisco, Big Manuel, Little Manuel, Anthony Portuguis Gracia, Peter Santomee, Jan Francisco, Little Anthony; and American names: Jan de Fort Orange. Mayken was the only woman among these first arrivals whose name survives. Spanish and Dutch naming practices provided slaves with a saint's first name while the second name identified ethnic and place origins. The use of two names did not automatically signal acculturation into European society, as Angolans regularly took patronymics at home. Moreover, several of the names proclaimed their bearers as Africans. Others, such as Jan Rodrigues, were members of the Atlantic community.[7]

By 1630, the tiny colony held roughly three hundred European residents, most of whom were Walloon, and the small assemblage of blacks. Twenty male and thirty female Africans, also captured from the Spanish, worked on a plantation at Pavonia, across the Hudson River. They were the first black residents of New Jersey. Other slaves belonged to settlers at the South (Delaware) River colony. Very little is known about the identity of the enslaved Africans in these short-lived colonies. (Wappinger Indians destroyed Pavonia in 1643.) It is likely, however, that the bulk of enslaved Africans at either station were Creoles captured by pirates from Spanish ships. Though it paid higher wages than in Europe, the Dutch West India Company attracted families from Holland to the colony by giving favorable land grants and by promising in 1630 to garner black laborers for "Patroons, Colonists and other farmers."[8]

From the earliest years, blacks were core laborers in the struggling colony. At first, they worked for the company. Overseer Jacob Stoffelson described their tasks as cutting timber and building "the Large House as well as the Guardhouse, splitting palisades, clearing land, burning lime," and harvesting grain. There are later references to their labors in resodding the exterior of the fort, constructing a wagon road, and rebuilding the fences to protect against the English. Paulus Heymans, a white man, supervised the company blacks from 1647 until his resignation in 1654. The Dutch West India Company built a house and a hospital for its slaves which lasted at least until the late 1650s. Their importance is attested in a request by Governor Peter Stuyvesant for additional slaves in 1660: "They ought to be stout and strong fellows, fit for immediate employment on this fortress and other works; also, if required, in war against the wild barbarians, either to pursue them when retreating, or else to carry some of the soldiers' baggage." Later, the governor indicated that a new shipment of slaves was necessary "to procure provisions and all sorts of timber work, fix ox carts, and a new rosmill."[9]

Their legal status in the colony was unclear. They were not free; no laborer in the colony was. Very few Africans came to the colony voluntarily; most sweated as slaves for the company. At the same time, Holland did not recognize slavery at home, and chattel bondage had not yet emerged in the laws of any North American territory. Nor did race determine whether a person was free or in bondage. The Dutch West India Company kept both its white and black servants in bondage. The majority of white servants were engaged for as long as seven years, during which time they were little better off than the Angolan slaves.[10] Further, the Africans came from societies in which slavery was a fluid institution. In African legal systems enslaved people were revenue-producing property. Africans accepted that their labor might be captured in a war or could be used as demonstration of loyalty to a ruler. At the same time, slaves in Africa could hold a variety of statuses. In Angola, in particular, slaves were torn from their own kin groups, who lacked land, and made dependents of landowners and corporate authorities. Although under Angolan traditions, slaves performed the most burdensome tasks, they could look forward to better conditions and were not always distinguishable from servants, who were nominally free. African slave captives could usually expect manumission themselves or freedom for their offspring. Carrying these attitudes into the New World, they probably regarded themselves as at least equal to "lower servants."[11]

That ambivalence was revealed in one of the first labor appeals in the New World. Five blacks traveled in 1635 from New Amsterdam to Holland to seek a settlement on their salaries of eight guilders per month, wages comparable to those of white laborers. They were apparently successful because in 1639 the company paid blacks for building the fort.[12] Another indication that the first arrivals were hardly docile was the frequency of their appearances in local courts.[13] Few New Amsterdamers were as litigious as Anthony Jansen van Vaes, one of a handful of local blacks in New Amsterdam who arrived as a free person. Anthony Jansen van Vaes, "a mollato noted for his size and strength," lived in New Amsterdam with his Dutch wife and was the first nonindigenous resident of Gravesend on Long Island. After several public controversies involving the couple, the company banned the Jansens from Manhattan but granted them two hundred acres near

Portrait of New Amsterdam, 1643. This generic image represented several Atlantic ports in the early seventeenth century but was particularly appropriate for the emerging slave society in New Amsterdam. (Print Collection, Miriam and Ira D. Wallach Division of Art, Prints, and Photographs, New York Public Library, Astor, Lenox and Tilden Foundations)

Coney Island. Despite his official exile, Jansen later returned to Manhattan, acquired property, and worked as an independent merchant.[14] A second free black also demonstrated the fluidity of race relations and statuses in the fledgling colony. Jan de Fries, baptized on August 25, 1647, was the son of a Dutch sea captain, Johan de Fries, and a black woman named Swartinne. After his father's death, de Vries inherited his property, held in trust for him by Paul D'Angola and Clara Criole, two former slaves of the captain. Despite the loss of some of his property to his father's creditors, Jan de Fries became a landowner on the outskirts of New York City. He was a member of the Dutch Reformed Church, in which he was married to Ariantje Dircks of Albany and in which they baptized their four children between 1682 and 1689. Later de Fries became an original patentee of Tappan, New Jersey, where his descendants lived for many generations. Although Governor Willem Kieft decreed in 1638 that Dutch settlers must refrain from "Adulterous intercourse with Heathens [and] Blacks," the presence of de Fries and Jansen in New Amsterdam indicates that intermarriage occurred in the tiny colony.[15]

The company demonstrated through legal actions that it considered the Angolans' status to be lower than that of white laborers. When Gysbert Cornelissen Beyerlandt was convicted of public disturbance and wounding a soldier in the fort, he was sentenced to "work with the Negroes" until he could be transported to the colony on the South River to serve the company there. Later Nicholas Albertsen was punished for deserting his ship and betrothed bride by having his head shaved. He was then flogged and sentenced "to work two years with the Negroes."[16]

Their ambivalent status did not deter this first generation of African Americans from creating a community based on personal freedom, landownership, religion, and local institutions. New Amsterdam was a smaller version of the African and West Indian ports from which they had originated. In Luanda, Elmina, and Curaçao, they had grown up around local markets and seafarers' taverns where they had encountered Europeans working for slaving companies as sailors, artisans, and laborers. The presence of familiar cultural sites and people made community formation easier for the Africans. If landownership was rare in Africa, they quickly adapted to it in the New World.[17]

By 1639, black neighborhoods appeared on contemporary maps. One of several slave work sites known as Quartier van de Swarten de Comp Slaves existed on the East River opposite Hog Island (later Roosevelt). A free black community had already been established on the land north of the Fresh Water Pond.[18] Beginning in 1644, the Dutch West India Company emancipated its laborers, but with the condition that their children would be enslaved. Historians have viewed this action as a desire by the company to be free of responsibility for aging slaves.[19] Evidence indicates that blacks traded their labor, augmented by military service, for freedom. In the Kieft War of 1640, company slaves "armed with small ax and half-pike," fought against the Indians.[20] On February 25, 1644, Manuel de Gerrit and ten other Negroes with their wives gained freedom on condition that each of the men pay the government yearly thirty skepels (twenty-two and a half bushels) of maize, wheat, peas, or beans and one fat hog valued at thirty guilders and that their children "already in existence or hereafter born, shall be slaves." Through this important clause, which colonists in New Amsterdam at first protested, Dutch officials ruled that slavery would descend through the mother, a practice that became standard in America. In the next few years, the company recognized the "long and faithful service" of blacks by manumitting them, usually with a form of quitrent attached to the grant, making customary the belief that former slaves owed obligations to their old masters.[21]

Company slaves were not the only ones to attain freedom. Other enslaved blacks were freed by their masters. Paul D'Angola and Clara Criole were privately emancipated by their master, the black sea captain Jan De Fries. Nor were all the emancipated blacks male. Three black females petitioned the company for their freedom in 1663; on April 19, 1663, Mayken received her liberty, "she having served as a slave since the year 1628."[22] Ascento Angola, Christopher Santone, Peter Petersen Criole, Anthony Criole, Lewis Guinea, Jan Guinea, Solomon Petersen, and Basije Petersen successfully petitioned the court for full freedom, indicating that half-freedom was unacceptable to them.[23] These examples and the lengthy terms of service for all emancipated blacks were indications that any freedom would be hard earned and only after many years of service. Theirs were the first gradual emancipations.

Landownership glued the black community together. The Dutch West India Company recognized African land claims on the Bowery Road near the Fresh Water Pond by 1643. The first known landowner was Domingo Antony, who received his land on Manhattan Island, "towards the land of Tomas Sandersen," near the Bowery Road. Shortly after, Anthony Portuguese, Manuel Trumpeter, and Big Manuel acquired land nearby. One surviving deed demonstrates that these former slaves were given freehold rights similar to those of Dutch residents. Governor Willem Kieft granted Simon Congo land "by the west of the land of Jan Celes between this land and a thicket, having on the east side Peter Santome." The deed acknowledged Congo's complete "power, authority & order over the forewritten parcel of land to build on, to live on, in the use of, as he does with all others of his patrimonie lands and effects." In 1646, the government agreed to clear the land and "make it fit for the plow." Land rights were hereditary. The widow of Andries D'Angola, for example, held land situated between that of Peter Tamboer and Fonteyn Briel. She was one of twelve black women to own property during the Dutch era.[24]

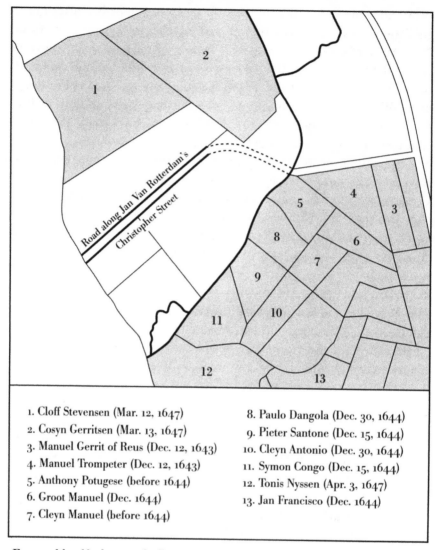

1. Cloff Stevensen (Mar. 12, 1647)
2. Cosyn Gerritsen (Mar. 13, 1647)
3. Manuel Gerrit of Reus (Dec. 12, 1643)
4. Manuel Trompeter (Dec. 12, 1643)
5. Anthony Potugese (before 1644)
6. Groot Manuel (Dec. 1644)
7. Cleyn Manuel (before 1644)

8. Paulo Dangola (Dec. 30, 1644)
9. Pieter Santone (Dec. 15, 1644)
10. Cleyn Antonio (Dec. 30, 1644)
11. Symon Congo (Dec. 15, 1644)
12. Tonis Nyssen (Apr. 3, 1647)
13. Jan Francisco (Dec. 1644)

Farms of free blacks near the Bowery in the 1640s. (Based on information from the Museum of the City of New York)

The black community grew in the late 1650s, and the farms of free blacks dotted the Bowery from present-day Prince Street to Astor Place. On the future corner of Bowery and Houston was the farm of Christoffel Samsone; just beyond his were those of Manuel de Ros, then Pieter Tamboer, Fransico Cartagena, Assento, Claes de Neger, Groote Manuel, and ten others. By the time all Angolan land claims were recognized in the early English period, at least thirty blacks had become independent landowners on Manhattan Island.[25]

A weekly market located near the crossroads of the roads to Fort Orange and New England was the centerpiece of this community. The market featured weekly sales of "Beef, Pork, Butter, Cheese, turnips, carrots, cabbage and other country produce" and annual fairs for cattle and hogs "on the beach by or near the house of Mr. Hans Kierstede," adjacent to the "Negro Lands."[26] Such local markets combined Dutch and African traditions. They were public spaces created as much by culture as by convenience or rational economics. Strangers and citizens — Indians, blacks, and Dutch — traded, sold, drank, gambled, and competed in games of skill.[27] In New Netherland, markets allowed commercial and symbolic exchange for African men and women. To Africans, the market, like the crossroads, was the home of the trickster god, where human experiences took on uncountable possibilities. Markets were meeting grounds where kinsmen, friends, and lovers could trade, drink, and dance. In such places cultures melded as people winked at social restraints.[28]

It is noteworthy that the first blacks in New Amsterdam came from urban African cultures with active market economies. The Angolan capital, Luanda, was a cosmopolitan city with numerous markets. Andrew Battel, an English sailor captured by the Portuguese near Brazil in 1590, then transported to Angola, spent much of the next twenty years there. In the capital he described "a great market which met at noon each day. The market featured palm-cloths, victuals including flesh, hens, fish, wine, oil, corn, and copper and ivory." In Luanda, Dutch and Angolans learned to trade at the markets, first in commodities and later in human chattel.[29]

Other institutions anchored the black community in New Amsterdam. In the late 1650s, the provincial council established a hospital near the Bowery to serve sick soldiers and Negroes in the employ of the Dutch West India Company. A cornerstone of the black community was the "negro burying ground," established in the late 1630s at the corner of Broadway and Chambers Street. Lasting until the late 1780s, the burial ground provided the black population of the city with a sacred center.[30]

Hardly sacred but no less important were taverns, in which blacks and whites could revel with little supervision and which dotted the streets of the grubby little city. In these bars, lonely men could demonstrate their honor, dignity, and strength to each other, forgetting for a moment the alienation of the isolated port where they lived. In a case that illustrates the rough-and-tumble ambience of these groggeries, on

January 24, 1641, the court of assizes convicted eight blacks of killing Jan Premero, another black, in a tavern brawl. The prisoners pled guilty, were condemned, then drew lots to determine "who shall suffer death." The sentence fell upon Manuel Gerrit, the Giant, who was to be hanged until dead "as an example to all malefactors." As Manuel was standing on the gallows and the hangman turned off the ladder, "The above, negro, having two strong halters around his neck, both of which broke, whereupon all the bystanders called out, Mercy, which was accordingly granted."[31] The incident is remarkable in several ways. First, it was a sign of the disorderly conduct present at local taverns, behavior that would prompt strict (if ineffective) laws a few years later. Second, the desperate need for labor ensured that but one of the prisoners would pay for the group's crime. Third, the use of magical proof showed how premodern judicial methods determined guilt. The Angolans were familiar with the use of lots to determine guilt. The traditional Kongo-Angolan method for determining guilt was to force the prisoner to ingest a beverage known as the "Bonde Drink." His status was determined by his ability to drink and then urinate the strong herbal juice. This method differed from the Dutch procedure, but both ethnic groups relied on supernatural forces to reveal a person's guilt or innocence. Agreement on judicial procedure existed, then, "below the level of consciousness," as a common assumption about divine intervention in a trial. Use of supernatural proofs would recur in future generations of Africans and Dutch.[32]

In a pattern echoed over succeeding generations, Africans had to look beyond their home cultures to build families. Of 306 adult blacks imported into New Amsterdam between 1626 and 1664, 174 were male and 132 were female. This imbalance (reversed after 1700) indicates how the slave trade and the local economy hampered finding partners of the same race. While sex ratios perhaps improved by the 1660s, when the children of the first black residents achieved maturity, it is doubtful that enough children were born to ensure reproduction of black society in New Amsterdam. At least twenty-six marriages between blacks were performed in the Dutch Reformed Church between 1641 and 1664. Only one couple was identified as slaves; the rest presumably were free.[33]

Between 1639 and 1655, blacks brought twenty-nine male and twenty female children for baptism in the church.[34] Africans, much like the many other ethnic groups in a diverse society, used selective adaptation of language, religious rituals, family formation, and landownership because they were necessary for survival and mobility. Dutch became the lingua franca as blacks embraced those customs that would benefit them the most. This conscious choice did not obliterate their origins; a telling fact is that all the witnesses to the baptisms of black children were other Africans.[35] In the uncertain social environment of New Amsterdam, Africans retained the cultural traditions of their past. Marriage certificates and deeds indicate the patterns of African extended families. In 1661, Emanuel Petersen and Dorothy Angola, both free Negroes, successfully "prayed for a certificate of freedom for a lad named Anthony Angola," whom they adopted as an infant and then raised and educated. Similarly, Domingo Angola applied in 1663 for the freedom of Christina, a baptized daughter of the deceased Manuel Trumpeter and Antonya, his wife. The Dutch authorities replied that Christina could go free provided either a replacement was found or three hundred guilders paid. Their appeal met a friendly response from the prosperous miller Govert Loockermans, who paid the three hundred guilders to free Christina.[36]

Dutch magnanimity toward the Angolans had its limits. The Dutch magistrates clearly would not tolerate sexual difference. As in Puritan New England, homosexuality was mercilessly punished. In one case, the Dutch magistrates displayed a judicial ferocity toward black defendants that would become common in the future. The second conviction of Jan Creoli, a Negro, for sodomy on June 25, 1646, showed the harsh methods of justice used in the colony. Using the elaborate and fierce punishments enacted by the States of Holland, the court ordered the prisoner to be "conveyed to the place of public execution and there choked to death and burnt to ashes." The Dutch abused corpses to drive home their implacable justice. Manuel Congo, a ten-year-old lad "on whom the abominable crime was committed," was "tied to a stake, and faggots piled around him, for justice sake . . . to be flogged." Although very severe, the sentences were in accordance with Kongo-Angolan beliefs, where, as with the Dutch, law intersected with cosmology.[37]

In short, this first generation of Africans in New Netherland made the best of their exile to this remote colonial outpost. They worked through any chattel obligation to the Dutch West India Company and used the Reformed Church for rituals of great personal and group value. They became landowners and created a small but vibrant community within Dutch culture. Their group identity best resembled the confraternities or brotherhoods found among Kongolese and Angolan

blacks living in Brazil. They largely governed themselves as an association, a method the company judged a useful means of self-control.
Though their activities were not as visible as those of later black associations in New York, members did take on serious issues such as child
rearing, punishment, and, though they were a small, elite minority,
provided a supportive model for newly arrived, enslaved Africans.[38]

The Religious Construction of Slavery

Enslavement of Africans became the future mode of race relations
in New Netherland and, later, under English rule. Previous scholars
have used economic interpretations to describe this passage in North
America. Following the lead of Edmund Morgan, historians contend
that shortages of laborers, desire for a docile labor force, and promotion of the international slave trade by imperial governments were
the engines of developing slave societies. Certainly they were in New
Netherland. The Dutch West India Company required inexpensive
laborers to meet its own needs. Beginning in 1629 and repeatedly over
the next thirty years, the company also made promises to import
and sell slaves to allure prospective farmers from Holland. Eventually,
traffic in humans became its own justification as the company sought
profits in New Amsterdam and local merchants and farmers sought
human chattel to work on their property.[39]

Less understood is how slavery required torturous interpretations
of Christianity, new understandings that would permanently alienate master and slave. David Brion Davis and Winthrop Jordan have
revealed the theological roots of slavery, but they have emphasized
political and ideological developments.[40] In the colonial period, religion
was the deepest currency among individuals and between individuals
and the state. In New Amsterdam, the influence of the Dutch Reformed Church was critical and complex. The conflict began with legal
difficulties when the colony was founded. The Dutch West India Company lacked the legal power to legislate slavery and thus introduced
chattel bondage without formal directives from the States-General in
Holland. Just a few years before settlement, however, a major doctrinal synod offered theological justification for enslavement in the colonies. In 1618, at the Council of Dordrecht (Dort in English) in Holland,
European Protestants gathered to hammer out a theology that would
greatly affect the future of Dutch settlement and the texture of race
relations in North America. This was the last general meeting of Reformed churches and included representatives from the Netherlands,

England, Scotland, the German states, and Geneva. The Canons of Dort affirmed predestinarianism, limited atonement, the irresistibility of grace, and the perseverance of the saints. An underlying agenda was to stem the rising power of Arminians, or defenders of the doctrine of free will. Religious conservatives worried that free choice gave individuals the power to determine their own salvation, rendering obsolete the church polity so carefully constructed by John Calvin. The orthodox faction, headed by Professor Franciscus Gomarus, and thus known as Gomarians, quickly routed the Arminians and reestablished a hierarchical theological order. The Gomarians condemned the Arminians as heretics and barred ministers and theologians who refused to accept the new orthodoxy.[41]

Decisions made at the Council of Dort strongly affected New Netherland. Politically, the new orthodoxy was important because the Gomarians favored the emerging plans for the West India Company and a settlement in America.[42] The Council of Dort's orthodoxy confirmed a hierarchical election, predestined by God. Sinners, among whom followers of African beliefs were decidedly the lowest, could be saved only by accepting the will of God—as interpreted by the elect—and by the mystery of the faith.[43]

A key, but unsettled, question was the conversion of heathens. Like their counterparts in Puritan New England, the Dutch Reformed in New Amsterdam doubted that pagans could be saved in this lifetime but had to content themselves that "by the same grace of God, they know and feele, that in their hearts they beleeve and loue their Saviour." In short, Africans could never be truly Christian, but they could approach grace. All agreed that the path to emancipation lay in conversion to the Reformed Church. Manumission was a meritorious act in the eyes of God. Slaves or servants were encouraged to work out terms to purchase themselves from their masters. The church insisted that masters be responsible for slave baptism.[44] True Christians had to offer slaves access to Christian faith. Because the Council of Dort and the Dutch West India Company were so intertwined, such declarations amounted to government policy, which mixed a paternalist ideology of servitude composed of power, wealth with a desire to convert, and a belief in hierarchy.[45]

Unceasing controversy arose over the legitimacy of baptism for slaves. The Council of Dort's deliberations on pagan baptism troubled relations between masters, clerics, and enslaved blacks for the next two centuries. The synod debated the fundamental question of whether slaves should be baptized, incorporated into the master's family, and then freed. Baptism was a first step toward salvation, but true grace was impossible until after death. In a signal measure that gave immense power to slave masters, the synod gave Reformed laity the power to choose whether household servants would be baptized. The Reformed head of household, not the church or the parents of the child, who could also be unconverted adults, had the primary responsibility for baptizing slaves and heathens. That declaration gave colonial slaveholders in the New World patriarchal power over children, servants, and slaves. Considered in Dutch society to be the bedrock and saving grace of its culture, the patriarchal family was the crucible through which rude matter and beastliness could be redeemed. The fate of African Americans' souls, indeed of their mortal bodies, was thereby placed in the hands of the family patriarch, who regarded unrelated servants as legally dependent on him. The edict effectively created the personality of a pietistic, domineering slave master who fiercely regarded governance of slaves as family business, traits also present in the matriarch, who often had great power over the family's slaves.[46] As a result, each owner was left to make his or her own determination, meaning that Arminianism had, in fact, crept into the crucial issue of conversion. Eventually, this would cause sharp disagreements between government officials and clerics seeking to proselytize blacks and settlers hoping to secure valuable slave labor without threat of losing their investment.

Further confusion arose when a Swiss theologian, Giovanni Deodatus, argued that "those baptized should enjoy right of liberty with all other Christians" and should not be sold. Slaves arriving in the United Provinces were automatically emancipated. In contrast, in the New World, while there was no timetable for the proper age of baptism, or for freeing a Christianized slave, or for determining how that precept should be enforced, enslaved blacks could easily understand the equation between baptism and liberty. In a religious environment in which baptism was analogous to legal enfranchisement, the stakes were immensely high for both masters and slaves.[47]

The Dutch West India Company was unsure about the legality of enslaving Christians permanently, however, and wanted all residents of the colony to accept Christ. Ostensibly, the Reformed Church was the sole permissible denomination in the colony. In the original terms of settlement in 1624, the Dutch West India Company announced that the Reformed Church should be the official theology of the colony, though that dictum soon proved impossible to enforce. After the arrival of the Walloons, other European pietist denominations, including Lutherans, Swedish Reformed, Puritans, and others, settled in the colony. Many of them came from rural provinces of Holland or from other countries where popular attitudes maintained that Christianized slaves should be freed. The Angolans had probably converted to Roman Catholicism before their arrival in New Amsterdam. The Reformed faith did have a monopoly in one area: only the religious edifices of its church were allowed in New Netherland until the 1650s. Some dissidents quietly joined the Reformed congregation. To keep the peace and allow some observance of other creeds, the Reformed Church used a concept of the "hidden church" to allow other denominations to borrow time in the sanctuary. Because religion was the clearest avenue to freedom and civil equality, the first blacks in New Netherland sought membership in the state church.[48]

Because the Synod of Dort permitted local ministers the right to refuse baptism and allowed clerics to own slaves and deny them Christian fellowship, slavery gained a de facto legality in New Amsterdam, thereby opening clerics to pressure from their parishioners to do little about the fate of Africans. The historical assessment of clerical attitudes about slavery has accentuated their racism and dependence on the Dutch West India Company and the inability of ministers to perceive any incompatibility between their beliefs and slavery.[49]

One answer came from a lengthy treatise, *'t Geestelijk roer van't coopmans schip* (The spiritual rudder of the merchants' ship), published in 1638 by the Reformed minister Godefridus Cornelisz Udemans. An early Dutch pietist who attended the Synod of Dort, Udemans emphasized in his work the importance of scriptural meditation, humility, and repentance as steps in the development of Christian life. Immensely popular in the New World, his book was a famous companion for lonely seamen throughout the seventeenth century. It also commented specifically on the purchase and enslavement of Christians. Addressing his thoughts to both India companies, Udemans argued that Christians could be sold as slaves only if they were captured in a just war or purchased for a correct price from their parents or other competent masters, "as is related that this ordinarily occurs in Angola," a principal source for Dutch slaves. Udemans was an early proponent of the "fortunate fall," arguing that slavery benefited Africans by exposing them to Protestant Christianity and keeping them from "popish mischief."[50]

Udemans's interpretation of the enslavement of Christians caused a split between the Dutch West India Company and its American colonists. The company, seeking to reconcile the Synod of Dort's mandates on pagan baptism with the allure of the slave trade, saw no contradiction in the purchase and sale of Christians. In contrast, pietist settlers, while eager to obtain slaves, remained anxious about converting their chattel and possibly losing them. For example, in a remonstrance against Peter Stuyvesant delivered to the company in 1649, settlers argued that "if they (the slaves) want to submit themselves to the lovely yoke of our Lord Jesus Christ, Christian love requires that they be discharged from the yoke of human slavery."[51] Dutch families arriving in New Amsterdam surely recognized that this conflict worked against their self-interest. In the future, settlers would solve this problem simply by refusing to let their slaves anywhere near a church pulpit.

Initially, Dutch Reformed Church efforts to convert Africans in New Amsterdam depended heavily on the dominie, or minister, who was an employee of the Dutch West India Company. The first Dutch cleric, Dominie Jonas Michaelius, had helped create a Dutch Reformed presence in West Africa before coming to New Netherland, but he showed little interest in black souls in his new post, where he derided Angolan women as "lazy, useless thieving trash."[52] After his departure, relations between the Dutch Reformed Church and local Angolans improved. In 1638, Dominie Everardus Bogardus of New Amsterdam wrote asking church authorities in Holland to send a schoolmaster "to teach and train the youth of both Dutch and blacks in the knowledge of Jesus Christ." In 1641 the elders and deacons of the New Netherland church reported to the Classis in Amsterdam that the "Negroes, living among the colonists, come nearer thereto, and give better hope," of conversion.[53]

Given the social consequences of the Synod of Dort, it was unlikely that Reformed ministers would agree to baptize black children without some assurance that their freedom was in the offing. As the company imported more blacks as lifetime slaves and sold them to private owners, Reformed clerics became leery about performing a rite that had powerful social and legal consequences. Also, although clerical reports suggest that blacks were eager to be baptized, the requirements included a solid understanding of the basic beliefs of the Reformed Church and patience with the solemn, unemotional sermons. The orthodoxy issued from the Synod of Dort ensured a strict hierarchical order in which blacks were far down the ranks. Blacks owned by patriarchal masters had the tough task of convincing the family head of the necessity of catechism and church membership. Together, these reasons were early signs that Christian denominations would make only partial headway in converting African Americans.

Public anxiety over the black equation of baptism and freedom curbed the willingness of Dutch Reformed members to catechize their slaves. Dutch ministers shared that fear. For example, Dominie Henricus Selijns, who ministered to Governor Peter Stuyvesant's bouweries (farms), was very reluctant to baptize the governor's forty slaves. Church officials back home in Amsterdam instructed Selijns that slaves be carefully catechized and allowed to confess but not baptized until the parents abandoned heathenism for Christianity. Selijns responded that "the Negroes occasionally request that we should baptize their children, but we have refused to do so, partly on account of their lack of knowledge and of faith, and partly because of the worldly and perverse aims on the part of the said Negroes. They wanted nothing else than to deliver their children from bodily slavery, without striving for piety and Christian virtues. Nevertheless, when it was seemly to do so we have to the best of our ability taken much trouble in private and public catechizing. This has borne but little fruit among the elder people who have no faculty of comprehension, but there is some hope for the youth who have improved reasonably well." In future years, baptism of blacks occurred sporadically in rural areas in Flatbush and Gravesend in Brooklyn and Hackensack in Bergen County.[54]

By denying blacks the sacrament of baptism, the Dutch removed an important ideological barrier to servitude. The effect of these theological rationalizations on blacks were twofold. Baptism remained an elusive talisman of freedom for blacks who seized upon divisions in the white community over baptism as hopeful evidence that its liberating beauties could be restored. The new policies also focused attention on the masters' convictions. Calvinist pietism was highly individualistic. Every master or mistress was to decide whether to catechize the family's slaves. In turn, every slave had to determine whether his or her master had ushered the way to Christian baptism or stood intransigent in the doorway.

As the Dutch curbed baptism of blacks to avoid the threat of emancipation, Africans became unrecorded spectators in the Reformed churches. The Reformed Church discouraged lay preaching and approached theological disputes in a distinctly paternalist manner, di-

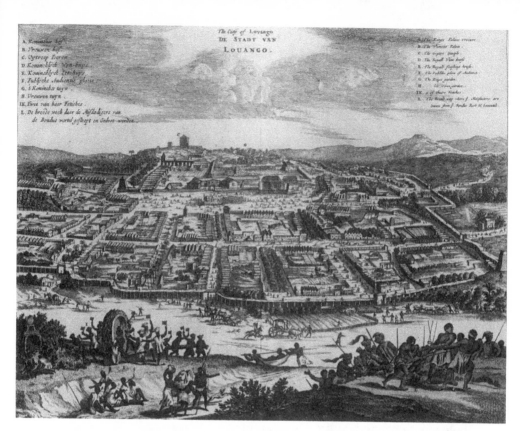

City of Loango (Luanda), 1670. Luanda was the port of origin for many Creole and saltwater slaves in the mid-seventeenth century and one of the principal slave depots on the West African coast. (From John Ogilby, Africa, *1671. Photograph courtesy of the Division of Rare and Manuscript Collections, Cornell University Library.)*

minishing any black contributions.[55] Blacks' participation in religious affairs became limited to annual public rituals. The liturgical year in New Netherland was richly celebratory and preserved traditional pietism in the church. In particular, the Dutch observed Pinkster, their version of Pentecost, as a sanctified revival of the early Christian church. Pinkster was already known to Africans. Even before arriving in New Netherland, Africans were exposed to Roman Catholic instruction from missionaries. Kongolese royalty became Catholic during the sixteenth century after conversion by Jesuits and Capuchin clergy, and so slaves exported from Luanda in the seventeenth century had been exposed to Christianity. Catholic missionaries in the Kongo regarded all aspects of the culture of the target country that were not directly contrary to the fundamental doctrine of the church as immaterial and left them unchanged. Thus blacks in New Amsterdam coming from Angola had a syncretic rather than an assimilated understanding of Christianity.[56] This alchemy is visible in the anxieties European divines expressed over African use of the holiday. The Capuchin monk Denis De Carli baptized several Angolans on Pentecost Sunday, then watched with apprehension as "They fell a playing upon several instruments, a Dancing and a Shouting So Loud that they might be heard half a league off." [57]

Pinkster was celebrated in New Amsterdam as early as 1628.[58] In the New World, Pinkster celebrants met on Sunday and Pentecost Monday and kept Tuesday as a holiday, creating a long weekend holiday for slaves. Pinkster was a time of interracial celebration when African and Dutch music and dance intertwined and wine and ale flowed freely. Sundays were also free times for slaves. New Amsterdam was not as determined as New England to keep the Sabbath holy. Although the Dutch did attempt to cease all work, amusements, and drinking during worship, the city magistrates refused to publish Stuyvesant's decree that the entire twenty-four hours of the Sabbath be holy, declaring it to be too severe and contrary to the rights of the homeland.[59]

Opening New Amsterdam to the Slave Trade

Economics and local politics in the struggling colony pushed the Reformed Church to add further religious qualifications to the edicts from Dort about the fate of Africans. In 1640, the company repeated its earlier promise to provide patroons and colonists with as many blacks as possible. Both company and colonists seemed to agree on the desirability of buying slaves. As labor needs pressed heavily on the colony, Governor Peter Stuyvesant strove to make New Amsterdam the principal slave port of North America, again forcing the Dutch to face the contradictions of morality and economics. The paucity of free blacks in the colony and the difficulty in attracting single immigrants from home required the Dutch West India Company to find more coercive measures to increase the number of laborers. By now, the company recognized the value of enslaved labor. In 1644, Governor Willem Kieft observed that "Negroes would accomplish more work for their masters and at less expense, than [Dutch] farm servants, who must be bribed to go thither by a great deal of money and promises." Apparently local residents agreed. The next year, the colonists repeated their wish for a greater supply of enslaved blacks. As younger families with small children settled in the colony, they became ready customers for newly imported slaves.[60]

Reassured by Udemans's teachings and pushed by colonial needs for labor, the company increased its participation in the Atlantic slave trade. Over thirty years, the Dutch slave trade moved from random acquisition of blacks, often freemen, stolen by pirates from Spanish and Portuguese ships, to purchase of slaves from the West Indies and Brazil and direct importation from Angola and the Guinea Coast. The Dutch had entered the slave trade in Africa in the late sixteenth century, borrowing methods of the Portuguese in Lower West Africa. From 1504 through 1650, European slave traders in Africa bargained with local leaders and depended on native interpreters.[61] Within that trade system, the West India Company and its black employees in New Amsterdam interacted in ways that afforded both acculturation and ethnic identity.

Kongo-Angolan resistance to Portuguese domination continued throughout the period, but desire for European goods ensured a vigorous slave trade that exported an average of ten thousand blacks from Angola annually. By 1600 the slave trade was easily the most important marketing activity of Luanda. African wars produced the bulk of these slaves. Luanda slave merchants operated a chain of towns across Kongo, east to the Malebo Pool, and south to Matamba and Angola. Because neither the Portuguese nor their Dutch successors were allowed into the interior, they obtained slaves through tribute from subject leaders who gathered them by direct warfare, recovery of runaway slaves, or punishment of tax delinquents. By far the most important method was direct trade with ethnic chiefs. The coastal-bound Portuguese and Dutch slavers were highly dependent on local traders.[62]

Although New Netherland farmers continually demanded more slaves, the Dutch West India Company initially made only intermittent deliveries. The chief beneficiary was Governor Peter Stuyvesant, who employed forty slaves at the company farm north of the city. Stuyvesant, who earlier as a fledgling bureaucrat in Curaçao had argued for expansion of the slave trade to North America, oversaw the enlargement of human traffic from occasional to official as the company became the largest employer of a burgeoning slave force in New Netherland. At times, it leased slaves to private owners, a practice condemned by local residents, or sold slaves to English colonists in Virginia.[63]

Despite their misgivings, the acute labor shortage in New Amsterdam prompted private citizens to seek, often illicitly, the acquisition of slaves to labor in agriculture or for domestic use. A sign of the legitimacy of servitude in the young colony was local trafficking in slaves.[64] At the same time, settlers grew more accustomed to purchase of slaves from the international trade. The Dutch capture of Fort Elmina on the Guinea Coast in 1637 enabled them to acquire much of the Spanish slave trade in the New World.[65]

The allure of the slave trade also deepened the split between the monopoly of the Dutch West India Company and local traders. Governor Willem Kieft had attempted to shore up commercial regulations and sustain the company as a strong central government in the early 1640s, but his departure opened the door to smaller merchants to prosper by commerce in humans. As the colony approached a degree of economic maturity, company desires for monopoly control met furious opposition from an emerging elite. Arising from humble circumstances and prospering through intermarriage, these merchants sold slaves along with other commodities in the coastal trade of North America. Traveling to the West Indies and the Chesapeake, these traders earned sudden wealth by combining the slave trade with other forms of local commerce. Their successes created a new middle class in the colony with strong roots in the slave trade.[66]

Larger traders profited by access to the West African trade. The process of acquisition of slaves on the Guinea Coast resembled that in Angola. Elmina, the principal slave factory on the West Coast, was built by the Portuguese in 1442 and was surrounded by a town inhabited by company slaves and free blacks. The castle serviced a fairly large area with distinct yet related nationalities. Slaves came to New Amsterdam from up and down the West Coast of Africa from points as distant as Kongo and the Malaguetta Coast. The Ardra, Popo, and Whydah "nations" were important sources of slaves who possessed skills valuable in the frontier colony of New Netherland. Slaves cleared land and mined gold and worked as farm laborers, porters, craftsmen, herdsmen, brewers, guards or soldiers, traders, household servants, and attendants. A second enslaved group included debtors, apprentice household servants, boatmen, and fishermen.[67]

With the arrival of slaves from the Guinea Coast, the West India Company initiated sales to private citizens. That decision prompted an unexpected controversy that had international complications. In 1652 pirates arrived in New Amsterdam with forty-four slaves they had captured from Juan Gallardo Ferrera, a Spanish merchant. The

Dutch West India Company kept most of the adults and sold the rest to settlers, though the transactions violated long-recognized international agreements against kidnapping of freemen for use as slaves.[68] Gallardo traveled to New Amsterdam after relations between Spain and Holland improved to press his case for restitution and to reclaim his property. Greeted in New Amsterdam by his former slaves, who bore his initials branded on their skins, Gallardo identified thirty-seven blacks belonging to other Spanish citizens and himself.[69] Stuyvesant and the company owned ten slaves, which doubtless accounts for the governor's recalcitrance with Gallardo, but others now toiled for such individuals as "Jacob the Miller," who owned five, or were "in the possession of the Potter's son or daughter."[70] Rebuffed by Stuyvesant, who claimed that the slaves were legally purchased from a Captain Guert Tysen, who brought them to New Amsterdam as a war prize, Gallardo, after two years of frustration, took his case back home. The issue quickly escalated into an international controversy. In 1655, the ambassador of Spain complained to the States-General in Holland about kidnapping of blacks owned by Spanish citizens, a problem repeated again and again.[71] This incident is also significant because it reveals the presence of Spanish blacks in the colony. Many of the Spanish slaves kidnapped and sold in New Amsterdam in the 1640s and 1650s were Catholic. There was room for them to practice their faith surreptitiously in New Amsterdam. Unable to accept Reformed doctrines, they were able to celebrate their beliefs though the Dutch concept of the "hidden church" that allowed toleration of banned religions without official recognition.[72]

These intermittent arrivals left Dutch colonists unsatisfied. By 1654, local merchants convinced the Dutch West India Company to grant permission for slave trading with the Caribbean and Virginia, with a 10 percent duty on slaves resold to the Chesapeake. Dutch control of the slave trade in the French and English West Indian colonies and a near monopoly on trade with Barbados softened the loss of Brazil to the Portuguese in 1654. The Dutch acquisition of Curaçao in the West Indies gave them an important entrepôt for its slave cargoes. Not a plantation colony, Curaçao served primarily as a depot for the thriving slave trade. Nominally under the governance of Peter Stuyvesant, ruler of the New Netherland colony, Curaçao became a center of slave trading in the New World.[73]

During the 1650s, despite the assurances of the directors of the

West India Company that slaves would be supplied regularly to New Amsterdam for use there or for exportation to the "English and other neighbors," Stuyvesant was frequently reduced to begging his vice-governor, Mathias Beck, to direct slave ships to New Amsterdam. Stuyvesant believed that with the loss of Brazil, company officials in Amsterdam might view New Netherland as a new entrepôt for slave trading and thus bring enormous profits to New Amsterdam and at the same time satisfy local colonists' demands for slaves.[74]

After the Dutch West India Company permitted city merchants to trade in slaves as chattel, the number of enslaved Africans arriving in the city jumped sharply. Direct trade with Africa began on September 15, 1655, with the arrival in New Amsterdam of three hundred enslaved blacks. The ship master auctioned them off and netted above 1,200 florins for each slave. The following year three more vessels arrived after a stop in Curaçao. By agreement, two-thirds of each slave cargo came to New Amsterdam. Stuyvesant and local merchants sold many slaves to Virginia and Maryland, two English colonies that converted to unfree labor.[75]

Despite Stuyvesant's difficulties with his vice-governor, New Amsterdam was by 1660 the most important slave port with the largest population of slaves in North America.[76] Regularly scheduled shipments authorized by the company supplied the colony with cargoes of slaves from the Guinea Coast, primarily from Elmina. Between 1660 and 1664, New Netherland received at least four hundred slaves, primarily adult males, from Curaçao. The slave ships were charnel houses, where deaths of the captives averaged almost three a day. One vessel in 1659 lost 111 blacks during the voyage from Africa to the New World.[77]

Almost three hundred more slaves arrived in 1664 almost simultaneously with the English fleet sent to conquer New Amsterdam. The half-starved Negroes required, in Stuyvesant's estimation, over a hundred bushels of wheat weekly. Stuyvesant referred to the arrival as at "an unseasonable moment to our great embarrassment." They were, he lamented, old and rejected slaves from the West Indies.[78] Despite his anxieties, slave owners quickly bought them. The victorious English quickly did an audit to learn how the slaves had been dispersed. They learned that the 290 slaves were designated "to be employed solely in agriculture, which is the only means by which the State can be rendered flourishing . . . the slaves must be sold to our inhabitants on express condition that they will not be taken out of our district, but

Slave Trading in New Amsterdam. *A late nineteenth-century depiction of slave trading in the 1650s after Peter Stuyvesant succeeded in establishing New Amsterdam as the leading entrepôt for slaves in North America.* (Harper's Monthly Magazine, *1895)*

kept specially there and employed in husbandry." This new plan was a harbinger of the important role enslaved blacks would play in the agricultural economy of rural New York and East Jersey.[79]

Of the 290 slaves, 40 went to Peter Stuyvesant's bouwerie, and slave trader John de Decker took another 40 to sell in Albany. Many others probably went to Virginia, but records show that 19 adult males, 10 adult females, and 1 child were sold to prominent local Dutch burghers and Englishmen. These chattel labored in their houses as domestics. Anecdotal evidence suggests early signs of the tensions between masters and domestic servants. Writing to his brother Jan Baptist Van Rensselaer in 1659, Jeremias Van Rensselaer argued against sending his slave Andreis to Holland, noting that "it would be foolish to try to have him serve you in a free country, as he would be too proud to do that, I have noticed that in his manner." Van Rensselaer worried, "It is bad enough here to get him to do anything for anybody if I have not ordered him to do it . . . that sort of Negro is too treacherous." He urged his brother to buy a seasoned slave who "has always lived here with the Dutch people."[80] Other slaves worked adjacent to the free black community. Nicholas de Mayer, Govert Loockermans, and Jacob Leisler obtained slaves to use in mills at the Fresh Water Pond adjacent to the "negro land." Some slaves labored on large plantations outside of the city, such as Captain John Lawrence's plantation at Hempstead, Nicholas Verleith's farm in Bergen County, and Captain Thomas Willet's land in Queens County.[81]

At the close of Dutch rule, slavery was entrenched in the colonial urban economy. A tax list for New Amsterdam in 1664 indicated that nearly one out of eight citizens in the colony owned slaves. Of the thirty slaveholders (out of 254 taxpayers), half were in the wealthiest cohorts of the population, but slaves were also owned by tavern keepers, mariners, a butcher, and a turner. The slaveholders were English, French, and German as well as Dutch.[82]

By 1664, the African population was 800, or 10 percent of the population of the colony, and 375 in New Amsterdam, or approximately 25 percent of New Netherland's population of 1,500. This quarter of the colony's population was suffused throughout the society. Did the English then capture a slave society? By current definitions, New Netherland was not a slave society because slavery was an important part of the political economy but not the sole form of labor. In New Netherland and in the future New York, however, existed a slave society made up of Dutch farmers and their bondspeople, who would remain entangled for the next century and a half. The New York–East Jersey region differs from classical slave societies in the Chesapeake, Caribbean, and low-country Carolina in the ethnic diversity of slave owners. In other words, the English conquered a slave-owning culture within a larger society.[83]

Conclusions

The effect of Dutch rule on the establishment and future of slavery and African American culture in the region was profound. In the half-century before English conquest of the colony abruptly ended Dutch control in 1664, African and European peoples selectively adapted to each other's laws and mores and established cultural relationships that lasted far longer than the few decades of Dutch rule. Studying the mutual existence of free and enslaved Africans in New Amsterdam provides answers to key questions about black life in the region. For example, historians have often referred to the creation of slavery in New Netherland and New York as an "unthinking decision." A closer look shows that religious reasons shaped the conscious enslavement of Africans. Scholars have also described the rapid transformation of Africans into black Dutchmen, but the black experience was part of a diverse engagement among many peoples, which a Catholic priest famously called "Too Great a Mixture of Nations." Not only did blacks hold several ranks in the colony, but they also came from a wide range of places and interacted with Germans, Belgians, Swiss, Scandinavians, and English settlers as well as Dutch. One means for this interaction was religion. Africans encountered the official church, the Dutch Reformed, and Lutherans, Huguenots, Puritan, Swedish Reformed, and other pietist denominations. The mixture of peoples precluded consensus in the colony, ensuring that Dutch West India Company edicts often met with hostility from settlers and militated against agreement on a key issue like slavery.

Economic and demographic reasons also prompted the shift to slavery in the struggling colony. Single young Dutch men could be induced to migrate to the settlement, but after arrival in New Amsterdam, they quickly headed for the frontier to rent land or left for a more attractive colonial enterprise. Hoping that white laborers would quickly seek their own land if labor was available, as they had in Virginia, the company acquired more slaves.[84]

New Amsterdam was, like the Chesapeake, a society in which enslaved and free Africans lived and worked. As Ira Berlin has argued, members of the first generation of Creole blacks were sophisticated bargainers for freedom. Their talents, he contends, enabled them to earn freedom and even a limited prosperity in a relatively fluid racial atmosphere.[85] Slavery existed in New Amsterdam virtually from the onset, in small numbers at Pavonia, and, gradually, in larger numbers among private citizens. What changed were not the skills of Creoles at arbitrating freedom but the economic needs and aspirations of the Dutch West India Company and its ambitious colonists. Acceptance of slavery as an institution among the Dutch and the "mixture of nations" in New Amsterdam were facilitated by theological compromises among Puritan denominations in Europe. The lessons taught by the first generation of Africans in the region did not die after they earned their freedom. Rather, the Creoles represented an early example of how Africans quickly learned to seek freedom from fissures in European-American theology, law, politics, and diplomacy. One skill that would reappear constantly was the African ability to play the imperial government, in this case the Dutch West India Company, against the colonists.

But the direction of the young colony, as it changed ownership, was toward a slave society. As the labor needs of white merchants, artisans, and farmers grew, the Dutch West India Company, aided by pirates, imported slaves into the colony. Governor Peter Stuyvesant envisioned New Amsterdam as the supply depot for the slave owners of North America, an ambition hampered only by the voracious needs of West Indian and South American colonies. The decision of the Dutch Reformed Church to cease slave baptisms and curtail emancipation was a significant foundation for the codification of slavery in New Netherland. Local interpretations by Dutch and other Calvinist slave masters of the teachings of the Council of Dort deeply affected the texture of their relations with enslaved Africans.[86] The English capture of New Amsterdam in 1664 transformed the governance of the colony but scarcely altered its society. Dutch-speaking New Yorkers remained prominent throughout the region for the next century and a half. Less visible were the tiny number of free blacks who continued as a small but significant free population in New York City, Long Island, and East Jersey.[87]

CHAPTER 2

The Closing Vise of Slavery

1664–1714

A Free Black Society

In October 1679, Jasper Danckaerts, a Labadist traveler, observed about the Bowery in New York: "Upon both sides of this way were many habitations of negroes, mollattos and whites. These negroes were formerly the proper slaves of the (West India) company but in consequence of the frequent changes and conquests of the country, they have obtained their freedom, and settled themselves down where they thought proper and thus on this road, where they have ground enough to live on with their families." At least twenty-four blacks lived in this neighborhood. This second generation of Angolan farmers and their children worked small plots of land and sold vegetables at the nearby market. This area just north of the city retained its earlier title as the "negro land," stretching from the Bowery Road and the "cripple bush," or swamp, to Minetta Creek and the Hudson River and to the Stuyvesant farm, with its forty slaves.[1]

The new English government protected this small coterie of free blacks. The Articles of Capitulation, signed on August 27, 1664, specified that the new English government would respect current property and status relations in New Amsterdam and in Bergen County in East Jersey. On October 19, 1667, the new governor of New York, Richard Nicolls, also confirmed the manumissions and freeholds made in 1659 and 1660 to "divers negroes" along the Bowery Road.[2]

Freedom did not mean prosperity. Only one free black left a will, attesting a limited lifetime accumulation. Emancipated in 1664, Solomon Peters (Peiterszen) and his wife, Maria Anthony, lived for nearly thirty years on his Bowery farm. Their four children were baptized in the

Dutch Reformed Church. His will, proved in 1694, left all his land, home, and household goods to his wife. To his four sons he left his iron tools, implements of husbandry, guns, swords, pistols, and cash.[3]

Pressed by rising property taxes, the remnants of New Amsterdam's free black society gradually moved outside the city. Free blacks settled in Kings County (Brooklyn). Negroes Francisco and Anton joined Anthony the Turk as part of the first twenty-three settlers of Boswyck (Bushwyck) in 1660. "Bettie, a free negresse," was among the first settlers of New Utrecht. Abraham Jansen, James Van Luane, and "Black Hans" were other free black residents of the town of Brooklyn. Jan de Negro and Annetke Abrahams were members of the Dutch Reformed Church in Brooklyn in which they were married in the 1660s.[4]

Free blacks also spread into newly settled hinterlands of New Jersey. Three of the original shareholders in Tappan, New Jersey, were John De Vries Sr. and Jr. and Nicholas Manuels, free black farmers from Manhattan. Antony Van Salee's son Frans, the son-in-law of John De Vries, also moved from Brooklyn to Tappan. Samuel Francisco and the sons of Solomon Peters moved to the western portion of Bergen County.[5] Youngham Antonious Roberts, a freeborn black, purchased two hundred acres of land and became one of the first residents of Hackensack, New Jersey. Later, distressed at poor relations with Dutch farmers, he moved into the Mattawan Mountains. Another free black, Jochem Antony, was a member of the Bergen Dutch Reformed Church in 1679. The Van Doncks, a free black family, established a farm near Saddle River during this period.[6] In all, more than seventy-five free blacks lived in and around New York City in the late seventeenth century.

Free blacks reinforced their society through marriage in the late seventeenth century.[7] Francisco Bastienz wed Barbara Emanuels and Marrije Anthony married Salomon Pietese in the Dutch Reformed Church in 1686. Manuel Sanders, widower of Mary Sanders, married Maria Angola, widow of Christoffel Santomme, all free blacks. Blacks also purchased land from each other. A free black woman, Susannah Antony Roberts, purchased property from Anthony Portuguese.[8]

Masters and mistresses seldom emancipated their slaves, and the infrequency of manumissions doomed any substantial growth of the free black class. The first emancipation, granted by Anna Medford, a New York widow, freed her slave Frans in 1669 and gave him a small bit of land. Seven years later, Swaentie Janse, a Kings County widow, freed three slaves and promised "the boy Domingo" his freedom after fifteen years of service to her daughter. Such gradual freedom became the rule. For example, Mary Loockermans instructed that her slave Francis should be emancipated after the death of her daughter Elsie Leisler. Christiana Cappoens of New York City freed one slave immediately and made another wait until the death of her daughter for his liberty. In 1683 Lewis and Mary Morris consigned a slave named Maude to their daughter for eighteen years, after which Maude would receive several suits of clothing and her freedom. In 1702 Maude secured her emancipation. Between 1669 and 1712, a time when manumissions were private affairs, only eighteen deeds were granted, of which only four were given between 1701 and 1712, showing a hardening of slave owners' attitudes.[9]

Restricting Black Freedom

Under English governance, the civil liberties of Africans in the region narrowed sharply. Nicolls had made it clear that he recognized the value of slaves by ordering that Dutch farmers pay for recently arrived slaves immediately. These actions transferred governance of slavery from the Dutch West India Company, an administrative body, to the English Foreign Office.[10] Nicolls, who respected religious bias against enslaving white Christians, used New England laws to limit the terms for white indentured servants. That action clarified the issue for white servants, but the Duke of York's Laws confused the Africans' civil status. "No Christian," Governor Nicolls announced, borrowing from the Council of Dort and the writings of Udemans, "shall be kept in Bond-Slavery except such who shall be judged thereto by authority, or such as willingly have sold or shall sell themselves." He instructed that all instances of servitude be entered in the court of sessions for each district.[11]

Although Nicolls's instructions validated slave ownership, New York and East Jersey did not have fully developed slave laws until the first decade of the eighteenth century, nearly fifty years after the English takeover. Several factors influenced the colony's gradual transition into a slave society. The first was the English recognition of Dutch titles to African slaves after the conquest of 1664. Second was the influx of wealthy Barbadian planters and slave owners in the 1660s. Having already experienced significant slave rebellion in the West Indies, they arrived in New York and East Jersey prepared to respond to slave restiveness with the implacable repression they had honed in the Caribbean.[12]

A third development was the Crown government's attempt to base slave identity on race. On December 8, 1679, Governor Edmund Andros ruled that enslaving local American Indians was illegal but holding blacks in bondage was permissible. Such evidence led Winthrop Jordan to conclude that skin color was the factor determining freedom or bondage. Yet in New York and New Jersey, race was an issue complicated by ethnicity and religion. Despite the governor's edict, local masters continued to enslave Indians. Andros's edict also failed to solve the vexing diplomatic problem of kidnapped free Spanish Indians, a dilemma with international implications. Privateers' sales of Spanish Indians as slaves in New York contradicted English colonial policy. Diplomatic efforts by European nations to avoid enslavement of each other's citizens were rarely respected in the colonies. The legal dilemma of Spanish nationals resurfaced in 1687 when the New York Colonial Council ordered that "Christian Indians and children of Christian Parents brought from Campeche and Laverde Cruise (Vera Cruz)" be liberated. The next year the council ordered that Spanish Indian slaves professing Christianity be set free, provided they "were able to say the Lord's Prayer." The significance of this decision was long term. Slaves found that they could seek release from slavery by petitioning royal officials and by demonstrating knowledge of Christian theology. Nonetheless, sales of Indian slaves continued in New York and New Jersey during the 1680s. On the international level, this practice irritated the Crown's diplomatic relationships with Spain. Locally, it meant that slave traders ignored injunctions against enslaving Christians.[13]

Conflicts between English laws and colonial practice surfaced in judicial cases that demonstrated how eager whites were to ensnare blacks into servitude. To combat this tendency, free people appealed to the imperial government to protect their positions. A dispute between William Corwan, "an alleged free mullato," and Thomas Thatcher, who claimed Corwan as a slave, showed that laws still protected free blacks. Corwan bound himself as an indentured servant on February 12, 1677. A few months later problems developed between master and servant. A seaman from Jamaica, Robert Little, testified that Corwan was a freeman of Martinique and not a slave. Governor Anthony Brockholles ordered Thatcher to prove Corwan a slave in eight days and post a £1,000 security, or Corwan would be "declared free."[14] Despite this protection, the inexorable shift toward enslavement meant that the region was no longer a haven for free Africans.

Another divisive issue between Crown and colony was abuse of slaves. The Crown instructed Governor Thomas Dongan in 1686 to pass a law for "restraining of inhuman severities which by all masters or overseers may bee used toward their Christian servants, wherein provision is to bee made that ye willful killing of Indians and Negroes may be punished by death." Local authorities invoked the law only in the most horrific cases.[15] While such laws seemed to qualify the legal status of slavery, the personal actions of slaveholders began to take on a routine character. Although the Crown tried to protect enslaved people, masters began to sell, bequeath, or even give away slaves as wedding presents.[16]

The English Slave Trade

Although Crown officials issued contradictory edicts regarding slavery, the colonial population made the issue moot by grabbing any available chattel. The movement of the European population across the region created a demand for slaves. New York's principal merchants learned that much profit could be made by trading grain and flour for humans. The late seventeenth-century slave trade built on earlier patterns. Barbadians had for years been principal customers of Dutch slave traders, who brought the vast majority of the nearly ninety thousand slaves imported into Barbados before 1670.[17] When seasoned slaves from the Gold Coast, Bight of Benin, and Angola came to New York and East Jersey with their masters from Barbados, they met kinsmen already in the region. Those imported from the Kongo region mingled with their country people who had lived in New York for several generations. They came, however, from a region riven by civil wars and now surging with the angry, antislavery, restorationist crusade known as the Antonian movement, led by the charismatic Doña Beatriz Kimpa Vita. For the next several decades, any slave brought from the Kongo seemed to possess divine inspiration for resistance to bondage.[18]

Because the Royal African Company, formed as a monopoly in 1664 to supply slaves to English colonies, largely ignored New York and New Jersey, colonists obtained most slaves from local adventurers plying the Madagascar Coast, in single consignments from the West Indies, and directly from Africa.[19] Officially inhibited by the Royal African Company's monopoly over the West Coast of Africa, New Yorkers learned that government officials were less concerned with controlling the slave trade than with suppressing foreign imports and com-

Castle of El Mina, 1670. Located in present-day Ghana, this fort was the departure point from Africa for millions of enslaved blacks from the fifteenth century until the closing of the Atlantic slave trade. (From John Ogilby, Africa, *1671. Photograph courtesy of the Division of Rare and Manuscript Collections, Cornell University Library.)*

merce with Amsterdam. Accordingly, New Yorkers acquired slaves either from Madagascar or directly from the West Coast. In 1698, the *Prophet Daniel* was captured by pirates along the coast of Africa and its fifty slaves, intended for New York City, were eventually sold in Barbados. Stockholders who took the loss blamed the captain for detouring from his original route directly to New York. Enterprising merchants were hardly deterred by such setbacks. Around the same time, Frederick Philipse hired pirates Samuel Burgess and the famous William Kidd to bring slaves to New York or the Chesapeake. Philipse also used these new imports as laborers on his manor. Slaves from Madagascar were not acceptable to all New Yorkers. One slave trader claimed in 1698 that "the great quantity of slaves are come from Madagascar [which] makes slaves to sell very slow." [20]

The arrival of slaves from Madagascar had two unintended effects on African American society in New York. First, the pirated blacks were Catholic converts. At first slaves converting from Catholicism were freed, but later, in the 1650s, emancipations largely ceased. By the 1680s, the introduction of Madagascar people brought to New York Catholic slaves who would never attain liberty and who regarded their masters as violators of Christian rights. Catholic slaves were present among the first generation of Angolans in New Amsterdam, but they were eventually freed and at least nominally joined the Reformed Church. Now enslaved, Catholic blacks faced lifetimes of bondage with no religious assimilation. The second consequence was the effect of a highly diverse ethnic group. The Malagasy settled their island in several migratory movements from a variety of origins including Malay, Maori, Indians, Arabs, Persians, Jews, Phoenicians, Chinese, and Japanese. Representatives of this human potpourri were among the first of each background to appear in New York. Passers in the streets now encountered Africans whose looks also reflected Arab or Asian antecedents.[21]

At the same time, West Coast blacks arrived in New York and East Jersey. The slave trade gave a more African air to black society in and around New York. In addition to free blacks with creolized names, the records contain African names. The census of 1698 for rural counties around New York lists such names as Cuffe, Mingo, Sambo, Shantee, and Abashee. Some of Lewis Morris's slaves in Monmouth County, New Jersey, had African names.[22]

Growth and Settlement

Following the English conquest, New York City increased slowly to about forty-five hundred souls in 1690. A majority of the English immigrants occupied the top rungs of society, while Dutch merchants quickly accommodated the new rulers by adopting English ways. The middle and lower classes remained Dutch, with an admixture of Huguenots after 1690. New York was a small port town serving a limited regional population. Artisans and laborers depended on direct contact with customers in a city crammed into the tip of Manhattan Island. Stem families were the principal social units, melded into a wider network by church, occupation, and ethnicity. In an environment in which relations were often face-to-face, everyone knew who was free and enslaved.[23]

Between 1664 and 1698, the year of the first provincial census, the black population of New York City nearly doubled, from approximately 375 to 700 people. New Yorkers had become highly dependent on slave labor; nearly half of all Dutch male adults in the city owned slaves, with an average of 2.1 slaves per holding. Slightly less than 40 percent of English males, 13 percent of French, and 2 percent of Jewish males owned slaves. In all, 41 percent of all households in New York City held at least one slave. By 1703, black women outnumbered men by 397 to 233, setting a pattern that continued for over a century.[24]

A distinct pattern of urban slaveholding emerged by 1703. A total of 804 slaves lived in the city's six wards in 1703, but slaveholding was concentrated in the wealthiest wards. Of 212 households in the east ward, 96 owned slaves; of 118 households in the south ward, 62 held bondsmen and women; in the dock ward, the figures were 80 out of 124 and in the rural out ward, 25 of 51. In contrast, the artisan-dominated north and west wards contained 62 slave masters in 311 households. Across the city, 290 adult males and 279 females lived near each other. In 49 households, black adult males and females resided with children, while in 31 others, adult females lived with children. By 1703, even though their proportion of the population grew only slightly and their economic position worsened, the Dutch still constituted more than half of the slaveholders. Next in size were the English, followed by Huguenots and Jews.[25]

Only in 1700 did the royal government have any fixed idea of the number of slaves imported into New York. Between 1700 and 1703, the year of the first fully usable census, New Yorkers imported 217 slaves, all from the West Indies. Overall, between 1700 and 1715, New Yorkers imported 209 slaves from Africa and 278 from the West Indies.[26]

An internal slave trade also developed in this period. Masters swapped slaves for products or sold them outright. The Lloyd family of Lloyd's Neck in Queens County regularly sold slaves. Other masters found customers in other colonies. Jacob Leisler, for example, sold slaves to purchasers in Maryland.[27] Hiring of slaves was a development related to the slave trade. Although artisans frequently did not own slaves, they hired them as unfree wage laborers. New York City's economy focused on local and international trade, with artisans filling specific needs. Enslaved blacks worked as assistants to artisans and semiskilled tradesmen, as domestics, at shipyards, and on construction projects. If demand in one area slackened, slave masters could profitably hire out slaves. One New Yorker, Olfert Siortse, organized and leased groups of hired slaves. During the summer of 1697, Siortse leased from two to six slaves to merchant John Abeel to work on con-

Meal Market, 1711. This market was the site where enslaved blacks were auctioned to new owners or hired out for a period of time. (From Bruce, The Empire State in Three Centuries, *1:244.)*

struction projects. Slaves were sent over by the half-day, day, or week. Skilled blacks were identified by name and paid more. The municipal government was also a frequent hirer of slaves. There are many entries in the chamberlain's account book listing payment to blacks for their "hyre." For example, the city of New York paid "Mr. Papin 11s 6p for Negroes work" on May 17, 1691, and paid "Captain Saisler, 9s for Negroes Work." Between September 17 and 30, 1699, for example, the city paid over forty pounds for "negro hyre." The daily rate for black laborers was two shillings, six pence, slightly less than the three shillings paid to white laborers.[28]

In 1711, the municipal government established the Meal Market on the east side as a daily fair for hiring blacks. The institution of a hiring fair at the Meal Market indicates that masters routinized the practice and perhaps imported slaves for the purpose of speculating in the hiring market. However profitable for white slave masters, the practice of hiring created greater autonomy for black laborers. Enslaved blacks reached agreements with their masters which allowed hiring and could occasionally lead to purchase of freedom. For blacks, hiring ensured that they entered the cash economy with spending money for clothing, liquor, and entertainment.[29]

This widespread employment of slaves threatened to undermine the status of free white workers, who, in turn, were determined to confine blacks to unskilled labor. Whites segregated many tasks and kept blacks from rising to independent status. Citing English and Dutch traditions of labor monopoly, New York City carters and porters successfully petitioned the Common Council to bar slaves and free blacks from driving carts in the city. The council declared that "noe Negroe or other slave doe drive any Carte within the Citty under penalty of twenty shillings, to be payd by the Owner of the Slave Brewers Drays or Carriages for Beer, Only Excepted." Requests for waivers of the law proved futile. In 1684 Elsie Leisler petitioned the mayor's court on behalf of her husband, Jacob, the future revolutionary. Mrs. Leisler owned a mill and found it difficult to hire cartmen to "carry Wheat and other Corne." Because she owned a slave, "who is a Christian, being Baptized and Instructed in the Christian religion," she prayed that she be allowed to use her slave to drive her own horse and cart. The court ruled that the Leislers could cart their own goods, "but the cart must be driven by a white man." [30]

Nothing, of course, stopped white carters from owning or hiring blacks and using them on their jobs, while paying them approximately a third of a white's daily wages (a practice used during the construction of Trinity Church in the 1690s). A second indication of early segregation of work was in apprenticeship programs. In this primary means of vocational training, only one black was apprenticed to a master to learn his craft. These practices separated white artisans and licensed laborers from slaves by what David Roediger has called the wages of whiteness. [31]

Rural Life and Work

In the countryside, slaves rapidly became a core source of farm labor. Settled by Europeans in the last decades of the seventeenth century, farm communities in counties around New York and across the Hudson River in East Jersey employed enslaved black males extensively. From just a few scattered slaves at the time of the English conquest, the number of bondspeople soared to 576 in Kings, Queens, and Richmond Counties in 1698. In East Jersey the black population was around 120 in 1680, a figure that would rise to nearly 1,900 within fifty years. [32]

A major type of rural community was the manor. The English rulers awarded government-allotted enclaves to wealthy colonists to counterbalance the patroonships granted by the Dutch. Manors granted under English rule included the Fordham Manor in 1671, the Livingston

Manor in 1686, the Pelham Manor in 1687, Philipsbourough Manor in 1693, Van Cortlandt Manor and Morrisania in 1697, and Scarsdale in 1701. Although the English briefly promoted a resolution offering free grants of over one hundred acres to arriving families, most of these manors were occupied either by the owner or tenants. Lords of the manors commonly employed large groups of slaves on "gentlemen's farms." Barbadian immigrants were the largest contributors of slaves in the New York region in the late seventeenth century. Often close friends or relatives of council members, they received large grants, above two thousand acres, in the Monmouth region. Attracted by such favorable land terms, settlers from Barbados arrived in New Jersey and New York to establish plantations. For men like Lewis Morris and Colonel Thomas Berry, New Jersey was healthier, its coast more accessible to England than South Carolina, which was too hot and too close to the Spanish in East Florida. New Jersey proprietors offered the same generous terms that were used to entice settlers to South Carolina, promising 150 acres for each head of family, 150 for each manservant, and 75 for each female servant. An additional inducement ensured that indentured servants received 75 acres of land while slaves received none. Intended to lure New Englanders to East Jersey, this clause attracted Barbadians who owned large parcels of slaves. The first generation of New Jersey settlers from Barbados included John Berry, with thirty-two slaves near Hackensack, in Bergen County; Lewis Morris Sr., who operated a forge and mill in Monmouth County employing over sixty slaves; and William Sandford and Nathaniel Kingsland, who purchased a fifteen-thousand-acre tract near New Barbados in Bergen County.

The best-known slave manor was the Philipsbourough Manor. Frederick Philipse, the first lord of the manor, graduated from a stint as a carpenter for the Dutch West India Company in 1653 to plantation owner in Yonkers in 1672 and supplemented his earnings by slave trading. By 1693, he became the owner of almost two hundred square miles of land in Westchester, known as Philipsbourough Manor. At his death in 1702, his twenty-six slaves were divided between his son Adolphus and his grandson Frederick. Over the years, Adolphus had a total of twenty-seven people working on his mill. After the manor was consolidated following Frederick's death in 1752, the number of slaves was seventy-six. They toiled at the mills, the bakery, and the cooperage in addition to agricultural chores.[33]

While their roots lay in the sugar islands, gentleman slave masters could not reproduce in the mid-Atlantic the wealth extorted from enslaved labor further south. No staple crop of any great value developed from the gentlemen's farms. Rather, these holdings supplemented their dealings in trade, law, and politics. It is important, though, to remember that such men ran the two colonies for the next century and they never doubted the wisdom or sanctity of slavery. These men, together with other arrivals from Barbados, all brought slaves and cultivated their holdings. Their influence trickled down to lesser men as they sold bits of land to slaveholding Dutch farmers.[34]

The future of rural slaveholding was on middle-sized farms. East Jersey, sparsely settled by Europeans in the era of Dutch control, developed rapidly in the 1660s with the use of slave labor. The transition from the era of Dutch corporate to English proprietary and then imperial governance saw the arrival of a diverse group of immigrants. Dutch settlers, encompassing wide ethnic variations, were joined by Barbadian slave owners, English Quakers and Congregationalists, Scots-Irish Presbyterians, and French Huguenots. Land allocations and religious justification of slavery permitted each group to purchase and keep bondspeople. Although some of these farms were isolated, the vast majority were in agricultural communities of Dutch, Scottish, French, and English farmers. In 1698 in New Rochelle, New York, for example, Huguenot families owned 1 slave for every 2.3 adult males. Most of the Protestant refugees owned one or two slaves; others owned whole families.[35]

Even in the largest units, masters and mistresses considered slaves part of their extended families. Just as families formed the center of such agricultural societies, so too patriarchal control over bondspeople began at home. Ethnicity was an important factor in identifying slaveholders. Within ethnic groups certain families became known as masters of slaves. Intertwined by marriage and blood, these families lived fairly close to each other and often divided slaves and their children among them. Rather than create paternalist ties, such arrangements constituted real hazards for black families when masters died or when their children reached maturity and needed laborers.[36]

Many of these small units formed into agricultural towns, strikingly dependent on slavery. In the predominantly Dutch Kings County, over 40 percent of white households (129 of 317) contained slaves by 1698. Although percentages were generally lower in Queens County, in the Dutch community of Flushing, over 44 percent of families owned slaves. Smaller but significant percentages were evident in the West-

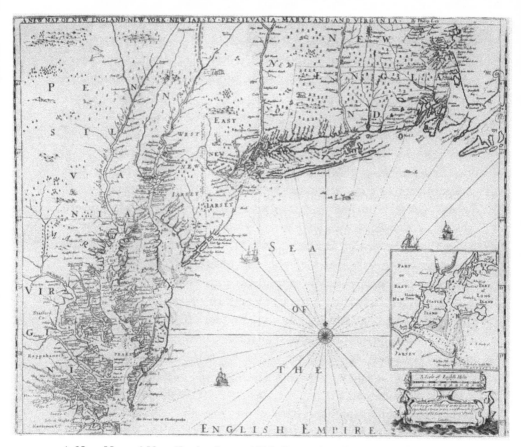

A New Map of New England, *ca. 1685. Portraying the northern portion of the Atlantic coastal colonies during the brief period of consolidation, this map offers one of the first accurate views of East Jersey. (Print Collection, Miriam and Ira D. Wallach Division of Art, Prints, and Photographs, New York Public Library, Astor, Lenox and Tilden Foundations)*

chester County towns of Fordham, New Rochelle, and Mamaroneck. In such rural New York towns, there was, as Vivienne J. Kruger notes, a positive correlation between landed wealth and slave ownership in each rank of society. Prosperous farmers with slaves owned more land generally, while even modest property owners gained an advantage from enslaved labor.[87]

Between 1664 and 1704, a Council of Proprietors ruled New Jersey, and its agents allocated patents to settlers according to their rank, size of family, and ethnicity. Dutch farmers who came before 1664 secured fairly small lots of about seventy-five acres. Later, in the 1690s, the Dutch moved south to the Raritan Valley and Monmouth County but still received only small land grants. Small holdings limited the upward mobility of farmers and hampered future generations. With little excess land available, Dutch children were forced either to work for parents long into life or to move west. If they stayed with their parents, Dutch farmers benefited from ownership of slaves; if the children moved west, a bondsman was essential to starting a new farm. Authorities were more liberal to English farmers arriving in the 1670s. Settlers in Newark in Essex County, founded in 1675, held freeholds of about one hundred acres. In the Monmouth Patent farms were more substantial, with grants averaging above three hundred acres.[38] New Englanders, encouraged by the Duke of York to settle in East Jersey, received larger farms of about two hundred acres. Coming from New England, where slaves were an expensive luxury, these settlers found enslaved labor a boon to their prosperity. In the 1690s, these migrants were joined by more Dutch, new arrivals from Scotland, and French Huguenots.[39]

East Jersey and rural New York became hinterlands, delivering food and fuel to the growing market in New York City. Farmers practiced a four-crop system of grains, meadowlands, fruits, and vegetables. Some land was spared for animals and hay. Additional diversification occurred, benefiting from a network of roads and deepwater rivers that cut across East Jersey from the ocean. Fishing was a profitable supplement, but even more important was the easy access from interior farms to urban markets. Distribution depots were also milling centers. Accessibility and low cost meant that most middlemen and shippers appear to have been local residents.[40]

Slave Culture and the Legal Response

By the first years of the eighteenth century blacks in and around New York faced a fundamental dilemma. Females lived in the cities, while males were generally restricted to the rural areas. Kings County (Brooklyn), where Anthony the Turk once lived in freedom, was the home in 1703 to 343 enslaved blacks, of whom 207 were male. In Richmond County, black males outnumbered females by over two to one. Similar imbalances existed in Queens and Westchester Counties.[41] At times, this imbalance would improve over the course of the century, but it would never even out. Black men had to roam away from home in search of female companionship while black women faced a lifetime of solitude working in the house of a white family. At the same time, Africans found the boundaries between countryside and city permeable.

Rural blacks traveled across land and water to join their urban compatriots in revelry, and colonial assemblies and town councils responded by passing a series of ineffective laws restricting their activities. Beginning with ordinances barring sales of alcohol in taverns to blacks by free blacks or poor whites, restrictions expanded to prevent holding funerals after dark, assemblages of blacks on Sundays, and use of weapons, and to special injunctions against purchasing stolen goods.[42]

Free blacks hosted a nascent slave culture in their impromptu, unlicensed taverns. In 1671 the magistrates complained to free blacks Domingo and Manuel Angola that "the free Negroes were from time to time entertaining sundry of the burghers' Negroes to the great damage of their owners." They were charged by the court henceforth "not to entertain any Servants or Helps, whether Christian or Negro on pain of forfeiting their freedom. . . . or harboring any Servants or helps longer than twenty-four hours." The pair was ordered to communicate the edict "to the remaining free negroes." [43]

Authorities tried vainly to halt slave celebrations. On April 24, 1691, New York City's Common Council outlawed sales of liquor to slaves without their masters' consent and a year later ordered the sheriff to give twenty lashes to any slaves found "playing or making any hooting or disorderly noise in the Street on the Lords Day or be found in any publick house." Slaves were barred from taverns on Sundays, and "whereas the frequent randivouzing of Negro slaves att the Houses of the free Negroes without the gates hath been the occasion of great discord," the city magistrates ordered that free blacks be fined six shillings for serving liquor to slaves. Such laws were virtually unenforceable, however, because white tapsters were also willing to make money by fencing stolen goods for slaves.[44]

Momentarily free from colonial religious and political control, blacks in the taverns created early forms of African American music and dance. Northern blacks during the colonial era constructed music for barroom frolics using banjos, drums, rattles, and horns and playing African songs mixed with European popular songs. As W. E. B. Du Bois has described it, such "veiled and inarticulate" music was rarely written down but frequently transmitted through the elders. Du Bois recalled a song heard by the fireside in his childhood, which came down from a distant West African ancestor: "Do bana coba, gene me, gene. Do bana coba, gene me, gene me! Ben d'nu-li, nu-li, nu-li, bene d'le." This may have been a Wolof song from the Senegambia about the confinement of captivity, but over time its exact meaning was lost. Black popular songs continually changed to suit the desires of the audience but mainly functioned as methods of overcoming despair. In contrast to the call-and-response of sacred black song, popular melodies offered an individualized complaint about life.[45]

White authorities took a dim view of these frolics. The grand jury first noted the problem in 1682 as a genuine threat to "Good Order and Discipline" when it complained of the "many Greate Evills and inconveniencys . . . occasioned and committed by Negroes and Indian slaves their frequent meetings and gathering themselves together in greate numbers of the Lords Days and att other unseasonable times using and exercising severall rude and unlawful sports and pastimes to the dishonour of God." The celebrations made other blacks the "Spectators of such Evill practices and thereby diverted from the more suitable and Pious Duty of the day." The court asked that the sheriff check that all slaves had passes from their masters and whip those without them.[46]

The Sunday gatherings are direct evidence of the survival of African traditions. Though arriving from disparate parts of Africa and the Caribbean, enslaved blacks formed "nations" or cultural units fusing religious beliefs and customary behaviors.[47] These units were similar to those travelers found in Africa. Nathaniel Uring, visiting Luanda in 1701, observed young blacks carousing and dancing on Sundays. Uring noted that "the young men and women often meet together in small companies by moon-light and Sing and Dance most part of the night, which they choose for coolness, it being too hot during the day for those kind of diversions. This custom of dancing is kept up in all our American plantations. On Sundays when they have leave to visit their friends they get together in small companies in the streets." Similarly, blacks in Barbados, the source for many New Jersey slaves in this period, reveled on Sundays and on special feast days, whether African or European.[48]

These events often occurred on European holy days. Among Africans there was no clear division between the sacred and the secular. As Jon Sensbach has observed, religion suffused and dominated every aspect of life. Accordingly, what Europeans saw as blasphemy of holy days was to Africans religious observance. Moreover, the European religious community in the region lacked consensus on Sabbath behavior. Presbyterians, an important denomination in East Jersey, did not keep the Sabbath. The Society of Friends regarded strict Sabbath-keeping as a relic of authoritarian New England. The Dutch often frolicked on Sundays and invoked order on the Sabbath only to corral their unruly servants.[49]

Black Sunday romps continued through the 1690s. The grand jury in Kings County complained on November 10, 1697, of "great concourse and Mobbing of Negroe Slaves from Yorke and other places to this Place on the Sabbath Day. . . . to the horror of the majority of His Majesty's Loyal Subjects." The court accused John Norton, ferryman, of transporting slaves from "yorke on the Sabbath Day" and urged that he be fined for each and every slave. Frustrated by similar problems the following year, the same court urged that "no Negroes, male or female, shall presume to go out their Majesty's habitations from one town to another without a Ticket on the Sabbath Day, under penalty of a whipping." In 1702 Lord Governor Bellomont (Richard Coote) asked the Board of Trade for a law regulating slaves, which "is become so necessary through the great insolency that sort of people are grown to." By 1706 in New York black frolics grew so threatening that Bellomont's successor, Viscount Cornbury (Edward Hyde) issued a warrant to the justices in Kings County giving them authority to break up illegal assemblages of blacks and including "the extraordinary command that if the negroes could not be taken they might be fired upon and killed."[50]

Blacks and whites joined together in the frolics of the slave culture. New York City followed the custom established centuries earlier in England of issuing alehouse licenses to widows and spinsters to keep them off the public dole. Such taverns were meeting grounds for slaves, places where they could fence stolen goods. Among the first of many indictments of widows and spinsters for selling liquor and receiving stolen goods from slaves, the grand jury charged Jannetje Barber with "entertaining of negroes" on October 7, 1699. Hester Blanck was presented to the grand jury for "encouraging the servt of Mr. Clarke to steale money and entertaining of negroes."[51] Beginning with Eric Hobsbawm, historians have come to regard such theft as a form of social resistance to attacks on customary rights. One problem with this approach is that historians infrequently find social bandits but encounter plenty of ordinary felons. Virtually every traveler's account, however biased, of African port society emphasizes the prevalence of stealing. Networks formed of paupers, vagabonds, and thieves similar to those found in Amsterdam, London, and the port cities along the Gold Coast. Later, however, as the threads of enslavement wove into a steel mesh, the activities of such criminals in New York became explicitly political.[52]

White authorities responded to this black resistance with a harsher slave code. Although slaves could not vote or hold office, ironically they influenced the creation of a criminal code reserved for them alone which reflected white anxieties about deep cultural differences.[53] In New York and East Jersey, laws were passed to punish receivers of stolen goods. New York City in 1681, New Jersey in 1682, and New York Colony in 1684 prohibited sales or purchases of any goods from slaves. The reason, stated in the East Jersey act, was that "it is found in daily experience, that negro and Indian slaves or servants under the pretense of trade or liberty to traffic, do frequently steal from their masters and others what they expose to sale at distance from their habitations." Believing that "without a receiver the thief would soon desert his practice," the governor and assembly outlawed "trade and traffique with any negro slave, or Indian slave or servant, for any rum, brandy, wine or other strong drink or any other goods, wares or commodities." Penalties for the purchaser included fines and, for the slave, a whipping.[54]

In both colonies, the stated legal penalty for felonious theft was death. In practice, punishment for crime against property was less rigorous. Benefit of the clergy usually mitigated the ultimate punishment, which meant that any slave demonstrating knowledge of Christianity received clemency. East Jersey magistrates followed New England law, using an escalating series of punishments. The first offense required a whipping and treble restitution, the second, branding of the hand or forehead, and the third, death. Penalties for theft in New York ranged from whippings while being dragged through town by a cart to hanging.[55]

Enslaved blacks advanced from pilfering trinkets to stealing themselves. Individual control over slaves was at best hazardous, and despite laws passed in New York forbidding flight from masters, blacks frequently escaped from servitude.[56] Governor Nicolls made the first "hue and cry" announcing a runaway slave in 1664. He proclaimed that "all persons within my government to bee ayding and assisting [to Mr. Yarmouth of New England] to find out said Negroe . . . to seize him and return him."[57] On October 2, 1679, the colony council responded to masters' complaints by establishing a sizable fine of £25 for harboring runaways and neglecting to send them home or to the magistrates.[58] Ten years later, the council heard a petition from the Dutch farmers of Harlem who complained of "a band of Negroes, who have runaway from their masters at New York and commit depredations on the inhabitants of the said village."[59]

Work practices on the frontier permitted moments of freedom. A few blacks found liberty at work. A Bergen County court of sessions held on September 15, 1680, learned that "negroes were sent to care for the hoggs," but as they could not return conveniently until morning, they cared for the hogs in the woods. Because the hogs did great damage to a Colonel Lawrence's property, the Negroes were sentenced to be "whipt, 20 lashes apiece, and their masters admonished to be aware of their whereabouts." The grand jury of Westchester County complained in 1692 that a group of black hogreeves "doe commonly goe into the woods with Gunns, Staves and Dogs; which may be the occasion for . . . losse and damage and that the Negroes have the liberty to Bye and Sell." The magistrates quickly ordered the practice to cease, assessed penalties against the owners of the slaves, and outlawed sale of "any Strong Drinke, to slaves without consent of their masters."[60]

Black men were not the only ones to seek liberty through flight. In 1699, Mando, a Negro woman, petitioned for her daughter's and her own freedom from Samuel Denton of Queens County. Mando claimed that Ann Wharton had promised her freedom after Wharton's death. Denton, who somehow gained Mando's services, refused to comply when Wharton died. Mando then escaped from Denton and fled to Westchester County. Subsequent efforts by Denton to regain Mando failed because the Westchester County sheriff "Cannot find the Negro woman."[61]

Mando was one of many enslaved blacks who left for the Indian territories. American Indian nations offered inviting frontiers. In 1679, Jacob, who spoke "Good English, Dutch, good Mohawk and Mohegan," ran away from his master, Sven Theunisse, who offered a reward for his capture in either "Indian or Christian territory."[62] The two colonies did not penetrate far into the interior of the continent and Amerindians rarely returned escaped slaves, particularly those with mixed blood. In the 1680s worried colonial authorities passed several laws concerning fugitive slaves aligning with nearby Indian tribes.[63] The problem became so acute that by 1705 the New York Assembly passed a law permitting the death penalty for any slave found more than forty miles north of Albany. The legislation was reaffirmed in 1725.[64]

A symptom of the growing tensions over enslavement was the rise in the frequency of slaves' attacks on their masters and on officials. Assailants faced harsh punishments. Prince, a slave who slapped Mayor William Merritt of New York City on the face in 1696, was sentenced to be carried to the "publick whipping post of this city and then to be stripped Naked from the middle upwards and there be tyed to the tale of a cart and being soe stripped and tyed shall be drawn round this City within the fortifications till he return to the said Whipping Post and at every corner of every street shall receive Eleeven lashes on his Body." [65]

Rural courts were even more brutal. They were quick to condemn and immune to appeal. Dutch predilection for torture and abuse of corpses influenced law in both colonies. Cuffy, a slave of Lewis Morris, was executed for arson, then disinterred and hung in chains in 1685. Murders by slaves were considered "petit treason," which provided legal and moral justification for the severity with which violators were punished. Governors and privy councils could award clemency only when the special courts had not already dispensed quick "justice." In rural courts three justices of the peace and six freeholders decided guilt or innocence. Summary justice was determined in a matter of hours. The court was first used in the trial of seven blacks "suspected to be guilty of the Horrid murder of Lewis Morris of Passage Point." Two slaves, Jeremie and Agebee, were accused of "shooting him through the body with a hand gun," in revenge for Morris's earlier murder of a Negro woman, which, despite pleas from blacks, the New Jersey courts refused to investigate. After a brief consultation, the court ordered Agebee and Jeremie to be hanged and a third, Oliver, whipped.[66]

European Religion

Such turbulent behavior convinced English authorities that local slaves need greater instruction in servility. When whippings and executions failed to cow the slave populace, the English turned to religion. There was much to be done. Neglect by the Dutch Reformed Church and lack of interest by newer congregations in the region left Africans virtually unchurched in Christian mores. In 1730, David Humphreys, reviewing the efforts in New York of the Society for the Propagation of the Gospel in Foreign Parts (SPG), the missionary wing of the Church of England, reported that in the last decades of the seventeenth century, "the Negroes were much discouraged from embracing the Christian religion. . . . Their marriages were performed by mutual consent only, without the blessings of the Church; they were buried by those of their owne country or Complexion in the common field, without any Christian office; perhaps some ridiculous Heathen rites were performed

The Closing Vise of Slavery { 53

at the Grave by some of their owne people. No notice was given of their being sick, that they might be visited, on the contrary, frequent Discourses were made in Conversation that they had no souls and perished as the Beasts."[67]

Humphreys's descriptions indicate that over a half-century after the arrival of the first nonindigenous settlers in the region, African religious practices were still prevalent among the colony's slaves and that little effort had been made to Christianize them. Newly arrived enslaved Africans had either been exposed to Catholicism, which the English loathed, or lacked any Christian experience. Religion, which James Axtell has termed "the invasion within," was the most potent tool for acculturation. In English society, as in other Protestant nations, baptism was a foremost ritual in any person's life cycle. Although the ceremony of baptism was fraught with ambiguity and ideological debate, there was no disagreement about its fundamental importance as the foundation of Christianity. Blacks coming into contact with Christian nations shared this view and regarded catechism and baptism as powerful steps toward free membership into society.[68]

The Church of England made the strongest institutional effort to convert Africans in the New York region. In contrast to the flagging or timorous efforts in the West Indies and the southern colonies,[69] the educational missions of the SPG in New York and New Jersey at first were powerful attempts at acculturation. Anglican efforts in North America began in the 1680s, employing the rite of baptism as the doorway to salvation for Africans. Theologian Morgan Godwyn took pains to assure nervous colonials that baptism did not require emancipation. Godwyn was emphatic about bringing Christianity to slaves; failure to do so, he argued, invited a secular, licentious reading of the Bible and God's intentions.[70] Secret instructions to royal governors contained orders to "facilitate and encourage the Conversion of Negroes and Indians to our Christian religion." The principal support for proselytizing blacks came from wealthy New Yorkers and Crown officials but from few other colonists. Puritans in particular had deep reservations about the lasting value of the baptism of pagans.[71]

That the Church of England was quite weak outside of New York City was evident early on. For example, when the Dutch briefly recaptured the city in 1674, magistrates instructed residents of surrounding towns to nominate a representative of the Reformed faith. All residents were ordered to worship according to the tenets of the Council of Dort. Extreme Labadist pietists attempted to ban celebration of Pinkster.

Even after the English retook the colony in 1675, Dutch pietism gained strength in rural parts. After the Glorious Revolution of 1688, English clerics determined to stamp the Anglican faith on the colony but had little success. Charles II's policy of awarding large grants of land to his supporters and the ensuing desire to populate proprietary colonies like New York and New Jersey required appealing to diverse groups of immigrants. Crown mercantilist legislation inevitably came into conflict with the established church by encouraging an environment open to dissenters. Thwarted, Anglican missionaries took aim at Indians and Africans.[72]

In 1703, the SPG's plans bore fruit when Elias Neau opened the first Anglican school for New York's blacks. Born a Huguenot in France in 1662, Neau fled to the West Indies with other French Protestants in 1679, married, and traveled in North America in the early 1690s. Captured by a French privateer while he was en route to a business trip to London in 1692, he served in the galleys and was later held in the prison in the Marseilles harbor. There he wrote a series of impassioned letters to correspondents in America. He was released in 1698 after the end of King William's War and migrated to New York City the following year. A slaveholder himself, Neau was a partner of a leading slave trader, John Cruger. In 1702 Neau published a classic text in Protestant pietism in which he described Christ as the vehicle for comprehending suffering and described his own imprisonment as the gift that brought him true religious understanding.[73]

In New York, Neau initiated catechism classes without formal permission from London, arguing that the city's principal churches did nothing for blacks: "There are a great number of slaves of both sexes of all ages who are without God and for whom there is no manner of care taken . . . while we are at devotions, the streets are fill'd with Negroes who Dance and Divert themselves for they are kept in the same manner as horses." He met his black scholars in his home, preparing a "room up two flights of stairs 48 foot in length and 22 in breadth with benches for them to sit on." Recognizing that few of his catechists were "masters of their own time," Neau rarely waited until all slaves had arrived. Using techniques of love festivals and sacred theater learned during his Huguenot upbringing, Neau began services with a public prayer in which "all of them fall down on their knees," reciting the church prayers in unison, "after which we make our remarks upon 8 or 10 verses of the scripture, especially the Gospel of St. John . . . prevailing with a great deal of Charity and afterwards . . . reflections with an Exhortation at the End on the Reformation of manners." [74] Compacting his efforts in a two-hour service, Neau generally conducted the principal parts, including catechism, Bible study, and liturgy, while the slaves stood listening. Neau then administered individual catechisms from one end of his attic to the other. When numbers were small, he made catechists stand up "when I speak to them." When more blacks attended, Neau catechized three at a time, using terms "suitable to the capacity of those to whom I apply myself." Successful acolytes learned the Lord's Prayer, the Anglican Creed, the Ten Commandments, and part of the shorter catechism. Neau had special success with psalm books from which "my catechumens sing as well as pray and we sing the new verses because 'tis that which is used in church." [75]

Neau and the slaves used a call-and-response method that merged the belief systems of Africans and Anglicans. In one letter to an Anglican official, Neau described a common prayer, using questions and answers to inculcate doctrine.

Q. How long since God had his being?
　　A. From Eternity.
Q. How long will he continue to be?
　　A. For ever.
Q. By whom does he Subsist?
　　A. By all folk.
Q. On Whom does he Depend?
　　A. On Nobody.
Q. Where is God?
　　A. Everywhere.
Q. Where is he Chiefly?
　　A. In Heaven.
Q. What does he Do there?
　　A. He governs all things.
Q. What does he Search?
　　A. The Heart of all Things.
Q. What does he behold?
　　A. All things.
Q. But why does he regard them?
　　A. To Judge Them.
Q. Who is with him?
　　A. The Saints and the Angels.

Q. What is his Throne?

A. Heaven.

Q. What is his Footstool?

A. The Earth.

Q. How does God Make Himself Known?

A. By his Works.

Q. How Afterwards?

A. By his words.

Q. Who Teaches us to Understand that?

A. The Holy Spirit.

Q. How Many Works are there of God?

A. Two Among Others.

Q. What is the First Work?

A. Creation.

Q. What is the Second?

A. Redemption.[76]

Neau's conceptions of God, the creation of the earth and man, the hereafter, and the works of the Savior contained in proverbs and brief prayers dovetailed neatly with African theology. While offering a new form of worship, Neau transmitted a patina of European theology that disguised retention of African theology. One crucial retention was the African concept of soul. A flexible, dual perception of soul made Africans capable of resolving opposing tendencies through an outward-bound personality while nurturing an interior "Little Man Inside Me." Africans, who saw everyone as a spiritual messenger, were well prepared culturally to assimilate the generalized theology Neau offered. The format was equally significant. Neau's prayers used concrete imagery, while staying in accord with easily understood ways of God. Important as well to Africans were charismatic priests. Neau's background, genuine commitment, and sympathetic experiences made him perfect for the part. Finally, rather than catechize blacks in the church, Neau used his own home, in which Africans, believing that any place had religious potential, could feel comfortable, in contrast to the parish of Trinity Church, where they were barely tolerated.[77]

Neau used the Gospel of St. John to emphasize the sufferings of Jesus, the importance of private family worship, the utility of despair, and millenarianism. His fusion of established and pietist tenets ensured that any local slave with the slightest religious experience could comprehend his messages. Neau's conception of Jesus offered the slave far greater hope and human dignity than the paternalist ideals his colleagues in the Church of England tried to instill or the denial of Christian hope inculcated by patriarchal masters. In his teachings, Jesus became a prophet of freedom for slaves. Neau encouraged the slaves to find their own rebirth in personal suffering and human tragedy. If Neau's assignment was to acculturate the Africans and create acceptance of their slave status, they interpreted his message differently. Doubtless many could see that Neau's captivity experience was analogous to their Middle Passage, a therapeutic device that helped Africans make the transition from local beliefs to the state church of Anglicanism.[78]

His Anglican colleagues regarded Neau as an unqualified intruder and felt his poor mastery of English limited meaningful success. Neau's linguistic deficiencies, combined with the uncertain fluency of the slaves, meant that his classes were conducted in a melange of Atlantic tongues. In a report to London, Neau apologized for his verbal shortcomings, which he admitted were a problem for teaching a clear understanding of theology, "especially to those who are Christians by birth."[79] To the dismay of his colleagues, Neau attended morning prayers infrequently, prompting Anglicans in New York to seek to replace him with a professional cleric. Neau responded that he "had nothing to do with any but the slaves, for that effect I have the Lord's approbation." The London authorities chose to back Neau; their support for Neau over the wishes of local Anglican clerics must have increased his prestige among Africans, who viewed him as favored by the king.[80]

Neau identified masters' fear that baptism mandated emancipation of slaves as the key problem for the school. He suggested that Parliament pass a law clarifying the issue, "according to the example of the French and Spanish who baptize all slaves without giving them temporal liberty."[81] Together with the Reverend William Vesey, the Trinity priest, Neau lobbied the New York Assembly to duplicate earlier laws in other colonies, which "confirmed the rights of masters over their slaves after baptism . . . for without that they will not suffer them to be instructed, for fear they should be baptized without their knowledge." Neau reported that masters threatened to sell slaves who asked to attend the school to Virginia and the West Indies.[82] In fact, Vesey did baptize enslaved blacks without their masters' knowledge. In 1706 and again in 1712, he acknowledged that "those who were baptized had it done to them without consent of their masters and there are . . . [some] who wish me ill and many negroes come to catechism unknown to their masters."[83]

Neau's first success came across the North (Hudson) River. In 1704, the New Jersey Assembly, led by Lewis Morris, proclaimed that "the baptizing of any Negro, Indian or Mulatto slave shall not be any reason or cause for setting them or any of them at liberty." Two years later the New York Assembly tacked onto general tax legislation a law that intended to end the "groundless opinion that hath spread itself throughout the colony" that baptism of slaves meant "that they would become free and ought to be set at liberty." Rather, the legislation declared that baptism "shall not be any cause or reason for the freeing them." Further, the law inscribed the lineage of slavery, providing that a child "shall follow the state and condition of the mother." An additional clause ordered that "no slave whatsoever in this colony shall at any time be admitted as a witness against any freeman" in any judicial matter.[84]

The laws showed the contradictions of Anglican liberalism. Intended to open the church to potential black adherents, they reduced blacks to the status of noncitizens, permitting the act of baptism to become a justification for racial bondage. Anglican officials expected little from the act, noting that its success with French and Dutch slaveholders was uncertain. The SPG secretary wondered that "there should be any people so narrow spirited and weighted in their opinions as to exclude their servants from the great advantage of becoming Christians." The only hope, the secretary concluded, was for Dutch and French pastors to urge their congregations to attend catechism classes.[85] Bishop William Fleetwood muddied the issue further in 1705 when he argued that law, religious or civil, had a higher authority than the will of the master. Fleetwood argued that masters had a moral obligation to permit their slaves access to religion. Such claims, of course, affronted pietist masters in dissenting denominations.[86] To blacks themselves, the law violated international codes about the manumitting powers of baptism. The Roman Catholic Church in the late seventeenth century experienced an antislavery movement affecting black populations in Brazil which centered on awarding freedom to anyone "who had received the water of holy baptism." Although the movement eventually foundered because of papal indifference, it showed the splits within Catholicism over baptism already observed among Protestant leaders and their flocks. Blacks, who regarded Euro-American religion in pragmatic and experiential ways, could readily understand where their best interests lay. Denial of the right of baptism would only create bitterness.[87]

Slaves flocked to the school, undeterred by the new law. The first students were the slaves of prominent New Yorkers, but enrollments soon shot up to over one hundred, many of whom were not slaves of wealthy families. Neau begged his superiors for cheap psalters and catechisms, requesting editions of the Lord's Prayer in the African languages of "Carmantie and Mandingo." Neau was aware that the cheap psalters were a powerful attraction. He continually asked the SPG secretary for more, noting that after he had dispensed many of the tracts, the slaves "did not continue to come, but I believe came only for the books."[88] Although he could identify the domestic servants of wealthy Anglicans, Neau found it "impossible to take all the Names for often several Sailors, Negroes and Indians from Bermuda and other places come to school when their vessels were in harbor." These transient students often arrived after services began and took "small tracts, books and catechisms so that they might learn at sea." Neau clearly was more interested in instructing blacks in Christian ways than in keeping tabs on their activities to reassure their masters. The traffic of anonymous, transient black pupils indicated that they were attending his lessons to gain literacy and to create their own versions of Christianity, both of which were still insurance against capital punishment.[89]

Despite Neau's efforts, the SPG worried that "the greatest part of the black people in New York remain unbaptized, thro' the indifference of their masters, notwithstanding the good laws that have been made . . . and the subsequent services of the Society." Neau turned to the governor for help. Responding to the schoolmaster's request for an endorsement in early 1712, Governor Robert Hunter issued a proclamation "to the effect that all slaves should be sent to Neau's school." On the eve of a slave conspiracy that rocked the colony, Trinity rector William Vesey refused to read the proclamation in church (although it was distributed widely), indicating sharp political disagreements toward black instruction, which could not have escaped notice among

Proclamation of Governor Hunter, 1711. Hunter's official proclamation ordered slave masters to allow their chattel to attend Anglican catechism classes. Deeply opposed by owners of dissenting denominations, the proclamation inspired hope and a sense of deprivation among blacks forbidden access by their masters. (Courtesy of the New-York Historical Society)

By His Excellency

Robert Hunter, Efq; Captain General and Governour in Chief of the Provinces of *New-York*, *New-Jerfey*, and all the Territories thereon depending in *America*, and Vice Admiral of the fame, &c.

A Proclamation.

COnfidering that true Religion and Piety are the only firm Foundations of the Profperity of any People, and Irreligion, Immorality and Prophanenefs the Caufes of their Mifery and Deftruction, are Truths attefted by the holy Scriptures, and confirmed by the Suffrages of all Ages.

Wherefore, that the Service of God may be advanced, his Judgments averted, and his Bleffings beftowed upon us, I have thought fit to Publifh this Proclamation, Strictly Charging and Requiring all Judges, Mayors, Sheriffs, Juftices of the Peace, Conftables, and all others whom it does or may concern, to be Vigilant and Strict in the faithful and impartial Execution of the Laws made againft Prophanation of the Lords Day, Curfing and Swearing, Blafphemy, Drunkennefs, Lewdnefs, and all other Immoral and diforderly Practices, which have too much obtain'd in this Province, to the Difhonour of Almighty God, and the great Scandal and Reproach of our holy Religion, the contagious Examples of bad Men having fo great a tendency to the Corruption of others vertuoufly difpofed, it's highly neceffary that all Perfons in Authority do apply themfelves with all care and diligence to the Suppreffing of the fame.

And to the intent that Chriftian Knowledge, Religion and good Manners may flourifh and increafe in this Province, I earneftly Recommend and Exhort that all Perfons Decently and Reverently attend the Worfhip of God on every Lords Day, and other Days fet a part for Religious Worfhip, and that all Heads of Families do promote the Service of God in their refpective Families, and inftruct their Children and Servants in the principles of Piety and Vertue.

That in this City of *New-York*, Where the *Venerable Society for Propagation of the Gofpel In Forreign Parts*, have in their great Zeal for the enlargement of Chrifts Church, appointed Mr. *Elias Neau*, a Perfon well qualified with Piety and Knowledge, to Catechife and Inftruct Children, Servants, Negro and Indian Slaves in the Knowledge of Jefus Chrift, That all Parents, Mafters and Miftriffes of Families, be affifting in the accomplifhing of a Work fo good and commendable, by fending and encouraging to go to fuch School of Inftruction, their Children and Servants, Negro and Indian Slaves.

I likewife order and Command, That this Proclamation may be read by every Minifter in this Province, in his refpective Church and Congregation, at leaft four times in every year, immediately after Divine Service, and that the Exhort and Incite their refpective Auditories to a fincere Practice of Piety and Virtue, and a Religious Obfervation of Gods holy Laws.

And I do hereby further Command, That the Judges or Juftices of the Peace in the refpective Counties of this Province, do caufe the fame likewife to be read at the Quarter-Seffions of the Peace in every County of this Province, immediately before the Charge be given to the Grand Jury, who are to be encouraged and talled on to difcover and prefent all fuch as fhall be guilty of the Breach of any the of Laws made againft Prophanenefs and Immorality. And all her Majefties Judges, Juftices of the Peace, Sheriffs, Conftables, and all other Officers whatfoever, within the aforefaid Province, as hereby Required and Commanded in their feveral and refpective Stations and Diftricts to fee that this Proclamation be duly obferved, as they will anfwer the contrary at their Peril.

Given under my Hand and Seal at Fort Anne in *New-York* this Twelfth Day of *January*, in the Tenth year of the Reign of our Soveraign Lady *ANNE*, by the Grace of God of *Great Britain*, *France* and *Ireland*, Queen, Defender of the Faith, &c. Annoq; Dom. 1711.

By his Excellency's Command,
GEO. CLARKE.

R.O. HUNTER.

God Save the Queen.

the enslaved population. On April 25, Neau reported that "Vesey refused to baptize a mulattress tho' she had a letter directing [him] to baptize her." The black woman was then baptized by the chaplain of the fort in his chapel. Baptism was a major issue in the revolt a few weeks later, after which the Reverend John Sharpe noted that "what is very observable the Persons whose Negroes have been found guilty are such as are declared opposers of Christianizing Negroes." Following the conspiracy, Elias Neau retreated to his rooms, canceled classes, and worried about possible involvement of his scholars: "(only one, Hendrick Hooglandt's slave, angry at his master's refusal to allow him baptism was involved)."[90] After the revolt was repressed, Neau reopened his school. Governor Robert Hunter and his wife endorsed Neau and his students with several visits. Without Hunter's patronage, it is unlikely that Neau's school would have survived.[91]

Neau's efforts to inculcate Christian religion in African slaves had mixed effects. His sincerity and willingness to allow Africans open admission surely gave the Church of England a better reputation among slaves than it deserved. It cannot be argued, however, even so early in the century, that his teachings reached all enslaved Africans locally or convinced them to submit docilely to their fates. In New York, he worked virtually alone. Though backed by the London bishopric and by the governor, he was opposed and disliked by other colonial clerics. His historical reputation is perhaps larger than his contemporary success. Jon Butler has contended that Anglican missions caused a holocaust of African religions in America.[92] Certainly, it is true that open worship was impossible because it threatened theological hegemony and undermined the authority of slave masters. It is possible, however, that local observers did not understand how blacks used Neau's classes for their own purpose. The eagerness of transient blacks to attend classes and grab reading material for their own purposes combined with the explicit threat of the weekly or holiday African celebrations and Neau's failure to erase them are perhaps the strongest, immediate contradictions of Butler's argument.

Other European faiths did not match Anglican efforts. The Dutch Reformed Church, easily the second strongest denomination in the region and in rural areas the most powerful, rejected its earlier efforts to proselytize among blacks. The church split at the close of the seventeenth century between urbanites willing to compromise with the official Church of England and pietists who resisted Anglicanism fiercely. Pietism was most influential in the Dutch counties of Bergen in East

Jersey and Kings in New York. In Bergen County, a pietist personality emerged in the aftermath of the Liesler Rebellion, which shook New York in the early 1690s. During the brutal repression by English authorities, Dutch pietists fled to Bergen, which was already overwhelmingly Dutch. As Randall Balmer has suggested, the rural pietist personality emerged among people of peripheral social status, and its ecstatic religious expression derived from inner light conversion. Proof of conversion was necessary for membership in churches governed by parishioners who valued charisma over learning and illumination over doctrine. Sacraments were reserved to the faithful, though they were incidental to spirituality. Identity was local and dependent on an "inner elect" who had withdrawn from the outer world. These qualities helped Bergen slaveholders resist Anglican calls to catechize their slaves. Elias Neau recognized this problem, explaining: "I have not catechized [in New Jersey] because they are almost all Dutch there and for they that live in town are afraid that their slaves may demand their freedom after Baptism, the country people certainly believe there is some other design upon them, besides depriving them of their slaves." No law passed by English authorities would convince these Dutch to ignore customary beliefs that baptism mandated emancipation. It was better, they decided, to keep slaves out of church and share religious experiences with them only at festivals, especially the ecstatic moments of Pinkster. For blacks, this meant that they would not receive the religious instruction given by Neau (with its concomitant gift of literacy), but they would be able to maintain their own religious faiths and encounter the Dutch and Huguenots in the magical days of Pinkster.[98]

Black Revolt

The good efforts of Elias Neau were insufficient to ease the anxieties of white colonists or to check the African urge to be free. So the two colonies created tougher laws. In 1704, New Jersey was the first of the two colonies to create a code noir when it passed "An Act for Regulating Negro, Indian and Mallato Slaves." Two years later, New York passed similar legislation. The first few clauses reasserted bans on sales to slaves and attempted to curtail blacks from straying by offering rewards to any white "so taking [up slaves] and carrying them to be whipped." Black theft was now threatening enough to require branding "on the most visible part of the left cheek near the nose, with the Letter (T) by the constable." Most controversial was the clause in the New Jersey laws which required that black rapists or even fornicators with white women be "castrated at the care and Charge of his Master or Mistress." The Privy Council in London quickly disallowed the law.[94]

The announcement of the code noir doubtless angered the slave population and spawned increased violence. On February 10, 1708, Lord Cornbury wrote the Board of Trade that "a most barbarous murder has been committed upon the family of one Hallet by an Indian Man Slave, and a Negro Woman, who have murdered their Master, Mistress and five children." One eyewitness reported the devastation at the Hallet home in Newtown, Long Island:

> William Hallet junior who labored at a place called Hellgate his wife and five children in a quarter of an hour were all murdered by one Indian slave whom he had up for 4 years. There was a negro woman Slave in the house who was to him in counseling him in this bloody matter. Both he and his wife have gone at Justice Hattely house with some others . . . about seven at night [Hallet and his wife] returned home and went to bed. . . . The slaves were watching their opportunity for they had to do it that night, and the house being something dark, [Sam] came into the house and had a axe laid behind the door and seeing his Master asleep took the axe and struck him first with the edge and then with the back of it. The first shook awakened his wife who was abed in the same room and she called murder, thereupon he struck her with the back of an axe on the head. There was one child lying in a box about 7 or 8 years of age. Those he murdered with the back of an axe and then drags the Young Child out from its murdered mother and Struck it on the head. The mother of the murdered child was also big with child.[95]

The slaves were taken and tried under a "special commission." The man was hung in gibbets and placed astride a sharp iron and the woman burned; "they have discovered two other Negroes their accomplices who have been tryed, condemned and executed."[96] As Herbert Aptheker has argued, the incident crossed the line between murder and rebellion. At least two slaves came from outside the household, and the affair was carefully planned and carried out with precision.[97] The murder sufficiently terrorized the legislative council that it passed acts for preventing conspiracies of slaves and providing compensation for loss of their "hostile property."[98]

As New York and New Jersey laws increasingly restricted black liberties, reaction and resistance grew. The Reverend John Sharpe reported to the SPG secretary on June 23, 1712, "Some negroes slaves here of the Nations of the Carmantee and Pappa, plotted to destroy all the whites, in order to obtain their freedom, and kept their conspiracy secret that there was not the least suspicion of it." Though "seasoned," these Coromantine, Angolan, and Yoruba slaves were hardly docile. One Antiguan planter, describing a revolt there in 1701, argued that the Cormantines "are not only the best and most faithful of our slaves but are really born Heroes. . . . Noe Man deserved a Cormantine that would not treat him like a Friend rather than a slave." [99]

African ethnicity and cosmology, further signs that African beliefs persisted in the colonies, were of great importance in the 1712 conspiracy. Conspirators, for example, used magic to protect themselves. Sharpe related that "a free negro who pretends sorcery gave them a powder to rub on their clothes which made them so confident," in the fashion of Coromantee beliefs that a priest must bless the warriors before they went to battle. The blacks initiated their plans on New Year's Day (March 25, old-style calendar), "tying themselves to secrecy by sucking the blood of each others hands." During the night of April 1, they set fire to a house, and when whites answered the alarm, "stood in the streets and shot down and stabbed as many as they could," murdering about eight and wounding about twelve more. [100]

White New Yorkers reacted brutally. After routing the remaining conspirators from the woods north of town, local authorities convened special courts, which were held through the remainder of April and May. After hurried trials, juries condemned twenty-one blacks and authorities executed eighteen. In one session the grand jury convicted twelve slaves of "using guns, clubbs, pistols, Staves, axes" to kill one Adrian Hooglandt. The convicted slaves were owned by masters of different classes, including three merchants, two butchers, a smith, a boatman, a mariner, a barber, and a widow. The condemned were executed through a variety of tortures, including "breaking on the wheel," burning, hanging in chains, and hanging by the neck. Bodies and heads were displayed for weeks in an attempt to convince the slaves that the souls of the slain martyrs had not returned to Africa, thus adding further deterrent to similar crimes. Though Winthrop Jordan has suggested that punishments for slave crimes in the North were much lighter than in southern colonies except in times of panic, the harsh punishments for the 1712 conspirators must be seen as continuing established patterns of repression. Worse, the number of capital punishments suggests that local authorities sanctioned racial revenge, thereby opening the door to more oppressive acts in the future. [101]

Paternalist leaders plainly wanted an end to the bloodshed. After observing "the most exemplary punishments inflicted that could be thought of," Governor Hunter attempted to put a halt to the executions. Hunter wanted New York to follow the methods used "in the West Indies where their laws against the slave are most severe, that in a case of conspiracy in which many are engaged a few only are executed for an example." He also believed that state evidence in New York, based on the testimony of two slaves, was weak. The governor recommended clemency for Mars, confronting the actions of May Bickley, the ambitious attorney general, whom Hunter regarded as a "busy, waspish man." After Mars was acquitted, Bickley indicted him a second and third time. Hunter also recommended clemency for Abigail, who had been convicted as accessory to the murder of Henry Brasier, but "pled her belly" because she was pregnant. He asked for mercy for several Spanish blacks who earlier had petitioned Hunter for their freedom as prisoners of privateers unlawfully held as slaves and set aside the convictions of Tom and Cuffee as accessories to the murders of Henry Brasier and Augustus Grasset on grounds of insufficient evidence. His final request for mercy was for Peter the Doctor, a free Negro laborer, believed to be the ringleader but never convicted.[102]

Hunter's actions sparked controversy. Bickley openly challenged the governor, sought his removal, and attempted to overturn his requests for pardons. Learning that the "Order of the Queen in Council . . . granting H.M. Pardon for Mars, a Negro and Hosea and John, two Spanish Indians" was the only positive news for blacks in New York and New Jersey. The pardon showed the Crown's respect for the rights of Spanish freemen unlawfully sold by privateers into slavery in New York.[103]

Hunter's relief when the pardons arrived from the Privy Council in early 1713 was almost palpable. He responded that the pardons "will enable me to struggle chearfully with all other difficulties, for indeed . . . a faction here had spread that I was disregarded at home and consequently speedily to be recalled." Hunter assured his employers that "your Lordships will never have reason from any act of mine to repent or be ashamed of your generous patronage."[104] The importance of Hunter's actions lies not only in his merciful character in contrast to the bloodthirsty New Yorkers, especially Bickley, but also in their appearance to black New Yorkers. Throughout the winter of 1712–13, while New York and Governor Hunter awaited the Crown decisions on the pardons, local desires to execute the remaining blacks in jail were strong. To any black watching the proceedings, the disharmony between Hunter and white New Yorkers demonstrated a fundamental split. Hunter's reprieves were only the first of many times that blacks would appeal to Crown officials for mercy or freedom against the legal determination of local magistrates and citizens.

Hunter then suggested that the New York Assembly avoid repetition of the "late Hellish Attempt of yor Slaves" by recognizing the "necessity of Putting that sort of men under better regulation by Some good law for that Purpose, and to take away the Root of that Evill, to Encourage the Importation of White Servants." If Hunter hoped for "better regulation," he would be bitterly disappointed. Early in the spring of 1713 Hunter forwarded new laws to London passed by the New York Assembly in response to the slave revolt. Hunter noted that the "Negro Act" was too severe, but after the late barbarous attempt of some of their slaves nothing less could please the people. Historians have repeated Hunter's observations, arguing that the laws passed on December 12, 1712, in New York and the following year in New Jersey were the final nails in the coffin of black freedom.[105]

The first four clauses of New York colony's laws reiterated injunctions against trading and against entertaining or selling liquor to slaves and gave masters permission to correct their chattel privately except in capital offenses. These clauses, repeated throughout court decisions and assembly complaints for the previous thirty years, were frustrated admissions of failure. White New Yorkers simply could not stop blacks from congregating, buying and selling goods, and having "frolics" at local taverns. The repetition of these complaints is simple testimony that whites, reacting to black indifference to civil law and to the explosive events of the spring of 1712, were unable either to police their slaves or to include them in the corporate body of society.

The key and cruelest clauses in the new legislation, to which Hunter objected strenuously and which the Privy Council attempted to disallow, were the restrictions on free blacks and on manumissions. This law attempted to forbid free blacks from selling liquor to slaves and ordered that "no Negro, Indian or Mallatto, that hereafter be made free, shall enjoy, hold or possess any Houses, Lands, Tenements, or Hereditaments in this colony." Although these laws did not affect the blacks already free in the colony, they ensured poverty for any newly manumitted slave. With a gratuitous slur that "it is found by Experience that the free Negroes of this colony are an Idle Slothful people and prove very often a charge on the place where they are," the assembly required that any master wishing to manumit a slave post a £200 surety and provide £20 annually to ensure the former slave's maintenance. The origin of this nefarious clause is obscure. Most free blacks in the colony were farmers, some with three generations of local reputation. Moreover, very few manumissions had occurred to this date in New York or New Jersey. The most careful scholars on the subject have turned up no more than a handful of grants.[106] It seems rather that the assembly's intentions were to define blacks as slaves and to strangle any pursuit of freedom.

Conclusions

In a half-century, then, New Yorkers along with their new neighbors in East Jersey had created a slave society. During this same period, colonists in the Chesapeake colonies and South Carolina shaped their slave societies. The difference between the mid-Atlantic and southern colonies was in the character of servitude, not the degree. In his masterful work on slavery in early America, Ira Berlin has concluded that the mid-Atlantic colonies could not support plantation regimes, despite the aspirations of gentry and small farmers. True, New York and East Jersey lagged far behind the Chesapeake, South Carolina, and the voracious sugar colonies in imports of slaves. Yet by 1700, slavery was a core legal, economic, and social system in New York and East Jersey. As free blacks found their rights being eroded, the number of enslaved Africans grew steadily. Employed and owned by skilled and semiskilled tradesmen, Africans performed difficult and menial labors in a status legally defined as inferior to that of their co-workers. European religious orders failed to acculturate Africans and convince them to accept their positions docilely. As they found avenues to freedom closed, ultimately, blacks reacted violently. In response, local authorities enacted harsh laws ensnaring future generations of Africans into permanent bondage—and unwittingly preparing for nastier conflicts in the future.[107]

CHAPTER 3

The Thirty-Year Rebellion

1714–1741

The Free Black Society Disappears

During the late seventeenth century, free blacks in New York and East Jersey were living examples of the pathways to African American liberty. By the early decades of the eighteenth century, such avenues had almost completely disappeared. The foremost effect of the punitive legislation passed following the 1712 rebellion was to restrict the presence of free blacks in the two colonies to an occasional émigré, scattered recipients of grants of emancipation, and the remnants of the seventeenth-century free people of color. The sad tale of Sam, slave of George Norton, a New York City butcher, shows how strong were the new obstacles to legal freedom. Governor Robert Hunter reported that Norton emancipated Sam by will in 1713 and bequeathed to him £30 and another slave. Norton acknowledged Sam's vital contribution to his prosperity and wished to establish him as a butcher in his old shop on Burger Street. Norton's executor, Captain Ebenezer Willson, however, refused to provide the £200 security for Sam or to provide the other provisions in the will, forcing him to remain in servitude. In 1717, Sam petitioned for release of the money. Sam complained that "Willson . . . will neither pay your poor petitioner the Thirty Pounds nor let him have said Negro Robin. . . . And yet in the winter when said Negro wants Cloaths he is forced to come to your poor petitioner for a supply. And so also when he is sick or lame he has come to your Petr several times and lain upon him for a month at a time. But so soon as he is well and able to work, Mr. Willson takes him away and imploys him in his own service." The petition demonstrated the inequities of the new law.

In addition to a failure to recognize blacks' dignity and independence, it opened them to exploitation by rapacious whites.[1]

Sam's plight prompted the Board of Trade in London to notify Hunter that it would "recommend the Act for punishing Negroes for disallowance unless the Assembly passes an amended act." The assembly responded by passing a new law stipulating that anyone ensuring that an emancipated black would not become a public charge could enter the security.[2] John Ellison, a joiner, and Thomas Slow, a merchant, agreed to stand bond for Norton in November 1717.[3] Nonetheless, the law served to inhibit black freedom. In future decades only a small number of free blacks received public funds.[4]

The property holdings of the few free blacks belie the slurs cast on them by the 1714 legislation. Solomon Peters, for example, accumulated a small estate in the seventeenth century. His son Solomon II, a property-owning farmer and artisan, died in 1724 and bequeathed to his widow, Maria Anthonis Portuguese, "all my houses and lands and household goods, as long as she lives." If she remarried, the property passed on to Peters's sons, who initially received "all my iron tools and implements of husbandry, and all my guns, pistols." Peters left £4 to his eldest son and 18 shillings to the others. It was a modest estate, surely, but equivalent to that of the average artisan or small farmer in the area. His nephew Lucas Peters fared less well and abandoned his wife, Mary, to the poorhouse in 1738.[5]

Other free blacks owned farms in East Jersey. The Van Doncks operated a small cattle farm near Tappan. Augustine Van Donck married Rachel Matthys in 1726. Their three children were baptized in the Dutch Reformed Church. Augustine and Rachel lived into the 1770s, leaving the farm in several parcels to their children, who maintained the farm into the nineteenth century. The De Vries (De Fries) and Manuel families, owners of small truck and cattle farms, were among the second generation of free black families who migrated from Manhattan to Bergen County in the 1680s.[6]

These holdovers from the seventeenth century were insufficient to maintain the growth of the free black class. The 1712 law requiring a £200 bond for emancipation and the revoking of black property rights virtually nullified any economic opportunities for free blacks. In addition, as white tradesmen, merchants, and farmers became dependent on slaves for labor, they were reluctant to let go of their most valuable movable property. As a result, manumissions were exceptionally rare in early eighteenth-century New York and East Jersey. The reasons for emancipation were individual, not systematic. Some wills freed one or two blacks but bequeathed others as slaves. Peter Woglum, a New York City yeoman, offered future emancipation to a black man and his wife, pending their good service to Woglum's widow; another black remained a slave forever. Woglum's slaves were baptized in the Lutheran Church, promising to "serve their masters and mistresses as they had done before." Samuel Thorne of Flushing freed "my old Negro wench, Dinah," leaving her a linen and a woolen spinning wheel,[7] but left another slave to his son. Elias Van Alary left his slave Caesar to his wife, Mary, ordering him freed after seven years and providing for a "suit of clothes fitting for a negro."[8] A few manumissions acknowledged blood ties. Leonard Brown, a farmer from Yonkers, acknowledged his paternity of "two Mullato children, Robert and Mary," and freed them after his death. In his will, Brown gave his children cash grants and apprenticed them to tradesmen. Thomas Hadden of Scarsdale left the use of his farm, animals, and wheat to "my wench Rose" for six years. Hadden left money to his "negro children" and ordered the executors to see that "all my negroes are to be free and the children bound out to trades" and "also to take some care that they are learnt to read."[9] Grateful masters rewarded faithful servants. Elias Nezreau of Jamaica, Queens, freed his "negro boy Augustine" to live in New York or London and financed his apprenticeship as a carpenter or cooper with a £20 grant to buy tools.[10] Occasionally free blacks were able to purchase, then emancipate, their families. John Fortune, a free black cooper in New York City, bought his wife, Marya, and her son Robin from Thomas Parcells of Barn Island for £40.[11]

Analysis of the probate records for New York for the first three decades after 1712 shows that slave owners, regardless of religion, occupation, residence, or sex, tended either to pass slaves along to relatives or to sell them to provide money for the family. Of 115 wills between 1712 and 1742, the largest numbers of bequests (forty-five) were to sons, with widows second (thirty-eight), daughters third (twenty-two), and nine instances of slaves ordered sold. Many slave owners divided their chattel among several members of their families. William Lawrence of Flushing left his wife two slaves, his son "one negro and two horses," and his daughter two Negroes. Others left money to make up for a lack of slaves. Mary Ricketts, widow, of New York City, left her youngest daughter "a negro woman and her daughter," while leaving £65 to her eldest daughter "to buy her a negro slave."[12] Masters promised gradual emancipation to ensure slave loyalty. William Walton, a wealthy merchant, freed his slaves only upon the future death of his wife, Cornelia. The slaves then would receive security of £14 per annum and "£25 when of age to purchase tools to enable them to carry on trades."[13]

Wills, which often legitimized long-term understandings, also reflect the relationships between masters and enslaved. John Arientsen, who owned a ferry in Brooklyn, left a Negro girl to his wife and others to his son but promised freedom for "two of my old Negroes, Sambo and his wife, Mary, [who] are to stay on the farm, and are not to be sold, and they are to have every Saturday afternoon to work for themselves." Masters sometimes awarded blacks money or commodities but not freedom. Hannah Titus left one slave "a small legacy and a bible." Other blacks were kept as slaves but given authority to find new masters. Jeannette Evans ordered that "my negro girl, Bess, aged 8, shall live where she sees fit." Quaker Robert Field of Newtown, Queens County, left several Negroes with the injunction that if any were sold, "they may choose their masters."[14] Though more liberal than other testimonials, such agreements nevertheless supported the edifice of slavery.

Enslaved blacks tried to use political splits to advance their freedom by appealing to Crown officials but were unsuccessful in petitions to local residents. Will, a thirty-two-year-old butcher and slave to Joris Elswort of New York City, escaped from his master and changed his name to William Archer. Barrister Jacob Rynier pled Archer's case so persuasively that Elswort declared himself ready to withdraw the case, "seeing the Supreme Court against him." Nonetheless, a jury decided against Archer, ordering that he should be prohibited from "pretending to be free." The court also ordered Rynier to cease carrying on such suits as "to encourage their rising and murdering their masters (of which we have lately most deplorable Examples)," a reference to the murder of the Hallet family in Newtown, Long Island.[15]

As a legal vise closed around free blacks, colonial lawmakers also made life harder for slaves. Additions to the 1712 act passed over the next three decades show sharpening fears within the slavocracy. Amendments included permission to "master and mistress" to punish slaves for infractions, short of "life or limb." The assembly repeated laws passed after the Hallet massacre of 1708. Any attack on a "Freeman or woman Professing Christianity" mandated immediate imprisonment and, potentially, a death sentence. To curtail flight and conspiracy, slaves found in groups of three or more without permits faced

City of New-York, _ss._

A LAW

For Regulating Negroes and Slaves in the Night Time.

BE It Ordained by the Mayor, Recorder, Aldermen and Affiftants of the City of New-York, convened in Common-Council, and it is hereby Ordained by the Authority of the fame, That from hence-forth no Negro, Mulatto or Indian Slave, above the Age of Fourteen Years, do prefume to be or appear in any of the Streets of this City, on the South-fide of the Frefh-Water, in the Night time, above an hour after Sun-fet; And that if any fuch Negro, Mulatto or Indian Slave or Slaves, as aforefaid, fhall be found in any of the Streets of this City, or in any other Place, on the South fide of the Frefh-Water, in the Night-time, above one hour after Sun-fet, without a Lanthorn and lighted Candle in it, fo as the light thereof may be plainly feen (and not in company with his, her or their Mafter or Miftrefs, or fome White Perfon or White Servant belonging to the Family whofe Slave he or fhe is, or in whofe Service he or fhe then are) That then and in fuch cafe it fhall and may be lawful for any of his Majefty's Subjects within the faid City to apprehend fuch Slave or Slaves, not having fuch Lanthorn and Candle, and forth-with carry him, her or them before the Mayor or Recorder, or any one of the Aldermen of the faid City (if at a feafonable hour) and if at an unfeafonable hour, to the Watch-houfe, there to be confined until the next Morning) who are hereby authorized, upon Proof of the Offence, to commit fuch Slave or Slaves to the common Goal, for fuch his, her or their Contempt, and there to remain until the Mafter, Miftrefs or Owner of every fuch Slave or Slaves, fhall pay to the Perfon or Perfons who apprehended and committed every fuch Slave or Slaves, the Sum of _Four Shillings_ current Money of _New-York_, for his, her or their pains and Trouble therein, with Reafonable Charges of Profecution.

And be it Further Ordained by the Authority aforefaid, That every Slave or Slaves that fhall be convicted of the Offence aforefaid, before he, fhe or they be difcharged out of Cuftody, fhall be Whipped at the Publick Whipping-Poft (not exceeding _Forty Lashes_) if defired by the Mafter or Owner of fuch Slave or Slaves.

Provided always, and it is the intent hereof, That if two or more Slaves (Not exceeding the Number of Three) be together in any lawful Employ or Labour for the Service of their Mafter or Miftrefs (and not otherwife) and only one of them have and carry fuch Lanthorn with a lighted Candle therein, the other Slaves in fuch Compay not carrying a Lanthorn and lighted Candle, fhall not be conftrued and intended to be within the meaning and Penalty of this Law, any thing in this Law contained to the contrary hereof in any wife notwithftanding. _Dated at the City-Hall this Two and Twentieth Day of April, in the fourth year of His Majefty's Reign, Annoq, Domini_ 1731.

By Order of Common Council,

Will. Sharpas, _Cl_

A Law for Regulating Negroes and Slaves in the Night Time, 1731. The law provided a summation of the Black Code, with the added injunction that slaves out after dark carry a lantern. It is a good example of a repressive but unenforceable law. (Broadside Collection, Rare Book Room, Miriam and Ira D. Wallach Division of Art, Prints, and Photographs, New York Public Library, Astor, Lenox and Tilden Foundations) forty lashes. Slave testimony was admitted only to inform on rebellious plans by other blacks.[16]

The Demography of Slavery

The bloodshed of the 1712 revolt did not deter white New Yorkers from seeking to import more slaves. Lawmakers did attempt to avoid importing West Indian "refuse" slaves in favor of African chattel. In the decades after 1712, the African population of New York and East Jersey more than doubled as enslaved blacks became the primary laborers for small farmers and urban artisans and domestics for the gentry and their widows. Most of this increase came from forced immigration from Africa, with lesser numbers from the West Indies.

By 1726, the black population of southern New York and East Jersey soared to over 5,500, with the largest concentrations in the counties of New York, Kings, and Queens in New York and Bergen, Somerset, and Monmouth in New Jersey. The most dramatic increases in the colony's countryside were in Queens County, where the black population tripled by 1723; Westchester, where it doubled between 1723 and 1737; and Kings, where blacks constituted a quarter of the population by 1737.[17] In New York City, the black population more than doubled from 630 in 1703 to 1,362 by 1723. After that, growth slowed, but blacks still amounted to over 16 percent of the total population in 1737.[18]

In New Jersey, the first full census in 1726 showed an increase in the proportion of blacks to over 10 percent of the population. Blacks formed significant portions of the population in these counties, ranging from 8 percent in Middlesex and Essex Counties to 18 percent in Bergen County in 1726. Boston slave traders brought other human chattel to New York City in the 1670s.[19] By 1738 the black population of the five easternmost counties of New Jersey increased to 3,071, more than double the estimates made two decades earlier. As in rural New York, the population was skewed toward males.[20]

Disease was an immediate problem for newly arrived Africans. Unaccustomed to northern winters and the region's contagious diseases, Africans quickly succumbed to common ailments such as measles and whooping cough and were devastated by more serious epidemics such as the yellow fever plague, which killed 10 percent of the city's black population in 1698 and struck again in 1731. Slaves were vulnerable because of their inadequate shelter, poor diet, and insufficient clothing, which were worsened by close living conditions, causing morbidity and mortality to rocket upward, creating, according to Ira Berlin, a demographic disaster that in turn necessitated increased imports.[21]

Six factors hindered creation of black nuclear families: small population size, low population density, unbalanced sex ratios, small slaveholdings, disease, and random distribution. The most striking problem was gender imbalance. Women still outnumbered men in New York City. The situation was reversed in the rural areas. Throughout the New York hinterland, males predominated. The most extreme example was Westchester County, where males outnumbered women by 445 to 227 in 1731. This imbalance clearly hurt chances for forming black families. Despite the soaring number of Africans in the two colonies, finding a mate and sustaining a stable marriage proved difficult for blacks.[22]

Slaves were spread throughout East Jersey with usually no more than three blacks per farm. Generally young males predominated, and gender imbalances in Monmouth County were nearly two to one and in Bergen County three to two. Growth rates averaged above 5 percent annually, and the black population of Somerset County increased by nearly 8 percent.[23] The clear preference for black males as agricultural laborers in rural areas meant that African males had to travel to town in search of female companionship, let alone marriage. Although the total black population was growing, the region was also expanding, making visits from the farther reaches more arduous than ever.[24]

The natural life cycle of enslaved blacks in and around New York was fraught with peril and paradox. Small farm and urban slaveholding meant that few bondspeople could expect to live with relatives for much of their lives. Masters regarded children, who constituted as much as 40 percent of all slaves, as unwanted dependents with little work value until after puberty. Pregnant women were regarded with disfavor. At the same time, masters frequently sold children with adults to enhance the deal. Few children lived with either parent after the age of six. Children were overrepresented in mortality rates.[25]

Slave marriage had no legal standing until 1809 so the best that most couples could hope for was to live fairly close to each other. Family slavery, so popular in East Jersey, meant that couples often had to seek permission from related patriarchal masters to spend any time together. The sexual imbalance required slaves to travel sizable distances for visits. Slave marriage around New York virtually meant a separated or mutilated union. As much as 13 percent of the region's slaves never found partners. Status was another factor; the rarity of free blacks in the region meant that almost all marriages were between slaves, which meant that masters ultimately decided whether the union would occur or continue. Slaves lucky enough to live under the same roof always had to worry about being sold separately. Venture Smith was sold away from his wife and child as punishment for running away. Later, Smith bought himself and his family; while they were enslaved, his wife and he shared a home for only seven of twenty-one years. Smith's case was unusual; the ordinary slave husband had to bargain with a master for visiting time to his wife and family. Restrictive laws and bad weather made visits all the harder.[26]

The problems incurred by human bondage meant that biological relationships had to transcend local boundaries, with "abroad" marriages and distant, scattered children. Enslaved residents often performed the practical, pedestrian tasks of rearing other people's children, making visits from actual parents a special event. What seemed disorderly behavior to slave masters was a simple acceptance of harsh reality and the building of a surrogate family. Such families were especially important in larger slave units of several unrelated adults and children.[27]

For Africans, the solution to these problems lay in their home culture. John Bartow, an SPG missionary in Westchester, noted in 1725 that "they marry after their heathen way." Unfortunately for Bartow's sensibilities, very few black marriages were held in Protestant churches in the colonial period, leaving ceremonial powers to Africans themselves. Christian neglect allowed for the retention of African traditions of polygamy. Serial marriage among blacks undoubtedly existed, with "polygamy contracted before baptism when none or neither of the wives will accept a divorce." The nature of slavery exacerbated this problem, argued the Reverend John Sharpe, for when one partner was sold one hundred miles away, they have "not the continence to persevere single." Their marriages were "performed by mutual consent without the blessing of the church." While some blacks agreed to "break by mutual consent their Negro Marriages as I may call it and marry a Christian spouse," Sharpe noted the difficulty of "how to proceed without giving scandal or matter of temptation."[28]

Polygamy, practiced in all the African cultures represented in New York and New Jersey, offered significant social insurance for black men and women. For rural males living in a region with a strong gender imbalance, polygamy offered release from sexual uncertainty and from anxiety over procreation. For women, the unmarried state was less worrisome than being childless. Rather than diminishing the family, as Anglicans fretted, polygamy actually fostered the power of the family group.[29]

Despite the obstacles to formation of nuclear families in the region stemming from small slaveholdings, distance between marital partners, slave sales, and gender imbalance, blacks did reproduce. The number of children per woman was approximately the same for white and black women throughout this era, and black women actually produced more children by 1746.[30] New York and New Jersey's slave populations were not growing as fast as those in South Carolina and Virginia, but the rate of increase closely matched that of the local white population. In counties where slavery was the most important labor form, such as Kings and Queens in New York and Bergen, Somerset, and Monmouth in New Jersey, the black population never dropped below 10 percent of the total population in the eighteenth century.[31]

The Slave Trade

When natural reproduction could not fill the economy's voracious desire for black chattel, masters turned to the international slave trade. When the Spanish government awarded English slave traders access to its West Indian colonies in 1714, the English quickly expanded their operations on the West Coast of Africa. The increased trade meant that more slaves were available to the mid-Atlantic colonies.[32] Whether shipped directly from Africa or the West Indies, almost seven thousand blacks entered New York and upward of six hundred passed through the port of Perth Amboy, New Jersey, between 1717 and 1757.[33]

Mid-Atlantic slave owners preferred to purchase slaves directly from Africa. After the slave revolt of 1712, the two colonial legislatures passed duties in 1714 discriminating against West Indian blacks in favor of Africans. This law was motivated by a perception that West Indian slaves were too prone to rebellion. Governor Hunter explained that the differential duty on West Indian slave imports was "to discourage an Importation to the Plantations, by which we are supplied with the refuse of their Negroes and such malefactors as would have suffered death in the Places from when they came, had not the avarice of their Owners, saved them from the Publick Justice by an Early Transportation from these parts; where they not often fail of repeating their Crimes."[34]

That desire did not immediately translate into reality, and the two colonies continued to rely on sources from the West Indies. From 1715 until 1741, the year of the next revolt, New Yorkers imported at least 3,411 slaves. The largest number came from Jamaica, then from the African coast, Barbados, and Antigua, colonies characterized by staple crop economies, heavy slave mortality, little cultural interaction between whites and blacks, and repression.[35] Many transactions involved young, healthy slaves, resident in the West Indies a few years and sent north on consignment in small lots.[36] Isaac Bobin, private secretary to Lieutenant Governor George Clarke, then secretary of the province of New York, conducted a search for the governor in the 1720s for a "Lusty Negro," who "in all Manner of Household Affairs is no Stranger." After one prospective purchase was rejected because of his ignorance of "matters belonging to the field," Bobin encouraged Clarke by noting that "vessels are dayly expected from the West Indies with negroes." Eventually Bobin acquired a "young Negro wench" in Perth Amboy. Three months later he was on the market again because the black woman "has a great itch to running away."[37]

Blacks brought in singly had very different passages than those imported by the hundreds. Ships bringing individual blacks to New York and New Jersey from the West Indies used them as sailors or hands. Such seafaring experience was not only invaluable to blacks planning future escapes but also brought them into contact with sympathetic whites. The social gap between colonial blacks and whites on the sea in this era was small.[38]

By the second decade of the eighteenth century, New York City merchants had established regular deliveries directly from Africa. Six vessels transported more than 100 Africans each per trip to New York and New Jersey between 1715 and 1741, all from the "Coast of Guinea."[39] Captain Dennis Downing of the *Crown Galley* had left Madagascar in early 1721 with 41 men, 31 women, 142 boys, and 40 girls, a tightly packed cargo of 254 humans. After a stop for supplies in Brazil, the vessel suffered an eight-week voyage to Barbados, by which time half of the slaves had died in the five months since departure. After a lengthy stop in Barbados, Downing arrived in New York with his cargo. His sales receipts show the wide variety of slave purchasers in the colony. Ninety-five New Yorkers stepped forward to buy 106 slaves; 11 slaves were too ill for sale. Most purchasers were prosperous citizens, including Joseph Reade, a merchant; Rip Van Dam, the longtime city recorder; Governor William Burnet; merchants Philip Schuyler and

William Beekman; and lawyer James Alexander. Other buyers were such ordinary New Yorkers as tavern keepers, farmers, and artisans.[40]

Encouraged by this international traffic, Francis Harrison, a customs official in New York City who had previously worked in the slave factories on the West Coast of Africa, offered a plan in 1724 to the English government for increasing shipments of slaves into New York. Harrison noted the small number of direct imports from Africa, chiefly because of the tariff and apprehensions of "pyrates." Imports into New York and New Jersey had been extremely slow in the past few years and "seldom more than 2 or 3 at a time." Conducting a census at his own expense, Harrison counted 34,393 white people and 6,171 "blacks young and old." From the latter total he deducted 445 free negroes (a very high estimate) and those "old and past service." He also subtracted 1,087 children under the age of eight. He concluded that 4,639 useful blacks remained in a proportion of two to eleven to the white population. In a colony where freeholders "manure no land but their own," Harrison identified slaves as the key "portion which young men have from their parents or received with their wives when they set out in the world." Harrison found little local interest in indentured servants. The people of New York "(especially the Dutch who are ¾ of this colony) are unwilling or rather in cases of necessity only take any white servants knowing by experience from their neighbors of Virginia & Maryland &ct that the worst in the world come out of Bridewell and Newgate." Freeholders, he wrote, were "so used to property and to Command, that they will rather starve than serve under any roof but their own." He forecast that easy profits could come by supplying "Negroes not exceeding 300 aged 14 to 28 or thereabouts" arriving in the summer to produce £45 to £46 and better per head. He contended that the only obstacle was the duty placed on direct imports.[41]

Although there is no official confirmation, Harrison's words of encouragement apparently found ready listeners in New York. In the second quarter of the eighteenth century, New York merchants preferred large shipments of slaves from Africa over those from the West Indies. In 1725, 59 slaves arrived from Africa in a Rhode Island slaver.[42] The *Catherine,* owned by John Watts of New York City and Arent Schuyler, a large slaveholder in Bergen County, landed in Perth Amboy in the summer of 1731 and in New York a few weeks later.[43] Two years later the *Catherine* returned with a second load of 100 slaves, docking at Perth Amboy and then New York City. The first stop was not only an attempt to spur shipping at the New Jersey port but also a means by which Schuyler, a large consumer and seller of slaves, could avoid the duty in the New York colony. The log for the second voyage of the *Catherine* shows the method of acquiring large shiploads of slaves for northern ports. The *Catherine* departed from New York on September 6, 1732. By November 24, 1732, Captain Jasper Farmer was negotiating along the West Coast of Africa, trading for 73 slaves, rice, and malagete pepper. After sailing along the coast for two weeks, the *Catherine*'s crew probed a river, purchasing wood, meat, and more slaves. The slavers bought humans all along the coast, eventually going as far south as Angola, from which it finally turned homeward with 257 slaves. Of these, 10 men, a woman, 4 boys, and 2 girls died en route. The boat landed 130 slaves in Perth Amboy and arrived in New York a few weeks later.[44]

The black immigrants of 1715–41, whether they arrived singly or in large parcels, reinforced African cultures in the New York and New Jersey region. While Barbados and Jamaica absorbed the greatest numbers of blacks from the West Coast of Africa, smaller ports such as New York City and Perth Amboy received both direct imports and seasoned slaves.[45] The national origins of these slaves were similar to those of previous generations of Africans in New York and East Jersey. Occasionally pirates brought in Madagascar slaves. The Gold Coast factories of Whydah and Elmina produced Kwa, Ewe, and Fanti nationals; from the Senegambia came Mandingoes, Fulas, Wolofs, and Jolas. From Benin and the area of Nigeria came primarily Aja, Yoruba, and, to a lesser extent, Nupe and Hausa. The southwest African ports of Luanda, Molembo, and Benguela sold slaves secured from the Kasanje, Mbondo, and Mbailundu regions of Angola and Kongo.[46] This rapid influx of Africans clearly disturbed colonial leaders. In 1734 Governor William Cosby's address to the colonial assembly stressed that "whilst the neighboring provinces are filled with honest, useful, laborious white people, the truest riches of a country, this province seems regardless of the vast disadvantages that attend too great importation of Negroes and convicts."[47]

The African societies producing these slaves were undergoing severe social dislocation. The "moving frontier" of slavery pushed further and further inland as new African political powers replaced and extirpated older cultures. Many of the slaves brought to New York and New Jersey were refugees from the turmoil in Africa and had barely escaped the hazards of the Middle Passage. They were survivors of sev-

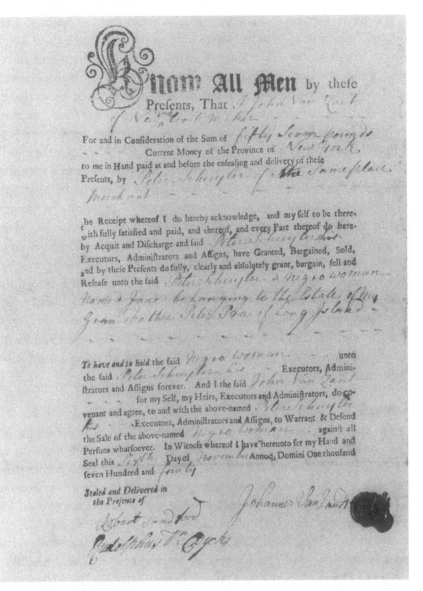

Bill of sale for a black woman, New York, 1740. A standard deed of sale, recording the purchase of one human being by another. (Courtesy of the New York State Library)

eral catastrophes, grimly resolute against the terrors of life. Although some arrived in America broken in body and spirit, others were determined to survive. Upon arrival in the mid-Atlantic, these Africans had more in common with each other than did the contentious melange of English, Scots-Irish, Dutch, Swedes, French, and Sephardic Jews who populated the region.[48]

Harder to document than the oceanic trade was the internal mar-keting of slaves at merchant houses such as Arent Schuyler's or Jacob Walton's and at the Meal Market in lower Manhattan, where slaves were hired out and sold permanently and in weekly transactions.[49] Sales could occur for many reasons. Slaves were used as currency and collateral, became security for mortgages, and were used to raise cash and repay debts. Masters often no longer needed their labor, sold women because they bore children, or sold children because they were not financial assets. Inability to control slaves' habits was a common reason for sales, suggesting that discontentment among bondspeople could force a transaction. Most slaves were sold individually, though at times efforts were made to preserve families. The price per slave ranged from £45 to £70 for healthy males and females. The success of private sales depended not only on the buyer's creditworthiness but on the slave's reputation or willingness to accept a new master. In the countryside, few slave sales were public. On Long Island, masters not only hired out and sold slaves but permitted slaves to seek new mas-ters themselves. The Lloyd family of Queens County consulted slaves about annual fees for hiring. Nearly 10 percent of Long Island sales were by blacks seeking to free family members.[50]

Work

The spread of slavery throughout New York and East Jersey meant that enslaved blacks could be found in virtually every segment of the economy. In the rural counties, most slaves did farm and domes-tic work. As slaves became the core workers in the rural environs of New York, their owners did not change the production process and create large southern-style plantations but used slaves as jacks-of-all-trades in house and field. New Jersey's farmers concentrated on grow-ing wheat, corn, and rye, as well as keeping orchards and meadow-lands. In Dutch communities, slaves herded cattle, pigs, and horses. Other chores included barrel-making, carting, shoemaking, carpentry, and preparing meats, poultry, and fish for cooking. On these farms, slaves labored next to free whites. The difference, of course, between enslaved and free wage laborers was mobility. Free wage laborers could choose masters, own land, and plan for the future. The only mobility for slaves occurred when they were sold. In the countryside, passed from one owner to the next, slaves learned new skills and often per-formed several tasks on a farm. The mercurial skills of rural slaves are evident in runaway notices. Stoffels, for instance, who fled from his mistress in Monmouth County in 1734, had experience as a house carpenter, cooper, wheelwright, and butcher. As Edgar McManus has observed, virtually the only difference between skilled free white and enslaved black workers was their degree of liberty. In the cities, urban slaves listed skills suitable for work in shipping yards, leather dressing, milling, stonework, shopkeeping, and even fine artisanry like goldsmithing. Some were skilled carpenters. Henry Lloyd reported an offer of a "Strong healthy Negro fellow," raised in a ship carpenter's yard as a "sawyer & boarer of holes and sometimes employ'd at the Smiths." Andrew Saxon, who fled from Jacobus Van Cortlandt of New York City in 1733, "is a carpenter and a cooper by trade, and has a Broad-Ax with him, a Two-foot rule, and a Howell-hovel." The diversity of such skills meant that, while identified as slaves by law, the identity of each bondsman and woman was often much more complicated than by reference to their work.[51]

White artisans resisted the trend toward diversity among slaves. One difficulty white tradesmen faced was the economic advantage to owners of hiring out their slaves. Sufficient numbers of blacks worked as coopers in New York City in 1737 to prompt local coopers to complain of the "pernicious custom of breeding slaves to trades whereby the honest and industrious tradesmen are reduced to poverty for want of employ." Lieutenant Governor Clarke agreed with them and condemned slave competition, which "forced many of us to seek their living in other countries." But the assembly refused to act. One occupation in New York City was able to restrict blacks. Carting, an integrated trade in Philadelphia and in southern cities, remained rigidly segregated in New York, keeping slaves and free blacks from working in this job.[52]

Advertisements for slave hiring were abundant in this period. Having valuable skills could earn enslaved blacks a degree of freedom. Jack, a slave of the Lloyd family, lived freely in New York City, provided that he paid his mistress £12 and supported himself. Hiring was also used to rid a family of a troublesome slave. Aurelia, a slave of the Lloyd family, was hired out as a spinner in 1726. After her term was finished, Aurelia refused to return to her master, Henry Lloyd, in Queens County. Lloyd angrily commented that he was "well used to Negroes resolutions" and agreed to let her be hired again. Although Aurelia was a valuable slave, Lloyd sold her three years later.[53]

Religion and Acculturation

As the African population grew, political need for acculturation to Christianity increased. For Anglican purposes, the slave revolt of 1712 was a disaster. Elias Neau now had to work under a cloud of suspicion, with William Vesey and Anglican colleagues regarding his methods as dangerous. In the aftermath of the revolt, missionaries reported distrust of baptism for political reasons.[54] In 1713, the chaplain of the fort, the Reverend John Sharpe, commented on the still prevalent belief among blacks that "Christianity would make them free," despite legislation designed to prevent that, arguing that only "Spanish Negroes and Mullatoes" could claim such emancipation. Sharpe also noted an argument that "Christianity makes them rather worse than better," a view greatly expanded by the "late barbarous massacre attempted by the blacks."[55] Missionaries in the countryside experienced sustained hostility from slave owners toward black baptism. In Westchester County, fifteen years after the revolt, James Wetmore reported to the SPG that "people don't trust [slaves] in companion any more" and noted that "some have pretense of going to catechism and have taken opportunity to absent themselves from their masters many days." To combat this tendency, masters instructed their slaves at home, saying that "the blacks learned more mischief than good" at the school.[56] The Reverend Robert Jenney of Rye, New York, argued that most masters regarded baptism of slaves as useless and damaging to order and that slaves saw baptism as a ticket to manumission. In 1726, the Reverend Thomas Stoddard in Brookhaven wrote that the "proprietors of the poor slaves are averse to baptism because of the 1712 conspiracy." Stoddard repeated rumors that the conspiracy was "secretly carried on for a year . . . and was executed by those who have been instructed."[57]

Tensions over his mission to blacks ended with Neau's death in 1722.[58] He had sustained the school despite social and bureaucratic opposition. For slaves, Neau was the epitome of godly governance. Although Neau did not question slavery and helped pass a law that protected the system, his school was a sympathetic world in which blacks could experience Christianity, learn the precious skills of reading and writing, and practice their beliefs openly and collectively.

After Neau's death, Vesey sought to change the direction of the school, asking the SPG for a priest "to officiate . . . with the children and servants." William Huddleston, appointed in 1722, kept a strict record of attendance and penalized tardiness by slaves, helping to dispel white prejudice against the school. Huddleston reported that "Swarms of Negroes come about my door and asking if I would be pleased to teach them and build on Mr. Neau's foundation." In 1726 Huddleston's successor, the Reverend James Wetmore, a cleric lacking any experience with slaves, reported that "few slaves . . . constantly attend" and left within a year to take a new post in Westchester County.[59] In the years that followed, a series of Anglican priests ministered to the slaves. The schoolmaster's job became a lowly rung on the career ladder for young Anglican clerics who performed the tasks with little enthusiasm and withdrew when a promotion beckoned. In their new jobs they rarely catechized blacks. In the decade after Neau's death, Anglicans gave little assistance to blacks.[60]

Most missionaries felt little obligation toward slaves and believed Neau succeeded largely because of his proximity to urban slaves. In a typical letter, John Thomas of Hempstead reminded the society that Neau's "business is wholly with the slaves at New York City where they live contiguously and where they come to his house."[61] Even after Neau's death, despite the reluctance of local missionaries to catechize blacks, the London offices of the SPG kept up a steady stream of instructions. In 1730 the bishop of London appealed to colonial clerics and slave owners to consider blacks "not barely as slaves and upon the same level with laboring beasts but as Men-Slaves and Women-Slaves, who have the same Frame and Faculties as yourselves and have Souls Capable of being made eternally happy, and Reason and Understanding to receive Instruction to it." Once again, imperial edicts conflicted with local perceptions and fears.[62]

Missionaries learned to accommodate local anxieties while fulfilling the orders of the faith. The Reverend Richard Charleton operated the Trinity Church school from 1733 until 1747. He kept meticulous attendance rosters, constructed a syllabus more palatable to the wishes of local slave masters, and did little without the consent of masters. The Trinity school became a training ground for carefully selected domestics, for whom education was more an advertisement of their employer's wealth and breeding than of their own abilities. Black scholars studied from a missionary library that included Bibles, Books of Common Prayer, church catechisms, and spelling books. These books, available in multiple copies for home study, were translated into Dutch, French, and Indian languages. Charleton's successes, he believed, inspired spiritual knowledge among the slaves which "might make many white people (who have had more happy opportunities of instruction) blush, were they present at their examinations."[63]

Seventy black students attended Charleton's school, and fifteen to twenty baptisms occurred annually. The skills required of candidates for baptism included literacy, memorization, and public theological explication. After Charleton's recovery from illness in mid-1744, he was assisted by Joseph Hildreth, who taught literacy through study of the Bible and psalm-singing. In 1747 Charleton, exhausted by his endeavors, transferred to Staten Island, where he served as cleric for St. Andrew's. He baptized blacks only occasionally in the years before his death in 1777.[64]

Blacks encountered various other European faiths. Members of the Society of Friends (Quakers), a denomination with heavy representation on Long Island and in mid-Jersey and influential in New York City, continued to use slaves on farms and in households. Although radical Friends such as John Hepburn and John Sandiford initiated a campaign to cleanse the church of slavery in this period, most Quakers kept their slaves. Indicative of this pattern is the fact that over half of the members of the Shrewsbury Meeting in Monmouth County bequeathed slaves to relatives before 1741. Quaker reforms were still in the future.[65]

Two European faiths were sufficiently open to black membership as to be considered interracial communities. The Lutheran Church, in particular, attracted rural blacks. Separated by language and culture from Anglican influences and strongly pietist in rural regions, Lutherans gave free blacks high-ranking positions in their churches. Arie Van Guinee came to New York City from Surinam as a free man in 1705 and, with his wife, joined the Lutheran congregation in New York City under the Reverend Justus Falckner. A few years later Van Guinee moved to the Raritan Valley in New Jersey, where he hosted the first recorded Lutheran service in the area in 1714. Van Guinee assisted in the baptisms of his niece and nephew. He and his family purchased sizable plots of land over the years, and he became a man of considerable means and influence in the church. In 1735 he married a second wife, Margareetje Peters, granddaughter of Solomon Peters, in Hackensack.[66] Lutheran liberality attracted other descendants of the original free blacks. Families whose children appear in church registers include the Matthys, Anthonys, Franciscos, and Peterses, whose ancestries can be traced to the first Angolans in the mid-seventeenth century. Other important Lutheran free black families included the Jacksons and Cromwells.[67]

The Moravian Church, whose American territory lay largely in Pennsylvania and in North Carolina, permitted black conversion in East Jersey. Andrew, the communicant member of the Moravian church in Bethlehem, Pennsylvania, prepared a memoir telling of his capture from the Igbo nation in what is now southeastern Nigeria and sale to a merchant in New York City in 1741. After being resold to a Moravian merchant named Thomas Noble, Andrew learned to read the Bible and finally convinced Noble to allow him to be baptized. The ceremony was held in Bethlehem, where Andrew joined the communal congregation and its choir. He married a free black Moravian named Magdalena with whom he had three children. He died in 1779.[68]

The Dutch Reformed Church was far less liberal. Cultural divisions between the urbane Church of England and rural Dutch pietism widened. Dark suspicions that slave baptism inspired the revolt of 1712 darkened Dutch pietist attitudes toward English rule and Anglicanism.[69] In rural East Jersey, Theodore Frelinghuysen's evangelical movement emphasized spiritual rebirth, but older beliefs such as predestinarianism restrained Dutch confidence in blacks' spiritual potential. Suspicion of Anglican missionary efforts centered around customary beliefs about baptism and emancipation.[70]

To avoid political entanglements, the Dutch used Pinkster, their version of Pentecost, as their primary religious interaction with Africans. Widely observed as a sacred and folk holiday throughout Europe, Pentecost ranks among the great festivals of Christianity.[71] Pinkster functioned both as an agriculturally based community gathering and as a deeply private religious occasion. Observance of Christ's sacrifice and resurrection occurred when the Holy Ghost rushed through the heart or home on a "Holy Wind," compelling powerful preaching and prophesying by males and females of any caste and provoking "speaking in tongues" by the participants. "Holy Wind" ecstasy happened when the participant, whether master or slave, became a "mouthpiece of God." [72]

The observance of Pinkster created a momentary equality and community among Africans and Dutch and was a safety valve for household tensions. More important, it served a greater purpose for Dutch and Africans. Ecstatic moments of the "Holy Wind" and speaking in tongues were a form of spiritual conversion which replaced church baptisms. Dutch slave owners could accept their slaves into the sanctity of the faith without apprehension about the effects of Anglican baptism on slaves' expectation of emancipation. Among slaves, moreover, Pinkster ceremonies sustained promises of sacred equality and nurtured their spiritual sensibility. Pinkster resembled the pietistic ceremonies at Elias Neau's school, differing from later Anglican education, which emphasized acculturation. Pinkster services did not require perfect English, literacy, or command of Scripture. Observed in nearly all the denominations in the mid-Atlantic, Pinkster or Whitsuntide became a social conversation among English, Dutch, German, and African cultures, a union possible only in New York and New Jersey.[73]

Blacks could also use Pinkster for their own purposes. A satire that appeared in the *New-York Weekly Journal* in 1737 noted use of African musical instruments during Pinkster. Africans from the Guinea Coast in particular were adept at drums and stringed instruments. Bangars, rattles, and fiddles were common at Pinkster festivals. Performance on the fiddle was very different from European methods, with a highly percussive style in which the musician plucked the bow energetically. Pinkster songs, with their emphasis on role reversal, complemented African songs and dances of derision. Finally, the use of several instruments at Pinkster created an orchestral style akin to the music of an African festival.[74]

The article noted that blacks were forming according to their "nations." Such nationhood did not allude to specific African ethnicity but to associations of blacks formed on shipboard or in the Americas. Most common in Latin America, nations were associations of people from similar African cultural areas who typically came together to bury the dead and conduct festivals. In a large celebration such as Pinkster, when the whole African American community might assemble, blacks divided up by these nations, which served otherwise as rudimentary self-help organizations and even as governments.[75]

Slave Culture and Black Revolt

Celebrations such as Pinkster are evidence that enslaved Africans in the mid-Atlantic were moving from tribal affiliation to a new concept of nationhood based on slave culture. The cruelest punishments by the master class could not suppress this emerging identity. Although in the years following the 1712 revolt, authorities stepped up the pace and level of punishments for black crime, poor whites and blacks were skirting the laws. Whippings in series were ordered for Nan and Tom, the Negro men of John Taylor, for "being drunk on the Sabbath."[76]

Although city authorities showed their zeal for prosecuting white fences and black thieves, the regularity of arrests demonstrates the ineffectiveness of the law as a deterrent. Two examples indicate the freedom blacks enjoyed at convivial alehouses. In August 1714 Mary Wakeum, a widow, was indicted for keeping an alehouse in the west ward, "where there is drinking, swearing, playing of unlawful games and entertaining of slaves." Peter the Doctor, who barely escaped execution during the 1712 conspiracy, was arrested and charged with entertaining Sarah, the slave of merchant William Walton, and other slaves in August 1715.[77]

Despite the laws against selling liquor to slaves, tavern keepers and grocers found the profits irresistible. In the countryside, blacks purchased rum without much difficulty. Account books from rural New Jersey record free blacks and slaves dropping by to pick up gallons of rum. Occasionally, the tapster noted the master's name; at other times he could not even identify the slave. In New York, masters' surveillance was sufficiently weak that magistrates issued periodic proclamations that blacks were not allowed out after dark without a lantern.[78] Stealing meat, grain, and other commodities was not simply a release of tension or means of survival, as has been described in histories of the southern slave experience. When mixed with rumors of impending royal action freeing the slaves, animosities between slave owners and their chattel, and the autonomy of isolated slave quarters, petty crime could lead to revolutionary action.[79]

The slave culture soon turned conspiratorial. Two slave plots were reported in the provinces between 1712 and 1741. The first was in 1721, when New York City's Common Council heard evidence, now lost, from several justices about a "supposed designed insurrection of the Negroes within this Citty." Over the next few years, various municipalities passed legislation in an attempt to curtail nocturnal gatherings of blacks. In 1731, for example, New York City's lawmakers required that any slave out after dark carry a lantern and barred meetings of more than three slaves. Consistent complaints are indicative of how ineffective such laws were.[80]

A more substantial plot occurred in Somerset County in eastern New Jersey in 1734. One Reynolds of Raritan uncovered the plot when speaking to a tipsy slave on the road. The slave informed Reynolds that the "Englishmen were generally a pack of Villains and Kept the Negroes as Slaves, Contrary to a Positive Order from King George, sent to the G—— of New York, to set them free, which they said the G——

intended to do but was prevented by his C—— and A——," which was the reason for the present disputes. Reynolds remonstrated with the slave, who told him that "he was as good a Man as himself, and that in a little time he should be convinced of it." Alarmed, Reynolds had the slave arrested. Quickly, "he and another Negro [were] taken up, Tryed, Condemned and one Hang'd." About thirty alleged conspirators were apprehended. Some "had their ears cut off and the others whipt. . . . Several of them had poison found about them." The *New-York Gazette* printed an extensive account of the plan and its causes. Examination revealed a plot "for every Negro in each family to rise at midnight, Cut the throats of their Masters and Sons, but not to meddle with the women, whom they intended to ravish and plunder the next day, and then set all the houses and barns on fire, kill all the draught horses and secure the best Saddle Horses for their flight towards the Indians in the French Interest." Blacks, reported the newspaper, "met at Colonel Thomas L——'s slave quarters which were a dangerous distance from his main house." These quarters were a "Rendevouze for the Negroes and . . . a pest to the neighborhood by encouraging the Neighbors Negroes to steal from their Masters both Beef, Pork, Wheat, Fowles, wherewith they [hold] feasts and junkets," in companies of many hundreds. It was at one of these feasts that their "Design of Rising was agreed." The chronicler went on to recall the "great calamity and Desolation there was in the City of New York some years since" and cited the recent uprisings on St. John's and Jamaica as examples of the "great fatality" which attends the "English Dominion in America," by "too great a Number of that Unchristian and barbarous People being imported and then too much indulged in their vices." The black population apparently believed that newly arrived governors had orders to free Christianized slaves, a rumor that sparked insurrection in Virginia in 1730.[81]

Equally threatening were slaves' attacks on their masters. On January 9, 1739, for example, in Rocky Hill, Somerset County, New Jersey, Robert Hooper's slave, "being ordered by the Overseer's wife to bring in some wood and make fire, he replied in a surly tone that he would make fire enough and pursued her with an axe." The woman succeeded in shutting the door against him but "unhappily locked her little son out, him the Negro struck so that the whole breadth of the Bitt of the Axe entered the Cavity of the body between the shoulders and the Lower part of the Neck." The slave then set fire to the barn, burning it and over one thousand bushels of grain. He was captured and burned at the stake three days later.[82] Another terror was poisoning. Two slaves were jailed and then executed for an attempt to poison a master near Trenton in March 1738. The pair was caught after trying to persuade a third slave of the "Efficacy of the Drug," telling him that "Mr. Trent, and two of his sons, Mr. Lambert and two of his wives and sundry other persons were removed by their slaves in this fashion," using "Arsenick and an unknown kind of root."[83]

Other violent crimes were severely punished. On January 20, 1734, a Mr. Vallet's Negro attempted "to ravish a young woman of 14–15 in New York City." When she recognized him, he "desisted and ran away." On Monday, January 21, he was apprehended; on "Tuesday he had his trial." In accordance with the Special Trials Act, three justices of the peace and six freeholders, using "some other evidence," convicted the slave. On Thursday, he was "burnt accordingly in the presence of numerous company of spectators, the great part of which were the black tribe."[84]

Colonists in New York and New Jersey also worried about slave revolts throughout the Western Hemisphere and off the coast of Africa. During the 1730s, local newspapers gave much coverage to reports about insurrections in Virginia, maroonage and impregnable slave forts in Jamaica, St. John's, St. Kitts, and Antigua, and uprisings on slave ships. By 1739, New York and other American colonies were caught in the middle of England's war with France and Spain. Known as King George's War or the War of Jenkins's Ear, the conflict made New Yorkers all the more anxious about international influence on their bondspeople.[85]

In this fearful context blacks in New York and New Jersey shook white society to its roots in the famous slave conspiracy of 1741. Whites suspected a plot after Fort George in New York City burned to the ground. In succeeding days, fires destroyed buildings in New York City and New Jersey and on Long Island. Firefighters in the city heard one slave mutter, "Fire, Fire, Scorch, Scorch, A LITTLE, damn it, By-And-By," then throw up his hands and laugh. Lieutenant Governor George Clarke reported to the Board of Trade that blacks in New York and New Jersey conspired to burn the fort and farms as a prelude to destruction of the town and massacre of the whites. He argued that blacks hatched their plans in taverns run by treasonous whites interested in criminal organization and conspiring with the Spanish. After detection of the conspiracy, New York's government tried dozens of slaves and four whites for capital offenses. Several blacks were burned

A
JOURNAL
OF THE
PROCEEDINGS
IN
The Detection of the Conspiracy
FORMED BY
Some *White* People, in Conjunction with *Negro* and other *Slaves*,

FOR
Burning the City of *NEW-YORK* in AMERICA,
And Murdering the Inhabitants.

Which Conspiracy was partly put in Execution, by Burning His Majesty's House in Fort GEORGE, within the said City, on Wednesday the Eighteenth of *March*, 1741. and setting Fire to several Dwelling and other Houses there, within a few Days succeeding. And by another Attempt made in Prosecution of the same infernal Scheme, by putting Fire between two other Dwelling-Houses within the said City, on the Fifteenth Day of *February*, 1742; which was accidentally and timely discovered and extinguished.

CONTAINING,

I. A NARRATIVE of the Trials, Condemnations, Executions, and Behaviour of the several Criminals, at the Gallows and Stake, with their *Speeches* and *Confessions*; with Notes, Observations and Reflections occasionally interspersed throughout the Whole.

II. AN APPENDIX, wherein is set forth some additional Evidence concerning the said Conspiracy and Conspirators, which has come to Light since their Trials and Executions.

III. LISTS of the several Persons (Whites and Blacks) committed on Account of the Conspiracy; and of the several Criminals executed; and of those transported, with the Places whereto.

By the Recorder of the City of NEW-YORK.

Quid facient Domini, audent cum talia Fures? Virg. Ecl.

NEW-YORK:
Printed by *James Parker*, at the New Printing-Office, 1744.

Title Page of Daniel Horsmanden's Journal of the Proceedings, *the famous account of the trials of enslaved blacks who conspired to take over New York City in 1741. The book is also an amazing source for black culture in mid-eighteenth-century America. (Courtesy of the Gilder Lehrman Collection on deposit at the Pierpont Morgan Library, New York, GLC 4205)* at the stake in Hackensack and Newark for arson connected with the events in New York City.[86]

Executions by immolation and hanging occurred almost daily for several months. In contrast to the insurrection of 1712, there was no division between colonial and imperial authorities. Lieutenant Governor Clarke, who had barely gained his post during fierce political battles in 1736, was not about to offend local authorities on this issue, as Robert Hunter had done in 1712. Clarke quickly issued a proclamation awarding £100, a pardon, and manumission to any slave giving important evidence. He extended the sessions of the New York Supreme Court long after their normal termination to complete the trials. In response to Clarke's transmission of several confessions by blacks and reports of the numerous executions, the Board of Trade in London applauded his efforts and hoped that they "put an effectual stop to this Pernicious Conspiracy." The board commended Clarke for the "severity you have shown to those concerned."[87]

Although the revolt has received much attention, until very recently few historians have credited slaves with a true conspiracy.[88] A significant exception was W. E. B. Du Bois, who, early in this century, described the 1741 episode as a prime example of the "movement of small knots of conspirators." Concentrating on environmental factors such as harsh winters and food shortages, local racial antagonisms, and the presence of kidnapped Spanish blacks, scholars now view the conspiracy as violent resistance against slavery.[89]

Criticism of Daniel Horsmanden's *Journal of the Proceedings in the Detection of the Conspiracy Formed by Some White People in Conjunction with Negro and Other Slaves for Burning the City of New York and Murdering the Inhabitants,* the official trial record, has focused on the testimony of an indentured servant named Mary Burton and on the witness of frightened slaves threatened with death penalties and thus eager to tell whites what they wished to hear. But much evidence rings with the authority of truth.[90] Horsmanden's *Journal* contains ample signs of a flourishing slave culture of drinking, dancing, and music playing. The *Journal* links theft, gambling, arson, murder, and poisoning to black resistance. Testimony by slaves and other witnesses also uncovers recurring tensions over the volatile issue of baptism and its linkages to emancipation. Horsmanden's *Journal* further indicates that, unlike in the 1712 revolt, whites played key roles. The conspirators included Irish, English, French, and Dutch in addition to Africans and Hispanic Americans. The conspiracy in New York can also be seen in the context of international disorder, linking it with slave revolts in South Carolina, Antigua, and Jamaica.

As Lieutenant Governor Clarke feared, the plot was hatched in the taverns and workplaces of poor whites and blacks. John Hughson, a tavern keeper and woodcutter, often spent time in the forests of New Jersey with teams of blacks "who brought him wood every night." At his tavern across the street from the homes of these black woodcutters, Hughson fenced stolen goods from blacks. His tavern became famous for its Sunday "great feasts," which began after church and continued long into the evening. Hughson served quarters of mutton, goose, and other fowl to be washed down with rum, punch, cider, and beer. Blacks flocked to Hughson's, Comfort's, and other alehouses on Sundays and holidays for parties featuring fiddles and dancing. After the merrymaking, Hughson and leading blacks swore new confederates into the conspiracy, using ceremonies involving kissing the Bible and Book of Common Prayer, showing knives, and stepping inside a chalk circle to swear allegiance until death.[91]

Most threatening to the Protestant colonials was the Catholicism of slaves. Ringleaders in the 1741 conspiracy included illegally enslaved Spanish Catholics. These slaves, who claimed freedom, were in a parcel Captain John Lush sold to Christopher Bancker in 1738. Bancker then sold the slaves to Nicholas Bayard and Cornelius Brower. The Spanish slaves' anger was especially directed against Lush, whom they regarded as a kidnapper. Sawney testified that they cursed, "pointing to captain Lush's house, d——m that son of b——, they would ruin the city and play the d——l with him." They promised to burn Lush's house, tie Lush to a beam, and "roast him like a side of beef." The Spanish blacks firmly believed that once Lush was killed, they could take over the country and assured other slaves that several hundred French and Spanish soldiers would soon arrive to complete the conquest.[92]

Spanish-speaking slaves carrying messages from South Carolina and Florida assured the rebellious slaves that once the English were overthrown, the Spanish would protect their newly won freedom. Governor James Oglethorpe of Georgia warned New Yorkers that Spanish "priests, under pretended appellations of physicians, dancing masters," provoked the slaves.[93] Roman Catholics, black or white, could cause dangerous problems among New York's bondspeople by baptizing them. Because many whites and blacks still believed that baptism mandated emancipation, conspirators adapted this Christian ritual for their own purposes. John Hughson used the Book of Common Prayer to baptize blacks and to swear fealty to the planned revolt. White anxieties about the misuse of church ritual climaxed at the trial of John Ury on charges of conspiring with New York City blacks to enable the Spanish to take over the city and institute Catholic rule. Ury's trial, which used the most extraneous evidence, nonetheless turned on the issue of whether Ury had administered the sacrament and baptized local blacks into the Catholic faith. Meeting in taverns, at street corners, and at the markets, blacks adapted Christian baptism to swear allegiance to their cause. The prosecutors charged Ury with baptizing Quack, a key slave conspirator, by drawing "a round ring on the floor with chalk . . . and [standing] in the middle of it with a cross, and [swearing] the negroes into the plot." Regardless of Ury's alleged guilt, such a ceremony was plausible to the prosecutors and to the condemned blacks.[94]

New Yorkers' fears about Catholicism placed the conspiracy in an international perspective. Such charges were reasonable to New Yorkers, who recalled that Spanish-speaking slaves were key figures in the 1712 revolt. Clarke reported to the Board of Trade that "the hand of popery is in it, for a Romish priest . . . was in full and clear evidence convicted of heavy and deep share in it besides Several other white men in prison . . . most of them . . . it is thought Irish Papists."[95] Black conspirators also remembered the 1712 rebellion. Though he was a young man then, Sawney recalled the summer of 1712, when "after the negroes told all they knew, then the white people hanged them." The method of rebellion, arson followed by murder of whites, was, as noted at the trial, exactly the pattern used in 1712.[96]

Conspiring blacks used any religious event to gather and promote rebellion. On Sundays, a perennial day for black frolicking, as many as thirty or forty slaves drank, gambled with dice or cocks, fiddled, and danced at Hughson's or Comfort's. Fortune, Wilkens's Negro, testified that "they had a dance there every other night." Slaves also resorted to Hughson's on market day and in idle moments. Wan, an Indian slave of Mr. Lowe, testified that he met John, a free Indian, late of Cornelius Cousine, at the waterside. John took him to Hughson and bought him a mug of beer. Primus, slave of one Debrosse, swore that a week before Christmas, "he met Ticklepitcher and Kelly's London on a Sunday. . . . gave them some punch, and they took a walk to a house on the North Side and called the man (Hughson) for liquor and they drank." Cajoe, alias Africa, recalled going the Saturday after New Year's to a house on the North River where "there were negroes dancing and fiddling," where he drank rum and talked of rebellion with other slaves from the city and country.[97]

On the special holiday of Pinkster blacks met to finalize their plans. Joseph North, a watchman, provided a memorable account of one holiday party. He found a "cabal of Negroes at Hughson's last Whitsuntide was twelve months; ten, twelve or fourteen of them, which they have intelligence of went down thither in order to disperse them; and when they came there, they went into the room where the Negroes were around a table, eating and drinking, for there was meat on the table, and knives and forks, and the Negroes were calling for what they wanted." It was at one such meeting that blacks planned the conspiracy. As Alfred Young and others have shown, the politicization of religious holidays was an important step in radicalizing the artisan communities. The holy days were occasions when license was normal, and the streets and taverns offered relative freedom from scrutiny.[98]

The authorities came to understand the perils of such gatherings. After discovery of the plot, on June 11, 1741, the New York Assembly passed laws regulating the numbers of "publick houses" and urged greater penalties for serving liquor to slaves and more effectual laws against illegal receipt of goods at taverns. The assembly stiffened the laws because "the great number of houses in which Negroes have been entertained" were the "principal Instrument to their Diabolical Villainy." While the conspiracy trials were in full swing, the justices took time at one session in mid-July 1741 to fine ten different tavern keepers for "keeping a disorderly house and entertaining negroes."[99] Conspiracy meetings occurred on street corners and at the markets. Several revels and plotting sessions were held in the Fields, the site of Pinkster celebrations, and where, twenty-five years later, Liberty Boys demonstrated against the Stamp Act.

Other sessions occurred at the homes of free Negroes. Adam, whose confession sparked innumerable other slaves to come forward and confess, recalled that Otello and Braveboy told him of the plot at the well by the Dutch Church "after they had come from a frolic at some free negro's house in Bowery-Land."[100] There are so many documented instances of such meetings that it seems impossible for the conspiracy to have been entirely fabricated by the authorities.

Blacks formed cabals that mixed crime and revolution. Among those meeting at Hughson's and Comfort's were the Geneva Club, the Long Bridge Boys, and the Smith's Fly Boys, maroons composed of runaways, and other rowdy slaves under the leadership of Caesar and Prince, who were the first blacks executed. At their immolation, authorities commented that "the negroes bore the character of very wicked fellows." Testimony revealed that the Geneva Boys, active since a famous robbery of gin from a tavern keeper six years before, had "the impudence to assume the style and titles of Free Masons," with officers and rules. In such a manner, the gang covered the tradition of "slave nations" (noted in the 1734 conspiracy and Pinkster celebrations) with a European fraternity. Black elections of kings, dismissed in the past as harmless, now were perceived as revolutionary. Witnesses testified that Caesar would become governor and Hughson king of New York after the revolution.[101]

Through such practices, the conspiracy advanced the process of nationalism among slaves. When the colonial New York and New Jersey assemblies outlawed the gathering of groups of African mourners or worshipers, black religious congregations were rare. Yet there were clear signs of national formations derived from ethnic, linguistic, and cultural affiliations that survived the Middle Passage at Pinkster festivals. Gary Nash's research has indicated the mixed ethnicity of the names of the conspirators. While English names were most common (30 percent), African and geographical nomenclature was equally present (30 percent). If degrees of acculturation had little impact, what mattered were interior feelings of nationality. The nations of "Mandingo and Carmantie" had already been detected among Elias Neau's students. Forbidden to practice their faith openly, Africans now adapted European rituals. They were able to do so because many came from cultures in which hidden or secret societies were common. As in South Carolina, where Margaret Washington has demonstrated the "poro and sande" secret societies thrived, so African-derived societies appeared in the New York conspiracy.[102]

The plot involved huge numbers of blacks. Prince's master, John Auboyneau, first discovered his slave's criminal behavior in March 1741, starting a chain reaction that unraveled the conspiracy.[103] Caesar and Prince planned to burn New York and overthrow the slave masters' rule. Members of black gangs had contacts with radical whites John and Mary Hughson, Margaret Kerry, and John Romme. Romme apparently knew of black gangs elsewhere. When he convinced slaves to burn their masters' homes, he promised to "send into the country for the rest of the negroes to help, because he could write and he knew several negroes in the country that could read." If the uprising failed,

Romme counseled, "he would make his escape, and go to North Carolina, Cape Fear, or into the Mohawks Country," all areas of maroon activity. Romme and Cuffee, slave of Adolphe Philipse, held similar beliefs about overcoming class oppression through revolt, arguing that "a great many people had too much, and others too little; that his old master had a great deal of money, but that, in a short time, he should have less and that he (Cuffee) would have more." These class-specific beliefs show that a powerful proletarian republicanism existed in the plot.[104]

Several black leaders stepped forth in the conspiracy. As in the 1712 revolt, a key figure was a black doctor. "Doctor Harry," who "had a few years before been forbid the town for malpractice in physic," was arrested, convicted, and burned on suspicion of poisoning. Will, "Ward's Negro," had "within a few years past, been concerned in two conspiracies, the first at St. John's, the last at Antigua." Will brought Harry, Quamino, and Worcester into the plot at the tavern in Jamaica, Long Island. After turning state's evidence in Antigua, he was sold to Providence, then came to New York. Will was involved for several reasons. He was angry that his master would not permit him to "come to his wife." Will said that "the negroes here were cowards, for they had no hearts as those at Antigua." The court sentenced him to be burned at the stake.[105] Black musicians were also an important element in the conspiracy and were present at virtually every frolic during which the conspirators planned the revolt. One fiddler, Braveboy, confessed on June 30 that Carpenter's Albany approached him about joining the conspiracy the previous summer and asserted that "they would have him, because he was a fiddler." [106]

Trials and punishments continued throughout the summer. White terror did not vanquish black aspirations for freedom. The failure of legal restrictions on black freedoms enacted in the aftermath of the slave revolt of 1712, the inability of Christian denominations to inculcate docility into bondspeople, and the severe social strains in households set the stage for the massive plot of 1741. Africans may have been acculturated to the mores of slave societies in New York and New Jersey, but shaking off the chains of bondage was their goal. As W. E. B. Du Bois has argued, the "fire of African freedom still burned in the veins of the slaves." [107] The horrific aftermath of the conspiracy did not cow them but prepared them for the next opportunity in 1775.

Conclusions

In his classic study of slavery in colonial South Carolina, Peter Wood demonstrated how heavy importation of slaves from Africa, combined with a brutally repressive slave system and absentee ownership, resulted in a bloody slave revolt at Stono in 1739.[108] Although there were few if any absentee masters in New York and East Jersey, the three decades between 1712 and 1741 saw continued imports of troublesome bondspeople from the West Indies followed by shiploads of unseasoned slaves directly from Africa. As white residents of New York and its rural environs turned to slaves as a core labor source, they provided for no way to release pressure. Whatever succor Elias Neau provided to his students was lost; no other denomination continued his work. Unhappy and turbulent young male slaves openly confronted patriarchal masters and mistresses in the rural areas, often with violent results. As blacks found freedom an ever-vanishing quality, they ran away, attacked their masters, and rebelled. One bloody revolt and a failed but potentially horrific conspiracy framed the African American experience in New York and East Jersey in the early eighteenth century. The decision by white slave masters to import slaves directly from Africa in preference to dangerous West Indian blacks they considered responsible for the 1712 revolt proved disastrously wrong. A glance at the list of slaves involved in the 1741 conspiracy shows a mix of African and Europeanized names. Neither acculturation nor unfamiliarity with European mores kept the slaves from conspiring. The heavy oppression by white authorities was as much an admission of failure as a flawed conception of justice. It was a stark truth that European-American institutions had not created a docile race of black slaves. Religion was particularly lacking in power and influence. Anglican efforts to acculturate blacks failed, as did pietist hopes that annual rituals would suffice. As sizable imports of slaves arrived from the West Coast of Africa, they rapidly formed "nations" with seasoned slaves. As white society closed the door on black freedom and kept it locked shut, the region's slaves responded with acts of individual resistance ranging from flight to murder. Gangs formed in city and countryside. Eventually, these bands turned conspiratorial and prepared with dissident whites to overthrow colonial society. Only the discovery of loose talk kept the 1741 plot from becoming the worst racial uprising in colonial North America. Time would tell if enslaved blacks in and around New York would have another opportunity.

CHAPTER 4

From Conspiracy to Revolution

1741–1776

The Black Rebellion Continues

The stream of executions throughout the summer and fall of 1741 did not calm white New Yorkers' anxieties. In January 1742, Lieutenant Governor George Clarke reported that "cabals of negroes" were causing great alarm. Although he expressed worry over conspiracies between New York and Charles Town, South Carolina, blacks, Clarke was especially concerned about local plans. He noted with "suspicion that the same villainous scheme was yet in execution, particularly in Queen's County, on Nassau alias Long Island." There blacks "about Christmas last" formed mock militia companies and "mustered and trained with the borrowed arms and accouterments of their masters." Clarke ordered that the blacks be chastised and informed city magistrates in New York that "the insolence of the negroes is as great, if not greater than ever, and they are not only suffered to have private, but even public meetings, in great numbers, without the least molestation or interruption from the magistrates and in defiance of . . . laws." Clarke ordered civic officials "to see the laws against negroes duly and punctually executed." The city government responded by indicting but not convicting two white tavern keepers. Shortly afterward, however, an arson conspiracy surfaced when several blacks were accused of attempting to set fire to their masters' homes. Confessions revealed that while gambling, slaves complained about masters' behavior and agreed to fire the houses, believing that "in firing the shed, that would fire the whole town, and the negroes in town with the negroes that were to come from Long Island, would murder the white people. . . . And then they would be rich like the Backarara [white people]" [1]

These were but the first of a series of black crimes throughout the 1740s which indicated worsening antagonisms between slaves and masters. White residents of New York and New Jersey raised immediate alarms of slave insurrection following a whiff of fire or whisper of insolence. Throughout 1742 examinations and trials of suspected conspirators continued whenever fires in the city and countryside burned buildings.[2] A sign of public disquiet was that New Yorkers no longer used slaves to fetch fresh water from upper Manhattan Island. As Dr. Alexander Hamilton explained, "When the Negroes went for tea they had their cabals and consultations."[3]

Black gangs terrorized rural communities. An incident in Westchester County in 1746 exposed the continued dangers of slave bands. A farmer there suspected several blacks of robbing his hen roost. He accosted them while they were at anchor in a small boat. Although they brandished a gun and warned him to stay away, he "resolved to go on board and search." One of the blacks pushed the gun into his mouth and shot him "in a grievous manner, but the gun being only loaded with Powder, which otherwise would have killed him outright, he now lies very ill. The slave was immediately committed to jail." Across the river in Bergen County, slaves assaulted masters with axes, poisoned them, and burned their barns.[4]

Problems with violent slaves surfaced everywhere. Newspaper reports told of black violence beginning on the slave ships crossing the Atlantic. The *New-York Weekly Post-Boy* reported how Captain Codd of the *Marlborough* three days off the Bight of Benin "had indulged 28 Gold Coast Negroes with their liberty on Deck for the sake of their assistance to navigate the ship." The slaves behaved for a considerable time "in a very civil manner," but when the crew went below to clean, the slaves on deck shot the captain to death, secured the deck and arms, and "were soon Masters of the Ship." The slaves then butchered thirty-five members of the crew, "except the Boatswain and Cabin boy whose lives they preserved to conduct the ship back again to the Bight of Benin." The crew of another English ship attempted to board the *Marlborough*, "but the Negroes were so expert at the great guns and small arms that they soon repelled" it. After some of the Africans succeeded in returning home, others took the ship and headed toward the southern coast of the continent. Such insurrections surely enhanced perceptions of rebellion among enslaved blacks hearing of them or reading about them in New York newspapers.[5]

Worried legislators in the two colonies resurrected old laws against conspiracy. In 1751 New Jersey's assembly passed legislation banning meetings of more than five blacks. New York's assembly followed suit in 1755. New York's proclamation warned: "It is well-known that . . . the Negroes in this city of New York and in other parts of this province have assembled . . . in Publick and Private . . . have uttered very insolent Expressions and in other ways misbehaved themselves."[6]

Free Blacks

In their zeal to stamp out black rebellion, New York and East Jersey legislators overlooked its principal cause. One quality was missing from the lives of African Americans in New York and East Jersey: freedom. As the number of emancipations dipped almost to insignificance and the older generations of free blacks moved away, liberty became very elusive. There were only a handful of manumissions in the decades before the American Revolution. One of the most remarkable was that of William Johnson of Jamaica, Queens County. Between 1741 and 1745, Johnson freed seven young men between the ages of seventeen and thirty, all of whom had his last name and had been raised in his home. Johnson eventually freed several more slaves at his death. Johnson's philanthropy was not, however, free. Two slaves were freed immediately but had to give him a quitrent of £4 annually; others paid similar sums. One slave who was freed after Johnson's death had to pay his executors £20. Betty, the sole female among the new free people, also received her master's home, barn, orchard, lands, and meadows as well as free use of his horses, mares, plows, harrows, wagons, and all of the corn and half the wheat on his farm. Such unparalleled generosity suggests a blood relationship.[7]

A second manumission was more standard. Eve Scurlock of New York City, a tavern keeper and victualler, freed her three slaves in 1754. She provided "Caesar with £4 and a pair of hand irons, and ½ the firewood, soap and candles, six plates, the English books and a small looking glass." Anthony received the "tools he commonly works with in the carpenter's trade." Ann received £3 and "some household utensils and my homespun clothes and the cupboard I put my clothes in." Scurlock's legacy is a good example of how difficult it was for well-meaning masters to free faithful slaves. The three slaves had to wait until the city government approved a £200 guarantee made by executors of the will, a process that took three years to accomplish—during which time Caesar, Anthony, and Ann remained slaves. On May 4, 1757, Mayor John Cruger, aldermen Philip Livingston, Simon Johnson, and Francis

Jilken, and justices Leonard Lispenard and William Coventry signed off on a document that attests to the gravity and thoroughness with which society regarded manumissions.[8]

Most masters freeing their slaves were members of the Society of Friends, but even they were initially intransigent about emancipation. Before 1740, only one Quaker manumission occurred in New York. Richard Hallet of Newtown, Long Island, freed his "negro man James" with the contingency that his sons support James if he slipped into poverty.[9] In New Jersey, because of the £200 rule, which required masters seeking to emancipate slaves to post a bond for that amount, most emancipations were conditional or deferred. George Williams of Shrewsbury, Monmouth County, who died in 1743, freed his "mullatto man when he reaches thirty years of age, giving him two suits of wearing clothes one new." Williams ordered that if the slave "takes bad ways, then my executors may sell him or do as they please with him."[10] Other masters required cash payments for their slaves' freedom. Thomas White of Shrewsbury, who died in 1748, instructed that "my negro man James is to serve my son Thomas for one years and after that if he thinks he can pay the sum of £5 a year to Thomas, the said Negro is to be set free."[11]

The good intentions of the departed slave master could be frustrated by corrupt executors even if a bond was secured in the will. In 1763, Isaac Johnson, a New York City shopkeeper, provided security for the emancipation of his fourteen-year-old "mollatto slave," Thomas Jackson, in his will. The bond was destroyed, however, and the executors of the will attempted to sell Jackson, a literate young man, "beyond the sea." Fortunately, "certain persons, from Motives of Humanity," paid Jackson's bond and warned "all persons against purchasing the said Thomas."[12]

Population Growth and the Slave Trade

Despite the terrors of the 1741 conspiracy, legislators decided that slave imports should continue but with fewer coming from the West Indies. In 1744, New Jersey's assembly passed a £10 duty on slave imports from the Caribbean, but the colony's council disallowed the law, declaring it a ban on all imports, which the "People of this Province in general (a few laborers excepted) and the Farmers in particular, would be greatly suffering by it." Slave masters in New York and East Jersey apparently decided they needed black labor enough to endure black misconduct, however dangerous. Despite insurrections at sea and peri-

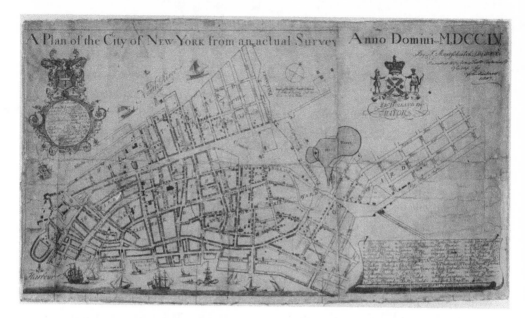

Plan of the City of New York *(Maerschalk or Duyckinck Plan), 1755. This detailed map of the City of New York shows the Negro Burial Ground just west of the Collect or Fresh Pond, on the right side of the map. (Courtesy of the New-York Historical Society)*

odic epidemics, imports and natural reproduction steadily enlarged the area's black population after 1750.[13]

In New York County the black population of 2,444 in 1746 grew to 3,200 by 1771. Curiously, between 1741 and 1756 the black population decreased from 2,444 to 2,272, suggesting a fearful reaction to the conspiracy of 1741 and perhaps the beginnings of a gradual movement to free wage labor. But the number of black males in the city increased and in 1756 achieved parity with women for the only time in the century. Older gender patterns and an increase in overall black population returned in the census of 1771.[14]

The proportion of blacks in the overall population remained over 16 percent in the southern five counties of New York. In Kings County, the black population increased from 645 to 783 in the three years between 1746 and 1749. At the same time, the number of males was nearly double that of females. By 1750 the black proportion of the total population was 34 percent in Kings, 19 in Richmond, and 18 in New York County.[15]

The increase in the local black population occurred primarily via the

African slave trade. After only a handful of direct import expeditions before 1747, New York City's African trade jumped in the quarter-century before the American Revolution. Evidence survives of at least 130 (possibly as many as 150) voyages between New York and Africa between 1748 and 1774.[16] James Lydon's figures on the size of this slave trade indicate that at least 2,800 of the 6,800 blacks imported as slaves into New York from 1701 to 1774 came directly from Africa.[17] Underwritten by leading city merchants, New York captains traveled along the coast of Africa, bartering powder, clothing, tobacco, and rum for humans. By the 1760s an English officer proclaimed that in New York there "are more Negroes than in any northern province."[18]

Upon arrival in New York City, slave traders sold their chattel at brokers' offices, at the Meal Market, on the wharf, or on board the ship. One newspaper advertisement announced the sale of "a Parcel of Likely Negro Men and Women also Negro boys and girls." Occasionally dealers included vague information about origins such as "imported from Africa," "the coast of Africa," "from Guinea," or "the Gambia." The lack of precise information suggests that older methods of combing the African coast in search of slaves prevailed, rather than a direct supply from a specific place.[19]

New Jersey attempted with little success to compete with New York as a slave-trading center. Most of its traffic in slaves was illegal. New Jersey had no duty on slave imports for most of the colonial period, making it convenient to smuggle slaves into New York and Pennsylvania. The governor of New Jersey informed the British Board of Trade in 1762 that "great numbers of Negroes are landed in the Province every Year in order to be run into New York and Pennsylvania besides overstocking this country with slaves." Between 1740 and 1757 at least 290 slaves were imported through Perth Amboy on vessels owned by such prosperous New Yorkers as John Watts, Henry and John Cruger, Samuel Bayard, John Johnson, and longtime New Jersey slaver John Schuyler. Thirty percent of these slaves came from Antigua, 25 percent from St. Christopher's and the coast of Africa (the latter in two loads in the 1750s), and lesser amounts from Jamaica, Rhode Island, Barbados, and North Carolina. After arriving in Perth Amboy, merchants kept the slaves in a barracks on Smith and Water Streets. Numbers of imports into Perth Amboy are sketchy at best because of the lack of duties.[20] New Jerseyans regarded the slave trade with increased concern. In 1769 legislators passed a duty on the importation of slaves in the hope that curtailing slave imports would attract more European laborers, reasoning that "Duties on the importation of Negroes in several of the neighboring colonies have been found beneficial to the introduction of sober industrious Foreigners . . . [and] promoting a Spirit of Industry among the Inhabitants." The act also continued a £200 bond for the manumission of slaves.[21]

Census data for East Jersey in the 1770s are fragmentary, but annual growth rates of blacks in Bergen County of 6.7 percent, Monmouth of 3 percent, and Somerset of 10.5 percent show a steady increase of the rural black population. By 1790, because there had been few imports into New Jersey since 1770, the black population was as follows: Bergen, 2,301, Monmouth, 1,596, Essex, 1,171, Middlesex, 1,318, Somerset, 1,810 (the latter a jump of 1,500 in forty-five years).[22]

In 1771 the southern five counties of New York had a black population of roughly 16,000; the 1745 black population in the five counties of eastern New Jersey was 3,200, so even modest growth in twenty-five years would bring that total to more than 5,000. By 1775, it can be safely be estimated, more than 21,000 blacks lived and worked within thirty miles of Manhattan.[23] The black population was by now a mixture of native-born, West Indian, and African peoples. A sense of this mixture can be gleaned from their names. The 1755 census of rural New York counties lists enslaved people with comic, English, classical, and African names.[24]

A thriving internal slave trade lessened the chances that slaves would spend their lives with the same masters, thus weakening paternalist ties. Among the best records for the internal trade are advertisements for fugitive slaves. To enhance recapture of escaped slaves, masters sometimes listed previous owners and the history of sales. For example, Hank escaped from John Mersereau, a carpenter living on Staten Island on January 8, 1761. Mersereau reported that Hank formerly belonged to Mr. LeRoux and Mr. Campbell, both of Tappan, Bergen County. Slaves brought from overseas were often swapped around the colonies. Lewis Francois, an escaped slave of William Smith Jr. of New York City, "lately belonged to Mr. Francis Phillips, after that to Mr. Henry Cuyler, to whom he came not long since from Jamaica." Norton Minors, a caulker and ship carpenter who had belonged to two merchants in New York City, was born in Newbury, Massachusetts, then sold to Mr. Craddock in Nevis, then brought to New York City. Minors, who was literate, finally escaped by joining the crew of a sloop bound for Louisbourg.[25]

Inheritance was another means of spreading slaves around the two colonies. Enslaved African Americans constituted much of the white population's valuable property. Slaves continued to be passed on from generation to generation. One of the most even distributions of slaves was in Robert Field's will in 1765. Field gave his wife "a negro boy and girl" and gave a slave to each of five sons. A grandson received a young slave, and Field's two daughters also received slaves. Such division among siblings created awful pain within slave families. In Purchase, New York, in 1764, a man, angry with his brother over division of the slave's time, declared that "he would cut him in two but he would have his half of him" and then killed the slave.[26]

Slaves at Work

Local economies depended on enslaved black laborers. Advertisements for slaves for sale announced broad-ranging abilities and emphasized that a slave was "fit for town or country." In New York City, in surrounding towns, and on large estates, female blacks worked as domestics. In rural regions, the vast majority of blacks, male and female, worked for small farmers. Advertisements for slaves in New Jersey newspapers in the mid-eighteenth century described over three-quarters as farmers. There was no distinction by sex because black men and women labored in the fields, cut firewood, and fed animals. Blacks were skilled at droving, hogreeving, and truck farming.[27]

Black laborers were becoming the principal labor supply, particularly in primarily Dutch counties. Two tax lists between 1751 and 1769 showed the overwhelming use of slaves in preference to single, free male laborers in Bergen and Somerset Counties. In Dutch-dominated Bergen County, slaves and servants outnumbered single men by 306 to 8 in 1751 and 422 to 34 in 1769. Likewise, in Somerset County the ratios were 378 to 94 in 1751 and 440 to 192 in 1769. The imbalances were not as great in Middlesex, Monmouth, and Essex, where Dutch farmers toiled alongside Scots, New Englanders, Huguenots, and Quakers. No county in East Jersey had more single white men available than slaves. By comparison, by 1769, Quaker-dominated West Jersey clearly preferred free wage labor over enslaved.[28]

Africans in New Jersey labored as farm workers with particular skills in raising cattle, hogs, and horses on small farms with limited slaveholdings.[29] In their diaries and account books, slave owners commented on slave methods and performance of work. Robert Livingston, for example, a large Hudson Valley slaveholder, used his slaves for a multitude of tasks. Slaves milled flour, sowed and harvested the fields, filled the furnace, and carted around the mine and ironworks as well as performing household duties.[30]

The slave census for rural New York in 1755 reveals the significance of broadly based small farm holdings. Data have survived for Kings and Westchester Counties. In town after town, the average number of adult slaves among 793 masters is only slightly over two. Vivienne J. Kruger's estimates of children bring the average family size to a low of 2.1 in North Castle, Westchester, and 5.3 in Pelham. Only six households in these counties had more than ten slaves. Larger plantations also meant older slaves. At Lewis Morris's farm in Morrisania, seventeen of twenty-six men were over the age of forty. In Monmouth County, single men and women were the predominant family type among slaveholdings in this period.[31]

In New York City, black laborers were ubiquitous. Blacks' presence along the docks caused the visiting Patrick M'Robert to exclaim: "It rather hurts a European eye to see so many Negro slaves upon the streets."[32] Blacks earned good money around the docks and wharves. White workers earned from four to six shillings each day, and blacks earned up to three shillings to six pence. As the ship neared its departure date, black wages rose to par with whites. In several cases, slaves even received cash and clothing from their lessors. One result of slave hire for boat work was a preponderance of black pilots and watermen on the rivers of New Jersey and on the Hudson.[33]

In the city and in larger towns, prosperous artisans and semiskilled workers often purchased or hired slaves as assistants. Sales notices and advertisements for runaway slaves often identified slaves as having three or four skills. Many blacks were seafarers and dock workers. Runaway notices commonly mentioned blacks as domestics, farmers, privateers, mariners, chimney sweeps, blacksmiths, bakers, coopers, shoemakers, carpenters, tailors, weavers, and barbers. There was evidence that blacks were concentrated in certain skills. In November 1743, the coopers of New York City petitioned the Common Council for relief against merchants who used "great numbers of slaves in that occupation, not only to supply their own occasions with casks, but likewise sell and dispose to others."[34] Blacks were often referred to simply as laborers. Seventeen of thirty blacks enlisted in the militia between 1755 and 1764 identified themselves as such, along with four Spanish mariners and assorted weavers, coopers, tanners, carpenters, tailors, and cordwainers.[35]

Another means for blacks to earn money in this period was mining, at which blacks from the Kongo and Angola were especially skilled. One of the largest mines, employing over two hundred slaves, was the Schuyler mine in lower Bergen County (discovered by an elderly black, whose reward was a "fancy dressing gown like his master and some pipe tobacco"). Mine owners were ready employers of whites and blacks and asked few questions about their backgrounds. In the mines, blacks worked with skilled and journeyman whites and indentured servants and in skilled positions at forges and blast furnaces. Others worked as teamsters, hauling pig iron from the forges to the cities. Blacks fled to mines and forges because of the better wages and greater freedom of movement.[36]

The plenitude of skills among rural and urban blacks in the region is an indication that historians cannot understand African American rural culture at this time solely by reference to a certain crop. Because blacks in and around New York worked at so many tasks and for a variety of masters, their labor experiences varied. People's tasks in life naturally affect their personalities, but the mixed crop economy in the rural regions and hiring practices in New York City meant great diversity in the experiences of enslaved blacks. According to whether they lived in Dutch or English households, enslaved blacks used different plows and wagons, herded different animals, and lived in varying styles of buildings. That variability existed in local politics as well. As they looked upon the world of work around them, blacks could not help but notice instability in the decades before the American Revolution. As the amount of improved land soared, turmoil ensued among the white population. Tenant farmers rioted regularly in the Hudson Valley and East Jersey. Landless whites began to move west, searching for potential landownership no longer possible close to New York City. Their departure increased reliance on black labor. In Bergen County, for example, slaves made up over 40 percent of the labor supply, a figure approached in nearby Somerset County.[37]

Labor practices created limited autonomy for enslaved blacks, who took part in the cash economy by picking up commodities for their masters at general stores. Roger Abrahams has shown that laboring for white slave owners did not deter African Americans from creating their own rhythms and cultural interpretation of work.[38] For slaves armed with a pass or with the familiar trust of whites, such duty meant easy passage within a particular region. Although masters were required to furnish slaves with passes, it is likely that over time few bothered, giving trusted slaves greater mobility. Because general stores frequently serviced large areas, delivery permitted rural blacks to travel freely into the city, and urban blacks could meet without suspicious gazes from whites.[39]

The regularity of such practices is evident from its abuses. In 1751 John Van Beverholdt advertised that "my Negro man named Gullen" had at various times borrowed money in Beverholdt's name under the pretense of paying for purchases at the market. Beverholdt informed readers that "money is given to him every night for that purpose." Slaves also served as messengers. A New York City cartman gave one slave a letter for delivery in Elizabethtown, New Jersey. Both slave and letter promptly disappeared. Masters seeking the return of fugitives sometimes mentioned a slave's notoriety. Sylvanus, who "was well-known in New York," was supposed to be about town in the daytime, "carrying in Wood for People to support himself." Pompey was "exceeding well-known in this city, having been used long ago with the Beer Waggon." Jacob, belonging to Henry Brasier of Hellgate, was "formerly known in [New York City] by the name of the Fu-Fu Negro or Money Digger." Charles was "well known in town and in Harlaem." Slaves could also use their passes to facilitate freedom. Prince, who could speak Dutch and English and lived in New Jersey, Long Island, and New York City, pretended to "fetch cattle for a Butcher in New York City" when he passed King's Bridge on his way north to freedom. Another slave deceived his master and embezzled "money sent with him to pay for goods, borrowed money and taken up goods in my name unknown to me. . . . I suppose by this Villanous Proceeding he had collected a considerable sum of money." These examples show how slaves gradually gained their masters' trust, then used that permission to snatch freedom.[40]

Black farm laborers also worked as hired hands or as independent agents. John Taylor of New York City hired a black to help barrel flour in 1766. John Pryor hired several blacks for work on building a house in Perth Amboy in 1762. Francis Filkin of Poughkeepsie hired out his slave at four shillings per day in the summertime and three shillings in the fall and winter. As general laborers, blacks appealed to a variety of employers. Jack and Sharp, slaves of George Janeway, a New York merchant, worked in the fields of Hackensack, New Jersey, then soon after boarded privateers for two-week journeys. At harvest time, Sharp "cradled" wheat for seven shillings a day. Hiring brought income to the slave owner; it also offered blacks the opportunity to roam the countryside in search of work.[41]

They found little competition from free white laborers. On the whole, Pennsylvania, Maryland, and Virginia were much more attractive to servants than New York and New Jersey. White laborers held monopolies over entrance to many trades. Enslaved blacks, unable by status and color to work independently, formed a pool of semiskilled employees for these tradesmen. Despite their need for a steady labor supply and fear of black conspiracy, officials in the mid-Atlantic avoided the transportation trade of convicts. Although indentured servants were very cheap, official prejudice in New York reflected the English elite fear of the urban poor. The main attraction in the region was not domestic labor but the iron mines where miners, colliers, quarrymen, carters, and woodcutters were in constant demand. Free blacks, hired slaves, and runaways fit part of the need, but ventures such as Peter Hasenclever's industrial center of five furnaces and seven forges deep in the Ramapo Mountains required a labor force of over five hundred men and their families. Although normally they worked only with whites of higher status, occasionally blacks labored side by side with indentured servants.[42]

Black females made up much of the enslaved workforce in the city, where they performed most of the domestic labor. By 1756, New York City had 695 female slaves older than sixteen years and 443 under that age, a total of 1,138 black women to serve a white population of 10,768.[43] Skill and status among domestics varied considerably. The occupation was generic and included a spectrum of workers from hairdressers to farm laborers. Domestics included house servants, barbers, farriers, launderers, weavers, spinners, and cooks.[44] Their experiences varied widely as well. The most fortunate usually lived in Anglican houses where they could ascend to positions of responsibility. In such houses chosen females attended the Trinity Church schools, wore clothing as expensive and well made as their masters and mistresses, and were well fed and housed. New Yorkers emulated European gentry, who displayed their wealth partly through well-dressed and educated servants.[45]

Although historians in the nineteenth century and since have emphasized the paternalist relations in New York households, male and female masters even in prosperous homes complained bitterly about slave behavior. Esther Edwards Burr, mother of Aaron, wrote a friend that she was "Exceedingly busy, expect company and our Negroes are gone to seek a master. Really my dear I shall be thankful if I can get rid of them."[46] A surly slave could upset even the wealthiest of white

Black Servant. *A nineteenth-century image of a colonial-era male domestic slave. A necessary adornment to any elite household, the domestic could create or destroy the tranquility of a home. Masters and mistresses in New York and East Jersey bargained with talented domestics by rewarding them with fine clothing, education, medical care, and other privileges. (*Harper's Monthly Magazine, *1876)*

households. Robert G. Livingston wrote his son Henry in 1751 about a pregnant female whom he had hoped would find another master but was concerned about her salability: "I do assure you that the only Reason I have to part with her, she has a devilish tongue and will be Mistress in any family unless she is Overpowered by a Master that can manage her." [47]

During the late colonial period, any closeness in living conditions between owners and masters disappeared. Bergen County, New Jersey, offers examples of three ranks. Accounts of the architecture of wealthier households reveal physical separation of master and slave.

Slave Housing in Old New York. *As part of the "kitchen family," enslaved blacks often lived literally above or near the house's cooking area. (*Harper's Monthly Magazine, *1876)*

Blacks were exiled either to the wing or, more often, a separate building in the rear of the farm. Real estate advertisements mention "Negro-Houses." Separate "Negro Kitchens" combined housing and cooking areas. A British lieutenant, Isaac Bangs, visited the home of the slave trader and miner Arent Schuyler just after the onset of the American Revolution. Bangs noted that though fifty to sixty slaves worked on the plantation, "I never saw more than 2 in the kitchen and those were waiters. Those who live in the Out House each have their particular Department and Regular Hours to work in." Bangs stated that "their Victuals is cooked at Certain Hours by their Owne Cooks." This arrangement discouraged intimacy between master and slave. Among the middling sorts, separation occurred within the home. In the house of Abraham Demaree of Closter in Bergen County, for example, two doors led from the main house into the slaves' wing. Cut into the panel of each door was a small square spy-light through which the master could survey his slaves.[48] In poorer Bergen homes, older parts of the house were used for a combination of kitchen and slave quarters. Slaves lived over ovens, in separate huts and barns, in crude tents, and even in caves.[49]

Although they often worked together, the daily experiences of white and black females were very different. White women were free, could marry legally, and could own property, rights unknown to most African American females. White women also owned black females. Widows often owned slaves through the institution of dower and were able to retain them even after remarriage, making slavery a form of dower. Among Dutch and English families, the principal slaveholders in the region, personal estates, especially slaves, were bequeathed almost entirely to Dutch widows and to nearly half of English widows. Ownership of slaves ensured a widow's ease late in life, and they could be sold to avoid debt.[50] For example, Annie Bergen of Brookland, Kings County, received the entire estate of her husband, Jacob, a farmer, which included several slaves. Jacob Bergen instructed that "if any of my negro slaves of either sex shall not behave themselves or are disobedient to their mistress," she had the power to sell them. Slaves often constituted a large share of the wife's dower. In other cases, the wife's ownership of the slaves was so limited that if she remarried, slaves reverted to the sons or daughters. This was especially true in Dutch counties, where husbands and wives held property in common and where wives owned slaves as movable estates. In his study of New York wills, David Narrett has determined that most widows received at least one slave for their personal use and that they tended to hold absolute ownership in their chattel. The distribution of slaves helped widows retain significant power within the family.[51]

In rural New Jersey, women either owned slaves outright through dower or inherited them.[52] The age of widows and the contingencies built into wills regarding remarriage meant that women were very likely to be slave owners for an extended period of time. Women were no more likely than men to free slaves in their wills. Even when widows emancipated slaves, often they were simply fulfilling their husbands' wish that manumission occur after her death. Masters frequently passed slaves to their daughters. While some fathers were attentive to primogeniture by awarding slaves to their sons as explicit birthrights, others distributed their chattel to daughters.[53] Such family customs had social ramifications. The majority of slaves received by widows were adult males, many of whom were in the prime of their lives; female ownership of husky young farm slaves heightened the need for community vigilance.[54]

Slave Culture

The yawning separation between blacks and whites manifested itself in the power of the slave culture. In the years that followed the conspiracy in 1741 many aspects of slave culture which threatened authority thrived. Taverns remained a refuge for thieves seeking to fence stolen goods. In one of many examples the court of general sessions indicted tavern keeper Matthew Maguire for "entertaining negroes and receiving stolen goods" in the summer of 1744 and then again two years later. The court of general sessions convicted Catherine O'Neal in 1765 of permitting "Negroes and others at unlawful times . . . Night and Day . . . drinking, tippling, whoring and misbehaving themselves to the great damage and common nuisance of all." [55]

White authority unsuccessfully governed a slave culture evident in taverns, alehouses, and dance halls, at markets, and at secret black gatherings in the woods, where conspiracies against the slave order were hatched. Black culture reflected the hardness of black life. Black dances, frolics, and marketing activities produced a culture that sustained autonomous black traditions and nurtured a rich internal ethnicity. [56]

One expression of this culture was the frequency of black fiddlers. Between 1741 and 1775 the most commonly mentioned talent in fugitive slave notices was fiddling, a skill that had special currency in the black tavern and dance hall community of New York City and at rural frolics. Of 776 runaways between 1741 and 1780, 39, or 5 percent, were fiddlers. Adding 3 drummers, 2 fifers, a French horn player, and 2 singers means that in 175 instances in which masters specified black skills, 47 fiddlers and other musicians accounted for 27 percent of skilled fugitives. A talented fiddler, or in African American terminology a "songster" or "music physician," could make a living singing and playing for fellow blacks. "Songsters," a term current by the late eighteenth century, bound together a broad range of secular music including social songs, comic songs, blues, and ballads. Such professional demands required extensive travel. In Africa, professional musicians toured up and down the West Coast, taking inspiration from polycultural sources. Similarly, in America, black traveling musicians drew from Scottish, Irish, and English vernacular music as well as African. There were other fugitives with intellectual talents. Scattered among the runaways in the mid-eighteenth century were three ministers, three doctors, two fortune tellers, and a watch seller. [57]

Mixed with these mysterious faculties was a predilection for alcohol

Ye Execution of Goff ye Neger of Mr. Cochins on ye Commons. *An undated portrait of the execution of a slave in New York City. (From* Valentine's Manual of the Corporation of the City of New York, *1860, collection of the author)*

consumption which frightened white authorities. Robert Livingston sought to sell his tempestuous city domestic to the country because "here there are so many Little Dram Shops that ruin half the Negroes in town."[58] On February 16, 1756, a newspaper reported "nine of the Ethiopian Breed (to wit, Negroes), belonging to this city, have been apprehended, committed, try'd and whipt at the whipping post for assembling and meeting together in an Illegal manner, on Sunday the 8th Instant." The town council also increased fines for entertaining slaves to £5 per violation and 40 shillings per offense for selling them liquor.[59] Regardless of these punishments, in 1767 the *Weekly Post-Boy* reported that "20 negroes received the Discipline of the Whip, at the Publick Post for preparing a "junketing frolic, designed at a poor white man's house in the Out-Ward, where two pigs ready for the fire and two gallons of wine awaited them." The newspaper editorialized, "It is such houses that ruin servants, as the Receiver is as bad as the Thief."[60]

The most concise information about the slave culture of New York and East Jersey comes from runaway notices in newspapers, which offer information about physical characteristics, origins, religion, occupations, and intentions.[61] Although wills in East Jersey occasionally noted the value of "negro bedding and cloathing" at less than £2, the best source of knowledge for African American clothing in this period is the runaway notices.[62] Blacks leaving their masters in rural regions were most likely to take just the homemade clothes on their backs. Such garments included leather or buckskin breeches, tow cloth and ozenbrig trousers and shirt, homespun overcoats, and leather hats. Blacks from the city had more plentiful and fancier clothing, including linen trousers, corduroy pants, beaver hats, and good new shoes. Like convicts, escaped slaves tried to steal as much clothing for their trips as possible. Multiple sets of clothes allowed greater deception and could easily be sold in the city markets.[63]

Among the least subjective observations were masters' comments on slaves' linguistic abilities. By the 1740s many slaves in New York and New Jersey spoke good English and Dutch. Spanish and French speakers were common. Many runaway notices indicated blacks' origins and language abilities. Several came from Madagascar, such as Cato, who ran away with another slave, Johnny, a cooper, and an indentured servant, John Watson. Cato and Johnny spoke good English and Dutch, a common linguistic combination among slaves; Johnny could also speak French.[64] Acculturated slaves with good linguistic skills were not the only ones who fled their masters. Newly arrived Africans speaking poor or no English were common fugitives. Popaw, who had "filed teeth and could not tell his master's name," surrendered himself "for want of sustenance."[65]

Runaway notices often mentioned personality traits of escaped slaves. Between 1740 and 1775 there was a marked increase in masters' comments about assertive slaves. During the 1740s the most common descriptions were "flatterer," "laugher," "cunning," "artful," and "liar." By the 1750s these adjectives were joined by "smooth tongued" and "sly." Charles Wray gave a vivid and telling description of his absconding slave, Jacob. The bondsman had a "lump on each shoulder by being flogg'd some time past; stoops forward in walking, and hangs down his head." Another slave, Charles, spoke good English, some French, and a little Spanish, but no Dutch. He had an "insinuating address, very apt to feign plausible Stories and may perhaps call himself a Free Negro." The 1760s saw frequent mention of "drinker" and "troublesome when drunk." Such descriptions suggest elements of African tricksters among runaways. Gathering together the master's possessions, using deceptive skills to avoid capture, the runaway, like the trickster, was what Robert Pelton has described as the image of the man "individually . . . seizing the fragments of his experiences and discovering in them an order sacred by its very wholeness . . . weaving together a fabric of meaning through the transforming power of his imagination." [66]

Advertisements for fugitives reveal much about slaves' survival skills. Joe fled from Augustine Reid in 1764 to New York City, where he "hired himself as a free man to a Butcher, in whose service he stayed that winter." The next year Joe hired himself to Mr. Oakley in Westchester for a year and a half. Reid, hearing about his slave in 1766, went to take him up, but "he getting notice of it, went off and is probably lurking or concealed in the Neighborhood, Long Island or New York." Slaves used fake passes to deceive potential captors writing passes themselves or getting assistance from sympathetic whites. Claus, thirty-five-year-old slave of Cornelius Newkirk of New York City, could "read and write both English and Dutch" and "it's likely will forge a pass." Caesar ran away from John Hobart of Eaton, Suffolk County, in 1765 in the company of "one Thomas Cornwall . . . who it is feared has forged a pass for the Negro." [67]

As slave literacy increased, the number of forged passes rose from two in the 1740s to thirteen in the 1750s to thirty-six between 1760 and 1770. Other slaves used masquerade to escape capture. A favorite means was changing names. Jem, the slave of Isaac Wilkins of Newark, "calls himself by the several names of James, Gaul, Mingo, Mink and Jim." Another slave changed his name and race. Jacob, of Upper Freehold, New Jersey, "has several times changed his name, calling himself James Start, and James Pratt, &ct. . . . he passes himself as an Indian." Jacob was very determined to leave his master as "he went from work at his plough and was without shoe or stocking and no other clothes but an Oznabrig Shirt and Trowsers, an Old ragged waistcoat and an old hat." Although poorly dressed, Jacob went to New York City on a sloop and "has since been seen in town." One slave faked his own death. Ben, slave of Elizabeth Finn of Bergen County, left his clothes by the shore of the Hackensack River, "which gives reason to suppose he took that method to deceive his master and prevent a search." Others found refuge among free blacks. Mary Ferrari of New York City, mistress of Cato, guessed that her escaped slave "is harbored by some of the Free Negroes." [68]

One of the most striking observations about the psychology of runaways was the frequent warning that the slave would "pretend to be free." The act of flight was in itself a statement of freedom. Once ab-

sconded, thirty-two fugitives between 1740 and 1770 used their guile
to convince the world of their self-emancipation. "Adonia, but called
by us Duca," a blacksmith belonging to Johannes Blauveldt of Orange
County, New York, was whipped in September 1762, then fled the next
day. Blauveldt informed the world that "He pretends to be free and
perhaps will get a pass for that Purpose." Slaves often helped each
other. Toby and Abraham of Upper Freehold, New Jersey, ran away in
1764. Abraham was literate, and "it is likely he will forge a pass and
pretend to want a new Master for himself and the other." [69]

Religion

Slaveholders in the region regarded forged passes as clear evidence
of the pernicious danger of exposing blacks to Christian education. The
cleavages between paternalist and patriarchal masters and their enslaved blacks was no more apparent than in religion. The paternalist
Church of England maintained its limited relationship with a few privi-
leged slaves. The Reverend Samuel Auchmuty succeeded Charleton as
instructor to the slaves at Trinity. He remained as catechist at Trinity
until 1764, a term that brought further growth and stability to the
school. Between 1747 and 1762 Auchmuty, though hampered by illness
and the recalcitrance of slave masters, averaged about fifty baptisms
each year. Auchmuty reported that his students "make no small profi-
ciency in the Christian religion." He instructed his scholars by making
them "repeat their catechism . . . also I endeavor to make them sen-
sible of the true meaning of every question, which naturally opens and
discovers to them the Christians scheme and the Duty and Obligation
they are under to live as Christians." Auchmuty's students learned to
read from books using symbols and pictures to give meaning to words.
Pupils memorized maxims broken into syllables. One key proverb ex-
horted "ser-vants to be o-be-di-ent unto their Mas-ters . . . Ser-vants
o-bey in all things your master ac-cording to the Flesh." The messages may have preached docility, but the Anglican persuasion that all
humankind was equal before God was a powerful antidote to the dis-
mal slave condition. In short, the Anglican schools and their curricula
became carefully constructed steps toward black initiation into white
society. [70]

Rev. Samuel Auchmuty's description of two candidates for baptism
in 1762 indicates the rise of an acculturated black leadership. He described the pair whom "I have admitted to the Holy Table, their characters being unexceptionable, and their knowledge of our most holy

religion, and their duty, very considerable for people of their color. They read well." Auchmuty also had two female students "at present under instruction, read well, are very desirous of tasting the heavenly feast." A few years later, Auchmuty described one such individual: "One of the blacks, a sincere good man in my absence reads such parts of the Church service as I have directed & then such sermons as I order, best adapted to their capacities." Auchmuty added that "an able instructor would (as indeed many of them are now) soon become qualified to instruct their own children." Now, the cleric affirmed, an educated class of blacks in New York City could reproduce itself.[71]

After 1760, the endeavors of Dr. Thomas Bray's associates supplemented Auchmuty's school. Auchmuty hired a schoolmistress to teach "reading, Spelling and writing" and announced the establishment of a "Free School near the New-Dutch Church." The school offered instruction of "thirty Negro Children, from 5 years old and upwards in reading, and in the Principles of Christianity, and likewise sewing and knitting under the inspection and care of the Clergy of the Church of England in this city."[72] The two schools thrived throughout the 1760s by placing constant pressure on reluctant slave masters. Joseph Hildreth read a catechism lecture every Sunday evening to an assemblage of about one hundred slaves and free blacks, offering prayers, general thanksgiving, and psalm singing.[73] Auchmuty estimated that each year he baptized "80 or 90 & often upwards of 100" slaves; the scholars, who were primarily the female domestics of wealthy New Yorkers, "constantly attend Divine Service not only on the Lord's Day but also on week days."[74]

In rural New York and New Jersey, Anglican clerics faced other frustrations. There was enormous opposition to their plans for an American bishopric. Colonial Americans deeply feared that such a move would further diminish freedom, and any proposal immediately aroused opposition. One critic argued that the church was largely composed of blacks, "almost all of whom are not Christians at all." Whether colonial Americans fretted about the potential power of the Anglican bishopric or about schools for slaves, such controversies were political as well as religious.[75]

Anglican missionaries in the hinterlands of New York faced local hostility and poor climate and road conditions, and they held deep-seated misgivings about baptism. The Reverend Robert Jenney, for example, withheld baptism from his own slaves because of "moral duties, in which most of their colour are very loose, but without which I cannot conceive that they have any title to Church membership, nor consequently to baptism." [76] In New Jersey, informal Anglican schools appeared only where the church had some presence. Anglican clerics in Monmouth, Essex, and Middlesex Counties sponsored catechism schools, but Bergen and Somerset residents, dominated by the Dutch Reformed Church, did not. The more rural an area, the more likely whites were to be antagonistic toward the Church of England.[77] Still, clerical accomplishments in New Jersey were impressive. Between 1740 and 1782 Anglican missionaries baptized at least 350 blacks in New Brunswick, Newark, Elizabethtown, and Perth Amboy.[78]

In seventy-five years of effort, the SPG had only limited success. One student of the SPG has estimated that there were an average of nineteen baptisms each year in the lower six counties of New York colony, from a total of 1,407 rites over seventy-five years, a figure which suggests that church participation was limited to a small minority of the enslaved blacks. Ira Berlin has concluded that even this figure was too generous. There were also troubling signs of racism among frustrated missionaries. It is doubtful that the Anglican catechism classes obliterated all traces of past African faiths. Scrubbing free the minds and souls of the continually arriving Africans would have required a much greater effort than that mounted by the timid Anglican divines.[79]

At the same time, the effects of Anglican catechism classes on local blacks were sizable. The presence of well-dressed, healthy, articulate servants in Anglican households was visible proof of the benefits of ties to the colonial aristocracy. Always in pursuit of the perfect servant, Anglican colonists favored their slaves with better treatment than many whites enjoyed. That did not ensure loyalty. Titus, for example, who ran away from Mary Elliston in New York City in 1756, was well-dressed, was described as "full of Talk, and can read and write well." Most black Anglican students were urban women, a group poorly represented in the lists of fugitives. Generally, however, Anglicans inadvertently offered receptive Africans access to the manners and presence of imperial power in the colony. To make any positive impression on the bigoted whites in the region, slaves had to be literate, which they could easily gain from Anglican classes. For those few males in Anglican classes, church training could advance their status. Accepting the tenets of Christianity, these slaves prepared for leadership, usually as ministers in the black community during the Revolution and afterward. The Talented Tenth, as W. E. B. Du Bois has described the most educated and assimilated portion of the African American population, descended from this group.

Politically, Anglican missionary efforts had important consequences. As the official church, its teachings stressed the prestige of royal and imperial bonds over local governance and the importance of sacred power over the temporal. Inadvertently, because of the better treatment received by the slaves of paternalist Anglicans and the occasional emancipation stemming from baptism, the church's behavior sustained the folk custom that admission to the church mandated freedom for slaves, an axiom still held by local blacks and pietist whites. Implicit in this tenet was the understanding that refusal of this rite placed slave masters in opposition to God and instilled among blacks a critique of slavery.[80]

As the Great Awakening disturbed religious orthodoxy in colonial America, the Dutch needed a stronger buttress against slaves' claims for equality. With very rare exceptions, Reformed churches still refused to baptize free or enslaved blacks. Members or not, blacks were constant, if rowdy, listeners at Sunday services. The Awakening's evangelical methods loosened the church's hierarchy and doubtless made black adherents question their lowly status.[81]

The new theologies required a new defense of slavery. One source came from abroad. In 1742, black theologian Jacobus Eliza Capetein offered a scriptural defense of slavery, which Wilson Moses has termed the "fortunate fall." In his dissertation at the University of Leyden in 1742, Capetein updated Udemans, arguing that slavery was positive because it exposed blacks to Christianity. Christian love, contended Capetein, prevented believers from treating their slaves cruelly and permitted masters to offer freedom after years of good behavior, although he acknowledged that the Gospel gave no express command for emancipation. Capetein's great erudition and his wholehearted embrace of slavery as a positive road to Christian enlightenment made his example irresistible to Dutch Reformed congregations. This message from a learned slave encapsulated the folk beliefs of generations of patriarchal Dutch slave masters.[82]

As evangelical churches joined Anglicans with gifts of baptism to blacks, urban Dutch Reformed intransigence faltered in the 1760s. Lambertus De Ronde, dominie of the First Dutch Church of New York City, became a primary proponent of black baptism. Lambertus, author of several theological exegeses, announced plans for a book of first truths for the slaves written in Dutch and "Negro English." No copies of this work have surfaced, but De Ronde did publish a simple primer on Dutch Reformed principles. Several points in this work spoke to De Ronde's perception of the place of African Americans in God's eyes. De Ronde argued that "full and perfect good" meant acceptance that one does "not belong to myself but unto the faithful savior Jesus Christ." Only those incorporated with Jesus Christ by the true and lively faith (the Reformed Church) could apply its benefits to themselves. On the important issue of baptism, which De Ronde saw "cleansing the impurities of the soul," he noted that it by no means disturbed the bodily condition.[83]

De Ronde's reforms occurred in New York City. In the surrounding countryside, whites and blacks brooded about baptism. Rather than encourage blacks to join in worship, slave owners informed their chattel that they were "like the beasts that perish; not informing us of God, heaven, or eternal punishments." Lacking souls, blacks had no reason to study religion. Blacks, in turn, still believing that religion could lead to freedom, condemned such masters as bad Christians.[84]

However Reformed members inculcated doctrine among slaves, salvation usually occurred outside of the church. This may be seen in the slave narrative of James Albert Ukawsaw Gronniosaw, who came to New York City as a slave from his home in Bournou, in the interior of the Gold Coast. After serving a Mr. Van Horne of New York City, Gronniosaw was sold to the Reverend Theodores Frelinghuysen of the Dutch Reformed Church, who instructed him in Christian prayer. He "made me kneel down and put my two hands together and every night and morning he did the same." Frelinghuysen taught Gronniosaw that God was his father and best friend. Gronniosaw answered that his father was in Bournou and asked the pastor to send him back. Sent to school, Gronniosaw apparently learned to read and became deeply impressed by a passage in Revelations 17, which told him, "Behold, he cometh in the clouds and every eye shall see him and Christ pierced him." His religious training confused and troubled the young slave, and he attempted suicide with a clasp-knife. He was especially troubled by the Calvinist messages he heard in church about God's determination to judge Ethiopia, Asia, and Africa. At night he heard the words, "Behold the lamb of God." His teacher rejoiced in his journey and prayed with him frequently. Gronniosaw found God while sitting under a tree one day: "A light inexpressible darted down from heaven and shone around me for the space of a minute." Rather than receiving God within the boundaries of a church and community, Gronniosaw got his revelation in the open air near a tree, a symbol of the presence of divinity in African culture. His private conversion enabled him to live as a slave in a white-dominated religion. At the same time, his inner light stemmed from an African conception of salvation.[85]

The attitudes of Dutch Reformed congregations toward slaves and chattel bondage created subtle effects. Their staunch opposition to slave baptism, church membership, and emancipation imparts the impression that the Dutch believed slaves had no souls. In the late colonial period, for example, the master of John Jea, a rural slave, informed him that Africans lacked souls.[86] At the same time, the intimacy and magical powers of the Pinkster experience performed within the home ensured compelling spiritual effects. The paradox of public refusal to convert slaves while sustaining sacred occasions at home generated a combination of European pietism and barely disguised Africanisms.

The Lutheran Church generally sustained its liberal inclusion of blacks. Lutherans held marriage ceremonies for free black families around Hackensack in Bergen County. Ceremonies included the rites of the marriage of Willem Smidt and Barbara Franssen of Hackensack and the marriage of Caspar Francis Van Sallee, the grandson of Anthony the Turk, and Johanna Cromwell, a free black, at Hackensack in 1746. By performing such rites without requiring deep personal investment, the Lutherans showed far greater liberality than any other denomination. The Lutherans also performed interracial marriages. On June 6, 1741, James Elsworth, an Englishman, and Mary Jorga, a "free Portuguese baptized negress who had received liberty of her mistress to marry," did so at the home of Nicolaus Emmings in Highland, New York.[87] The New York Lutheran synod performed numerous marriages in the late 1720s among slaves and between slaves and free blacks. On the frontier, however, Lutherans abandoned their commitment to interracial membership after a sexual scandal was alleged between an elderly pastor and his black servant.[88]

By the mid-eighteenth century, other European denominations questioned the morality of slavery. Chief among them were the Society of Friends, who earlier had been unrepentant slave owners and traders.[89] In 1758 the Philadelphia Meeting voted to move against slavery and to visit member slave owners to convince them to manumit their slaves and end any involvement with the slave trade. John Woolman, the leading Quaker abolitionist, visited New Jersey Friends in 1761 to encourage them to free their slaves. Another leading Friend, Daniel

Stanton, spoke out against slavery in large meetings in New Jersey and New York in the early 1760s. Such meetings were more open than regular services, and it is likely that slaves attended and heard the debate. Quakers worried greatly about abolitionists encouraging possible slave revolts. Even Anthony Benezet, anxious about a possible revolt, asked a London merchant to ensure that blacks could not obtain his pamphlets because "this was thought to be of too tender a nature to be exposed to view, in places where it might fall into the hands of the negroes."[90]

East Jersey Quakers, influenced by the conservative New York Meeting, lagged behind Philadelphia Friends on the issue of slavery. Although Friends increasingly manumitted their slaves by will in Monmouth County, they usually required a term of years or cash payments as forms of quitrents. Even in the Revolutionary era, only after numerous visits did the Quakers finally excommunicate three Shrewsbury slave owners who refused to manumit their slaves. That they waited until their own deaths and even then required payments by the slave to their heirs shows that Quaker slave owners were determined not to lose money over conscience. Their policies anticipated the gradual emancipation laws of the late eighteenth century.[91]

Once determined to end slavery, Friends were energetic about cleansing the souls of members and washing away the sin of slavery. Quakers were not, however, interested in the souls of black folk. Once a slave was free, Quaker interest waned. The Society of Friends was extremely reluctant to admit any blacks into its fellowship. Although much more liberal than Anglicans about ending slavery, the society was far more conservative about black membership.[92]

The importance of the Quakers lies not in their congregation with blacks but in their equation of slavery and immorality. The question of Christians enslaving fellow believers had arisen before, but the Anglicans and Dutch Reformed dodged the issue. The Quakers met it head-on, determining to erase slavery from their faith. What is important for our concerns is that blacks listened with great interest to Quaker debates in public and, privately, during visits to recalcitrant Friends. During the Revolution these visits had severe consequences.[93]

If the Quakers were reluctant to view blacks as potential equals at prayer, the rising evangelical sects embraced Africans as brothers and sisters. Blacks attended the love feasts and mass rallies of the Great Awakening to hear messages of personal and bodily salvation. Outside of New York the Great Awakening animated greater Presbyterian efforts among blacks. The "sacramental season," which occurred in late fall, included fasting and lengthy family orations and prayers. Like Pinkster in the Dutch Reformed Church, the Presbyterian sacramental season was uncharacteristically egalitarian. Love feasts, open to all, instilled a temporary equality before God. At the same time Presbyterians held a cautious and hesitant attitude toward criticism of slavery in the colonial period.[94]

Methodism, unlike earlier European religions, did not require catechism before baptism, making it very attractive to the great masses of unlettered whites and blacks. The Wesleyan church, making its greatest impact in America in the prerevolutionary decade, was still a wing of the Church of England. Early leaders considered themselves Anglicans. They combined the liberal paternalism with the Pentecostalism inherent in pietist sects. Their difference from the latter was the absence of the patriarchalism that characterized the Dutch Reformed, Huguenot, and even Presbyterian Churches. Of primary interest to theologically marginalized groups like blacks were the Methodists' methods, which emphasized universal salvation, experiential religion, and sanctification. Church fathers promoted the faith in person. Benjamin Abbott, his mentor Francis Asbury, and George Wesley himself counseled American Methodists. Asbury preached in New York City in 1771 and itinerated on Long Island and in New Jersey in 1772. Of one gathering in New York Asbury characteristically wrote: "To see the poor Negroes so affected, to see their sable countenances in our solemn assemblies and to hear them sing with cheerful melody their dear Redeemer's Praise, affected me much and made me ready to say of a faith I perceive God is no respecter of Persons." Asbury also counseled slave owners about freeing their bondsmen. Methodism gained more than five thousand converts in 1775. In New York, black females were among the first members of the Methodist Church. The beloved church sexton was Peter Williams Sr. Blacks flocked to Methodism in its formative years because it was openly antislavery, respected African spirituality, focused on immediate salvation, and sponsored a nascent black ministry.[95]

The black religious impulse was still masked by slavery. Unlike the South, where historians have found ample remains of African survivals,[96] evidence of African religious traditions in the North has been scanty. Africans did adapt Christianity to their own uses within the structures of European religions; black leaders and audiences appear through the interstices of Protestant rituals. There are glimpses in the colonial period of the creation of a black ministry, which arose like a phoenix after the American Revolution. Runaway notices provide evidence of black preachers. Andrew Saxon, who fled from Jacobus Van Cortlandt of New York City, "professeth himself to be a Roman Catholic." He marked his shirt and coat with a cross. Simon, who escaped from James Leonard of Middlesex County, New Jersey, in 1740, was accused of having "Pretended to be a Doctor and very religious and says he is a Churchman." In 1775, Major Prevost of Bergen County advertised for Mark and Jenney. Mark was "a preacher, short, black, and well set and speaks slow; the woman is rather lusty, has a cast in one eye, bad teeth, smooth tongued and very artful." Other fugitive blacks passing through the region were described as "professors of religion," "preaches to his color," and "makes a great show of religion, on which he has much to say." [97]

Runaway notices offer fragments of black autobiographies, and those shreds are filtered through suspicious white eyes. By the 1750s, blacks recorded their own stories and conversions to Christianity, narratives that offer the contours of a developing African American Christianity. In their narratives, blacks who lived or passed through New York and East Jersey displayed a powerful cynicism about life, understandable in anyone kidnapped from a homeland in Africa and enslaved in America. Hope and conversion occurred in several ways. The luckiest received schooling, as in the case of James Albert Ukawsaw Gronniosaw, who was fortunate to live in the household of Theodore Frelinghuysen. More commonly, as in the instances of Katy Schenck of Monmouth County and John Jea of Brooklyn, religious instruction came only from deep personal conviction and effort. Helping their desires was a newfound absorption of radical views of human duty and destiny which characterized evangelical thought. A particularly radical idea, which appears in Jea's narrative and the works of Boston King, Venture Smith, and John Marrant, was that Christian conversion was a vehicle for gaining freedom. Implicitly understood since the days of Dutch rule, this affirmation at once helped blacks endure slavery in the North and forced them to confront their masters and demand freedom.

Before that could happen, however, salvation was necessary. Most narrators recalled African life with the sadness of an exile. The reverence for African religion was replaced in virtually every colonial black narrative with a deep awe for the Christian ritual and the doctrine of reconciliation. Their religiosity, shown most cogently in Jupiter Hammond's poetry and in Jea's narrative, was overwhelming, quickly replacing godliness for loyalty to a master. The word of God appeared to each outside of a church, usually in a field or road, and inspired the narrator to ecstasy. The emotions expressed demonstrate that blacks felt that Christianity, if properly followed by true adherents, would lead to bodily freedom.[98]

Those with little contact with Christianity used the supernatural. Cunning men and women were skilled in magical powers. During the 1730s New Jersey slaves using African methods of poisoning terrorized their masters. Self-appointed black doctors were leaders in the revolts of 1712 and 1741. In the years just before the Revolution, Jack, from Bergen County, gained a reputation as a cunning man, who used charms to secure obedience from others. A cunning black woman named Charity was regarded as a witch who could cause a pregnant woman to give birth to a monster or cure sick children when doctors failed; Charity often transformed herself into a cat.[99]

There were additional instances of poisoning in the prerevolutionary decades. Peter Kalm recorded a witchcraft poisoning by black collaborators in New York in the late 1740s. He noted that "only a few of them know the secret . . . and the remedy" for the poisoning and they "employ [the poison] on brethren as behave well toward whites, are beloved by their masters, and separate from the countrymen, or do not like to converse with them." The poison could take several years to prove fatal, but the victim "knows that he is poisoned the day he gets it" and falls "into a consumptive state" for several years."[100] This African sacrament was used to punish slave masters.

Masters used horrific methods to punish slaves suspected of poisoning. Phyllis, a black slave in New York City, was committed to jail for "suspicion of poisoning her master." After five weeks' imprisonment she was discharged, after which her master confined her in a small room in his house "having a chain Bound around her arms and made fast to a partition." She refused to eat because the food he gave her "was full of worms." A neighbor, Susannah Romme, gave the woman some tea, which greatly angered the master, one "Lowder a Tailor." Lowder then refused her any drink or food; neighbors could hear Phyllis call for water all day and night. "Phyllis died of starvation while delivering a bastard child" in the room with a chain around her neck.[101]

Legal Resistance to Slavery

Unable to find avenues to freedom through religion, blacks turned to the imperial government. For example, Spanish blacks continued to sue for freedom in Crown courts. Even during times of revolt, Spanish blacks gained succor from colonial officials bent on judicial revenge. In the 1740s, in the aftermath of war between the English and Spanish, many slaves claimed status as free citizens of Spain and were freed by the Crown attorney general. Spanish slaves watched the international situation to sue for their freedom. While England and Spain were at war, pirating blacks in the Caribbean, then selling them in New York, was fair game. Once peace came, local slave traders and owners found themselves at odds with the imperial government. Suits for freedom by Spanish captives were always contentious, but now they demonstrated the growing split between local needs and imperial policies over slave trading. Spanish blacks used loopholes between colony and Crown policies to push their grievances.

New York pirates and fleet owners brought numerous captives before the court of admiralty in the early 1740s and met little initial opposition to their sales. In 1745, shortly after the court permitted sale of captive blacks, the Crown attorney general sought a reversal of that decision. The Crown pleaded that the two nations had entered into a cartel which prohibited such privateering in 1743. Furthermore, in retaliation for the privateers' activities, the Spanish government imprisoned sixty-nine English sailors. Negotiations between Spain and England over the next year secured an agreement to exchange hostages. In September 1746 the court of admiralty ordered freedom for the condemned slaves, accepting depositions from several that they were illegally enslaved. In response, the Spanish freed their English prisoners.[102]

Matters became complicated locally. Slave owners, perhaps aware that the Crown planned no compensation for their losses, began selling "Spanish mullattoes" out of the province. On October 15, 1746, the Crown did in fact reject masters' claims for compensation and freed the Spanish slaves unconditionally. Later that fall numerous Spaniards sailed for Havana, having secured freedom in a triumph of personal initiative and international law.[103]

The success of some Spanish prisoners encouraged others to file suit. By 1750, forty-five enslaved Spanish freemen placed their hopes with the Crown authorities in New York against local slaveholders. Soon after, the interim governor of Florida requested a Spanish captain in

New York to investigate their claims.[104] After reports flew back and forth across the Atlantic trying to resolve the crisis, the Board of Trade ordered that, upon the cessation of hostilities between Spain and England on August 9, 1748, all prizes were to be returned, freeing all forty-five slaves. The board ordered that the colonial government prosecute any persons involved in the kidnapping of one slave, Paul Mesqua, who had been sold in irons to Albany.[105]

The decision spurred further petitions. The Crown invariably sided with the aggrieved slave, and the slave master was left without his chattel or money. In one case Manuel de Cumana, a Spanish Indian, went to the home of John Tabor Kempe, attorney general for New York, seeking his freedom. Cumana had been captured while fishing in the West Indies, then brought to New York and sold to Abraham Pawling of Tappan, East Jersey. Such cases added further acrimony to relations between local slave masters and their Spanish chattel. With the 1741 conspiracy still in the forefront of many provincial minds, Catholicism, a key agent in the 1741 conspiracy, again became associated with freedom to slaves. In the case of Juan Miranda, a petition for freedom wound through the courts for over ten years, during which Miranda was nearly sold out of town, then the attorney general issued a warrant for the arrest of his master.[106] These cases indicate how, during the most legally confining periods of slavery, blacks secured freedom by using loopholes in the laws or international controversies to their advantage.

In the prerevolutionary decades, the experiences of Miranda and other Spanish slaves had an additional importance. The actions of the attorney general and the decisions of the court of admiralty taught slaves in New York and New Jersey that, under the right circumstances, international contention could lead to freedom. The diplomatic and military maneuvers of imperial nations would override the individual property rights of private, colonial citizens. Blacks learned that opportunities could arise in which they could manipulate opposing sides to gain liberty.

Fugitive Slaves

Fugitive slaves became a significant problem for white authorities between 1741 and 1775. Flight of a slave meant loss of a costly investment. The number of runaways increased steadily over the thirty-year period, rising from 64 fugitives between 1740 to 1750 to 123 the following decade and 141 in the 1760s, an average of 14 runaways each year, a rate comparable to that in the southern colonies. Males outnumbered females by 419 to 34. The median age for runaways was twenty-one, a year often marking the end of apprenticeship for white youths and the year generally agreed to be the onset of manhood.[107]

Rarely did masters know where their chattel fled. In only 176 of 776, or 22 percent of the cases, between 1711 and 1780 did masters offer a possible destination in runaway advertisements. Those places listed showed a general desire to put as much distance as possible between themselves and their master. Thirty-nine slaves sought refuge on a vessel; nineteen escaped to New York City or the woods on northern Manhattan Island; nine went into the swamps and woods of New Jersey; six traveled to live with the Indians; and five went to other colonies, including Connecticut, Pennsylvania, and Maryland. Seven escaped to Albany and beyond while two entered the military service. Only six went to former owners, to visit their families, or to their birthplaces. Slaves found employment in colonial port cities, where jobs as mariners were abundant. Flight to the sea became such a problem that by the late 1730s runaway advertisements routinely reminded captains of vessels of the harsh penalties and fines for harboring fugitives.[108]

Some runaways were captured, then escaped again. Sheriffs posted notices to masters of captured fugitives held in jails, giving them a designated time to collect their chattel and pay expenses before the slave was auctioned. In 1751, Thomas Smith, sheriff of Cape May County in southern New Jersey, picked up Jupiter Hazard, a twenty-seven-year-old slave recently escaped from Piscataway, Rhode Island. After giving particulars of Hazard's appearance, Smith noted that Hazard "seems to have traveled pretty much, for he gives a good account of Rhode Island, New York, Pennsylvania, Shrewsbury and other places." Bill, "a mullatto man" belonging to Dennis Hicks of Phillipsburg, Westchester County, was seen in New York and then was arrested in Litchfield, Connecticut. He escaped from the jail and was last seen headed for Massachusetts. Masters in southern colonies believed their slaves could make it to New York through paths along the Appalachian Mountains. Harry, who changed his named to Arnold, fled from his master in South Carolina and was "supposed to be in this province." Pero and Nero, "new negroes from the River Gambia," escaped from John Gartner of North Carolina, though they had little fluency in English. All three were arrested in Shrewsbury, New Jersey, in November 1765. Eight months later they escaped from John Morris, their jailer, "in a small boat, 16 feet keel, a black bottom and her wales painted brown, had 4 oars on board." [109]

As they had in 1741, the local authorities worried about slaves cooperating with enemies. Masters suspected the French of enticing blacks with promises of freedom during the Seven Years' War. A report in 1756 worried about "too great intimacy between the Negro slaves and the French neutrals in this province which may at this time tend to stir up the negroes to an insurrection when such numbers of our militia are detached to the frontiers against the French." [110] The Indian territories were generally safe for escaped slaves. Before the early 1770s, European settlers had not penetrated the North American continent more than two hundred miles inland. Major Indian confederations still held sway over the interior. Along the frontier of European expansion, black and red traded and intermarried. [111] Dutch and English authorities negotiated with Iroquois and other Indian nations for the return of escaped slaves with mixed success. At times, Amerindians were amenable but not energetic about chasing and returning runaways. By the 1740s sufficient numbers of blacks lived in the North American interior that the issue became more focused and threatening to Europeans.

Other advertisements indicated the bondsmen's dedication to their own freedom. Frank of Morris County, who spoke English, Dutch, Spanish, and Danish, was "artful and cunning" and escaped "twice from Persons who took him up." Frank received assistance from "two of Capt. Kennedy's Negroes." Sampson, slave of John Phillips of New York City, "has made a practice of running away and skulking in the woods near plantations." Pompey, slave of Robert Benson of New York City, had been "skulking about the docks ever since his running away and wants to go a privateering." Arch, from Somerset County, New Jersey, went "some back way to Albany, to meet some yellow free Negroes, which went by water at the same time, or else try to get aboard some vessel, as he attempted about 3 years ago below Philadelphia." Arch could write his own pass and read the Bible. [112]

Bondsmen escaped despite drastic measures by their masters. Caesar ran away from Isaac Freeman of Woodbridge, New Jersey, in February 1756, then escaped again in August 1756. Caesar wore a "pair of iron pothooks around his neck with a chain fastened to it that reached his feet." Quaco fled in 1761 wearing an "iron collar with two hooks to it, round his neck, a pair of Handcuffs with a chain to them, six feet long." [113]

Slaves often ran away with white indentured servants. Race counted for little among what Peter Linebaugh has called the picaresque proletariat. For example, four servants, "a white man and three Negroes," stole a large two-masted boat from George Mumford of Fisher's Island. Joseph Heday, a ruddy-complexioned native of Newark, wore a "red Whitney Great Coat, red and white flower'd serge jacket, a swan skin strip'd [jacket], a pair of leather breeches, a pair of trowsers and other clothes." One of the blacks, Fortune, wore similar clothing, including "a new cloth coloured Fly-Coat with a red lining, a Kersey Great Coat, three Kersey Jackets and breeches of a dark colour, a new pair of Chocolate coloured corded Drugges breeches, a pair of blue and white check'd trowsers, two pair of shoes, one of them new, several pair of stockings a Castor and a new felt hat." The others carried similar amounts of clothing. The quartet stole "a firkin of butter, weighs about 60 pound, two cheeses weighs 64 pounds and Bread for the same." [114] On at least five occasions, four or more blacks or blacks and whites fled together. Bood, Bristol, Jack, and Tom fled masters in New Jersey together, heading for the "indian towns upon Sasquehannah," where Bood had been "entertained by the Indians there several months." In 1763 four blacks, "Lester, Caesar, Mingo and Isaac," fled from William Bull of New York City, who offered to pardon them if they returned. Two slaves named Jack fled with Cuff from masters in Bergen County and Staten Island in 1757. Masters believed that servants enticed slaves to run away. Sam, of Trenton, was "enticed by one Isaac Randall, an apprentice"; the pair stole a bay gelding to escape to New York or Philadelphia, where they hoped to get on a privateer. Ham, an African slave, ran away with two servant men, Harbackkuck Eastwood and John Nickels, armed with fake passes and destined to receive assistance in Philadelphia. Men and women ran away to form families. "A short chubby fellow" ran away from John Decker of Staten Island to be with a "a negro wench of middle size, with child it is supposed they went together." Runaway combinations revealed interracial marriages. Ned of Lancaster County, Pennsylvania, ran away with Mary Woods, a white woman from New Jersey "by whom he had a child near 3 months old." Ned could read and write and "tis very likely he has procured a pass for them as man and wife." Domingo, a "Spanish Negro Man," fled in 1748 to hide in the swamps of Manhattan Island, near the home of Mary Carrey, "a white woman who used to harbour him at her lodgings near the Stockade." [115]

Crime and Violence

Despite pitiless laws and severe punishments, the laws against slave crime were ineffective. Although black theft was harshly punished in the post-1741 era, there was no sign of decrease. The confession of Hannah in 1760 reveals the methods and reasons for petty theft. She "crept into the House of John Newkirk of the Dock Ward, silversmith, hid herself in the loft till near the break of day, then came down stairs and went into the shop, taking as much Bristol Shiff muslim handkerchief and a small piece of calico as she could make her a gown and pettycoat." She then went to the tailors, where her theft was discovered and the goods returned to Mrs. Newkirk. Hannah stole the goods because "she was almost naked and her mistress would give her no clothes." Hannah received a pardon.[116]

Despite thievery by their chattel, some masters petitioned to avoid their slaves' execution during this period. Falmouth, property of Robert Gibb, was convicted of armed robbery and attempted murder in 1770, but his master's petition enabled him to avoid the gallows by a sentence of transportation to "any of the foreign West Indies."[117] Slaves cheated the hangman by robbing their masters and then escaping to parts unknown. Johan Jeremiah Myer, an indentured servant, and Tom, a mulatto man belonging to John Shepard of Shrewsbury, New Jersey, robbed Myer's master of "a considerable sum of money," then escaped.[118]

Relations between slaves and masters often became strained to the point of violence. Angry slaves raped their mistresses, burned their homes, and attacked and murdered their masters.[119] It was recognized that murders were a result of slaves' desires for freedom. A New York City news story in 1746 reported on a slave who murdered his master with an ax "to gain his liberty."[120] In 1750 in Amboy, East Jersey, Mrs. Obadiah Ayers was shot dead in her own house by her slave, "in conjunction with another New Negroe belonging to one of the neighbors." The pair plotted to steal guns and kill their masters and any other white they might encounter. They were burned for their crimes.[121]

In December 1752, at the fork of two rivers near Raritan, Somerset County, New Jersey, a condemned slave was burned at the stake for the murder of his master, Jacob Van Neste. Van Neste had angered the slave, described as "large and athletic," by taking some tobacco without his permission. When Van Neste returned home one evening, the slave struck his master with an ax as he dismounted at the stable door, nearly decapitating him. The next day, local farmers proved the bondsman's guilt by forcing him to touch the slain master's head, causing, according to eyewitness reports, blood to run from the corpse's nose and ears. The execution occurred the following morning at dawn.

Map of the Province of New-York, *1776. This military map shows the spread of settlements around what would become Greater New York. In 1771, 21,000 enslaved blacks lived within fifty miles of Manhattan Island. (Courtesy of the Division of Rare and Manuscript Collections, Cornell University Library.)*

Sheriff Abraham Van Doren of Somerset County orchestrated the killing, with drawn sword held high above his head while riding on his horse. Van Doren represented implacable authority to the audience of local farmers and their slaves, for whom the immolation was intended to be a horrific lesson of the futility of resistance. Onlookers reported that the slave "stood the fire with greatest intrepidity." Newspaper accounts related that as the flames covered his body, he shouted to the assembled blacks, "they have taken the root, but left the branches." [122]

The counterpoint to Van Doren's performance was a slave culture with strong African roots. In the West African societies from which many of the enslaved blacks came, adults were taught to have a "profound disdain for pain . . . to make a single cry would be a dishonor."

Through self-knowledge and courage, an African secured esteem from his peers. Mastery of pain was a major factor in the social integration of the individual. To the assembled slaves, the anonymous slave burned at Raritan was a hero, his memory recounted in the collective identity of resistance.[123]

The location of the incident at Raritan is also important. Authorities placed the execution at a river crossroads so that more people could view the auto-de-fé. To the assembled Africans, however, the crossroads represented the Four Moments of the Sun and brought to the surface of their consciousness pre-Christian beliefs symbolizing spiritual continuity and renaissance. The crossroads represented the deepest spiritual resistance to the brutal punishment, as a transient, restless people came together to hear the dying man's song of affirmation. Retold many times at work on farms, along the wharves, in forest retreats, and in taverns, such events congealed into the history of a people. Their inchoate emotions coalesced into fierce desires for insurrection and retold many times became deeply nurtured hurts that could be avenged during the American Revolution. W. E. B. Du Bois contended that an intense fire of African freedom flowed in the veins of these slaves, many of whom had arrived from Africa in the past few years.[124]

A Restless People

The early 1770s were filled with slave restlessness in New York and New Jersey. Blacks, listening to the Patriots' revolutionary demands, countered with petitions designed to end slavery just as white Americans grappled with the necessities of separation from England to guarantee their freedom. In Massachusetts, free blacks and slaves petitioned the colonial and later the state assembly to end slavery and include African Americans in constitutional debate. Rumors floated along the coast about the effects of the Somerset decision, which virtually ended slavery in England. An anonymous pamphleteer announced to enslaved blacks that English freedom was available to all simply "by setting a Foot on that happy Territory where slavery is forbidden to perch." [125] In New York and eastern New Jersey worsening racial relations prohibited such discussion. Rather, Patriots cautioned against any encouragement of black freedom and considered alternate means of dealing with the problem of slavery. In county after county, slave owners worried about slave uprisings.[126]

Made anxious by rumors of slave conspiracies, local authorities looked to past laws to curb unruly bondsmen. In New York City in

1773, the Common Council revived a law requiring white residents to detain for whipping any slave found in the streets after dark. In Queens County, Patriots reported disaffection among their slaves and worried about "enlisting negroes." Tensions between slaves and masters resulted in gruesome but familiar tragedies. In 1775 in New York City "two Tory Negroes" were hanged for "engaging to murder their masters who were supporters of Liberty." The plight of one slave master indicates the anxieties felt by many. William Livingston, soon to be governor of New Jersey, offered to sell a male slave, whom he described as good-natured, sober, "fit for a house negro & especially to tend a table." The one caveat was that while Livingston lived in New York City the slave "would be abroad at night after the Family was a bed and we never found by what avenue he went or returned." [127]

Slave resistance in colonial New York and East Jersey ranged from highly individual acts to moments of decisive, collective revolt, from petitions seeking relief from imperial governors to plots hatched in taprooms and on holidays. Members of African "nations" were involved as were highly acculturated, seasoned slaves. Opportunism characterized their approach to resistance. Viewed apart, these actions seem inchoate and aimless; taken together they were the actions of people ready to strike at any moment for their liberty. Current arguments about the onset of true African revolutions in North America contend that blacks did not think politically until the Haitian revolution of the 1790s. But the conspirators of 1741 and the angry, even nihilistic confrontations that followed in the next two decades were certainly signs that African Americans in New York and East Jersey were preparing to move against their white oppressors.[128]

Conclusions

Neither black nor white knew in the early 1770s that over the next decade a war for independence would engulf all Americans. Enslaved blacks and their masters in and around New York City found themselves on the rim of a whirlwind, as Patriot, British, and vigilante forces battled for land and position around New York, aptly described as the cockpit of the American Revolution. Lacking clairvoyance, black and white could look back over the past three decades since the bloodbath of 1741. White masters had learned little from that debacle. Voracious demands for labor brought thousands more Africans to the region, few of them acculturated or acquiescent to their bondage. European religions either shrank from a full drive to enclose blacks in their church memberships or tried to hide behind rituals, which were already proven to have double meanings for their bondspeople. Nor could ferocious laws cow the black population, which sustained its slave culture in a combination of nascent nationhood and semicriminal behavior. Only a fraction found sanctuary in European religion. A few Spanish blacks could appeal to Crown officials to gain emancipation. For the rest, the hardships of servitude, the hazards of family life, and demographics that sent young men careening around the countryside in search of female and other companionship could only further alienate them from their masters. The slave culture was an avenue to express their grievances. When the Revolution hit the region, young and old blacks were ready to make a move.

CHAPTER 5

The Black American Revolution

1776–1783

Running to Freedom

In 1779, Boston King fled from Virginia to New York City in search of freedom behind the British lines. He later related his escape in dramatic fashion:

As I was at prayer one evening, I thought the Lord Heard Me, and would mercifully deliver me. Therefore putting my confidence in him, about one o'clock in the morning, I went down to the river side and found the guards were either asleep or in the tavern. I instantly entered the water, but when I was a little distance from the opposite shore, I heard the sentinels disputing among themselves. One said, I am sure I saw a man cross the river. Another replied, there is no such thing. When I got a little distance from the shore I got down on my knees and thanked God for this deliverance. I traveled until five o'clock in the morning and then concealed myself until seven o'clock at night, when I proceeded forward thro' brushes and marshes for fear of being discovered. When I came to the river, opposite Staten Island, I found a boat, and altho it was near a whale-boat, I ventured into it and cutting the rope, I got safe over. The commanding officer, when informed of my case, gave me a passport and I proceeded to New York.[1]

King was one of thousands of blacks seeking liberty during the American Revolution. A British invitation to revolt helped inspire their enthusiasm. On November 7, 1775, after months of speculation and threats, John Murray, Lord Dunmore, governor of Virginia, proclaimed freedom to all "indented servants, negroes . . . willing to serve

His Majesty's forces to end the present rebellion." Dunmore's proclamation probably did more than any other British measure to spur uncommitted Americans into the camp of rebellion. In the North, angry Long Island farmers burned Dunmore, once governor of New York, in effigy and worried about slaves "being too fond of British troops." If the proclamation made stronger patriots of plantation owners and yeoman farmers, it turned many blacks into Tories. Hundreds of black fugitives in Virginia, Maryland, and the Carolinas accepted Dunmore's call to join his Ethiopian Regiment.[2]

Choosing Sides

African Americans in New York and East Jersey chose sides in the Revolution after much personal reflection. They knew that neither side was trustworthy. American Patriots did not encourage black hopes that the war would end slavery, and English promises of freedom often proved illusory. Military necessities forced Dunmore and British generals William Howe and Henry Clinton to make bold proclamations offering freedom to blacks willing to serve the king, but many Loyalists and British officers owned slaves and gave little support to their hopes for freedom. Blacks in New York and New Jersey, like their southern counterparts, viewed the Revolution as a triangular conflict. In her comprehensive history of southern blacks in the American Revolution, Sylvia Frey has emphasized the valiant efforts of African Americans often caught in the web of a treacherous British military apparatus. The British motives were often questionable, but African Americans made deliberate, conscious decisions about casting their fate with the Tories and were frequently able to gain liberty.[3]

The military situation around New York offered them ample opportunity. Military action from 1776 to 1783 was intermittent and seasonal, political and civil control over the rural environs of New York and New Jersey was uncertain, and primary authority often rested in vigilante committees. Depending on the proximity of either army, farmers in these counties were Whig or Tory. The counties around New York City constituted a neutral zone over which the two sides battled for food, forage, and fuel. Vigilante bands on both sides conducted guerrilla actions until the end of the war in late 1783. Conditions became so turbulent that masters leaving their homes told slaves to shift for themselves. As a result of the military uncertainties, enslaved blacks desiring freedom could easily attach themselves to marauding armies.[4]

The Patriots Reject Blacks

As the conflict unfolded, blacks who declared their willingness to fight met with sharply different reactions from Patriots and Tories. American Whigs vacillated between official rejection of the use of black troops and the pressure of local needs. Not only was there danger of black revolt, but also slaves were valuable property, made more so by the absence of white laborers serving in the army. In addition, most white Americans did not regard blacks as fit soldiers. Moreover, the Patriots, who believed that they were engaged in the conflict to avoid English enslavement of the colonies, realized that talk of liberty was dangerous if heard by America's actual slaves.[5]

Despite official objections, some blacks did serve in military roles for the Patriots throughout the war. General George Washington at first rejected all black recruits, then changed his mind after Dunmore's proclamation. Henry Laurens's proposal that the Continental Congress purchase slaves from their masters and then draft them was rejected; still, blacks filtered into the American forces. In smaller states such as Rhode Island and Connecticut blacks made up significant portions of the Patriot regiments.[6]

Some states permitted masters to send slaves as replacements in military service with promises of freedom to substitute slave-soldiers. New Jersey and New York blacks joined the Patriots in this way. In 1777 in Philadelphia, a writer using the pen name "Antibiastes" condemned such arrangements, arguing that "a general emancipation of the Slaves, enlisted in the army or the navy ought immediately to take place," with compensation for their masters.[7] Local examples show the abuses inherent in this system. Samuel Sutphin of Readington, Somerset County, New Jersey, enlisted in the militia in place of his master, Caspar Berger, who had purchased him from Guisbert Bogert for that purpose. Sutphin "agreed to the terms" and served in the militia from 1776 until 1780. He bore arms, drew guard duty, and served as a guide for the Continental army. He was in New York City when the HMS *Asia* fired on the city and later took part in the Battle of Long Island, escaping with the aid of a "colored man who took me from Long Island to Staten Island in a skiff." Sutphin fought in several battles against Indians over the next year in upstate New York, receiving a bullet in his leg. After the war, instead of giving Sutphin freedom, the duplicitous Berger sold him to Peter Ten Eyck. Eventually, the black veteran was sold to another master named Peter Sutphin. He worked out an arrangement with his new owner, adopted his name, and gradually

Peter Williams Sr. Beloved sexton of the John Street Methodist Church, Williams sided with the Patriots during the American Revolution. The church purchased him from a departing Loyalist master, after which Williams worked off the debt and freed himself. He was a founding member of the African Methodist Church. (Courtesy of the New-York Historical Society)

purchased his freedom after twenty years.[8] Though most New Jersey blacks fighting in support of the Americans came from the southern part of the state, there were individual men of color who served with the Patriot forces. A black New Yorker, Peter Williams Sr. may have served the Patriots and, according to his son, the esteemed Episcopal cleric was a devout supporter of the Americans.[9]

Patriot blacks served in support roles as the "men behind the men with the guns." Patriots requisitioned slave labor to fortify New York City and Long Island in preparation for the British invasion in 1776.[10] On March 20, 1776, William Alexander (Lord Stirling) and the Committee of the Provincial Congress of New York, preparing for the defense of the city, ordered all masters to bring their slaves equipped with entrenching tools to build fortifications. Sarah Henry, a black woman from New Rochelle, recalled seventy-five years later that on July 9, 1776, after a reading of the Declaration of Independence, Patriots destroyed the king's statue, "the head cut off with an ax and stuck to the top of one of the iron rails that surround the statue and afterwards carried through the city in a cart."[11] A few weeks later the British warship *Asia* opened hostilities, bombarding the city from the harbor. Many Patriots had already fled north, some leaving their slaves behind to fend for themselves. Others took their slaves with them.[12]

New Yorkers disregarded recommendations that future abolition of slavery be included in the state constitution of 1777, but in New Jersey, Patriot governor William Livingston, influenced by a lengthy correspondence with Quaker Samuel Allinson, considered asking the state assembly to abolish slavery. After private discussions in 1778 with key legislators he wrote Allinson: "I have the pleasure to be entirely of your sentiments; I sent a message to the Assembly the very last session to lay the foundations for their manumission, but the house thought of us in too critical a situation to enter on the consideration of it at the present time, desired me in a private way as far as my influence extends to push the matter till it is affected being convinced that the practice is utterly inconsistent with the principles of Christianity & humanity & in America, who have almost idolized liberty, particularly odious and disgraceful."[13]

Blacks in New York and New Jersey found little hope for the abolition of slavery from religious denominations. The Society of Friends continued its appeals to end lifetime servitude, but, as the Quakers were neutral in the war, few Patriots regarded their appeals favorably. In most denominations, enforced silence about slavery was the rule. In 1778, the abolitionist minister Jacob Green of Hanover Presbyterian Church in New Jersey sermonized that "however free we may be from British oppression, I venture to say, we shall have inward convulsions, contentions, oppressions and various calamities . . . till we wash our hands of the guilt of negro slavery." As a mob formed outside the church to intimidate the pastor, Green thundered, "Can it be believed that a people contending for liberty should at the same time be supporting slavery? Is not freedom, the natural, inalienable right of all? What says Congress in their Declaration of Independence? I cannot but think that our Practicing Negro Slavery is the most crying sin in our land." His church was sacked and Green was silenced.[14]

Patriots were also chary of emancipating blacks. Emancipation by will during the American Revolutionary period remained as rare as in preceding eras. Of 227 recorded wills in New York State and New Jersey between 1775 and 1783, 190, or 83 percent, bequeathed slaves to kin or ordered them sold to pay debts or provide a financial estate.[15] Other masters granted limited forms of emancipation. Seven percent bequeathed slaves the right to choose new masters, with executors reserving the right to make the sales. Peter Jay, of Rye, father of the future chief justice, gave two blacks, Zilpha and Mary, "in consideration of their long service the choice of masters among my sons." Ten percent of wills provided conditional freedom. Typical of such contracts was that of Daniel White, a physician from Westchester, who "makes negro wench Hagar free at the end of the American War & her children and other negroes (except as my wife shall need them) will be free at age 21." Showing the fragility of such promises, Nathan Underhill of Westchester left several blacks to his nephew and friend and initially freed Abraham, Phyllis, and Peggy. Later Underhill wrote a codicil stating that Peggy had misbehaved and so should be sold.[16] Manumissions by Quakers, like those of other slave masters in the area, did not forecast immediate emancipation as much as pave the way for gradual freedom. Some Quaker emancipations were private. Isaac Corlies gained his freedom from Will Mott, a Quaker from Great Neck, Long Island. His wife, Hagar Corlies, also became free by manumission from Quaker Joseph Hewlett of Great Neck.[17]

Choosing the British

As Patriots hesitated or refused to include blacks in the battle for freedom, many African Americans sided with the British. The famous Moravian minister Henry M. Muhlenberg realized early in the war that the Negroes "secretly wished the British army might win, for then all Negro slaves will gain their freedom. It is said that this sentiment is universal amongst all the Negroes in America." Muhlenberg complained that "Barbarous Indians & Negroes are being enticed by the so-called Christians with gifts and promises." As the first year of the war unfolded, Patriots worried about a full-scale black revolution. In early 1776, Charles Lee wrote of the need to impose military order over the black population of Virginia, noting that "dominion over the black is based upon opinion, lose that and authority will fall." [18]

Evidence of the validity of Patriot concerns quickly emerged. After Dunmore's defeat in Norfolk, Virginia, in early 1776, he sailed for New York City, arriving at Staten Island on August 13, 1776. Accompanying him were some one hundred men, the "remains of the Aetheopian Regiment." On Staten Island, these black soldiers joined with other refugee blacks to create a regiment rumored in reports to General Nathanael Greene to be over eight hundred strong. Many fell in the Battle of Long Island in the summer of 1776 as part of the English force that mounted an attack on the fortifications at Brooklyn Heights.[19]

By September 1776, General William Howe's British regulars and Hessian troops had swept across Long Island and New York City and established a toehold at New Barbados Neck in Bergen County. During this time, blacks fled their masters to work within the British lines.[20] Freeborn blacks also joined the British, finding work in the Wagon Master General's Department or as woodcutters.[21]

During the disastrous American retreat across New Jersey in the autumn of 1776, more blacks joined the English forces. General George Washington first stationed his troops at Hackensack, then retreated in November 1776, leaving the town open to British control. Lord Cornwallis and his forces arrived at daybreak on November 20, 1776, forcing Washington and his army at Hackensack, pinned between the advancing British to the east and the Passaic and Saddle Rivers to the west and lacking a single entrenching tool, to retreat south and west. Washington was troubled by a lack of recruits as his army limped into West Jersey. As the Americans retreated, at least five slaves took advantage of the chaos to defect to the British.[22] These fugitive blacks were immediately put into action. In the wake of the American retreat on November 23, 1776, Tories and fugitive blacks sacked the homes of Patriots in Schraalenburgh in Bergen County, increasing local hostilities.[23] When each army was positioned for winter, the British raided the Bergen County townships of Closter, Tenafly, and Tappan to secure cattle and forage.[24]

By the close of 1776 the British had opened a wide offensive line stretching from Tappan to Monmouth County. Blacks in Middlesex County joined the advancing British army. Local slave owners complained of British soldiers "continually forming with Numbers of our Negroes."[25] In a letter written in 1776, the Reverend Alexander Mac-Whorter of Newark wrote anxiously: "Great have been the ravages committed by the British troops in this part of the country. . . . One Thomas Hayes, who lived about three miles out of town, as peaceable and inoffensive a man as in the State of New Jersey, was murdered by one of their Negroes, who run him through the body with his sword. He also cut and slashed his aged uncle in such a manner that he is not yet recovered of his wounds, though received about three months ago. The same fellow stabbed Nathan Baldwin in the neighborhood, who recovered."[26]

Coupled with rising royalist sentiment in New Jersey, black defections caused the Patriot cause to falter until Washington's badly needed victories at Trenton and Princeton.[27] As the British retreated back to New York City, blacks accompanied them.[28] During the skirmishes of early spring, more blacks left masters in Essex, Morris, and Middlesex Counties, New Jersey, and in Westchester County, New

York.[29] Though New Jersey had a patrol system, there is little indication that escaped slaves were easily captured in the chaotic years of the Revolution. Acquackanonk (Passaic), New Jersey, was across the Hudson River from New York, yet whole families from there sought refuge in British-occupied Manhattan in the early years of the war, safe from their masters. Owners persistent in their search had several possible avenues. On occasion, constables lodged suspected runaways in jails until the master fetched them, a profitable venture for the officers. Negotiation with the British commander, General William Howe, was possible, but with uncertain success. Other owners simply crossed into the British lines to seek return of escaped slaves. Patriots would send captured blacks to work gangs or assign them to new owners.[30]

Soon the Americans devised harsh penalties for blacks seeking to join the British. Captured fugitives were tortured or shot. Boston King described one slave arrested for trying to escape from his master: "He had been taken prisoner and attempted to make his escape, but was caught twelve miles off. They tied him to the tail of a horse and in this manner brought him back to Brunswick. When I saw him his feet were fastened in the stocks and at night his hands also."[31] Even these punishments did not deter blacks intent on joining the British. After fighting broke out, John Thompson, a freeborn black from Long Island, offered his services to Edmund Fanning, secretary to Governor William Tryon of New York. Fanning put him to work carrying secret correspondence between British vessels and David Mathews, Loyalist mayor of New York City. Thompson was apprehended and jailed for two months in Newark, New Jersey. Somehow he escaped, reenlisted with the British, and served for several years in the King's American Regiment and later in the Royal Navy.[32]

Black Religion in Occupied New York

As in the colonial period, alliances between the British and blacks were built on religious foundations. Although the war seriously hampered religious observance, blacks and whites worshiped together. In 1776 as the American army fled New York City, a wounded British soldier observed returning Loyalists, particularly Anglicans, "mother and children, grandfather and grandchildren, etc. down to the black children of the slaves, hugging and kissing each other." Anglicans were generally loyal, particularly in New York and New Jersey, where support for the SPG and a bishopric was strong. While black and white Anglicans celebrated British control, a plot to destroy the city was afoot.

Charles Inglis reported to his SPG directors in London in 1776, "Several rebels secreted themselves in the houses. . . . The weather being very dry and the Wind blowing fresh on Saturday, they set fire to the city in several places at one time, between 12 and 1 o'clock in the morning. The fire raged with the utmost fury and its destructive Progress consumed about one thousand houses, or a fourth part of the city." [33]

The fire destroyed Trinity Church and its charity school for blacks and forced Anglicans to borrow the Dutch Reformed Church for their services. The school for blacks reopened: "Mr. Hildreth opened his school, his scholars collected and . . . The Number of Negroes is the same." Inglis reported to the SPG that "Mr. Bull regularly catechizes the Negroes on Sunday after the Evening Service, and the Reverend Mr. Walters, a worthy clergyman from Boston, generally gives them a Lecture or Sermon at the same time." Bull reported that many of the black refugees became communicants. By 1778 the rebuilt Trinity Church began to hold marriage ceremonies for freed slave couples. Another Anglican missionary, Abraham Beach, used flags of truce to travel from a refuge in New York City to New Brunswick, New Jersey, where he baptized six blacks each year. [34]

The fusion of Christian and black religion continued apace. One example was the free black leader Stephen Bleucke, who arrived in New York City in the late 1760s with his wife, Margaret, and became the head of the black Loyalists in the wartime city. Bleucke, described as an impressive, educated man, was the culmination of Anglican missionary efforts toward blacks. A member of the church and the leader of his people, Bleucke became very important in British postwar plans for black Loyalists. [35]

In the King's Service

Beginning with Dunmore's Ethiopian Regiment, the British quickly put black fugitives to work at paramilitary duties. Commissioned by General Henry Clinton on April 2, 1776, in New York City, the Black Pioneers served as guards, pilots, spies, and Indian interpreters. They performed executions and were able horsemen, hunters, and drummers. [36] Two white officers commanded companies of Pioneers in the Carolinas, Virginia, and New York, which included three black sergeants, three black corporals, and thirty-two black privates. Pay was generally equal to that of white Loyalist infantry. [37] In May 1776, George Martin, the white captain of the Pioneers, swore a group of blacks into the British army on board a ship in the Cape Fear River in North Carolina. The oath briefly noted that volunteers entered the company without compulsion and that applicants would faithfully serve the British army. In August 1776 the Black Pioneer company assisted the carpenters preparing fortifications in New York. With the company were fifteen women and eight children. Thomas Peters, who was sworn in on November 14, 1776, by Alderman William Waddell in New York City, remembered promises from the officers that after the war they would be "at our own liberty to do & provide for ourselves." [38]

General Henry Clinton remained interested in the welfare of the Black Pioneers. In the initial stages of a relationship that lasted beyond the war, Clinton wrote his then commanding officer, Sir William Howe, on January 11, 1777, of the needs for funds for uniforms for the "black company." During the 1778 campaign Clinton placed the Black Pioneers on the list of persons "victualled at the Commissary General's Provision Stores," a privilege they retained throughout the war.[39]

Among Black Pioneers who spied for the British was Benjamin Whitecuff, freeborn on Long Island, who joined the British forces on Staten Island in 1776 and worked for General Clinton as a spy for two years, earning over fifteen guineas in that time. Caught by the Patriots near Cranbury, New Jersey, Whitecuff was hanged. The Americans left him dangling and still alive. A few minutes later he was rescued by an English regiment. Whitecuff proceeded to Staten Island, then went to Virginia. Captured in Boston by the Americans, Whitecuff was again condemned to be hanged. Fortunately for him, the British recaptured him a second time and sent him to England for refuge. Although he announced his intention to emigrate to Sierra Leone, he stayed in London. Later he served the British in the siege of Gibraltar.[40]

In addition to the officially recognized Black Pioneer company, an informal but highly effective black military force was known as the "followers of the Army and Flag." These were escaped slaves and free blacks expert in guerrilla warfare and very useful for softening up Patriot militias with nighttime raids or securing much-needed livestock for the English garrison in New York City.[41]

The "followers of the army" resembled several historic British slave regiments. First were "Black Shot" organizations of whole units of armed slaves. Used in Jamaica in the 1740s and again in the 1780s, the Black Shot was usually a temporary military force. A second type were Black Corps, special military units of free blacks, mulattos, and recently freed slaves. Black Corps were auxiliaries to other militia units or organized as rangers who could transfer between colonies to meet special crises. A third type were black sailors employed in all the major European navies and merchant marines. Black pilots were invaluable in guiding warships along treacherous colonial coasts and inland waterways.[42]

Blacks helped the British cause around New York in support companies as well. Freedom permitted access to paid work, possible during the colonial period but now far more open. One hundred twenty blacks worked as laborers in the Quartermaster General's Department, for the wagon master, or in the Forage and Provision Departments of the army. Although the British paid these laborers less than they did white Loyalists, wartime necessity permitted desegregation of several occupations such as cartman, wagon driver, and carpenter. As the labor shortage worsened, blacks commanded the same inflationary wages as whites.[43] There was work and security in New York City or in Staten Island, where, one Hessian reported, "various blacks are just as free as the whites." In 1779 the Black Pioneers made about £60 every six months supplying the quartermaster general.[44] Tory blacks served as personal servants. For an escaped slave, offering one's services to a British officer was a good way to avoid recapture by a pursuing master.[45]

Privateering offered limitless possibilities to self-emancipated blacks. New York City and Perth Amboy were the home ports for innumerable vessels with letters of marque, entitling masters to raid Patriot boats or ports. With a constant need for sailors on these often dangerous voyages, ship captains were hardly choosy about hiring black sailors.[46]

Another area of wartime opportunity was in private business. Some of this was quite exploitative. The Royal Chimney Sweep in New York City kept half a dozen blacks, each of whom swept at least twenty chimneys a day. For each chimney "his master receives £2, the negro gets nothing but coarse food and rags." In contrast to these abusive arrangements, wages at the Faulkner Brewery in New York were generally high. "James, a negroe boy," earned £1 and 8 shillings per week in February 1778; the other six blacks working regularly at Faulkner earned about 6 to 7 shillings per day.[47]

A few blacks prospered in Revolutionary New York. Samuel Burke, who served as a "batman," or military servant to a cavalry officer, married a "free Dutch Mollatto woman" in New York City. They purchased a very good house and garden with furniture in the city. Burke served in numerous battles before leaving for England in 1783. His wealth was fleeting, however. Destitute, his wife dead, and his papers lost at the Battle of Charleston, Burke made artificial flowers in London. He estimated his New York City losses at £350 for the house and garden and £45 for possessions such as a mahogany bedstead, a feather bed, six chairs, a looking glass, and dishes and plates.[48]

As the war continued, the British promised freedom in exchange for black military service. In July 1779 Henry Clinton issued a proclamation promising to "every Negro who shall desert the Rebell Standard full security to follow within these lines any Occupation which he shall think Proper."[49] The American reaction to this invitation was ridicule. A New Jersey poet wrote:

> A proclamation oft of late he sends
> To thieves and rogues who are only his friends
> Those he invites; all colours he attacks
> But deference pays to *Ethiopian Blacks*.[50]

Clinton's promise of sanctuary, widely circulated in Loyalist newspapers, set off a rush of black enlistments.[51] The British government offered some judicial equality to its black soldiers. One white Loyalist, Micah Williams, was arrested for kicking Quamino, a black driver. Quamino lifted his complaint only after Williams publicly apologized.[52]

In 1779, a British census-taker counted 1,951 blacks living in the city, or about 16 percent of the total population of 12,408. For New Jersey the best sources are the tax ratables for 1778 and 1780, which offer a partial estimate of 1,788 slaves in the six eastern counties surrounding New York. Both tallies are indications that the chaos of the war made blacks highly unaccountable.[53]

In fact, the war did create many possibilities for blacks to live independently of whites. Blacks in New York City lived in "Negro barracks" at 18 Broadway, 10 Church Street, 18 Great George Street, 8 Skinner Street, and 36 St. James Street and in Brooklyn near the navy yard and the wagon yard. These dormitories were crowded: sixty-four laborers shared one set of five and a half rooms, seventy-eight others had six and a half rooms and thirty-seven Black Pioneers shared three and a half rooms. A meager one lamp and one pint of oil or one pound of candles were allowed per room each week. Thomas A. Jones, the Loyalist historian, groused that excellent housing that could have been rented profitably to deserving white Loyalists, with profits used to support the war effort, was being wasted on refugee blacks. Black housing may not have been as luxurious as Jones suggested. A young runaway was "supposed to be in the houses behind the college, where his mother lives," a neighborhood partially destroyed in the fire of 1776, where many lived in tents.[54]

No longer restricted by anxious colonials, the slave culture appeared openly. New York was the scene of "Ethiopian Balls" in which African Americans and British officers and soldiers freely mingled to the music of black fiddlers and banjo players. The music season began in the late fall. Black tavern life flourished. African Americans joined British soldiers, especially in horse racing, which spiced life in occupied New York. Americans satirized the familiarity between the British and the blacks in a biting commentary on an interracial ball held in 1778. The writer described General William Howe's review of the Royal African Regiment: "The contest for pre-eminence between Quaco and Sambo was long and obstinate. It is evident that Sambo has the thickest lips and the whitest teeth, but his Excellency's partiality is in favor of Quaco as he has honored him with the command; at the entertainment lately given by the officers of the Royal African Regiment, his Excellency opened the ball with Colonel Quaco's Lady and danced very gracefully to the music of a full orchestra of banjoes and hurdy-gurdies. How far the superior beauty of Colonel Quaco's Lady may have contributed to his promotion is uncertain."[55]

Despite the contradictions in British attitudes, during 1778 slaves openly declared plans to join the British. Patriot Richard Varick, writing his friend Philip Van Rensselaer, echoed many slave masters in Bergen County who felt the loss of slaves: "In the beginning of the war, my father had two middle-aged negroes and wenches—he has lost the wench. . . . One negro died and the last wench and one negro left with the enemy to my mother's distress." Not only were blacks leaving their masters, but it was becoming harder to purchase replacements because slave imports had ceased. In their wills, masters inflated the value of their slaves. In Middlesex County, hard hit by British raids, inventories listed slaves suddenly worth £600 for a man, £375 for a young girl, and £400 for a boy.[56]

Runaway slaves found refuge among the black gangs in blockhouses that lined the Hudson River. These gangs raided Bergen County homes at will in early 1779. Major Tom Ward formed a squad of black wood-cutters and foragers at the blockhouses at Fort Lee and Bergen Neck; these bands were "of great assistance in supplying the Garrison with fuel." Ward's blacks, the Black Pioneers, and the Black Brigade all took part in quick probes in Essex, Monmouth, and Bergen Counties.

Colonel Cuff commanded fugitive blacks garrisoned at a blockhouse on the Hudson River near Dobbs Ferry. Other New Jerseyans worried about a slave plot in Elizabethtown, promoted by British officers.[57]

In Monmouth County, New Jersey, Colonel Tye, formerly Titus, who escaped from John Corlies of Shrewsbury at the beginning of the war, returned to terrorize his master and other Patriots. In 1779 and 1780, Tye and his "motley crew" raided Monmouth County homes and farms at will, capturing Patriots and bringing them to the British in return for rewards. Tye and his men proved invaluable to the beleaguered British in New York City during the harsh winter of 1779–80. Slipping undetected into the towns and farms of Monmouth, Tye and his men carried off cattle, forage, and plate. The exploits of Tye and other black guerrillas around the neutral zone enabled innumerable blacks to escape their masters.[58]

The waves of refugees in New York City disturbed both sides. On May 25, 1780, the British major general James Patterson wrote the Loyalist ferrymaster Abraham Cuyler that "not only male but female Negroes with their children take advantage of your port in New Jersey to run away from masters and come into the city where they must become a burden to the town. . . . Be so good as to prevent their passing the North [Hudson] River as far as it is in your power to do it." American officials warned Bergen and Monmouth residents that "it may be dangerous to the community to permit Negroes to reside near enemy lines . . . remove them to some more remote part of the state." To shore up local defenses, New Jersey governor William Livingston again declared martial law. Undaunted, in early June 1780 "twenty-nine Negroes of both sexes deserted . . . from Bergen County." Their method was to flee with the interracial guerrilla bands sent out to forage in Bergen County. Blacks could leave through ferry landings at Fort Lee, Bull's Ferry, and Fort Delancey at New Barbados Neck, where blockhouses manned by refugees and black soldiers guarded access to New York City. A "Negro Fort" perched near Kingsbridge on northern Manhattan Island, and a British army report said that Tom Ward's black stronghold was placed "upon the banks of the North River." Designed to cart wood for the army, this post was "secured with a blockhouse, two pieces of cannon, a stockade in front." Protected by the blockhouse, fugitive blacks rolled logs down a natural gorge at Weehawken, tied the logs together, and floated them across the Hudson River to freedom in New York City.[59]

The raids of Ward's Blacks from Bull's Ferry left Schraalenburgh and Tappan in Bergen County devastated but helped black brothers and sisters escape down the roads from Tappan and Hackensack to freedom inside the British lines.[60] Individual Patriots lived in fear of their lives after Ward apparently hired three of the blacks, including "little Will, owned by Van Ryper," to kill a creditor in Bergen. Patriots caught the three blacks and hanged them in the swamp north of Brown's Ferry Road; their bodies were left hanging in the air for weeks, an act of desecration that terrified blacks viewed as preventing their souls from returning to Africa. Despite this insult, the black fort withstood attacks. The Continental army's attempt in July 1780 to blast the black woodcutters and gangs out of Bull's Ferry met with a crushing defeat.[61]

As the war wound down in the mid-Atlantic region, trade resumed between New York and New Jersey. Blockhouses on the Hudson River and Sandy Hook, operated by blacks, became important regulators for the British. Inspired by desires for freedom, bold, courageous, and resourceful blacks with British protection made life very dangerous for their former masters. In the strife-torn neutral zone, the blacks represented civil authority. To proclaim their loyalty, the Black Pioneers sent a New Year's greeting to Henry Clinton on January 1, 1781, wishing him "the greatest success in all your Public and Private undertakings." The British demonstrated approval of their actions in a visit to the Fort Lee blockhouse by Prince William Henry, third son of George III, and later William IV, in September 1781.[62]

In the early 1780s, the Black Pioneers and the Black Brigade propped up the fading hopes of local Loyalists. Despite Cornwallis's defeat in 1781, Loyalists refused to go quietly, and they raided Long Island and New Jersey constantly. Ward's plunderers from Bergen Neck attacked Patriot positions in Hackensack and Closter several times in the summer of 1781. On June 5, 1782, forty whites and forty blacks known as the Armed Boat Company landed at Forked River, New Jersey, plundered Patriot homes, and burned several saltworks.[63] These forays, which doubtless raised the spirits of black and white Loyalists, contributed half of a seething cauldron of emotions that would spill over into the postwar period. It is difficult to blame the black Loyalists for continuing the fight, but white Patriots had long memories and did not easily forgive.

The Cost to Slave Owners

Crown protection of blacks had never pleased the region's slave masters. It was doubtless more irritating now that the war had become costly for them. Patriots were not the only masters to suffer the loss of valuable bondspeople. During 1777 the Continental Congress and state governments seized Loyalist property, an act that divided New Jersey and New York societies as much as the fighting. In addition to selling off land, houses, and livestock, American officials took slaves. Auctioning blacks and supplying them to American forces made confiscation agents the most active slave marketers during the war. As the various Loyalist claims made after the war attest, dozens of blacks found themselves with new masters. For example, Abraham Van Buskirk, a leading Loyalist of Bergen County, lost "1 negroe named Sam, 20, a miller, taken by the rebels; 1 negroe named Primus 19 by trade a carpenter, 2 negroes named Caesar and Quashee carpenters and millers, all taken by the rebels." Van Buskirk also lost "Two who were taken when he left home.... One was taken in a fishing boat in 1778 & he cannot say what became of him." Van Buskirk gave another "his freedom so that he might not be taken & believe he is still at liberty." The greatest single loss to a Loyalist came from an act of philanthropy. Oliver De Lancey, who took command of a British brigade of fifteen hundred Loyalists in 1779, freed twenty-three slaves on his farm in Bloomingdale on New York Island rather than have them confiscated by Patriots.[64]

Not all black laborers found freedom behind British lines. Because the international slave trade avoided war-torn New York City, internal traffic in slaves soared. The market was especially strong for domestics. Of 161 slaves offered for sale in the *Royal Gazette* between 1778 and 1783, 117, or 72 percent, performed domestic services ranging from general housework to gardening and hairdressing. At the close of the war, a departing Loyalist described a thirty-two-year-old black woman as "remarkable for being a good Cook, House Wench, perfectly sober and honest." She had lived with the family for twenty-four years. Accompanying her were three children, "a fine, healthy boy, 16 years of age, who can cook and attend table with any of his age and complexion in this country, and one other boy, who is equal in his attendance at the tea-table, and can not be equaled in Parisian graces in the bowing way, he is 12 years of age." The third child was a daughter, "well made and handsome and fit for the Lady's toilet." Other advertisements showed cooperation between slaves and masters. One mistress offered a married black woman with four children for sale as a group.[65]

The Perils of Peace

Peace negotiations between the Americans and the British in 1783 encouraged slave masters to petition British commander in chief Guy Carleton for permission to enter New York City to recapture fugitive blacks. Former slave Boston King described the terror of seeing old masters from the South and from Philadelphia and New Jersey seizing former slaves off the streets. King wrote: "The dreadful rumour filled us all with inexpressible anguish and horror . . . for some days we lost our appetite for food and sleep departed from our eyes."[66]

Only the protection of the British army kept nearly four thousand blacks in New York City safe from their former masters. Carleton eventually decided that blacks who responded to proclamations from the British general before 1782 were free and entitled to protection. Events in South Carolina were deeply influential. Lieutenant General Alexander Leslie wrote Carleton in June 1782 that "there are many who have been very useful, both at the Siege of Savannah and here, some of them have been guides and from their loyalty have been promised their freedom."[67] Such service convinced Carleton that blacks deserved protection and transportation to Nova Scotia. Boston King recalled that Carleton's decision meant that "each of us received a certificate from the commanding officer at New-York, which dispelled all our fears and filled us with gratitude." Infuriated, Washington and the other Patriots argued with Carleton, initiating a dispute that lasted for thirty years.[68]

The Black Pioneers were on the English payroll in New York City from mid-1782 until their departure in the fall of 1783, and Carleton approved quarterly payments through the Pioneers' officers and payments to independent pilots and spies until the Pioneers sailed for Nova Scotia.[69] Carleton clearly valued the Pioneers for he ordered them to remain in New York City until November 1783 to regulate the interim period. He also recommended that on reaching Nova Scotia, the Pioneers be awarded twenty acres of land each.[70]

Despite the British protection, American slave owners persisted in chasing former slaves. One remarkable incident demonstrates the black response. Captain Hessius from Totowa Falls went into New York City with a companion named Van Houten in early July 1782 to "enquire about some runaway negroes." On his return, Hessius "was beset and murdered by about 12 or 15 of Wards' Blacks not far from Bergen," described as "followers of the army." Though several were convicted, General Carleton, reviewing the case, commuted their punishment from death to transportation to the West Indies. The incident demonstrated the militancy with which blacks responded to attempts at reenslavement.[71]

Carleton dealt harshly with residents of New York City who aided slave masters intent upon recapturing escaped slaves. Thomas Willis, a police employee, was convicted of forcing Caesar, "a Negro, who came to New York City under a proclamation," onto a vessel that carried him to Elizabethtown in return for a gold coin. Willis had tied Caesar's hands behind his back and driven him through the streets, beating him with a stick. After fining him fifty guineas, Carleton ordered Willis exiled from the city immediately. In a similar incident, the slave of Jacob Duryea of Dutchess County refused to return with his master from New York City after making a delivery. After Duryea tied the slave to his boat, the slave was rescued on the Hudson River by Colonel Cuff and helpful Hessian soldiers. The slave was freed and Duryea taken back to New York City and court-martialed.[72]

While General George Washington and Carleton quarreled about the meaning of Clause Seven in the peace treaty, which called for the return of all Patriot property, including slaves, New York City blacks, like their counterparts in Savannah and Charleston, fled the city before the British evacuation, scheduled for November 1783. Fifty-six blacks were among 501 persons sailing from New York City bound for Halifax in October 1782.[73]

Carleton finally decided to honor black loyalty and wrote Washington on May 12, 1783, that "in the case of the Negroes declared free previous to my arrival. . . . I had no right to deprive them of that liberty." Under pressure from Washington, Carleton agreed to list each black émigré from New York City, providing names, ages, brief descriptions, origins, status, and date of arrival. Such information, the authorities reasoned, might be useful should the dispute ever entail compensation. The list of 3,000 included 1,336 men, 914 women, and 750 children. About 65 percent were from the southern colonies, 19 percent from the middle colonies, 5 percent from New England, and the rest were of unknown origins. Most had different surnames than their previous owners, indicating either several masters during a lifetime or a desire to separate their identity from that of the slave owner.[74] Almost 60 percent of blacks leaving New York City at the end of the war did so in family units, a huge jump over colonial era patterns for fugitive slaves.[75]

Many blacks traveled to Nova Scotia as indentured servants of Loyalists. Loyalists still believed in slavery, which meant that some blacks apparently exchanged one master for another. Others were more fortunate. General Samuel Birch, who issued the coveted passes to Nova Scotia, recognized any claims to freedom that predated 1782. Refugees entitled to passes had to have certificates of good character, and blacks in the guardhouse imprisoned for crimes ranging from theft to arson and murder were excluded.[76] Black declarations indicate how long some escaped slaves had eluded their masters. John, for example, a member of the elite Black Brigade, was but thirteen when he left his master, Jacob Fortune, in 1776. Isaac Taylor, another Black Brigade veteran, left John Van Horn in late 1775 at the age of fourteen.[77] Not all blacks in New York City succeeded in their efforts to go to Nova Scotia. Some blacks were incarcerated in the provost marshal's prison for assault and arson.[78]

Responding to American protests, the British set up a board of inquiry to handle slave owners' claims. The board's rulings often resulted in the recapture of former slaves even from boats ready to leave the New York Harbor. Meeting at Fraunces Tavern on July 24, 1783, the board heard the case of Gerrard Beeckman versus two black children, Peter and Elizabeth, "lately embarked with their Father for Nova Scotia and brought on shore for examination." Beeckman claimed that Pierre Van Cortlandt of Westchester County gave him the two children in 1777 but that Samuel Dobson, the children's father, came to Van Cortlandt's house and brought them to New York City. Apparently because the children were too young to answer any proclamation, the board awarded them to Beeckman. In another case, the board ordered Betty from Aquackanonck, New Jersey, though possessing a certificate from Samuel Birch, removed from a ship in the harbor to answer a claim by her former master, Thomas Smith. Smith argued that Betty had escaped only the previous April. Despite her protests that she "came within the British lines under the Sanction and claims the Privilege of the Proclamation," the board ordered her returned to New Jersey. A third case in which a wife and three children stayed behind while the husband went into the British service resulted in freedom for the man but continued bondage for his family. In several cases in which blacks clearly demonstrated that they came under British protection, the board declared that it lacked authority to determine their fate. American military officials were further hampered by claimants who were unwilling to journey to New York City.[79]

Americans suspected that the British did not report many fugitives and that the compilation of three thousand names was too small. The muster book of the Black Pioneers at Birchtown in Nova Scotia in 1784 suggests that American suspicions were correct. Stephen Bleucke, leader of the Black Pioneers, commanded the first division of Pioneers, which included forty-one men, thirty-eight women, and twenty-six children, none of whom were listed as passengers of *L'Abondance*.[80] Similar gaps appear in the muster rolls of George Travelle's company. Travelle, who escaped from his master in Bergen County in 1779, led a company of blacks from Bergen and Essex Counties. Some of their names appear in the embarkation lists, but others do not.[81] Other blacks left New York under different auspices. Bill Richmond, for example, born in Castelton, Staten Island, in 1763, was abandoned by his Loyalist master. Richmond attached himself to the future Duke of Northumberland, who took the lad home to England with him. There Richmond took an apprenticeship as a cabinetmaker. His love of gaudy clothing attracted bullies whom Richmond dispatched easily. His prowess as a boxer became known in 1791 when he decisively defeated the much larger Docky Moore. Ultimately, he lost to the champion Tom Cribb in a famous bout in 1805. Five years later, Richmond trained the great black pugilist Tom Molineaux for his battle against the English champion, Tom Cribb. Richmond remained one of the most honored boxers in England, fighting until he reached the age of fifty-six.[82]

When the British agreed to turn over New York City officially to the Americans on November 25, 1783, the Black Brigade was the sole group of Loyalist blacks left in the city. Many Americans, including vengeful slave masters, were unwilling to wait that long. One American ship in the harbor received much of the wrath of the remaining Loyalists. On October 28 the *Pennsylvania Packet* reported that "capt. Stewart's vessel, with the colours of the United States of America flying, was boarded by the Canaille, who, in a riotous manner, tore [it] down and carried [it] through the streets in triumph, attended by a Chosen group of blacks, seamen and loyalist leather-aprons."[83] With complete evacuation just weeks away, the Black Brigade's ire was unquenched. When they finally departed on November 30, 1783, the Black Brigade was the last British group to leave New York City.

Conclusions

African Americans did not end slavery in New York and New Jersey by their valiant mobilization during the American Revolution. Patriots in New York and New Jersey clung fiercely to slavery out of fear and necessity. Despite choosing the losing side in the American Revolution, though, African Americans could look back at the years between 1775 and 1783 with powerful feelings of accomplishment. Despite harsh penalties and constant surveillance, black runaways were a persistent and expensive problem. The numbers of them who fled greatly exceeded those in any previous era, nearly four times the amount known in the previous seventy years in the region.[84] At least three thousand of them, former slaves and free blacks, left bondage and discrimination behind for hopes of a new life in Nova Scotia. Those numbers, combined with the estimates of twenty-five thousand to fifty-five thousand fugitives from the southern states, add up to the largest black escape in the history of North American slavery.

The first fugitives arrived in New York City in 1776; the last who were permitted to leave with a certificate from General Birch gained sanctuary in 1782. None were free less than two years; many tasted liberty for as long as seven. That emancipation was hard-earned. The British proclaimed liberty to slaves to undermine the American military and economic strength, and blacks came to New York prepared to serve. The great majority purchased their liberty with service as soldiers, guides, woodcutters, sailors, cooks, washerwomen, cartmen, wagoneers, and foragers. Nor were they wholly subject to British command. A self-contained black leadership emerged during the war. The actions of Colonel Tye and his "motley crew" and Tom Ward's blacks demonstrate the importance of black raiders in gathering valuable supplies for the beleaguered English garrison in 1779 and 1780 and policing the Hudson River from blockhouses. In the neutral zone, where neither army held sway, African Americans held their own and at times seemed the most established authority. One important fact of life in New York during the evacuation period was that slave masters seeking to regain their chattel did so at the risk of their lives.

Given a chance by the conflict, blacks in New York formed a community. Living in tents, abandoned houses, shops, and British barracks, African Americans in New York in 1779 worked, held church services or attended Trinity Church, drank in their own bars, and held celebration dances. Their years of experience in New York helped blacks establish a society in Nova Scotia and, later, in Sierra Leone. Within this community emerged the most visible black leadership yet to appear in North America. Among the black Loyalists living in or passing through New York during the war were Stephen Bleucke, Boston King, Thomas Peters, Moses Wilkinson, David George, Cato Perkins, and other ministers who would lead exiled African Americans in their hegira around the Atlantic basin. It would be years before remaining blacks in New York and East Jersey could replace their commanding presences.[85] How deeply influenced black liberation plans were by religion can be seen in the remarkable dream of Murphy Stiel, a sergeant in the Black Pioneers. Stiel was in the barracks at Water Street when he heard "a Voice like a Man's (but saw no body)." The voice commanded Stiel to deliver a message to Sir Henry Clinton, commander in chief of British forces, that he should warn General George Washington to surrender "himself and his Troops to the King's Army" or else God's wrath would fall upon them. God's anger, Murphy explained, would mean that all the "Blacks in America" would fight against the Patriots. Stiel was compelled by the voice to tell Clinton that "for that the Lord would be on their Side." This amazing conflation of secular military goals and evangelical Christianity reveals the spiritual faith with which blacks empowered their struggle against the Patriots.[86]

The war also gave aspiring black females an opportunity to declare themselves free. Previously, fugitives had to "pretend to be free" by use of forged passes and freedom papers. When the British registered applicants for transfer to Nova Scotia, a surprising number of free women stepped forward. The English were often dubious about such claims, but 56 black women, 46 black men, 16 boys, and 13 girls presented themselves for passage as free people. Seventeen of the women were from New York, another 19 from Queens. These numbers are possible, but the 8 from Bergen County seems high. The total of 131 from the region meant that virtually every black person who could claim to be free chose to leave for Nova Scotia. Whatever the inflation in the numbers, unquestionably a sizable contingent of ambitious blacks elected for exile.[87]

Finally, the black experience in New York and New Jersey during the American Revolution demonstrated that African Americans fought for many of the same liberties as whites. Blacks sought freedom from bondage, greater political liberty, and access to land and opportunity, goals that were intrinsic to American republicanism in decades to come. Former slaves and free people of color around the Atlantic, inspired by their accomplishments during the Revolution and deeply imbued with the promise of freedom, created their own black republicanism from the ashes of war.

Blacks in New York and East Jersey who did not join the exodus to Nova Scotia, England, or the West Indies faced an uncertain future.

The valiant efforts of the black Loyalists had not toppled slavery; indeed, after the Revolution, the system of servitude, though under attack, was as strong as ever. The disorganized economies of the two states depended more than ever on the labor of enslaved blacks. Opposition to slavery was, for the moment, discredited. Blacks themselves would have to choose between the new American republicanism and their own sense of nationality.

CHAPTER 6

Gradually Free

1783–1804

White Freedom and Black Enslavement

The army of the United States of America entered New York City on November 25, 1783, a date commemorated throughout the nineteenth century as Evacuation Day. On that morning American troops paraded from Harlem on the Bowery into the city before thousands of cheering citizens. After a brief difficulty removing the English flag from atop a greased flagpole, Patriots raised the American banner symbolizing the city's transition from colonial to republican rule. Out in New York Harbor, the Black Brigade watched from the last British ship before it sailed away on November 30. The position of the Black Brigade ironically symbolized the peripheral status of African Americans in local freedom festivities.[1]

The postwar celebrations held as much danger as promise to local African Americans. Flush with military success, anxious about an economy denied access to traditional markets in England and the West Indies, and sorting out definitions of loyal citizenry, Patriots in the city and countryside had little interest in expanding the liberties of blacks. In New York City, Mayor James Duane and the Common Council, while reorganizing city government, quickly reinstated colonial laws governing slavery. This action matched earlier legislative confirmation of servitude by the state governments of New York and New Jersey. Black support of the British was not forgiven. One writer cursed black emancipation as "the total subversion of our liberties." The Negroes, "in combinations with their friends, the Quakers, would give every assistance to our enemies as . . . in the late contest, when they fought against us by whole regiments and the Quakers at the same time supported every measure of Great Britain to enslave us." New Jersey citizens expressed similar attitudes, contending that Quakers were pro-British and guilty of "poisoning the minds of our slaves." Opponents of abolition argued that it was a Quaker plot to give blacks the vote and control the state. Other antiabolitionist sentiment rested on age-old fears that free blacks would be unable to support themselves.[2]

African Americans, while feeling the tug of the rhetoric of revolutionary egalitarianism and liberty, had to focus on obtaining individual freedom and on constructing institutions outside of politics and inside of religious institutions. Both efforts required trial and failure before success in the early days of the nineteenth century. Generally they received little advice from the Patriots and were shut out of politics. In a heavily armed, vengeful white society, the conspiracies and rebellions of the past seventy years seemed more dangerous than ever. The loss of black leadership to Nova Scotia and beyond also dampened prospects for insurrections, though individual acts of defiance continued. There were, moreover, some grounds for optimism. Abetted by elite whites, blacks in New York and New Jersey gradually won precious liberty and established a community culture based on personal freedom, religion, and civic institutions. They were unable to duplicate the landowner-ship of the early seventeenth-century generation because property around New York became inaccessible to the poor, whether black or white. A second saga is the black success in obtaining individual liberty in the postrevolutionary decades. A lingering question was whether their future lay in the United States or in exile, as hundreds of black Loyalists had so recently chosen. In time, blacks learned to identify with the United States, though that emotion was always precarious.[3]

Chaos of the War and the Black Population

The departure of several hundred African Americans from New York and New Jersey to Nova Scotia created noticeable decreases in the immediate postwar black population of the two states. New York County's black population declined by 1,034 between the 1771 and the 1786 censuses. New York City returned to its prewar population by 1790 when the first national census counted 3,092 blacks in the city. Of this total, 1,036 were free, an unprecedented number and percentage unknown since the first decades of the city's existence. Yet 2,056 black people remained in bondage. Among male slave owners, merchants, retailers, and artisans predominated; widows were the largest group among women. Although skilled workers abandoned slavery in

Philadelphia, in New York City they remained the largest single group among slave owners. Even when masters freed their slaves, the emancipated blacks did not automatically become independent. As Shane White has demonstrated, 246 free blacks lived in white households in 1790, mostly among artisans and merchants.[4]

After the first difficult years, the black population of New York jumped sharply. By 1800, the free black population of the city was 3,333, or 56 percent of the total population of 5,867 people of color. The number of enslaved African Americans in the city grew to 2,534, a 25 percent increase. The next ten years saw a second leap in the number of blacks in New York. While the number of slaves decreased to 1,446, that of free blacks more than doubled to 7,470. That growth meant that most of the city's people of color were free. In twenty years, the proportion of enslaved blacks had dropped from 66 to 16 percent. The total population of the city tripled in those two decades, reaching 90,000 by 1810, but blacks remained nearly 10 percent of the city's populace, a significant portion.[5]

Similar growth did not occur in the rural areas. In Westchester County, the postwar black population dipped by 2,190 and did not approach its prewar levels until 1830. Slavery flourished in localities with Dutch majorities such as Bergen in New Jersey and Kings and Queens in New York. In Richmond and in the rural parts of Kings County, almost 60 percent of the white households in 1790 used black laborers, most of them enslaved. Households containing more than ten slaves were common. Kings, Queens, and Richmond Counties, where Dutch farmers remained the most steadfast slaveholders, experienced only slight growth between 1771 and 1790, indicating the losses of the Revolutionary years. Kings County had the largest slaveholdings with households of more than ten quite common. Nearly 40 percent of the households in Kings, Queens, and Richmond Counties owned slaves, a higher ratio than in South Carolina, North Carolina, or Maryland.[6]

The census of 1790 in New Jersey counted over eight thousand blacks in the five eastern counties. The proportion of free blacks in the overall population ranged from lows of 7.5 percent in Somerset and 7.7 percent in Bergen to a high of 18 percent in Monmouth. The number of slaveholders in Bergen County actually increased in the postrevolutionary era. In Hackensack township, slaveholders listed as taxpayers increased from sixty-five in 1789 to seventy-nine in 1792 and ninety by 1800. Slavery on small farms increased dramatically in newer, western towns in New Jersey. The number of slave masters jumped from twenty-five in 1784 to sixty-two in Franklin township and ninety in Harrington township by 1802. In Somerset County, slavery grew even faster, at about 10 percent a year. By 1790, blacks were more than 15 percent of the county's population.[7]

The routine commerce of slavery continued unabated in the postwar years. Sales, leasing, and hiring all resumed with little interruption. One of the most active participants in this commerce was John Peter De Lancey, a prominent farmer and political figure in Westchester County. Between 1790 and 1808, De Lancey recorded the purchase of more than twenty slaves in fifteen different transactions, buying slaves for life or until conclusion of their gradual emancipation.[8]

As in the colonial era, slaves were easily the most valuable possession of farmers, especially when free white laborers were becoming increasingly scarce. In the five eastern New Jersey counties of Bergen, Essex, Somerset, Middlesex, and Monmouth, the average acreage of individual farms was at most 70 in Shrewsbury and as little as 42 near Newark. In comparison with prosperous farms in Chester County, Pennsylvania, which averaged over 130 acres, small farmers in eastern New Jersey eked out only a subsistence. At a time of reduced land-holdings, owning slaves made the difference between prosperity and hardship. Slave masters held more cattle, horses, and acreage than non-slaveholders. In Hackensack, Bergen, Harrington, and New Barbados slave owners owned four times as many horses and cattle as non-slave owners. These differences became critical as Dutch farmers were hit hard by declining land fertility; those with any cash moved west into Somerset County. The others clung to their small freeholds. The same pattern occurred in the largely Dutch counties of Queens, Kings, and Richmond in New York State. Only in Westchester County did confiscation offer any real democratization of land, while in the Dutch counties, the upper classes and speculators purchased more than half of the land sold.[9]

Religion also played a larger part in the chances that a black person could become free. Large numbers of free blacks lived in those areas where Quakers, Anglicans, and Presbyterians were a significant proportion of the population. In Upper Freehold, a Quaker stronghold, and Shrewsbury, where Friends lived near Anglicans and Presbyterians, more than one hundred freedpeople lived, as opposed to a dozen in Dutch-dominated Freehold.[10] Whatever impulse toward emancipation existed among whites came primarily from members of the paternalist denominations.

The Manumission Society

Virtually the only whites openly campaigning for the emancipation of slaves were members of the New York Manumission Society formed in 1785 by congregants of the Church of England and the Society of Friends. The society served several important purposes. First, it attempted to persuade slave owners of the "injustice and Cruelty of their former conduct." Using verbal persuasion, letters, and readings of the English abolitionist Thomas Clarkson's essay on slavery, the society sought to convince slave owners of the virtues of gradual emancipation. More forcefully, it brought suit against kidnappers of slaves and interfered with slave sales. In 1789, Manumission Society member Lawrence Embree was indicted for preventing a constable from putting a runaway slave named Molly on a boat to send her home to her master. When the constable "got near the boat, the defendant and some of his friends took hold of him and others saved Molly." Despite clear violation of the law, the prosecutor withdrew the charge. The society's activities became federal crimes with passage of the Fugitive Slave Act of 1793, which empowered slave catchers to enter northern states to retrieve escaped bondspeople and required citizens to help them. The society claimed that between 1792 and 1814, it liberated 429 African American slaves. It also provided a registry for free blacks wishing to leave precious freedom papers in a secure place. Finally, the Manumission Society acted as a political conduit between black voters and the Federalist Party. Blacks acquired antislavery materials from the society, which distributed three hundred copies of Thomas Clarkson's *Essay on Slavery* and Granville Sharpe's reports on the fledgling colony in Sierra Leone. The society paid for publication of "Slavery" by "A Free Negro," an important early black abolitionist appeal that appeared in the *American Museum* in 1788.[11]

The society won an important victory in the late 1790s by ending the city government's practice of correcting disorderly slaves at the request of their masters. This method, a carryover from the colonial period, was widely used in the 1790s. According to a city report in 1799, the law was also used regularly to bring runaway slaves from other areas into the Bridewell jail to await retrieval by their masters. That year the Manumission Society successfully petitioned the city government to end the practice.[12]

Slave ownership by key members was a sharp contradiction of the society's liberalism. Important statesmen and philanthropic members, including future chief justice John Jay, Judge James Duane, and Senator Rufus King, proposed legislation favoring abolition of slavery while retaining their own bondspeople. Nearly all planned gradual emancipation for their slaves, a process that could take twenty years.

Recently, historians have viewed the society very critically. Shane White, for example, has contended that the Manumission Society did nothing to end slavery in New York. Another argument suggests that the society forced free blacks into accepting dependent status even as free laborers by requiring registration before black children could attend the African Free School. Countering these views is Rob Weston's argument that Alexander Hamilton and other Manumission Society members made up a liberal wing of the merchant class, which by now owned the majority of slaves in the city. In Weston's view, Hamilton's ambitions to join the top ranks of urban society mandated his ownership of slaves. Hamilton's ability to juggle self-interest, ambition, and lofty ideals of reform perhaps epitomizes the contradictions of the society. It was at once interested in modernity yet clung to traditional markers of status. The society's significance lies less in its members' halting, neocolonial liberalism than in its support for African Americans' legal actions for freedom, its hot-minded vigilance against dangerous slave catchers, its lobbying of recalcitrant slave masters, and its registry for freedom papers. It is noteworthy that the society's assistance to fugitive slaves placed it in violation of the 1793 Fugitive Slave Act, which carried substantial penalties. Finally, the society earned an important victory by convincing the municipal government to halt the practice of disciplining slaves.[13]

Across the river, the New Jersey Society for the Abolition of Slavery had more modest gains, primarily in defending the rights of free blacks and winning some important cases for slaves wrongfully kept from freedom. In one such case, Quamini of Morris County sued his new master, William Leddell, for his freedom, claiming that his former master, the now deceased Captain Augustine Bayles of Morris, had promised him that "if he would be honest, faithful and industrious, he would never serve another master." After Bayles's death, his widow remarried and her new husband, Thomas Faircloth, tried to sell Quamini to Leddell. The court ruled that Bayles's deathbed promise to Quamini made him a free man. In this case, as in others sponsored by the society, abolitionist whites assisted blacks intent on liberty.[14]

A few enlightened masters freed their slaves by public testimony. Moses Bloomfield set the tone on July 4, 1783. Bloomfield, joined by his fourteen slaves, mounted a platform in Woodbridge, New Jersey, during a celebration to mark the close of the war. Bloomfield declared, "As a nation, we are free and independent—all men are created equal, and why should these, my fellow-citizens—my equals, be held in bondage? From this day forth they are emancipated and I here declare them free and absolved from all servitude to me or my posterity." Bloomfield then asked the newly freed blacks if any intended to rely on public support. One held up his left hand and, with his right hand, drew a line across the middle joint of his fingers and proclaimed: "Neber, massa, Neber, so long as any of dese fingers are left above dese jints." [15]

Debating Emancipation

Stalled during the American Revolution and put on hold just after the war, talk of abolition of slavery returned as the two states settled into a peacetime normality. The legal end of slavery took time, but by 1799 in New York and 1804 in New Jersey, state legislatures passed gradual emancipation acts that initiated the end of chattel bondage. Scholars have sharply debated the reasons for this change. Leon Litwack and Arthur Zilversmit contend that postrevolutionary ideology could not tolerate the contradictions of slavery. Robin Blackburn revived this argument, showing that Federalists and Democratic-Republicans needed to demonstrate Revolutionary egalitarianism. Edgar McManus offers a similar argument though observing that economic needs slowed the extinction of slavery. Gary Nash, in his own work and in collaboration with Jean Soderlund, has attacked the ideological failure of postrevolutionary republicanism and argues that the economic decline of slavery was hastened by the rush to accept free wage labor. Shane White contends that emancipation occurred as a result of electoral redistribution in 1798, massive migration of New Englanders into western portions of New York State, and an identity crisis among slaveholding Dutch.[16] In my view, slavery ended in New York and New Jersey because of the cooperation of elite paternalists in the New York Manumission Society and the unceasing efforts of blacks themselves to end their slavery. Even then, servitude continued for several decades.

Early political discussions about abolition were not encouraging. In 1785 the New York State legislature debated the abolition of slavery. Opposed by small and large slaveholders, the bill failed in part because legislators attached noxious clauses to it such as the revocation of the suffrage granted inadvertently to blacks in the constitution of 1777. Other conservative corrections of the constitution included nullifying the right of blacks to testify in courts against whites and the right to marry a white without being fined. Although the legislature passed the bill, its governing body, the Council of Revision, rejected it because of the extra clauses.

There were incremental achievements in this legislative session. First was the prohibition of the sale of slaves in the state. Second, the legislature lifted the requirement in place since 1712 requiring masters to post a £200 bond before freeing a slave. The bond was replaced by a certificate from the local overseer of the poor. Once local poor officials certified that a slave was at least twenty-one and less than fifty years of age and capable of self-maintenance, his owner could free him without further obligation. The bond continued for slaves over fifty years of age.[17] None of these laws undermined the legal framework of slavery. Indeed, in 1788 the New York legislature reaffirmed the 1730 slave codes, making but a single concession to the arguments of the newly formed New York Manumission Society by making it illegal to buy or receive a slave with the intent to export him. Penalties were £100 and freedom for the slave.[18]

In New Jersey, Governor William Livingston, frustrated by pro-slavery forces during the Revolution, pushed through a ban in 1786 on importation of slaves from Africa or the West Indies. (Slave owners could still import bondspeople from other states, however.) The act also ended the £200 bond on manumissions, requiring only that masters freeing slaves between the ages of twenty-one and thirty-five provide some monetary security that none would become public charges. Although it greatly liberalized manumissions, the law did not immediately increase emancipations. In 1788 Livingston secured an amendment to the ban on the slave trade which instructed owners not to remove their slaves out of the state. An additional clause required masters to teach slaves who were born after passage of the act to read.[19]

Among the factors that protected slavery in the North was the complacent belief that it was milder than in the South or the West Indies. One anonymous New Yorker, writing in 1796, denounced slavery in America as "abominably unjust, inconsistent and ridiculous," showing that the Revolution, "tho truly great and glorious, is by no means so thorough." Still, he argued, slavery in New York and New Jersey was "mild (if any slave can be said to receive mild treatment), compared with what they receive in the southern states." Blacks in the North were "better clothed and fed and could avoid excessive whipping." Probably in no part of the world, concluded the author, "do slaves live so comfortable as here."[20]

Abolitionists in New York and New Jersey continued their appeals in the 1790s. Their efforts were set back in 1794 when the New Jersey Assembly passed a bill making it harder for slaves to gain their freedom through the courts. Joseph Bloomfield, head of the New Jersey abolition society, advanced a gradual emancipation bill the same year, but it was quickly defeated. In New York, prospects remained dreary despite the election of John Jay, a stalwart member of the Manumission Society, to the governorship in 1795. A bill for gradual emancipation failed in committee when the opposition argued that it would be "unjust and unconstitutional to deprive any citizen or citizens . . . of their property without compensation." Despite these legislative defeats, popular opinion and party newspapers became more cautious about the abolition issue. In truth, ideological justification for slavery in New York and New Jersey had vanished. Speaking to the New York Manumission Society, member E. H. Smith directly linked slavery with barbarous civilizations "of the rude edges of the world" and derided defenders of it as "deserters from the cause of revolution." Republicans admitted that slavery was incompatible with the Declaration of Independence. The Republican *Argus* reminded readers that blacks "had died on the field of battle bravely fighting for that liberty and independence we this day enjoy."[21]

After years of controversy, New York finally enacted a gradual emancipation act in 1799. The law, which did not affect any slaves born before July 4, 1799, provided that all black children born after that date would be free after serving the masters of their mothers until they were twenty-eight (males) and twenty-five (females). To pacify slave owners who claimed that the state was robbing them of their property, the law allowed them to abandon black children a year after their birth. Such children would be considered paupers, bound out to service by the overseers of the poor. New York State agreed to pay a maintenance fee of $3.50 a month for each child even if the caretaker was the former slave owner. Masters thus earned a sizable return for their acts of conscience; in effect, the abandonment clause was a hidden form of compensated abolition. The law passed despite splits in both parties. The abandonment clause quickly became costly: by 1804 the state had paid over $20,000 for the program, causing the senate and assembly to agree to revoke it.[22]

Under the New York law, slave masters could still bring their chattel into the city by applying to the mayor of New York City. In 1803 and 1804, masters and mistresses from southern states and the West Indies informed Mayor De Witt Clinton of New York City of their intention to bring slaves into the city and take up permanent residence. He assured them that no action would be taken against them.[23]

After many defeats, the New Jersey Assembly finally passed a gradual emancipation act in February 1804, which duplicated the gradual emancipation and abandonment clauses in the New York act. (Without those restrictions, the abolition act would not have passed.) By 1807, payments to masters caring for abandoned infants mounted to $12,000, or 30 percent of the state's budget. Most petitions sought the repeal of the entire abolition law rather than of the abandonment clause. Bergen County slave owners charged that abolition was "unconstitutional, impolitic and unjustly severe" and would "endanger the community." Opponents of slavery withstood such arguments, however. In no small part, the distant prospect of emancipation (no slave would be free for at least twenty years) lessened the concern of whites. That was the limit to reform in New Jersey, where slavery did not become illegal until 1865.[24]

Legal Freedom

Obtaining legal freedom required patience. In New York, manumission by will was rare in the first years after the Revolution. Of thirty-seven wills involving transfer of slave property, only three grants occurred between 1784 and 1786. New York wills retained colonial patterns making women the overwhelming recipients of slave inheritances. Manumissions were usually conditional. Lawrence Roome of Staten Island freed his slave Michael provided that "he bring to my executors a sum sufficient in case of casualties or old age." In contrast, Samuel Van Horne of New York City made his "slave Hester, her daughter also named Hester and Chance free" with annual stipends of £25.[25]

Manumissions in New York City increased in the 1790s. With gradual emancipation on the horizon, freedom was granted in fifteen of twenty-four wills involving the fate of enslaved blacks. The dominant patterns of inheritance still provided widows and daughters with slaves, with sons receiving fewer than half. Gradual emancipation was the rule. For example, John Baker, formerly a resident of Virginia but living in the seventh ward of New York at the time of his death in 1796, committed "the care of all my negro servants unto my wife, to retain them in her service, or to provide other masters or mistresses for them or to free them, but none of them shall be sold." Baker added that "it is then my pleasure that they become free after my wife's decease," with a dollar a week for support. William Walton, a prominent politician and merchant, freed his eleven slaves "after the decease or remarriage of my wife." Masters and mistresses also continued to allot money for maintenance of their slaves. Cornelius Clopper of New York left interest-bearing bonds worth £1,000 to provide sustenance for his six slaves.[26]

The greatest number of manumissions in the postrevolutionary period came while masters were still alive. Such deeds of manumission freed 1,837 slaves between 1785 and 1831; only 313 of these, however, came before 1799. These deeds derived from the conscience of the master, agreement between slave and owner, and slaves' persistent efforts to obtain freedom. Blacks bargained with their masters to change their status from permanent to term chattel and were able to set exact dates for the end of their bondage, even if they were resold. Philanthropic whites sometimes purchased slaves with the express plan of freeing them after a short term of service. The Manumission Society helped blacks arrange such sales, which became an inducement to slaves to serve their masters well during an era of changing labor methods. Blacks also purchased themselves, members of their family, and friends.[27] More than seventy slaves in East Jersey bought their own freedom, received assistance from relatives, or became indentured servants for a limited time. Fifty-two of these purchased their own or their relatives' freedom. Arrangements were made with masters to borrow money or time against bondage. An example of such contracts was the experience of Jack Earnest, a slave living near Harrington, Bergen County, New Jersey. Born in 1770, Jack was originally a slave of the Gesner family of Lower Closter near the Palisades. Nicholas Gesner purchased Jack from his father in 1793. A year later Jack "desired a paper to seek a new master," despite Gesner's promises to free him after seven or eight years. A brother-in-law of Gesner's, Jacob Conklin, promised Jack Earnest freedom after seven years and land, and Gesner's warnings about Conklin's duplicity eventually proved true when Jack was denied freedom after the promised seven years. He was freed only after a third white, Peter Willsey, paid Conklin $100 for his security. By 1806, Jack Earnest was a free man and owned five acres of land in Harrington.[28]

Manumissions were equally rare in postrevolutionary East Jersey; Monmouth County, with large Anglican and Quaker populations, had the greatest number of emancipations, but other counties lagged far behind. In some instances, masters or mistresses awarded freedom to one slave but not others. For example, in 1788 William Stone, of Wood-bridge, Middlesex County, gave his slave Cato to his wife with the proviso that he would be free at the age of thirty but did not free an aged female, two other women, and a boy.[29] Occasionally, masters gave slaves property along with their freedom. Joan Blair, a widow from Piscataway, Middlesex County, freed her slave, Tom, and gave him £50, a wagon, tools, two horses, and land at Raritan.[30]

In most instances, however, masters simply passed their slaves on to descendants. A master's death could break up families. Dispersal of slaves among members of a family made the stability and emotional life of a black family more dependent on the financial situation of an owner. Dispersal by will increased the chances of further sales and worsened the conditions for families. Peter Vreland of Essex County equitably distributed fifteen slaves among seven members of his family in 1795, separating children from mothers and husbands from wives.[31]

As they had in the colonial period, African Americans used the judicial system to gain liberty in the postrevolutionary years. Precedent came from the American desire to deprive Loyalists of their property. The British left slaves behind, the most productive of whom were sold by the Commissioners of Forfeitures between 1784 and 1786. The rest, primarily aged slaves, were freed in 1786. The state accepted the burden of their care, franchising support out to local overseers of the poor or to independent contractors. From available records, expenditures seem parsimonious. Annual support for Tone, formerly the slave of Daniel Kissam of North Hempstead, for example, amounted to £18 for medical care, a blanket, one pair of stockings and shoes, a coffin, and burial expenses. The widow Mary Fowler spent £9, reimbursed by the town of Eastchester over three years, for the care of Nero. Such minute sums mounted. New York State spent over $7,000 on such support between 1785 and the late 1850s when the last of former British slaves died. These expenditures demonstrate exactly what colonial legislatures feared, that maintaining aged free blacks would be costly. Productive blacks remained enslaved while superannuated African Americans were discarded, in this case by masters who left the country.[32]

Runaway Slaves

Blacks ran away to New York City, left on vessels, or joined the military; the city was the most popular destination for runaway slaves. Most runaways were young men, trying to pass as free. Nearly 40 percent of the twelve hundred runaway notices examined by Shane White indicate the city as the probable destination.[33] Several runaway notices show the lingering effect of the Revolution. Prince, from Blooming-Grove in upper Manhattan, fled his master using the discharge of a "Continental Army Negro named Cuff Govender," which he bought from a free black. Brock, also known as Tom, was "probably lurking about New York City until he can get passage to Nova Scotia," warned his master in December 1785. In a notice in May 1784, the master of Scipio complained that he "ran away in 1776 to the British but got him back again." John Peter De Lancey made more familiar complaints when he advertised his slave Simon or Sam as "speaks remarkably quick and is in general very evil, fond of horses and wenches."[34]

Some successful runaways celebrated their freedom by taking new names such as Thomas Paine, Royal Cromwell, and New Year Evans. The greatest number chose anonymous labels such as Johnson, Williams, and Thomas to cloak their past. Fugitives arriving in New York City bought secondhand clothing in shops and on the wharfs or, if necessary, stole it. An underground economy arose whose rootless character can be illustrated in the defense of Oliver Quadron, a sailor accused of stealing a pea coat. Quadron testified that he "slept where he wished because he had no money"; he bought his pea coat "from a stranger near the Fly Market."[35] Runaway slaves gave the city streets a more cosmopolitan air. Most fugitives spoke passable English, mixed with African, Dutch, and other tongues known as "negro English or Dutch." With the addition of African French from Saint Domingue in the 1790s, urban language became a cosmopolitan patois.[36]

The number of blacks who ran away from their masters reached a peak in the last few years before enactment of gradual emancipation. Nearly a third of the 1,232 self-emancipated people of color enumerated by Shane White took flight between 1796 and 1800. Not coincidentally, this was also the period when masters recorded the highest numbers of deeds of emancipation. The 1790s saw as well the arrival of newly freed people from Saint Domingue. Understood in the context of unceasing lobbying to end slavery by the two manumission societies, abetted by formation of a free black community in New York City, Boston, and Philadelphia and in the rural areas, these patterns reveal a widespread contest between masters and slaves in the last few years of the century. The two manumission societies could enable legislation with long-term effects, but the immediate battle was within the slave-holding households. Inside the home, blacks and whites negotiated a personal emancipation.[37]

The results of these negotiations were twofold. If slaves wished to quit their masters completely, they could expect no assistance whatsoever. Obviously this was true for fugitives, but those who left the home were also shunned. Butcher Frederick De Voe freed Jack, one of the best dancers in the Catherine Market, and gave him a new suit. De Voe informed Jack that "if you will go home with me, you shall never know want, but if you leave me now, my home shall never more know you." Jack refused to go with his master and stayed to dance at the Catherine Market.[38]

The other response was to gain civil but not personal independence. Shane White has uncovered substantial degrees of dependence among newly freed blacks in New York City, a pattern that existed in rural areas as well. Under this plan, free blacks either stayed with their old masters or moved into the home of another. Given that the dominant work in the city was domestic and that building of middle-class housing was booming in this period, this work arrangement makes sense. It also meant that free blacks often had to labor alongside slaves in about one in three white households using enslaved workers. White has also demonstrated that the economic profile of such employers was virtually the same as that of slaveholders.[39]

The Constricted Lives of Rural Free Blacks

Rural free blacks faced an even more difficult future. The percentages of free blacks was far lower in the countryside, and masters were fiercely intransigent. Ethnicity, religion, economics, and custom all played roles in determining a black person's chances for freedom. Lacking political power and credit and with tiny incomes, unable to buy land, free blacks combined hiring out their backs to white farmers with part-time labor on their own minuscule plots of land. For example, Jack Earnest became the first resident of a small black community called Skunk Hollow near the New York–New Jersey border in Bergen County in 1806. He was followed by thirty or more families in the next few years. Many of the residents of Skunk Hollow were former slaves in Bergen County who bore names reflecting that bondage. The difficulty was that none of them owned sufficient property to gain more than a subsistence income. The same was true in other free black communities that developed in Monmouth, Middlesex, and several southern New Jersey counties. In Westchester County, New York, emancipated slaves clustered in a community referred to as "the Hills," outside of Harrison, New York, where they tended miniature farms.[40]

Even Jack's small freehold was exceptional. In the countryside, blacks remained in prerevolutionary roles as farmhands and domestics.[41] Land prices soared in the counties near the city. Lenders for mortgages were scarce for white and black applicants; over one-third of the principal was due immediately and the rest had to be paid off quickly. Under the best of conditions, plans to purchase land required total commitment of wages for several years, making a freehold out of the reach of free blacks.[42]

Some free blacks, who were primarily independent farmers, owned modest homes. The French traveler Brissot de Warville visited some of them in 1788 and was "impressed by the good clothes, their well-kept log cabins and their many children, while the eye of the philosopher lyes with pleasure on these homes where tyranny causes not tears to flow." The chief problem for free blacks, de Warville argued, was white prejudice. Advancement was difficult for free people because "whites who have the money are not willing to lend to a Negro." Whether one was a shopkeeper or farmer, lack of credit limited opportunity.[43]

Even the most paternalist, liberal whites did little to advance the status of free blacks. Members of the Society of Friends in East Jersey pitched in to help Sampson Adams build his house in the late 1780s. Still, Adams, who was able to accumulate some land and personal property, had to hire out as a day laborer for white farmers to make ends meet.[44] Adams was lucky and more independent than most. In the rural areas at the close of the nineteenth century, many free blacks had to accept continued dependence as "cottagers" on the farms of prosperous whites. In an economic pattern that increased over the next twenty years, free blacks bargained their labor for sustenance with white farmers, who also owned slaves.[45]

Black Society in the City

In the 1780s hundreds of former slaves from the countryside moved to the city looking for economic opportunities and a richer cultural life. Between 1771 and 1800, the number of free blacks living in New York City increased from a little over 100 to 3,500, despite the loss of several hundred who fled to Nova Scotia with the British.[46] In New York City, independent blacks clustered in the Montgomerie, north, and out wards, where 506 free people lived in 118 houses. The greatest concentration was in the Montgomerie ward, where almost half of the free blacks tabulated in the 1790 census lived. More than one-third of this population lived on Fair Street, with sizable communities on nearby

Beekman and Gold Streets. Other ties were made through boarding, a common practice for both white artisans and blacks. In the out ward, for example, William, a free black, presided over a household of fourteen and another free man of color named Ranger over a house of eleven. Owning a boardinghouse was an early form of empowerment for black females. In the north ward, Hannah, a free woman, owned a house occupied by twelve people. In the three wards, there were eleven houses in which more than nine people lived. Black boardinghouse keepers also earned cash caring for the poor. The almshouse paid "Black Jenney Cook," for example, five dollars a week for boarding a black woman and her three children and twelve shillings six pence for boarding another impoverished family.[47] In 1800, as the city reorganized its wards numerically, black neighborhoods emerged in the working-class wards around the Collect or Fresh Water Pond. No longer bucolic, the pond was in the center of a marshy, mosquito-infested industrial area where blacks and whites rubbed shoulders in the streets.[48]

Fugitives from the Haitian revolution made up part of this rising black population. While the bulk of refugees from the revolution settled in Charleston, hundreds more came north to New York and East Jersey. One reason they moved was slavery. The Duc de la Rochfoucauld-Liancourt reported that "the liberty of keeping Negro-slaves and the general opinion of the country in favor of slavery, have brought into New Jersey, a number of French emigrants from St. Domingue, who have set their Negroes at liberty." Haitian slaves were mostly from Angola and from a society riven by marronage and rebellion. Their struggle strongly affected the French abolition of slavery in remaining colonies, which occurred on February 4, 1794, and freed more than seven hundred thousand people in the West Indies. Saint Domingue slaves were quick to get into trouble as runaways, as participants in the 1796 arson scare, and as members of a major riot against kidnappers in 1801. For some Haitian blacks, the transfer to a new slave society was too traumatic and they committed suicide.[49]

Haitian blacks renewed African cultural styles in the city. Creoles and "Coal black Negresses" proudly flounced through the streets richly clad in West Indian and African colors. Black New Yorkers heard with pride the news from Saint Domingue of the creation of the first black state in the Western Hemisphere. While some whites trembled at the news from Haiti, others blamed every act of black autonomy in America on the troubling news from the West Indies. Soon white New

Yorkers echoed the anxious racism of South Carolinians about slave revolts.[50]

City Work

In New York City service provided the largest area of employment. Many blacks, male and female, worked as domestics, often living in the homes of their former owners. Almost one thousand free blacks lived in white households in 1800. Some were former slaves who preferred the security of the master's home for food, shelter, and employment. Jupiter Hammond declared that "liberty was a great thing" and "worth seeking" but asserted, "for my own part, I do not wish to be free." Another slave accepted his bondage because "I have a wife and children; my master takes care of them." The slave went on to say he rejoiced in his bondage because his master and he read the Bible together.[51] Not all slaves were so content. Slave disobedience made Joanna Van Cortlandt regard herself as "the slave of slaves," and her husband rushed to sell them as "wicked servants who practice only wickedness." Another slave regularly disappeared to fiddle at frolics.[52]

Formerly limited as the slaves and assistants of white artisans, in the postrevolutionary period black artisans served the African American community. Over one-third of the male free black heads of households in New York City in 1800 worked as carpenters, coopers, cabinetmakers, upholsterers, sailmakers, butchers, and bakers. Blacks were also able to make inroads in a few semiskilled, licensed occupations. Though still barred from carting, one of the largest and most lucrative of entry-level positions in the city, African Americans replaced whites in such lowly but indispensable posts as chimney sweeps and porters. Blacks also took control of the emerging occupation of hackney coach driver; benefiting from Federalist patronage, they received priority in obtaining licenses.[53]

Newly freed blacks received no invitations to join white artisan groups. As in the days of slavery, mechanics' societies worked vigorously to maintain segregated occupations. Nor were the ideologies of the political parties helpful. Even the most radical republican émigrés quickly adopted proslavery attitudes.[54] Such discrimination was not limited to the Republican-minded mechanics. The arch Federalist Alexander Hamilton, though a charter member of the Manumission Society, completely ignored free blacks in 1791 when constructing his plans for an industrial society. In passages that presaged the great immigration movements of the nineteenth century, Hamilton urged

Americans to offer "foreign artists . . . moral certainty of employment and encouragement" so that, as in the past, they would flock to America. He thereby ignored a sizable group of potential artisans. Rather than look to training free blacks, Hamilton affirmed the need to entice European workers.[55]

Not all blacks arriving in New York City found employment. The almshouse and Bridewell housed numerous blacks (and whites) in the 1790s who were unable to fend for themselves. Rapacious masters in New Jersey and rural New York freed aged or sick chattel and then abandoned them in the streets of New York City. In 1795, "several french negroes" from Haiti were left at the almshouse by their masters and lived in rags. When the board of managers was about to release the Haitians as free men, their masters appeared to claim them. By 1797, the almshouse decided that boarding sickly slaves was "not agreeable to the design of the institution." The almshouse also served as a source of supply for masters seeking servants. Farmers and artisans seeking apprentices and homeowners wanting servants came to the almshouse to indenture young blacks (and whites). At times these arrangements failed and servants reappeared at the almshouse telling tales of brutality. Jacob White, a nineteen-year-old black, came to New York City and was apprenticed to a black sweep master, George Gray. White lost both feet from exposure to the harsh winter and the almshouse pursued Gray for support money.[56]

Slave Crime

Slave restiveness was very evident in the postrevolutionary era. Higher expectations stymied by harsher economic realities, especially during the depression of the late 1780s, made some blacks turn to petty crime. The District Attorney's Indictment Papers are filled with citations for theft of such articles as clothing, bushels of wheat, small amounts of money, oars, buckles, and shoes. By the late 1790s New York State began supplementing public whippings for such crimes with jail terms, opening a penitentiary in Greenwich Village, which was soon filled. By 1800 the jail held ninety whites and forty-four blacks, a proportion of blacks far greater than their percentage of the overall population. Sentences for theft ranged from three months for petty larceny to four years or more for second offenses of grand larceny.[57]

In Bergen County, New Jersey, black men assaulted white men on three different occasions between June 1793 and October 1795. Penalties were as harsh as in the colonial era. In January 1801, two slaves,

Ned and Pero, were found guilty in Bergen of larceny and ordered whipped from place to place throughout the county during the course of a month. Each week they were whipped at a new location: the court-house, Pond's Church, Hoppertown, and New Bridge, for a total of four hundred lashes. Ned died from his whippings.[58]

Arson was another black weapon against white society. Three slaves in Bergen County burned down the homes of their masters between 1796 and 1801. Across the river Lewis Morris wrote his son in 1796 that "we have had the most terrible fire lately in New York it has burnt the whole block from Stuart's Store to the Fly Market upwards of 60 houses many attempts have been made since to set fire to the town all exclaim against the freedom of the Negroes it has been fatal to that business." Morris's apprehensions were correct. The *New York Minerva* published an alarm that Lewis Ogden's slave set the fire and that other attempts were planned. The newspaper warned, "Double your night-watch and confine your servants."[59]

Religion and Black Freedom

In the years after the American Revolution, the reorganized Episco-pal Church stayed in the vanguard of black conversion. Trinity Church in New York City became a center for black marriages. After conduct-ing a few ceremonies during the Revolution, Trinity Church clerics Samuel Provoost and Benjamin Moore officiated at thirty to forty mar-riages between blacks annually through 1806. Some of the ceremonies joined together free blacks and slaves given permission to marry by their masters.[60]

Despite the blessings of such rites, African Americans felt stymied in the Anglican faith. Although Episcopalians strongly believed that blacks were capable of true understanding of Christian faith, they were very reluctant to promote black leaders. For example, Peter Wil-liams Jr., trained by the Episcopalians in the 1790s, did not become a priest until 1826, despite his obvious erudition and high status among blacks. As part of their mission effort to retain black interest, Trinity and the uptown St. Paul's Parish of Bloomingdale opened Sunday schools for blacks with the purpose of "influencing many children who would otherwise be but profane violators of the sanctity of God's Holy Day."[61] But desegregation of Episcopal Church ritual was not uni-versal. Episcopalian parishes including St. Mark's in the Bowery, St. Peter's Church in New Brunswick, New Jersey, St. George's, and Christ

Church of Flushing, Long Island, baptized very few blacks in the years after the Revolution.[62]

The Episcopalians did, however, create an institution for blacks with far-reaching implications. The African Free School, founded in 1789, was a direct descendant of the charity schools administered by Anglican missionaries in the colonial period. Within four years 160 students were enrolled; by the close of the century, about 140 students of both sexes stood for examinations. The African Free School was supported by city tax revenue. In the next few decades it became the foremost vehicle to success for aspiring blacks.[63]

Reform occurred, however gradually, even in the Dutch Reformed Church. Officially segregated since the 1660s, the church began accepting black communicants soon after the Revolution. The church constitution of 1792 resolved that "no difference exists between bond and free in the Church of Christ; slaves or blacks when admitted to the church possess the same privileges as other members; their infant children are entitled to baptism and ministers who deny them any Christian privilege are to be reprimanded." In the early postrevolutionary years, black members were usually servants or slaves of white worshipers. Several new communicants, however, were free blacks, with certificates of membership from Dutch Reformed parishes in outlying regions. The Dutch Reformed Church also performed marriages either among slaves, between slaves and free blacks, or among free people, and the Dutch Reformed cemetery accepted several black burials. Still, black membership in the Dutch Reformed Church, though far greater than in the colonial era, remained small compared with the number of African Americans owned by the Dutch. Colonial-era splits between rural pietists and urban paternalists affected this reform. The new liberalism was largely confined to the city.[64]

The experience of one slave demonstrates how contentious the issue of baptism remained between Dutch masters and their bondsmen. John Jea, an African who preached in New York and New Jersey in the 1790s, claimed that an angel taught him to read the Bible in Dutch and English. Following this miracle, Jea, who lacked permission from his master, persuaded a Presbyterian minister to baptize him. According to Jea, the laws of New York State required his Dutch Reformed master to emancipate him. His master, who had informed Jea that he did not need religious instruction because he lacked a soul, became enraged at this event though he eventually freed Jea. No such law existed, of course, but Jea's error demonstrates how contentious an issue slave baptism remained after the Revolution.[65]

Presbyterian churches in New York City and New Jersey welcomed several free blacks during the 1780s, while other Presbyterian churches waited until the second decade of the nineteenth century to admit blacks. In South Hempstead, Long Island, Christ's Presbyterian Church neither admitted nor married blacks until 1810. More active was the Old Tennant Church of Freehold, New Jersey, which accepted around five slaves and free blacks as members in the first decades after the Revolution. Significantly, however, the Old Tennant Church created a new plan for seating in 1790 and permitted no blacks on the main floor. Black Presbyterians' anger over "negro pews" kept African American membership low. Racist ministers also plagued the Presbyterians, especially in New Jersey, where the southern-oriented Princeton Theological Seminary produced most church leaders. Ashbel Green, one of the most respected members of the Presbyterian Synod, declared slavery "a gross violation of sacred rights" but argued that the "number of slaves, their ignorance and vicious habits, render immediate emancipation inconsistent alike with the safety and happiness of masters and slaves." The New York Synod also flinched at the idea of immediate emancipation. There, Presbyterians worried that newly freed blacks "may be in many respects more dangerous to the community" than slaves. The synod encouraged masters to provide "such good education as to prepare them for the better enjoyment of the future." If emancipation was gradual, freedom would best occur in Africa, an early sign of the colonization movement that would dominate church policy in the antebellum period.[66]

The Methodist Church, whose English founders were abolitionists, gained numerous black adherents in the last years of the colonial era and continued to accept blacks after the war. The Methodists combined American Revolutionary egalitarianism with their own evangelical "conscience" concerns, and, in 1782, passed a rule excluding slaveholders. The Methodist Church attracted charismatic black preachers, licensed and otherwise.[67] The limitations of the Methodist Church, easily the most liberal toward blacks, are indicative of the difficulties Protestant sects had with a black membership. As Nathan O. Hatch has argued, the Methodist Church's position toward blacks was torn by the paradox of its egalitarianism on the one hand and its racism on the other. Increasing white discomfort with black membership meant less tolerance following the Revolution. In the 1790s, Methodists amended the constitutional ban against slaveholding to apply only when slavery was "contrary to the laws of the state." Methodist ministers and their flocks in the South and West welcomed masters but excluded their slaves. The Methodists limited the authority and status of black ministers.[68]

Black Churches

The limited leadership of the parent church notwithstanding, Methodism offered African Americans the greatest room for growth and religious self-expression. In the 1795, the John Street Methodist Church in Manhattan had 155 black members enrolled in eight worship classes; only two of the classes included males, a total of 34. As in other denominations, female adherents were most numerous. Class number 31, led by a white preacher, Cornelius Warner, was filled with black males who soon would found the African Methodist Episcopal (AME) Zion Church. The roster included James Varick, Abraham Thompson, William Miller, William Hamilton, Francis Jacobs, Thomas Miller, George Moore, George White, Thomas Cook, David Bias, and Samuel Pointer, whose words and writings became significant instruments in the formation of the black community in New York City and beyond.[69]

The first indication of a separate black religious organization came in New York City in 1795 when a group of free blacks, calling themselves the African Society, petitioned the Common Council for assistance to purchase land in the seventh ward for a burial ground. The group's leaders complained that they were not allowed to incorporate as a religious body. They petitioned for assistance to "procure a place for the erection of a place of divine worship and the interment of the People of Colour." This last request hit a positive note with the council, which for seven years had been vexed by speculators' encroachments on the Old Negro Burial Ground behind the almshouse on Bowery Lane. Land investors had chipped away at the cemetery, in operation since the 1640s, and the city wanted closure of the problem. It granted £100 to the African Society to create a new church and graveyard. The same year, angered by continued white racism against the Haitian revolution and by the incessant irritation of "black pews," Peter Williams Sr. led the black congregation out of the John Street Church to hold separate meetings. Six years later, this group of dissident black Methodists constructed the African Methodist Episcopal Zion Church on a lot at Church and Leonard Streets. The church obtained a charter from a bishop, James Varick.[70]

Peter Williams Jr. The leading black minister in New York for decades, Williams attempted a conciliatory line between a nascent black nationalism and the racism of Episcopalian officials. He was a key figure in many of the important events and movements in black New York between 1800 and his death in 1840. (Courtesy of John H. Hewitt)

The creation of the African Methodist Episcopal Zion Church in 1796 led to other black congregations. The first of these in New York was the Abyssinian Baptist Church, formed by former members of the Gold Street First Baptist Church in 1807. The Reverend Thomas Paul, founder of the First African Baptist Church in Boston, mediated the split between white and black worshipers at Gold Street and became the first minister of Abyssinian Baptist when he led four men and twelve women plus three new members out of Gold Street to form the new church. In 1810 the congregation selected Josiah Bishop of Portsmouth, New Hampshire, as its minister.[71]

African American churches provided emotional support in the face of uncertainty and disappointment and enforced the norms and values of society. Black churches in the early nineteenth century engaged in gospels of moral improvement, charity, and benevolence. They offered peace, hope, and tranquillity through Christ. They used religion and the Scripture in black protest against slavery and racial caste and to emphasize the universal equality of humans.[72]

The careers of two black ministers in this era demonstrate the parameters of black religious zeal. George White, who arrived in New York City in the early 1790s, took part in a famous class for black leaders at the John Street Methodist Church and preached on Long Island and in Westchester County and rural New Jersey. His goal was to be licensed by the Methodist Church as an ordained minister. During this pilgrimage he suffered many disheartening rejections from the Methodist hierarchy, gaining his license only after a dozen years of trying. He remained, however, very faithful to the Methodist faith. In contrast, John Jea, a less educated but more charismatic preacher, itinerated throughout rural New Jersey in the 1790s, preaching to crowds of enslaved and free blacks. Jea preached a theology of rebirth by linking the story of Lazarus with the aspirations of an emerging free black congregation. Jea disdained denominational affiliation and eventually left the New York area for crusades that took him to South America, the Far East, England, Ireland, and France. His prophetic messages appealed to blacks and whites; his methods anticipated the Pentecostal styles popular among black male and female preachers around New York from the 1830s on. Unlike White, Jea refused to be confined by the judgments of the Methodist hierarchy.[73]

Black churches were intrinsic parts of a developing black community. Concentration of blacks enabled the growth of black churches as did their imposed segregation in the lower classes. Independent black churches were part of an overall construction of benevolent societies, literary and political forums, and occupational structures. An important reason for independence was that the black ministry was engaged in the struggle to end slavery, a process that brought cooperation from few sympathetic whites. In contrast, blacks warmly embraced the radical views of man's destiny and duty which characterized evangelical Christian thought in this era. Unlike the South, however, where such theology also enabled blacks to endure slavery precisely because doctrine promised eventual deliverance without the demands of resistance, blacks in the North employed their beliefs as proof of equality and requisite liberty.[74]

Conclusions

In sum, the postrevolutionary years produced a very gradual abolition of slavery. Given the attitudes of slave masters, especially in the rural regions, the laws of 1799 and 1804 were major accomplishments by a coalition of liberal-minded whites in the abolition societies and by blacks themselves. Emancipation-minded whites came from the Society of Friends and Episcopalians, or reconstituted Anglicans, the most paternalist denominations in the region. Methodists, who originally were antislavery, began to shrink from emancipation by the 1790s. Opposed to abolition were the patriarchal sects, especially the Dutch Reformed and Huguenot. Less than half of the impetus toward emancipation came from whites. Freedom at the death of a master or by deed of manumission accounted for only a minority of free blacks in New York City and a fraction in the countryside. The primary drive came from blacks who did not restrict their push for freedom to politics and the court but voted with their feet by flight from rural pietist farmers to the more liberal, if paternalist, world of New York City. There were limits to the city's liberalism, and African Americans found sustained discrimination in the trades. Gradually, African Americans constructed communities based on the independent black churches. Still, slavery cast a shadow over their efforts.

CHAPTER 7
Making a Free People

1804–1827

The years following the passage of gradual emancipation acts in New York and New Jersey saw the emergence of a sturdy, free black class in New York City. Their rural cousins, by contrast, were stymied by worsening racism, an obdurate political economy, and still-potent vestiges of slavery. As their fortunes diverged, urban and rural blacks experienced the heady draughts of freedom differently. In the city, the nascent free black middle class regarded memories of Africa with reverence while striving to gain greater civil rights. They organized churches and benevolent societies and held celebrations to laud their own freedoms, to oppose slavery elsewhere, and to demand citizenship. In the countryside such open representations were impossible in the face of racism; accordingly, rural blacks took painstakingly slow paths toward economic independence while constructing societies shielded from white authority.[1]

Urban blacks formed their own political movements in commemoration of heroic aspects of their history. The black benevolent association movement, which grew out of religious and political movements, became a significant vehicle for black political expression. The New York City African Society for Mutual Relief, which started initially as a burial society in 1808, then incorporated in 1810, admitted any who came recommended by a member. A visible outgrowth of the confraternities of the colonial period, the African Society acted as a benevolent society. Benefits included two dollars a week for members during the first three months of illness, declining to twelve shillings for the next three months. Widows received twenty dollars per year. Wedded to the gospel of moral improvement, the society also attempted to regulate members' behavior, threatening to expel any recipient "spending his time in a brothel, in gambling or tippling." Membership came from the black middle class. The first president, William Hamilton, was a house carpenter; the first secretary, Henry Sipkins, was a mechanic. Other occupations represented on the first membership rolls included bootmakers, a pickle manufacturer, a soap chandler, an innkeeper, and eight ministers, including William Miller, James Varick, Christopher Rush, Peter Williams Jr., Thomas Paul, Samuel Cornish, Theodore S. Wright, John T. Raymond, and Timothy Eaton. Soon finding itself "incapable of helping or affording assistance to every indigent African who came their way," the society nevertheless survived and by 1819 had over $500 worth of bank stock. The society invested heavily and successfully in real estate and became one of the most important features of New York black society.[2]

Benevolent societies and churches were the sites for black political celebration and strategy. On each occasion, speakers enunciated important themes in African American history. Peter Williams Jr., speaking at a celebration of the abolition of the Atlantic slave trade in 1808, reviewed the history of that trade, described the Middle Passage, and praised the abolitionist efforts of Anthony Benezet and John Woolman. He anticipated the day when "Ethiopia shall stretch forth her hands . . . on the whole African race . . . and promote the luxuriant growth of knowledge and virtue." Williams's discourse emphasized the special importance of history to the African American and looked to Africa for future inspiration and knowledge. Williams made it clear that slavery was a lesson which African Americans should never forget. Joseph Sidney offered similar sentiments in an address before the Wilberforce Society a year later. Rebutting critics of black equality, Sidney listed the contributions of Ignatius Sancho and Phillis Wheatley and the contemporary importance of William Hamilton and James Varick. Commemoration of the closure of the slave trade became an annual event for free blacks. In 1809 the celebration included an oration by Henry Sipkins which reviewed the history of Africa and the Portuguese, Spanish, English, and Dutch slave trades.[3] In 1813 George Lawrence, speaking in the African Methodist Episcopal Church, attacked recent concepts of racial inferiority. Two years later, William Hamilton, the society's first president, gave a strongly nationalist oration commemorating the anniversary. Hamilton offered a lengthy history of Africa and its degradation by Portuguese and Spanish slave traders.

He noted that some African nations "have painted their devil in the complexion of the white man." If one viewed the history of the slave trade, Hamilton argued, the choice of a likeness could not have been better.[4] Hamilton's strong words suggested the growing breach between whites and blacks in Jeffersonian New York. As racial lines hardened, African Americans took solace in reconstructing their history.[5]

Further inspiration from Africa came from renewed contact with the exiled black Loyalists. The famed black sea captain Paul Cuffe returned from several voyages with reports of former slaves now living as free landowners in Africa. Cuffe met with leading black New Yorkers to tell them of the exploits of their brethren in Sierra Leone, some of whom hailed from New York and East Jersey.[6] Reverence for African history and its message was evident in memorial services. Peter Williams spoke before the congregation of the African Methodist Episcopal Institution on October 21, 1817, in memory of the recently deceased Cuffe, giving a short biography of his life, his involvement in the petition of 1780 seeking black suffrage in Massachusetts, his assistance in forming the benevolent society, and his participation in the Sierra Leone colonization project.[7]

Blacks also learned of their heritage from the English translation of the French Bishop Henri Gregoire's essay on black intellectual and moral faculties. Published in Brooklyn in 1810, Gregoire's book corrected racial fallacies by citing the talents of fifteen Africans. He offered detailed information about many little-known blacks and powerful commentary on the bravery of black maroons and the establishment of the Sierra Leone colony.[8]

In addition to the rhetorical celebrations, there was stepped-up, confrontational abolitionism. On several occasions, Quaker Isaac Hopper helped East Jersey slaves escape their masters. Black New Yorkers themselves rioted against slave catchers, or "blackbirds," who were intent upon returning runaways to their masters. In 1819 a crowd of forty blacks mobbed John Hall, who had seized a fugitive slave, Thomas Harlett. (The attempt to save Harlett failed when the city marshal took the slave to the City Hall to prepare his return to slavery.) In 1826 a much larger mob of blacks surrounded the City Hall, trying to intercept slave catchers taking slaves back to Virginia. The crowd attacked a police escort for the slave catchers and several witnesses, hurling bricks, sticks, and stones. One member of the crowd hit a policeman in the face with a brick. After the police chased the mob out of City

Hall Park, they pursued a white man down nearby Ann Street, shouting, "Kill Him, Kill Him!" The authorities sentenced several leading rioters to year-long prison terms.[9]

In New Jersey in 1820, a brave free black named Richard Dean used the courts to secure freedom for an enslaved female. Using a method later popular in New York City, Dean observed the arrest of Phebe, who had been the slave of a Captain D. Roff. That worthy had taken her to New York but had failed to register her so she was able to claim her freedom. Years later, Phebe traveled to Newark to visit her mother (a free woman). Roff, abetted by Judge Crane of Newark, seized her as a runaway and had her imprisoned. Dean then swore out a writ of habeas corpus, which was honored by the court in New Brunswick. Dean next served the writ on Roff and the jailer. The court in New Brunswick ruled that no law existed which would permit the imprisonment of a slave and ordered her freed.[10]

By such actions blacks showed their willingness to demand true egalitarian behavior from white society and so keep the promises of the American Revolution alive. Those who lived in New York and East Jersey seemed determined to make the best of America. Indeed, personal names showed how deeply they identified with American life. By 1820, over 80 percent of the forenames of slaves and free blacks in the city were English. Allegiance was pronounced in public ways. On August 13, 1814, "one hundred and fifty free colored people and seventy members of the Asbury African Church" volunteered to help build fortifications in Brooklyn to defend New York City against possible British attack in the War of 1812. The following week a notice from "A Citizen of Colour" appeared in the *New York Evening Post*. The "Citizen" argued that it was the "duty of every coloured man, resident in this city to volunteer." In New York, he claimed, "we dwell in safety and pursue our honest callings." In the near future, New York would, the "Citizen" forecast, "not include a single slave." He concluded that "we have now an opportunity of shewing that we are not ungrateful . . . but are willing to exert ourselves . . . for the protection of our beloved state."[11] The black volunteers joined many other artisan and community groups in a massive show of patriotism. Two thousand blacks from New York and New Jersey enlisted in a new regiment and in the American navy to fight the British. (Black sailors from New York and New Jersey were the most numerous among captives at Dartmoor prison in England.) In contrast, in the southern states, slave support for the British was notorious. While blacks in Maryland and Virginia greeted

British invaders with open arms hoping for liberation from bondage, northern blacks, allied with the Federalists, generally supported the American side.[12]

A Painfully Slow Emancipation

Although gradual emancipation laws in New York and New Jersey limited the future of slavery, masters retained possession for as long as possible and used various subterfuges to extract income from their chattel. For example, the abandonment law allowed masters to free infant children of slaves born after July 4, 1804, then renounce rights to their future labor in exchange for three dollars a month for support of the children. Support for abandoned slaves burdened state budgets until repeal of the program in 1812, after which masters began the nefarious practice of selling slaves about to be freed to southern states, where their bondage became permanent. Isaac Holmes, an English traveler, described large profits made by masters willing to sell slaves in New Orleans. Masters evaded the 1788 law forbidding such sales by finding justices of the peace willing to agree that the slaves assented to their sale. Middlesex County inhabitants petitioned in 1820 for an efficient law "to prevent kidnappers and carrying from the State blacks and other people of colour" and succeeded in establishing legislation barring sales. Clauses permitting sales when the slave had lived in the state five years or the master obtained a full license weakened the bill. Masters prosecuted slaves for spurious reasons to gain permission to sell them to the South.[13]

Thus gradual emancipation laws did not produce instant civil liberties for free blacks. A compilation of New York State laws in 1806 showed the mixed character of the judicial and legislative attack on slavery. Certain noxious clauses favored slavery. These included gradual emancipation, refusal of the right of slaves to testify, and permission to slaveholders to bring slaves into the state for up to six months without penalty. Injunctions against sale of liquor to slaves without their masters' consent and the harboring of fugitives continued. There were some progressive aspects to these laws. Slaves could be liberated because of improper importation or exportation or fraud and receive compensation for abandonment. Within the next few years, New York extended the power to contract marriages indissoluble by the master, the right to own property, the right to testify in court, and the right to a jury trial in all felony cases.[14]

While state assemblies thrashed out the tortured end of servitude, they instituted laws that sharply curtailed black political freedoms. In 1807 New Jersey lawmakers closed loopholes in the constitution of 1777 which permitted blacks and women to vote. A new law provided that no one should vote "unless such person be a free, white male citizen." New York's assembly, led by Republicans eager to disfranchise blacks they considered a permanent opposition, placed a $250 bond on annual voting permits for free blacks in 1821. By 1828 there were only 298 black voters in New York in a total population of 29,701 African Americans.[15]

Blacks fared even less well with the judiciary than in the legislature. In 1807 the New York Supreme Court disallowed the claim for freedom of Sable, a New Jersey slave brought into New York by her master and sold after his death. Sable complained that such action violated the 1785 law barring importation of blacks for quick sales. The court disagreed, placing a higher value on inheritance rights than on the right of a slave to freedom. In a similar case a few years later the New York Supreme Court denied freedom to a slave sold for debt. In both cases the court ruled that involuntary benefits to heirs or creditors should not be denied. In New Jersey, the case of *State v. Quick* showed the overwhelming power of the rights of slave owners. Quick was purchased in New York, then brought into New Jersey. Quick sued for freedom, arguing that the transfer violated New York State laws. Judge William Pennington noted, however, that Quick was resident in New York for two years before his removal; thus his purchase was not an attempt to evade the New York law. Quick remained a slave.[16]

Abolitionist attempts to speed up the end of slavery met staunch resistance in both states. For several years after 1804, masters in Bergen County, New Jersey, petitioned the state assembly to repeal the emancipation acts. Although abolitionists were able to rebuff these attempts, their strength was clearly waning. The New Jersey Society for Promoting the Abolition of Slavery was the first to falter. In 1807 it was already too weak to prevent the assembly from abolishing black suffrage. The society held its last meeting in 1809. In New York, the Abolition Society's fervor also cooled after passage of gradual emancipation.

Fortunately, a small group within the New York Manumission Society continued to petition for reform and to hasten the end of slavery.[17] One of the society's leading members was Daniel Tompkins, reelected governor of New York State in 1810, who, although a Republican, asked the state assembly for "extinction of slavery." But support for expediting total emancipation rested almost solely in the waning Federalist

Party, and Republicans concentrated on curbing the black vote to cut Federalist margins of victory, as in 1813 when the Federalists were swept back into power on the strength of "the votes of three hundred Negroes in the city of New York." Afterward, Republicans, overriding the opposition of the Federalist Council of Revision, required black voters to bring elaborate registration forms to the polls.

In 1817, Governor Tompkins, in his last session before becoming vice president of the United States under James Monroe, pushed through a law emancipating all blacks born before July 4, 1799, as of July 4, 1827. Masters no longer had to guarantee maintenance for aged slaves. Although the act freed slaves born before 1799, many others were still subject to gradual emancipation. Still, the law sealed the extinction of slavery in New York.[18]

The Rise of Freedom in the City

By 1810, free blacks outnumbered slaves by 8,137 to 1,686 in New York City. Thirty-two percent of the state's black population lived in the city. Females, working as domestics, continued to be the majority of New York's black population. In 1820, of 10,886 free people and 518 slaves in the city, females outnumbered males by 6,174 to 4,194. In the wards, this imbalance was even more striking. In the prosperous second ward in 1816, for example, free black women outnumbered their male counterparts by 392 to 162; there were 56 female slaves and 25 male slaves. By 1819, free females accounted for 343 of the ward's free black population of 452 people. Also, the black population of New York City was overwhelmingly young. In 1820, free black males under forty-five years of age outnumbered their elders by 3,588 to 606 while females under forty-five outnumbered women above that age by 5,340 to 834.[19]

Very gradually, blacks in New York City made the transition into independent households. In a local census of 1813, 275 free black males and 467 free females lived in the prosperous first ward along with 91 male and 138 female slaves, both clear signs of dependent housing. In contrast, the sixth ward, home to much of the city's black middle class, contained 517 free males and 718 free females, with only 13 male and 24 female slaves. The 1813 census also showed the continued feminization of slavery. Of the city's 976 slaves, 694, or 71 percent, were female. By 1820 nearly two-thirds of New York City's blacks lived in independent households.[20]

Boarding enhanced the shift toward independent black households. In contrast with Boston and Philadelphia, where such arrangements were rare, over 50 percent of New York City's black households contained unrelated boarders. Both parents lived in over 80 percent of black households with children under age fourteen. Of 527 black children under fourteen listed in the census for 1820, 505, or 96 percent, lived in two-parent households. Black families were much smaller in freedom than in slavery. New York's black population was quite young, with 80 percent under forty-four years of age. The 1809 law legalizing marriages gave blacks even further autonomy. The law made all children born of pre-1809 marriages legitimate and prompted widespread marriages between slaves and freed blacks. Such unions created legal problems which blacks quickly took to court in hopes of securing further freedoms.[21]

By 1816, free blacks had established neighborhoods in the fifth, sixth, and eighth wards, ranging from the Five Points north and west to the Hudson River, all close to the site of the original community of the seventeenth century. The initial traces of this integrated, vibrant community were apparent in the second decade of the century. One could walk down Reed Street in the fifth ward and see Primus Sackett, a sixty-seven-year-old coachman living with his wife and sharing the home with a widow and an Irish stonecutter. Around the corner on Duane Street lived David Seafield, another coachman, his wife, Phillis, and two daughters; sharing the home were an assemblage of New Yorkers including a widow, two independent women, and a white grocer named George Morrison. In the same neighborhood were Francis Kirwen and Benjamin Boe, two young black jewelers. The point of these brief references is that the black community sported a wide variety of working people of mixed races and statuses. Although living conditions were often poor, there was an incredible vitality to the neighborhood which would spawn the creative, dynamic leaders of the next generation.[22]

Of 12,575 blacks in New York in 1825, 6,109, or 48 percent, lived in these three wards. Blacks clustered together in houses often containing five or more families. Nine black families lived at 54 Lombardy Street. Further south, a population of over 1,000 blacks lived in the wealthy first ward and the newly developed bourgeois tenth. In these

Title page of the "African Free School Notebook" (vol. 3), 1822. Drawn by a student at the school, this sketch of the African Free School commemorates the institution which, despite the paternalism and racism of its white leaders, delivered a generation of African American leaders. (Courtesy of the New-York Historical Society)

John Burns "The ... N° 2.

New York African Free School,

ERECTED IN THE YEAR 1815.

By the

New York Society for promoting the Manumission

of Slaves.

Officers of the Society.

Cadwallader D. Colden President.

Valentine Seaman 1st Vice Pres.t, George Newbold 2nd Vice Pres.t

John Murray Jun.r Treasurer.

Jeremiah Thompson Secre.y, Thomas Tucker Assis.t Secre.y.

Trustees of the School.

John. Murray Jun.r Chairman, Thomas Collins Secre.y

Benj.n S. Collins, Robert C. Cornell, T. F. Jenkins,
Valentine Seaman, Willet Seaman, Jeremiah Thompson,
Thomas Tucker, William King, George T. White,
Samuel Wood.

Teacher.
Charles C. Andrews.

and smaller wards black domestics lived in the homes of their employers.[23]

The conditions of life in black neighborhoods were very dangerous. Investigators blamed overcrowding and dwelling in cellars as the main cause of death for blacks during the yellow fever epidemics of the 1820s. Of 119 blacks who lived in cellars around Bancker Street, 54 became ill and 24 died from "Banker-Street Fever," a bilious typhus fever. Forty-eight blacks lived in cellars on Bancker, Lombardy, and Pike Streets. Of these, 33 became ill and 14 died. No whites living in apartments above the cellars died. Consumption was another deadly predator on African Americans, killing over 10 percent of blacks affected with it in the late 1820s. Other dangerous diseases were pneumonia and bronchitis. Black death rates were considerably higher than those for whites in the 1820s. In 1824 black deaths amounted to 718 out of 4,341, or 16.5 percent. The next year they were 875 out of 5,018, or 17.4 percent. The nature of disease and the death rates in these black urban neighborhoods rivaled conditions on southern plantations.[24]

The Urban Black Middle Class

New York City housed the most viable black community in the region. Well-educated, articulate black intellectuals, many of them from the ranks of the clergy, led a black community focused on evangelical religion and cooperative associations and politically motivated to end slavery in the region and attack it nationally. Black leaders in New York began consciously to create an African American intellectual tradition. By the 1820s, this leadership cadre was publishing newspapers, writing pamphlets, opining on a variety of political topics, and sustaining a cultural enlightenment.

A nascent black middle class emerged in New York City with estimated family incomes ranging up to $10,000. Blacks established churches, ran small businesses, and worked unceasingly to end slavery and to improve black civil rights. Whether they lived in white households or were independent, blacks had marketable skills. In 1816, blacks living in white households in the eighth ward, though nominally dependent, worked for butchers, printers, grocers, papermakers, shoemakers, goldsmiths, and tallow chandlers. It must be presumed that such blacks helped their masters in these businesses. More encouraging were the members of free, independent skilled people of color. Over one-third of blacks appearing in the directories of 1800 and 1810 were artisans. Many of these skilled blacks worked for whites, but some were private businessmen. A visiting Englishwoman named Mrs. Felton noticed that blacks were "never behind in rivaling whites." Barred from many white occupations, those blacks created their own workforce of carpenters, coopers, cabinetmakers, upholsterers, butchers, sailmakers, and bakers.[25]

This black middle class also patronized fledgling black theaters. In the 1820s, William Henry Brown, a West Indian former seaman, offered entertainment in his tea and ice cream garden in his backyard on Thomas Street, which he called the African Grove. It had avenues for strolling, refreshment boxes seating four or more persons, and a long room for the theater. He served ice cream, punch, and other relishes and had a band to entertain guests. One auditor reported in a local newspaper the easy and informed conversation of the relaxed couples. He overheard discussions of the war between the Greeks and the Turks, the many wives of the bey of Algiers, the decline of Ballston and Saratoga because of the recent arrival of many southerners, and the necessity of voting Federalist.[26]

Later Brown converted his upper apartments into a theater seating three to four hundred people. Brown's initial theatrical performances at the African Grove presented *Richard III* to racially mixed audiences separated by a curtain. Mrs. Felton observed a performance in which William Hewlett, Brown's first star actor, "in order to please his audience, whenever the word 'York' appeared, politely accommodated his language by altering the text to say 'New York.'" In addition to Shakespeare, the African Grove presented controversial plays. Brown wrote a now-lost play called *The Drama of King Shotaway*, which was "founded on facts taken from the Insurrection of the Caravos in the Island of St. Vincent in 1795." Hewlett played the leading role of the Carib chieftain Shotaway.[27]

After Brown attempted to move the Grove into the white theater district, white toughs invaded the "African theater" in August 1822 to "break it up root and branch," destroying much of the property and stripping and beating the actors, actresses, and proprietor. The police arrested and jailed the actors. A magistrate permitted their release only after they agreed not to play Shakespeare. Their actual offense was competing with the white-operated Park Theater next door. Brown tried a second time with a theater on Mercer Street; again, however, gangs vandalized the theater. Although the black company fought back against the assailants, eventually the theater company filed for bankruptcy. Hewlett and the aspiring actor Ira Aldridge then

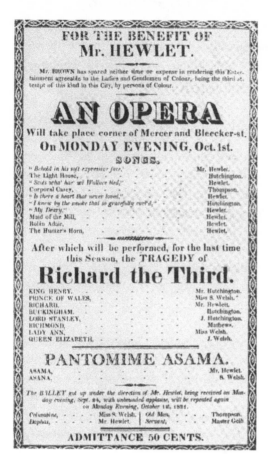

traveled to Europe. Aldridge stayed on the Continent to become one of Europe's greatest actors. Hewlett returned to face further racism, and his career declined to presenting demeaning farces. Mobs and the police continued to harass the African Grove until it was finally closed in 1829. Meanwhile, a black theater on De Lancey Street and the Haitian Retreat on Broadway at Prince Street struggled to survive, but the racism that dashed Brown's and Hewlett's hopes and sent Aldridge into exile placed a low ceiling on the aspirations of black theater for generations to come.[28]

A cornerstone of the black middle class was the nation's first African American newspaper, *Freedom's Journal,* whose inaugural issue appeared on March 16, 1827. Founded in the home of Boston Crummell, a New York oysterman, member of the African Mutual Society, and father of philosopher Alexander Crummell, the *Journal* devoted itself to "useful knowledge of every kind and everything that relates to

Africa shall find a ready admission to our columns." Its editor, Samuel Cornish, initiated the paper partly in angry reaction at unceasing white journalistic racism and unthinking support for the American Colonization Society (ACS). Even more ominous than the crude negrophobia of the newspapers was the calm reasoning of colonizationist editors who assumed that African Americans had no future in the United States. The *Freedom's Journal* was a rallying point for the black community. Early issues were devoted to Paul Cuffe and Phillis Wheatley.[29] Cornish, a firm believer in the gospel of moral improvement, included favorable stories on black education and quarreled convincingly with popular prejudice that blacks were an inordinate percentage of almshouse clients by showing the good work of the African Society of Mutual Relief.[30]

Cornish's strong attacks on the American Colonization Society pained his white colleagues in the Presbyterian Church, many of whom were the principal supporters of the movement. Princeton Theological Seminary professors Archibald Alexander and Samuel Miller warned Cornish that continued attacks would alienate white support for the newspaper and for the First Colored Presbyterian Church, where Cornish was still pastor. In response, Cornish resigned his pastorate. After building the newspaper up to twelve hundred subscribers, he left the editorship to his partner, John Russwurm. Fifteen months later Russwurm abandoned the paper and accepted a post as administrator of Liberia's school system.

Russwurm's decision scandalized many blacks, who felt he was a pawn of the ACS, but racism in America was clearly the compelling reason for his departure. In his valedictory editorial, Russwurm wrote that blacks did not create prejudices and "they were not in our power to remove." He wrote later that he felt blacks should not stay in the United States and "bear the degradation which brands every man of color and their children after them." He believed that full citizenship in America for blacks was "utterly impossible in the nature of things." However despairing, Russwurm anticipated the first signs of change in African American opposition to colonization.[31]

At the time, Russwurm's attitudes were not shared by the bulk of middle-class black New Yorkers. Early efforts by black New Yorkers to travel to Africa to settle ended in illness and death. The eventual decision to turn against colonization was more ideological. By 1828, for example, the African Society had turned against colonization. William L. Jennings, former president of the society and a successful New York tailor, declared that America "is the land of our birth. . . . It is a land in which our fathers have suffered and toiled." The black man's relation with Africa, he argued, is the "same as the white man's with Europe"; both races were American in "habit, manners, passions, dispositions." Africa, he concluded, was "as foreign to us as Europe is to them." [32]

Samuel Cornish immediately formed a second newspaper, the *Rights of All*, which concentrated on economic and political themes. Although it lasted only six months, the *Rights of All* took a stand in the evolving debate over monopolistic licenses in New York City and the need for expanded rights for all citizens. Licenses as carters, porters, and peddlers, Cornish argued cogently, would allow blacks, like other poor New Yorkers, an opportunity to earn an income in all seasons. White monopoly of these licenses was unfair and contrary to the ideals of the American Revolution. Cornish also campaigned against the $250 suffrage bond, gave extensive coverage to antiabolitionist riots in Ohio, and maintained a steady fire at the American Colonization Society. Cornish was unable to sustain the personal losses incurred by publication, and the paper died in October 1829. [33]

City Work and Culture

Black New York's wage force in the 1820s remained primarily female, a characteristic that did not lend itself to deference. To the dismay of employers, the faithful servant became a distant memory. Restlessness and freedom of spirit undermined presumptions of deference and loyalty to paternalist masters. Higher wages for their services, increased demand, and republican pride combined to create a "love for incessant change." As Captain Basil Hall, a Scottish visitor, observed, "Of this insolence of servants I saw daily examples." Pierre Van Cortlandt described his suffering mother as "the Slave to Slaves." Her servants, he declared, "practice only wickedness." The Society for the Encouragement of Faithful Domestic Servants, formed in 1826 to increase stability in the occupation, offered Bibles and cash premiums to steadfast servants. It awarded twenty-five dollars to servants with ten or more years of continuous service to a single master, but most of its grants were to women with three or less years on one job. To its dismay, when the society created a registry to supplant corrupt job referral agencies known as intelligence offices, initial requirements of one year of constant employment disqualified virtually all two thousand applicants. [34]

The paternalist influence of conservative, elite New Yorkers dominated the society. In his diary John Pintard described model servants worthy of recognition. His cook, Tamar Fulmeter, after eighteen years of service, had saved about $600 and owned a "premium Bible." The chambermaid, who also owned a "premium Bible," taught Pintard's grandson the Lord's Prayer. All four of the family domestics attended either white or black churches. Nonetheless, only one servant had been with the family longer than two years. Even the pious servant felt free to switch masters.[35]

Many free blacks remained domestics in white households. Such servants became part of paternalist lore. Eliza Schuyler recalled the family servant, Prince, whom Philip Schuyler purchased out of debtor's prison and who "proved a good and reliable slave, preparing food and lodging." Easily the most saintly servant was the legendary Pierre Toussaint. Born in Haiti in 1766, Toussaint arrived in New York City with his master in 1787. There he was apprenticed to a hairdresser and, though still enslaved, set up a successful salon of his own. Even though he made enough money to purchase his freedom, Toussaint chose to stay with his mistress until she freed him on her deathbed. As his fame grew and his services became known to nobility throughout Europe, Toussaint remained loyal to his former owners, supporting their daughter. He purchased the freedom of his wife, his sister, and his daughter. After his daughter's untimely death in 1829, Toussaint dedicated his life to philanthropy and became the most notable black person in the New York diocese in the antebellum era. Yet even faithful servants faced insecurity. Francis, a "man of color," who worked for eight years as domestic to Mrs. Francis Pearsall, made $144 a year and at one point even had his children laboring for her. In 1819, though, she decided to save money, fired Francis and his family, and replaced them with Shepherd Stay, another man of color, and paid him $120 a year.[36]

The paternalist world of domestics is perhaps best illustrated by the activities of the Manumission Society, which apprenticed young blacks seeking to enter the domestic trade. The society went to the orphan's court, made deals with presiding magistrates, and then placed the youngsters with families. From there, ambitious blacks could potentially rise. Black caterers and restaurant managers trained as domestics. Nor was the domestic trade simple. Robert Roberts, a black butler from Boston, wrote an extensive directory of tasks for the house servant. General skills included dressing, cleaning, cooking, and presenting meals, proper communications with employers, special cleansing methods, and knowledge of recipes.[37]

Pierre Toussaint. Toussaint was among the leading hairdressers in the city. He purchased his wife and daughter's freedom and later loaned money to his former mistress. (Courtesy of the New-York Historical Society)

Younger female domestics were far more assertive, negotiating with employers for control over their time and personal lives. John Pintard's servant Hannah, for example, won the key concession of keeping her infant children with her until she decided to leave his household to join her recently emancipated husband. After Hannah left, Pintard, desperate for help and unwilling to hire "unprincipled, unqualified and thieving white women," hired another African American servant, Tamar, and, after negotiation, was forced to employ her daughter

Nancy. Tamar's high skills and integrity made Pintard accept her demands despite her "violent temper."[38]

The Society for the Encouragement of Faithful Domestic Servants charted the origins of the roughly two thousand servants who registered at its offices. This number is but a sample of the twenty to thirty thousand domestics in the city, but it demonstrates that newly arrived Irish women were replacing black servants. The society counted 259 Americans, 1,279 Irish, 126 English, 18 Scottish and Welsh, 15 Germans, 7 French, and 460 "People of Color." Three-quarters of the domestics were female.[39]

The transition from black to Irish domestic help would rapidly increase in future decades. American attitudes about domestic or drudge work worsened in this period, calling into question historical arguments about the transition from enslavement to free labor. The arrival of the Irish perhaps pushed some native-born workers upward but clearly had a negative effect on New York City blacks, especially women. As Jonathan Glickstein has pointed out, Americans separated the quality of mental and drudge work in this period. If, as New York's homeowners determined, black women were no longer suitable for household chores, their place in the work world became tenuous and haphazard. As William J. Wilson has contended, occupations for urban blacks can simply disappear, a pattern that first occurred among African American domestics in the 1820s.[40]

If black domestics were gradually being squeezed out by newcomers, they were not going quietly. Better wages for domestics and the influence of Haitian blacks added a fashionable flair to the custom of Sunday gatherings. Castle Clinton and Broadway seemed "something like Hyde Park" to visitor C. F. Arfwedson. The tourist noted that "the women wear bonnets, decorated with plumes, ribbons and flowers of a thousand different colours." The men "are attired like real French *petit-maitres manques*, their coats are so open the shirt sticks out under the armpits; the waistcoats are of all colours of the rainbow; the hat is carelessly put off to one side; the gloves are yellow, and every dandy carried a smart cane." Known as "belles and beaux," young blacks courted each other on Sundays. Mrs. Frances Trollope watched a "young Negro in the extreme of fashion, accompanied by a black beau, whose toilet was equally studied; eye glass, guard chain, nothing was omitted; he walked beside her uncovered and with an air of most total devotion."[41] During the 1820s, black servants held annual balls, at

Black and White Beaux, *1826. As a black middle class emerged in the 1820s, well-dressed young couples like this one paraded on Broadway and at Castle Garden. (From* Frances Trollope, Domestic Manners of the Americans, *Vol. 2. Courtesy of the New-York Historical Society.)*

which they dressed, according to highly critical white observers, in "tawdry elegance" and arrived in coaches driven by white coachmen. The balls were further evidence of a burgeoning high life among lower-class blacks.

White observers often looked at such events with derision. Writers scoffed at black pretensions; caricaturists lampooned black dress mercilessly. Such satire did not sit well with more middle class blacks, especially those with religious and political aspirations, who condemned the balls as exhibitions that rendered the race as "laughing stocks." These comments suggest a class-based division within the African American community. As Shane White and Graham White have pointed out, some blacks abused the very idea of community by practicing confidence schemes or by stealing and committing violent acts against other African Americans. Certainly the black newspapers railed against the balls, processions, and flamboyant personal behavior as shameful. Given the very low wages and humble occupations of all blacks in antebellum New York, their condemnations sprang not so much from rank as from religious orientation. Sean Wilentz, among others, has charted the distances between white master craftsmen and journeyman artisans. That income gap did not exist among blacks. The African Americans who made up the fragile middle class in New York, and in the rural areas for that matter, generally came from service jobs where they constantly encountered genteel whites. These blacks, especially the leaders, were well-educated graduates of the African Free School and had literary ambitions and political aspirations.[42]

By contrast, playful African Americans were usually less educated, more likely to have abandoned contact with pietistic whites, and involved in the secular remnants of the slave culture. They should not, however, be dismissed. With their ubiquitous presence, gaudy clothing, extravagant hair styles, loud public performances, and predilection for nighttime entertainment, young black males and females were creating an urban street style with powerful modern connotations. Anticipating Mose and Lize, the Bowery b'hoys and g'hals evoked by Sean Wilentz and Christine Stansell, black domestics mixed with unemployed semi-criminals create a type of curbside tough who set the urban styles in clothing, hair, music, and walk. New York City and its rural environs have seldom been credited as being the formative centers of black culture, but in the antebellum years more professional black musicians lived there than in any other city in the nation. The hurly-burly world of the Five Points and other gathering places set the tone for later African American street culture.[43]

Much of this urban musical scene stemmed from work. For example, blacks with political connections could gain work in licensed trades such as chimney sweeps, porters, and hackney coach drivers. Chimney sweeping was fully regulated with a system of apprentices and journeymen. These trades were highly visible in the city streets. One observer in 1824 noted the bizarre appearance and high-pitched screams of the sweeps. Peering out of his window at 4 A.M. he watched the head sweep, dressed in "an immense mahoganny coloured shawl," carrying besoms (a broom made with twigs) with his apprentices. He listened intently to their cries, which combined English, Dutch, and African tongues: "Ek Ho, yaw, Ah hikko yek! E Oh! Yekko Kik aw!"[44]

Such behavior often offended public sensibilities. Chimney sweeps were fined if their apprentices screamed too loudly in the streets. Citizens made more serious accusations against night soil cleaners. An 1817 petition complained that "a number of vagabond negroes" who performed the work "scream through the streets at all hours of the night"

Butter and milk seller. Hundreds of rural blacks, like this man, brought country produce into the city to sell from wagons. Their cries filled the morning air. (Nicolino Calyo, The Butter and Milk Man, *1840–44, watercolor, 10¼ × 14", Museum of the City of New York, Gift of Francis P. Garvan)*

using "shockingly indecent" expressions. The privy cleaners, the petitioners claimed, spent their first shillings on rum and often "drop[ped] their loads" in the poorer parts of the city. However justified these complaints were, the offending black workers were placing their personal stamp on the city streets.[45]

Although blacks worked as porters and chimney sweeps, they were not allowed to practice many other trades licensed by the city and held exclusively by whites. Exclusion of blacks from carting affected ancillary trades. In 1819, for example, the city magistrates prosecuted William Williams, a "man of color," for carrying a trunk for hire without a license. Unable to secure a license or pay the five-dollar fine, Williams was sent to debtor's prison for nonpayment.[46]

Beneath the independent freedmen class was a large working class of poorer servants, laborers, and seamen. One of the most important occupations for free or enslaved blacks in New York and New Jersey at the turn of the nineteenth century was seafaring. Long a refuge for fugitive slaves or the choice of many free blacks and slaves on hire, seafaring labor ranged from work on privateers and tiny coastal crafts to large transoceanic vessels. The New York shipping market was booming in the late eighteenth century, and the merchant marine was a ready employer of African Americans. Seafaring was another escape route for fugitive blacks. Nearly 20 percent of the black seamen seeking citizenship papers at the port of Philadelphia were from New Jersey, a figure much larger than the free black population of the state. Whaling ships on Long Island hired blacks.[47]

African Americans held about 18 percent of the able-bodied seamen's posts on private ships out of New York City between 1800 and 1825, and as many as 16 percent of the 120 ships out of New York in 1818 used all-black crews. With the extraordinarily uncommon exception of Paul Cuffe, blacks were rarely officers on ships. Nevertheless, black sailors found autonomy on ships. Black sailors lived in the fo'c'sle, a part of the ships by custom off-limits to the captain and his officers. Similarly, the dog watch at twilight time was free of managerial interference. In the kitchens, black cooks controlled the ship's food.[48]

Working as able-bodied seamen and cooks, black crews added a picaresque air to lower-class society. When on shore in New York City, many mariners worked as laborers on the docks. The ferry stairs and the wharf on Sundays were the scene of fighting, quarreling, and the most profane language expressed by gambling "men boys and negroes." Seafaring took New York blacks all around the world. When Peter Wheeler returned to New York after each voyage, he would jump ashore, "slap my hand on my pocket and say that's my own and if I hauled out my turnip [watch], why it ticked for me and not for master." [49]

Seafaring was often the only resort for aspiring black males. Charles C. Andrews, principal of the African Free School, made navigational skills an important part of the curriculum, teaching male students to calculate longitude and latitude and chart the sun's declination.[50] But black sailors, though they formed a Colored Seamen's Home in New York in 1840, faced rising prejudice and declining berths. The United States Navy limited their numbers to no more than "five per cent of the whole number of white persons enlisted . . . and absolutely no slaves." In the merchant marine, the proportion of blacks declined from 8.5 percent to less than 6 percent and most berths were only as cooks or stewards. Jobs at sea became fewer and fewer for blacks. African American seamen in New York tried to stem this segregation by organizing a refuge. Within ten years, the Seaman's Home offered sanctuary to about 450 black sailors each year. This number included destitute mariners, who received relief in board and clothing.[51]

Further down the social ladder were the dependent poor, especially the old. The announcement of a pension for Revolutionary War veterans produced applications from several aged soldiers. Fortune Freeman, Artillo Freeman, and Prince Vaughan, who fought in the Battles of Saratoga, White Plains, and Monmouth, now lived in poverty in New York City. Vaughan, who had enlisted in the black regiment commanded by Colonel Greene in 1778, now kept an oyster stand and had no family or children to support him. Artillo Freeman, who claimed to be ninety-nine years old, supported his wife, aged eighty-eight, and a crippled daughter by picking oakum.[52]

Black street musicians, long a part of the urban scene, found their creative dances and songs bastardized while white imitators, with access to musical halls and theaters, made substantial amounts of money. Irish "b'hoys," observing black hot corn women, made room in the streets for their girlfriends to supplant their black sisters who sang the virtues of their vegetables and prepared foods.[53]

At the bottom of the social ladder was the swirling, transient mass of poorer blacks, residing in cellars, making ends meet with odd jobs and petty crime, and unable to rise above bare poverty. Not all could make ends meet in the metropolis, and in the first decade of the nineteenth century New York City transported vagrant blacks to the city line, a revival of colonial eviction of paupers. In 1805 the superintendent of the almshouse recommended closer examination and possible expulsion to their former homes of free blacks drifting into the city from the provinces. During 1808 the city transported nineteen criminals, including thieves and prostitutes, as well as seven families, four insane, and six aged or lame blacks.[54] On May 23 and 24, 1808, the city transported William Butler and his family of five back to Rockaway and evicted John Valentine and his family from Long Island. The almshouse was one of the few refuges for aged, abandoned slaves who might otherwise have been transported. Between 1815 and 1826 the almshouse averaged over one hundred black inmates per year or roughly 8 percent of the total population of blacks in the city. Some made lengthy stays. Abigail Dodson, a slave of a New York sea captain, lost her sight in 1813, was admitted to the almshouse the following year, and remained there until 1844, when she entered the Colored Home. Almshouse keepers could be tragically careless. In 1818 they coffined one black, Job Young, ill with typhus, while he was still alive and breathing.[55]

Construction of the state penitentiary in Greenwich Village and enlargement of the jail at the notorious neighborhood known as the Five Points accompanied a transformation of penal attitudes toward blacks. As masters' powers over slaves waned, the state took over punishment, performing whippings and incarcerating blacks. Imprisoned in 1820 were blacks convicted of petty larceny, vagrancy, and "disorderly conduct," a euphemism for prostitution. Blacks were also imprisoned for debt. Sentences ranged from sixty days for first offenses by black women to ninety days for burglary by black males. Second offenses earned much lengthier terms of five years and more even for minor theft. (Sharing the cells with blacks in 1820 were fourteen white men imprisoned for slave trading.)[56]

The black poor found themselves in frequent conflict with newly arrived Irish in the Five Points. When the two groups lived in close proximity, often in the same building, there were numerous open battles. In one instance, a black landlord named William Edwards attempted to evict an Irish tenant, Andrew Mickle, on May Day, the time when leases traditionally expired. Unable to get any police help during an election, Edwards hired several other blacks to help evict Mickle. When Edwards and his associates began hurling his furniture into the street, Mickle rallied a crowd of several hundred and attacked Edwards, crying, "Kill the negroes!" During the ensuing trial for mobbing, despite his correct legal position, Edwards lost the case.[57]

Unemployed young blacks formed gangs reminiscent of the colonial era. In 1816 Isaac Fraser and George Vanderpool joined a gang led by Richard Parcells. The gang's method was to set fires and then rob stores during the ensuing tumult. One night in late 1815 while at the circus, they decided to "have a scortch," to burn down the city "for the object of stealing and plundering." They set ablaze a stable on Lombardy Street near Bancker and then broke into a grocery, stole a few dollars, and divided the money in a dance hall. Caught soon after, Fraser and Vanderpool were convicted on the testimony of Parcells. Sentenced to death, Vanderpool was converted in prison by the noted missionary the Reverend John Stanford. Under the rope, Fraser and Vanderpool were separated when Governor Tompkins's reprieve arrived for the convert. As in the colonial era, clerical intervention saved the converted while those unconverted were sent to hang.[58]

In response to the growing hard times, some black women turned to prostitution. clustering primarily in the east, dock, and west wards of New York City.[59] On weekends prostitutes received from fifteen to twenty-five men and earned up to fifty dollars, far more than they

Five Points, 1827. *The crowds filling the intersection of five streets in the Sixth Ward generated a raucous popular culture and presaged what Walt Whitman called "a grand American opera." The Five Points, where blacks and whites mixed freely, was the most integrated part of New York City outside of the Toombs and was the nineteenth-century antecedent of Times Square. (From* Valentine's Manual of the Corporation of the City of New York, *1860, collection of the author)*

could earn in domestic labor. In a city where black females outnumbered men by almost two to one in 1820, love for sale was a refuge for discharged domestics. Paid sex was also the one area of life that crossed racial barriers. The Five Points district, home of the poorest blacks and Irish immigrants, was the location of many interracial bordellos. (The original Five Points was formed by the intersections of Cross, Anthony, Little Water, Orange, and Mulberry Streets around a triangular area about an acre in size. In the center of the area was a small park called Paradise Square.) Brothels were usually close to pleasure gardens and theaters, creating a blend of culture and sex.[60]

A comical case that touched on the deep sexual anxieties of the times was the assault trial of Captain James Dunn, a white man, in 1808. Dunn approached Sylvia Patterson on the street, followed her home, and attempted to seduce her. She told him she was a married woman and not interested. Dunn plied Sylvia Patterson with drink and tried to give her a watch. James Patterson, her husband, suddenly returned, found "the bed tumbled," and threatened to hit Dunn, who offered a bribe of $200 to Patterson, who refused and charged Dunn with assault and intent to seduce. During the trial witnesses told the jury that the two Pattersons were not married and that Sylvia Patterson had been in the hospital several times for "venereal rheumatism." The jury found Dunn guilty and fined him one dollar, having decided the Pattersons were playing a confidence game.[61]

Other members of this rowdy black underclass presented continual problems for middle-class New Yorkers. In 1810 and in 1819 "sundry inhabitants" complained of blacks living on Bancker Street who disturbed Sunday worshipers by nude bathing, profanity, and "immoralities." In August 1819, neighbors in Greenwich Village complained about "certain persons of colour practicing as Musicians with Drums and other instruments."[62]

Inevitably, poverty begat violence in the black community. The Reverend John Stanford visited a black woman in the hospital "badly mangled by her husband, who, deranged in mind by the stimulant effects of ardent spirits," decided one night that Jesus ordered him to sacrifice her. He stabbed her in several places in the head, throat, body, and hands. Her groans were heard in the morning by the family who lived above their cellar apartment. Despite the attack, the woman was unwilling to make a complaint against her husband, fearing he might be executed. A second woman, Ann Sands, was beaten by her husband three days after he was freed from prison for a previous charge.[63]

New York City became, as in colonial days, the gathering place for slave culture. Blacks traveled into town from all over the region. Ward Stafford, a shipyard preacher, noted that more blacks "pass in some of these boats on the Sabbath than during the whole week."[64] Their primary destinations were the city markets, which attracted a picaresque array of hucksters, peddlers, and hawkers crying out their products. Many slaves accompanied the wives of Jersey farmers, who sold milk, vegetables, and cider to supplement their subsistence farms. Others were widows, given hucksters' licenses to keep them off the public dole; they sold hot chocolate and cakes and often fenced stolen goods. Blacks hawked vegetables, sweets, firewood, and animal skins. Among the most famous black street sellers was the pious Mary Simpson Washington. Freed by the first president after he left New York for the new capital, Washington first gained notoriety for her selfless behavior distributing a curative "sheep's head soup" during the yellow fever epidemic of 1793. Later, New Yorkers paraded to her little shop on Chatham Street to eat her "Washington Cake," which she prepared

Hot corn seller. Mary Simpson Washington was the prototype of black and white women who sold candied corn ears to the masses on street corners. The songs of these women were plaintive and beautiful. (Nicolino Calyo, Hot Corn Seller, *collection of the author)*

on the president's birthday. She adorned a table on the street with a picture of her hero and a small leather trunk inscribed with the initials "G.W." and proudly displayed a Bible signed by him. On more ordinary occasions, her freshly made hot corn delighted New Yorkers for decades. At her death in 1834 she was mourned by city residents.[65] Mary Simpson Washington's example spawned a host of black and white imitators who sold hot corn on the city's sidewalks. Rural black women brought green corn in from the country and sold it from midsummer to late autumn. Boiled in the husk and lightly salted, the corn was sold for a penny an ear. Hot corn girls, who became the stuff of legend, sang plaintive songs:

> You who have money, (alas I have none,)
> Come buy my lily white corn, and let me go home.[66]

After sunset following a day of bartering, the night brought dances, music, and gambling. The New York City Common Council's attempts to bar blacks from selling at the markets failed. On any weekend or holiday, blacks gathered together anything that might sell, from roots, berries, and herbs, to birds, fish, clams, and oysters, then rushed off to join brothers and sisters at the markets.[67] The most notorious features of the markets were the black dance contests which seemed to observers directly derived from African tradition. At the Catherine Market, blacks from Tappan, New Jersey, danced for prizes against the champions "Ned," slave of Martin Ryerson, or "Bobolink Bob, from

Long Island." After selling their masters' produce at the Bear Market, slaves would "shin it" to the Catherine Market for the competition. Blacks dressed their hair for the contests. Tappan blacks had their "plaited forelocks tied up with tea-lead." Long Island blacks usually tied their hair up in a queue, with dried eelskins. Other times they combed it about their heads and shoulders in the fashion of a wig. A butcher would sponsor the initial prize, and the competition was on. Blacks brought their own "shingles," or dancing boards about five to six feet long, of large width, with good spring. Dance styles included "turning around and shying off" around a designated spot; "shakedowns were next." Assistants held down the board while the dancer showed his art accompanied by clapping hands or heel taps. These dances, practiced at home on a barn door or at frolics, lasted all night, with shouts urging on the competitors.[68]

This underclass black culture had its roots in the slave culture of the colonial period. Though most of the region's black inhabitants were no longer enslaved (a significant number were), their culture sustained characteristics of older social patterns. Like their enslaved ancestors, they were frustrated by an inability to rise in society yet found refuge in music, dance, and style located in tavern and street life. Anticipating the blues life of the twentieth-century black poor, antebellum blacks lived and played hard and saw and took part in sudden outbursts of violence. Denied the steady lives of prosperous whites and a few blacks, they instead shaped a vibrant popular culture that lasts to the present day.[69]

Religion

As the notoriety of the Five Points grew, individual clergymen and church missions made efforts to clean up the area. The Reverends Ezra Stiles Ely and John Stanford preached the Gospel to the bottom of society, working in the city hospital, almshouse, state prison, the Bridewell, the orphan asylum, debtor's prison, and lunatic asylum. In each place they encountered African Americans in dire need of solace. Stanford became famous for saving hardened criminals. He also performed numerous rites of marriage in hospitals and prisons for African Americans. Individual clergymen created bridges between white and black society through their missionary efforts.[70]

The most active denominations were the most paternalist. Episcopalians and Presbyterians poured their energies into missions, Sunday schools, and free schools. However well-meaning, these efforts reeked of racial condescension and a recalcitrance toward sharing power or responsibility with blacks. With the exception of the Society of Friends, Protestant sects rarely condemned slavery and were likely to welcome slaveholders into congregations without comment.[71] A final problem was that white churches rarely admitted blacks who lacked familial connections. In all the denominations, black members usually were servants or slaves of white members.[72]

Lingering discrimination and Episcopalian unwillingness to condemn slavery caused black members of Trinity Church to split off and form St. Philip's Episcopal Church in 1809. After several years in which a white lay reader served the church, Peter Williams Jr. became pastor of the church. Named after the biblical saint who evangelized among Africans, St. Philip's drew its membership from the elite of free black society. Its first baptismal book lists accountants, hairdressers, masons, and speculators.[73]

Racial antagonism and conservative theological positions on slavery cost white congregations any remaining hold they might have had on black worshipers. The Dutch Reformed Church and African Americans quickly parted. An attempt to establish a black Sunday school for blacks in the church failed after a few years. A black version of the Dutch Reformed Church opened in 1826, with Mark Jordan as the first minister. The church held services in a schoolroom at Duane and Hudson Streets. Two years later Jordan lost his license and the church collapsed.[74]

Even the Methodist Church, its ardor toward blacks cooling, became troubled by racism. The problem was the continued failure of the church to promote talented blacks into clerical leadership. Not until 1809 did Francis Asbury, for example, promote Richard Allen, the preeminent black Methodist since the 1790s, and New Yorkers Abraham Thompson and James Varick to the fairly low post of deacon.[75] Overt racism drove blacks from Methodist churches. One prime example was the Old Sand Street Methodist Episcopal Church of Brooklyn, founded in 1787. The initial membership lists held fifty-one whites, including all officers, sixteen black males, and ten black females. The church remained interracial until 1818, when blacks, angered by the Reverend Alexander McClain's racist sermons, created a subsidiary congregation and then split off entirely in 1820 to form the African Asbury Methodist Episcopal Church. The final split occurred when the Old Sand Street congregation requested that the African Asbury Church partially support McClain's salary in the parent church. After that, only six blacks remained in the Old Sand Street Church.[76]

Colonization

In 1816 the Reverend Robert Finley, a white Presbyterian minister from Basking Ridge, New Jersey, published *Thoughts on the Colonization of Free Blacks,* which argued for the voluntary removal of free blacks from the United States because they would never be accorded racial equality. Finley may not have been the founder of the American Colonization Society (in fact, there is strong evidence that Virginian Charles Fenton Mercer holds that dubious honor), but Finley's experiences in Somerset County convinced him that distributing Bibles and tracts did little to alter the blacks' social status or equality: "Every thing connected with their condition, including their colour, is against them." Finley's words echoed prerevolutionary demands from Somerset that blacks be exiled. Now, Finley found agreement among other New Jersey Presbyterians, including Princeton University professors, politicians, and ministers. Colonization quickly became a missionary obligation of whites to compensate for the crimes of slavery and to bring Christianity to Africa. This enthusiasm enabled Finley to form the region's branch of the American Colonization Society the following year, attracting sincere liberals as well as conservative racists. Its members included Charles Andrews, director of the African Free School in New York City, William Leete Stone, editor of the *New York Commercial Advertiser,* and Senator Rufus King. Whites viewed colonization from several perspectives: as a means of ridding the country of unwanted free blacks and keeping out Africans captured from slavers, for promoting missions, and to help American merchants gain a foothold in Africa. Rather than work with black projects for emigration to Haiti and Canada (both considered to be little more than havens for runaways), whites insisted on the aggressive finality of the African option.[77]

By the 1820s white congregations in the North regarded emancipation and the end of slavery as God's Will but feared the consequences of universal and immediate manumission. An orator at the Dutch Reformed Church in New York City in 1824 asked whether free blacks' lives were "much, if at all better than in the state of slavery." Sending blacks "to the land of their ancestors" seemed the only humane way to end slavery. Similarly, the organizers of the American Colonization

Society in New Jersey noted the dangers of general emancipation until "some suitable place beyond the limits of the United States had been prepared for the reception" of free blacks. This misguided benevolence masked deeper racist fears. In the same statement, the colonizationists worried that the black population of New Jersey, which they estimated at twenty thousand, would threaten the whole of the population "with a moral and political pestilence." The only answer was to take the "enormous mass of revolting wretchedness and deadly pollution" out of the state. Unless colonization occurred, gradual freedom, with blacks denied the vote and civil rights, would "provoke a civil and servile war."[78]

The Spread of Black Theology

Rejecting colonization and the patriarchal messages from white denominations, African Methodist Episcopal churches built on their early efforts and constructed several meetinghouses in New York City. Schisms developed in 1801 when two original members, Abram Thompson and June Scott, "induced by the expectation of filthy lucre," tried to form an independent church called the Union Society. After that failed, followers of Bishop Richard Allen formed the Asbury Methodist Church in 1817. In 1820 the black Methodists split off from the parent white church. In 1820 representatives from the Zion and Asbury Churches met together to write *The Doctrines and Discipline of the African Methodist Church in America*. The introduction to the *Doctrines* spoke openly about the reasons for the split with Methodism. As long as blacks stayed in the white church, "our preachers would never be able to enjoy those privileges . . . of those called of God to preach," for access to the clergy was limited by color. Establishing the African Methodist Church required "an itinerant plan" and advancement of black preachers *"according to our judgment of the necessity."* The use of black ministers would "induce many of our African brethren to attend on divine worship who are yet careless about their eternal welfare." The movement quickly spread throughout the Northeast, and the following year, restive black congregations held a conference of northeastern black Methodists, enlarging the circles of black religious connections. While the main reason for separation was to avoid racism in the parent church, another intent was to create a new class of black Methodist preachers.[79]

Black Methodist music was a combination of orthodox hymns with alterations and supplementary lines appropriate for an African American audience. Beginning with Richard Allen's collection of spiritual songs printed in Philadelphia and widely distributed throughout New Jersey, black Methodists added refrain lines not permitted in official Protestant hymnody. Similarly, black Methodist congregations chose hymnal tunes according to the occasion rather than relying on standard instructions. The line between sacred and secular black music often blurred. White Protestant critic John F. Watson complained that mid-Atlantic Methodists were generally too noisy but that blacks were especially exuberant for their "practice of singing in out places of public and society worship, *merry* airs adapted from old songs, to hymns of our composing; most often miserable as poetry and senseless as matter. . . . Most frequently [these hymns are] composed and first sung by the illiterate *blacks* of the society." [80]

African Methodist Episcopal churches developed rapidly throughout eastern New Jersey. Bushtown AME came first in 1807 through an informal congregation formed in Princeton in 1800. In the next fifteen years itinerant black ministers such as George White traveled throughout New Jersey, and in 1817 Richard Allen founded churches in Princeton and Trenton. In 1822 blacks organized the Clinton AME Zion Church in Newark. By 1820 there were over seven hundred church members in New York and eastern New Jersey. That year the AME Zion Church held its first annual conference in New York City with ministers attending from Harlem, Newark, and Flushing, Long Island. The event grew steadily with preachers coming from upstate, Pennsylvania, and New Jersey throughout the 1820s. [81]

Black Education in the City

Even after the rupture between white Protestant denominations and African Americans, the two sides remained intertwined by education. The most paternalist white schools were among the most successful. Trinity Church reopened its charity school for blacks in 1787, renaming it the African Free School. The New York Manumission Society paid expenses for all 47 scholars. The school prospered throughout the next few decades and served over 2,300 students by 1814. In 1800 its 110 scholars made it the largest school in the city. [82] Anglicans also provided blacks with education through Sunday schools, offshoots of the charity school. St. James Parish in Bloomingdale in upper Manhattan started a Sunday school for blacks in 1815 with the express purpose of "influencing many children who would otherwise be but profane violators of the sanctity of God's Holy Day." Sunday school at St. Paul's, St.

Mark's, St. Luke's, and other New York Episcopal parishes continued colonial era methods of teaching literacy through memorized biblical passages, hymns, and catechisms. The schools were oriented toward children, but adults were welcome.[83]

In the first decades of the nineteenth century, blacks were still highly dependent on European culture for education. Closely tied to the political powers of church and benevolent societies was the increased importance of the African Free School. In 1813, the school began receiving city and county funds. Four more such schools opened by 1827, and a female school opened in 1831. The free schools taught a basic curriculum of reading, writing, and ciphering supplemented by poetry, drawing, and public speaking. Judging by scrapbooks of award-winning assignments, the students performed admirably. School rules reinforced discipline. C. D. Arfwedson observed one class in which "rebellious urchins looked up to the black teacher with a confidence that proved at once that she filled the situation with dignity . . . a word from her lips struck awe in the numbers of noisy boys quarreling about a space of a quarter of an inch in their seats." Scholars were required to attend church and read the Scripture and were continually warned about minor sins of lying, dishonesty, profanity, and "cruelty to beasts." The school used the Lancastrian system of education, which employed student monitors to assist in instruction. Benjamin Shaw visited the Free School in 1817 and observed "an African prince in one corner attentively copying the alphabet; a young man of fourteen reciting passages from the best authors, suiting actions to words; another answering difficult questions in geography." Although Shaw concluded that the school's graduates proved the "poor despised African as capable of every intellectual improvement," white society was not receptive. As one graduate complained, after graduation, "No one will employ me; white boys won't work with me at all. . . . Drudgery and servitude . . . are my prospective portion." Still, the African Free School was the training ground of future African American leaders. Among its most illustrious graduates were James McCune Smith, Ira Aldridge, Peter Williams Jr., James Varick, and Thomas Sydney. The school encouraged students after graduation to consider apprenticeships in trades arranged by the Manumission Society, but these were generally as servants and farmhands.[84] Limited job placement was not the only reason blacks became disaffected from the African Free School. Its pedagogical methods proved unsatisfactory for independent-minded blacks. Unhappy with the rigid curriculum of the Free School and its Lancastrian system, which taught blacks "to answer like parrots," B. F. Hughes started a school for colored children of both sexes. It had a larger curriculum than the African Free School and provided instruction in reading, writing, history, arithmetic, English grammar, and geography.[85]

Other schools aimed at older blacks. In the 1820s, the Clarkson Benevolent Association sponsored a school for aged black women who wished to learn how to read and write. The testimonies of the elderly students, ranging in age from sixty-eight to over one hundred years, were living reminders of the days of general slavery in New York. For example, Billy and Cathy, born in 1738, told of their days of slavery on Long Island. Belinda Lucas, "about 100," came to Antigua from Africa and was sold several times before coming to New York City as a small girl. She bought her freedom in the 1770s and owned a house.[86]

When municipal governments opened schools, segregation was the norm. In 1817 the Brooklyn public school opened with segregated classrooms. Forty-five black scholars studied in a classroom separate from 190 white pupils. Black parents paid $1.00 per month versus $1.50 for whites, suggesting that, after books, stationery, and fuel were paid for, little was left for the black teacher. Pupils without funds were admitted free.[87]

Black Education in New Jersey

Despite legislation requiring that masters educate slaves before manumitting them, black education in New Jersey started late. The Society of Friends opened the first schools for emancipated blacks in the 1790s.[88] These schools soon closed, and the next attempts did not occur until after the onset of gradual emancipation. The Presbyterian Church of New Jersey founded an African School in Parsippany in 1817 to train black missionaries for the colonization movement and received financial support from blacks. The New Brunswick African Association, founded January 1, 1817, devoted its funds "exclusively to the school lately formed by the Synod of New York and New Jersey known by the name of the African School for the purpose of educating young men of colour." The association consisted of thirty-four men and twelve women with officers "chosen from males only." It met every month, collecting fifty cents from each subscriber. Speakers such as Jeremiah Gloucester of Philadelphia, a black clergyman, lauded the association's efforts and reminded "Africa's sons and daughters" that "forty or fifty years ago," all were enslaved. Gloucester beseeched his audience to teach their children of the contributions of Woolman and Benezet and the sufferings of past generations. He proclaimed that a "star was rising over Africa," which would produce among its peoples "philosophers . . . mathematicians and preachers of the ever-lasting gospel."[89]

Other black schools opened in New Jersey outside of the colonization movement. In 1826 the AME Zion Church in Newark offered common school courses in reading, writing, and ciphering to black youths and adults. The following year Abraham and John King started a "Colored School" in Newark that operated until 1909.[90]

Rural Work and Culture

In the New York countryside, freedom was a relative condition because many free blacks lived in white households and were employed as domestics and farmhands. In largely Dutch Kings and Richmond Counties, the number of enslaved blacks remained sizable until 1820. Dutch farmers in these counties tenaciously held onto their farms by using valuable slave labor. As late as 1820, only 55 percent of Kings County blacks and a minuscule 13 percent of blacks in Richmond County were free, against 95 percent in New York County and over 80 percent in Queens and Westchester Counties. Most free blacks in Kings and Richmond Counties were young, an effect of gradual emancipation and abandonment. In contrast, blacks older than forty-five years remained slaves in 1820, doubtless because masters were unwilling to accept responsibility for their maintenance otherwise.[91]

Economic patterns in the postrevolutionary period remained constant in the early national period. In 1814, for example, slaveholders in Bergen County owned four times as many cattle and three times as many horses as nonslaveholders. While slave owners constituted less than 15 percent of the taxpayers in Hackensack, they owned 30 percent of the improved acreage. Average acreage for slave owners in Hackensack was 107 versus 29 for non-slave owners. In New Barbados, slave owners owned 40 percent of the improved land but were only 15 percent of the taxpayers. These patterns were also true in newer, western townships. In Franklin township in 1814, thirty-nine slaveholders with an average of one slave each, or 6 percent of the town's taxpayers, owned 13 percent of the improved land. The average holding was 90 acres versus 38 acres for nonslaveholders.[92]

In rural areas prosperous blacks owned property through purchase or received gifts of land and money from former owners. Many took second careers as mariners, oystering, or as cooks on steamboats and ocean vessels in order to compile wealth. One black town, Seneca Village, sprouted in upper Manhattan, in present-day Central Park. In Seneca Village, black artisans and laborers owned homes amid German and Irish neighbors. In New Jersey a tiny black middle class included grocers, church sextons, farmers, and barbers.[93]

Poorer blacks worked as independent laborers on farms. White farmers hired blacks on a seasonal basis, paying them an average of $70 for six months' labor plus food and washing. Blacks could add income by selling firewood and hay and for cartage to the markets. John Baxter of Flatlands allowed his servants to cut fire wood, to crab, and to fish and then take their produce to New York City for market. Additional perquisites included tuition for the "negro school and time off for Pinkster."[94] James Hawkhurst, a Queens County truck farmer, hired black laborers to perform various chores by the season.[95] Farmwork changed little in this period, so that condition of employment was the primary difference between hired hands and slaves. Slaves worked next to free people. Masters regularly hired out slaves. Masters also boarded abandoned free people, receiving an average of two dollars each month.[96]

As in the city, the harsh work regimens produced a tough nighttime culture. In rural New Jersey, Sylvia Du Bois's nightclub near Hopewell, Somerset County, was an interracial milieu where cockfights, fox chases, prizefights, and prostitution took place. Du Bois recalled her early days when she could "cross my feet ninety-nine times in a minute and never miss the time, strike heel or to with equal ease and go thru the figures as nimble as a witch." In the long winters, Du Bois remembered, "we had frolics almost every week; we'd hardly get over one frolic when we'd begin to fix for another." There was always music: "We was sure to have a fiddle and a frolic . . . I could dance all night." Another important occasion for drinking was the house-raising, a neighborly exercise that often ended in fistfights. Du Bois said Training Day, or the general militia muster "was the biggest day." New Jersey blacks "were out to general training . . . and then we'd have some rum and then you'd hear them laugh a mile and when they got into a fit, you'd hear them yell more than five miles."[97]

Pinkster became a largely black holiday early in the nineteenth century. Dance and musical competitions focused on this most important festival. Preparation for Pinkster preoccupied blacks for weeks, dur-

Sylvia Du Bois (right) and her daughter Elizabeth Alexander, 1882. Long after her days of dancing in taverns and at training days were over, Sylvia Du Bois narrated her classic account of life as a rural female slave. She was the country cousin of the Black and White Beaux and of Toko. (From the Collections of the Hunterdon County Historical Society)

ing which they came to markets around the region to sell cheap goods to raise money for the event. At the four-day holiday, hucksters sold cakes and ale at booths. There was a mock election of a monarch. Usually, King Charley, a slave of a "respectable merchant prince of the Hudson," governed Pinkster. Charley was originally from Angola and was tall, dignified, and athletic, despite his seventy years. He wore a republican costume composed of an broadcloth scarlet coat, yellow buckskin shoes, a tricornered cocked hat, and a jacket formerly worn by a "British brigadier of the olden time." The music was profoundly African. Charley led the "Toto" dance, with music from drums made from eel pots. Women along the sidelines clapped "with their ungloved hands, in strict accordance with the eel-pot melody." Other blacks accompanied the music with whistling known as "negro Pinkster music." The dance went on and on with Charley in the midst of it, "until the shades of night and morning almost mingled together." On successive days poorer Dutch joined the party with much resulting drunkenness and fistfights.[98]

Celebrating the End of Slavery

African American communities in New York and New Jersey made great strides between 1804 and 1827, culminating in 1827, when the African American community turned out to celebrate the final abolition of slavery in New York State. The *Freedom's Journal* began commentary on the great day several months in advance. Two weeks before July 4, it announced two celebrations. To avoid confrontation with displeased white republicans, blacks would celebrate the end of slavery privately on the Fourth of July. The next day, blacks held a grand procession, an oration, and a public dinner. On July 4, 1827, emancipation day in New York, the Reverend William Hamilton proclaimed from the pulpit of the African Zion Church at Leonard and Church Streets in downtown Manhattan that "this day has the State of New York regenerated itself. . . . This day has She been cleansed of a most foul, poisonous and damnable stain." Celebrants filled the church with banners bearing the names of antislavery advocates. Hamilton saluted the black Loyalists, recalling that they "obtained their liberty, by leaving the country at the close of the war." The following day two thousand blacks marched from St. John's Park to the Zion Church to hear an oration at a dinner on Wall Street. James McCune Smith later recalled the procession, which he attended in his youth. Grand marshal for the parade was Samuel Hardenburgh:

A splendid looking black man, mounted on a milk-white steed, then his aids on horseback, dashing up and down the line; then the orator of the day, also mounted, with a handsome scroll, appearing like a baton in his right hand, then in due order, splendidly dressed in scarfs of silk with gold-edgings, and with colored bands of music and their banners appropriately lettered and painted, followed, The New York African Society for Mutual Relief, the Wilberforce Benevolent Society, and the Clarkson Benevolent Society; then the people five or six abreast from grown men to small boys. The sidewalks were crowded with the wives, daughters, sisters and mothers of the celebrants, representing every state in the Union, and not a few with gay bandanna handkerchiefs, betraying their West Indian birth. Nor was Africa underrepresented. Hundreds who survived the middle passage and a youth in slavery joined in the joyful procession.

A visitor, James Buckingham, described the huge parade: "Some hundreds of the black and coloured, extremely well-dressed and wearing sashes and ribbons, paraded the city in martial array, with the accompaniment of music." The only difficulty came from the "insulting behavior of many of the coachmen and carters . . . unblushingly displayed so as to interrupt the progress and order of the procession, although we did not witness a single provocation." [99] Numerous black churches held private celebrations the following day. On Staten Island blacks from all over Long Island and New Jersey sang old songs, "praised the lord," and set off firecrackers. Approximately twenty-eight hundred blacks were freed from masters who held them in bondage until the bitter end.[100]

Conclusions

Though New York African Americans won final emancipation in 1827, they still lacked such important civil rights as universal suffrage, trial by jury for fugitives, and access to licensed occupations. In New Jersey despite gradual emancipation over two thousand blacks were still enslaved in 1830; the rest lacked the vote and general civil rights. The processions capped a quarter-century of struggle. The twenty-eight years between the enactment of gradual emancipation and the closure of slavery in New York were marked by numerous African American commemorations of the abolition of the slave trade and black participation in the War of 1812, when they showed deep feelings of patriotism. Black freedom celebrations revealed a "double consciousness" toward American culture. Participants in parades and memorial services seemed torn about their identity as Americans or as displaced Africans.[101] Certainly the American system worked at an important level. Slavery as an institution was finished in New York and in decline in New Jersey. Black New Yorkers established churches, benevolent societies, and newspapers and worked at their chosen occupations. Yet growing political oppression, increasing immiseration, and rising social hostility called the permanence of those accomplishments into question. Blacks responded by reinvigorating their ties to Africa. The emancipation celebration was surprising for the degree of Africanity displayed. Various African societies attended the procession, and former slaves joined the march or cheered from the sidewalks. On a deeper level, however, the personas of Samuel Hardenburgh and William Hamilton may be linked with the coronations at Pinkster. Heavily adorned with sashes and ribbons, splendidly dressed, Hardenburgh and Hamilton stepped forward as noble leaders for the day, just as King Charley did at Pinkster and elected kings and presidents did in black New England celebrations. The close of slavery was a further extension of the Enlightenment ideals and the republicanism of the American Revolution. The mixture of European liberal thought and African cultural resistance carried African Americans in New York and New Jersey through the hazards of the antebellum years. Under the cloak of those belief systems, however, lay a bedrock of Africanity upon which black intellectuals and ordinary people formed their lives. In the next thirty years, black New Yorkers and New Jerseyans strove to amplify their freedoms. As the promises of the American Revolution declined, blacks turned more and more to Africa.[102]

Gradual emancipation did not immediately alter the occupational structure of African Americans in New York and East Jersey. As in the colonial era, females in the city and towns found work as domestics, while black males labored as farmers, sailors, and artisans. Unlike the colonial period, blacks could work at chosen occupations, even if they were restricted to the African American community. In addition, blacks could own property, move about, and associate with each other far more freely. Despite the hazards of racism and discrimination, African Americans made large strides toward the creation of a genuine community, only hinted at in the colonial and Revolutionary periods. Whereas class was a murky category in the colonial period, distinct ranks appeared in black society by 1830. However bourgeois the black middle class in New York and New Jersey was, it remained committed to social and political change. For poorer blacks, culture included the hurly-burly world of taverns and dance halls in the city and the rousing festival of Pinkster in the rural regions. Whites in New York did not generally celebrate the end of slavery. The newspaper the *New York Commercial Advocate*, which would become an enemy of black aspirations, cautioned that the abolition of slavery in New York would cause an influx of runaway slaves from New Jersey, "encouraged by emissaries from this state," and worried that the public would have to support those "who are too indolent or vicious to seek regular employment" until there would be "overflowing Bridewells, penitentiaries, and alms houses [arising] from the vagrant act not being supported more strictly." Such public racism shocked the Marquis de Lafayette when the French hero of the American Revolution visited New York City in 1824. He recalled, with sadness, how, during the Revolution, "blacks and whites messed together without hesitation." [103]

CHAPTER 8

The Black Renaissance
amidst White Racism

1827–1860

The abolition of slavery in New York meant only that the African American drive for equality had reached a new level with many tasks uncompleted. Over two thousand black people were still enslaved in New Jersey. In New York, racism became a major force in the aftermath of slavery. European travelers, intent on understanding the new American society, were appalled at the treatment of blacks in the city. The Englishman Henry Fearon noted that the "most degraded white will not walk in the streets with a black." E. S. Abdy observed a Frenchman "pelted with brickbats for speaking with a black." A visiting Englishwoman, Mrs. Felton, wrote that dogs were trained to bark at blacks and a parrot cursed every passing black.[1]

The most violent expression of this negrophobia occurred in the antiabolitionist riots of 1834. Several events preceded the outbreak. Troubles arose in early July, when Lewis Tappan, the noted abolitionist, ushered Samuel Cornish into his pew at the Laight Street Presbyterian Church in Greenwich Village. When the congregation objected, Samuel Cox, the minister, who had recently recanted his support for the colonization society, sought to calm the controversy. In a midweek lecture he warned against human prejudice and asked his congregation how white Jesus might have been. In response, racist editors accused the minister of claiming that Jesus was black. On July 4, Lewis and Arthur Tappan, along with several black ministers, scheduled a celebration of the emancipation of slaves in New York at the Chatham Street Chapel. After bigoted newspapers published nasty diatribes against interracial couples, angry crowds surged from the chapel to the nearby Bowery Theater to threaten an actor who allegedly made anti-American comments. Dissuaded from the attack by a popular actor, the mob flooded into the nearby home of Arthur Tappan. Warned in advance of their intentions, Tappan fled. The crowd sacked his house and burned his furniture in the street.

The next night the mob, which included both young toughs and middle-class citizens, hurled bricks at the home of an abolitionist Presbyterian minister. The crowd's greatest anger spilled over in the black districts. Rumors that Peter Williams Jr. had officiated at an interracial marriage prompted mobs to invade St. Philip's African Episcopal Church, destroy its furniture, and demolish the organ. White mobs attacked blacks and their homes throughout the Five Points, where Caucasian families were warned to stand near candles in their windows so that rioters could see them and not destroy their homes. Prominent New York blacks, warned of the mob's plans to attack their homes, asked the city for protection. Thomas Downing, the best-known black caterer in the city, and Hester Lane, a black philanthropist, sent notes to Mayor Cornelius Lawrence. City officials did very little to stop the violence until it threatened "respectable" parts of town. Not until two nights later could troops put down the violence. By its end, the rioters had destroyed St. Philip's Church, a black school, at least a dozen black homes, and the churches of Cox and a second white abolitionist, Henry G. Ludlow. Rioters aimed their hatred against black institutions and homes but less so at individuals. Scholars have often remarked about the spread of this virulent, dangerous racism. James Brewer Stewart, for example, has argued that the 1830s saw the emergence of a modern American society, bifurcated by race. However true, this argument does not do full justice to the remarkable efforts by poor and middle-class African Americans in New York to battle the twin evils of northern racism and southern slavery, whether through the abolitionist movement or in local civil rights struggles.[2]

The Persistence of Slavery

In the aftermath of the riots, blacks had to realize how much work remained to be done. Slavery was not just a southern sin but was practiced locally. The saddest examples were in New Jersey, where, although 90 percent of the state's blacks were free, 1,059 men and 1,195 women remained enslaved in 1830. Seventy percent (1,596) of these people lived in East New Jersey; 584 slaves were right across the Hudson River in Bergen County. Ten years later, 419 blacks remained slaves in New Jersey, of which 118 males and 104 females were in Bergen County. As late as 1850, 236 blacks were enslaved in New Jersey.[3]

When New Jersey blacks gained their freedom, they left their old homes. In Bergen County, as the slave population dropped from 1,683 in 1820 to 222 in 1840, the free black population first rose from 1,059 to 1,894 in 1830, then dropped to 1,529 in 1840, not regaining its 1830 level until 1900. Monmouth and Essex Counties sustained little or no black population growth between 1820 and 1850. In Middlesex County the black population dropped from 2,045 in 1820 to 1,380 in 1850. In New Jersey, the number of blacks increased by only 1,701 persons between 1820 and 1840, reaching 25,000 in the entire state as late as 1860. Between 1790 and 1860 New Jersey's blacks declined from 7.7 percent of the state's population to 3.4 percent. A carryover from the colonial period was imbalance of the sexes. In the largely agricultural counties of Bergen, Monmouth, and Somerset males outnumbered females, while in the more urbanized Essex and Middlesex Counties, females outnumbered men. Further, the aftermath of slavery in rural New Jersey left many blacks dependent on their masters. While these usually were male farm laborers, dependent females also outnumbered black women living on their own land. Ten years later the situation had improved very little. Only by 1860 were blacks in Monmouth County able to become independent and begin to work in trades. In Bergen County, the situation was even worse. Of 1,879 free blacks, 1,185 lived on the property of whites just before the Civil War.[4]

The abolition of slavery was only one of several tasks facing black society. The situation in New Jersey was complicated by the dominance of the American Colonization Society in any discourse over slavery and the black future. In New York, white racism grew stronger in the 1830s with sharper and more violent opposition to blacks in the trades, housing and transport, churches, schools, and on the streets. Crossing racial lines in antebellum New York City invited a fight. Change was even more difficult to achieve in New Jersey, where congressmen supported southern efforts to recapture fugitive slaves. These social dilemmas make the accomplishments of the rising black middle class all the more remarkable. During the 1830s, black activist intellectuals revived newspapers, published magazines and pamphlets, worked unceasingly against local denial of civil rights and national tolerance of slavery, and created a political force to prepare the road to freedom. Though much of this activity was confined to New York City, such efforts found their way into the smallest corners of rural New York and

New Jersey. Despite general poverty and lack of opportunity, fragile black middle classes emerged, standing on the accomplishments of the first postrevolutionary generation.[5]

Black Life in the City

In New York, lagging employment, a seesaw economy, and stark discrimination in most occupations stymied black demographic growth. Meanwhile, soaring white immigration rates meant the percentages of African Americans in the total society dropped precipitously. New York's black population was packed into the adjacent fifth and eighth wards, which abutted the notorious sixth ward, home of the Five Points district just north of City Hall. The 1852 directory showed 1,344 listings of black families at 479 locations, an average of 2.81 listings per address. Only one-seventh of those listed lived alone, while 45 percent lived with at least five other adults, and 12 percent lived among nine others. In Brooklyn, more than half of the city's blacks lived in the second ward. Few blacks in New York owned property worth more than $1,000. Although black females owned a disproportionate amount of property, few held any valued at more than $3,000.[6]

The percentage of blacks in the population of New York City declined still further after 1840. In that census, blacks totaled 16,358 in a citywide count of 312,710, and by 1845 the total population rose to 371,223 but the number of blacks decreased to 13,004. In 1860 the black population of New York City was down to 12,574, or less than 2 percent of the total of 813,669. The preponderance of women over men grew larger in 1860, when females composed 56 percent of the black population; among blacks of the childbearing years between fifteen and forty, females outnumbered males in New York County by 4,267 to 2,672. Despite the abundance of females, however, the percentage of black women with children was ten points less than that of white women with children.[7]

Mortality statistics for blacks show that poverty-related and occupational causes far exceeded old age. Coroners' reports compiled by Kenneth Scott for the years 1823–42 show especially the debilitating effects of poverty. In a sad recollection of the problems of the 1720s, pulmonary diseases, including tuberculosis, pleurisy, pneumonia, and hemorrhages of the lungs, were the leading causes of death among New York African Americans, especially among the young. Accidental drowning was the second largest cause, with blacks perishing in the sea, off the docks, and in rivers and streams. Another major killer was intemperance, which affected males and females equally. Sarah Cornell took an overdose of opium in June 1828 at the age of eighteen. Mary Grant, born in Dutchess County in 1810, committed suicide with opium in New York City in the winter of 1835. Children died from neglect, convulsions, and suffocation. Between 1825 and 1829 black death rates were an alarmingly high 56.1 per 1,000.[8]

Black death rates declined in comparison with those of the general population by the 1850s, but the causes of death remained depressingly similar to those in earlier decades. Accidents and poverty-related diseases of cholera, consumption, and dysentery led the causes of death in New York City and East Jersey. Perhaps the one bright spot was the drop in deaths from intemperance.[9] Blacks were ten times more likely to wind up in jail than whites. The ratio of white convicts to the whole population was 1 to 2,056 in 1840 while that of blacks was 1 to 142. Despite their declining percentage of the overall population, blacks constituted almost 12 percent of New York's 7,000 inmates and over one-third of New Jersey's 152 convicts.[10]

There was little of the flow of black people from other regions and continents that had characterized the earlier periods. One key reason was, of course, the close of the Atlantic slave trade. Additionally, there was little economically to attract blacks to New York, other than as a short stop on the way to freedom elsewhere. In 1840, 85 percent of free blacks in New Jersey and 77 percent in New York were born in the state. Of the 21 percent living in New York but born elsewhere, easily the highest number were from New Jersey, followed by Virginia and Pennsylvania. There were a few positive demographics. In 1840, New York ranked second in the nation to Maryland in the number of free blacks, but slipped to fourth in 1850. New York City outranked New Orleans in numbers of free black families by nearly a thousand. New Jersey ranked seventh in the number of blacks in 1840 and 1850, despite ranking eighteenth and nineteenth in total population. Newark and Jersey City were the homes of a small black middle class. Few were propertied. In Jersey City only six blacks owned land, with values ranging from $500 to $3,000. New York was the location of some of the largest black churches in America. Abyssinian, Ebenezer, and Zion Baptist, Shiloh Presbyterian, and St. Philip's Episcopal Church had congregations numbering in the several hundreds.[11]

City Work

The highly public nature of certain occupations gave a misleading character to New York's black life. Black entrepreneurs dominated certain food trades. Thomas Downing's Oyster Bar on Broad Street was the most famous in New York. Blacks and whites coming into New York from the north were welcome at Cato's Tavern, about four miles from town. The distinguished Irish actor Tyrone Power proclaimed that after several breakfasts at Cato's he acquired "added respect for the great man and increased regard for his excellent entertainment." Other food entrepreneurs included Thomas M. Jackson, the fashionable caterer, and many hucksters, peddlers, traders, market men, dealers, and oystermen who constituted almost 30 percent of the black workforce. Such occupations depended heavily on other blacks for support and held little possibility of upward mobility.[12]

In other, more numerous trades, blacks experienced exclusion and replacement. One of the most dramatic developments was the supplanting of black women in the city by Irish domestics in the 1840s and 1850s. Unlike native-born women of the earlier nineteenth century, Irish women had few qualms about domestic service. By the late 1830s they had pushed black women into specialized jobs in the retinues of the wealthy as laundresses, charwomen, and maids. By 1855 blacks working in domestic or related jobs, including waiters and laundresses, accounted for less than 1,000 of the 31,000 domestic workers in the city.[13] Of the 3,337 blacks enumerated in the census of 1850, 808 were personal servants. Other common occupations for blacks were coachman, barber, and cook. Thirty-four percent of all black males over the age of fifteen were laborers. The remainder included 434 mariners, 33 butchers, 24 farmers, 15 market men, 23 tailors, and 23 shoemakers. There were only tiny numbers in community trades such as bakers, blacksmiths, carpenters, coopers, ink-makers, and printers.[14]

Even though the city's population and economy created greater demand for transport workers, blacks were unable to break into the segregated trade of carting. By the late 1830s this entry-level trade employed over four thousand New Yorkers, particularly newly arrived Irish. Though social and judicial attitudes stemming from the workingmen's movement of 1829 softened support for restrictive licenses, custom and the demands of political patronage stood in the way of black carters. In 1836 a free black named William S. Hewlett, a porter, sought a cartman's license, using forty firms as character references.

He was described as "a worthy man, honest, temperate, of amiable disposition, muscular frame and good address being a member of the Society of Friends." Unimpressed, the mayor, Cornelius Lawrence, turned down his application "on the grounds of public opinion." Lawrence's vision was doubtless affected by the profitable business his shipping firm carried on with southern customers. Three years later, Anthony Provost, a black man described as having "as good a horse and cart as was to be seen on the dock" and supported in his application for a license by some of the wealthy leather dealers and even by some cartmen, sought permission to drive a cart. The mayor informed him that it was "not customary for colored men to drive carts in the city." Provost challenged this belief by driving without a license. After white carters complained, Provost was forced to sell his horse and cart and "betake himself to a more menial employment." The *Colored American*, New York's black newspaper, exploded in anger over the issue, dismissing Lawrence's explanation that he was "protecting" Provost, demanding carting licenses for blacks as their republican right. Samuel Cornish's newspaper appealed to the carters' sense of fairness, pleading, "It is disgraceful to oppress in this manner." The newspaper charged the mayor and carters with supporting southerners by keeping the black man down: "We will keep them poor . . . lest they should arise and give your doctrine the lie." The newspaper appealed to the next mayor, Aaron Clarke, to use his authority to prevent physical attacks on black carters. Only in the 1850s did Mayor Fernando Wood issue carting licenses to blacks. Even so, by 1855 the census showed only about fifty black cartmen in a trade that employed more than eight thousand men.[15]

By 1855 the industrial trades were overwhelmingly Irish. In brewing, for example, the Irish outnumbered blacks by 52 to 2; in cooperage, 413 to 6; in hat making, 289 to 1; among tinsmiths, 263 to 7; and among tailors, 4,171 to 24.[16] Blacks were somewhat more successful in trade union organization. In 1850 African American laborers, the largest percentage of the black male working class, formed the American League of Colored Laborers, seeking to correspond with similar groups in other cities. William Hamilton of the Union Place Hotel chaired the formation of the interracial Waiters' Protective Union Society in 1853. In an attempt to standardize wages across the industry, the society's rules required a minimum wage of eighteen dollars per month. Like blacks in other cities, African Americans in New York faced violent competition

On the waterfront, ca. 1850. This sketch shows a moment of leisure for black and white wharfingers in the forest of masts along New York's waterfront. (H. G. Cantzler, Sketchbook 1849–51, Print Collection, Miriam and Ira D. Wallach Division of Art, Prints, and Photographs, New York Public Library. Astor, Lenox and Tilden Foundations)

in the workplace from newly arrived Irish. In a battle over stevedores' jobs in 1853, Irish and blacks fought along the wharves of the North and East Rivers.[17]

Generally excluded from respectable trades, some blacks turned to gambling and prostitution. One police raid in the early 1840s resulted in the arrest of forty-two individuals in "various low negro gambling houses and brothels in the 5th and 6th wards." In 1840, "gentlemen from the Astor House and Carleton House" joined "yellow and black males and dingy and sooty females without respect to persons or regard to color" in a game of keno supervised by a "colored Baptist clergyman." The same year the police indicted one William Thompson, a "huge black man," for keeping a disorderly house at 479 Broome Street which featured "yellow females in front of the house in the street exposing their persons indecently." In the census of that year, one-sixth of the nearly four hundred prostitutes in the fifth ward were black.[18]

Charles Dickens's chronicle of a visit to Almack's tavern in 1842 revealed for middle-class readers the existence of a thriving black popular culture. The landlady, a "buxom fat mulatto woman with sparkling eyes, whose head was daintily ornamented with a handkerchief of many colors," welcomed Dickens into the tavern. The landlord, "attired in a smart blue jacket, like a ship's steward, with a thick gold ring upon his finger, and around his neck, a gleaming golden watch-guard," escorted Dickens to the dance floor for a "regular break-down." The English writer recorded that a "corpulent black fiddler and his friend, who played the tambourine," played a "lively measure" on the stage. Two demure young women set the dance, after which gentlemen and ladies performed their own gait. Steps included the "single shuffle, double shuffle cut, cut and cross-cut," until the fiddler retired from the room to thundering applause. Another visitor to a black tavern noted the syncretic style of music: "In the negro melodies you catch a strain of what has been metamorphosed from such Scotch or Irish tune, into somewhat of a chiming jiggish air." Such bars were also hotbeds of gambling.[19]

Reportage of such music venues coincided with another development stemming from black culture. Blackface minstrelsy, a process in which white performers blackened their faces and performed a derisive version of African American music, emerged in this period as a major form of American music. As scholars have relentlessly argued, blackface minstrelsy was a means by which white working-class singers and their audiences could openly display racism and distance themselves from their black counterparts. While true, the emphasis on the racial disharmony of minstrelsy and white accounts of black music misses an important point. During the antebellum period, black orchestras in New York were creating what Walt Whitman described as a "grand American opera." Descendants of similar artists in New York dating back to the seventeenth century, black bands in the taverns of the Five Points were advancing a black performance style that resonates to the present day. Whatever their self-perceived social betters thought of it, minstrelsy and bar music were created for and by African Americans and sympathetic whites.[20]

The Five Points also housed ordinary blacks living and working in fairly close harmony with Irish, Chinese, Germans, Jews, and Poles. Tolerance in the area was so great that while a hint of interracial love might spark riots in other wards, the Five Points was home to married couples of African and Irish descent. Living these precarious lives, blacks carved out public spaces for themselves in an area where two

Toko, *ca. 1845. A representation of the young black dandies who frequented the Five Points and became the prototype for the Bowery B'hoys and modern street characters. (Courtesy of the New-York Historical Society)*

hundred years before, the first generation of New York's people of color lived, worked, and were buried.[21]

Black Work in the Rural Counties

Free black owners of businesses were rare in the rural counties. Black and white entrepreneurs worked together in the oystering community in Sandy Ground, Staten Island, in the late 1840s. There whites and African Americans worked in relative harmony in a self-regulated artisan occupation interdependent with farmers, laborers, entrepreneurs, small shop owners, customers, and provisioners. The first black in the area was Thomas Holmes, who operated a ferry between Staten Island and Blazing Star, New Jersey. Most of the Sandy Ground blacks came from Maryland, and they owned small skiffs costing from twenty to fifty dollars.[22]

Few rural blacks secured independent economic status. Adrian Van Brunce of Brooklyn had an extensive "kitchen family" of twenty-six blacks working on his farm. Van Brunce employed men and women year-round. In the summer blacks plowed, manured, and planted vegetables and grains. They hoed and threshed salt grass, carted manure,

Sam the Witch Doctor and Yon the Fiddler. In the highly traditional, agricultural world of Bergen County, a mere ten miles from the Five Points, men such as these mixed the African spirit world with North American magic. (From John Hosey Osborn, Life in the Old Dutch Homesteads *[Paramus, N.J.: Highway Printing, 1967].)*

and occasionally marketed truck. While the blacks worked on his farm, Van Brunce was free to travel about, visit friends, go to funerals, attend church, and go to New York City. During the fall, Van Brunce laid off his white workers and assigned blacks various tasks in the fields such as digging potatoes, weeding the fields, and working with the oxen. On rainy days they worked in the cellar. There was no Christmas holiday on the Van Brunce farm, where Michael, Harry, and George worked in the fields. In the middle of the winter, "all hands are at work in the woods." Van Brunce's farm presents a vision of unchanging, seasonal labor at low rates of pay.[23]

By mid-century, however, blacks owned farms even where slavery left the longest shadow. Ceasor Jackson of Washington township, Bergen County, New Jersey, left a modest estate of $164 at his death. The most valuable possession of Jackson, descendant of a free black family living in Bergen since the late 1690s, was a cow worth $60. His other property, typical of the small farmer of the era, included such household goods as a wheelbarrow, a grain cradle, forks and rakes, a wagon, and the year's crop of corn, hay, and oats. In more pluralistic Monmouth County, a tiny black middle class emerged. By mid-century, accumulations of property reached over $5,000 for the most prosperous black families. Others left such articles as chairs, candlesticks, mirrors, and carpeting in their wills.[24]

In New Jersey, newly freed blacks began moving into suburban areas around the developing urban centers. Black women commuted short distances to service occupations in cities such as Newark while their husbands remained in agricultural work just outside of town. By 1860 unskilled blacks worked as laborers or domestics in Newark, along with a tiny number of artisans, small businessmen, and professionals. As in New York City, blacks faced competition from recently arrived Irish. As this migration continued, blacks left their historic homelands, where work had disappeared. Bergen County had the largest rural black population in the colonial period. As blacks attained freedom, they left Bergen. Between 1830 and 1860, the county's black population dropped from 2,457 to 1,656 souls.[25]

Religion

In the past, white churches had provided some amelioration to blacks for their painful existence. Even this changed for the worse in the antebellum years as white churches spent much of their efforts promoting colonization. Black attitudes toward colonization were ambivalent at first, but by the 1830s virtually all of the black intellectual class opposed it.[26]

White churches retreated from any confrontation with slavery. Despite some local abolitionism, the Presbyterians, among the largest employers of black servants in the two states, favored emigration to Sierra Leone and Liberia. Their rhetoric circulated primarily among the whites-only New Jersey Society for the Abolition of Slavery and in house organs of the movement. Episcopalians, Methodists, and Presbyterians all refused to condemn slaveholding among members. The Dutch Reformed Church continued to defend slavery, based on biblical readings. The fewer than one hundred black Catholics faced deep racial discrimination from the local diocese and from Irish parishioners.[27]

Protestant churches continued to use "negro pews" to separate white and black parishioners. When James W. C. Pennington went to the South Baptist Church in New York City to hear the famed minister Shepherd Knapp preach, ushers led him to a seat just inside the door and distant from the pulpit. Pennington concluded that it was fruitless to "get right in church" as long as services were conducted on "man-hating principles." In no instance did blacks gain any semblance of parity or achieve more than nominal membership.[28]

Aside from promoting colonization, white churches limited their energies to schools and philanthropy. Whites concerned about the black poor offered succor to the aged and orphaned in institutions such as the Colored Home or the Orphan Asylum. These institutions were part of the benevolent movement that enabled caring whites to show mercy toward bereft but worthy blacks while instructing them in Christianity.[29] The Orphan Asylum, established in 1835, was frequently a pathetic antechamber to death. Many children arrived at the asylum so weakened by pulmonary diseases that they quickly died. Healthier children were often "half-orphans," with the father missing and the mother "living at service." Known parents paid the asylum two dollars per month for the child's maintenance. Usually, the asylum apprenticed such children to rural parts or "at service." [30]

Blacks rarely found comfort in old age and faced segregation in government charities. The New York City almshouse gave blacks room only in the cellar. By 1847, 280 blacks had received support at the Colored Home, founded by wealthy philanthropists in New York City in 1839 and incorporated in 1844 at Avenue A and First Avenue.[31]

Battling Slavery

The aftermath of the 1834 riots showed the deep cleavage between Protestant officials and black religious leaders. The Episcopalian bishop Benjamin T. Onderdonk humiliated the venerable Peter Williams Jr. by ordering him to renounce any affiliation with antislavery. Williams unhappily accepted the edict, hoping to maintain some connection between the black and white branches of the church. His response to Onderdonk's demands for servility were remarkably republican. In his classic statement, Williams noted that his father was born on Beekman Street and had never lived farther away from New York than Albany. Williams Sr. had been a staunch patriot who refused British bribes for information about American activities. He was doubly joyful about American victory and the Methodist purchase of his bondage. He passed patriotism along to his son with talk that "filled my soul with an ardent love for the American government." Achieving the pastorate of St. Philips, Peter Williams Jr. "felt a burning desire to be useful to my brethren and to my country," despite having to live on "the scanty pittance of a colored minister." [32]

Black and white abolitionists used two methods of confronting racism in the churches. One was "pray-ins" in which blacks intentionally occupied pews reserved for whites. In Newark, New Jersey, a white minister was fired for walking to church with a black servant woman, then seating her in a pew with his wife.[33] The second method was to withdraw from segregated sects. As the era of Revolutionary egalitarianism waned, even the Society of Friends used separate seating for the "black people." Sarah M. Douglass recalled leaving the Quakers because "I do not like to sit on a back bench and be treated with contempt." Although black servants were regularly catechized and marriage ceremonies were available to any black, white churches had long lost the resolve to oppose the membership of slaveholders. Denominations with large tolerance for human imperfection, including Roman Catholics and Episcopalians, shied away from abolitionist condemnation of slave owners as sinners. Denominations with hierarchical structures were slow to change ecclesiastical policy and silenced antislavery debate quickly. Protestant denominations were reluctant to embrace the evangelical morality of the abolitionists and preferred the remote task of colonization.[34]

Despairing that qualified black youth found colleges closed to them and were thus unable to train for the ministry, Williams and others promoted a "Manual Labor College or High School, for ourselves." Beyond that innocent attempt at self-betterment, however, Williams had little contact with the Anti-Slavery Society's efforts. Though elected to its Board of Managers, he refused to serve and sat in the gallery at meetings. Submitting his resignation from antislavery groups, Williams demonstrated the impossible contradiction of compliance with Episcopalian rule, on the one hand, and black improvement, on the other. Episcopalian racism required submissive blacks in its church, and Williams was never allowed to sit as a member of the Diocesean Convention. St. Philips was never represented in church conclaves. Williams, bowing to the demands of the white Episcopalians, lost his reputation among blacks. Only after his death were reform-minded blacks able to effect any changes in the segregated denomination.[35]

White Protestant sects continually provided reasons for republican-minded blacks to leave the parent churches and establish their own congregations. In 1837 Samuel Cornish Jr., who labored faithfully in the Presbyterian Church, listed in twenty-one editorials in the *Colored American* complaints about white racism against blacks. Pay discrimination, bureaucratic snubs, and a lack of association between white and black ministers exacerbated the sores caused by the "negro pews." [36] The answer was to withdraw from white denominations. By the 1830s black churches were the bedrock of the African American community. The Methodist African Union built a permanent site in 1840 for its members. In Brooklyn, the High Street AME had a membership of three hundred by 1849. Annual Methodist conferences, initiated in 1820, by 1840 attracted participants from as far away as Ithaca, Buffalo, Rochester, and Syracuse. In New Jersey black churches opened in over a dozen little towns throughout the 1830s. Initially these churches used itinerants, but gradually they hired permanent ministers to serve congregations. The Trenton, New Jersey, AME conference, for instance, employed a staff of ten ministers and exhorters to preach in small congregations. The conference established tight discipline, expelling ministers and parishioners alike for doctrinal errors or moral offenses.[37] The development of a black church network opened career paths for ambitious blacks. During a period when discrimination cut short black ambitions in virtually every other field, African American churches and the antislavery movement provided vertical mobility.[38]

Black New Yorkers rejected the colonization movement. Believing that "the natural tendency of colonization is to retard emancipation," black leaders held meetings in 1831 in New York, Brooklyn, and Trenton, denouncing the American Colonization Society for its racism. In New York City, Samuel Ennals, chair of the meeting, blasted the ACS for its denigration of free black character, noting that whites know only "the unfortunate portion of our peoples whose characters are scrutinized by them as judges of the courts . . . their patrician principles prevent an intercourse with men of the middle ranks of society." In Trenton, the Reverend Lewis Cork, in a meeting at the Mount Zion Church in November 1831, described the ACS as "the most inveterate foe for both free and slave men of color." A committee of the Trenton meeting made several strong points joining theological proof with political. Developing a series of questions, the committee asked why, if the Gospel of Jesus Christ was calculated to be revolutionary among blacks, it should be spread in Africa; what gentlemen, having freed their slaves, were murdered by them; what cost there was to states that manumitted slaves; and what neighborhood, "where education and general information has been disseminated among the people of color, is the worse for it?" On Long Island, the Reverend Edward Cephas Africanus wrote of the "indissoluble bonds" between the free black man and the slave. Africanus vowed that the four million were one and that "we shall remain here at home until liberty is proclaimed throughout the land." [39]

Certain other colonization projects were supported even after blacks disavowed emigration to Liberia. In New York, Peter Williams Jr. shifted his support for Liberian colonization to asylums in Wilberforce, Canada. New York representatives to the first Negro conventions initially supported emigration to Canada or Haiti, even as they condemned the American Colonization Society. Gradually though, Bishop Richard Allen and his adherents convinced others to oppose colonization on principle. In 1834 a mass meeting of blacks in New York City decreed a solemn protest against colonization, which, "acknowledging our wrongs, commits a greater by vilifying us." [40]

The organizing thrusts against the colonization movement and white racism spurred independent black efforts in other areas, especially schools. Blacks reacted with bitterness to the pro-colonization attitudes of the longtime head of the African Free School, Charles Andrews, and consequently more than 150 scholars left the school. (Blacks were unwilling to let the school go entirely because standards were lower at the public schools.) [41]

Blacks similarly deserted the white-sponsored Sunday schools in New York and New Jersey. In 1821, two groups, the Female Union Society for the Promotion of Sabbath Schools and the New-York Sunday-School Union Society, educated 663 black adults in reading and writing, more than 95 percent of their total student body. Adult blacks, excluded from most forms of public schooling, sought opportunities for literacy at the Sunday schools with a disposition "for receiving instruction and intenseness of application." As the free public school movement spread in the early 1830s, however, white Sunday schools gradually dropped literacy classes in favor of concentration on strictly religious training. Without the promise of literacy and irritated by rising white racism, black adults dropped out and formed their own schools. In Elizabeth and Newark, New Jersey, the formation of an African church and school led to the wholesale withdrawal of blacks from a Presbyterian-sponsored Sunday school. [42]

The debate over schools split the black community in two. Supporters of common schools with whites had to counter both white segregationists and blacks who preferred separate schools. Integrationists argued that segregated schools were inherently unjust and received unequal resources. In response, advocates of separate institutions complained about the insults and stereotypes suffered by black youths in common schools and about the paucity of black teachers in these schools, which adversely affected black professional mobility. Initially unable to compromise on such profoundly separate views, black activists in New York reached a compromise when a black supervisory board controlled free public schools in 1841. Still, such facilities remained inadequate. In Newark, the faculty at black public schools, which were housed in churches, were primarily preachers.[43]

White Protestant sects also disappointed blacks seeking higher education. Outstanding graduates of the African Free School, including Charles B. Ray, James McCune Smith, Alexander Crummell, Charles Lewis Reason, and Isaiah De Grasse, found overwhelming discrimination on the young nation's campuses. Ray entered Wesleyan University in Middletown, Connecticut, but was driven away by student protests. De Grasse was admitted to the Episcopal Theological Seminary in 1837 but was asked to leave because "the reception of a colored young man might deprive [the school] of pecuniary benefits and prevent Southern gentlemen from connecting themselves with the school of divinity." Reason was barred from the seminary "except as a listener." [44]

Black Schools

Stymied by segregated schools, blacks planned their own. Their first efforts met with failure. In 1831, Peter Williams Jr. initiated the first black high school for the study of classics. The white press ridiculed this ambition by asking why servants needed to read Virgil or Horace. After Williams's attempt collapsed, in 1833 black ministers Christopher Rush, Thomas L. Jennings, Theodore S. Wright, Benjamin Hughes, and Peter Vogelsang formed the Phoenix Society. Assisted financially by Arthur Tappan, the Phoenix members planned to visit every black family in the ward, learning of their educational needs and convincing them to join the society. The group made plans for lending libraries and lyceums, hoping to attract and identify "young men of talents and good moral character." [45]

Two years later several young black men of promise, including Henry Highland Garnet, William H. Day, and David Ruggles, formed the Garrison Literary and Benevolent Association of New York. In 1836, with help from Gerrit Smith, the group started a black secondary academy. Again, however, funds proved insufficient and the school failed within a year. A third high school, the New York Select Academy, lasted only for several months in 1840. On Long Island the Reverend Edward Cephas Africanus taught at a small school for blacks along with his brother Selah H. Africanus. Though Rev. Africanus disliked teaching, he accepted the responsibility because to refuse "would be refusing to build up my own people and place."[46]

Not until the late 1840s, when the black-managed Society for Education among Colored Children ran several schools, was there secondary education for blacks in the city. In 1853 its schools were absorbed by the New York City Board of Education. By this time there were nine black public schools scattered about Manhattan and some in surrounding counties. White racism discouraged any attempt at integrated education. In Queens County, black attendance at public schools prompted white flight. Despite such difficulties, more than seventy-five hundred young blacks attended schools in New York and New Jersey in 1850.[47]

In New Jersey, black schools were still largely run by the colonization movement. The Parsippany School, founded in 1817, was still a presence, and the Presbyterian Sunday school movements promoted colonization. In Princeton, New Jersey, white teachers and a black librarian at the Sabbath school instructed 55 black male and 82 female students. The students' names, Van Horne, Ten Eyck, Schenck, Scudder, Wycoff, and Stockton, reflected a long-standing relationship with prominent New Jersey Presbyterian families. Teachers were drawn from Princeton Theological Seminary. With such an abundant supply, teacher-student ratios were quite good with 17 faculty for 130 scholars. Students paid tuition by giving pennies each day. The day's curriculum started with the Ten Commandments, followed by the lesson of the day, catechizing, and prayers. Despite reports of problems in the new African states, twenty-four New Jersey blacks emigrated between 1820 and 1853.[48]

The Ethiopian Manifesto

In 1829 Robert Alexander Young's firebrand pamphlet, the *Ethiopian Manifesto*, trumpeted the onset of militant black resistance. Little is known about Young. He lived on Lombardy Street at the corner of Scammel near the Five Points and published his *Manifesto* six months before David Walker's more famous *Appeal*, a book also well-known to black New Yorkers. The *Manifesto* was uncompromising in its demands for the end of slavery before a race war became necessary. First, Young reminded "Ethiopians" that they "enjoy but few of your rights of government." "Born free of the will allotted me by the freedom of God," Young claimed the right of a "universal freedom to every son and daughter descended from the black God." Revolution would come when a messiah, a "white man appeared on earth bearing in himself the semblance of his former race." This messiah would "call together the black people as a nation. He would appear to be white, but be born of a black woman. Another sign "peculiar in his make" was the "two middle toes on each of his feet . . . webbed and bearded." All Ethiopians should give such a man their pledge. The messiah would make the slaveholders, "thou task inflictor against the rights of man," learn that their hour was nigh, "when poverty would appear a blessing," as Africans reclaimed their birthrights and deliverance from all worldly evil. The *Manifesto* was signed "Rednaxlen . . . dated from the Ethiopian's Rock in the 37th Year from its Foundation."[49]

The *Manifesto*, with its mystical imagery and violent attack on slavery, offers a glimpse of a radical millenarianism present in New York City in the 1830s. Young's work, among the first to call for a reassembling of an African people, anticipates such radical twentieth-century mystics as Marcus Garvey, Malcolm X, and Minister Louis Farrakhan, whose racial interpretations of the origins of the species perceived whites as evil offshoots of a universal African people. Written at a time when white racism and oppression were growing in New York, Young's *Manifesto* demonstrated the radicalism of the wholly disfranchised. Unlike Pennington, Garnet, Cornish, and other black abolitionists who worked within the political framework of Euro-American society, Young was racially divorced from such solutions. His millenarianism may have been more acceptable to the common black on the street than were the international and cosmopolitan efforts of better-educated black radicals.[50]

The Committee of Vigilance

Radical black abolitionism quickly found expression in black resistance to local cooperation with southern slaveholders. In 1835, black New Yorkers formed a Committee of Vigilance. David Ruggles, William Johnson, George Barker, Robert Brown, and J. W. Higgins created this composite of abolitionist groups, businessmen, and churches to assist bondsmen in need. The Committee of Vigilance had a strong board, including ministers Charles Ray, Christopher Rush, and Samuel Edwards, and shared membership with the African Society of Mutual Relief. Members in both organizations included James White, Ray, Rush, William Tracy, Charles B. Hatch, and Henry Graves. The Committee of Vigilance had a financial agent, William Johnson, and met once a month in the Medical Hall on Crosby Street. Believing that the antislavery societies were not sufficient to battle proslavery forces, the committee concentrated its efforts on blacks recently arrived from the South who needed counsel, on kidnapped blacks, and on those in danger of kidnapping. It took legal action against slave catchers and reported the presence of slave ships in New York Harbor.[51]

The Committee of Vigilance grew out of street brawls between slave catchers and blacks defending runaways. Two years earlier blacks had fought in the streets with police officers while trying to rescue two runaways from the city courts.[52] Such battles increased after the riots of 1834. This street-level warfare centered on police protection of slave catchers (known as kidnappers or "blackbirds"). With the cooperation of New York City's judicial and police forces, blackbirds seized blacks on the streets, chained them, and, in a matter of hours, swept them aboard a ship bound for the South. In one instance, George Jones, a respectable free man, was arrested by the police on the pretext of "assault and battery." At first he declined to answer the citation but was convinced by his employers to appear. Jones, on the testimony of several known kidnappers, was declared a slave by the city recorder, Richard Riker. In less than three hours, Jones went from freedom to being "bound in chains, dragged through the streets, like a beast to the shambles." Even such defeats led to increased black self-esteem. As James Horton has pointed out, radical black abolitionism became a key component of an emerging sense of black manhood in this period.[53]

One escaped black aided by the Committee of Vigilance was Frederick Douglass. The exultant joy Douglass felt upon arrival in New York City soon gave way to loneliness and fear. Douglass encountered a fellow fugitive who warned him of slave catchers in the city. Fearing that his old master would hunt for him there, Douglass avoided the shipyards. Nearly broke and lonely, Douglass dodged slave catchers everywhere. Fortunately, he confided in a black sailor who took him to David Ruggles. Sheltered by Ruggles in his editorial rooms, Douglas called for his fiancée, Ann Murray, and married her in Ruggles's print shop a few days later. Rev. James W. C. Pennington, the self-educated former blacksmith who had fled from Maryland ten years before, performed the marriage ceremony. Two days later, the Douglasses were off to New Bedford. Other runaways were less fortunate. For example, Moses Roper escaped from bondage in the South by ship but was beaten by white sailors. After arriving in New York City, he drifted from job to job and finally abandoned the city for work on the canals.[54]

The committee also visited ships to offer assistance to enslaved blacks. Mahommah Gardo Baquaqua recalled his emancipation in the harbor of New York City in 1838. Baquaqua had arrived in New York as an enslaved sailor, and "a great many colored-persons came aboard the vessel to determine if we were free." The captain assured the visitors that all were free but preferred to remain on the boat. Baquaqua decided that given a second chance he would declare his desire to be free in fact. The captain, hearing of his intentions, put him in irons. The slave escaped and, wandering through the city streets, was arrested by a watchman. After some discussion Baquaqua was returned to the boat. In the nick of time abolitionist lawyers arrived and informed the captain that all on board were free. Baquaqua was returned to jail, then secreted out to freedom in Massachusetts.[55]

The Committee of Vigilance remained active after Ruggles's departure in 1840. Slaves seeking freedom came to New York from all over the South on their way to Canada. In the fifth annual report of the Committee of Vigilance in 1842, President Theodore S. Wright told of blacks who came through the Appalachian Mountains from Louisiana, speaking very little English and on their way to Canada. While "conductors" helped many along well-trod roads, others arrived in the city by themselves, without money, friends, or home. The city was filled with watchmen, carters, shopkeepers, and other citizens happy to ensnare a runaway in hopes of a share of the reward.[56]

Braving these dangers, by the 1840s, blacks and sympathetic whites had worked out an underground railroad, which shepherded fugitive blacks from the South to freedom in the northern states and Canada. Several routes ran through New Jersey. The most heavily frequented began at Bordentown and went through New Brunswick and Jersey City into New York. There escaped slaves either went north on through trains to Syracuse, New York, and Canada or used other routes into New England. This traffic meant considerable danger to conductors as well as passengers because neither New York nor New Jersey ever passed personal liberty laws; Jersey also sanctioned the 1850 Fugitive Slave Act, which mandated sizable penalties for aiding the flight of enslaved people.[57]

The street-level vigilance paid dividends in the 1840s and 1850s. In 1846 a slave stowaway named George Kirk entered New York Harbor on a ship from Georgia. The captain of the ship, citing Georgia laws on runaways, ordered Kirk confined "in chains" in the ship's hold. The black activist Louis Napoleon, who spent a great deal of time on New York's docks watching and listening for situations like Kirk's, quickly swore out a writ of habeas corpus and obtained excellent legal counsel through antislavery societies. They charged that Georgia's slave-catching laws did not apply outside the state, that the actual owner was not present, and that the captain lacked power in New York State to arrest Kirk. Judge John W. Edmonds freed the stowaway.[58]

Six years later Louis Napoleon discovered a Virginia couple in a New York hotel with eight slaves. The couple, Jonathan Lemmons and his wife, were passing through New York for three days on a round-about route to Texas. Napoleon petitioned for a writ of habeas corpus before Judge Elijah Paine of the superior court, who ordered the slaves brought before him. The slaves were placed in jail for the weekend. After a week of legal wrangling, Paine freed them under an 1841 act which he interpreted as emancipating any slave who touched the soil of New York. Louis Napoleon led the former slaves out of the courtroom to a cheering crowd of blacks. Before the stunned Lemmons could muster any appeal, the newly freed blacks were whisked away to Canada and permanent freedom. Prosouthern sympathizers raised $5,000 to compensate the Lemmons and to reassure the slave states that New York was not run by abolitionists. The Lemmons then formally manumitted the slaves before departing with the money. Their suit against the city was eventually dismissed in 1860. Their antagonist, Louis Napoleon, worked in a tradition of street-wise amateur black lawyers who were quick to exploit holes in the legal structure of slavery to free themselves and other blacks.[59]

Militant blacks used nonviolent methods to counter segregation on horse cars, railroad cars, and steamboats. The Reverend Charles B. Ray, the general agent of the *Colored American,* and Philip Bell, its publisher, took a steamboat ride up the Hudson to Newburgh, campaigning for subscriptions to the newspaper. At teatime, they repaired to the dining cabin. There a steward refused them service and said tea was available for them only in the kitchen. After some discussion, the captain arrived and supported his employee. Ray and Bell answered that they could not be the agents of their own degradation and refused to eat, but retained their seats at the table. To break segregation on railroads, demonstrators used various tactics from massive "ride-ins" to boycotts. Though only temporarily successful, these methods confronted Jacksonian America with its racism.[60]

Female Activism

The intellectual and political activism in the 1830s was primarily male. At a time when middle-class black women were required to work in a supportive role, few stepped onto the stage of history. An early indication of black female dissatisfaction with this condition appeared in the *Freedom's Journal* in the summer of 1827. A letter from "Matilda" asked the editors to recommend education for females as well as males. Matilda beseeched mothers to give their daughters "a knowledge of cookery and the various mysteries of pudding-making" but to remember that it was their "bounded duty, to store their daughters minds with useful learning. . . . They should be made to devote their leisure time to reading books." Matilda could not have been pleased by the gender attitudes expressed in an editorial in the *Freedom's Journal:* "Women are not formed for great cares themselves, but to soften ours." Women's place was in the home, "confined within the narrow limits of domestic assiduity." Those who strayed did so "without grace."[61]

In the 1830s the African Dorcas Society was joined by other women's groups, and by 1834 New York had a Colored Ladies' Literary Society, made up of the elite of the black community, the wives and daughters of prominent black ministers, teachers, and businessmen. A member, Elizabeth Jennings, wrote that the society intended to prove "the mind is the greatest and great care should be taken to improve it with diligence."[62]

Women were important conductors on the Underground Railroad. One important way station in New York City was the Colored Sailors' Home, where Mary Marshall Lyons, the owner's wife, fed and disguised more than one thousand refugees. Hester Lane, who accumulated a little money as an innovative wall decorator, purchased slaves from the South. After purchasing a girl of eleven years for $100, Lane liberated a boy of fourteen for $200, a man of thirty for $280, and a sickly family for $140. Lane became deeply involved with those she purchased. She was present at one girl's birth, later assisted at her marriage, attended the birth of her four children, and ultimately assisted at her funeral. She purchased and freed eleven people and helped the adults financially and ensured the education of the children.[63]

The strongest female voices of the 1830s were those of unlicensed preachers and exhorters. The most widely known of these women was Sojourner Truth. Born Isabel Van Wagenen in Ulster County in 1797, Truth toiled as a field hand and domestic for several masters. Eventually freed after some hard bargaining in 1827, she drifted into New

York City and became associated with the Matthias cult, whose sexual misdeeds shocked New Yorkers in 1834. Truth had already given herself to the service of God during a revelation at Pinkster upstate. Now, after the debacle over Matthias, which included a dismissed murder charge against her, she devoted herself to evangelical preaching and antislavery speeches. Immensely popular in the 1840s, she itinerated throughout the nation.[64]

Other female preachers kept a narrower compass. Barred from leading organized black churches, female ministers excelled at outdoor camp meetings. Jarena Lee of Cape May, New Jersey, began as an exhorter in the Presbyterian Church. Initially a member of a Philadelphia Presbyterian church, she recoiled from the paternalistic racism she experienced. Deciding that white church membership was not for her, she experienced a call one night from God to preach. Bishop Richard Allen informed her that the Methodist discipline "did not call for women preachers." Lee remained silent for eight years, then rose during a church service to interpret the Book of Jonah to a surprised audience. She was defended by Allen, who reversed his earlier criticisms. Lee became a preacher at camp meetings throughout New Jersey.[65] Julia Pell, a black female preacher, held forth at the Methodist church on Elizabeth Street in New York City in 1841. Pell began her service with great moderation, "gradually rising in her tones, till she arrived at the shouting pitch, common with Methodists." Pell's words rushed out of her mouth "with a huskiness of effort." Her theme was resurrection and the Day of Judgment. She described God bidding all the angels in heaven to hush their golden harps. Pell cried, "Let the mountains be filled with silence. Let the sea stop its roaring and the earth be still, until my people are free. God instructed Gabriel to find a messiah to lead his people and warned him not to be discouraged for the messiah would come out of the right hand of God." Lydia Maria Child, an observer, felt Pell's power over her spirit as the audience went to higher degrees of enthusiasm, culminating in shouts of praise and thanksgiving. The audience's emotion vented itself in murmuring, stamping, shouting, and wailing. "It was like the uproar of a sea lashed by the winds."[66]

Julia Foote, born in Schenectady, New York, in 1823, received a vision of God who presented her with a scroll, reading, "Thee I have chosen to preach my Gospel without delay." Although she previously was opposed to preaching by women, Foote itinerated throughout upstate New York and New Jersey.[67] Women preachers quickly began to sound antislavery themes. Miss Paulyon lectured extensively in New York for almost a decade, beginning her speeches with a narrative of her early slave life, "calling forth many tears, especially from the female portion of the audience." Her critical descriptions of racial caste were "frequently interrupted with shouts of applause." Paulyon did not describe her escape from slavery "as it might involve certain parties who aided her." That had occurred when she was sixteen, "suffering hunger, thirst and cold on her journey," and since her arrival in the North, she had learned "needlework, geography, arithmetic, grammar, painting, . . . all through her own exertions." Paulyon also wrote poetry and composed songs, including one entitled the "Slave's Farewell, at which many eyes filled with tears." [68]

Organized Black Politics

The movement for black schools heightened the need for an expanded black political presence. Shut out of politics, blacks attempted to create a shadow government to oppose colonization and fight slavery in the South. In 1834 the Negro Convention, after years of meetings in Philadelphia, staged a conference in New York City, where William Hamilton, president of the Fourth Annual Convention of the Free People of Colour, described the American Colonization Society as "evil minded." Hamilton accused the colonizationists of saying one thing in the South, another in the North. He argued that they describe "us as the most corrupt, vicious and abandoned; then again we are kind, meek and gentle." In the late 1830s David Ruggles, head of the New York City Committee of Vigilance, a defender of runaway blacks, bitterly attacked the colonizationist movement. Responding to colonizationist claims that the New York Antislavery Society was responsible for the 1834 riots, Ruggles described such logic as "mere slang, altogether too stale to rise." Why not blame the abolitionists, he asked, for the cholera and yellow fever epidemics? In New York City Samuel Cornish and Theodore S. Wright bitterly attacked the colonization supporters in 1840. They attempted to attend a convention of the ACS but were shut out of the meeting. The ACS, they argued, contemplated removal of blacks from "the land of our birth," without challenging slavery. As proof, they cited the membership of such slave owners as John Randolph and Henry Clay. They described the ACS as "packed with prejudice," especially the belief that the Christianization of heathens was a failure.[69]

As in the colonial period, blacks had keen eyes for truly sympathetic whites. The African benevolent societies mourned the death of Elias Hicks in 1830, listening to an oration by Barnabas Bates at the Zion Chapel in New York City in which Bates reviewed the career of the antislavery Quaker from Hempstead, Long Island, who had freed his slaves just before the Revolution. During the food crisis in the Revolution, Hicks had sold supplies to blacks on Long Island for half price. After the war he was a leading advocate of abolition. Bates congratulated the African societies for their decision to honor Hicks with a benevolent society in his name. The oration offers insights into the question of African and European sources for the antislavery movement. Blacks commemorated the memory of John Woolman, Benjamin Rush, John Clarkson, William Wilberforce, Anthony Benezet, Henri Gregoire, and other Euro-American abolitionists by naming self-help societies after them. At the same time, they thought of themselves as Africans and explored the continent's contributions to American and world civilization. Blacks welcomed William Lloyd Garrison's conversion from gradual to immediate abolitionism. Formerly a committed colonizationist, Garrison in the 1830s established the important antislavery newspaper the *Liberator*. Blacks quickly became subscribers and agents and contributed hundreds of essays and letters to its columns. Garrison and other highly educated reformers were not the only whites supporting antislavery. Artisans and shopkeepers formed substantial parts of antislavery society membership.[70]

Building on the efforts of Peter Williams Jr. and other early ministers, black clergymen confidently and courageously took up the antislavery crusade. Most ministers in rural New York and New Jersey attended small flocks in deeply conservative towns. In New York City, graduates of the African Free School mingled with charismatic fugitives and sons of black artisans to form a dazzling cohort of activist ministers. Most were tied to organized Protestant churches, though invariably the parent church caused deep alienation by its callous racism. Samuel Cornish was as vulnerable to insult as an itinerant exhorter risking his life in the border states. Still, antislavery activity occurred in the most benighted counties of East Jersey and in the highly paid pulpit of Henry Highland Garnet, who received $700 annually from the American Missionary Association. The vast majority were lay ministers used because of a paucity of trained clergy. When ministers were present, their effect was substantial. As Carol George has observed, if the lay people vied for control of budget, ministerial selection, and program, still the local preacher remained a role model and symbolic center for the community. By the 1830s, black ministers and laymen universally agreed that slavery was sinful in the eyes of God.[71]

Blacks continued to work throughout this period to regain the vote without restriction. Largely disfranchised by the $250 bond set in 1821, blacks used political and patriotic appeals to urge expansion of the electorate. In 1838 Thomas Jennings, Henry Sipkins, Charles L. Reason, Philip A. Bell, and Charles B. Ray led the formation of the Political Improvement Association and the Political Association of New York (which later merged), both committed to the elimination of discriminatory suffrage and to encouraging black political activity. When these efforts failed to sway the white majority, which refused to enfranchise blacks in New York State, organizers turned to other methods. Among these was public recollection of the contributions by blacks in American wars, a favorite theme even for pacifist abolitionists. In 1851 excavations for the foundations of a large retail store in lower Manhattan uncovered a tangle of human bones. The relics were "shovelled up with the earth they had rested in, carted off and emptied into the sea to fill up a chasm, and make the foundation for a warehouse." The bones were those of "colored American soldiers, who fell in the disastrous battles of Long Island, in 1776," now treated "as the rubbish of the town." William Wells Brown conjectured that "were they bones of white men they would have been honored with sumptuous burial anew and the purchased prayers and preaching of Christian divines." [72] Henry Highland Garnet gave tribute to the "colored men who stood by the fathers of the country. . . . No Monumental piles distinguish their 'dreamless beds.' " In 1836, William Yates contrasted these contributions with the inequity of New York laws stemming from the electoral bond. Denial of this basic citizenship right cost blacks trial by jury and the right to teach in public schools, serve in civil office, drive a cart, and enroll in the militia. Blacks, he protested, were not even legally allowed to own fishing vessels. Yates argued that earlier New Yorkers, including the revered De Witt Clinton, did not intend such discrimination, recalling Clinton's award of a passport for Peter Williams Jr.[73]

Politically, blacks had little to offer. Perhaps a thousand could vote across New York State. Fewer still could vote in New Jersey. Although the Whig Party gave lip service to black demands, it also defended the interests of the cartmen. The Democrats offered no hope to blacks, but the tiny Liberty Party showed some promise. Reform measures seeking to remove the property qualification suffered overwhelming defeats in the legislature in 1837 and 1846.[74]

The national political scene offered little to blacks. None of the four candidates for president and vice president in 1840 were remotely acceptable to black abolitionists. The *Colored American* analyzed the careers of Martin Van Buren and William Henry Harrison and declared both inveterate foes of equality and black rights. Formation of the Liberty Party did not spark much hope. As Thomas Van Rensselaer noted in the *Colored American*, though the professed object of the Liberty Party was "to secure the rights of the colored men in THIS Country," the party was unwilling to run any black candidates. While the Liberty Party may be pardoned because politicians run to win and black candidates had no chance, to African American audiences, the abolitionist party was just another whites-only group. Such alienation spurred calls for radical action. James McCune Smith, in a reprint of David Walker's *Appeal*, wrote in 1841 that insurrection was the "legitimate fruit of slavery, against which it was a spontaneous rebellion." Two years later, Henry Highland Garnet, speaking before the 1843 National Negro Convention, urged the slaves to revolt against their masters. He argued that the time had come "when you must act for yourself. . . . Rather die Freemen than live to be Slaves." [75]

Black Newspapers

Radical speakers could now be heard because of the rise of a black press. In January 1837 Samuel Cornish founded a second newspaper, first called the *Weekly Advocate*, then renamed the *Colored American*. The newspaper announced themes familiar to Cornish's philosophies: the desperate need for better and more widespread black education; black self-elevation through thrift, diligence, and temperance; attacks on the American Colonization Society; exposure of white oppression and dreams of a better life in rural America. Cornish chose the name, as he stated in the first issue, to emphasize the free blacks' right to stay in America. Reflecting the contributions of David Ruggles, it publicized political battles for black civil rights and local battles against slave catchers. Far better financed than previous efforts and encouraged by the steady growth of radical white abolitionism, the *Colored American* soon became the paper of record for African Americans. Linked to other cities through traveling agents, it reported antislavery actions across the country and became a bulletin board for black conventions. It inspired other black newspapers, including the militant *Ram's Horn*, edited by Willis Augustus Hodges, and the equally uncompromising

Alarm Bell, edited by the poet Alfred Gibbs Campbell of Paterson, New Jersey.[76]

Ending Slavery in New Jersey

Despite the activities of men like Campbell, rural blacks did not enjoy the intellectual freedom found in the city, despite the oppression there. New Jersey's labor relations were symptomatic of the state's poor legal climate for blacks. Slavery was still legal, and laws were passed in 1837 requiring the registration of all free blacks. Blacks from other states who wished to reside in New Jersey had to present proof of emancipation. Gradually, however, abolitionist lawyers chipped away at the remainder of the slave codes. In 1837, for instance, the New Jersey Assembly ordered jury trials for alleged fugitives. By 1840 the New York legislature also required jury trials at all state fugitive proceedings, provided counsel for alleged fugitives, and prohibited quick and arbitrary extradition procedures.[77]

Still, the apparatus of enslavement continued untouched at the local level. In New Jersey, masters still advertised for runaway slaves, as shown by an example in Monmouth County as late as 1857. Masters and mistresses routinely sold enslaved people for the time they had left to serve under gradual emancipation. Dependency rates remained high. Nor was there any reprieve late in life as slave owners passed enslaved people on to their heirs. Without a fundamental change in the laws, these patterns would have continued for decades.[78]

In 1845, a white lawyer named Alvan Stewart instituted a creative suit against slavery in New Jersey, arguing that an "all-men-are-by-nature-free-and-independent" clause in the state constitution of 1844 made severe laws governing black apprentices unconstitutional. Stewart lost when the courts declared that abstract propositions in the state bill of rights did not undercut the status of property. The following year New Jersey's legislature finally transformed all remaining slaves into indentured servants, to be supported for life by their masters and with larger degrees of freedom. New Jersey did retain, however, the right of slave owners to bring the "usual number" of household slaves into the state for visits.[79]

New Jersey blacks had founded an antislavery society in Newark in the 1830s, and in the next decade the movement in Jersey became more militant as black ministers and political figures concentrated on the dearth of civil rights and the repugnant leftovers of slavery. In 1849, the first Negro Convention in the state prompted unsuccessful appeals to the legislature by black activists from Monmouth and Middlesex Counties to give blacks the vote. Like their counterparts in New York, black males in New Jersey were not enfranchised until passage of the Fifteenth Amendment to the federal Constitution in 1870; females, of course, had to wait until ratification of the Nineteenth Amendment in 1920.

Declining Fortunes in the 1850s

The forty years after 1810 saw sustained, vigorous, hard-won improvements for free blacks in the region. In contrast, the 1850s were a time of severe trial for African Americans in New York and East Jersey. The federal Fugitive Slave Act of 1850, which required northern citizens to help return fugitive slaves to the South, so discouraged blacks in the region that many moved to Canada in search of security. Major black churches in New York and New Jersey lost nearly 20 percent of their memberships to Canada between 1848 and 1851. New York City's black population was able to rally together in the James Hamlet case in 1850. Hamlet, then working as a porter in the city, was arrested and deported to Maryland after the act was passed. The black community gathered together and raised $800 to purchase his freedom. Hamlet returned to the city to a rousing demonstration in his honor. After that came only bad news. In 1854 the Kansas-Nebraska Act repealed the Missouri Compromise and opened the western territories to slavery. The severest blow came in 1857, when a Supreme Court decision in the case of Dred Scott disallowed any notions of black citizenship in the United States. Chief Justice Roger Taney's determination that black men were never intended to be citizens under the Constitution also widened southern claims about slavery. Taney's decision reopened questions about the rights of southerners to bring their human chattel into northern states, or, worse, to buy and sell them there. Blacks in the North could easily foresee that seven decades of gradual emancipation and freedom could be quickly reversed. Added to the open racism voiced in northern journalism and the worsening racial climate, the case caused leading black intellectuals to spend more time in hospitable England while others reconsidered emigration to Africa.[80]

In the 1850s blacks, believing that inflation had lightened the burden of the $250 bond, stepped up the drive to get out the vote. Even so, by 1855 the maximum potential black voting bloc numbered less than five thousand. Even that small number offended many whites.

The Democratic Party used black efforts to slur the Whigs and Republicans, claiming that removing the property qualification would permit the opposition to add laws restricting the rights of the foreign born. Republican responses avoided public support for black efforts. To little avail, pamphlets, issued by black groups seeking to get out the vote, recounted past accomplishments of New York blacks in the military service and in business and social organizations and humbly pointed out that simple justice demanded abolition of the property requirements. Both parties chose to ignore these pleas, and the restrictions against black suffrage passed in New York and New Jersey decades before remained until passage of the Fifteenth Amendment.[81]

In 1857 the New York legislature, deeply angered by the recent Dred Scott decision, passed resolutions barring slavery "in any form for any time however short" in the state and announcing that the Dred Scott decision "impaired the confidence and respect of the people of this state" in the national Supreme Court. The same year the state supreme court upheld Paine's decision in the Lemmons case, which ended New York's comity with southern states.[82]

A sign of enmity was that New York State in the 1850s tolerated a revival of the illegal slave trade, despite the potential of capital punishment for convicted offenders. Confiscation of slave ships in New York was rare, and officials winked at slave trading. Dummy corporations concealed the trade in human flesh. Quietly working out of a small office on Pearl Street and guarded by lawyers specializing in admiralty law, Portuguese slave traders outfitted vessels bound for Angola thirty or forty times a year. A well-publicized trial in 1855 did little to stop the trade. Certain legal decisions actually protected the rights of slave traders. Only the captain or owner of a slave ship could be prosecuted, and if the owner was an agent for a third party he could be prosecuted only under the mild terms of the act of 1794. Confessions were allowed only for a specific voyage, and no past demonstrations of guilt were admissible. In 1857 an agricultural boom in Cuba sent prices for smuggled slaves soaring. The most careful student of this trade has counted at least fifty-seven slave ships fitted out in New York City between 1857 and 1860. The trade continued into the Civil War. Such commerce made the Fugitive Slave Act of 1850 and local discrimination more threatening than ever for black New Yorkers.[83]

Rethinking Africa

Despite the deep aversion of black intellectuals to the colonization movement, they began to rethink the potential of Africa, partly in an attempt to reclaim the legacies of the African past. The fugitive black-smith turned Presbyterian minister James W. C. Pennington wrote the first black history of the world, emphasizing the contributions of Africans. Ordinary blacks embraced a vernacular use of African burial traditions. As an implicit part of organizations such as the African Society for Mutual Relief, originally established as a burial society, by the 1840s African Americans in New York and East Jersey began to decorate their most sacred ground by African methods. This is most apparent in cemetery markings. As a statement of African national-ism, black churches in the antebellum period established graveyards, often using conscious recollections of African burial practices. Early nineteenth-century black cemeteries existed in New York City, in up-state New York, and in Monmouth and Bergen Counties, New Jersey. Suggestions of West African death rites are evident in black funer-ary objects in Bergen County cemeteries. At Gethsemane Cemetery in Little Falls, New Jersey, graves are covered with pieces of broken white pottery; one contains pipes reaching from the grave to the surface.[84]

In Kongo faith, white symbolizes the land of the dead, while the broken pottery was placed to provide the departed with objects to use beyond the grave. Pipes on a grave permit communication between the deceased and the living. Such objects, common in Kongo societies, act, as Robert Farris Thompson has observed, to impose the wisdom of the dead upon the living. The pipes suggest underground travel to the world of the ancestors beneath or beyond the sea. Such tombs become "ritual earthworks, conceptual doors to another universe, an intricate field of mediatory signs." In a cemetery, trees, each with its own special symbolic importance, indicate the hardiness of the elders' spirits and resistance to the force of time. In New York City, black parents deco-rated the graves of their children with glass boxes containing favored toys, including "woolly dogs and lambs, and little wooden houses." Similar grave markings are in black cemeteries in Staten Island and the African Methodist Episcopal Church cemetery in Holmdel, Mon-mouth County.[85]

Sagging political and legal fortunes by the mid-1850s spurred lead-ing black intellectuals to reconsider emigration to Africa. It was one of the paradoxes of the decade that, as blacks rejected colonization plans, they moved closer to an Afrocentric perception of history. An

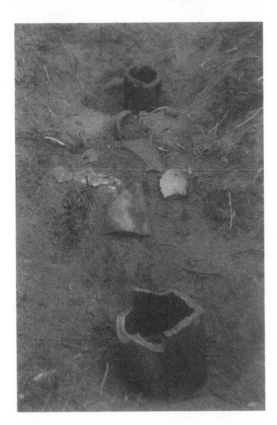

Porter family grave site at Gethsemane Cemetery, Little Ferry, New Jersey. The pipes and scattered pottery at this grave site represent a vernacular re-creation of the African past of the interred. (Courtesy of Arnold Brown)

important influence was the Amistad case of 1840, which freed a group of enslaved blacks from a slave ship that ran aground off Long Island. This celebrated trial convinced several black New York ministers that missionary efforts for Africa were necessary. James W. C. Pennington led an array of black preachers instrumental in the 1840s in the formation of the American Missionary Association. Numerous black preachers around New York City served as managers of the movement.[86]

Liberia became a focus for black Americans seeking to disprove white claims that Africa had made no achievements to civilization. In 1859, 144 blacks from New York and 33 from New Jersey emigrated to Liberia. Though a few black ministers became spokesmen for the ACS, for most interest in Africa was not a rapprochement with the society but combined growing awareness of African culture with despair for black fortunes in the United States.[87]

Martin Delaney was a key figure in this transition. Espousing black self-help and moral reform philosophies prevalent in African American thought throughout the century, Delaney initially held the worldview that energetic and responsible blacks could, by acquiring material wealth and standing in the United States, overcome the degradation of slavery. Delaney adopted the views of agrarian nationalist Lewis Woodson that all blacks suffered from "a prejudice of caste." Within a few years, incidents of personal humiliation by racist whites pushed him to accept emigration as the sole solution. Stung by passage of the Fugitive Slave Act of 1850 and by student demands for his expulsion from Harvard Medical School, Delaney emerged in 1852 as the major exponent of nationalist-emigrationist thought. After denouncing the American Colonization Society, Delaney argued that the perilous state of blacks in America required emigration. In a nation that denied them citizenship, Delaney wrote, "it would be folly" to pretend that the future bore any possibilities of employment or civil rights. He urged blacks to consider Central America, South America, the British West Indies, anywhere with nonwhite majorities capable of withstanding American imperial designs. Abolitionist measures in the United States, he concluded bitterly, were only paternalist. Initially not interested in Africa, Delaney visited the continent during the 1850s and left deeply impressed by Yoruba culture.[88]

Alexander Crummell promoted colonization as part of the Christian mission, a major theme in black religious thought since the 1790s. In a speech in Monrovia, Liberia, he argued that the duty of free blacks in America toward Africans derived not from their color but from their Christianity. While "Africa lies low and is wretched," self-love among adventurous, enterprising, and aspiring blacks could lead to trade for the many raw materials of West Africa, "all of which now flows into the coffers of the white man." Crummell believed that blacks should form associations to trade with the interior of the continent.[89]

The Reverend Edward Wilmot Blyden provided companionship for African American intellectuals in Liberia. Originally from St. Thomas and sponsored by a Presbyterian minister from Newtown, Long Island, Blyden came to study in New York City in the late 1840s but found "deep seated prejudice against my race, exercising so controlling an influence in the institutions of learning, that admission was impossible." After Blyden was refused entrance to Rutgers University, he attended church services at the Dutch Reformed congregation in New York City. There, he heard a speaker declare that efforts to uplift the African were fruitless. Blyden then decided to migrate to Monrovia, Liberia, for high school. By 1862 Blyden and Alexander Crummell became the first professors at Liberia College. Blyden argued in a book of essays that "republican government is nowhere more thoroughly carried out" than in Liberia. He visited New York City to raise funds for Liberia and to serve as commissioner for the American Colonization Society in New York.[90]

The *Anglo-African* magazine, founded by Thomas Hamilton of Brooklyn in 1858, increased black interest in emigration. It featured important articles by James McCune Smith on Thomas Jefferson, James Pennington's history of the slave trade, William C. Nell on black Revolutionary War veterans, and a very significant analysis of census returns. The magazine was the first publisher of Martin Delaney's novel *Blake*. The *Anglo-African* championed race pride and opened its columns to favorable commentary on emigration and Yoruba culture.[91]

Anglo-African editorials on the eve of the Civil War showed the deepening alienation of black intellectuals. One writer stated that "my duty and destiny are in Africa." Others complained of "despicable meanness" by the American government toward Liberia. Among some blacks, emigration to Haiti, not seriously discussed since the early 1830s, reappeared as a solution to the crisis. For a writer calling himself "Volunteer," Haiti was not just an escape from racism but a base from which the émigrés could attack the slave states. "Volunteer" described Haiti as a "nucleus of power to the black," in which slave dealers and slaveholders could be hanged as "surely as they are caught." [92]

Conclusions

During the antebellum decades black life in and around New York City was deeply paradoxical. Black activists and intellectuals published newspapers, books, pamphlets, and poems, made speeches, and organized political conventions, libraries, schools, and book clubs. The admirable David Ruggles led the organization of the Committee of Vigilance, the most visible tip of the Underground Railroad. Black ministers and activists emblazoned their names on the unceasing war against the twin evils of slavery and racism. There had never been a generation of black crusaders like them before, and there would not be again until the 1960s.

At the same time, the black population of New York City and the surrounding countryside suffered grievous losses. Racism became an open ideological weapon used by major political parties and by any ordinary white with a tiny grievance. The black community was mobbed in 1834. In the rural counties, African Americans were just beginning to advance beyond dependence and the shadow of enslavement. Amazingly, there were still slaves in New Jersey and masters were still advertising for fugitive bondsmen at the close of the 1850s. Politically, the bright hopes of the 1830s darkened in the turbulent decade of the 1850s. The Fugitive Slave Act of 1850 and the Dred Scott decision of 1857 convinced many blacks in the region to head for Canada or to sign up with the colonization movement. As a result, the black population dropped as much as 25 percent in the city and did no better than stay even in the surrounding counties.

On the eve of the Civil War, African Americans in New York and East Jersey pondered the question of identity. After three-quarters of a century of activism and struggle to gain liberties and rights owned by white males, African Americans felt the deepest despair about future prospects. Their fullest destiny seemed not to be the democratic society of the United States but rather the republic of Liberia. Beset by disappointment, blacks in New York and New Jersey looked inward to their African heritage to overcome their disillusion with America.

Epilogue

Between six and seven o'clock on the morning of July 13, 1863, thousands of white New Yorkers demonstrated before the Ninth District Marshal's Office at Third Avenue and Forty-Seventh Street, where military officials had scheduled a draft lottery for the Union army. At the lottery office, rioters forced suspension of the draft, compelled the city's businesses to close, and harassed the offices of Horace Greeley, editor of the *New York Tribune* and embodiment of the antislavery cause. After Greeley failed to appear, the huge crowd dispersed into various parts of the city. Having closed down the draft, some of the original rioters felt they had accomplished their purpose and went home, but by evening one group of rioters, led by a southern agent named Andrews, set fire to the Colored Orphan Asylum on Fifth Avenue and beat several black men and boys.[1]

What started as an antidraft demonstration quickly turned into a race riot. Mobs attacked blacks returning home from work and destroyed black homes and boardinghouses. Realizing the danger, blacks fled the city for Long Island, New Jersey, and upper parts of Manhattan. Some fled to Weeksville, a black community in Brooklyn, or camped out in the woods along the Harlem River, in Queens County, and in the Elysian Fields in Hoboken. Over seven hundred found refuge in the Central Police Precinct. At the Twentieth Precinct, which protected the children from the Colored Orphan Asylum, only a few disabled or elderly patrolmen guarded the building. Fortunately, the armed crowd did not know this. The mob attacked the homes of leading Republicans, beat blacks in the street, and burned and sacked black neighborhoods. As armed men held up travelers, hackmen charged extortionate rates for transport out of town.[2]

On Tuesday, July 14, the rioters continued to beat and kill virtually any black who came their way. A black seaman, William Williams, was stomped to death at the corner of Leroy and Washington Streets on the lower West Side after asking for directions to a grocery shop. Angry whites kicked out his eyes, stabbed him while on the ground, and then crushed his chest with a flagstone. Roaming bands of men beat or threatened black sailors, robbed African American boardinghouses, destroyed interracial brothels, and attacked ordinary black

Playground of the Colored Orphan Asylum, New York. The Draft Rioters of 1863 vented their wrath against the federal government by destroying the home of these black orphans. (Courtesy of the New-York Historical Society)

neighborhoods. A mob clubbed a black woman, her daughter, and grandson to death with a cart rung. (Three days after these murders, First Sergeant Robert J. Simmons of the Fifty-fourth Massachusetts Colored Troops, the son and brother of the dead women, was captured and severely wounded at Fort Wagner, South Carolina.) The infinite number of streets in the city worked against interference by the police and militia. The burning of the Colored Orphan Asylum the day before alerted vigilantes who were able to protect the Good Shepherd Home (formerly the Colored Home) on Second Avenue and Sixty-Fifth Street. Quick action helped preserve such targets as St. Luke's Hospital, Columbia University, and various homes in Yorkville. Throughout the day, rioters shouted their support for the Confederacy and slavery.

Blacks resisted fiercely. William Wells Brown found eight sturdy black women in a tenement on Thompson Street preparing several boilers with a mixture of water, soap, and ashes they referred to as the "King of Pain." The women asserted to Brown that if the rioters invaded the building, "We'll fling hot water on 'em an' scald dar very harts out." In another remarkable scene, blacks on a rooftop on Mac-Dougald Street armed with rifles stood off the mob while singing psalms.[3]

On Wednesday, after a city judge outlawed the draft, mobs continued to brutalize the city's black population. A mob wandering near Herald Square spotted black shoemaker James Costello, beat him to death, and then hung him from a lamppost. Mobs told black women at Sixth Avenue and Thirty-Second Street to leave their homes before they were torched. A gang of rioters told one woman to "go in and get everything you have in there out and don't never show your face in this street again." The mob looted and burned empty homes of blacks. In the afternoon some rioters discovered Abraham Franklin, a crippled black coachman, on Twenty-Seventh Street and Seventh Avenue, dragged him down the street to a lamppost, and lynched him. After military officers cut down the coachman, the mob hoisted him up again. After the body was taken down a second time, a small boy grabbed it by the genitals and dragged it down the street to the cheers of the crowd. Several other lynchings occurred during the early evening. Despite the Seventh Regiment's use of howitzers to battle the mob, blacks were unsafe anywhere in the city.[4]

By Thursday 4,000 federal troops had arrived to reinforce and occupy the city. By the time they achieved a semblance of order, at least 105 people were killed. Another 128 soldiers, police, and civilians were wounded. Three hundred fifty rioters, the vast majority Irish semiskilled and unskilled workers, were arrested. Although a few were professional brawlers, arrestees ranged from a Copperhead (southern sympathizer) professor from Columbia to ordinary working-class New Yorkers. They worked the streets in bands of 20 to 30 concentrating on blacks and sympathetic Republicans. In New Jersey, Union sympathizers feared similar rioting in the aftermath of the week in New York and urged the Supreme Court to settle the legality of the draft.[5]

There had been serious warnings of violence for some time. Just before the attack on Fort Sumter, New York's mayor Fernando Wood sent a message to the Common Council calling for the secession of the city; New York's Democratic Party was openly pro-South and spoke defiantly of secession. Copperhead newspapers proclaimed white supremacy. In New Jersey prosouthern attitudes were strongest in areas where slavery had flourished. There were riots in local army camps where desertions were rampant. White New Yorkers grew steadily more hostile to blacks, and, while unhappy about the inequities of the draft, they were especially antagonistic to visions of black troops. As early as 1861 blacks in New York organized a militia to prepare for a call from the Union army. The *Weekly Anglo-African* reported that "a party of colored men made their appearance on Broadway, a few days since, with drum and fife, and bearing the American flag, and attempted to march up the street." A crowd took away their drum and flag and informed them that "niggers could not be allowed to carry that flag!" Later, the sheriff ordered them to disband because he could no longer guarantee their safety. Protestant and Catholic clergy alike enunciated support for the South and slavery and espoused doctrines of black inferiority. Politicians argued the constitutionality of slavery, and many recalled the prewar illicit slave trade with nostalgia.[6]

Few charges against rioters resulted in convictions. The Common Council nullified the draft in a resolution granting $300 to any fireman, policeman, member of the militia, or indigent New Yorker who needed a deferment, but despite overwhelming evidence that they suffered the most, blacks received no public aid. Blacks who made claims through the Riots Claims Commission found that examiners disallowed their appeals for spurious reasons such as abandoning their property without waiting for the rioters to attack or failure to place precise values on property. The Merchants' Relief Committee, however, raised $42,000 to help black victims of the riot. Among men, the committee helped 1,267 laborers and longshoremen, 177 whitewashers, 176 cartmen, 250 waiters, 124 porters, 97 sailors and assorted coachmen, cooks, and chimney sweeps, and 20 butchers. Among women, the Association for the Improvement of the Condition of the Poor assisted 2,924 "Day's Work Women" (domestics), 664 monthly servants, 163 seamstresses, 106 cooks, 19 hucksters, and those in several other occupations.[7]

Blacks slowly returned to their jobs. Although there was some movement among upper-class New Yorkers to discharge their Irish servants and replace them with blacks, other blacks, especially longshoremen, found employment scarce. Street beatings of young blacks continued throughout the summer. Horace Greeley's *Tribune* noted that a number of blacks had left the city "never to return."[8]

Early historical interpretations accentuated the riot's anarchic qualities but offered some sympathy for the rioters' grievances against the federal government and its selective draft.[9] More recently, Iver Bernstein's *New York City Draft Riots* places the events of July 1863 within a transforming social order in which industrialists, shrewd politicians, and aroused Irish were displacing an alliance of the older, mercantile elite and New York's African Americans. This argument slights the importance of blacks in the city's society and history.[10]

The riot was only the largest in a series of battles between blacks and whites who were sympathetic to the southern cause and jealous of blacks in the workforce. Assaults on black workers had occurred in Brooklyn the preceding September, in March along the waterfront, and on May 29, when some Irish longshoremen beat up blacks at pier 9. Just before the riots, white longshoremen worried over rumors that three carloads of black strikebreakers were en route to New York City.[11] These assaults occurred within a fabric of intense racial antagonism dating back to the riots of 1834. Economic woes had exacerbated the situation as living conditions deteriorated badly after 1860. Under runaway inflation New York City saw extremes of wealth and poverty; war-rich contractors and their wives paraded their ostentatious luxury.[12] Irish laborers seemed determined to drive out black competition. Having undermined blacks in several occupations, the Irish had little interest in fighting a war for black emancipation. One New Yorker, Maria Daly, the wife of a well-to-do Irish-born Democratic judge in New York, explained that the Irish were angry at the draft because they believed that abolitionists would replace them with "good, faithful, colored servants," forcing the Irish into the poorhouses. Mrs. Daly felt sorrow for the "cruelties" inflicted upon the blacks but hoped they would "give the Negro a lesson, for since the war commenced, they have been so insolent as to be unbearable." Republicans, in contrast, believed the Draft Riots were the embodiment of Democratic treason against the northern war effort. In this view, antiabolitionism equaled war, riot, and murder.[13]

The rioters were also battling against the growing numbers of black enlistments in the Union navy. Although blacks were effectively barred from service in the Union army until 1863, they were welcomed into the naval service from the beginning of the war. Throughout the first years

Middle-class black woman, New York City, 1860s. Sometime during the Civil War, this young African American woman had her portrait made at a shop on lower Broadway, an act characteristic of a flourishing middle-class black sensibility. (Collection of the author)

of the Civil War, black seamen from New York and New Jersey led other states in numbers of enlistees. In 1861 and 1862, 339 blacks from New York and 66 from New Jersey joined the navy. The *Anglo-African* crystallized the black community's support for naval enlistments in an editorial on September 14, 1861, which argued that aiding the Union helped "to secure our own liberty." Although the newspaper acknowledged that the North was not fighting for black liberty, "circumstances have been so arranged by the decrees of Providence, that in struggling for their own nationality, they are forced to defend our rights." In February 1863, when Congress passed the Supplementary Enrollment Act welcoming "all able-bodied male colored persons, between the ages of twenty and forty-five years, and residents of the United States" into the military, the rush was on. In all, 1,126 blacks from New York and 362 from New Jersey accounted for over 15 percent of the total black enlistments in the Union navy.[14]

Republican support for black aspirations descended from a long-term compact between elite white and black New Yorkers. Abraham Lincoln's Emancipation Proclamation paved the way for black troops to enter the war on the side of the Union and play a crucial part in crushing the Confederacy. Blacks openly celebrated the Emancipation Proclamation at Henry Highland Garnet's Shiloh Presbyterian Church and antagonized the prosouthern white working classes. The decision to enroll large numbers of blacks in the Union army, urged continually by leading black abolitionists, was very unpopular among white New Yorkers, but once it took effect, it had devastating effects on the Confederate cause. In New York, the Union League began a campaign to shift the burden of the draft away from the Irish to African Americans. After Horace Greeley, William Cullen Bryant, and Peter Cooper visited Abraham Lincoln in May 1863 to seek black enlistments, Republicans held several mass rallies to support black troops.

In March 1864, one hundred thousand New Yorkers turned out in Union Square to watch the Union League present colors to the black Twentieth Regiment, about to embark for the war. The elite Union League pointedly associated the black regiment with the highest patriotism. Recruitment of black soldiers proved easy in New York City because African Americans believed the war to be a crusade against slavery and approached their commitment with great self-respect. Recruits came from every strata of black New York and New Jersey society. By the close of the war 4,125 black New Yorkers and 1,185 from New Jersey served in the Union army.[15]

African Americans continued their zeal for equality while serving in the military forces. One issue was equal pay. A New York State father wrote the secretary of war that his son, a black sergeant, was a "truly Loyal Boy," who believed "there is something wrong in relation to his receiving only Seven dollars per month pay" at a time when whites earned at least thirteen dollars.[16]

After being undercounted in the partial census of 1865, the black population of the region steadily increased. By 1870 the population of black New York City rose to 13,072. Increases occurred in Queens, Kings, Richmond, and Suffolk. Black populations in Monmouth, Essex, Bergen, and Middlesex Counties all rose. Despite the ravages of the Draft Riots, most of the black population in New York remained in the older neighborhoods through the 1860s. In 1870 41.5 percent of black New Yorkers still lived below Houston Street.[17]

Positive changes occurred in local civil rights. In 1864, a few months after the first black troops left, a streetcar conductor evicted the widow of a black soldier from the Eighth Avenue Line. Threatened by a suit from the Union League, the company quickly abandoned discrimination on the streetcars of the city, a reform demanded for several decades. Within days, public outcry forced the train companies to reverse this odious policy.[18]

The *New York World* published a survey in 1867 of black New York City which demonstrated the stability of the community. Black churches and the African Society for Mutual Relief retained their memberships. Elite blacks were bankers, merchants, printers, and notaries. Black schoolteachers, carpenters, waiters, cooks, domestics, caterers, and nurses made up a stable black middle class while poorer African Americans worked as laundresses, whitewashers, coachmen, and carters in lower-class positions. As in previous decades, thieves and prostitutes and fortune-tellers composed a black lumpen-proletariat. Most lived in wards adjacent to the Bowery. Late in the nineteenth century blacks finally abandoned this sacred ground for newer areas in the northern part of the city. In the final analysis, however, blacks in New York and New Jersey remained a permanent part of the city and its rural environs through the sacred and slave cultures' hard-won victories over the course of two and a half centuries. The Draft Riots and their aftermath demonstrated that African Americans would fight for their rights. Their conversation with the larger white society spoke with an American tongue inspired by an African soul.[19]

Appendix

Table 1. White and African American Population of New York and East Jersey, 1703–1775

		Total Population	White (%)	Black (%)	Male/Female (Black)	Mean Annual % Increase Black
New York						
1703	New York	4,375	3,745 (85.6)	630 (14.4)	233/397	—
	Kings	1,912	1,569 (82.1)	343 (17.9)	207/136	—
	Queens	4,392	3,968 (90.3)	424 (9.7)	215/209	—
	Westchester	1,946	1,709 (87.8)	198 (10.2)	124/74	—
	Richmond	504	407 (80.8)	97 (19.2)	64/33	—
	Total	13,129	11,398 (86.8)	1,692 (13.2)	843/849	—
1723	New York	7,248	5,886 (81.2)	1,362 (18.8)	628/734	5.81
	Kings	2,218	1,774 (79.8)	444 (20.2)	254/190	1.47
	Queens	7,191	6,068 (84.4)	1,123 (15.6)	621/502	8.24
	Westchester	4,409	3,961 (89.8)	448 (10.2)	247/201	6.32
	Richmond	1,506	1,251 (83.1)	255 (16.9)	150/105	8.15
	Total	22,572	18,940 (83.9)	3,632 (16.1)	1,900/1,732	
1731	New York	8,622	7,045 (81.7)	1,577 (18.3)	785/792	1.98
	Kings	2,150	1,658 (77.1)	492 (22.9)	270/222	1.35
	Queens	7,995	6,731 (84.2)	1,264 (15.8)	702/562	1.58
	Westchester	6,033	5,341 (88.5)	692 (11.5)	445/247	6.81
	Richmond	1,817	1,513 (83.3)	304 (16.7)	162/142	2.4
	Total	26,617	22,288 (83.7)	4,329 (16.3)	2,364/1,965	

	Total Population	White (%)	Black (%)	Male/Female (Black)	Mean Annual % Increase Black
1737					
New York	10,664	8,945 (83.9)	1,719 (16.1)	903/816	1.5
Kings	2,348	1,784 (76.0)	564 (24)	294/270	2.43
Queens	9,059	7,748 (85.5)	1,311 (14.5)	714/597	0.62
Westchester	6,745	5,894 (87.4)	851 (12.6)	457/394	3.83
Richmond	1,889	1,540 (81.5)	349 (18.5)	184/165	2.47
Total	30,705	25,911 (84.4)	4,794 (15.6)	2,552/2,242	
1746					
New York	11,717	9,273 (79.1)	2,444 (20.9)	1,140/1,304	4.69
Kings	2,331	1,686 (72.3)	645 (27.7)	339/306	1.6
Queens	9,640	7,996 (82.9)	1,644 (17.1)	892/752	2.82
Westchester	9,235	8,563 (92.7)	672 (7.3)	394/278	-2.33
Richmond	2,073	1,691 (81.6)	382 (18.4)	193/189	1.06
Total	34,996	29,209 (83.5)	5,787 (16.5)	2,958/2,829	
1749					
New York	13,294	10,926 (82.2)	2,368 (17.8)	1,111/1,257	-1.03
Kings	2,283	1,500 (65.7)	783 (34.3)	497/286	7.13
Queens	8,040	6,617 (82.3)	1,423 (17.7)	729/594	-4.47
Westchester	10,703	9,547 (89.2)	1,156 (10.8)	639/517	24
Richmond	2,154	1,745 (81.0)	409 (19.0)	218/191	2.37
Total	36,474	30,335 (83.2)	6,139 (16.8)	3,194/2,845	

continued

Table 1. *continued*

		Total Population	White (%)	Black (%)	Male/Female (Black)	Mean Annual % Increase Black
1756	New York	13,040	10,768 (82.6)	2,272 (17.3)	1,140/1,138	−.59
	Kings	2,707	1,862 (68.8)	845 (31.2)	447/398	1.13
	Queens	10,786	8,617 (79.9)	2,169 (20.1)	1,199/970	7.49
	Westchester	13,257	11,919 (89.9)	1,338 (10.1)	791/547	2.24
	Richmond	2,132	1,667 (78.2)	465 (21.8)	267/198	1.96
	Total	41,922	34,833 (83.1)	7,089 (16.9)	3,844/3,251	
1771	New York	21,863	18,726 (85.7)	3,137 (14.3)	1,500/1,637	2.54
	Kings	3,623	2,461 (67.9)	1,162 (32.1)	606/556	2.5
	Queens	10,980	8,744 (79.6)	2,236 (20.4)	1,156/1,080	0.21
	Westchester	21,745	18,315 (84.2)	3,430 (15.8)	1,777/1,653	10.43
	Richmond	2,847	2,253 (79.1)	594 (20.9)	351/243	1.85
	Total	61,058	50,499 (82.7)	10,559 (17.3)	5,390/5,169	
New Jersey						
1715	New Jersey	22,500	21,000 (93.3)	1,500 (6.7)		—
1726	Bergen	2,673	2,181 (81.6)	492 (18.4)	273/219	—
	Essex	4,230	3,922 (92.7)	308 (7.3)	162/145	—
	Middlesex	4,009	3,706 (92.4)	303 (7.6)	163/140	—
	Monmouth	4,879	4,446 (91.1)	433 (8.9)	258/175	—
	Somerset	2,271	1,892 (83.3)	379 (16.7)	213/166	—
	Total	18,062	16,147 (89.4)	1,915 (10.6)	1,069/845	—

		Total Population	White (%)	Black (%)	Male/Female (Black)	Mean Annual % Increase Black
1738	Bergen	4,095	3,289 (80.3)	806 (19.7)	443/363	5.32
	Essex	7,019	6,644 (94.7)	375 (5.3)	198/177	1.82
	Middlesex	4,764	4,261 (89.4)	503 (10.6)	272/231	5.5
	Monmouth	6,086	5,431 (89.2)	655 (10.8)	362/293	4.28
	Somerset	4,505	3,773 (83.8)	732 (16.2)	425/307	7.76
	Total	26,469	23,398 (88.4)	3,071 (11.6)	1,700/1,371	
1745	Bergen	3,006	2,390 (79.5)	616 (20.5)	379/237	-3.37
	Essex	6,988	6,543 (93.6)	445 (6.4)	244/201	2.67
	Middlesex	7,612	6,733 (88.5)	879 (11.5)	483/396	10.69
	Monmouth	8,627	7,728 (89.6)	899 (10.4)	513/386	5.33
	Somerset	3,239	2,896 (89.4)	343 (10.6)	194/149	-7.59
	Total	29,472	26,290 (89.2)	3,182 (10.8)	1,813/1,369	

Sources: Greene and Harrington, *American Population before the Federal Census of 1790*, 88–112; Wacker, *Land and People*, 189–205.

Table 2. Fugitive Blacks by County, New York and East Jersey, 1775–1783

	1775	1776	1777	1778	1779	1780	1781	1782	1783	No Date	Total
NEW YORK											
New York											
Adult Male	2	4	—	9	17	7	14	11	13	5	82
Adult Female	0	1	—	4	8	4	8	7	4	3	39
Boys	—	—	—	10	8	9	7	15	9	3	62
Girls	—	—	1	2	2	1	4	4	3	0	17
Kings											
Adult Male	1	1	—	—	—	—	—	—	—	1	3
Adult Female	—	—	—	—	—	—	—	—	—	—	0
Boys	—	—	—	—	—	—	—	—	—	1	1
Girls	—	—	—	1	—	—	—	—	—	—	1
Queens											
Adult Male	1	2	—	1	3	1	3	1	2	5	18
Adult Female	5	—	—	—	—	—	1	—	—	3	9
Boys	—	—	—	1	2	—	—	—	—	4	7
Girls	—	—	—	—	—	—	—	—	—	3	3
Richmond											
Adult Male	—	—	—	—	—	—	—	—	—	1	1
Adult Female	—	—	—	—	—	—	—	—	—	—	0
Boys	—	—	—	—	—	—	—	—	—	—	0
Girls	—	—	—	—	—	—	—	—	—	—	0
Westchester											
Adult Male	—	10	5	3	5	—	1	—	—	1	25
Adult Female	—	5	2	1	—	—	—	—	—	1	9
Boys	—	1	2	—	—	—	—	—	—	1	4
Girls	—	3	—	1	—	—	—	—	—	—	4
Total New York											
Adult Male	4	17	5	13	25	8	18	12	15	13	130
Adult Female	5	6	2	5	8	4	9	7	4	7	57
Boys	—	1	2	11	10	9	7	15	9	9	73
Girls	—	3	1	4	2	1	4	4	3	3	25
Total	9	27	10	33	45	22	38	38	31	32	285
NEW JERSEY											
Bergen											
Adult Male	2	9	7	16	14	7	1	—	—	—	56
Adult Female	1	5	4	2	15	2	2	1	—	—	32
Boys	—	—	—	2	4	1	1	—	—	—	8
Girls	—	1	—	—	3	1	—	—	—	—	5

Table 2. *continued*

	1775	1776	1777	1778	1779	1780	1781	1782	1783	No Date	Total
ssex											
Adult Male	2	8	3	6	1	2	—	—	—	—	22
Adult Female	—	3	1	1	—	2	—	—	—	—	7
Boys	—	—	—	—	—	1	—	—	—	—	1
Girls	—	—	—	—	—	2	—	—	—	—	2
Middlesex											
Adult Male	2	12	3	9	8	3	2	—	—	—	39
Adult Female	1	5	1	4	7	2	2	—	—	—	22
Boys	—	2	—	1	2	1	1	—	—	—	7
Girls	—	1	—	—	3	—	—	—	—	—	4
Monmouth											
Adult Male	1	6	2	4	5	—	1	—	—	—	19
Adult Female	1	—	1	4	—	—	—	—	—	—	6
Boys	—	—	1	2	1	1	—	—	—	—	5
Girls	—	—	—	—	—	—	—	—	—	—	0
Somerset											
Adult Male	1	—	—	—	2	1	—	—	—	—	4
Adult Female	—	—	—	—	—	—	—	—	—	—	0
Boys	—	—	—	—	—	1	—	—	—	—	1
Girls	—	—	—	—	—	—	—	—	—	—	0
Total New Jersey											
Adult Male	8	35	15	35	30	13	4	—	—	—	140
Adult Female	3	13	7	11	22	6	4	1	—	—	67
Boys	—	2	1	5	7	5	2	—	—	—	22
Girls	—	2	—	—	6	3	—	—	—	—	11
Total	11	52	23	51	65	27	10	1	—	—	240
Total New York and New Jersey											
Adult Male	12	52	20	48	55	21	22	12	15	13	270
Adult Female	8	19	9	16	30	10	13	8	4	7	124
Boys	—	3	3	16	17	14	9	15	9	9	95
Girls	—	5	1	4	8	4	4	4	3	3	36
Total	20	79	33	84	110	49	48	39	31	32	525

Sources: Hodges, ed., *Black Loyalist Directory; New York Royal Gazette*, 1775–83; *New Jersey Journal*, 1775–83.

Table 3. Free People of Color in "Book of Negro" from New York and
East Jersey, 1775–1783

	Free Adult Male	Free Adult Female	Free Boy	Free Girl	Total
New York	19	17	2	1	39
Kings	—	—	—	—	0
Queens	8	19	8	8	43
Westchester	4	3	2	—	9
Staten Island	—	2	—	1	3
Total New York	31	41	12	10	94
Bergen	1	8	1	—	10
Essex	5	4	3	3	15
Middlesex	5	—	—	—	5
Monmouth	4	3	—	—	7
Somerset	—	—	—	—	0
Total New Jersey	15	15	4	3	37
Grand Total	46	56	16	13	131

Source: Hodges, ed., *Black Loyalist Directory.*

Table 4. Population of New York and East Jersey, 1790–1860

	New York	Kings	Queens	Richmond	Westchester	Bergen	Middlesex	Essex	Monmouth	Somerset
1790										
Whites	28,133	3,017	12,897	2,942	22,227	10,108	14,498	16,454	14,969	10,339
Free blacks	1,036	46	808	127	357	192	140	160	353	147
Slaves	2,056	1,432	2,309	759	1,419	2,301	1,318	1,171	1,596	1,810
1800										
Whites	51,796	3,929	13,934	3,802	25,687	12,929	16,063	20,550	17,771	10,777
Free blacks	3,333	332	1,431	83	482	202	263	198	468	175
Slaves	2,534	1,479	1,528	675	1,259	2,825	1,564	1,521	1,633	1,863
1810										
Whites	82,743	6,450	16,173	4,636	28,343	13,368	18,418	24,097	20,014	17,382
Free blacks	7,470	735	2,354	274	948	785	665	758	632	1,859
Slaves	1,446	1,118	809	437	982	2,180	1,298	1,129	1,504	448
1820										
Whites	120,350	9,821	18,735	5,582	31,621					
Free blacks	10,368	882	2,648	78	1,636	1,059	1,033	1,390	982	1,487
Slaves	518	879	559	532	205	1,683	1,012	659	1,248	1,122
1830										
Whites	188,613	18,528		6,530		19,934	19,425	39,754	26,934	13,897
Free blacks	13,976	2,007		507		2,478	1,818	1,939	2,072	1,859
Slaves	17	—	—	—	—	584	309	218	227	448

continued

Table 4. continued

	New York	Kings	Queens	Richmond	Westchester	Bergen	Middlesex	Essex	Monmouth	Somerset
1840										
Whites	296,352	44,251	24,419	10,272	45,805	11,472	20,330	42,693	30,664	15,698
Free blacks	16,358	2,743	3,499	483	2,297	1,529	1,535	1,908	2,180	1,652
Slaves	—	—	—	—	—	222	28	20	85	105
1850										
Whites	501,732	134,817	33,382	14,471	56,188	13,060	27,255	71,616	27,915	17,950
Free blacks	13,815	4,065	3,451	590	2,075	1,624	1,369	2,328	2,323	1,711
Slaves	—	—	—	—	—	41	11	6	75	31
1860										
Whites	801,095	274,123	54,004	24,833	97,227	19,955	33,504	97,120	36,688	20,460
Free blacks	12,574	4,999	3,387	659	2,270	1,663	1,307	1,757	2,658	1,588
Slaves	—	—	—	—	—	—	1	—	—	9

Sources: Rosenwaike, *Population History of New York City*; Wright, *Afro-Americans in New Jersey*, 81–87; *Abstract of the Returns of the Fifth Census; Compendium of the Enumeration of the Inhabitants . . . for 1840*; De Bow, comp., *Statistical View of the United States; A Century of Population Growth*. For corrections in the New York City Census, see White, *Somewhat More Independent*, 26.

Notes

ABBREVIATIONS

AO   Audit Office, Loyalist Claims, Public Record Office, London.

BAP   *The Black Abolitionist Papers*, ed. Peter Ripley et al., 5 vols. (Chapel Hill: University of North Carolina Press, 1985–92).

CN-YHS   *Collections of the New-York Historical Society*

DANB   *Dictionary of American Negro Biography*, ed. Rayford W. Logan and Michael R. Winston (New York: Norton, 1982).

Doc. Hist.   *The Documentary History of the State of New York*, ed. E. B. O'Callaghan, 4 vols. (Albany, 1850–51).

Docs. Rel.   *Documents Relative to the Colonial History of the State of New York*, ed. E. B. O'Callaghan, 15 vols. (Albany, 1856–87).

Ec. Rec.   *Ecclesiastical Records of the State of New York*, ed. Edward T. Corbin, 7 vols. (Albany, 1901–16).

MCC, 1675–1776   *Minutes of the Common Council of the City of New York, 1675–1776*, ed. Herbert L. Osgood, 8 vols. (New York, 1905).

MCC, 1784–1831   *Minutes of the Common Council of the City of New York, 1784–1831*, 22 vols. (New York: Published by the City of New York, 1917).

MCNY   Museum of the City of New York.

NJA   New Jersey Archives.

N-JHS   New-Jersey Historical Society.

N.Y. Col. Mss.   New York Colonial Manuscripts, New York State Archives, Albany, New York.

N-YHS   New-York Historical Society.

NYMA   New York Municipal Archives.

NYPL   New York Public Library.

PRO   Public Record Office, London.

RNA   *The Records of New Amsterdam from 1653 to 1674*, ed. Bertold Fernow, 7 vols. (New York, 1897).

SPG   Society for the Propagation of the Gospel in Foreign Parts

Wills   *Abstracts of Wills on File in the Surrogate's Office*, 17 vols. In *Collections of the New-York Historical Society* (New York, 1893–1913).

INTRODUCTION

1 Alampi, ed., *Gale State Rankings Reporter*, 76; Slater and Hall, eds., *1994 County and City Extra*, 780. For a useful discussion of Rodrigues's role as an interpreter and indications of a potential black predecessor named Metthieu Da Costa, see Bakker, "First African into New Netherland."

2 See White, *Somewhat More Independent;* McManus, *History of Negro Slavery;* Ottley, *Negro in New York.* Here I follow the methods presented in Berlin, "Time, Space," and Meinig, *Atlantic America.* Scholarly approaches to issues of slavery, race, and black life in the mid-Atlantic states have changed markedly in recent years. Before 1980, studies focused on the economic and institutional aspects of northern slavery and on the ideological dimensions of white opposition to slaveholding. Now, historians are studying the world slaves and free blacks made themselves and the social and familial contexts of their lives. See Bodle, "Themes and Directions," 382.

3 Schwarz, *Jarring Interest.* For Monmouth, see Hodges, *Slavery and Freedom.* Bronx County was not created until 1912. In this book, New York and Westchester Counties encompassed most of present-day Bronx. See Long, *New York*, 33.

4 My use of the words *paternalist* and *patriarchal* differs from those employed by historians of southern slavery, who employ such terms to describe economic behavior by masters toward slaves. For a review of the vast literature about such relationships, see Morris, "Articulation of Two Worlds." As shown in this book, master-slave relations in the North were additionally heavily affected by religion, ethnicity, and class, as well as time and place.

5 For discussion of tricksters in African culture, see Pelton, *Trickster in West Africa.* On slave culture, see Stuckey, *Slave Culture*, 3–98.

6 Fields, *Slavery and Freedom on the Middle Ground*, 40–63; Wade, *Slavery in the Cities.*

CHAPTER ONE

1 For Rodrigues and the Dutch explorers, see Hart, ed., *Prehistory of the New Netherland Company*, 17–39, 80–82. See also Bachman, *Peltries or Plantation*, 9, 62–63, 75, 80. For the trade agreement, see "Jacob Eelkens, Agreement with Indians," Mss. 14164, New York Colonial Documents, New York State Archives.

2 For Esteban Gomez, see Burrows and Wallace, *Gotham*, 11. For the importance of African seamen, see Rawley, *Transatlantic Slave Trade*, 29–31, 32–37, 82; Miller, "Congo-Angolan Slave Trade," 14–21; Berlin, *Many Thousands Gone.* John Thornton has reemphasized the Africanness of Atlantic Creoles and the prevalence of military experience among them in his "African Experience of the '20 and Odd Negroes' Arriving in Virginia in 1619," 421–22, 434.

3 Rink, *Holland on the Hudson*, 143–44.

4 Ibid., 144.

5 For previous treatments, see McManus, *History of Negro Slavery*, 13; Mc-Manus, *Black Bondage in the North*, 8; Higgenbotham, *In the Matter of Color*, 100-112; Goodfriend, "Burghers and Blacks"; Wageman, "Corporate Slavery in New Netherland"; Jordan, *White over Black*, 60. For an interesting discussion of whether the first blacks arrived in New Amsterdam in 1626 or several years later, see Swan, "First Africans."

6 Though I have occasional differences with his interpretations, I have benefited greatly from Ira Berlin's *Many Thousands Gone*, esp. chap. 2.

7 O'Callaghan, ed., *Laws and Ordinances*, 36-37; Kruger, "Born to Run," 48-50. For Angolan naming patterns, see Thornton, "Central African Names." For a brief description of these and other early black arrivals, see Dickenson, comp., "Abstracts of Early Black Manhattanites."

8 Stokes, *Iconography*, 4:94; Weslager, *English on the Delaware*, 70, 190-91. For Pavonia, see Jameson, ed., *Narratives*, 379, and Swan, "The Other Fort Amsterdam," 21-22.

9 Goodfriend, "Burghers and Blacks," 130-32; Swan, "The Other Fort Amsterdam," 29; Donnan, ed., *Documents*, 3:421, 429.

10 For general discussion of the massive powers that the West India Company held over white laborers, see Wright, "Local Government in Colonial New York," 18, 24-26. For private controls, see the many contracts in van Laer, ed., *Van Rensselaer Bowier Manuscripts*, 186-90, 288, 332, 678-82; Morris, *Government and Labor*, 441; Van Den Bogaart, "Servant Migration to New Netherland," 67-97.

11 Thornton, *Africa and Africans*, 74-79, 99-107; Iliffe, *African Poor*, 53; Gray, *Black Christians and White Missionaries*, 18-19; for lower servants, see Towner, *A Good Master*, 23-51.

12 "Records of the Old West India Company," no. 14, Vol. 80, folio 93, Amsterdam, on microfilm in Archives of the First West India Company, Inventory number 14, folio 93v., Algemeen Rijksarchief, the Hague. See also Berlin, *Many Thousands Gone*, 52. For report and payments, see Scott and Stryker-Rodda, eds., *New York Historical Manuscripts* 1:112, 123.

13 Van Laer, *Netherland Council Minutes*, 4:53, 61; Fernow, ed., *Minutes of the Orphanmasters Court*, 1:46.

14 Herskowitz, "Troublesome Turk"; Hoff, "Frans Abramse Van Sale."

15 On de Fries, see Cohen, *Ramapo Mountain People*, 27-30, and Hoff, "De Vries," 345-53. For a third free black, see Bergen, *Register*, 344-45. For Kieft's decree, see O'Callaghan, ed., *Laws and Ordinances*, 12.

16 For these and other cases, see O'Callaghan, ed., *Calendar of Historical Manuscripts*, 1:66, 89, 194-95, 198, 228.

17 See the excellent discussion in Berlin, *Many Thousands Gone*, 50. For rarity of landownership, see Thornton, *Africa and Africans*, 74-76.

18 For the Hog Island site, see Burrows and Wallace, *Gotham*, 32. Stokes, *Iconography*, 6:73-77, 120-24, 136-37. See Goodfriend, "Burghers and Blacks," 130, and Swan, "The Other Fort Amsterdam," 31-32.

19 Kruger, "Born to Run," 49; McManus, *History of Negro Slavery*, 13. See the discussion of this problem in Van Den Boogaart, "Servant Migration," 65–70.

20 See McManus, *History of Negro Slavery*, 11–12; *Docs. Rel.*, 1:415.

21 See O'Callaghan, ed., *Calendar of Historical Manuscripts*, 1:45, 87, 105, 242, 262, 269; *Docs. Rel.*, 1:302, 343. See also *Year Book of the Holland Society of New York, 1901*, 125–31. For emancipation of castle slaves at Elmina, see Postma, *Dutch in the Atlantic Slave Trade*, 54–55.

22 For discussion of these cases, see Kruger, "Born to Run," 52–53.

23 O'Callaghan, ed., *Calendar of Historical Manuscripts*, 1:269.

24 The deed is in Miscellaneous Real Estate Papers, Box 6, File 1, Trinity Church Archives. For other grants, see *Year Book of the Holland Society of New York, 1901*, 125–27, 129–31, and Gehring, ed., *New York Historical Manuscripts*, 36, 48, 55–56. Fourteen blacks received such grants in the late 1640s. For black female property holders, see Dickenson, comp., "Abstracts of Early Black Manhattanites."

25 Stokes, *Iconography*, 4:265–66. The others were Luycas Pieterse, Solomon Peters, Willem Antonio Portuguis, Manuel Sanders, Assento Angola, Antony Angola, Francisco Negro, Manuel Neger, and Anne Negrinne. For land claims, see ibid., 6:70–77, 120–44. See also Dickenson, comp., "Abstracts of Early Black Manhattanites."

26 Stokes, *Iconography*, 2:344–46, 6:73; *RNA*, 1:251, 346; O'Callaghan, *Laws and Ordinances*, 29, 89.

27 Merwick, *Possessing Albany*, 81–90; Agnew, *Worlds Apart*, 20–27, 32–34.

28 For a study of the symbolic values of markets in African society, see Belasco, *The Entrepreneur as Culture Hero*, 20–35, 77–84, 88–90, 120–24, and in African American society see Lhamon, *Raising Cain*, 2–4.

29 Ravenstein, ed., *Strange Adventures of Andrew Battel*, 43–44. John Ogilby, plagiarizing the work of Montanus and O. Dapper in the early 1670s, described Luanda: "It hath wide broad streets, of which the inhabitants take great care. They stand in great order and are neatly planted with Palmeto-Trees and Bananas . . . in the middle of which you come to a great Market-Place by which stands the King's Court." Luanda had many skilled artisans, including weavers, smiths, cap-makers, potters, bead-makers, fishermen, canoe-makers, merchants and traders. See Ogilby, *Africa*, 491–92, 499, 503. Dapper, *Description de l'Afrique*, 424–26, 490–566; De Carli, "Voyage," in Churchill, *Collection of Voyages*, 1:485. See also Birmingham, *Trade and Conflict*, 45, 183–210; Martin, *External Trade of the Loargo Coast*, 35–36; Law, *Slave Coast of West Africa*, 70–156.

30 Stokes, *Iconography*, 2:207,197, 4:88, 130, 193. This burying ground was uncovered during excavation for a new federal office building in 1991. For a discussion of the site and subsequent controversy, see *New York Times*, October 9, 1991, August 9, 1992, February 29, 1993; Hansen and McGowan, *Breaking Ground, Breaking Silence*, 1–23.

31 O'Callaghan, ed., *Calendar of Historical Manuscripts*, 1:74. For a similar case involving guilt by lot, see Christoph, Scott, and Stryker-Rodder, eds.,

New York Historical Manuscripts, 2:495–96. For a discussion of the male culture of taverns in early Dutch culture, see Spierenburg, "Knife-Fighting and Popular Codes of Honor in Early Modern Amsterdam," 112–17. For agreement on this form of cultural interplay, see Thornton, *Africa and Africans,* 191–95, 246–54.

32 For tavern laws, see *New York Colonial Documents,* 4:6, 27–29, 497. For African methods of proof, see Ravenstein, ed., *Strange Adventures of Andrew Battel,* 23, and Father Jerome Merolla da Sorrento, "A Capuchin and Apostolick Missioner in the Year 1682. A Voyage to Congo and Several other Countires Chiefly in Southern Africa," in Churchill, *Collection of Voyages,* 1:554–55. For the concept of agreement below the level of consciousness, see Mintz and Price, *Anthropological Approach,* 5–6. For African methods of determining guilt, see Ogilby, *Africa,* 491–92, and Ravenstein, ed., *Strange Adventures of Andrew Battel,* 59–61.

33 Kruger, "Born to Run," 45–46.

34 For marriages, see Goodfriend, "Black Families in New Netherland," 96–99. For baptisms, see "Reformed Dutch Church, New York, Baptisms, 1639–1800," 1:10–27. For the idea of self-sustaining families, see Thornton, *Africa and Africans,* 168.

35 For the use of selective adaptation and diversity of the colony, see Cohen, *Dutch-American Farm,* 15–19, 31, and Gray, *Black Christians and White Missionaries,* 4–6. Cohen does not make the argument about Africans used above. On baptisms, see Kruger, "Born to Run," 47–48.

36 Kruger, "Born to Run," 44–45, 51; Stokes, *Iconography,* 6:60–74; O'Callaghan, ed., *Calendar of Historical Manuscripts,* 1:222. See Christoph, Scott, and Stryker-Rodda, eds., *New York Historical Manuscripts,* 2:22–23, 256.

37 For this case, see O'Callaghan, ed., *Calendar of Historical Manuscripts,* 1:103. For a case involving a white man and black child, see Christoph, Scott, and Stryker-Rodda, eds., *New York Historical Documents,* 4:480–81. For a similar case involving a white sailor who was drowned in a sack in the river in 1660, see ibid., 1:211, 213. The orphan boy upon whom the crime was committed was flogged and transported. For Dutch precedent, see Schama, *Embarrassment of Riches,* 601. For Dutch preference for exemplary punishment, see Spierenburg, *Spectacle of Suffering,* 44–45, 56–58. For acceptance of cosmology in African judicial procedures, see Thompson and Cornet, *Four Moments of the Sun,* 40.

38 Gray, *Black Christians and White Missionaries,* 13–15; Thornton, *Africa and Africans,* 183–87.

39 Morgan, *American Slavery American Freedom;* Berlin, *Many Thousands Gone;* Blackburn, *Making of New World Slavery.* The best works on New Amsterdam are Goodfriend, "Burghers and Blacks," and Swan, "The Other Fort Amsterdam."

40 Davis, *Problem of Slavery in Western Culture,* 165–217; Jordan, *White over Black,* 18–19.

41 *Judgement of the Synode Holden at Dort.* For lack of law, see Watson, *Slave Law in the Americas,* 102–14. For apposite discussions of the Synod of Dort,

see Rink, *Holland on the Hudson*, 17–18; Smith, *Religion and Trade in New Netherland*, 60–64; Sprunger, *Dutch Puritanism*, 355–57; Old, *Shaping of the Reformed Baptismal Rite*, 216–27 and Patterson, *Slavery and Social Death*, 276.

42 Rink, *Holland on the Hudson*, 62. Perhaps the Gomarians would have been less supportive had they realized that the synod actually enhanced Arminian power by publicizing its theology among lay Christians. The cross-fertilization of English, Scottish, and Dutch pietism coalesced in the New World, affirming freedom of choice and individual conversion. These components of pietism stirred significant disagreements between company and settler policies over many issues, including slavery. See Martin, *Tongues of Fire*, 20–21.

43 For the Dutch on Catholicism, see Price, *Culture and Society in the Dutch Republic*, 27–34; Geyl, *Revolt of the Netherlands*, 1–26. Many slaves from the Spanish Caribbean were baptized. See Klein, "Anglicanism, Catholicism, and the Negro Slave," 137–90.

44 Klein, "Anglicanism, Catholicism, and the Negro Slave," 141–57; Thornton, *Africa and Africans*, 269; Schell, *Children of Bondage*, 333. Religious requirements for manumission have been studied more thoroughly elsewhere. For example, in Cape Town, South Africa, slaves followed a specific track of acculturation toward freedom. Requirements included fluency in Dutch and membership in the Dutch Reformed Church. Each freeman paid annual dues of one hundred florins. See Boeseken, *Slaves and Free Blacks at the Cape*, 81–82; Ross, *Cape of Torments;* Worden, *Slavery in Dutch South Africa*, 97, 143–44.

45 *Judgement of the Synode Holden at Dort*, 38–41.

46 Schell, *Children of Bondage*, 333. For the power of the patriarch in Dutch society, see Schama, *Embarrassment of Riches*, 388–89. For Puritan evocation of patriarchal power in the New World, see Norton, *Founding Mothers and Fathers*, especially her comments on maternal attitudes toward servants, 170–71, and as familial authorities, 289–95. For a master's power over servants, see Steinfeld, *Invention of Free Labor*, 56.

47 Schell, *Children of Bondage*, 332–35. For automatic emancipation in the Netherlands, see Drescher, "Long Goodbye," 49.

48 For pietist settlers, see Cohen, *Dutch-American Farm*, 16–18; Sprunger, *Dutch Puritanism*, 53, 111, 292–96, 364; van Laer, ed., *Documents Relating to New Netherland in the Henry E. Huntington Library*, 2; Pratt, *Religion, Politics and Diversity*, 3–24.

49 Smith, *Religion and Trade*, 126–27.

50 Udemans, *'t Geestelijk roer van't coopmans schip*. On Udemans, see Stoeffler, *Rise of Evangelical Pietism*, 126–27. For his popularity, see Tanis, *Dutch Calvinist Pietism*, 35.

51 *Docs. Rel.*, 1:302. For the company's response, see 1:343.

52 "Letter of Reverend Jonas Michaelius," in Jameson, ed., *Narratives*, 129.

53 See DeJong, *Dutch Reformed Church in the American Colonies*, 163–69, and

"Dutch Reformed Church and Negro Slavery in Colonial America." For hope of conversion, see *Ec. Rec.*, 1:142, 150. Despite this quote, there was little evidence to suggest that the Dutch Reformed schools provided much instruction to blacks. See Kirkpatrick, *Dutch Schools of New Netherland and Colonial New York*, 143–60.

54 Kruger, "Born to Run," 48; Cohen, "In Search of Carolus Africanus Rex"; Cohen, *Ramapo Mountain People*, chap. 2; *Ec. Rec.* 1:548, 554; Stokes, *Iconography*, 4:239.

55 For discussion of the conservatism of the Dutch Reformed Church in New Netherland, see Smith, *Religion and Trade*, 79–82, 131–55.

56 For discussion of the syncretic nature of religion in Kongo, see MacGaffey, *Religion and Society in Central Africa*, 200–208; Thornton, "The Development of an African Catholic Church in the Kingdom of the Kongo, 1491–1750," 152–57. For conversions in Africa, see De Carli, "A Voyage to Congo," in Churchill, *Collection of Voyages*, 1:491–503. On African Christianity before and during the process of enslavement, see Balandier, *Daily Life in the Kingdom of the Kongo*, 81; Thornton, "On the Trail of Voodoo: African Christianity in Africa and the Americas," 261–79.

57 R. R. F. F. Michelangelo and Denis De Carli, "A Voyage to Congo in the Years 1666 and 1667," in Churchill, *Collection of Voyages*, 1:492–93. For Pinkster in Dutch culture, see Schama, *Embarrassment of Riches*, 185–88.

58 For mention of Pinkster in 1628, see "Letter of Reverend Jonas Michaelius, 1628," in Jameson, ed., *Narratives*, 130. For mention in 1645, see *New York Colonial Documents*, 4:294.

59 *Ec. Rec.*, 1:488, 656–58; Stokes, *Iconography*, 4:130. For Pentecost in Africa, see Sorrento, "A Capuchin and Apostolick Missioner," in Churchill, *Collection of Voyages*, 1:573. For Pinkster in New Netherland, see Merwick, *Possessing Albany*, 74–76, and Cohen, *Dutch-American Farm*, 160–63. For Sabbath, see Solberg, *Redeem the Time*, 7–22. For discussion of masters' obligations to let slaves have holidays, see Klein, "Anglicanism, Catholicism, and the Negro Slave," 148–49, 151.

60 *Docs. Rel.* 1:123, 154, 162.

61 Postma, *Dutch in Atlantic Slave Trade*, 11–14; Kea, *Settlements, Trade and Politics*, 308–10.

62 Birmingham, *Trade and Conflict*, 44–48, 53–54, 62–63, 78–80, 88–90, 104; Thornton, *Kingdom of Kongo*, 6–10; Hilton, *Kingdom of Kongo*, 94–96, 141–62; Snelgrove, *New Account*, 72, 79, 159.

63 Goodfriend, "Burghers and Blacks," 132–34; Swan, "The Other Fort Amsterdam," 20; Postma, *Dutch in the Atlantic Slave Trade*, 10–12. For sales to Virginia, see Breen and Innes, "*Myne Owne Ground*," 70–71, and Matson, *Merchants and Empire*, 76.

64 O'Callaghan, ed., *Calendar of Historical Manuscripts*, 101–4, 127–29.

65 *Docs. Rel.*, 1:162, 364, 500, 302; Scott and Stryker-Rodda, eds., *New York Historical Manuscripts*, 2:58, 158. For conquest of Luanda, see Hilton, *Kingdom of Kongo*, 142–62; Postma, *Dutch in the Atlantic Slave Trade*, 17–18.

66 Matson, *Merchants and Empire*, 19–24, 26–29.

67 Kea, *Settlements, Trade and Politics*, 51–94, 105–8; Thornton, *Africa and Africans*, 180–91.

68 Donnan, ed., *Documents*, 3:410–11, 416–17; Goodfriend, "Burghers and Blacks," 128–29, 132; Kruger, "Born to Run," 35–36, 57. For discussion of the crime of kidnapping in its historical context and the 1652 incident in particular, see Riddell, "Observations on Slavery and Privateering," 337–40, 357–67.

69 Raesley, *Portrait of New Netherland*, 160–61.

70 *Docs. Rec.*, 9:31.

71 *Docs. Rel.*, 1:577–81, 2:1–4, 23–47.

72 Smith, *Religion and Trade*, 101–2, 113.

73 See Goodfriend, "Burghers and Blacks," 135–36; Matson, *Merchants and Empire*, 74–76; Curtin, *Atlantic Slave Trade*, 55, 117; Goslinga, *Dutch in the Caribbean*, 368–69; Boxer, *Dutch in Brazil*, 83–84. Johannes Postma argues that Curacao quickly became one of the most important slave depots in the New World. See his *Dutch in the Atlantic Slave Trade*, 19–20.

74 O'Callaghan, ed., *Calendar of Historical Manuscripts*, 1:275, 278, 289–90, 293, 295, 302, 307, 331–34; O'Callaghan, ed., *Voyages*, 100–120. For agreement on Stuyvesant's plans, see Emmer, "History of the Dutch Slave Trade," 734.

75 Rink, *Holland on the Hudson*, 163–64; Matson, *Merchants and Empire*, 76.

76 For development of Dutch slave trading, see Matson, *Merchants and Empire*, 76–78, 357 n. 6; Rawley, *Transatlantic Slave Trade*, 85–97; Goslinga, *Dutch in the Carribbean*, 344; Vogt, *Portuguese Rule on the Gold Coast*, 164–90; Van Den Boogaart and Emmer, "Dutch Participation in the Atlantic Slave Trade," 373.

77 Manning, "Slave Trade in the Bight of Benin, 1640–1890," in *Uncommon Market*, ed., Gemery and Hogendorn, 107–43; for certification of 153 male and 137 female slaves on August 14, 1664, see O'Callaghan, ed., *Voyages*, 8–12; see also Postma, *Dutch in the Atlantic Slave Trade*, 239–60.

78 Donnan, ed., *Documents*, 2:156–58, 213–14, 218, 371, 430, 474, 495, 504, 521. See also Berlin, *Many Thousands Gone*, 48.

79 *Docs. Rel.*, 1:122.

80 Van Laer, ed., *Correspondence of Jeremias van Rensselaer*, 167, 175.

81 For list of purchasers, see Donnan, ed., *Documents*, 3:428. For information on purchasers, see Stokes, *Iconography*, 2:308–9, 4:230, 236 and "Burghers and Freemen," 14, 19, 21, 25, 39, 42. For sale to De Decker, see *Wills*, 1:82–83. De Decker had to petition for ten of the slaves who were impounded by the new British government; whether he received them is unknown.

82 Goodfriend, "Burghers and Blacks," 142–43.

83 For the estimate of population, see Van Den Boogaart, "Servant Migration," 58. For conclusions about attractiveness of the colony, see Rink, *Holland on the Hudson*, 156–57. For slave societies and societies with slaves, see Berlin, *Many Thousands Gone*, 8. Berlin argues on page 50 that New Am-

sterdam rested on slave labor more than the Chesapeake colonies, a conclusion with which I concur.

84 For the agreement by the West India Company to provide to each patroon "twelve black men and women out of the prizes in which Negroes shall be found, for the advancement of the Colonies in New Netherland," see "New Project of Freedom and Exemptions," in *Docs. Rel.* 1:123, 154, 162, 364, 157, 500; and for the promise see *Ec. Rec.* 1:79. For the Virginia experience, see Morgan, *American Slavery American Freedom*, 108–96.

85 Berlin, "From Creole to African," and Berlin, *Many Thousands Gone*, 52–53.

86 For the continued effect of the Council of Dort, see Fabend, "Synod of Dort."

87 Kruger, "Born to Run," 52–55; Cohen, *Ramapo Mountain People*, chap. 2; "Bushwyck Town Records, 1660–1875," 7, 69, NYMA.

CHAPTER TWO

1 Jameson, ed., *Journal of Jasper Danckaerts*, 65; Christoph and Christoph, eds. *Andros Papers*, 1:350–51. For twenty-four blacks, see Scott and Stryker-Rodda, eds., *Denizations*, 86.

2 For confirmation, see Stokes, *Iconography*, 4:266; O'Callaghan, ed., *Calendar of New York Colonial Manuscripts*, 4, 29; and for Bergen, see Hodges, *Slavery, Freedom, and Culture*, 37. For the articles of capitulation, see *Docs. Rel.*, 2:250–53. For discussion of the transfer, see Smith, *History of the Province of New York*, 1:24–34; Ritchie, *Duke's Province* 1–24; Kammen, *Colonial New York*, 73–80. The following year an English Assembly composed of New Englanders who migrated to Long Island ratified the governor's laws concerning slavery with a proviso patterned after the Massachusetts law of 1641. See Jordan, *White over Black*, 84.

3 Kruger, "Born to Run," 55.

4 Herskovitz, "Troublesome Turk," 299–310; Hoff, "Swan Janse Van Luane."

5 Nordstrom, "Slavery in a New York County," 145–47. Old Tappan is on the northern edge of New Jersey; Tappan is now in Rockland County, New York.

6 For Roberts, see Wacker, *Land and People*, 203. For Jochem Antony, see *Year Book of the Holland Society of New York, 1915*, 62, 83. For the Van Doncks, see Durie, *Kakiat Patent*, 50–52. The Van Donck holdings lasted until well after the American Revolution.

7 *RNA*, 5:337, 340. For other cases involving blacks testifying, see *RNA*, 3:42, 5:172; 7:11.

8 "Records of Dominie Henricus Selijns of New York, 1686–1687," 13–14; *RNA*, 6:335; Hoff, "Colonial Black Family."

9 For Medford and Janse, see Kruger, "Born to Run," 592–94. See "Will of Mary Jansen Lockermans," July 22, 1678, Voorhees, ed., *Leisler Papers*, forthcoming, and Will of Christiana Cappoens, June 17, 1687, Maass Col-

lection, Fales Library, New York University. For Maude, see "Burghers and Freemen," 601.

10 For the changeover, see Burrows and Wallace, *Gotham*, 71–80.

11 *Colonial Laws* 1:18.

12 On Barbadian arrivals, see Pomfret, *Colonial New Jersey*, 29, and Wacker, *Land and People*, 191. For conditions in Barbados, see Rawley, *Transatlantic Slave Trade*, 85–92. For the rebellious nature of Barbadian slaves, see Beckles, *Black Rebellion in Barbadoes*, 25–52. See also Jordan, *White over Black*, 84.

13 Jordan, *White over Black*, 94–98; Fernow, ed., *Calendar of Council Minutes*, 55, 60–61, 89; Lauber, *Indian Slavery*, 113–17; Petition of Philip and Dego Degaue, two Negroes of the Spanish Main, Claiming to be Freemen, February 25, 1684, N.Y. Col. Mss., 21:121, and Petition to the Governor from the Mayor and Alderman of City of New York demanding the release of a free-born Indian woman, native of Curacoa, now held as a slave by Edward Antill, December 28,1701, N.Y. Col. Mss., 44:23; O'Callaghan, ed., *Calendar of Historical Manuscripts*, 2:81–82.

14 Order Respecting William Corwan, an alleged free mullatto, April 6, 1677, N.Y. Col. Mss., 26:49–51; O'Callaghan, ed., *Calendar of Historical Manuscripts*, 2:56; Christoph and Christoph, *Andros Papers*, 2:55–57. Little's testimony is the first recorded instance of a white sailor testifying for a black slave, evidence of the frequently noted affinity between sailors and slaves. For other cases, see Petition of Quamino, a free Negro, April 19, 1699, N.Y. Col. Mss. 42:177; O'Callaghan, ed., *Calendar of Historical Manuscripts*, 2:268; Christoph and Christoph, *Andros Papers*, 1:13; Bolster, *Black Jacks*, 15.

15 Morris, *Government and Labor*, 478. For inquests, see N.Y. Col. Mss., 17:9, and O'Callaghan, ed., *Calendar of Historical Manuscripts*, 2:117.

16 For sale, see Deed for Negro Woman and two children, Martha De Hart to Paulus Linhard, May 13, 1693; for inheritance, see William Lawrence Inventory, April 27, 1680; for wedding present, see Deed of Gift by William Sandford to Richard Berry and Nidernia Sandford, June 14, 1682, for ownership of Will and his wife, Nama, all in N-YHS.

17 Israel, *Dutch Primacy in the Seventeenth Century*, 239–40.

18 Thornton, *Kongolese Saint Anthony*, 10–31; Gray, *Black Christians and White Missionaries*, 19–22.

19 For neglect of New York and New Jersey by the Royal African Company, see Rawley, *Transatlantic Slave Trade*, 386; Davies, *Royal African Company*, 100; Lydon, "New York and the Slave Trade," 376. Curtin, *Atlantic Slave Trade*, 143, argues that "the safest course is simply to disregard the slave imports of the northern colonies." For New York merchants in the slave trade, see Matson, *Merchants and Empire*, 61.

20 For discussion of the Madagascar slave trade, see Ritchie, *Captain Kidd*, 112–14. See also Rawley, *Atlantic Slave Trade*, 11, 280–81, Curtin, *Atlantic Slave Trade*, 130, 144, 240–41; Judd, "Frederick Philipse and the Madagascar Trade"; Platt, "The East India Company and the Madagascar Trade";

Donnan, ed., *Documents*, 3:439–43; Matson, *Merchants and Empire*, 58–63. See also Depositions of William Johnson and Peter Lockcourt Concerning ye Ship Charles Being at & Coming from Guinny, 1685, National Archives, Mid-Atlantic Region, New York City. See also "Narrative of John Cruger," in Valentine, *Manual of the Corporation of the City of New York for 1853*, 406–8. For quote, see Van Cortlandt Letter Book, 1698–1700, N-YHS.

21 Kent, *Early Kingdoms in Madagascar*, 34–60.

22 Hodges, *Slavery and Freedom*.

23 For the social context of New York's growth, see Goodfriend, *Before the Melting Pot*; Kammen, *Colonial New York*, 73–100; Nash, *Urban Crucible*, 3–36; Archdeacon, *New York City*.

24 Goodfriend, *Before the Melting Pot*, 76; Kruger, "Born to Run," 128–34. A yellow fever epidemic in 1702 caused a drop in the black population of New York City from 700 in 1698 to 630 in 1703. See Duffy, *History of Public Health*, 1:54, 58, 69.

25 Goodfriend, *Before the Melting Pot*, 76; Archdeacon, *New York City*, 41, 51–52, 62, 89–90; Ritchie, *Duke's Province*, 150–52; Matson, *Merchants and Empire*, 137.

26 Donnan, ed., *Documents*, 3:444; Goodfriend, *Before the Melting Pot*, 113.

27 Barck, ed., *Papers of the Lloyd Family*, 1:109–10, 113, 115; Christoph and Christoph, eds., *Andros Papers*, 1:149–50, 230, 2:62, 88, 482. For Leisler, see Jacob Leisler v. Mark Cordea, October 15, 1679, *Leisler Papers*, forthcoming.

28 Chamberlain's Records for the City of New York, 1690–1700, Trinity Church Audit Book, 1696–1730, and John Abeel Account Book, 1697–99, Box 2, Neilson Papers, Alexander Library. For agreement about treatment, see Barck, ed., *Papers of Lloyd Family*, 1:105, 147, 161, 181, 187.

29 Morris, *Select Cases*, 237–40; Kruger, "Born to Run," 100–103. For the Meal Market, see *MCC, 1675–1776*, 1:458.

30 For the legislation, see *MCC, 1675–1776*, 1:136–37. For discussion of this action and others favoring whites, see Morris, *Government and Labor*, 182–84, and Hodges, *New York City Cartmen*, 25, 31, 35, 103, 152, 158–59. For the Leisler petition see Petition of Elsie Leysler on ye Behalf of her Husband Jacob Leysler, March 21, 1683/4, *Leisler Papers*, forthcoming.

31 Hodges, *New York City Cartmen*, 26; Morris, *Government and Labor*, 183. For the decision to use blacks on the construction project at Trinity Church, see First Recorded Minutes Regarding the Building of Trinity Church, 1695, Trinity Church Archives. For slave hire in the countryside, see John Bowne Account Book, 12, 20, 26, NYPL. For black apprentice, see "Burghers and Freemen," 569. See also Roediger, *Wages of Whiteness*, 19–43.

32 McManus, *Black Bondage in the North*, 208, 212; Wacker, *Land and People*, 191.

33 Kruger, "Born to Run," 150–56.

34 See Scot, *Model of Government*, 209–15; Pomfret, *Colonial New Jersey*, 22–31; Wacker and Clemens, *Land Use*, 89–92; Wacker, *Land and People*, 190–91; McManus, *Black Bondage in the North*, 41. Kim, *Landlord and Tenant*, 8–

15; Cohen, *Dutch-American Farm*, 74–76; Inventory of Lewis Morris, N.Y. Col. Mss, 14577. A student of Morris's early life in New Jersey notes that he arrived with thirty-eight to forty slaves in 1677, increasing that number by 50 percent by his death in 1691. See Strassburger, "Origins and Establishment of the Morris Family," 67. For Lewis Morris, the nephew, see his Account Book, 1690-98, NJA, and Miller, "Census of Fordham and Adjacent Places, 1698," 218–19. See *Wills*, 1:108 (John Lawrence), 181 (Lewis Morris), 317–18 (Thomas Noell), 322 (William Smith), 325 (Mathew Howell); and for James Graham, see *Docs. Rel.*, 4:847. For Mitchell Smith, see Monnette, *First Settlers*, 24; Wacker, *Land and People*, 263–64, 304–5, 377–78.

35 Landsman, *Scotland and Its First American Colony*, 72–99; Butler, *Huguenots in America*, 149–50.

36 Hodges, *Slavery and Freedom*, 16–20. See the lengthy discussion of the power of the family in New England slavery in Melish, *Disowning Slavery*, 26–34.

37 Kruger, "Born to Run," 90–94.

38 For the moderate size of Dutch slaveholding farms for this period, see ibid., 94–95, 128–40.

39 For New Jersey, see Pomfret, *Colonial New Jersey*, 22–92; Wacker, *Land and People*, 121–221; Landsman, *Scotland and Its First American Colony*, 31–163.

40 See also Pomfret, *Colonial New Jersey*, 9–11; Ryan, "Six Towns," 37–33; Wacker, *Land and People*, 126–30.

41 Goodfriend, *Before the Melting Pot*, 113.

42 Greenberg, *Crime and Law Enforcement*, 44–45.

43 For these incidents, see Stokes, *Iconography*, 4:27; *RNA*, 6:286; Minutes of the Mayor's Court, December 7, 1680, NYPL.

44 *MCC, 1675–1776*, 1:222–24, 276–77. See also Morris, *Select Cases*, 408–9.

45 Du Bois, *Souls of Black Folk*, 183–86.

46 *MCC, 1765–1776*, 1:277.

47 For "nations," see Thornton, "African Background to American Colonization," 59–60.

48 Uring, *History of the Voyages and Travels*, 46–47. For dancing and drinking in the West Indies during this period, see Ligon, *True and Exact History;* Bosman, *New and Accurate Description*, 189–91.

49 Solberg, *Redeem the Time*, 197–222; Sensbach, *Separate Canaan*, 6.

50 Kings County Court and Road Records, 41, 46–47, 60, 74–76, 81–82, NYMA. Miscellaneous Conveyances of Kings County, 3:70, NYMA.

51 "Minute Book of the New York Supreme Court of Judicature, April 4, 1693–April 1, 1701, 43, 113, 172, County Clerk's Office, New York City. For other cases Rex v. Peter Melott, August 1695; Rex v. Katherine Marchand, May 2, 1693; Rex v. Lydia Rose, May 2, August 3, 1693; Rex v. John Kissine, November 4, 1697; Rex v. Aron Cornelius Van Schaick, fined £5, May 3 and 4, 1698; Rex v. Francis Cooley, August 3, 1698; Rex v. Albertus Ringo and Richard Pleastead, fined 50 shillings each, February 8, 1699/1700; Rex v. John Gardner, August 6, 1706. Gardner was forced out of business. See later Rex v. Mary Lyndsey, August 2 and November 2, 1710; Rex v. Elizabeth Green for fencing and entertaining, November 8, 1710; Rex v. Elizabeth

Ranger, November 6, 1711, all in Court of Quarter Sessions, County Clerk's Office, New York City.

52 On thieving, see Bosman, *New and Accurate Description*, 116–18, 352–55, 427. On theft as social resistance, see Ray B. Kea, "I Am Here to Plunder on the General Road," in Crummey, *Banditing, Rebellion, and Social Protest*, 109–32.

53 On thieving, see Genovese, *Roll, Jordan, Roll*, 607–11. On Virginia, see Schwarz, *Twice Condemned*, 16–17. On effectiveness, see Greenberg, "Crime, Law Enforcement and Social Control in Colonial America," 300, 321.

54 For the New York City laws, see *MCC, 1675–1776*, 1:85–86, 93, 139. The first laws against trade were interspersed with injunctions against serving alcohol to blacks. For New Jersey legislation, see Leaming and Spicer, *Grants, Concessions*, 254–55. For New York law, see Lincoln, ed., *Colonial Laws of New York*, 1:157.

55 Greenberg, *Crime and Law Enforcement*, 115–17; Goebel and Naughton, *Law Enforcement in Colonial New York*, 705–7; N.Y. Col. Mss. 22:135, 140; Christoph, Scott, and Stryker-Rodda, eds., *New York Historical Manuscripts*, 1:495–96; Mayor's Court Minutes, April 16, 1679, September 21 and 23, 1680, as quoted in Peterson and Edwards, *New York City as an Eighteenth Century Municipality*, 198.

56 Lincoln, ed., *Laws of New York*, 1:157–58.

57 *Colonial Records of New York*, 122. In his proclamation Nicolls offered the first available description of a slave and his clothing: "The Negroe is a lusty young fellow about 20 years of age, hee was cloathed in a red waistecoat, a pair of linen breeches, somewhat worne, a grey felt hat, but no shoes or stockings." These hues and cries are collected in Hodges and Brown, eds., *"Pretends to Be Free,"* 321–29.

58 N.Y. Col. Mss., 28:129, 142, 38:3, 35:113.

59 N.Y. Col. Mss., 36:14.

60 For the Bergen County incident, see N.Y. Col. Mss., 29:218, and Christoph and Christoph, eds., *Andros Papers*, 3:395–96. For the Westchester incident, see Fox, ed., *Minutes of the Court of Sessions*, 66–67. For laws, see Leaming and Spicer, *Grants, Concessions*, 341–42. The act was passed in 1694, indicating that problems with hogreeves continued.

61 O'Callaghan, ed., *Calendar of Historical Manuscripts*, 2:270, 285, 289, 305, 371, 375, 383, 394, 409. See also Christoph and Christoph, eds., *Andros Papers*, 1:207–9; Barck, ed., *Papers of the Lloyd Family*, 144.

62 N.Y. Col. Mss., 28:127.

63 Lincoln, ed., *Colonial Laws of New York*, 1:157; Cooley, *Study of Slavery in New Jersey*, 32; McManus, *Black Bondage in the North*, 108–11.

64 Lincoln, ed., *Colonial Laws of New York*, 1:582–84, 880; Cornbury to Board of Trade, November 20, 1705, *Doc. Rel.*, 4:11, 168; N.Y. Col. Mss. 50:114, 134; Greenberg, *Law and Crime Enforcement*, 46.

65 Minute Book of the New York Supreme Court of Judicature, 1693–1701, 13, County Clerk's Office, New York City. See also Stokes, *Iconography*, 4:32, and McKee, *Labor in Colonial New York*, 43–144.

66 For the extensive powers of the local justices, see Greenberg, *Crime and Law Enforcement*, 34, 174–77; Goebel and Naughton, *Law Enforcement in Colonial New York*, 118, 120, 134, 425, 472–76. For such crimes, see, for example, N.Y. Col. Mss., 27:61, 86; O'Callaghan, *Calendar of Hisorical Manuscripts*, 1:259, 264; Christoph and Christoph, eds., *Andros Papers*, 2:291–92. For the Morris case, see Edsall, ed., *Journal of the Courts of Common Right*, 282–85.

67 Humphreys, *Account of the Endeavours*, 238–39.

68 Axtell, *Invasion Within;* Cressy, *Birth, Marriage and Death*, 98–100; Klingberg, *Anglican Humanitarianism*, 122–23.

69 On this point, see Washington, *Peculiar People*, 67–74, 96–97; Davis, *Problem of Slavery in Western Culture*, 210–22.

70 Godwyn, *Negro's & Indians Advocate*. On Godwyn, see Vaughan, *Roots of American Racism*, 55–82.

71 Lords Commissioners of Trade and Plantation to Archbishop of Canterbury, October 25, 1700, SPG Papers, Rhodes Library, Oxford Univrsity, 13:3–4; Extract from the Instructions to Earl Clarendon when Lord Cornbury & Governor of New York, January 1, 1702/3, SPG Letter Book B:1 (Appendix); *Ec. Rec.*, 2:954, 1034. For Puritan reservations, see Cressy, *Birth, Marriage and Death*, 111–13.

72 For the Dutch, see Balmer, *Perfect Babel*, 15, 25. For Whitsun, see Cressey, *Bonfires and Bells*, 6, 8. For the Anglicans and their frustrations, see Bonomi, *Under the Cope of Heaven*, 31, and Butler, *Awash in a Sea of Faith*, 101–5.

73 For Neau's background and published work, see Butler, *Huguenots in America*, 160–65. For the partnership, see Elias Neau and John Cruger Account Book, N-JHS.

74 For the radical quality of Huguenot beliefs, see Garrett, *Spirit Possession and Popular Religion*, 35–55. For quotes see Elias Neau to Treasurer, July 10, 1703, Lambeth Palace Papers, 13:28, Rhodes Library, Oxford University; Neau to Hodges, June 22, 1704, SPG Letter Book A II, 1, and Neau to John Chamberlayne, New York, June 22, 1707, A 3, 80, SPG Papers, Rhodes Library, Oxford University.

75 Neau to Secretary, February 27, 1709, Letter Book A 4:121A, July 5, 1709, Letter Book A 4:151, SPG Papers, Rhodes Library, Oxford University.

76 Neau to Woodward, September 15, 1704, Lambeth Palace Papers, 13:56–66, Rhodes Library, Oxford University.

77 Mbiti, *African Religions and Philosophies*, 3–5, 20, 30–33, 36–43, 50–88, 93; Sobel, *Trabelin' On*, 14–15, 22–37; Hefner, "Rationality of Conversion," 22; Raboteau, *Slave Religion*, 87–89. For priest figures and prayer in African culture, see Hale, *Scribe, Griot, and Novelist*, 32–37, and Horton, "African Conversion," 87–88.

78 Hefner, "Rationality of Conversion," 28.

79 See Linebaugh, "All the Atlantic Mountains Shook," and Sobel, *Trabelin' On*, 35–37, for the formation of pidgin language and preservation of African cultures. See Elias Neau to Treasurer, April 15, 1704, A 13:48; SPG Papers, Rhodes Library, Oxford University.

80 For bureaucratic infighting, see Vesey to Secretary, October 26, 1704, Let-

ter Book A 2: 35–36, SPG Papers, Rhodes Library, Oxford University. For Neau's concern about language, see ibid., 13:65–66. For African perceptions of the relations of priests and kings, see Hale, *Scribe, Griot, and Novelist*, 28–29.

81 Translation of Elias Neau to John Chamberlayne, New York, October 3, 1705, in Letter Book A 2 124–26, SPG Papers, Rhodes Library, Oxford University.

82 Neau to Secretary, April 30, 1708, Letter Book A 2:167, ibid. For examples of popular prejudice toward slave baptism at this time, see *Journal of the Life of Thomas Story*, 176–77; John Cotton to Unknown Minister, September 9, 1699, Pierpont Morgan Library. Cotton may have been opposed for personal reasons. In 1711, he wrote the Reverend Rowland Cotton that "Negroes and other servants grow so intolerant that I am afraid what the issue will be" (John Cotton to Rowland Cotton, October 27, 1711, ibid.). For English cases, see Shyllon, *Black People in Britain*, 17–19.

83 Klingberg, *Anglican Humanitarianism*, 127, 130, 132.

84 Trott, ed., *Laws of the British Plantations*, 257; *Colonial Laws of New York*, 1:597–98; *Ec. Rec.*, 3:1673; *Journal of the Legislative Council*, 1:243–45; McManus, *Black Bondage in the North*, 101–2. Neau forwarded the laws to the SPG secretary, offering hope that it would "help the instruction of slaves." See Neau to Secretary, July 22, 1707, Letter Book A 3, 80, SPG Papers, Rhodes Library, Oxford University.

85 Secretary to Neau, June 3, 1707, Lambeth Palace Papers, 14:2, Rhodes Library, Oxford University.

86 Fleetwood, *Relative Duties of Parents and Children*, 273, 277, 289. I am interpreting Fleetwood's message very differently than Butler does in *Awash in a Sea of Faith*, 135–38, 141–42.

87 Gray, *Black Christians and White Missionaries*, 22–26.

88 Neau to Chamberlayne, New York, August 24, 1708, Letter Book A 4, 68, SPG Papers, Rhodes Library, Oxford University.

89 Neau to Secretary, n.d. (1715), Letter Book A 10:162–64, 196–98, ibid.

90 Secretary to Neau, May 24, 1711, Lambeth Palace Papers, 14:248; Neau to Secretary, February 21, 1712, Letter Book A 7:143–46, SPG Papers, Rhodes Library, Oxford University.

91 Neau to Secretary De La Matre, n.d. (1713), Letter Book A 8:42; Neau to Mr. Chamberlayne, September 2, 1713, Letter Book A 8:41, SPG Papers, Rhodes Library, Oxford University.

92 Butler, *Awash in a Sea of Faith*, 129–63.

93 Hodges, *Slavery, Freedom, and Culture*, 37; Balmer, *Perfect Babel*, 101; Neau to Secretary, August 5, 1708, Letter Book A 3:128, SPG Papers, Rhodes Library, Oxford University.

94 Bush, comp., *Laws of the Royal Colony of New Jersey*, 2:28–30. In 1709 the Privy Council disallowed a New Jersey law of 1708 requiring castration for black rapists, noting that such punishment "was never allowed by or known in the Laws of this Kingdom." For the Privy Council action, see Lords of Trade to Governor Hunter, December 23, 1709, *Docs. Rel.*, 5:57. For discus-

sion of Privy Council actions toward excessively severe punishments, see Russell, *Review of American Colonial Legislation*, 144–47.

95 Letter first published in *New York Genealogical and Biographical Record* 22 (1891): 128. For another Anglican view, see Mr. Urquhart to the Secretary, February 4, 1707/8, Letter Book A 3:176, SPG Papers, Rhodes Library, Oxford University.

96 *Docs. Rel.*, 5:39. See also *Boston Weekly News-Letter*, February 9, 23, 1708.

97 Aptheker, *American Negro Slave Revolts*, 109.

98 *Journal of the Legislative Council*, 1:269–71, 274; McKee, *Labor in Colonial New York*, 149–50.

99 Donnan, ed., *Documents*, 1:398.

100 John Sharpe to [secretary], New York, June 23, 1712, Letter Book A 7:215–18, SPG Papers, Rhodes Library, Oxford University. For Coromantine use of priests, see Bosman, *New and Accurate Description*, 151. For a full description, see Governor Hunter to Lords of Trade, June 23, 1712, *Docs. Rel.*, 5:340–42. Elias Neau also wrote a full account of the uprising, but unfortunately that letter is lost. See Neau to Secretary, October 15, 1712, Letter Book A 7:39, SPG Papers, Rhodes Library, Oxford University. For agreement on the importance of ethnicity, see Goodfriend, *Before the Melting Pot*, 122.

101 See Neau to Secretary, October 15, 1712, Letter Book A 7:39, SPG Papers, Rhodes Library, Oxford University. For the 1712 revolt, see Scott, "Slave Insurrection." For the grand jury proceeding, see New York City Coroner's Jury, Verdict of the Jury that Adrian Hooglandt Died from Wounds Inflicted by certain Named Negro Slaves during the Insurrection of April 7, Signed by the Coroner and Jury, April 9, 1712, NYPL. See Jordan, *White over Black*, 105.

102 For these actions, see Hunter to Lords of Trade, June 23, 1712, *Docs. Rel.*, 5:341–42; *Journal of the Legislative Council*, 1:333–34; Scott, "Slave Insurrection," 63–66; N.Y. Col. Mss. 58:24–25, New York State Library, and Lustig, *Robert Hunter*, 103–6.

103 For the queen's pardon, see Sainsbury et al., eds. *Calendar of State Papers*, 33:37, 71.

104 Hunter to Lords of Trade, July 18, 1713, *Docs. Rel.*, 5:367.

105 For the acts, see *Colonial Laws of New York*, 1:761–67; Allinson, ed., *Acts of the General Assembly*, 18–22; Bush, comp., *Laws of the Royal Colony*, 2:136–40. For the Hunter quote, see *Journal of the Legislative Council*, 1:333. For comments, see Baseler, *"Asylum for Mankind,"* 78–79. Localities also adopted severe restrictions. See, for example, the New Brunswick Statute Book, 1733–1745, Alexander Library. For historical views on restrictions occasioned by the slave revolt, see Scott, "Slave Insurrection," 71–72; McManus, *History of Negro Slavery*, 80–82, 125; Zilversmit, *First Emancipation*, 3–33; Greenberg, *Crime and Law Enforcement*, 33. For New Jersey's laws, see Pomfret, *Colonial New Jersey*, 92–93; Cooley, *Study of Slavery in New Jersey*, 32–35; Price, *Freedom Not Far Distant*, 1–15.

106 For the paucity of manumissions before 1712, see Kruger, "Born to Run," 593, indicating eighteen manumissions between 1669 and 1712. Soderlund, *Quakers and Slavery*, 119, notes that in 1720, John Lippincott, a Shrewsbury Quaker, was the first to manumit his slave by will; by 1739, four of ten Quakers had freed slaves in wills. In contrast, only one non-Quaker, a French Protestant, freed his slaves before 1739.

107 Berlin, *Many Thousands Gone*, 56.

CHAPTER THREE

1 Sam's petition is quoted in full in Morgan, *Slavery in New York*, 11–12. For proof of this freedom, see Minutes of the Quarter Sessions, May 3, 1715–February 1, 1721, Columbia University Special Collections, November 6, 1717.

2 For the letter to Hunter, see *Docs. Rel.*, 5:457. For Norton's will, see *Wills*, 2:151. For the effect of Sam's petition, see Parish Transcripts, September 5, 1717, Folder 158, N-YHS, and Sainburg et al., eds., *Calendar of State Papers*, 49.

3 For the bond by Ellison and Slow, see Minutes of the General Quarter Sessions of the Peace, November 6, 1717, County Clerk's Office, New York City. For a similar case, see Parish Transcripts, June 15, 1725, Folder 154, N-YHS.

4 The churchwardens' accounts for New York City show one grant in 1738 of £1, 16 shillings, 3 pence for a "negro wench." See Audited Accounts of Church Wardens of New York City, Received and Disbursed for the Minister and Poor-House, 1714, 1723–26, 1738, N-YHS. See also Scott, "Church Wardens and the Poor."

5 *Wills*, 2:293. See also Goodfriend, *Beyond the Melting Pot*, 116. For a full list of recipients of poor relief mentioning a few blacks, see Scott, "Church Wardens and the Poor," 53–54. For other free blacks, see Klingberg, *Anglican Humanitarianism*, 137, and *New-York Weekly Journal*, September 6, 1736.

6 Durie, *Kakiat Patent*, 50–51; Cohen, *Ramapo Mountain People*, 36–39.

7 Wills, 3:72. For Woglum baptisms, see "Baptismal Record of Church Protestant Lutheran Congregation," 44. For other emancipations, see *Wills* 3:72, 244.

8 *Wills*, 3:92.

9 *Wills*, 6:53–54.

10 *Wills*, 2:6, 40, 75.

11 Yoshpe, "Records of Slave Manumission," 82.

12 *Wills*, 2:213-14, 3:379; Narrett, *Inheritance and Family Life*, 85–88, 186–92.

13 *Wills*, 7:179–81, 8:32.

14 *Wills*, 2:304, 364, 372, 3:26, 36; for Robert Field, see *Wills*, 3:174–75. See also *Wills*, 5:99, 159, 293, 6:1, 258, 7:173, 8:11, 86, 118, 327, 335; See also Robert G. Livingston to Henry J. Livingston, June 18, 1751, 55, N-YHS.

15 N.Y. Col. Mss., 50:115, 134, 54:21. For Archer's later adventures with the law, see Goebel and Naughton, *Law Enforcement in Colonial New York*, 279, 752. For further discussion of this case, see Goodfriend, *Before the Melting Pot*, 124-25. For the murder of the Hallet family, see Chapter 2.

16 *Acts of the General Assembly of the Province of New-Jersey*, 45, 60-65, 68, 81, 135, 183.

17 Davis, "New York's Long Black Line"; Wacker, *Land and People*, 190-93; McManus, *History of Negro Slavery*, 197; Wells, *Population of the British Colonies*, 112-14, 133-34.

18 Yearly increases in many counties were substantial. The black population in Queens County increased over 8 percent annually. In New York County, it jumped by almost 6 percent each year between 1703 and 1723. For a full account, see Appendix Table 1. Even between 1731, the year of a devastating smallpox epidemic, and 1737, the county saw increases of 1.5 percent annually. See Duffy, *History of Public Health*, 1:54, 58, 69.

19 Kruger, "Born to Run," 131; Wacker, *Land and People*, 190. For Boston traders, see Sanbom, "Angola and Elizabeth."

20 See Appendix Table 1 and McManus, *Black Bondage in the North*, 208-9, 212-13.

21 Berlin, *Many Thousands Gone*, 184-85.

22 Kruger, "Born to Run," 128; Berlin, *Many Thousands Gone*, 184. Du Bois, *Black North*, 5.

23 Kruger, "Born to Run," 133-38; Wacker, *Land and People*, 191-92, 201; Wells, *Population of the British Colonies*, 122-23, 138-40.

24 Kruger, "Born to Run," 200-261; Nash and Soderlund, *Freedom by Degrees*, 23-25, 28-29.

25 Kruger, "Born to Run," 262-87.

26 Ibid., 320-60.

27 See the excellent discussion of this ibid., 180-84. For a sophisticated discussion of slave families in a southern county with conditions similar to the New York region, see Stevenson, *Life in Black and White*.

28 The Reverend Robert Jenney to the Secretary, November 19, 1725, Letter Book A 19:187-90; Neau to Secretary, July 2, 1718, Letter Book A 13:397, SPG Papers, Rhodes Library, Oxford University; Sharpe, "Reverend John Sharpe's Proposals," 354-57.

29 Ekechin, "African Polygamy and Western Christian Ethnocentrism," 329-51; Berlin, *Many Thousands Gone*, 189, cites an Anglican chaplain who complained that black people shunned Christianity "because of their polygamy contracted before baptism where none or neither of the wives also will accept divorce."

30 Kruger, "Born to Run," 425-27, 592-93; McKee, *Labor in Colonial New York*, 133.

31 Wells, *Population of the British Colonies*, 116-17, 135. For a very different conclusion on family development, see Kruger, "Born to Run," 133-34. For percentages, see Wacker, *Land and People*, 190; Davis, "New York's Long Black Line," 44, 49, 52-53. For growth in South Carolina, see Menard, "Afri-

canization of the Lowcountry Labor Force"; Kulikoff, "Origins of Afro-American Society."

32 *Asiento;* Rawley, *Transatlantic Slave Trade,* 67–69; Goslinga, "Curacao as a Slave-Trading Center."

33 Lydon, "New York and the Slave Trade"; Donnan, ed., *Documents,* 3:511–12; Wax, "Preferences for Slaves in Colonial America," 380.

34 *Journal of the Legislative Council,* 433–34.

35 For New York trade patterns, see Steele, *English Atlantic,* 68–70. On Barbados, see Beckles, *White Servitude and Black Slavery;* Dunn, "Servants and Slaves," 164–66, 173–75. For Africanity, see Patterson, *Sociology of Slavery,* 113–32, 160–99. For revolts, see *Genuine Narrative of the Intended Conspiracy of the Negroes at Antigua;* Craton, *Testing the Chains,* 67–81, 105, 140; Gaspar, *Bondsmen and Rebels.*

36 For delivery of slaves in small parcels, see Minchton, "Slave Trade of Bristol," 42. For discussion of heavy mortality, see Dunn, "Servants and Slaves," 174–75; Sheridan, *Sugar and Slavery.* For discussion of the youthfulness of New York slave imports, see Rawley, *Transatlantic Slave Trade,* 390–91.

37 *Letters of Isaac Bobin,* 39, 96, 116, 143, 148, 152; O'Callaghan, ed., *Calendar of Historical Manuscripts,* 2:452–54, 476–81, 490, 496. See also "Cadwallader Colden Papers," 1:39, 8:183, 198, 200, 202, 9:157.

38 Bolster, *Black Jacks,* 7–44.

39 Donnan, ed., *Documents,* 3:464, 472. Lydon, "New York and the Slave Trade," expands on Donnan, finding additional voyages from Africa but none of over a hundred slaves. The *Dragon* arrived on August 23 with 106 slaves, the *Postillion* on September 12 with 100, and the *Catherine and Mary* the same day with 60. Identification of the origin of the Madagascar slaves comes from Elias Neau to Secretary, June 22, 1721, Letter Book A 15:95, SPG Papers, Rhodes Library, Oxford University. See also Matson, *Merchants and Empire,* 148.

40 Nathan Simpson Letter Books, C104–14, 85, PRO. For extensive research into the PRO records of slave trading by New York merchants, see Matson, *Merchants and Empire,* 60–62, 202–3. For a discussion of the limited role of Jewish merchants in the slave trade, see Faber, *Jews, Slaves, and the Slave Trade,* 132–35.

41 Harrison, "Observations Humbly," Bodleian Library.

42 Donnan, ed., *Documents,* 479; Lydon, "New York Slave Trade," 382. On rise of the African trade, see Matson, *Merchants and Empire,* 142–45, 202–3.

43 Donnan, ed., *Documents,* 492, 511.

44 Christopher Bancker Ledger Book, 196, N-YHS; Levitt, *For Want of Trade,* 96, 105; David Provoost Duty Statement, State Historical Society of Wisconsin; Donnan, ed., *Documents,* 3:492, 511; Log of the Ship *Catherine,* 1733, N-JHS. For this method of slave trading, see Manning, *Slavery, Colonialism, and Economic Growth,* 30–40.

45 Rawley, *Transatlantic Slave Trade,* 166–68, 387–90.

46 Manning, *Slavery, Colonialism, and Economic Growth,* 30–34; Miller, *Way of Death,* 10, 24, 277–79; Rawley, *Transatlantic Slave Trade,* 109–23; Inikori,

ed., *Forced Migration;* Lovejoy, "Volume of the Atlantic Slave Trade," 473–501. Lovejoy argues that the Bight of Benin and Angola were especially important for the period 1711–40.

47 *New-York Gazette,* April 22–29, 1734. Very few convicts were brought into New York. See Ekirch, *Bound for America,* 112–13.

48 For analysis of the social changes in Africa, see Flynn, *Asante and Its Neighbors,* 20–44; Searing, *West African Slavery;* Miller, *Way of Death,* 140–73. For the character of the mid-Atlantic population, see Berlin, *Many Thousands Gone,* 191.

49 McManus, *History of Negro Slavery,* 29–30; Nash, *Urban Crucible,* 107.

50 Kruger, "Born to Run," 200–206; Barck, ed., *Papers of the Lloyd Family,* 1:234, 258, 310–11, 368. For prices, see Zilversmit, *First Emancipation,* 232–33.

51 On New Jersey farms, see Wacker and Clemens, *Land Use in Early New Jersey,* 143, 208, and Berlin, *Many Thousands Gone,* 177–79, 184. On urban skills, see McManus, *History of Negro Slavery,* 46; Nash, *Urban Crucible,* 108–10. For runaway advertisements, see Hodges and Brown, eds. *"Pretends to Be Free,"* 3–17; for Lloyd slaves, see Barck, ed., *Papers of the Lloyd Family,* 2:261 (Jack), 560–61 (carpenter).

52 McManus, *History of Negro Slavery,* 49; for cartmen, see Hodges, *New York City Cartmen,* 35.

53 Barck, ed., *Papers of the Lloyd Family,* 1:261; for Aurelia, see ibid., 258, 277, 282–83, 307.

54 Neau did not reveal Vesey's reaction for several years until a serious dispute arose between them. See Elias Neau to Mr. Taylor, December 6, 1715, Letter Book A 11:293–94, SPG Papers, Rhodes Library, Oxford University. See also Neau to Secretary, June 22, 1721, Letter Book A 15:95; Neau to Secretary, April 2, 1722, Letter Book A 16:196, and Neau to Secretary De La Matre, n.d. (1713), Letter Book A 8:42, ibid. In 1717 Vesey tried unsuccessfully to fire Neau. For memorials defending Neau see Letter Book A 13:44, 48 (1718) and Governor Robert Hunter and Nine Clergy on Behalf of Neau, July 2, 1718, Letter Book A 13:424, ibid. For Neau's own defense, see Neau to Secretary, July 2, 1718, Letter Book A 13:397, ibid.

55 Sharpe, "Reverend John Sharpe's Proposals," 348–58.

56 Rev. James Wetmore to Secretary, December 3, 1726, Letter Book A 19:190–94, 395–96, SPG Papers, Rhodes Library, Oxford University.

57 Rev. Thomas Stoddard to Secretary, October 1725, Letter Book A 19:404–6; Stoddard to Secretary, November 5, 1729, Letter Book B 1:Appendix A; Rev. James Wetmore to David Humphreys, February 30, 1727, Letter Book A 30:207–20, ibid.

58 Neau did not free his slave in his will. See *Wills* 2:254–55.

59 Rev. William Vesey to Secretary, December 20, 1726, Letter Book A 19:421–22, SPG Papers, Rhodes Library, Oxford University. For Wetmore's appointment, see Vesey to the Society, November 16, 1724, Letter Book A 18:201–2; Mr. Wetmore to Society, November 7, 1724, Letter Book A 18:202–6, ibid. For his brief experience at Trinity, see Mr. Wetmore to the

Society, May 14, 1725, Letter Book A 19:262, and William Vesey to the Society, July 5, 1726, Letter Book A 19:170–72, ibid.

60 See William Vesey to Secretary, December 26, 1726, Letter Book A 19:421–22; Rev. Thomas Colgan to Secretary, January 23, 1726/27, Letter Book A 19:430–31; Colgan to Secretary, July 1731, Letter Book A 23:330–36; Rev. Richard Charleton to Secretary, June 5, 1733, Letter Book A 24:462, ibid.

61 John Thomas to Secretary John Chamberlayne, Hempstead, June 12, 1709, in Letter Book A 5:9; see also Mr. Muirston to Secretary, January 9, 1707/08, Letter Book A 3:168, ibid.

62 Humphreys, *Account*, 27–30.

63 Charleton to Philip Bearcroft, New York, November 11, 1740, and Charleton to Bearcroft, New York, October 30, 1741, as quoted in Klingberg, *Anglican Humanitarianism*, 144–45. For comment on servants, see McKendrick, Brewer, and Plumb, *Birth of a Consumer Society*, 58–59.

64 Rev. Richard Charleton to Society, March 28, 1743, Letter Book B 11:146; Charleton to Society, September 30, 1743, Letter Book B 11:147; Charleton to Society, March 26, 1745, Letter Book B 13:217, 219, SPG Papers, Rhodes Library, Oxford University. Charleton baptized nine blacks in thirty years in Staten Island. See Davis et al., *Church of St. Andrew Richmond*, 128–29.

65 Hodges, *Slavery and Freedom*, 70–72; Soderlund, *Quakers and Slavery*, 112–48.

66 For Arie Van Guinee and his family, see Hodges, "The Pastor and the Prostitute."

67 Kenn Stryker-Rodda, "Baptisms of the Lutheran Church of New York City," *New York Genealogical and Biographical Record* (1967–72), 97–102; "First Communions in the Lutheran Church of New York City, 1704–1769," *New York Genealogical and Biographical Record* 104 (1973): 28–52, 109–15, 181–86, 212–14. See also Hodges, "The Pastor and the Prostitute."

68 Thorpe, "Chattel with a Soul." For a general history of black Moravians, see Sensbach, *Separate Canaan*. For the concept of interracial communities, see Sensbach, "Interracial Sects."

69 Pointer, *Protestant Pluralism and the New York Experience*, 15–27; Balmer, *Perfect Babel of Confusion*, 72–99; Bonomi, *Under the Cope of Heaven*, 73–74.

70 For religious divisions between governor and citizens in New York, see Goodfriend, "Social Dimensions of Congregational Life in Colonial New York City," 255. For Dutch pietism and isolation, see Tanis, "Reformed Pietism in Colonial America," 48–56.

71 Weiser, *Handbook of Christian Feasts*, 246–54.

72 Bernard, "Die Pinksterfees in Die Kerklike Jaar," 14–22, 24–25, 32, 40, 45–46, 48, 54, 57.

73 Ibid., 106.

74 *New-York Weekly Journal*, March 7, 14, 21, 18, 1737. See also Dom Rex v. Mary Holst, November 4, 1718, Court of General Quarter Sessions, *New-York Weekly Journal*, June 12, 1738. For agreement on the concept of African "nations," see Berlin, *Many Thousands Gone*, 189–90.

75 See Thornton, *Africa and Africans*, 184–204; Gray, *Black Christians and White Missionaries*, 13–15.

76 Minutes of the Quarter Sessions, November 6, 1717, April 5, 1719, Columbia University Rare Book Room. For the increase in whippings, see McKee, *Labor in Colonial New York*, 133–34.

77 Queen v. Mary Wakeum, August 4, 1714, Court of Quarter Sessions, County Clerk's Office, New York City. See also indictments of John Webb, victualler, May 6, 1713; Queen v. John MacCloud, August 2, 1715; Queen v. "Doctor Peter," August 2, 1715; Queen v. Winnifred Douglass, August 6, 1718; Queen v. Thomas Codman, William Carr, Isiah Bartless, and Jacob Garriott, August 6, 1718; Queen v. Mary Holst, November 4, 1718, and February 4, 1719, for receiving stolen rings and other gold items; King v. Judith Peters, November 4, 1724; King v. John Wallace, May 4, 1737, all in Court of General Quarter Sessions, County Clerk's Office. See also Morris, *Select Cases*, 327–29, and Conroy, *Public Houses*, 125–26.

78 Greenberg, *Crime and Law Enforcement*, 59, 74. For the proclamation, see A Law for Regulating Negroes and Slaves in the Night Time, April 22, 1731, Broadside Collection, NYPL.

79 For accounts of this conspiracy, see *Weekly Rehearsal*, February 11, April 8, 1734; *New-York Weekly Journal*, March 25, 1734; *American Weekly Mercury*, March 5, 1734. For discussion that stealing worked to the advantage of slave masters by reinforcing negative stereotypes and accommodation, see Genovese, *Roll, Jordan, Roll*, 599–610.

80 *MCC, 1675–1776*, 3:254; Kruger, "Born to Run," 331–34.

81 *New-York Weekly Gazette*, November 30–December 7, December 13–20, 1730. For the influence of this rumor in the Antigua revolt of 1737, see *New-York Weekly Gazette*, March 22–28, 1737.

82 *Boston Weekly News-Letter*, January 18–25, 1739; *New-York Weekly Journal*, January 19, 1739.

83 *Pennsylvania Gazette*, February 28–March 7, 1738. For the executions, see *Boston Evening Post*, June 19, 1738. For the deadly impact of the trial on a small boy, see *Pennsylvania Gazette*, June 8–15, 1738.

84 *New-York Weekly Gazette*, January 21–28, 1734; *New-York Weekly Journal*, January 28, 1734. For punishment of whites, see Greenberg, *Crime and Law Enforcement*, 110–11. The issue became embroiled in the Zenger controversy. See *New York Gazette*, January 21–February 4, February 11–18, 1734; *New-York Weekly Journal*, January 28, February 4, 1734.

85 For Virginia, see *New-York Weekly Gazette*, November 30–December 7, December 13–30, 1730. For maroonage, see *New-York Weekly Gazette*, October 16–23, 1732; *New-York Weekly Journal*, March 11, 1734, May 3–10, 1734; extensive coverage of attempts to suppress slave rebellions in St. John's and Jamaica and Spanish efforts to aid blacks in *New-York Weekly Gazette*, September 23–30, 1734, and *New-York Weekly Journal*, October 14, 1734, May 28, 1739. For reports of impregnable slave forts, see *New-York Weekly Gazette*, November 25–December 2, 1734. For the Antigua revolt, see lengthy discussions in *New-York Weekly Gazette*, February 22–March 1,

1737, and *New-York Weekly Journal,* April 4, 11, 25, 1737. For reports of a slave ship insurrection, see *New-York Weekly Gazette,* December 13–30, 1730, September 4–11, 1732; *New-York Weekly Journal,* July 29, 1734.

86 For quote see Horsmanden, *Journal,* 27. For the Hackensack conspiracy, see *Minutes of the Justices and Freeholders of Bergen County,* 36–40. For Essex County, see Hatfield, *History of Elizabeth, New Jersey,* 364. For Clarke's letter, see *Journal of the Commissioners for Trade and Plantations,* 49, 396, 400, 412; CO 5/1086; CO 5/1194, PRO; Extract of a Letter from Mr. Clarke . . . to the Board of Trade, June 20, 1741, CO 5/1086, no. 26, and Minutes of the Council, April 11, 1741, CO 5/1194, pp. 83, 92–97, PRO.

87 CO 5/1086, p. 26; CO 5/1126, pp. 67–68, 93, 106–13; CO 5/1213, pp. 68, 76, PRO. See also *Ec. Rec.,* 4:2356–57, 2363–65. For Clarke's shaky position in local politics, see Bonomi, *Factious People,* 132–35.

88 Horsmanden, *Journal.*

89 See Du Bois, *Economic Co-Operation among Negro Americans,* 25; Launitz-Shurer, "Slave Resistance in Colonial New York"; Davis, *Rumor of Revolt;* Davis, "These Enemies of Their Own Household"; Burrows and Wallace, *Gotham,* 159–64; Du Bois, *Black North,* 14.

90 Davis, *Rumor of Revolt,* 265–68. For discussion of popular culture present in Horsmanden, *Journal,* see Launitz-Shurer, "Slave Resistance in Colonial New York," 146–48. See also Rediker and Linebaugh, "Many-Headed Hydra," 225–52.

91 See Horsmanden, *Journal,* 59, 106, 135, 205, 208, for Christmas meetings; 68, 94 for Easter; 130, 131, 163 for Whitsuntide. Virtually every confession included narration of past visits to ceremonies at Hughson's. For some of the most evocative, see ibid., 71–72, 83–86, 91–93, 131, 149, 158–59, 160–61, 206.

92 Horsmanden, *Journal,* 117, 147, 159, 179–86. For sales to Nicholas Bayard and Cornelius Brower, see Christopher Bancker Ledger Book, 196, 204, 206, 210–11, N-YHS. For slave participation in the 1741 insurrection, see Horsmanden, *Journal,* 48, 133, 257.

93 Horsmanden, *Journal,* 350–51, 383–86.

94 For extended descriptions of baptisms, see the trial of John Ury, ibid., 338–75.

95 Clarke to Board of Trade, August 24, 1741, CO 5/1059 part 2, Bundle 66, PRO.

96 Horsmanden, *Journal,* 59, 80; Report of Lt. Governor Clarke to Board of Trade, August 10, 1741, CO 5/1194, no. 101, PRO.

97 Horsmanden, *Journal,* 194, 195, 226. For location of the tavern, see Watson, *Annals and Occurrences,* 297. For other reports of Sunday gatherings, see Horsmanden, *Journal,* 58–59, 147, 249, 250.

98 Horsmanden, *Journal,* 58–60, 70, 103, 110–30, 172–73; Davis, *Rumor of Revolt,* 104–5. For the marriage of folk activity and political activities, see Young, "English Plebeian Culture and Eighteenth-Century American Radicalism," and Waldstreicher, *In the Midst of Perpetual Fetes,* 21–22.

99 Horsmanden, *Journal,* 330. In another instance, a huge frolic occurred "in

the fields (. . . they had been at some free negroe's house in Bowery-land.)"
It was at such ordinary meetings, staples of slave life in the city, that black
leaders discussed insurrection and recruited followers. See Votes of the Assembly of New York from March 1739–29 October 1742, p. 68, CO 5/1213,
PRO.

100 For meetings in the street and markets, see Horsmanden, *Journal*, 93, 117,
132, 211, 232, 246–47, 252, 259. For meeting in the Fields, see 119. For frolics
of free Negroes, see 233, 256–57.

101 Horsmanden, *Journal*, 66–67, 91; Du Bois, *Black North*, 18.

102 See Thornton, *Africa and Africans*, 184–205; Washington, *"Peculiar People,"*
46–50, 289–90; Nash, "Forging Freedom," 23; Gomez, *Exchanging Our
Country Marks*, 94–100. One of the conspirators, Will, came from Antigua,
where the secret societies played a part in a slave conspiracy in 1737.

103 Horsmanden, *Journal*, 67, 69, 93–94. For Prince's arrest, see "John Cruger
to Watchman. . . . Order Remitting Prince to Gaol at the Request of his
Master, March 9, 1741, in Francis, *Old New York*, 9:31.

104 Horsmanden, *Journal*, 42, 60.

105 For rumors, see Horsmanden, *Journal*, 206, 225. For Will, see 206, 212, 265.

106 For slaves of the attorney general and aldermen, see Horsmanden, *Jour-
nal;* for trials and confessions of Albany, Anthony, Caesar, Cuffee, Otello,
Pompey, and for fiddling at frolics, 110–11, 134, 151, 164, 222–25, 233, 249.
For Doctor Harry, see 286–87, 325. For Braveboy, see ibid., 255–56.

107 Du Bois, *Souls of Black Folk*, 84.

108 Wood, *Black Majority*.

CHAPTER FOUR

1 Horsmanden, *Journal*, 179, 386–90. See reports of similar acts of arson in
Ulster County and Schnectady in *New-York Weekly Journal*, February 22,
1742, and in Schenectady in 1747 in *New-York Weekly Post-Boy*, March 16,
1747.

2 See the series of examinations in Horsmanden, *Journal*, 400–420. As with
all great works of history, the *Journal* was remaindered a few years after
publication at three shillings a copy, or one-third the original cost. See *New-
York Weekly Post-Boy*, October 17, 1748.

3 Bridenbaugh, ed., *Itinerarium of Dr. Alexander Hamilton*, 88.

4 *New-York Weekly Post-Boy*, December 29, 1746. For a similar gang in Ulster
County, see *New-York Weekly Post-Boy*, October 29, 1753. For Bergen, see
Hodges, *Slavery, Freedom, and Culture*, 42.

5 These uprisings were reported in New York newspapers. See the *Weekly
Post-Boy*, April 30, 1753. For other slave mutinies, see *Weekly Post-Boy*,
March 18, 1754, August 21, 1766. For the importance of these mutinies to
enslaved blacks, see Sale, *Slumbering Volcano*.

6 Neville, *Acts of the General Assembly*, 443–44; N.Y. Col. Mss., February 5,
1755, 80; *New-York Weekly Post-Boy*, February 10, 1755; Stokes, *Iconography*,
4:664. See also Hodges, *Slavery and Freedom*, 64–65.

7 *Wills*, 4:244; Kruger, "Born to Run," 592–99.

8 See Bond of Eve Scurlock Will, Court of General Sessions, May 3, 1757; for approval see Philip Livingston, Document Signed, May 4, 1757. For similar action, see Bond of Joseph Murray to free Caesar and Mary, August 4, 1757, Court of General Quarter Sessions of the Peace, County Clerk's Office, New York City. For other manumissions, see *Wills*, 4:409, 436, 5:42, 7:36, 148.

9 *Wills*, 7:266, 413.

10 Monmouth County Will No. 1193, NJA. For other wills requiring time and good behavior, see John Lippincott, Monmouth County Will No. 1413; John Lippincott of Shrewsbury, No. 1537; William Evelman, No. 2341; John Horsefell, No. 2785, ibid.

11 Thomas White, Monmouth County Will, No. 1459; see also Richard Stout, No. 1671; Dr. Wolfer Harbee, No. 2086, ibid.

12 *New York Gazette* (Weyman's), July 18, 1763.

13 For the duty, see Wax, "Preferences for Slaves in Colonial America," 380; Goodfriend, *Before the Melting Pot*, 113.

14 The most convenient source for the these numbers is McManus, *Black Bondage in the North*, 209–12.

15 Davis, "New York's Long Black Line," 44; Harrington and Greene, *American Population*, 91; Kruger, "Born to Run," 131; McManus, *Black Bondage in the North*, 208–9, 212–13.

16 Rawley, *Transatlantic Slave Trade*, 386–87; Lydon, "New York and the Slave Trade," 375–95.

17 Lydon, "New York and the Slave Trade," 387, 393. Lydon believes that as many as 7,400 blacks may have entered the port during these years.

18 Philip Livingston and Sons, Book of Trade for the Slave Ship Rhode Island on a Voyage to Sierra Leone, January–July 1749, listing goods bartered for slaves and the number of slaves who died on the Return Voyage, N-YHS; "Letter Book of John Watts," 31; Rawley, *Transatlantic Slave Trade*, 390; McKee, *Labor in Colonial New York*, 117. For the English officer, see "Journal of an Officer." For African names in the census of 1755, see Kruger, "Born to Run," 88.

19 For sales notices, see *New-York Weekly Post-Boy*, July 31, 1749, May 13, August 26, 1751, June 8, 1752, August 1, 1757, August 7, 1758, July 17, 1760.

20 Donnan, ed., *Documents*, 3:511.

21 Engrossed Act to Lay a Duty on the Importation of Slaves, 1769, Misc. Mss., N-YHS. See also Baseler, *"Asylum for Mankind,"* 234.

22 Wacker, *Land and People*, 290–95; McManus, *Black Bondage in the North*, 211–13.

23 This estimate is based on the 1771 census for New York and for birth and increase rates in Wacker, *Land and People*, 192–93.

24 *Docs. Rel.*, 4:845–63.

25 For Hank, see *New-York Weekly Post-Boy*, January 8, 1761; for Lewis Francois, see *Weekly Post-Boy*, November 5, 1753; for Norton Minors, see *Weekly Post-Boy*, November 20, 1760. See also *Pennsylvania Journal* (Philadelphia), November 29, 1750. For other sales, see Judd, ed., *Correspondence of the Van*

Cortlandt Family, 4:434–38; Barck, ed., Papers of the Lloyd Family, 1:501–2, 516, 584–85, 723, 735–36, 779; Philip Livingston, Document Signed, November 29, 1760, Pierpont Morgan Library; Deed of Sale for Negro Boy Boam, July 12, 1758, and Bill of Sale, May 5, 1755, New York State Library and Archives; Beekman Family Papers, N-YHS; Bill of Sale, August 12, 1760, Misc. Mss. Flushing, N-YHS; Bill of Sale, September 29, 1761, Dean Family Papers, N-YHS; Bill of Sale, April 24, 1766, Harry Dickenson Papers, N-YHS.

26 Wills, 7:120–21, 255. For the incident at Purchase, see Stanton, Journal of the Life, 149–50. See also Conveyance of Slaves, 1765, Miscellaneous Conveyances of Kings County, NYMA.

27 Wacker and Clemens, Land Use, 99–101.

28 Wacker, "New Jersey Tax-Ratable List of 1751," 32–34; Wacker and Clemens, Land Use, 100.

29 Nash and Soderlund, Freedom by Degrees, 24.

30 Kierner, Traders and Gentlefolk, 60, 63, 98.

31 Kruger, "Born to Run," 13–16; Doc. Hist, 2:852–68; Hodges, Slavery and Freedom, 18–20.

32 M'Robert, "Tour." See also O'Conor, ed., A Servant, 49; Burnaby, Travels through the Middle Settlements, 110; "Journal of an Officer," 414.

33 Charles Nicoll Day Book, N-YHS. For another instance of a black sailor in this period, see Alexander MacDougall Papers, Box 1, Mss. Manuscripts, N-YHS, and New-York Mercury, April 17, 1758; for hiring out, see Thomas Witter Account Book, N-YHS; Inventory and Administration of the Estate of Adolph Philipse, NYPL. For frequent drownings, see "Inquisitions on the Dead," 1:12, 133, 154, 188, 201, 206, 211, NJA.

34 Parish Transcripts, November 1743, folder 156, N-YHS.

35 Muster Rolls of the New-York Provincial Troops, 1755–1764, 60–64, 74, 80, 112, 288, 292, 298, 304, 310, 328, 368.

36 MacFayden, "Schuyler Copper Mines," 15.

37 Wacker and Clemens, Land Use, 70, 89–92, 99; Cohen, Dutch-American Farm, 123–30; Countryman, People in Revolution, 37–46. For the concept of a single crop, see Morgan, Slave Counterpoint, 194–96.

38 Abrahams, Singing the Master, 131–54.

39 For examples of blacks picking up commodities at stores, see Scott, "John Evert Van Allen's Account Book," 10–16; Samuel Deall Account Book, N-YHS; Ledger of Doctor Elias Cornelius, New York Genealogical and Biographical Record (1980–81), 111–12; Nathaniel Holmes' Day Book; Charles Nicoll Day Book, N-YHS; Stryker-Rodda, "Janeway Account Books."

40 New-York Weekly Post-Boy, November 4, 1751. For Prince, see New-York Weekly Post-Boy, August 28, 1758. For Pompey, see New-York Weekly Post-Boy, July 26, 1756; for Jacob, see New-York Weekly Post-Boy, March 13, 1769; for messenger incident, see Pennsylvania Gazette, June 26, 1760; for Charles, see New-York Weekly Post-Boy, November 6, 1760. For Sylvanus, see New-York Weekly Post-Boy, October 14, 1762. For the embezzler, see New-York Weekly Post-Boy, April 19, 1762.

41 John Taylor Day-Book, N-YHS; John Pryor Account Books, N-YHS; Van Shaick Papers, Folder 7, New York State Library and Archives; James Beekman Account Book, N-YHS; Stryker-Rodda, ed., "Account Book of George Janeway"; Ann Elizabeth Schuyler Account Book, N-YHS.

42 For monopolies of trades, see Morris, *Government and Labor*, 50–125, and Hodges, *New York City Cartmen*. For indentured servants, see McKee, *Labor in Colonial New York*, 89–113, and Klepp and Smith, eds., *The Infortunate*.

43 Nash, *Urban Crucible*, 194. Males were also used as domestics. See, for example, *Pennsylvania Journal* (Philadelphia), October 13, 1763; *New-York Weekly Post-Boy*, September 6, 1764; *New-York Mercury*, June 8, 1771.

44 For a full description of domestic duties, see *New-York Weekly Journal*, April 15, 1734.

45 Charles Nicoll Day Book, N-YHS. Nicoll did a steady business selling shoes to such masters as John Lamb, Joseph Allicock, Francis Welsh, Jon Taylor, William Brown, and Captain Randall, among others. "For medical care," see Daybook of an Unidentified New York Pharmacist, N-YHS.

46 Karlsen and Crumpacker, eds., *Journal of Esther Edwards Burr*, 104. See also Dunlap, *History of the Rise and Progress*, 1:288; Graydon, *Manners of a Life*, 247–49; Freiburg, ed., *Journal of Madam Knight*, 20–21; Barck, ed., *Papers of the Lloyd Family*, 258, 261, 262, 270, 282–83, 707–9, 713–19.

47 Robert G. Livingston to Henry J. Livingston, June 18, 1751, N-YHS. See also Bridenbaugh, ed., *Itinararium of Dr. Alexander Hamilton*, 186.

48 For Dutch architecture, see Bailey, *Pre-Revolutionary Dutch Houses*, 269–381, esp. 272–75, 288, 306, 314, 326–27, 370, 377; for slaves living in caves and tents, see Hodges, *Slavery, Freedom, and Culture*, 39–40.

49 See Bailey, *Pre-Revolutionary Dutch Houses*, 288, and Reynolds, *Dutch Houses in the Hudson Valley*, 14. For "Negro kitchens" see *New-York Weekly Post-Boy*, December 19, 1748. See also *Journal of Lieutenant Isaac Bangs*, 51, and "Inventory and Administration of the Estate of Adolph Philipse," NYPL.

50 Narrett, *Inheritance and Family Life*, 119–24, 134–44, 151–70, 337–41.

51 *Wills*, 7:64, 179, 201, 243, 253, 287, 357, 395, 8:57, 135. For New York, see Narrett, *Inheritance and Family Life*, 188–90, and Cohen, *Dutch-American Farm*, 138–42. For the persistence of widows' power, see Goodfriend, *Before the Melting Pot*, 181–86; Hershkowitz, *Wills of Early New York Jews*, 21–23, 44, 60–66, 80, 87–88, 179, and Nash and Soderlund, *Freedom by Degrees*, 58–59.

52 *Wills*, 3:8, 26, 36, 53, 152, 197, 201–2, 8:21, 213, 235, 343, 349, 379.

53 For testators' use of primogeniture transferring slaves in wills, see *Wills*, 4:20, 22, 6:13, 168, 304, 329, 8:29, 137, 141. For discussion of the use of primogeniture in New York Colony, see Narrett, *Inheritance and Family Life*, 221–34. For New Jersey, see Landsman, *Scotland and Its First American Colony*, 155–58. For widows and remarriage, see Wells, *Population of the British Colonies*, 81, and Kruger, "Born to Run," 217–18.

54 Soderlund, *Quakers and Slavery*, 108, 114–20.

55 King v. Matthew Maguire, May 3, 4, 1744, May 7, 1746, King v. Catherine

O'Neal, October Term, 1765, Parchment K-249, Court of General Quarter Sessions of the Peace, County Clerk's Office, New York City. See also King v. Henry Smith, February 9, May 3, 1749; King v. Philip Miller, July Term 1772; King v. Heston Campbell, October 26, 1773, ibid. See also King v. Cornelius Edison, John Crawford, John Brown, and Aeneas, a Mollatto Slave, October 23, 1771, Parchment K-274; King v. Tawney, July 29, 1762; King v. Scipio, January Term 1774, Parchment K-227; King v. Jenney, July Term 1755, Parchment K-359. For other cases see Parchments K-500, K-510, K-470, K-511, K-662, K-473, and K-517 all in County Clerk's Parchments, County Clerk's Office, New York City.

56 Du Bois, *Souls of Black Folk*, 46; Roberts, *From Trickster to Badman;* Levine, *Black Culture and Black Consciousness*, 297.

57 Hodges and Brown, eds., *"Pretends to Be Free,"* xxii. All subsequent newspaper citations may be found in this volume, organized by date. For advertisements of fiddlers, see *New-York Weekly Post-Boy*, July 11, 1748, June 12, 1752, January 31, June 6, October 10, 1757, July 24, December 11, 1758, April 29, August 26, 1762; *Pennsylvania Gazette*, May 9, 1751, April 15, 1756; *New-York Mercury*, May 14, 1764.

58 Robert G. Livingston to Henry J. Livingston, N-YHS.

59 *New-York Weekly Post-Boy*, February 16, 1756.

60 *New-York Weekly Post-Boy*, November 19, 1767.

61 Mullin, *Flight and Rebellion*, 36–58; White, "Question of Style."

62 See, for example, Monmouth County Wills, 1253, 1709, 1839, 4509, 5187, NJA.

63 Ekirch, *Bound for America*, 199–201; Prude, "To Look Upon the 'Lower Sort.' "

64 *New-York Weekly Journal*, May 10, 1736.

65 *American Weekly Mercury*, July 14, 1726.

66 For Jacob, see *New-York Weekly Post-Boy*, March 22, 1764. Pelton, *Trickster in West Africa*, 255–56.

67 For Joe, see *New-York Weekly Journal*, June 26, 1766; for Claus, see *New-York Weekly Post-Boy*, July 4, 1757; for Caesar, see *New-York Weekly Post-Boy*, December 5, 1765.

68 For Jem, see *Pennsylvania Chronicle*, July 8, 1771; for Jacob, see *New-York Mercury*, September 10, 1764; for Ben, see *New-York Weekly Post-Boy*, September 4, 1766; for Cate, see *New-York Weekly Post-Boy*, June 27, 1765. For masquerade among convicts, see Ekirch, *Bound for America*, 201.

69 For Adonia, see *New-York Weekly Post-Boy*, September 30, 1762; for Toby and Abraham, see *Pennsylvania Gazette*, May 31, 1764.

70 Unfortunately, Auchmuty's book of baptisms burned in a fire, but his frequent reports to the SPG show constant attention to baptisms. See the various letters from Auchmuty to the society in Letter Book B 19:67, B 20:56–57, B 2:1–5, 7, 58, SPG Papers, Rhodes Library, Oxford University. For means of instruction, see *British Instructor*, 3. In the text the author identified himself as a former missionary who wrote the book "to induce numbers of poor negroes to read."

71 For the first quote, see Klingberg, *Anglican Humanitarianism*, 149; for the second, see Rev. Samuel Auchmuty to Rev. John Waring, New York, October 20, 1774, in Van Horne, ed., *Religious Philanthropy*, 322.

72 For announcement of the free school, see *New-York Mercury*, August 4, September 15, 1760. See also Rev. Samuel Auchmuty to Rev. John Waring, New York, April 19, 1763, in Van Horne, ed., *Religious Philanthropy*, 197.

73 Thompson, *Thomas Bray*; Bray, *Missionalia*.

74 For quotes, see Van Horne, *Religious Philanthropy*, 166–70, 197; "Records of Trinity Parish: Baptisms," 77–79, Trinity Church Archives.

75 For discussion of the controversy over the Anglican plans for a bishopric, see Bridenbaugh, *Mitre and Sceptre*, 116–71. For the critic, see *Pennsylvania Journal*, March 31, June 23, 1768.

76 Bolton, *History of the Protestant Episcopal Church*, 39–40, 63; Moore, *History of St. George's Church*, 52–56, 69.

77 For locations, see Burr, *Anglican Church in New Jersey*, 224–28, 485; Vibert, "The S.P.G," 208. For antagonism, see Wacker, *Land and People*, 187–89; Burr, *Anglican Church in New Jersey*, 95.

78 William Skinner to Rev. D. Bearcroft, January 9, 1749, SPG Transcripts, Alexander Library; Burr, *Anglican Church in New Jersey*, 29, 32, 72, 86, 225–27.

79 Kruger, "Born to Run," 74–77. Kruger estimates that the SPG baptized 1,407 blacks between 1705 and 1780; Berlin, *Many Thousands Gone*, 61. For racism, see Hodges, *Slavery and Freedom*, 69.

80 For Titus, see Hodges and Brown, eds. *"Pretends to Be Free,"* 60; for comments, see Hodges, *Slavery and Freedom*, 70–71.

81 Leiby, *United Churches of Hackensack and Schraalenburgh*, 244; Messler, *Forty Years at Raritan*.

82 There is little work on Capetein. For the best single discussion, see Bartels, "Jacobus Eliza Capetein." See Moses, *Wings of Ethiopia*, 142.

83 De Ronde, *System*, 7, 33, 92, 111. For reference to the primer for blacks, see Corwin, "The Church and the Negroes in Colonial Days," 399–400.

84 Hodges, ed., *Black Itinerants*, 39, 90; Hodges, *Slavery and Freedom*, 78–80.

85 Gronniosaw, *Narrative of the Most Remarkable Particulars*, 27, 30–31, 33–40, 45–47; Thompson, *Flash of the Spirit*, 6; Zahan, *Religion, Spirituality, and Thought*, 27–28. For a similar account, see Hodges, *Slavery and Freedom*, 78–80.

86 Hodges, ed., *Black Itinerants*, 90.

87 See "Some Early Records of the Lutheran Church of New York," in *Year Book of the Holland Society of New York, 1902*, 8, 14–15, 17, 19, 20–22; "New York Lutheran Church Book, 1704–1723," *Year Book of the Holland Society of New York, 1903*, 6, 8, 15.

88 "New York Lutheran Church Book," *Year Book of the Holland Society of New York, 1903*, 17, 20–22. For the sex scandal, see Hodges, "The Pastor and the Prostitute."

89 Soderlund, *Quakers and Slavery*, 54–86.

90 For the Benezet quote, see Fladeland, *Men and Brothers*, 15–16. For Wool-

man, see Moulton, ed., *Journal and Major Essays of John Woolman*, 18, 52, 95–99, 107–8, 117. See also Stanton, *Journal*, 111, 145–48, 152–55.

91 For the Society of Friends in New Jersey, see Wacker, *Land and People*, 178–83. For the conservatism of the New York Meeting, see Oblong (Pawling) Monthly Meeting, 126, 141–45, Haviland Record Center, New York City; Cox, *Quakerism in the City of New York*, 57–62; Aptheker, "Quakers and Negro Slavery," 350; Soderlund, *Quakers and Slavery*, 122–24; Kruger, "Born to Run," 609–11.

92 See Cadbury, "Negro Membership in the Society of Friends"; Soderlund, *Quakers and Slavery*, 177.

93 See, for example, Hodges, *Slavery and Freedom*, 91–93.

94 See Schmidt, *Holy Fairs*, 69–85, 196. For slavery, see Kull, "Presbyterian Attitudes."

95 Clark, ed., *Journal and Letters of Francis Asbury*, 1:9, 25, 43; Maser and Maag, eds., *Journal of Joseph Pilmore*, 74, 96, 131. See also Hodges, ed. *Black Itinerants*, 10–44, and Walls, *African Methodist Episcopal Zion Church*, 40–41.

96 Joyner, *Down by the Riverside*, 141–71; Washington, *Peculiar People*, 47–52.

97 For Andrew Saxon, see *New-York Gazette*, October 1, 1733; for Simon, see *Pennsylvania Gazette*, September 11, 1740; for Mark and Jenney, see *Rivington's New-York Gazetteer*, June 8, 1775. For other religious blacks, see Smith and Wojtowicz, eds., *Blacks Who Stole Themselves*, 97, 110, 120, 124, 125, 152.

98 Hodges, ed., *Black Itinerants*, 22, 114–17; Caretta, ed., *Unchained Voices;* Smith, "Slavery and Theology."

99 For Jack, see Leiby, *Revolutionary War in the Hackensack Valley*, 200–202. For poisoning, see *Pennsylvania Gazette*, February 7, 1737; *New-York Weekly Post-Boy*, June 4, 1744; for Caro, see *New-York Weekly Post-Boy*, March 22, 1756, August 1, 1757; for Charity, see Irvis, "Negro Tales from Eastern New York," 166–68. See also Yvonne Chireau, "The Uses of the Supernatural: Toward a History of Black Women's Magical Practices," in Juster and McFarlane, eds., *Mighty Baptism*, 171–88.

100 For the Kalm quote, see Piersen, *Black Yankees*, 82–83. For other poisonings, see *New-York Weekly Post-Boy*, June 4, 1744; "Official Records of Bergen County, in the Clerk's Office," 179; *Pennsylvania Journal*, March 10, 1754; *New-York Weekly Post-Boy*, February 11, 1751.

101 Case of Phyllis, Negro Slave of New York City, October 22, 1748, Coroner's Proceedings in the City and County of New York, Columbia University Rare Book Room.

102 N.Y. Col. Mss., 75:55, 56, 68, 70, 74, 79–80; Parish Transcripts, Folder 162, N-YHS; Hough, *Reports of the Cases of the Vice Admiralty*, 29–33, 199.

103 Fernow, ed., *Calendar of Council Minutes*, 358, 366; N.Y. Col. Mss., 75:81, 86, 93, 128; Parish Transcripts, Folder 162, N-YHS. See also the Petition of Juan de Costa a free mulatto subject to the King of Portugal, N.Y. Col. Mss. 89:158–64.

104 Parish Transcripts, Folder 160, N-YHS; N.Y. Col. Mss., 76:16. For the Spanish request, see Interim Governor [of Florida] Fulgencio Garcia de Solis to

Marquesta de la Ensaenada [governor of Cuba], August 25, 1752, in *ramo Gobierno: Santo Domingo, leagajo* 58-1-33, document 23, Archivo de Indias, Seville.

105 Parish Transcripts, Folder 160, N-YHS.

106 Parish Transcripts, 10–18, Folder 160, N-YHS; N.Y. Col. Mss., 77:70, 98, 80:148, 85:27, 63, 84. For the Miranda petition and affidavits see Testimony of Grace Pinhorne and Jacobus Kingsland, John Tabor Kempe Papers, N-YHS; Minute Book of the New York Supreme Court of Judicature, and County Clerk's Parchments, P-159, E-6, October Term 1758, in County Clerk's Office, New York City; *New-York Weekly Post-Boy,* July 24, 1758. For similar cases see *Narrative of the Uncommon Sufferings and Surprising Deliverance of Briton Hammond,* 7, 10, 13–14; Case of Simon Moore, a Free Negro, and Letter to the Mayor of New York City, August 6, 1772, Kempe Papers, N-YHS.

107 Hodges and Brown, eds., *"Pretends to Be Free."*

108 Greenberg, *Crime and Law Enforcement,* 45–46.

109 For Jupiter Hazard, see *Pennsylvania Gazette,* June 13, 1751; for Bill, see *Weekly Post-Boy,* August 27, 1759; for Arnold, see *Weekly Post-Boy,* November 20, 1760; for Nero and Pero, see *Pennsylvania Gazette,* November 8, 21, 1765, *New-York Weekly Post-Boy,* June 5, 1766. For transported convicts and the desire to return to England, see Ekirch, *Bound for America,* 206–7.

110 Parish Transcripts, Folder 160, N-YHS; David Jones to Archibald Kennedy, August 15, 1757, Fort Neck, Long Island, Emmet Collection, NYPL; for another incident, see Hodges, *Slavery and Freedom,* 65.

111 Muster Rolls of the New-York Provincial Troops, 1755–1764, 60–74, 304; *Wills,* 8:63–64.

112 For Frank, see *New-York Journal or General Advertiser,* December 8, 1768; for Sampson, see *Pennsylvania Journal,* January 28, 1752; for Arch, see *Pennsylvania Chronicle,* October 8, 1770.

113 For Caesar, see *New-York Weekly Post-Boy,* August 30, 1756; for Quaco, see *Pennsylvania Journal,* August 20, 1761. For other uses of iron collars, see the cases of Harry, *New-York Weekly Post-Boy,* December 31, 1759, and Cyrus, *New-York Weekly Post-Boy,* October 15, 1761.

114 For ads, see *New-York Weekly Journal,* August 6, 1750; *Pennsylvania Gazette,* September 6, 1750; *New-York Weekly Post-Boy,* October 15, 1753, April 1, 1754, March 1, 1756, July 24, 1758.

115 For Bood and others, see *Pennsylvania Gazette,* June 21, 1759; for the four fugitives from William Bull, see *New-York Weekly Post-Boy,* October 27, 1763. For two Jacks, see *New-York Weekly Post-Boy,* June 6, 1757; for Sam and Isaac Randall, see *Pennsylvania Gazette,* October 31, 1745; for servants and slave, see *Pennsylvania Journal,* October 4, 1770; for the man and woman, see *New-York Weekly Post-Boy,* July 5, 1756; for Ned and Mary, see *Pennsylvania Gazette,* October 31, 1771; for Domingo and Mary Carrey, see *New-York Weekly Post-Boy,* June 27, 1748.

116 *New-York Weekly Post-Boy,* February 17, 1767, October 28, November 4, 1751; *New-York Weekly Journal,* February 4, 1744/45. See also King v. Nep-

tune, a Negro Man Slave, October 28, 1773, Court of Quarter Sessions, County Clerk's Office, New York City; King v. Quack, September 30, 1769, Ancient Indictments, Bergen County Historical Society; *New-York Weekly Post-Boy*, May 7, 1767. For Hannah, see N.Y. Col. Mss., 60:117, July 3, 1760.

117 King v. Falmouth, August 3, 1770, Parchment K-314, County Clerk's Office, New York City; O'Callaghan, ed., *Calendar of Historical Manuscripts*, 2:719; Benjamin Douglas to the King, Recognizance Pursuant to the Condition of the Pardon of a Negroe Man Named Falmouth, Misc. Mss, B. Douglas, November 28, 1770, N-YHS. For other petitions for pardons, see O'Callaghan, ed., *Calendar of Historical Manuscripts*, 2:719, 735, 756, 808, 812, 820, 822, 823, 834.

118 For Myer and Tom, see *New-York Weekly Post-Boy*, March 1, 1756. See also *New York Gazette, or the Weekly Post-Boy*, March 18, 1751.

119 For rapes, see *Pennsylvania Gazette*, December 14, 1744, and *Pennsylvania Chronicle*, March 20, 1767. For murders, see *New-York Weekly Post-Boy*, May 16, 1746/47; *Pennsylvania Gazette*, April 19, 1770. See also *New-York Journal or General Advertiser*, October 16, 1766.

120 *New-York Weekly Journal*, February 10, 1746. See also the report from Santo Domingo of a mutiny of blacks whose reason was "that they were born free men and made slaves by the English during the war and had no other way of getting their freedom," in *New-York Weekly Post-Boy*, January 23, 1748/49. See also report of the "arrival in New York of Captain Hammond with the effects of *HMS Polly* which was mutinied by three Spanish Negroes who murdered all the whites on board," in *New-York Weekly Post-Boy*, July 24, 1749.

121 *New-York Gazette Revived in the Weekly Post-Boy*, July 2, 1750. For other murders, see *New-York Journal or General Advertiser*, October 1, 29, 1767; *Pennsylvania Gazette*, October 1, 1767. See also the report of the murder of a mistress in Orangeburg, New York, in 1763 by a slave who then dressed up in his master's clothes and burned down the house. He was then arrested and burned. See *New-York Weekly Post-Boy*, April 7, 1763. In 1764 a slave tried to kill his master with a scythe. See *New-York Weekly Post-Boy*, April 16, 1764. In 1767, Cuff, slave of Daniel Hart of Hopewell, Hunterdon County, axed his master and young son, then committed suicide in the woods. "His dead body was burnt the day after." See *New-York Weekly Journal*, October 29, 1767; *Pennsylvania Gazette*, October 22, 1767. For other attacks on slave masters in New Jersey during this period, see *American Weekly Mercury*, January 14, 1729; *New-York Weekly Journal*, January 1, 1739; *New-York Weekly Post-Boy*, December 29, 1746, March 16, 1747, January 23, 1749, July 2, 1750, and February 11, 1751.

122 *New-York Gazette and Weekly Post-Boy*, December 25, 1752; *Pennsylvania Gazette*, January 9, 1753; Mellick, *Story of an Old Farm*, 226. Although the slave's dying words, as quoted in press accounts, reversed the botanical function of root and branches, they nonetheless provided a powerful message of resistance and hope, which I why I have chosen to use them as

an epigraph for this work. For a similar incident a dozen years later, see Hodges, *Slavery, Freedom, and Culture,* 42.

123 For these concepts, see Zahan, *Religion, Spirituality, and Thought,* 110–12; Du Bois, *Souls of Black Folk,* 46. For discussion of the importance of such events in the collective resistance and historical memory of a slave group, see Price, *First-Time,* 5–8, 12.

124 For the importance of the crossroads, see Washington, *"Peculiar People,"* 52–53; Stuckey, *Slave Culture,* 6–37, 40; MacGaffey, *Religion and Society,* 12, 116–19, 121; Thompson and Cornet, *Four Moments of the Sun,* 27–28, 42–47; Thompson, *Flash of the Spirit,* 103–58. For African American literature, see Gates, *Signifying Monkey,* 6, 31, 41, 64–65. For Du Bois, see *Souls of Black Folk,* 47.

125 For the most recent work on these petitions, see Davis, "Emancipation Rhetoric." For the effect of Somerset, see Drayton, *Some Fugitive Thoughts.*

126 Hodges, *Slavery and Freedom,* 93–94; Price, *Freedom Not Far Distant,* 56–60. For Livingston, see William Livingston to Unknown, November 21, 1774, Pierpont Morgan Library.

127 *New York Gazeteer,* December 9, 1773, February 16, 1775; *New-York Weekly Post-Boy,* June 25, 1772. For hanging of blacks, see *New England Chronicle,* June 1, 1775.

128 See the useful interpretation of such actions in Glassman, "The Bondsman's New Clothes," and Wood, "Liberty Is Sweet," 149–85.

CHAPTER FIVE

1 "Memoirs of Mr. Boston King," 109–10; Hodges, ed., *Black Loyalist Directory,* 86.

2 For the text of Dunmore's Proclamation, see Force, *American Archives,* 4th ser., 3:1185–87, and Berkeley, *Dunmore's Proclamation.* For the best discussion of the proclamation and events leading up to it, see Quarles, *Negro in the American Revolution,* 18–31, and Frey, *Water from the Rock,* 63, 67, 114. For the effect of Dunmore's proclamation, see Morris, "Class Struggle and the American Revolution," 18. For literary evidence of fears, see Laycock, *Fall of British Tyranny.* For the debate over Dunmore's proclamation in Parliament, see Simmons and Thomas, eds., *Proceedings and Debates,* 6:96, 105, 438, 565. For payroll of the Ethiopian Regiment, see Lord Dunmmore's Account of Expenses, PRO.

3 See Frey, *Water from the Rock,* esp. chap. 4.

4 Countryman, *People in Revolution;* Leiby, *Revolutionary War;* Lundlin, *Cockpit of the Revolution;* Kruger, "Born to Run," 660.

5 Robinson, *Slavery in the Structure of American Politics,* 54–98; Okoye, "Chattel Slavery."

6 The best review of American use of blacks remains Quarles, *Negro in the American Revolution,* 68–111.

7 Antibiastes, *Observations.* Free blacks occasionally joined the American

forces. For local examples, see Nell, *Colored Patriots*, 160–63, and Quarles, *Negro in the American Revolution*, 59–64.

8 Price, *Freedom Not Far Distant*, 63–67. Another black from eastern New Jersey, Samuel Charleton of English Neighborhood, Bergen County, substituted for his master as a teamster in George Washington's baggage train. Hagar, a black woman from Newark, cooked meals for Washington. Cudjoe, a slave from Newark, fought in the Battle of Monmouth. See Nell, *Colored Patriots*, 162–65; Quarles, *Negro in the American Revolution*, 77–79.

9 For James Array, see Hoff, "Colonial Black Family." Williams is quoted in Rock and Gilje, eds., *Keepers of the Revolution*, 214–15.

10 Quarles, *Negro in the American Revolution*, 94–99.

11 "Regulations for Defense of New-York City Agreed upon by Lord Stirling and the Committee of the Provincial Congress of New York," March 20, 1776, as quoted in Duer, *Life of William Alexander*, 145–46, 152; Thompson, *Sketches of the History*, 36–37; Andrew Hunter, War Diary, Princeton University Library; Charles Inglis Papers, MG 1, vol. 479:4, 13, Public Archives of Nova Scotia.

12 New York Minutes of the Committee of Safety, July 18, 1776, Peter Force Collection, 8d, Reel 53, Item 114, Library of Congress; Schaukirk, *Occupation of New York City by the British*, 2–3.

13 Quarles, *Negro in the American Revolution*, 49; Prince et al., eds. *Papers of William Livingston*, 2:387–88.

14 Thayer, *Colonial and Revolutionary Morris County*, 217–18; Thompson, "Slavery and Presbyterianism in the Revolutionary Era."

15 Quarles, *Negro in the American Revolution*, 34–48. These figures are derived from *Wills*, vols. 9–12.

16 *Wills*, 9:64, 84, 121–24, 135–36, 10:92–93, 12:131, 182. For other emancipations, see 10:99, 100. For Peter Jay, see 9:262. For other conditional wills, usually by Quakers, see Shrewsbury Scrapbook, 1, 9, 11–21, Haviland Record Center; Soderlund, *Quakers and Slavery*, 122–26; A Record of the Discharge of the Negroes Set at Liberty by Friends of the Westbury Monthly Meeting, 1–10, Haviland Record Center.

17 See *Wills*, 1:24, 32; Manumission Statement of Israel Young, April 9, 1779, Samuel Jones Papers, State Historical Society of Wisconsin; Indenture, 1782, between the Superintendent of Police of Long Island and Captain John Pebbles for the Servitude of a Negro Boy, in Cunningham of Thornton Muniments, Scottish Record Office, Edinburgh. One black published his own views on his emancipation. See *New-Jersey Gazette*, January 26, February 2, 23, March 1, 8, June 25, December 23, 1780.

18 See Nelson, *American Tory*, 111–12; Muhlenberg quoted in Tappert and Doberstein, *Journals of Henry Melchior Muhlenberg*, 3:53, 105.

19 Nathanael Greene to George Washington, July 21, 1776, in Force, *American Archives*, 5th ser., 1:486. A captured slave named Strickland gave Greene this figure. See also Force, *American Archives*, 1:862, 949, for intelligence about Dunmore's moves.

20 See "Cornelius Lydecker Diary for 1776," 60; Hodges, ed., *Black Loyalist*

Directory; "A Book of Registers and Copy of Inventory of Damages Done by the Enemy and the Adherents to the Inhabitants of the County of Middlesex, 1776–82, NJA. For other black fugitives, see "A Mechanic to Bernardus LeGrange, June 1776, Middlesex County" in Gerlach, *New Jersey in the American Revolution,* 239–42; *Pennsylvania Gazette,* September 26, 1776; Countryman, *People in Revolution,* 171–72. December 1776 was a particularly costly month for New Jersey slaveholders. Fifteen Middlesex County blacks and four from Bergen County fled their masters to join the British army. See "A Book of Registers," Middlesex, 143, 152, 173, 180, 187, 214, 284, 329, and Bergen County, 3, 12, 13, 27, NJA.

21 For employment of blacks, see Force, *American Archives,* 5th ser., 1:486, 2:252, 3:109, 266; "Proceedings of a Board of General Officers of the British Army at New-York, 1781," 112, 118, 125–26, 130–31, 134, 136–39, 141–42, 174, 210; General Return of the Wagoneers and Owners and Cooks in Rochambeau's Army," Wadsworth Papers, N-YHS. For other examples, see Leiby, *Revolutionary War in the Hackensack Valley,* 200–202, and Clayton, *History of Bergen County,* 344. For general conditions in New York City, see Albion and Dodson, eds., *Journal of Philip Vickers Fithian,* 204–10.

22 See Appendix Table 2; Lundlin, *Cockpit of the Revolution,* 143–45; Pettengill, ed., *Letters from America,* 177; Leiby, *Revolutionary War in the Hackensack Valley,* 75–87; Andrew Hunter, War Diary, Princeton University Library.

23 Leiby, *Revolutionary War in the Hackensack Valley,* 93–99.

24 Damages Done by the British in Bergen County, 1776–82, 3,12, 27, NJA.

25 Ibid., Essex County (Acquackanonck), 25, 38, 40, 41, 52, (Newark), 23, 39, (Springfield), 3; Somerset County, 47, 141, 153, 181, 185.

26 "Reverend Alexander MacWhorter's Letter," quoted in Price, *Freedom Not Far Distant,* 69–71; see also Atkinson, *History of Newark,* 101.

27 A Book of Registers, Middlesex, 1, 10, 27, 31, 54, 133, 143, 152, 163, 173, 178, 180, 187, 214, 218, 284, 329, NJA; Hodges, ed., *Black Loyalist Directory;* Lundlin, *Cockpit of the Revolution,* 153–59; Collins, ed., *Brief Narrative of the Ravages of the British and the Hessians,* 24.

28 Calhoon, *Loyalist Perception,* 151. For the controversy around Howe, see Howe, *Narrative of Lieutenant Sir William Howe,* 8, 37–40, 63–67, and Tarleton, Letters Relating to Military Movements in New Jersey, Princeton University Library.

29 For a discussion of the massive amounts of goods taken by the armies, see *New-Jersey Journal,* August 4, 1829; O'Callaghan, ed., *Calendar of Historical Manuscripts,* 2:114, 120, 124; Syrett et al., eds. *Papers of Alexander Hamilton,* 1:283–84, and "Minutes of the Committee," 202, 223.

30 See, for example, Sam, Sarah, and daughter Sarah Van Nostrandt of the Black Brigade in Hodges, ed., *Black Loyalist Directory,* 43, 209; Prince and his wife, Margaret, son Mintard, daughter, Elizabeth, and son-in-law Samuel Van Nostrandt of Second River and Acquackanonk, ibid., 43. For lodging in jails, see *Minutes of the Council of Safety of the State of New Jersey,* 43, 52. For negotiations with the British, see Stryker, ed., *Minutes of the Provincial Congress,* 516–17; Stryker, ed., *Calendar of Historical Manu-*

scripts Relating to the War of Revolution, 1:432. For Howe's meeting with sixty Loyalists from Shrewsbury, July 7, 1776, see Davies, *Documents of the American Revolution,* 12:158–59, and Clute, *Annals of Staten Island,* 85. For Patriot measures, see Prince, ed., *Papers of William Livingston,* 1:377. Livingston satirically described the British army as including eighty-five hundred blacks. See ibid., 232. For work gangs, see "Minutes of the Committee and of the First Commission for Detecting and Defeating Conspiracies in the State of New York," 166, 179, 270, 340.

31 See the various arrests for consorting with the enemy in Ancient Indictments, Bergen County Historical Society; Prince, ed., *Papers of William Livingston* 2:80, 111; AO 15/493; "Memoirs of Mr. Boston King," 109–10.

32 See Todd W. Braisted, "The Black Pioneers and Others: The Military Role of Black Loyalists in the American War for Independence," in Pullis, ed., *Moving On.*

33 For a description of the fire, see Thomas Moffat Diary, Peter Force Collections, 8d, Reel 53, Item 106, Library of Congress, and Schaukirk, *Occupation of New York City,* 253–55. For Anglican Loyalism, see Holmes, "The Episcopal Church and the American Revolution."

34 See Lydekker, *Life and Letters of Charles Inglis,* 183–86, 193, 207; Midwinter, "The S.P.G and the Church in the American Colonies," 78–79, 81. See also Pointer, "Religious Life in New York during the Revolutionary War," esp. 361–64. For marriages in Trinity Church, see Register of Marriages, 1:104–7, Trinity Church Archives. For Beach, see Stowe, "The Reverend Abraham Beach, D.D." Only one other denomination performed rituals for blacks in the war-torn city. A Lutheran pastor baptized seven blacks recently arrived from the South and performed two marriages for blacks in New York City during the Revolution. See Stryker-Rodda, "Baptisms of the Lutheran Church, New York City, from 1725," *New York Genealogical and Biographical Record,* 97–103 (1966–72), 44, 157–58, 217, 219, 222–23. For Lutheran baptisms and marriages of blacks in New Jersey, see Johnson, ed., *Journal and Biography of Nicholas Collin,* 251, 258, 282.

35 Bleucke's career may be followed in Hodges, ed. *Black Loyalist Directory,* xxiii–xxv, xxxiv, 88.

36 Quarles, *Negro in the American Revolution,* 134–54. For black executions of Hessian soldiers, see "Intelligence," November 6, 1782, Green Manuscripts, Clements Library.

37 See Quarles, *Negro in the American Revolution,* 94–97, 134–57. For discovery of conspiracy, see Edsall, ed., *Journal of John Charles Philip Von Kraft,* 104. For tracking Hessians, see Atwood, *Hessians,* 193. For use of blacks as spies, see Secret Intelligence, July 21–November 10, 1778, British Memo Book, USR Accession 748, Library of Congress. For rescuing soldiers, see Frederick Mackensie Papers, 5, Clements Library. For blacks' assistance to Tarleton, see Randall, "Tarleton's Legion," 3–5. For blacks joining Hessians, see Jones, "Black Hessians"; Edsall, ed., *Journal of John Charles Philip Van Kraft,* 83; and Henry B. Livingston to Governor Trumbull, in Force, *American Archives,* 5th ser., 2:252. For company organization, see the many

pay vouchers for the Black Pioneers in the British Headquarters Papers, PRO/55/57, folio 6492; PRO 30/55/57, folio 6480; PRO 30/55/79, folio 8918; Return of Strength and Distribution of His Majesty's Provincial Troops, 1779, Cortlandt Skinner Papers, Library of Congress. Further evidence of the Black Pioneers' presence in New York from August 1779 until June 1780 comes from the account book of a brewer, William D. Faulkner, who supplied beer to the British troops and sold more than 260 gallons to the Black Pioneers in that time. See William D. Faulkner Account Book, 1773-90, 76, 110, 112-19, 130, 139-46, Faulkner Manuscripts, N-YHS.

38 Return of Troops in the North Fit for Duty, April 2, 1776, Clinton Papers 19:40; The State of the Black Company of Pioneers as Given up by Captain Martin to Capt. Stewart, July 13, 1777, ibid., 41:29, Clements Library; Frederick Mackensie Papers, vol. 1, May 10, August 19, 1776, Clements Library; Raymond, "Muster Roll of the Queen's Rangers," 243, 250; "Muster Roll of Butler's Rangers," 13, 16; Wilson, Loyal Blacks, 34; Nash, Forging Freedom. For Black Pioneers arriving in Canada, see Allen, ed., Loyal Americans, 12, 14, 71, 83. See also Walker, Black Loyalists, 1-17, and Wilson, Loyal Blacks, 1-41. For officers, see Davies, ed., Documents of the American Revolution, 21:227-50, and especially Raymond, "Muster Rolls of Loyalist Officer Corps," 256, 258, 263, 269, 270.

39 Sir Henry Clinton to Sir William Howe, January 11, 1777, Newport, Rhode Island, Clinton Papers, 20:13, Clements Library, and Wanted for Cloathing 500 Negroes, ibid., 233:42; Abstract of the Numbers of Men, Women, Children and Wagoneers Victualled at the Commissary General's Provision Stores, July 20, 1778, ibid., 37:18, 37, 39. See also "Abstract of Men, Women, & Children Victualled on Long Island, 24-30 January, 1780, Mackensie Papers, vol. 2, Clements Library; Account Book of the British Army, N-YHS; Letter Book of Brigadier-General James Patterson, Royal Artillery Institute, Woolwich Arsenal, London.

40 List of the Names of Negroes belonging to Capt. Martin's Company, whom they Belonged to, and the Respective Places They Lived At, Gold Star Manuscripts, 30, Clements Library; Transcript for Benjamin Whitecuff, AO 41/223; Egerton, Royal Commission, 132; "Minutes of the Committee," 265, 271-72, 443: Ernst, "Long Island Black Tory." See also "Family Record of Abraham Hasbrouck," 34-41. See also the Loyalist Claim of David Key, black shoemaker of New York, AO 41/555.

41 Extract of General Orders Given by His Excellency General Henry Clinton, Commander in Chief of the Army in America, Mackensie Letter Book E, Clements Library, and Order of the Superintentent General of the Police of the City of New York and its Dependencies Authorized by Major General Jones Commanding the Forces by Proclamation, Patterson Papers, MD 963/7, Royal Artillery Library, Woolwich Arsenal, London.

42 For black sailors and pilots, see Quarles, Negro in the American Revolution, 83-90.

43 See Kelby, ed., "Orderly Book of Three Battalions of Loyalists," 369, 372, 379, 410, 425, 2:104-5; Jones, History of New York, 1:334. See also Quarles,

Negro in the American Revolution, 94–110, 156, and Morris, *Government and Labor,* 306–7. See also black reminiscences in Dann, *Memories of the War for Independence,* 46–48, 390–99. These black wagoneers were the first of their race to drive legally in New York City.

44 British Army Quartermaster General Accounts, Box 52, N-YHS; Abstracts of 200 days pay Forage to the General and Staff of the British Army for the Campaign of 1779, and Return of the Clerk's Storekeepers, Wagon-Masters, Conductors and Laborers, July 1, 1781, PRO 30/55/31, folio 125. For fraud, see Jones, *History of New York,* 1:334.

45 Quarles, *Negro in the American Revolution,* 94–111.

46 Crew List for Brigantine Swallow, Box 1, Folder 10, Elliott Papers, New York State Archives; *Archives of the State of New Jersey,* 2d ser., 5 (1971): 435, 436.

47 For chimney sweeps, see Pettengill, ed., *Letters from America,* 232–33. It should be noted, however, that this was the first black entrance into this trade, one they would dominate in the early nineteenth century. See Chapter 6. For work at the brewery, see William D. Faulkner, Brewer, Ledger Book D, 1773–1790, N-YHS.

48 AO 4/539. See also Braisted, "The Black Pioneers and Others," in Pullis, ed., *Moving On.*

49 For Howe's proclamation, see Wilson, *Loyal Blacks,* 29. Clinton's proclamation ran in the *Royal Gazette,* July 3, 1779–September 25, 1779. For the original order, see Clinton Papers 62:28, Clements Library.

50 See *New-Jersey Journal,* July 20, 1779. Like Patriot commanders, British officers were sometimes inconsistent about offering places in their armies to blacks. Oliver De Lancey, for example, a Loyalist given a key position in the British army, declared in 1777 that "all Negroes Mullattoes and other Improper Persons who have been admitted to the Corps be immediately discharged." See Kelby, ed., "Orderly Book of Three Battalions of Loyalists," 6. For other songs and poetry related to the black Loyalist experience, see Kallich, *British Poetry and the American Revolution,* 72–73, 76.

51 "Proclamation of Sir Henry Clinton, K.B.," *Royal Gazette,* July 3, 1779–January 7, 1780. For numbers, see Appendix Table 2.

52 Wilson, *Loyal Blacks,* 65.

53 Box 4, Folio 2, Elliott Papers, New York State Library.

54 For black charity, see Inquisition on the Body of Jones, a black man, August 21, 1783, PRO 30/55/78, folio 8773. For black housing, see Rent Memorandum Book for the South, Dock and West Wards, March 5–June 23, 1778, 31:44, Clinton Papers. Jones, *History of New York during the Revolutionary War,* 2:76; Stone, *History of New York City,* 232; for crowding and rations, see Wilson, *Loyal Blacks,* 64; Kruger, "Born to Run," 674. For the runaway, see *New-York Gazetteer,* January 24, 1778. For reference to Negro barracks near the wagon yard, see Inquisition on the Death of Jenney, October 20, 1783, PRO 30/55/84, document 9400.

55 For black fiddlers, see Sabine, ed., *New York Diary of Lieutenant Jabez*

Fitch, 218; *New-York Gazetteer*, May 20, December 22, 1778, June 3, 1779. For the music season, see *Royal Gazette*, January 5, 1782. For blacks skilled in horse racing, see *New-York Gazetteer*, November 18, 1778. For drummers, see Silverman, *Cultural History of the American Revolution*, 147; "Brunswick Contingent in America," 224. For a Royal African Regiment Ball, see *New-Jersey Gazette*, April 8, 1778. For American ridicule of British multiracial forces, see *Freeman's Journal*, March 22, 1777.

56 *Archives of the State of New Jersey*, 2:365–77, 3:73–74, 185, 235, 273, 437, 610–11. Palsits, ed., *Minutes of the Commissioners*, 1:142–43; Richard Varick to Philip Van Rensselaer, October 30, 1778, Varick Papers, N-YHS. For wills, see Middlesex County wills 5703 and 5758, NJA. Other Patriots worried about their slaves' lack of loyalty. See Hawkins, *Adventures of Christopher Hawkins*, 99–100. For other blacks, see Palsits, ed., *Minutes of the Commissioners*, 1:304–5, 2:454–55. In October a black man was arrested and discharged by General Schuyler on suspicion of going over to the enemy, urged by a "man named Shepherd who is one of the People called Shaking Quakers." See ibid., 2:555. In 1781 several blacks were arrested for conspiring to flee to Canada. See ibid., 702–3.

57 Leiby, *Revolution in the Hackensack Valley*, 190–99. See Clayton, *History of Bergen and Passaic Counties*, 56–66; Demarest and Demarest, *Demarest Family*, 67–68; Taylor, *The History of Teaneck*, 34. See also *Royal Gazette*, May 12, 1779. For formation of Ward's blacks see Undated Memorandum Book, Elliott Papers, 83–89, New York State Library, and Braisted, "Black Pioneers and Others." For Colonel Cuff's blockhouse at Dobbs Ferry, see Martin, *Private Yankee Doodle Dandy*, 205. For the Elizabethtown plot, see *New-York Gazette and Weekly Mercury*, June 20, 1779.

58 The exploits of Tye and his band are fully covered in Hodges, *Slavery and Freedom*, 92–106.

59 For letter to Cuyler, see Letter Book of James Patterson, in *CN-YHS*, 397; for the American warning see *New-Jersey Gazette*, June 5, 1780; for martial law, see Prince, ed., *Papers of William Livingston*, 3:421; for slaves running away, see *Burlington New-Jersey Journal*, June 13, 1780, and *Pennsylvania Evening Post* (Philadelphia), June 23, 1780. For the blockhouse, see Sergeant George Beckwith to Major John Andre, June 20, 1780, Clinton Papers, 105:20, Clements Library, and for similar letters, see ibid., 105:36, 54, 106:1, 13, 37. For "Negro Fort," see *Rivington's New-York Gazetteer*, December 6, 1777. For method of escape, see Van Winkle, *Old Bergen*, 122.

60 Leiby, *Revolutionary War in Hackensack*, 256–58; Quarles, *Negro in the American Revolution*, 147–48. For a biography of Tom Ward, see Jones, *Loyalists of New Jersey*, 240.

61 Hodges, "Black Revolt."

62 Ibid. For the Black Pioneers' New Year's greeting, see Clinton Papers, 138:10, Clements Library.

63 Hodges, "Black Revolt," and Braisted, "Black Pioneers and Others."

64 AO 15/272–76, 15/499–503, 18/235, 38/5–9, 44/65. See also AO 18/561,

18/609, 20/178, 43/203, and 40/309 for other large confiscations. For De Lancey, see Kruger, "Born to Run," 648–49.

65 *Royal Gazette*, February 13, 1779, September 20, October 8, 29, 1783.

66 For requests, see John Harbeck to Carleton, April 14, 1783, CO 50/152; Nicholas Jamieson to Lt. Governor Elliott, April 22, 1783, CO 25/93; John Willoughby, a Virginian, to Carleton, April 28, 1783, in pursuit of three hundred slaves, CO 52/69; Wilson, *Loyal Blacks*, 51–52. See also Peter D. Vroom to General Carleton, Petition to Secure Runaway Negro, ca. 1782–83, N-JHS. One agent, Ralph Wormley, charged £48 for returning thirty-one slaves to Virginia. See Ralph Wormley to John Robinson, April 19, 1782, Library of Congress; "Memoirs of Mr. Boston King," 155.

67 See Lt. General Alexander Leslie to Carleton, June 27, 1782, N-YHS, and James Moncrief to Henry Clinton, March 13, 1782, Moncrief Letter Book, 1780–1782, Clements Library. Intelligence given to General Nathanael Greene refers to British use of "black dragoons" and "Ethiopian Dragoons" in South Carolina. See Green Manuscripts, November 6, 1782, Clements Library.

68 King, "Memoirs of Mr. Boston King," 155; Lindsay, "Diplomatic Relations"; Wilson, *Loyal Blacks*, 53–55. For a summary of Carleton's decision, see PRO 30/8/344/109–11.

69 PRO 30/55/47, 52, 58, 63.

70 Document 6480, Carleton Papers, Public Archives of Nova Scotia.

71 For the murder of Hessius, see Rev. Dirck Romeyn to Richard Varick, July 20, 1782, Varick Papers, N-YHS, and Guy Carleton Orderly Book, 44–45, Mackensie Papers, Bound Volume F, Clements Library. For a slave's refusal to return with his master, see "An Excerpt from a Letter on the Banks of the Hudson, July 9, 1783," in Valentine, *Manual of the City of New York for 1870*, 808–9. See also Brown, ed., *Baroness von Riedesell*, 112–13.

72 Guy Carleton Orderly Book, Mackensie Papers, 138, 166, Clements Library; Valentine, *Manual of the City of New York for 1870*, 794; Wilson, *Loyal Blacks*, 65.

73 For a good account, see Quarles, *Negro in the American Revolution*, 160–81. For the vessel bound for Halifax, see its shipping manifest, October 20, 1782, PRO 30/ 55/52, p. 5938.

74 Carleton to Washington, May 12, 1783, PRO 30/55/69, p. 7666. See the excellent summation of the negotiations between Carleton and Washington in Wilson, *Loyal Blacks*, 41–57; Walker, *Black Loyalists*, 10–12; Quarles, *Negro in the American Revolution*, 167. Although three thousand blacks went to Nova Scotia, others departed for Germany and Great Britain, and an even greater number left from Charles Town and Savannah for Jamaica. For their experience in London and other English cities, see Norton, "Fate of Some Black Loyalists of the American Revolution," 402–3; Gretchen Holbrook Gerzina, "Black Loyalists in London," in Pullis, ed., *Moving On;* Hodges, ed., *Black Loyalist Directory*. For Jamaica, see John Pullis, "Bridging Troubled Waters: Black Loyalists in Jamaica," in Pullis, ed., *Moving On*.

75 See, for example, Hodges, ed., *Black Loyalist Directory*, 81, 102, 132, 202.

For percentages, see Kruger, "Born to Run," 668–70. For the mechanics of departure, see Syrett, *Shipping and the American War,* 238–41.

76 Board of Commissioners for Superintending British Embarkation, Peter Force Collection, Series 8d, Item 14, Library of Congress; Scott, "Prisoners of the Provost Marshall," 15.

77 Hodges, ed., *Black Loyalist Directory,* 209, 212, for John, Isaac Taylor, and the Freelands.

78 See Six Cargo Manifests Showing that Negroes were not taken from the city without permission, 1783, Box 2, Folder 13, Elliott Papers, NYSL. For blacks in jail, see "Monthly List of Prisoners Confined in Provost," *Royal Gazette,* August 6, 1783, and Provost's Report, September 29, 1783, PRO 30/55/97, 99. For harsh punishments, see "Kemble Papers," 183, 193.

79 Board of Commissioners Superintending British Embarcation, July 15, 24, August 2, 7, 1783, Peter Force Collection, Library of Congress; also available in PRO 30/55/100; for American claimants' problems, see CO 30/55/70 and CO 30/55/73. There has been much speculation about whether Samuel Fraunces was black. For a thorough if inconclusive discussion, see Rice, *Early American Taverns,* 147–48, n 1.

80 Muster Book of Free Blacks, Settlement of Birchtown, 1–4, Public Archives of Canada, Ottawa.

81 Ibid., 42–46.

82 Fleischer, *Black Dynamite,* 1:22–30. Richmond later trained Sam Robinson, a black New Yorker who migrated to England to box. See ibid., 1:51–54. For Richmond and Molineaux, see Egan, *Boxiana,* 360–71, 392, 432–40, and Fleischer, *Black Dynamite,* 1:22–30. For Richmond and Robinson, see ibid., 51–54.

83 *Pennsylvania Packet* (Philadelphia), October 28, 1783.

84 See Hodges and Brown, eds., *"Pretends to Be Free,"* and Hodges, ed., *Black Loyalist Directory.*

85 On the experiences of these black Loyalists, see the introduction to Hodges, ed., *Black Loyalist Directory.*

86 Clinton Papers, vol. 170, item 27, as quoted in Braisted, "Black Pioneers and Others."

87 Totals derived from Hodges, ed., *Black Loyalist Directory* and Appendix Table 3.

CHAPTER SIX

1 See Pomerantz, *New York City,* 17. For festivities, see Waldstreicher, *In the Midst of Perpetual Fetes,* chap. 1.

2 For anouncement of laws, see *New York Packet,* March 3, 11, May 8, 1784, and *MCC, 1784–1831,* 1:11, 16, 17, 31. For belief in treason of blacks, see *New York Packet,* April 4, 1785. For leading studies about the end of slavery in the two states, see Zilversmit, *First Emancipation;* McManus, *Black Bondage in the North;* Litwack, *North of Slavery;* White, *Somewhat More Independent;* Melish, *Disowning Slavery.*

3 For community culture in this period and problems securing land, see Hodges, *Slavery and Freedom,* 113–47.

4 White, *Somewhat More Independent,* 7–8, 11. White has corrected the total federal census figures for 1790.

5 Ibid., 26.

6 For analysis of counties, see Moss, *Slavery on Long Island,* 264–70; Kruger, "Born to Run," 752–65; White, *Somewhat More Independent,* 22–23; Potter, "Growth of Population in America," 641.

7 For these numbers, see Wacker, *Land and People,* 190–93, and Hodges, *Slavery, Freedom, and Culture,* 51–52. For tax ratables, see the series from 1778 to 1820 in NJA.

8 See De Lancey Family Papers, MCNY, for his many purchases.

9 For Dutch opposition to abolition, see Main, *Political Parties before the Constitution,* 142–43; Ryan, "Six Towns," 261–76, 280–85, 290; Kruger, "Born to Run," 743–46; Bernard, *Retrospections of America,* 51; Stuart, *Tour of the United States of America,* 379. The Dutch were very reluctant abolitionists internationally. For examples of sales, see Cornelius Hoogeboom to John Hathaway, May 4, 1790, Misc. Mss. Slavery, N-YHS; Receipt of $200 for sale of Negro boy to Peter Gansevoort, February 6, 1796, Gansevoort Papers, N-YHS.

10 For general discussion, see Hodges, *Slavery and Freedom,* 130. See also Tax Rateables for 1787, Shrewsbury Township, NJA; *Return of the Whole Persons within the Several Districts of the United States . . . for the Year 1790,* 39; *Return of the Whole Numbers of People within the Several Districts of the United States. . . . for the Year 1800,* 45; *Heads of Families,* 96–98.

11 New York City Manumission Society Standing Committee Reports, 1785–95; "Statement of the Number of Africans and their Descendants Enjoying Freedom, having Been Released from Unjust Slavery, through the execution of the Standing Committee," in New York Manumission Society Papers, N-YHS; Moseley, "History of the New-York Manumission Society," 1–2, 18, 170–74, 99–100, 107; Fladeland, *Men and Brothers,* 40–41, 80–85; People v. Lawrence Embree, November 5, 1789, New York City Mayor's Court Records, 1789–90, NYPL. For registrations, see Kruger, "Born to Run," 736–37. For political contact, see Fox, "Negro Vote in Old New York," 252–55. For text by "A Free Negro," see Woodson, *Negro Orators,* 25–30. For the 1793 act, see Finkelman, "Kidnapping of John Davis."

12 For confinement in the Bridewell, see *MCC, 1784–1831,* 1:558, 559, 563, 2:614, 3:16, 353, 440, 465, 691, 749, 4:402, 422, 435, 7:344, 350–51, 373–74, 386, 711, 770, 9:474, 493–94, 742, 765; for the Manumission Society proposal, see ibid., 3:440; for runaway report, see Prisoners brought into the Bridewell, August 1, 1799–January 2, 1800, Papers of the Common Council, Box 19, File 1800–1801, NYMA.

13 Alexander, "Federal Officeholders in New York State." For recent criticism of the society, see White, *Somewhat More Independent,* 81–88. For the argument that the society channeled workers, see Harris, "Creating the African

American Working Class." For a counterargument, see Weston, "Alexander Hamilton and the Abolition of Slavery," 41–43. For the 1793 act, see Siebert, *Underground Railroad,* 274.

14 Catteral, *Judicial Cases,* 4:319–50. For the black response, see *Niles' National Register,* October 9, 1847. For Quamini and other emancipated blacks, see Bloomfield, ed., *Cases Adjudged,* 10–12, 16–17. For the society, see *Constitution of the New-Jersey Society for Promoting the Abolition of Slavery.*

15 Nell, *Colored Patriots,* 164–65.

16 See Litwack, *North of Slavery,* 6–7; McManus, *Black Bondage in the North,* 167–70; Nash, *Race and Revolution,* 25–70; Nash and Soderlund, *Freedom by Degrees,* 79, White, *Somewhat More Independent,* 84; Blackburn, *Overthrow of Colonial Slavery,* 273–75.

17 Lincoln, *Messages from the Governors,* 2:237–39; Main, *Political Parties before the Constitution,* 142; Zilversmit, *First Emancipation,* 146–52; Freeman, *Free Negro in Antebellum New York,* 17–21; Pomerantz, *New York City,* 221–22; Kruger, "Born to Run," 726–29.

18 For the ban on the external slave trade and end of the manumission bond in New Jersey, see *Acts of the General Assembly,* 239–40. Price, *Freedom Not Far Distant,* 73–85; Du Bois, *Suppression of the African Slave Trade,* 227, 230–31, 240.

19 Prince, ed., *Papers of William Livingston,* 5:255.

20 *Reflections on the Inconsistency of Man Particularly Exemplified in the Practice of Slavery in the United States,* 8, 15.

21 See Zilversmit, *First Emancipation,* 178–81; Smith, "Discourse Delivered April 11, 1798," 6–8, 15–16; Burrows and Wallace, *Gotham,* 347–49.

22 Ibid., 183–84; Kruger, "Born to Run," 824–51.

23 See Petitions of Alexandrine Fleguy, William Bernan, Mary Warden, Elizabeth Hamersley, Magliore Baillard, John Joseph Boyreau, Jacque DeCamp, Jacques Petit de Vievigne, Loin Dubue, Adrian Depeyrat, and Rev. Lane Jones to Mayor De Witt Clinton, 1803–5, Queensborough Public Library.

24 Zilversmit, *First Emancipation,* 209–22.

25 *Wills,* 13:35, 194, 237, 305, 317, 347; White, *Somewhat More Independent,* 29.

26 Manumissions occurred in seven out of thirty-seven wills probated involving slaves between 1786 and 1792. Of sixty-nine slaves transferred, women (wives, daughters, stepdaughters, nieces, and sisters) received forty-five, or 65 percent. See *Wills,* 14:136, 159, 175, 190, 202, 240, 224. For Baker's will, see ibid., 15:25–28. For Walton, 15:32; Clopper, 15:53–54; Helme, 15:96; Kip, 15:104–5. For other emancipations, see 15:25, 74, 110, 128, 167, 173, 199, 220, 231.

27 Kruger, "Born to Run," 750–60; Berlin, *Many Thousands Gone,* 235.

28 Kruger, "Born to Run," 762–66; McMahon, *Jack Was Earnest,* 3, 5, 9–11.

29 See Middlesex County will 7351, NJA. See also Bergen County will 2588, Essex County will 7178, and Middlesex wills 7723, 7743, 8047, 9483, ibid.

30 Will of Joan Blair, Middlesex will 6703, ibid.

31 See Essex County will 8262. See also Monmouth County will 5587, ibid.

32 For care of emancipated slaves of Loyalists, see Kruger, "Born to Run," 680–88, and Yoshpe, *Disposition of Loyalist Estates*, 91–93. For freedom of Patriot blacks, see Price, *Freedom Not Far Distant*, 72–73.

33 White, *Somewhat More Independent*, 125–33, and Kruger, "Born to Run," 226–35.

34 *New York Packet*, May 5, September 16, 1784, February 21, 1785, December 22, 1785; De Lancey Family Papers, 40.190.63, MCNY.

35 White, *Somewhat More Independent*, 188–202; for Oliver Quadron, see Hodges, "Black Society," 24. For an account of a whole family fleeing New York, see Mars, *Life of James Mars*, 4–5.

36 See *New York Packet*, May 8, 1784. See also Society for Apprehending of Slaves, Constitution and Minutes, Shawangunk, Ulster County, May 21, 1796, Mss. 11155, New York State Library. For runaways, see Jacob Van Schaick to Jacob Gordon, June 12, 1786, Van Schaick Papers, ibid.

37 For runaways and personal contracts, see White, *Somewhat More Independent*, 141–47.

38 De Voe, *Market Book*, 344–45.

39 White, *Somewhat More Independent*, 44–55.

40 McMahon, *Jack Was Earnest*, 11, 15, 19, 21; Geismar, *Archaeology of Social Distingration*, 18–21; Cohen, *Ramapo Mountain People*, 42–49; Caro, "The Hills" in the Mid-Nineteenth Century.

41 Judd, ed., *Correspondence of the Van Cortlandt Family*, 3:45, 118–19, 122, 591.

42 Hodges, *Slavery and Freedom*, 119; Hodges, *Slavery, Freedom, and Culture*, 51–52; Wacker and Clemens, *Land Use*, 97, 99; White, *Somewhat More Independent*, 52–53.

43 Warville, *New Travels*, 232. See also Jeremy, ed., *Henry Wansey*, 91, and Main, *Social Structure of Revolutionary America*, 198.

44 Hodges, *Slavery and Freedom*, 131–33.

45 Ibid., 161–65; Hodges, *Slavery, Freedom, and Culture*, Appendix; White, *Somewhat More Independent*, 51–54.

46 Zelinsky, "Population Geography of the Free Negro," 386–401; Nash, "Forging Freedom," 285–88.

47 For census data, see *Heads of Families*, 119–31. For concentration in Montgomerie ward, see Rothschild, *New York City Neighborhoods*, 100. For discussion of boardinghouses, see Blackmar, *Manhattan for Rent*, 60, 63, 88, 134–35, and Horton, *Free People of Color*, 32–34, 112, 175. For "Black Jenney," see "Minutes of the Alms House and Bridewell," 229–30, NYPL.

48 White, *Somewhat More Independent*, 174–77.

49 For analysis of the rebellious nature of Saint Domingue slaves and their origins, see Fouchard, *Haitian Maroons*, 13–181. For the quote, see Rochefoucauld-Liancourt, *Travels*, 1:544, 2:29–30. For discussion of Saint Domingue migration, see White, *Somewhat More Independent*, 155, and Berlin, *Many Thousands Gone*, 243. For discussion of the 1801 riot, see Gilje, *Road to Mobocracy*, 147–49. For suicide, see *New York Daily Advertiser*, August 31, 1807, and *Reflections on Slavery*.

50 For discussion of the fears of Americans about incoming Haitian blacks, see

Link, *Democratic-Republican Societies,* 173, and Davis, "American Equality and Foreign Revolutions," 747–49.

51 *An Address to the Negroes in the State of New-York by Jupiter Hammond,* 9–10; for Bible reading, see *Authentic Account of the Conversion and Experience of a Negro.*

52 Judd, ed., *Correspondence of the Van Cortlandt Family,* 2:513, 595.

53 White, *Somewhat More Independent,* 157–63. For chimney sweeps, see List of Licensed Chimney-Sweeps, 1799, Licenses Folder, 1799, NYMA, and Gilje and Rock, eds., *Keepers of the Revolution,* 221–24; for hackney coach drivers, see Rock, *Artisans of the New Republic,* 217–18.

54 Durey, *Transatlantic Radicals,* 282–84.

55 [Alexander Hamilton] "Report on Manufactures," in *Papers on Public Credit, Commerce, and Finance,* 206–10.

56 "Minutes of the Alms House and Bridewell," 46, 55–56, 78, 110, 117, 120, 185, 188, 199, 203, 247, 249, 256, 262, 263, NYPL. This form of indentureship differs from the use of apprenticeship as gradual emancipation described for Philadelphia in Salinger, *"To Serve Well and Faithfully,"* 3–4, 146–48. New York's method is closer to the original intent of apprenticeship although gradual emancipation in New York and New Jersey approximated temporary bondage.

57 People v. Nancy, February 7, 1794; People v. Lewis, February 7, 1794; People v. Tom, July 22, 1795; People v. Jack, August 1, 1794; People v. George, Negro Man Slave of John Van Dyck, New York City, April 20, 1792; People v. Harry of White Plains, January 1, 1795; People v. Harry, December 10, 1791. See District Attorney Indictment Papers, NYMA; see also People v. Nancy, August 31, 1790, Minutes of the Mayor's Court, NYPL. See also New York Court of Oyer and Terminer, 1785–1801, Queensborough Public Library. For a complete list of offenders, see "A General List of All Persons Indicted & Convicted in the City and County of New York from the end of the American Revolution to the Year 1820," Microfilm Reel N-YR 1015, Roll 5, ibid. For discussion of larceny upstate, see Coventry, "Memoirs of an Immigrant," 1:167, New York State Library and Archives. For discussion of thievery in New Jersey, see Mellick, *Story of an Old Farm,* 633. For runaways, see The Corporation of the City of New York to the Constables, Marshals and Watchmen for Prisoners Brought into the Bridewell, by them Respectively, 1799–1801, Common Council Papers, 1800–1801, Box 19, NYMA. For the state prison, see Eddy, *Account of the State Prison,* 84–87, and Lewis, *From Newgate to Dannemora.*

58 Bergen County Court Indictments, June term, 1793, October term 1795. See also People v. Port, a Negro Man Slave, March 4, 1785 sentenced to 200 lashes for beating the wife of Daniel McCormick, Parchment P-1001, County Clerk's Office, New York City; People v. Tom, April 19, 1792, for riot, "accused of throwing a great many rocks at Alexander Lamb, Constable, New York City," ibid. See also Conviction of Abby Leonard, a Negro Woman Slave for Assault on Rosannah Wallace, May 5–9, 1798, District Attorney Indictment Papers, Box 2, NYMA. See also ibid., Box 3, for several

more assault cases, and Coventry, "Memoirs of an Immigrant," 1:446, New York State Library and Archives, for black gangs in the woods.

59 Munsell, *Annals of Albany,* 3:161–63; Lewis Morris to Son, December 29, 1796, No. 15765, New York State Library and Archives; *New-York Minerva,* December 14, 1796; for another arson by a black, see *Elizabeth-Town Federal Republican,* September 27, 1803.

60 Register of Marriages, 1:104, 107, 149–295, Trinity Church Archives.

61 For an example of Anglican optimism about blacks, see *Authentic Account of the Conversion and Experience of a Negro.* For an extensive discussion of the problems black ministers had with parent churches, see Hodges, ed., *Black Itinerants.* For Sunday schools, see Brewer, *History of Religious Education,* 104, 164.

62 "Records of St. Mark's Church in the Bowery," 71:337, 72:85, 164–66; "Records of St. Peter's Episcopal Church," 112; Scott, ed., "Record of St. George's Episcopal Church," 110:3–6; Scott, ed., "Records of St. George's Episcopal Church," 112:41–44; "Records of the Marriages and Baptisms as Contained in the First Book of Records of Christ Church," 42:322; Davis et al., *The Church of St. Andrew, Richmond, Staten Island,* 129; "Baptismal Record of St. John's Church, Elizabeth, New Jersey," 6:1–8. For Williams, see Hewitt, "Peter Williams, Jr.," 119–23.

63 White, *Somewhat More Independent,* 116.

64 For the constitution, see *Tricentenary Studies of the Reformed Church,* 401; Luidens, "Americanization of the Dutch Reformed Church," 331. See also "Records of the Reformed Dutch Church in the City of New York," 61:277–79, 373–80, 62:41–45; "Marriages from 1801–1866 in the Dutch Reformed Church, New York City," 70:35–40, 171–72, 277–79, 385–88, 71:187, 300–301, 394–99; "Burials in the Dutch Church, New York," 32, 73; "Church of Brooklyn," in *Year Book of the Holland Society of New York 1897,* 141; "Records of the Reformed Dutch Church of Harlem," 117:228–33, 118:31–32; "Baptismal Records of Reformed Dutch Church of Cortlandtown," 33.

65 Hodges, ed., *Black Itinerants,* 22, 114–17.

66 For black Presbyterians, see "Records of the First and Second Presbyterian Churches in the City of New York," 18:170, 20:177, 179, 181; Robinson, *Testimony and Practice,* 16, 27–29; "Christ's Presbyterian Church at South Hempstead, Long Island, Marriages," 242–54; "Records of the Presbyterian Church, Newtown (Elmhurst) Queens County, Long Island," 291, 393–98; "Baptismal Records of Basking Ridge Presbyterian Church, Somerset County," 23, 36–38; "Bound Brook, New Jersey, Presbyterian Church Records," 66; "Records of the First Presbyterian Church of Cranbury," 60.

67 Wakeley, *Lost Chapters Recovered,* 438–80; Hatch, *Democratization of American Christianity,* 106; Mathews, *Slavery and Methodism,* 5, 9–10.

68 Hatch, *Democratization of American Christianity,* 106–8.

69 Walls, *African Methodist Episcopal Zion Church,* 47–48.

70 For petition of the African Society, see *MCC, 1784–1831,* 2:112, 151, 158, and Walls, *African Methodist Episcopal Zion Church,* 47. For problems over the Old Negro Burial Ground, see *MCC, 1784–1831,* 1:554, 598, 610, 663, 709–

10, 739, 769, 2:22, 134, 218, 221, 252, 264, and Miner, *Tour Around New York City*, 145.

71 Smith, *Climbing Jacob's Ladder*, 39–40.

72 Fordham, *Major Themes in Northern Black Religious Thought*, 29–30.

73 Hodges, ed., *Black Itinerants*. For black ministers on Long Island, see Day, *Making a Way to Freedom*, 113.

74 Gravely, "Rise of African American Churches"; Smith, "Slavery and Theology," 497–98.

CHAPTER SEVEN

1 See Litwack, *North of Slavery;* Curry, *Free Black in Urban America;* Waldstreicher, *In the Midst of Perpetual Fetes*, 323–35.

2 *Constitution of the New-York African Society for Mutual Relief*, 3–4, 7; *New York African Society for Mutual Relief;* Zuille, *Historical Sketch of the New York African Society*, 5, 10, 16; Scottron, "New York African Society for Mutual Relief." See also Perlman, "Organizations of the Free Negro in New York City"; Wilder, "The Rise and Influence of the New York African Society." For confraternities, see Gray, *Black Christians and White Missionaries*, 13–17; Walker, *History of Black Business*, 97–98.

3 Sipkins, *Oration*, 9–14.

4 Williams, *Descendant of Africa*, 13–19, 22, 26; Sidney, *Oration*. See also Hamilton, *Address to the New York African Society for Mutual Relief;* [Sipkins], *Oration;* [Miller], *Sermon on the Abolition of the Slave Trade;* Carman, *Oration;* Hamilton, *Oration on the Abolition of the Slave Trade*, 8–9, 11; Lawrence, *Oration*. See the discussion of the term "African" during this period in Stuckey, *Slave Culture*, 200–202, and Gravely, "Dialectic of Double-Consciousness."

5 For other societies in this period, see *Constitution of the New-York African Clarkson Association;* Mohl, *Poverty in New York*, 154; Sterling, *We Are Your Sisters*, 110; Perlman, "Organizations of the Free Negro," 185–86. There may have been early versions of black fraternal organizations in New Jersey in this period. See Morgan, *History of the Knights of Pythias*.

6 See Hodges, ed., *Black Loyalist Directory;* Wiggins, ed., *Captain Paul Cuffe's Logs and Letters*.

7 Williams, *Discourse Delivered on the Death of Captain Paul Cuffee*, 5–6, 10–11, 16.

8 Gregoire, *Essay Concerning the Intellectual and Moral Faculties and Literature of Negroes*.

9 See Child, *Isaac Hopper*, 164–89. For riots, see *New York Evening Post*, September 20, 21, October 17, 1826; Gilje, *Road to Mobocracy*, 149–51. Blacks could be conservative on some issues. See, for example, *Oration Delivered at the Fifteenth Annual Celebration of the New-York African Society*, 1, 6–7, 12–13, 15–17.

10 *Niles' Register* 18 (July 8, 1820): 344.

11 For black volunteers, see Guernsey, *New York City and Vicinity during the War of 1812*, 1:210–11, and *New York Evening Post*, August 20, 1814. See also White, " 'We Dwell in Safety,' " 445–46. For names, see Nash, "Forging Freedom," 23. See Du Bois, *Black North*, 7.

12 For black sailors, see Fabel, "Self-Help in Dartmoor," 169, and Admiralty Records 103/87, PRO.

13 See discussion of laws in Wright, "New Jersey Laws and the Negro," 178–80; McManus, *Black Bondage in the North*, 181–84; Schneider, *History of Public Welfare in New York State*, 206–9. For tales of kidnapping, see *Niles' Register* 14 (June 13, 1818): 280, 15 (December 12, 1818): 268. For the fate of New Jersey slaves sold to the South, see Malone, *Sweet Chariot*, 100–103. For other slave trade arrests in New York City, see *New-York City Hall Recorder*, 4:172–74.

14 *Laws Relative to Slaves and the Slave-Trade*, 1–5, 10–11, 20–25; Wiecek, *Sources of Anti-Slavery Constitutionalism*, 89–90; Kruger, "Born to Run," 347–56.

15 McManus, *Black Bondage in the North*, 184–85; Litwack, *North of Slavery*, 75; Field, *Politics of Race in New York*, 32–36; Fox, "Negro Vote," 259–60.

16 Finkelman, *Imperfect Union*, 74–77.

17 Wright, "New Jersey Laws and the Negro," 177; Zilversmit, *First Emancipation*, 208–9.

18 *Public Papers of Daniel D. Tompkins*, 1:20, 106; *Laws Relative to Slaves and Servants by the Legislature of New-York;* Lincoln, *Messages from the Governors*, 2:693, 880–81; Zilversmit, *First Emancipation*, 213–15; Fox, "Negro Vote," 257–60.

19 Lee and Lalli, "Population," 33–34, 37; Jury Lists, second ward, 1816, 1819, Microfilm AR-9, Queensborough Public Library.

20 For New York population statistics, see *MCC, 1784–1831*, 7:689, 702; Nash, "Forging Freedom," 285–86, 290, 302–3; White, " 'We Dwell in Safety,' " 452–53; Rosenwaike, *Population History of New York City*, 25; Kruger, "Born to Run," 745–50.

21 Nash, "Forging Freedom," 303–4, 306–7; Kruger, "Born to Run," 348, 351, 354.

22 Jury Lists, fifth ward, 1816, Microfilm AR-9, Queensborough Public Library.

23 Jury Lists, seventh ward, 1819, ibid. For statistics, see *Colored American*, March 25, 1837.

24 The figures are 117 out of 820 affected in 1826, 100 out of 729 in 1828, and 99 of 906 in 1828. See *Statement of Facts Relative to the Late Fever*, 4, 7, 14; *New York Daily Advertiser*, September 19, 1820; *New York Commerical Advertiser*, November 22, 1823. See Duffy, "Account of the Epidemical Fevers," 360; Griscom, *Sanitary Conditions of the Laboring Population of New York*, 14–15, 18.

25 Jury Lists, eight ward, 1816, Microfilm AR-9, Queensborough Public Library; Freeman, *The Free Negro in New York City*, 27; Kruger, "Born to Run," 887–91, 949–58.

26 *New York National Advocate,* August 3, 21, 1821. See Bank, *Theater Culture in America,* 96–97, 113; Southern, *Music of Black Americans,* 116–22; White and White, *Stylin',* 93–95.

27 Over, "New York's African Theater," 7–13; O'Dell, *Annals of the New York Stage,* 1:2, 32, 70–71, 224, 293, 3:70. See also *Memoirs and Theatrical Career of Ira Aldridge.*

28 Hay, *African American Theater,* 6–10; Gilje, *Road to Mobocracy,* 157; Gronowicz, *Race and Class Politics,* 89–91.

29 *Freedom's Journal,* March 16, 23, 30, April 6, 20, June 27, 1827. For Cornish, see Swift, *Black Prophets,* 27–30; *BAP,* 3:95. For Boston Crummell, see Moses, *Alexander Crummell,* 12–13, and Zuille, *Historical Sketch of the New York African Mutual Society,* 28.

30 *Freedom's Journal,* February 14, 1828.

31 Russwarm introduced these ideas in his graduation speech from Bowdoin College. See *Eastern Argus* (Maine), September 12, 1826, in John Russwurm File, Schomburg Center. For other material, see Swift, *Black Prophets,* 39–41; Miller, *Search for Black Nationality,* 88–91; Kinshasa, *Emigration vs. Assimilation,* 73–76; Smith, *Sojourners in Search of Freedom,* 87–89; *BAP,* 3:71–74; Campbell, *Maryland in Africa,* 50, 122–72; *Freedom's Journal,* March 14, 1829.

32 For early reports of illness, see *New York National Advocate,* September 4, 5, 1823; for Jennings, see *Freedom's Journal,* April 4, 1828.

33 Swift, *Black Prophets,* 42–43.

34 *First Annual Report of the Society for the Encouragement of Faithful Domestic Servants,* 2–4; for insolence, see Still, *Mirror for Gotham,* 106; Peter Gansevoort to William Walker, n.d., ca. 1807-8, Gansevoort Papers, N-YHS; *New York National Advocate,* March 2, 1825. For the early effort using Bibles, see Minutes of the Society for the Prevention of Pauperism, N-YHS.

35 John Pintard to Daria Paton, February 11, 1828, Pintard Papers, N-YHS.

36 Wilson J. Moses, "Pierre Toussaint," in Salzman, ed., *Enclyclopedia of African American Culture,* 4:2666. See also Sheehan and O'Dell, *Pierre Toussaint,* 65–90, 140–80; Ryan, *Old St. Peter's,* 210–15. The Pierre Touissant Papers at NYPL are filled with testimonials to his skills written in many languages by wealthy Europeans. For Francis, see Mrs. Francis Pearsall, Record Book of Servant's Wages, MCNY.

37 Kruger, "Born to Run," 909–13; White, *Somewhat More Independent,* 183–88; Richmond, *African Servant,* 3, 4; Litwack, *North of Slavery,* 153–86; Blackmar, *Manhattan for Rent,* 119–23; Stansell, *City of Women,* 156–57; for apprenticeships, see "Nineteenth Century Apprenticeship Register," 1–8; Roberts, *House Servants' Directory.*

38 For negotiations between Pintard and Tamar, see Blackmar, *Manhattan for Rent,* 119. For a similar example, see Harriet Fenno Rodman to Maria Fenno Hoffman, September 3, 1804, Box 1, 60, Fenno-Hoffman Papers, Clements Library.

39 *First Annual Report of the Society for the Encouragement of Faithful Domestic Servants,* 8.

40 Glickstein, *Concepts of Free Labor in Antebellum America*, 99–104, 155; Wilson, *When Work Disappears.*

41 Fearon, *Sketches of America*, 9; Hamilton, *Men and Manners in America*, 1:12, 56, 60; Dunk H. Sill, Biography of a Slave, N-YHS; Lambert, *Travels through Canada and the United States*, 1:107. For examples of brutality, see *Trial of Amos Broad*, 6–7, 11. For other cases of brutality, see Janson, *Stranger in America*, 384–85, and Gilje, *Road to Mobocracy*, 214–20.

42 White and White, *Stylin'*, 101–4; *New York National Advocate*, March 18, 1825; Wilentz, *Chants Democratic.*

43 For Mose and Lize, see Wilentz, *Chants Democratic*, 300–301; Stansell, *City of Women.* I have been influenced about the rise of popular black street style by Southern, *Music of Black Americans*, 116–25; Lhamon, *Raising Cain*, 1–56; White and White, *Stylin'*, 37–63; Roberts, *From Trickster to Badman.*

44 For regulated trades, see *MCC, 1784–1831*, 3:473, 493, 505, 589. For chimney sweeps, see *MCC, 1784–1831*, 3:473, 493, 589, 603, 684, 658, 5:673, 681, 8:613, 620, 625, 700; and List of Licensed Chimney Sweeps, and Common Council Papers, 1818, NYMA; and Gilje and Rock, " 'Sweep O!,' " 507–38. For cries, see Still, "New York City in 1824," 137–69.

45 Protest against the Conduct of Nightmen, August 12, 1817, City Clerk Papers, NYMA, in Rock, ed., *New York City Artisan*, 38–40; Rock and Gilje, *Keepers of the Revolution*, 318–24; White and White, *Stylin'*, 90.

46 Petition of William Williams, a Man of Color, June 28, 1819, Police Committee Folder, NYMA.

47 For New Jersey seamen in Philadelphia, see Smith, *"Lower Sort,"* 156–59.

48 Bolster, " 'To Feel Like a Man,' " 1185. For Paul Cuffe, see Thomas, *Rise to Be a People.* For other materials on black seamen working out of New York City, see Foner and Lewis, *Black Worker to 1869*, 196–214. Seafaring was among the most dangerous of occupations. See Inquisitions on the Bodies of Jack and James, October 5, 1797; Thomas, a Negro, August 24, 1787; John Harriott and Israel, December 22, 1787; Will, July 15, 1790, all in Coroner's Reports, County Clerk's Office, New York City, and Minutes of the Alms House and Bridewell, 1791–97, 22, 27, 76, NYPL.

49 Petition to City Inspector, June 13, 1803, Common Council Papers, Box 21, NYMA; Bolster, " 'To Feel Like a Man.' " For cosmopolitan sailors, see Blaine, *Excursion*, 3–4. For escape, see *Life of William Grimes*, 53–61, and Trumbull, *Life and Adventures of Robert*, 18–23. For a benevolent society, see *Constitution of the African Marine Society.* See also Wheeler, *Chains and Freedom*, 165–69, and Hodges, ed., *Black Itinerants.*

50 Washington, ed., *Narrative of Sojourner Truth; Life, Trial and Confessions of Thomas Jones;* Andrews, *History of the New-York African Free Schools*, 10–12, 86–90. Eddy, *Life of Jacob Hodges*, 4–6, 93–94; *African Repository* 18 (1842): 360–64.

51 Bolster, " 'To Feel Like a Man' "; Langley, "Negro in the Navy"; Foner and Lewis, *Black Worker*, 1:209–11, 285; for the colored retreat, see Duffy, *History of Public Health*, 1:490–91.

52 See Petitions of Artillo and Fortune Freeman and Prince Vaughan to the Mayor's Court, 1820, Miscellaneous Mss., Queensborough Public Library.

53 For developments in music, see Saxton, "Blackface Minstrelsy." For huckstering, see Stansell, *City of Women*, 202–3. Robinson, *Hot Corn*, features a white heroine in a job traditionally held by blacks. For the rise of white entertainers using black faces and songs, see Toll, *Blacking Up*, 30.

54 List of Vagrants Transported from New York Port, 1808, Alms House Collection, Vol. 89, and Census of Alms House Admissions, 1814–1815, Microfilm 257, Roll 28, NYMA; Alms House Report, 1805, Box 24, Common Council Papers, NYMA.

55 *MCC, 1784–1831*, 8:204. See also Alms House Census, 1817–1820, Alms House Collection, NYMA. For numbers and percentages, see "John Stanford's Almshouse Census, 1816–1826," in Mohl, *Poverty in New York*, 87. For Abigail Dodson, see Thompson, *Sketches of the History*, 32. For Job Young, see *MCC, 1784–1831*, 9:624–28.

56 See Bridewell Penitentiary File, August 1820, NYMA. See also District Attorney Indictment Papers, August 1820, NYMA. For debt imprisonment, see Record of Visits to the Debtor's Gaol, 1805–1815, Humane Society Papers, N-YHS. For lengthier terms, see Gardiner, *New York Reporter*, 1:9–11, 2:52–53, 59; *New York National Advocate*, October 5, 1821.

57 Gilje, *Road to Mobocracy*, 160–166; New York Court of Oyer and Terminer, 1808–1826, Microfilm, Queensborough Public Library, 154–58; A General List of All Persons Indicted and Convicted in the City and County of New York from the End of the American Revolution to the Year 1820, Microfilm N-YR 1015, Roll 5, Queensborough Public Library.

58 *Confessions of Isaac Fraser and George Vanderpool;* Sommers, *Memoir of Reverend John Stanford*, 234–40; Report to Society for Supporting the Gospel among the Poor, 1820, Stanford Papers, N-YHS. See also conviction of Rosanna Butler for arson in Box 95 (1819), Penitentiary Records, NYMA.

59 Gilfoyle, *City of Eros*, 58–64; "Minutes of the Alms House," 77, Alms House Collection, NYMA; *New York Evening Post*, May 29, 1815, July 9, 1822, March 27, 1830. My thanks to George A. Thompson Jr. for these references.

60 *First Annual Report of the Executive Committee of the New York Magadalene Society*, 6, 15; Gilfoyle, *City of Eros*, 40, 58–59, 62–65, 84–85, 104–8; White, " 'We Dwell in Safety,' " 459. For the sex ratio, see Kruger, "Born to Run," 312.

61 *Trial of Captain James Dunn*. For another case involving interracial sex and assault, see *Faithful Report on the Trial of Doctor William Little*. There was even one black transvestite working as a prostitute. See Burrows and Wallace, *Gotham*, 797, and Gilfoyle, *City of Eros*, 136–37.

62 *MCC, 1784–1831*, 10:452, 501; Petition of Hector Scott and David Bethune, April 16, 1810, Common Council Papers, NYMA. See also *New York Evening Post*, May 29, 1815, July 9, 1822, March 27, 1830. For urban examples, see *Murders! Report of the trial of James Johnson*, 1–3, 5–9; New York Court of Oyer and Terminer, 1808–26, 108–15, Queensborough Public Library; Ely,

Visits of Mercy, 1:32–33, 43, 52–54; *New York National Advocate,* July 9, 1822.

63 Stansell, *City of Women,* 79–83; Ely, *Visits of Mercy* 1:51, 221; District Attorney Indictment Records, May 11, 1820, NYMA.

64 For blacks on ferries, see Stafford, *New Missionary Field,* 13–16; see also Eddis, *Letters from America,* 426–27.

65 Nugent, "Mary Simpson Washington," Typescript, 1939, Schomburg Center.

66 Day, *New York Street Cries in Rhyme,* 18.

67 For "spectacle of market," see Agnew, *Worlds Apart,* 149; White, *Sierra Leone's Settler Women Traders,* 17–34. For an account of a black woman who walked to market from Little Ferry to Newark daily, see Arnold Brown, "The Elizabeth Sutliff Dulfer Story," typescript, Bergen County Historical Society.

68 The material on market dancing comes from DeVoe, *Market Book,* 344–45. For a fine discussion, see Lhamon, *Raising Cain,* 1–56. See also Cohen, "In Search of Carolus Africanus Rex," 156–57, and White, "Question of Style."

69 Lhamon, *Raising Cain;* White and White, *Stylin';* Hodges, "'Desirable Companions and Lovers.'"

70 Ely, *Visits of Mercy;* John Stanford Papers, N-YHS, excerpted in *New-York Historical Society Quarterly* 21 (1937): 22–30; Sommers, *Memoir of the Reverend John Stanford.*

71 Trendel, "John Jay II," 239; Bennett, "Black Episcopalians," 239–43; Reimers, "Negro Bishops and Diocesan Segregation," 236. For study of the mission and Sunday school movement, see Rosenberg, *Religion and the Rise of the American City,* 52–61, 84–86, 95, 125–36; Sommers, *Memoirs of the Reverend John Stanford,* 112, 218–35; Ely, *Visits of Mercy,* 1:166–71, 221–38. For discussion of the debate among Protestants about slavery, see Carwardine, *Evangelicals and Politics in Antebellum America,* 155–65.

72 For domestics, see Anstice, *History of the St. George's Church,* 485–89, which I checked alphabetically against *Longworth's American Almanac.*

73 St. Philip's Record Book of Baptisms, Schomburg Center; Hirsch, "Negro and New York," 441–42; Hewitt, "Peter Williams, Jr.," 105–8.

74 For Sunday school, see Mandeville, *Golden Memories,* 12–13.

75 See, for example, the prescient points in Woodson, *History of the Negro Church,* 78–83. For an update on these ideas, see Hatch, *Democratization of American Christianity,* 96–98; 103–10.

76 Warriner, *Old Sand Street Methodist Episcopal Church of Brooklyn,* 6–7, 21–22, 46; Taylor, *Black Churches of Brooklyn,* 9–10. McClain published a racist tract titled *Slavery Defended from Slavery.*

77 Fladeland, *Men and Brothers,* 91–98; Brown, *Biography of the Reverend Robert Finley,* 35–60; Frederickson, *Black Image in the White Mind,* 1–43; Quarles, *Black Abolitionists,* 4–8. For a correction of the origins of the ACS, see Egerton, "Its Origin Is Not a Little Curious."

78 McMurray, *Sermon,* 15–19; *Proceedings of a Meeting Held at Princeton, New Jersey, July 14, 1824.*

79 *Doctrines and Discipline of the African Methodist Church in America*, iii–iv; [Rush], *Short Account*, 27–29, 31, 37–40; Woodson, *History of the Negro Church*, 70–74.

80 Southern, *Music of Black Americans*, 85–90; Watson, *Methodist Error.*

81 Morgan, *Morgan's History*, 12–13, 65, 73, 89, 94; Hodges, ed., *Black Itinerants;* Drew, *North-side View of Slavery*, 32–37, 174; Williams, "Blacks, Colonization, and Antislavery"; Pawley, *Negro Church in New Jersey*, 27–30. By 1836 New York City alone had twelve churches and 750 members. See Payne, *Semi-Centenary and Retrospection of the African Methodist Church*, 23, 31. For the spread of AME Zion to Brooklyn, see Taylor, *Black Churches of Brooklyn*, 9–12.

82 Statement of the Number of Children Educated at the African Free School at the Expense of the Manumission Society, New York Manumission Society Papers, N-YHS; Mosely, "History of the New-York Manumission Society," 174–200; Andrews, *History of the New-York African Free Schools*, 8–9, 31; African Free School Records, 1:4–10, N-YHS; Mohl, "Education as Social Control in New York City." For the number of scholars and financial assistance, see *MCC, 1784–1831*, 2:296, 401, 452, 608, 620, 3:12, 564.

83 Brewer, *History of Religious Education*, 104, 164, 169–70, 172. For a brief attempt to educate black males, see New York (N.Y.) Records of the Association for the Instruction of Colored Male Adults, American Antiquarian Society.

84 Barnett, "Educational Activities"; Stuckey, *Slave Culture*, 145–47; Freeman, *Free Negro*, 319–28 Mohl, *Poverty in New York*, 176–78; African Free School Records, N-YHS; *African Repository* 6 (1831): 302–5; Andrews, *History of the New-York African Free Schools*, 65, 118–23; *Address to the Parents and Gurdians of the Children*, 13–16. For the Shaw quote, see Kaestle, *Pillars of the Republic*, 38–39. For a list of apprentices, see Nineteenth Century Apprenticeship Register, New York City, 115:1–8, N-YHS.

85 *Freedom's Journal*, April 6, 1827.

86 Mott, *Biographical Sketches*, 66–70, 74–80, 109–32.

87 Mabee, *Black Education*, 51–52. For a different emphasis on these schools, see Swan, "Did Brooklyn Blacks Have Unusual Control."

88 Woody, *Quaker Education*, 266–80.

89 Constitution of the African Association of New Brunswick, New Jersey, Adopted January 1, 1817, Alexander Library; *Address to the Public on the African School*, 1–3. See also Williams, *Discourse Delivered on the Death of Captain Paul Cuffee*, 16.

90 Wright, *Afro-Americans in New Jersey*, 30–32.

91 Kruger, "Born to Run," 742–49.

92 Tax Ratables, NJA.

93 For Seneca Village, see Blackmar and Rosenzweig, *The Park and the People*, 64–73. For New Jersey, see Anna Bustill Smith, "Reminiscences of the Coloured People of Princeton, New Jersey, 1800-1900," typescript, Alexander Library, 2–3, and Hodges, *Slavery and Freedom.*

94 Adriance Van Brunt of Brooklyn, Diary, NYPL; James Hawkhurst, Jour-

nal, NYPL; Stephen Vail Journals, Historic Speedwell, Morristown, N.J.; John Baxter of Flatlands, Diaries, 3:2, 18–19, 4:48, passim for innumerable work notations, Brooklyn Historical Society; Augustus Griffin Diaries, 1:125–26, Brooklyn Historical Society; Farm Accounts of Robert Drummond, Alexander Library; John Neilson Farm Diary, 1802–32, Box 1, Neilson Papers, ibid.

95 James Hawkhurst, Account Book and Journal, NYPL; Unidentified Account Book, Brookhaven, Long Island, N-YHS; Day Book of Charles Nicoll, N-YHS; Ledger of Daniel Schenck of Monmouth County, 30, 58, 61–65, 77, Alexander Library; James Tallman's Ledger from Monmouth County, 6, 13, 20, ibid. For examination of the transition from bonded to free wage labor, see Paul G. E. Clemens and Lucy Simler, "Rural Labor and the Farm Household in Chester County, Pennsylvania, 1750–1820," in Innes, ed., *Work and Labor in Early America*, 106–44.

96 "Extracts of John Baxter's Journal of Daily Activities and Related Events Pertaining to Slaves, January, 1790–February, 1830," and "Extracts from Dr. Samuel Thompson's Journal of Daily Activities and Related Events Pertaining to Slaves, March 1800–January, 1801," in Moss, *Slavery on Long Island*, 322–24.

97 Larison, ed., *Syvia Du Bois*, 65–68,103–5. For Christmas, see Strickland, *Journal of a Tour*, 63–64. For frolics, see Mellick, *Story of an Old Farm*, 607.

98 Pleat and Underwood, "Pinkster Ode Albany," and article on Pinkster in *Albany Centinel*, June 13, 1803, as quoted in White, *Somewhat More Independent*, 100–101. For blacks selling goods to raise money and comment on whistling, see Furman, *Antiquities of Long Island*, 266; Dunlap, *Diary of William Dunlap;* DeVoe, *Market Book.*

99 *Freedom's Journal*, April 20, July 6, 1827, June 22, 1826; Hamilton, *Oration at the African Zion Church*. See also Gilje and Rock, *Keepers of the Revolution*, 241–42; Lorini, "Public Rituals," 18–23; Bernhard, *Travels through North America*, 1:126; Garnet, *Memorial Discourse;* [Buckingham] *Citizen*, 310–14; Hall, *Travels in North America*, 110–11. White, "Proud Day," 39–41.

100 For the celebration on Staten Island and numbers freed, see Kruger, "Born to Run," 780–83.

101 Gravely, "Dialect of Double-Consciousness," 302–3.

102 Stuckey, *Slave Culture*, 144; Pierson, *Black Yankees*, 117–43.

103 *New York Commercial Advertiser*, September 22, 1827. For Lafayette, see Du Bois, *Black North*, 7.

CHAPTER EIGHT

1 Fearon, *Sketches of America*, 60; Abdy, *Journal of a Residence and Tour*, 1:302; Felton, *American Life*, 58. For other racial incidents, see Marryat, *Diary in America*, 150; Nevins and Thomas, eds., *Diary of George Templeton Strong*, 1:100, 199–200, 217. The famed black dancers frequently suffered public humiliation. See George D. Parnham to the Common Council,

July 25, 1837, Misc. Mss., Schomburg Center. Even the revered black Catholic Pierre Toussaint was publicly insulted. See Sheehan and O'Dell, *Pierre Toussaint*, 178–82, 214–16.

2 For descriptions of the mob violence, see Headley, *Great Riots of New York*, 79–97; Hewitt, "Sacking of St. Philip's Church"; Kerber, "Abolitionists and Amalgamators"; Richards, *"Gentlemen of Property and Standing,"* 113–22, 126, 152–54; Swift, *Black Prophets*, 66–69; Curry, *Free Black*, 101; Gilje, *Road to Mobocracy*, 162–73. For letters from prominent blacks, see 1834 Riot Folder, Misc. Mss., N-YHS. Gilje's discussion of the riot comes closest to my point of view, arguing that while the composition of the rioters was largely unskilled and in competition with black laborers for work, the focus of rage was on black institutions and attempted to "root out blacks as an alien group" (*Road to Mobocracy*, p. 167). I am unpersuaded by the explanation that such mobbing can be excused as a class-oriented attempt to evict potential competition or as nose-thumbing at the Tappans. For recent discussion of the emergence of modern racist society, see Stewart, "Emergence of Racial Modernity." I agree with Stewart on the racism in the 1834 riots. See ibid., 200.

3 New Jersey's black population is conveniently summarized in Wright, *Afro-Americans in New Jersey*, 80–98, and Wacker, *Land and People*, 210.

4 Hodges, *Slavery and Freedom*, 171–203; Hodges, *Slavery, Freedom, and Culture*, 146.

5 Litwack, *North of Slavery*. For William Lloyd Garrison and black activists, see Pease and Pease, *They Who Would Be Free*, 7–9, 13; Swift, *Black Prophets*, 93; *BAP*, 3:8–19.

6 For numbers, see *Abstract of the Returns of the Fifth Census*, 11; *Compendium of the Enumeration of the Inhabitants and Statistics of the United States . . . for 1840*, 21; U.S. Census Office, *Fifth Census or Enumeration of the Inhabitants of the United States, 1830*, 51; *New York State Census for 1835*, 26; De Bow, *Statistical View*, 64. For free black ownership of slaves, see Woodson, *Free Negro Owners of Slaves*, 23. For population and property in New York City, see Curry, *Free Black*, 2–13, 37–40, 269; Rosenwaike, *Population History of New York City*, 32–45.

7 United States Census Office, *Sixth Census of Enumeration of the Inhabitants of the United States . . . 1840*, 114; *New York State Census for 1845;* United States Census Office, *Population of the United States in 1860*, 324–25, 337; Wright, *Afro-Americans in New Jersey*, 35–37; Rosenwaike, *Population History of New York City*, 36–45; Curry, *Free Black*, 40–41, 53–54, 73, 79; Ernst, *Immigrant Life in New York City*, 41, 235. New York City housing remained far less segregated than that in Boston, Philadelphia, and Baltimore. See Berlin, *Slaves without Masters*, 257.

8 Scott, comp., "Coroner's Reports for New York City, 1823–1842." For Monmouth County, see Hodges, *Slavery and Freedom*. For death rates, see Duffy, *History of Public Health*, 1:536–37; Curry, *Free Black*, 137–42. For children, see Book of Indentures of the Association for the Benefit of the Colored Orphan Asylum, vol. 1, N-YHS.

9 De Bow, comp., *Mortality Statistics of the Seventh Census of the United States*, 161–63, 171–87.

10 De Bow, *Statistical View*, 166–67; Curry, *Free Black*, 113–16.

11 De Bow, *Statistical View*, 65, 67, 79–80, 97; Shaw, *Making of an Immigrant City*, 29–30.

12 Gilje and Rock, eds., *Keepers of the Revolution*, 234–35; Curry, *Free Black*, 23–25. For the story of a Brooklyn black entrepreneur, see Gatewood, ed., *Free Man of Color*, 39–40, 43–53, 74–79. On Cato, see Kaplan, "The World of the B'hoys," 27–28.

13 Stansell, *City of Women*, 157; Gilje and Rock, eds., *Keepers of the Revolution*, 211.

14 De Bow, *Statistical View*, 80–81.

15 *Colored American*, September 16, 1837; De Bow, *Statistical View*, 80. For Lawrence, see Willet and Lawrence Account Book, Arents Rare Book Room.

16 For divisions of labor, see Stott, *Workers in the Metropolis*, 92, 145. For comparisons between Irish and blacks, see Groneman, "Bloudy Ould Sixth," 444–45, and Ernst, *Immigrant Life in New York City*, 213–17.

17 Foner and Lewis, *Black Worker*, 1:178–79, 191–94, 245.

18 Curry, *Free Black*, 117–18; Sanger, *History of Prostitution*, 580; for the keno game, see *New York Daily Express*, December 10, 1840; for Thompson, see *New York Daily Express*, December 10, 1840, January 5, 1841.

19 Dickens, *American Notes*, 43. For a return visit, see Blumin, ed., *New York by Gaslight*, 140–49.

20 Lhamon, *Raising Cain*, 38–46. For the Whitman quote, see Hodges, "Muscle and Pluck." For interpretations of race, see Lott, *Love and Theft;* Melish, *Disowning Slavery.*

21 See Hodges, "Desirable Companions and Lovers," 107–25, and Ryan, *Civic Wars*, 35–60.

22 For a description of black oystermen at work, see Sutcliff, *Travels in Some Parts of North America*, 115–16.

23 Adrian Van Brunce of Brooklyn, Diary, NYPL. See also James Hawkhurst, Journal, NYPL; John Baxter of Flatlands Diaries, Brooklyn Historical Society; Eddy, *Life of Jacob Hodges*, 6–7; Dickenson, *Census Occupations*, for large categories of black farm laborers. See also Stephen Vail Journals, Historic Speedwell, Morristown, N.J.

24 For Bergen County, see Hodges, *Slavery, Freedom, and Culture*, 56–58. For Monmouth, see Hodges, *Slavery and Freedom*, 181.

25 Wacker, "Patterns and Problems," 54–62; Hodges, *Slavery, Freedom, and Culture*, 146–48.

26 Klips, "Institutionalizing the Poor," 276; Thompson, *Sketches of the History*, 18–19, 28–29, 33, 36, 70–72.

27 For Presbyterians, see Howard, *Conscience and Slavery*, 32–36; How, *Slaveholding Not Sinful*. For Methodists, see Hagood, *The Colored Man in the Methodist Episcopal Church*, 35–83. For black Catholics, see Dolan, *Immigrant Church*, 24–25.

28 Pennington, *Text Book of the Origin and History of the Coloured People*, 81–85. See also Newcomb, *"Negro Pew."*

29 For this development, see Ginsberg, *Women and the Work of Benevolence;* Howard, *Conscience and Slavery*, 29–100.

30 Book of Indentures of the Association for the Benefit of the Colored Orphan Asylum, N-YHS. See also Newark Alms House Records, N-JHS.

31 Klips, "Institutionalizing the Poor," 268–75. For the ages of blacks in the Colored Home, see *Annual Report of the Society for the Support of the Colored Home* and *Report of the Resident Physician of the Colored Home;* De Bow, *Statistical View*, 68–69.

32 See Benjamin T. Onderdonk to Rev. Peter Williams, July 12, 1834 and Rev. Mr. Williams to the Citizens of New York, July 14, 1834, reprinted in Woodson, *Mind of the Negro*, 629–34.

33 Mabee, *Black Freedom*, 127–30.

34 For commentary on the Negro Pew, see *Ram's Horn*, November 5, 1847. For discussion of white religious bias during this period, see Quarles, *Black Abolitonists*, 71; Litwack, *North of Slavery*, 202–10; McKivigan, *War against Proslavery Religion*, 44–46, 51–55. For an example of black use of white churches by servants, see "Christ's Presbyterian Church at South Hempstead, Long Island, Marriages," 242–46, 251–54.

35 "Williams to the Citizens," in Woodson, *Mind of the Negro*, 633–34; *African Repository*, July 14, 1834. For exclusion of Williams from the diocese, see [Jay], *Caste and Slavery*, 14, and Hewitt, "Peter Williams, Jr.," 119–23. For later reforms, see Hewitt, "Unresting the Waters."

36 See, for example, *Liberator*, September 1, 1837.

37 For black congregations, see Greenleaf, *History of the Churches of All Denominations*, 327–29; Rush, *Short Account of the A.M.E. Zion Church*, 87–89, 92–93; *Minutes of the General and Annual Conference of the A.M.E. Zion Church*, 18, 27; Morgan, *Morgan's History*, 57–71; Day, *Making a Way to Freedom*, 54–56, 125–26; *Articles of Faith*. For itinerant ministers, see *Narrative of the Life of Reverend Noah Davis*, 56, and *Brief Miscellaneous Narrative*, 70–74. For the Trenton conference, see Trenton, New Jersey, Circuit of the African Methodist Church, 1828–1848, Carter G. Woodson Papers, Microfilm, Reel 4, Library of Congress.

38 See, for example, Ward, *Autobiography*, 3–26, 28–54; *DANB*, 631–32; Morgan, *Morgan's History*, 12–81; Hood, *One Hundred Years;* Drew, *North-side View of Slavery*, 32–37.

39 Garrison, *Thoughts on African Colonization*, Appendix, 12–15, 23–28, 46–52. For Africanus, see Ward, *Momento*, 15.

40 Bell, *Survey of the Negro Convention Movement*, 16–18, 30–35; Bell, ed., *Proceedings of the National Negro Conventions;* Williams, *A Discourse Delivered in St. Philip's Church*, 1–3, 10–13; "A Colored Citizen of Brooklyn," in Woodson, *Mind of the Negro*, 238; *Liberator*, February 12, 1831, as quoted in Aptheker, ed., *Documentary History*, 109. For the lingering appeal of Haiti, see Hunt, *Haiti's Influence*, 160–63.

41 Mabee, *Black Education in New York State*, 20–23; Rury, "New York African

Free School"; Kaestle, *Pillars of the Republic*, 174–76; *African Repository* 10 (1830): 23–27; Taylor, "A Sketch of Religious Experiences in and around New York City," Misc. Mss. 1858, Library of Congress. For whites visiting the Free School, see Washburn, ed., *Diary of Michael Floy, Jr.*, 44, 213, 219, 222–25.

42 Boylan, *Sunday School*, 24–29; Anderson, "Negro Education," 119–25.

43 Kaestle, *Pillars of the Republic*, 179–80; Dann, *Black Press*, 293–97; Anderson, "Negro Education," 140–45.

44 See Sterling, *Speak Out in Thunder Tones*, 91–96; Mabee, *Black Education*, 30–34. For Reason, see Sherman, *Invisible Poets*, 27.

45 Porter, "Organized Educational Activities of Negro Literary Societies," 564–69; *African Repository* 11 (1835): 146.

46 Ward, *Momento*, 4.

47 Mabee, *Black Education*, 55–65, 73–77; Aptheker, ed., *Documentary History*, 141, 153; Pease and Pease, *They Who Would Be Free*, 134–36; Swift, *Black Prophets*, 60–63. For the program of the Phoenix Literary Society, see Foner and Lewis, *Black Worker*, 1:251. For statistics, see De Bow, *Seventh Census*, lix.

48 Princeton, New Jersey, Presbyterian School (Colored), 1852–56, Records of the Sabbath School, Princeton University Library; Seaton, "Colonies and Reluctant Colonists." Sunday schools were still popular in New York. See Mabee, *Black Education*, 35–47.

49 Young, *Ethiopian Manifesto*, 1–2, 5, 8–9, 10–11. For comment on reassembling Africans, see Stuckey, *Going through the Storm*, 87–88. On David Walker, see Hinks, *To Awaken My Afflicted Brethren*, 95–98, 162.

50 Walker was also well-known in New York. See *Freedom's Journal*, March 16, 1827, July 27, 1827, among many others; for discussion, see Litwack, *North of Slavery*, 232–35, and Swift, *Black Prophets*, 45.

51 [Ruggles]. *First Annual Report of the New York Committee of Vigilance*, 13–17, 20–31, 66–70, and *Philanthropist* 44 (1835): 2–5. For other reports of slave ships in New York City during this period, see Eltis and Richardson, *Economic Growth*, 114, 127, 145, 157–58, 161.

52 Swift, *Black Prophets*, 77; for the 1832 riot, see Gilje, *Road to Mobocracy*, 152–53; Gooch, *America and the Americans*, 74–77.

53 David Ruggles, in *Liberator*, August 6, 1836, in *BAP*, 3:168–80; Horton, *Free People of Color*, 80–98.

54 Douglass, *My Bondage and My Freedom*, 206–7, and [Douglass], *Life and Times*, 230–31. For discussion, see Quarles, *Frederick Douglass*, 8–9. See Porter, "David Ruggles," 23–50; Pennington, *Fugitive Blacksmith;* Foner, ed., *Life and Writings of Frederick Douglass*, 1:23. For Roper, see *Narrative of the Adventures and Escape of Moses Roper*, 8–10.

55 "The Adventures of Mahommah Gardo Bequaqua," in Austin, *African Muslims*, 634–37.

56 *Fifth Annual Report of the New York Committee of Vigilance*, frontispiece for Board of Directors, 12, 13–18, and "Circular of the New-York State Vigi-

lance Committee," Rush Rhees Library, University of Rochester; Dann, *Black Press*, 324–28; *BAP*, 3:284–88. For stories of fugitives, see also Cheseboro, "Fugitive Slaves," Rush Rhees Library, University of Rochester. For membership of the African Mutual Society in 1830s and 1840s, see Zuille, *Historical Sketch of the New York African Society*, 27–33.

57 Siebert, *Underground Railroad*, 123–30.

58 Finkelman, *Imperfect Union*, 134–36. See also *Life and Adventures of James Williams*, 9–13, 16–19.

59 Finkelman, *Imperfect Union*, 296–98, and *Report of the Lemmon Slave Case*.

60 For these and numerous other illustrations, see Mabee, *Black Freedom*, 91–128.

61 For Matilda, see *Freedom's Journal*, August 10, 1827. For the opposition to colonization, see Miller, *Search for Black Nationality*, 82–89, and Bell, *Survey of the Negro Convention Movement*, 9–13.

62 Porter, "Organized Educational Activities of Negro Literary Societies." See also the experiences of Maria Stewart in Sterling, *We Are Your Sisters*, 111–13. For discussion of women's place, see Horton, *Free People of Color*, 99–103; Reed, *Platform for Change*, 76–79; Boylan, "Benevolence and Antislavery Activity," 119–38.

63 Abdy, *Journal of a Residence and Tour*, 2:32–33. For another instance of family purchasing by a benevolent black, see *New York Transcript*, February 5, 1836; *New York Commercial Advertiser*, February 8, March 29, 1836; Jeffrey, *Great Silent Army*, 183.

64 See Washington, ed., *Narrative of Sojourner Truth*.

65 "The Life and Religious Experience of Jarena Lee," in Andrews, ed., *Sisters of the Spirit*, 35–37, 42–45.

66 Child, *Letters from New York*, 65–68; Child, *Issac T. Hopper*, 385. See also Peterson, *"Doers of the Word,"* 81, 86, 95, 113.

67 "A Brand Plucked from the Fire: An Autobiographical Sketch by Mrs. Julia A. J. Foote," in Andrews, ed., *Sisters of the Spirit*, 200–203, 212–13, 219. See also in the same volume, "Memoirs of the Life, Religious Experience, Ministerial Travels and Labors of Mrs. Zilpha Elaw," 56, 65, 103–13; Washington, ed., *Narrative of Sojourner Truth*, 116–20.

68 For female itinerants, see Bogin and Loewenberg, *Black Women in Nineteenth Century American Life*, 128–32, 142–46, 174; Washington, ed., *Narrative of Sojourner Truth*; Brekus, *Strangers and Pilgrims*, 133–35, 143–46, 277–81.

69 Hamilton, *Address to the Fourth Annual Convention of the Free People of Color*, 5. For Wright, see *Colored American*, October 4, 1837; Ruggles, *Antidote*, 2–3, 14–15, 17–20; Cornish and Wright, *Colonization Scheme Considered*, 3, 5–8, 17–22.

70 Bates, *Remarks on the Character and Exertions of Elias Hicks*, 13–14. *BAP*, 3:9–13. For a different view of the balance of European and African influences on black abolitionists, see Moses, *Alexander Crummell*, 7–12. For an assessment of the early black literary societies, see Porter, "Organized Edu-

cational Activities of Negro Literary Societies," 555–76. For antislavery activists, see Jentz, "Antislavery Constituency in Jacksonian New York City."

71 George, "Widening the Circle," 75–99; Fordham, *Major Themes*, 111–37.

72 Nell, *Colored Patriots*, 150–53; Curry, *Free Black*, 218–22.

73 Yates, *Rights of Colored Men to Suffrage*, 1, 61–62, 86–87.

74 Sewall, *Ballots for Freedom*, 172–75.

75 For comments on the election of 1840 and the Liberty Party, see *Colored American*, September 12, October 3, 10, 1840; Smith, *Lecture on the Haytian Revolutions*, 15; Garnet, *Walker's Appeal;* and Garnet, *Past and the Present Condition*. On the Liberty Party's failures with blacks, see Sewall, *Ballots for Freedom*, 95–101.

76 Swift, *Black Prophets*, 82–87; *BAP*, 3:216–27; Litwack, *North of Slavery*, 238; Dann, *Black Press*, 123–26. For the *Alarm Bell*, see Sherman, *Invisible Poets*, 75–79. For choice of name, see Stuckey, *Slave Culture*, 206–9.

77 Wiecek, *Sources of Anti-Slavery Constitutionalism*, 198–99. In 1843 an angry mob blocked a southern slave master from taking his captured slave back home, though the master was aided by knife-wielding Princeton University students. He was forced to sell the enslaved man to a philanthropic lady, who then allowed the now indentured servant to purchase his freedom in five years. See *Niles' National Register* 64 (August 12, 1843): 384.

78 See Hodges, *Slavery and Freedom*, 178–81; Hodges, *Slavery, Freedom, and Culture*, 56–58.

79 Stewart, *Legal Argument;* Wiecek, *Sources of Anti-Slavery Constitutionalism*, 256–57; Callegio, "Negro's Legal Status," 171–73.

80 For general discussion, see Gronowicz, *Race and Class Politics*, 129–73. On the Hamlet case, see [Hamlet], *Fugitive-Slave Bill*.

81 See the extended discussion of these developments in Field, *Politics of Race*, 45–75, 103–10, 214–20; Swift, *Black Prophets*, 128, 135–38; Foner, "Racial Attitudes." For black votes, see Benson, *Concept of Jacksonian Democracy*, 179–81. See also Finkelman, "Protection of Black Rights in Seward's New York," for an argument that black rights were not wholly negated in this period.

82 Finkelman, *Imperfect Union*, 300–312.

83 Howard, *American Slavers and the Federal Law*, 49–57, 127–29, 164–69, 249–52; Ward, *The Royal Navy and the Slavers*, 138–51.

84 Reynolds, *Dutch Houses in the Hudson Valley;* Hodges, *Slavery, Freedom, and Culture*, 58; Hodges, *Slavery and Freedom*, 187–89; Moses, *Afrotopia*. For Pennington, see Howe, *Afrocentrism*, 37; Hobsbawm and Ranger, *Invention of Tradition*, 1–6.

85 For discussion of burial practices, see Washington, *Peculiar People*, 45–58, 311–18, and Vlach, *The Afro-American Tradition in Decorative Arts*, 139–48. See also Thompson and Cornet, *Four Moments of the Sun*, 181–91, esp. 181 for white pottery and 192–94 on the significance of pipes. For black cemeteries, see The Old Slave Cemetery, Cedar Street, Bergenfield, Notebook, 1987, Bergen County Historical Society; grave site at Gethsemane,

Little Ferry, New Jersey. For toys on graves, see Bishop, *Englishwoman in America*, 378.

86 Easton, *Treatise on the Intellectual Character*, 12–24.

87 For the number of blacks emigrating, see *Memorial of Semi-Centennial*, 182–90. For changing perceptions, see Swift, *Black Prophets*, 164–66, 244–65; Day, *Making a Way to Freedom*, 114. For black ministers in the ACS, see Peterson, *Looking Glass*, 90–100.

88 De Laney, *Condition, Elevation, Emigration, and Destiny;* Delaney, "Why We Must Emigrate," in Foner and Lewis, *Black Worker*, 1:365. See also Miller, *Search for Black Nationality*, 119–30, 187–99, and Moses, *Golden Age of Black Nationalism*, 35–36, 150–53, 187–93, 198.

89 Crummell, *Duty of a Rising Christian State*, 6–9. 19. See generally the collection by Crummell, *Future of Africa*.

90 Blyden, *Liberia's Offering;* Holder, *Blyden of Liberia*, 23–25, 87–94.

91 *Anglo-American*, 1859, 20, 30, 33–36, 65–68, 93, 98–100, 235–38; Miller, *Search for Black Nationality*, 170; Moses, *Golden Age of Black Nationalism*, 32–33.

92 Dann, *Black Press*, 264–66.

EPILOGUE

1 *War of the Rebellion*, 37, pt. 2: 875–914. See also Quarles, *Negro in the Civil War*, 237–47; McKay, *Civil War and New York City*, 197–202; Bernstein, *New York City Draft Riots*, 20–23; Cook, *Armies of the Street*, 55–67, 77; Asbury, *Gangs of New York*, 118–73; Headley, *Great Riots of New York*, 152–60; *Bloody Week!*, 8, 30.

2 *Report of the Committee of Merchants for the Relief of Colored People*, 24–25; Cook, *Armies of the Street*, 81–95.

3 *War of the Rebellion*, 886–87; Cook, *Armies of the Street*, 97–98, 121, 126, 132–36. For the eight women, see Quarles, *Negro in the Civil War*, 241. For psalm-singing resistance, see Hammond, ed., *Diary of a Union Lady*, 249–50. For reports on these incidents, see Foner and Lewis, *Black Worker*, 1:287–300. For Simmons, see Glatthaar, *Forged in Battle*, 240–41.

4 *War of the Rebellion*, 907; *Report of the Committee of Merchants for the Relief of Colored People*, 17–19; Cook, *Armies of the Street*, 136, 141, 152–53; Foner and Lewis, *Black Worker*, 1:292.

5 Cook, *Armies of the Street*, 194–99; *War of the Rebellion*, 935–38; McKay, *Civil War in New York City*, 20–21. For suppression of the riots, see Richardson, *New York Police*, 133–44.

6 For a careful analysis of these patterns derived from contemporary newspapers, see Lee, *Discontent in New York City*, 16–17, 20–31, 43–60, 105–8, 126–35, 147–53, and Montgomery, *Beyond Equality*, 102–7. For Wood's message, see McKay, *Civil War in New York City*, 33. For black militia, see *Weekly Anglo-African*, May 4, 1861; Quarles, *Negro in the Civil War*, 27, 29. For prosouthern views, see Wright, *Secession Movement in the Middle Atlantic States*, 98–124, 166–205. For the unchurched quality of the Catho-

lic Church's reaction, see Dolan, *Immigrant Church*, 24–26, 56–58. See also Berlin et. al., *Freedom*, 97.

7 *Report of the Committee of Merchants for the Relief of Colored People*, 9–12; Cook, *Armies of the Street*, 174–75; McKay, *Civil War in New York City*, 208–10; Bernstein, *New York City Draft Riots*, 56; Foner and Lewis, *Black Worker*, 289–91.

8 Bernstein, *New York City Draft Riots*, 66.

9 Headley, *Great Riots of New York*, 142–45; Barnes, *Draft Riots in New York;* Stoddard, *Volcano under the City;* Leonard, *Three Days' Reign of Terror*.

10 In addition to Cook and Bernstein, see the treatment in Ernst, *Immigrant Life in New York City*, 174, which was the first book to argue that the Draft Riots were a manifestation of working-class discontent. See also Montgomery, *Beyond Equality*, 107.

11 See articles cited in Foner and Lewis, *Black Worker*, 284–87. See also Glatthaar, *Forged in Battle*, 196–97, and McKay, *Civil War in New York City*, 159, 196–97.

12 Lee, *Discontent in New York*, 165–227.

13 Hammond, ed., *Diary of a Union Lady*, 182–83, and Lee, *Discontent in New York City*.

14 See Valuska, *Afro-American in the Union Navy*, 31, 56, 74, 144–47; *Weekly Anglo-African*, September 4, 1861. Valuska counted 9,610 blacks, or 8 percent of the total number of sailors in the Union navy, revising Herbert Aptheker's estimate of 25 percent but not substantially challenging Aptheker's comments about the influence or importance of black naval enlistments. See Aptheker, "Negro in the Union Navy." In 1864, 278 men from New York and 146 from New Jersey joined the navy; in 1865, 78 and 10 came from New York and New Jersey.

15 For efforts to recruit blacks into the Union army, see O'Reilly, *First Organization of Colored Troops in the State of New York*, 4–7; Douglass, *Life and Writings of Frederick Douglass*, 3:14, 35–39, 95–98; Blight, *Frederick Douglass' Civil War*, 80–88; Glatthaar, *Forged in Battle*, 71–80, 108–9, 201–3, 272; Cornish, *Sable Arm*, 253–54. For black celebrations, see Quarles, *Negro in the Civil War*, 143, 162–63. For numbers, see Hargrove, *Black Union Soldiers in the Civil War*, 206.

16 Berlin, ed., *Freedom*, 374–75, 668–70, 680; Glatthaar, *Forged in Battle*, 169–76; Price, *Freedom Not Far Distant*, 125–27.

17 Bernstein, *New York Draft Riots*, 66–68; Field, *Politics of Race*, 158; *Compendium of the Ninth Census*, 74–77; Scheiner, *Negro Mecca*, 16–20, 87–93; Rosenwaike, *Population History of New York City*, 60, 72, 77.

18 See discussion of this movement in McPherson, *Struggle for Equality*, 231–33.

19 For black elites, see Gatewood, *Aristocrats of Color*, 103–7, 277–79. For survey, see *New York World*, March 16, 1867, as printed in Thelen and Fishel, "Reconstruction in the North," 405–40. See also Du Bois, *Black North*, 8–14.

Bibliography

MANUSCRIPT SOURCES

Alexander Library, Rutgers University, New Brunswick, New Jersey
  Constitution of the African Association of New Brunswick, New Jersey,
    Adopted January 1, 1817.
  Drummond, Robert. Farm Accounts, 1822–56, Shrewsbury, New Jersey.
  Neilson Papers.
  New Brunswick Statute Book, 1733–45.
  Schenck, Daniel, of Monmouth County. Ledger, 1799–1801.
  Smith, Anna Bustill. "Reminiscences of the Colored People of Princeton,
    New Jersey, 1800–1900." Typescript.
  Society for the Propagation of the Gospel in Foreign Parts. Transcripts.
  Tallman, James. Ledger from Monmouth County, 1800–1801.
Algemeen Rijksarchief, The Hague, Netherlands
  Records of the Old West India Company.
American Antiquarian Society, Worcester, Mass.
  New York (N.Y.) Records of the Association for the Instruction of Coloured
    Male Adults, 1816–19.
Archivo de Indias, Seville, Spain
  Interim Governor [of Florida] Fulgencio Garcia de Solis to Marquesta de la
    Ensaenada [governor of Cuba], August 25, 1752, in *ramo* Gobierno:
    Santo Domingo, *leagajo* 58-1-33, document 23.
Arents Rare Book Room, Syracuse University, Syracuse, New York
  Willet and Lawrence Account Book, 1819–32.
Bergen County Historical Society, River Edge, New Jersey
  Ancient Indictments, 1700–1775.
  Bergen County Court Indictments, June term 1793–October term 1795.
  Brown, Arnold. "The Elizabeth Sutliff Dilfer Story." Typescript.
  The Old Slave Cemetery, Cedar Street, Bergenfield, Notebook, 1987.
Bodleian Library, Oxford University
  Harrison, Francis. "Observations Humbly Offered to His Grace the Duke
    of Chandos Sharing the Advantages Which the Royal African Company
    May Receive by Settling an Agency in order to Supply that Province,
    the Colonists at East and West Jersey, Connecticut, Rhode Island,
    Narragansett, and the Southwest Parts of New England with Slaves."
    Mss. Gough Somersetshire 7 (S.C. 18217).
British Museum Manuscript Room, London
  Journal of an Officer Who Travelled Over Part of the West Indies, and
    of North America in the Course of 1764, 1765. Kings Manuscripts,
    vol. 213:39.

Brooklyn Historical Society, Brooklyn, New York
  Baxter, John, of Flatlands, Diaries, 1790–1835.
  Griffin, Augustus. Diaries, 1792–1850, 2 vols.
Clements Library, University of Michigan, Ann Arbor
  Clinton Papers.
  Fenno-Hoffman Papers.
  Gold Star Manuscripts.
  Green Manuscripts.
  Mackensie, Frederick. Papers.
  Moncrief Letter Book.
Columbia University, Special Collections, Rare Book Room, New York City
  Coroner's Proceedings in the City and County of New York, 1747–58.
  Minutes of the Quarter Sessions, May 3, 1715–February 1, 1721.
County Clerk's Office, New York City
  Coroner's Reports.
  County Clerk's Parchments, Court of General Sessions.
  Minute Book of the New York Supreme Court of Judicature, April 19,
      1757–August 2, 1760.
  Minutes of the Court of General Quarter Sessions of the Peace, 1691–1776.
Fales Library, New York University, New York City
  Maass Collection.
Haviland Record Center, New York City.
  Oblong (Pawling) Monthly Meeting, 1757–81.
  A Record of the Discharge of the Negroes Set at Liberty by Friends of the
      Westbury Monthly Meeting.
  Shrewsbury Scrapbook.
Historic Speedwell, Morristown, New Jersey
  Vail, Stephen. Journals, 1829–32.
Library of Congress, Washington, D.C.
  Board of Commissioners for Superintending British Embarcation,
      Force Manuscripts.
  Force, Peter. Collection.
  Ralph Wormley to John Robinson, April 19, 1782, Misc. Mss.
  Secret Intelligence, July 21–November 10, 1778, British Memo Book.
  Skinner, Cortlandt. Papers.
  Taylor, Jeremiah. "A Sketch of Religious Experiences in and around
      New York City, 1811–1858." Misc. Mss. 1858.
  Woodson, Carter G. Papers.
Museum of the City of New York
  De Lancey Family Papers.
  Pearsall, Mrs. Francis. Record Book, 1807–20.
National Archives–Mid-Atlantic Division, Special Collections, New York City
  Depositions of William Johnson and Peter Lockcourt Concerning ye Ship
      Charles Being at & Coming from Guinny, 1685.
New Jersey Department of State, Records and Archives, Trenton
  Bergen, Essex, Middlesex, Monmouth, and Somerset County Wills.

Books of Registers and Copy of Inventory of Damages Done by the Enemy
and the Adherents to the Inhabitants of the County of Bergen, Essex,
Middlesex, Somset, 1776–1782.

Inquisitions on the Dead. 4 vols.

Morris, Lewis. Account Book, 1690–98.

Tax Ratables, 1779–1814.

New-Jersey Historical Society, Newark

Engrossed Act to Lay a Duty on the Importation of Slaves, 1769.

Log of the Ship *Catherine*.

Neau, Elias, and John Cruger. Account Book.

Newark Alms House Records, 1854–58.

Peter D. Vroom to General Carleton, Petition to Secure Runaway Negro,
1782–83.

Tax Ratables, 1779–1814.

New-York Historical Society, New York City

Account Book of the British Army, 1776–82.

African Free School Records.

Audited Accounts of the Church Wardens of New York City, Received and
Disbursed for the Minister and Poor-House, 1714, 1723–26, 1738.

Bancker, Christopher. Ledger Book, 1718–55.

Beekman, James. Account Book of Personal Affairs, 1761–98.

Beekman Family Papers.

Book of Indentures of the Association for the Benefit of the Colored
Orphan Asylum, 1835–66.

British Army Quartermaster General Accounts.

Croesen Family Papers.

Daybook of an Unidentified New York Physician or Pharmacist.

Deall, Samuel. Account Book, 1756–78.

Dean Family Papers.

Dickenson, Harry. Papers.

1834 Riot Folder, Misc. Mss.

Faulkner Manscripts.

Gansevoort Papers.

Humane Society Papers.

Janeway, George. Account Book. 1768–99.

Kempe, John Tabor. Papers.

Lt. General Alexander Leslie to Sir Guy Carleton, June 27, 1782.

Livingston, Philip, and Sons. Book of Trade for the Slave Ship Rhode
Island on a Voyage to Sierra Leone, January–July 1749, listing goods
bartered for slaves and the number of slaves who died on the
Return Voyage.

Minutes of the Society for the Prevention of Pauperism, 1819–22.

Misc. Mss. B. Douglas.

Misc. Mss. Castleton.

Misc. Mss. Flushing, New York.

Misc. Mss. New York Inventories.

Misc. Mss. John Smith of Mastic, New York.

Misc. Mss. Slavery.

New-York Manumission Society. Papers.

Nicoll, Charles. Day Book, November 1758–August 15, 1768.

Parish Transcripts.

Pintard Papers.

Pryor, John. Account Books, 1762–67.

Robert G. Livingston to Henry J. Livingston, June 18, 1751.

Sandford, William. Papers.

Schuyler, Ann Elizabeth. Account Book, 1737–60, Schuyler Manuscripts.

Sill, Dunk H. Biography of a Slave.

Stanford, John. Papers.

Taylor, John. Day-Book, 1762–65.

Unidentified Account Book, Brookhaven, Long Island, 1774–1814.

Van Cortlandt Letter Book, 1698–1700.

Varick Papers.

Wadsworth Papers.

Witter, Thomas. Account Book, 1747–68.

New York Municipal Archives, New York City

Alms House Collection.

Bridewell Penitentiary File.

Bushwyck Town Records, 1660–1875.

Common Council of New York City. Papers, 1664–1831.

District Attorney Indictment Papers.

List of Licensed Chimney-Sweeps, 1799.

Miscellaneous Conveyances of Kings County.

Penitentiary Records.

Police Committee Folder, 1819.

New York Public Library, New York City

Bowne, John. Account Book, 1649–1703.

Emmet Collection.

Hawkhurst, James. Account Book and Journal, 1797–1851.

Inventory and Administration of the Estate of Adolph Philipse, 1749–63.

A Law for Regulating Negroes and Slaves in the Night Time, April 22, 1731.

Minutes of the Alms House and Bridewell.

Minutes of the Mayor's Court, 1789–90.

New York City Mayor's Court Records.

Toussaint, Pierre. Papers.

Van Brunt, Adriance, of Brooklyn. Diary, 1828–30.

Verdict of the Jury that Adrian Hooglandt Died from Wounds Inflicted by Certain Named Negro Slaves during the Insurrection of April 7, Signed by the Coroner and Jury, April 19, 1712.

New York State Library and Archives, Albany, New York

Conveyance, 1765, Archives No. 17534.

Coventry, Alexander. "Memoirs of an Immigrant."

Deed of Sale of Negro Boy Boam, Archives No. 5122.

Elliott Papers.

New York Colonial Documents.

New York Colonial Manuscripts. 101 vols.

Registry of Children and Manumission Papers, 1800–1806, Yonkers.

Society for Apprehending of Slaves, Constitution and Minutes,
    Shawangunk, Ulster County

Van Schaick Family Papers.

Pierpont Morgan Library, Gilder Lehrman Papers, New York City

Champion, Richard. Certification of Freedom of Negro Peter,
    November 27, 1786.

Compton, Harry. Deed of Purchase, November 13, 1803.

Cotton, John, to Rowland Cotton, October 27, 1711.

Cotton, John, to Unknown, September 9, 1699.

Livingston, Philip. Document Signed, May 4, 1757.

Livingston, Philip. Document Signed, November 29, 1760.

Livingston, William, to Unknown, November 21, 1774.

Rhea, Jonathan. Manumission Deed, April 13, 1813.

Princeton University Library, Princeton, New Jersey

Hunter, Andrew. War Diary.

Princeton, New Jersey, Presbyterian School (Colored), 1852–56, Records of
    the Sabbath School.

Tarleton, Banastre. Letters Relating to Military Movements in New Jersey,
    1776.

Public Archives of Canada, Ottawa

Muster Book of Free Blacks, Settlement of Birchtown, 1784.

Public Archives of Nova Scotia

Carleton, Sir Guy. Papers.

Inglis, Charles. Papers.

Public Record Office, London

Abstracts of 200 days pay Forage to the General and Staff of the British
    Army for the Campaign of 1779, PRO 30/55.

British Headquarters Papers, PRO 55/57.

Lord Dunmore's Account of Expenses, 1775–83, Audit Office 16/44.

Return of the Clerk's Storekeepers, Wagon Masters, Conductors, and
    Laborers, July 1,1781.

Simpson, Nathan. Letter Books.

United Kingdom, Colonial Office Papers, 5th ser., Records of the Customs
    Collectors, Records of Entrances and Clearances at the Port of
    New York, 1715–64.

Queensborough Public Library, Flushing, New York

A General List of All Persons Indicted and Convicted in the City and
    County of New York from the End of the American Revolution to
    the Year 1820.

Jury Lists for New York City, 1814, 1816, 1817, 1819, 1821.

Miscellaneous Mss.
New York Court of Oyer and Terminer, 1785–1801, 1808–26.
Petitions to Mayor De Witt Clinton.
Rhodes Library, Oxford University
Lambeth Palace Papers.
Papers of the Society for the Propagation of the Gospel in Foreign Parts.
Royal Artillery Institute, Woolwich Arsenal, London
Patterson, Brigadier-General James. Letter Book, 1777–78.
Patterson Papers.
Rush Rhees Library, University of Rochester, Rochester, New York
Cheseboro, Francis Worden. "Fugitive Slaves: Recollections of the
Underground Railroad." Typescript.
Circular of the New-York State Vigilance Committee.
Schomburg Center, New York Public Library, New York City
"Mary Simpson Washington." Typescript. 1939.
Parnham, George D., to Common Council, Misc. Mss., July 25, 1837.
Russwurm, John. File.
St. Philip's Record of Baptisms, 1818–1969.
Scottish Record Office, Edinburgh
Cunnningham of Thornton Muniments.
State Historical Society of Wisconsin, Madison
Jones, Samuel. Papers.
Provoost, David. Duty Statement, 1715.
Trinity Church Archives, New York City
First Recorded Minutes Regarding the Building of Trinity Church, 1695.
Miscellaneous Real Estate Papers.
Records of Trinity Church. Baptisms.
Register of Marriages, vol. 1.
Trinity Church Audit Book, 1696–1730.

PRINTED PRIMARY MATERIALS

[Aaron]. *The Light and Truth of Slavery: Aaron's History.* Worcester, Mass.:
Published at Worcester for Aaron, 1844.
Abdy, Edward. S. *Journal of a Residence and Tour in the United States of North
America from April, 1833 to October, 1834.* 3 vols. London: J. Murray, 1835.
Acts of the General Assembly of New Jersey, 1786 (10th Session). Trenton,
N.J.: I. Collins, 1786.
An Address to the Negroes in the State of New-York by Jupiter Hammond. New
York: Carroll and Patterson, 1792.
*An Address to the Parents and Guardians of the Children Belonging to the New-
York African Free School by the Trustees of the Institution.* New York: Samuel
Wood and Sons, 1818.
*An Address to the Public on the African School Lately Established under the Care of
the Synod of New-York and New Jersey.* New York: J. Seymour, 1816.

Albion, Robert G., and Dodson, Leonidas, eds. *Journal of Philip Vickers Fithian, 1775–1776.* Princeton: Princeton University Press, 1934.

Allinson, Samuel, ed. *Acts of the General Assembly of the Province of New-Jersey from the Surrender of the Government to Queen Anne, on the 17th Day of April, in the year of our Lord, 1702 to the 14th Day of January 1776.* Burlington, N.J.: Isaac Collins, 1776.

Andrews, Charles W. *History of the New-York African Free Schools.* New York: Mahlon Day, 1830.

Annual Report of the Society for the Support of the Colored Home with the Laws and Regulations. 21 vols. New York: J. Trow, 1838–60.

Antibiastes. *Observations on the Slaves and Indented Servants, Inlisted in the Army and Navy of the United States.* Philadelphia: Styner and Cist, 1777.

Archives of the State of New Jersey. 48 vols. Newark: Printed for the State of New Jersey, 1880–1949.

Articles of Faith, Church Discipline and By-Laws of the Abyssinian Baptist Church in the City of New York. New York: J. Post, 1833.

The Asiento, Or the Contract for Allowing the Subjects of Great Britain the Liberty of Importing Negroes into Spanish America, Signed by the Catholic King at Madrid, March 26, 1713. London: John Baskett, 1713.

An Authentic Account of the Conversion and Experience of a Negro, Extracted from a Letter Written by a Gentleman who was Secretary of Lord H——— during Part of the late American War. London: T. Wilkens, 1790.

"Baptismal Records of Basking Ridge Presbyterian Church, Somerset County, 1795–1817." *Genealogical Magazine of New Jersey* 7 (1931): 23, 36–38.

"Baptismal Records of Church Protestant Lutheran Congregation of New York, Nova Caesaria, Albany, and Other Parts Belonging thereto in North America, by Reverend Justus Falckner." In *Year Book of the Holland Society of America,* 1903. New York: The Society, 1903.

"Baptismal Records of Reformed Dutch Church of Cortlandtown, Westchester County." *New York Genealogical and Biographical Record* 75 (1945): 33.

"Baptismal Records of St. John's Church, Elizabeth, New Jersey." *Genealogical Magazine of New Jersey* 6 (1930): 1–8.

Barck, Dorothy, ed. *Papers of the Lloyd Family of the Manor of Queens Village, Lloyd's Neck, Long Island, New York, 1654–1826.* 2 vols. *Collections of the New York-Historical Society.* New York: Printed for the Society, 1926–27.

Barnes, David. *The Draft Riots in New York, July 1863.* New York: Baker & Godwin, 1863.

Bates, Barnabas. *Remarks on the Character and Exertions of Elias Hicks in the Abolition of Slavery; Being an Address Delivered before the African Benevolent Societies in Zion's Chapel, March 15, 1830.* New York: Mitchell and Davis, 1830.

Bell, Howard Holman, ed. *Proceedings of the National Negro Conventions, 1830–1864.* New York: Arno Press, 1969.

Bernard, John. *Retrospections of America, 1797–1811.* New York: Harper's, 1887.

Bernhard, Karl, Duke of Saxe Weimar-Eisenach. *Travels through North America during the Years 1825 and 1826.* 2 vols. London: Carey, Lea, and Carey, 1826.

Bishop, Lucy [Isabella Bird]. *An Englishwoman in America.* London: John Murray, 1856.

Blaine, William N. *An Excursion through the United States and Canada during the Years 1822-1823.* London: Baldwin, Cradock and Joy, 1824.

The Bloody Week! Riot, Murder & Arson Containing a Full Account of the Wholesale Outrage on Life and Property Prepared from Official Sources by Eye Witnesses with Portraits of "Andrews" the Leader and "Rosa" His Eleventh Street Mistress. New York: Coutant and Baker, 1863.

Bloomfield, Joseph, ed. *Cases Adjudged in the Supreme Court of New-Jersey Relative to the Manumission of Negroes.* Burlington, N.J.: Isaac Neale for the New-Jersey Society for the Abolition of Slavery, 1795.

Blumin, Stuart, ed. *New York by Gaslight and Other Urban Sketches by George G. Foster.* Berkeley: University of California Press, 1991.

Blyden, Reverend Edward Wilmot. *Liberia's Offering: Being Addresses, Sermons, Etc.* New York: J. A. Gray, 1862.

Bosman, William. *A New and Accurate Description of the Coast of Guinea.* London: J. Knapton, 1705.

"Bound Brook, New Jersey, Presbyterian Church Records, 1805-1810." *Genealogical Magazine of New Jersey* 37 (1962): 65-70.

Bray, Thomas. *Missionalia; or, A Collection of Missionary Pieces Relating to the Conversion of the Heathen; Both the African Negroes and American Indians.* London: W. Roberts, 1727.

Bridenbaugh, Carl, ed. *The Intinerarium of Dr. Alexander Hamilton, 1744.* Chapel Hill: University of North Carolina Press, 1948.

A Brief Miscellaneous Narrative of the More Early Part of the Life of Levin Tilmon, Pastor of a Colored Methodist Congregational Church in the City of New York Written by Himself. Jersey City, N.J.: W. W. and L. A. Pratt, 1853.

The British Instructor or the First Book for Children Being a Plain and Easy Guide to the English Language. . . . London: J. Andrew Oliver for Thomas Field, Bookseller, 1763.

Brown, Isaac V. *Biography of the Reverend Robert Finley, D.D., of Basking Ridge, New Jersey.* 2d ed. Philadelphia: J. W. Moore, 1857.

Brown, Marvin L. Jr., ed. *Baroness von Riedesel and the American Revolution.* Chapel Hill: University of North Carolina Press for the Institute of Early American History and Culture, 1965.

"The Brunswick Contingent in America, 1776-1783." *Pennsylvania Magazine of Biography and History* 40 (1891): 218-24.

[Buckingham, James]. *A Citizen of the World: America and the Americans.* New York: Harper's, 1873.

"Burghers and Freemen." In *Collections of the New-York Historical Society,* 18. New York: Printed for the Society, 1880.

"Burials in the Dutch Church, New York." *New York Genealogical and Biographical Record* 77 (1945): 26-37.

Burnaby, Reverend Andrew A. M. *Travels through the Middle Settlements of North America in the Years 1759 and 1760.* London: Printed for T. Payne, 1775.

Bush, Bernard, comp. *Laws of the Royal Colony of New Jersey, 1704–1775.* 5 vols. Trenton, N.J.: New Jersey State Library, 1975–86.

"Cadwallader Colden Papers." In *Collections of the New-York Historical Society for the Years 1917–1923.* New York: Printed for the Society, 1917–23.

Carman, Adam. *An Oration Delivered at the Fourth Anniversary of the Abolition of the Slave Trade in the Methodist Episcopal Church in Second-Street, January 1, 1811.* New York: C. Totten, 1811.

Catterral, Helen. *Judicial Cases Concerning American Slavery and the Negro.* 5 vols. Washington, D.C.: Carnegie Institution of Washington, 1936.

"Chamberlain's Records for the City of New York, 1690–1700." In *Collections of the New-York Historical Society for 1912.* New York: Printed for the Society, 1912.

Child, Lydia Maria. *Isaac T. Hopper: A True Life.* Boston: John P. Jewett, 1853.

———. *Letters from New York.* 2d ser. New York: C. S. Francis, 1843.

Christoph, Peter R., and Florence A. Christoph, eds. *The Andros Papers.* 3 vols. Syracuse, N.Y.: Syracuse University Press, 1989–91.

Christoph, Peter, Kenneth Scott, and Kenn Stryker-Rodda, eds. *New York Historical Manuscripts: Dutch Kingston Papers.* 2 vols. Baltimore: Genealogical Publishing, 1976.

"Christ's Presbyterian Church at South Hempstead, Long Island, Marriages." *New York Genealogical and Biographical Record* 53 (1922): 242–54.

Churchill, John. *A Collection of Voyages and Travels Some Now First Published in English.* . . . 6 vols., 3d ed. London: Printed by Assignment from Messrs. Churchill for Henry Lintot and John Osborn, 1744.

Clark, Elmer T., ed. *The Journal and Letters of Francis Asbury.* 3 vols. London: Epworth Press, 1958.

Collins, Varnum Lansing, ed. *A Brief Narrative of the Ravages of the British and the Hessians at Princeton in 1776–77.* Princeton: University Library, 1906.

Colonial Laws of New York from the Year 1664 to the Revolution. 5 vols. Albany: J. B. Lyon, 1894–96.

"Colonial Records of New York: General Entries, 1664–1665." *State Library Bulletin* 2 (May 1899).

The Commissioners of the Alms-House vs. Alexander Whistelo, a Black Man Being a Remarkable Case of Bastardy. . . . New York: David Longworth, 1808.

The Confessions of Isaac Fraser and George Vanderpool under Sentence of Death, for Arson, with Some Account of Thomas Burke for the Murder of His Wife Sentence to Be Executed on Friday, 19 January 1816. New York: Elias Gould, 1816.

Constitution of the African Marine Society. New York: John C. Totten, 1810.

Constitution of the New-Jersey Society for Promoting the Abolition of Slavery to Which Is Annexed, Extracts from a Law of New-Jersey, Passed 2nd March,

1786, and Supplement to the Same, Passed 26th November, 1788. Burlington, N.J.: Printed for the Society by Isaac Neale, 1788.

Constitution of the New-York African Clarkson Association. New York: E. Conrad, 1825.

Constitution of the New-York African Society for Mutual Relief, Passed June 8, 1808. New York: Printed for the Society, 1808.

"Cornelius Lydecker Diary for 1776." *Papers and Proceedings of the Bergen County Historical Society* 11 (1915–16): 66–68.

Cornish, Samuel E., and Theodore S. Wright. *The Colonization Scheme Considered in Its Rejection by the Colored People in Its Tendency to Uphold Case—in Its Unfitness for Christianity and Civilizing the Aborigines of Africa and for Putting a Stop to the African Slave Trade*. Newark, N.J.: A. Guest, 1848.

Corwin, Edward T., ed. *Ecclesiastical Records of the State of New York*. 7 vols. Albany: J. B. Lyon, 1901–16.

Crummell, Alexander. *The Duty of a Rising Christian State to the World's Well-Being and Civilization and the Means by Which It May Perform the Same, the Annual Oration before the Common Council and Citizens of Monrovia, Liberia, July 26, 1855*. London: Wertheim and MacIntosh, 1856.

———, ed. *The Future of Africa, Being Addresses, Sermons, Etc. Etc. Delivered in the Republic of Liberia*. 2d ed. New York: C. Scribner, 1862.

Dapper, Olfert. *Description de l'Afrique*. Amsterdam, Netherlands: Wolfgan, Waesberge, Boom, and Van Someren, 1670.

Davies, K. G., ed. *Documents of the American Revolution, 1770–1783*. Colonial Office Series. 21 vols. Shannon: Irish University Press, 1972–81.

Day, Mahlon. *New York Street Cries in Rhyme*. New York: Mahlon Day, 1825.

De Laney, Martin R. *The Condition, Elevation, Emigration, and Destiny of the Colored People of the United States, Politically Considered*. Philadelphia: M. R. DeLaney, 1852.

De Ronde, Lambertus. *A System Containing the Principle of the Christian Religion; Suitable to the Heidelburg Catechism; by Plain Questions and Answers Useful for the Information of All Persons in the True Confession of Faith; And Necessary for Their Preparation for That Awful and Solemn Ordinance, the Lord's Supper*. New York: H. Gaine, 1763.

DeVoe, Thomas F. *The Market Book*. New York: Printed for the Author, 1860.

Dickens, Charles. *American Notes for General Circulation*. Boston: Ticknor & Fields, 1867.

Dickinson, Richard, comp. "Abstracts of Early Black Manhattanites." *New York Genealogical and Biographical Record* 116 (1985): 100–105, 169–74.

The Doctrines and Discipline of the African Methodist Church in America, Established in the City of New York, October 25, 1820. New York: C. Rush and George Collins for the A.M.E. Church in America, 1820.

Donnan, Elizabeth, ed. *Documents Illustrative of the History of the Slave Trade to America*. 4 vols. Washington, D.C.: Carnegie Institution of Washington, 1930.

[Douglass, Frederick]. *Life and Times of Frederick Doulgass Written by Himself,*

His Early Life as a Slave, His Escape from Bondage and His Complete History to the Present Time. Hartford, Conn: Park, 1882.

———. *Life and Writings of Frederick Douglass*. 5 vols. Edited by Philip Foner. New York: International Publishers, 1950.

———. *My Bondage and My Freedom*. New York: Miller, Orton & Mulligan, 1855.

[Drayton, William Henry]. *Some Fugitive Thoughts on a Letter Signed Freeman, Addressed to the Deputies Assembled at the High Court of Congress, in Philadelphia. By a Black Settler*. South Carolina: 1774.

Drew, Benjamin. *A North-side View of Slavery: The Refugee or Narrative of the Fugitive Slave in Canada*. Boston: J. P. Jewett, 1856.

Duer, William C. *The Life of William Alexander, Earl of Stirling*. New York: Published for the New-Jersey Historical Society by Wiley & Putnam, 1847.

Dunlap, William C. *Diary of William Dunlap*. New York: New-York Historical Society, 1930–32.

———. *History of the New Netherlands, and New York*. 2 vols. New York: Harper & Brothers, 1839.

Easton, Hosea. *A Treatise on the Intellectual Character and Art and Political Condition of the Colored People of the United States and Prejudices Exercised against Them*. Boston: I. Knapp, 1837.

Eddis, William. *Letters from America, Historical and Descriptive Comprising Occurrences from 1769–1787 Inclusive*. London: Printed for the Author, 1792.

Eddy, A. D. *The Life of Jacob Hodges, an African Negro Who Died in Canandaigua, New York, February, 1842*. Philadelphia: American Sunday School Union, 1842.

Eddy, Thomas. *An Account of the State Prison or Penitentiary House in the City of New York*. New York: Isaac Collins and Sons, 1801.

Edsall, Preston W., ed. *Journal of the Courts of Common Right and Chancery of East New Jersey, 1683–1702*. Philadelphia: American Legal History Society, 1937.

Edsall, Thomas H., ed. *Journal of John Charles Philip Von Kraft, 1776–1784*. New York: New-York Historical Society, 1888.

Egan, Pierce. *Boxiana: Sketches of Ancient and Modern Pugilism*. London: G. Smeeton, 1812.

Ely, Reverend Ezra Stiles. *Visits of Mercy; or the Journals of the Reverend Ezra Stiles Ely, D.D., Written While He Was Stated Preacher to the Hospital and Alms House in the City of New York*. 2 vols., 6th ed. Philadelphia: Samuel F. Bradford, 1829.

"An Excerpt from a Letter on the Banks of the Hudson, July 9, 1783." In *Manual of the Corporation of the City of New York*, edited by David T. Valentine. New York: City of New York, 1870.

A Faithful Report on the Trial of Doctor William Little on an Indictment for an Assault and Battery Committed upon the Body of His Lawful Wife, Mrs. Jane Little, a Black Lady. 2d ed. New York: Printed for the Purchasers, 1808.

"Family Record of Abraham Hasbrouck." *New York Genealogical and Biographical Record* 71 (1941): 34–41.

Fearon, Henry B. *Sketches of America: A Narrative of a Journey of Five Thousand Miles.* 3d ed. London: Longman, Hurst, Rees, Orme, and Brown, 1819.

Felton, Mrs. *American Life: A Narrative of Two Years' City and Country Residence in the United States.* Hull, U.K.: J. Hutchinson, 1838.

Fernow, Bertold, ed. *Calendar of Council Minutes, 1668-1783.* Albany: University of the State of New York, 1902.

———. *Minutes of the Orphanmasters Court of New Amsterdam, 1655-1663.* 2 vols. New York: F. W. Harper, 1907.

———. *Records of the City of New Amsterdam from 1653 to 1774, Anno Domini.* 7 vols. New York: Knickerbocker Press, 1907.

Fifth Annual Report of the New York Committee of Vigilance for the Year 1842. New York: The Committte, G. Vale, Jun., 1842.

The First Annual Report of the Executive Committee of the New York Magdalene Society, Instituted January 1, 1830. New York: J. T. West, 1831.

First Annual Report of the Society for the Encouragement of Faithful Domestic Servants in New York. New York: D. Fanshaw, at the American Tract Society's House, 1826.

Fleetwood, William. *The Relative Duties of Parents and Children, Husbands and Wives, Masters and Servants.* 2d ed. London: Printed for John Hooke, 1716.

Foner, Philip, ed. *The Life and Writings of Frederick Douglass.* 5 vols. New York: International Publishers, 1950.

Foner, Philip, and Ronald L. Lewis. *The Black Worker.* 5 vols. Philadelphia: Temple University Press, 1978.

———. *The Black Worker to 1869.* Philadelphia: Temple University Press, 1978.

Foner, Philip S., and George E. Walker. *Proceedings of the Black National and State Conventions, 1865-1900.* Philadelphia: Temple University Press, 1986.

———, eds. *Proceedings of the Black State Conventions, 1840-1865.* 2 vols. Philadelphia: Temple University Press, 1979.

Force, Peter. *American Archives.* 4th and 5th ser. Washington, D.C.: Prepared and Published under Authority of an Act of Congress, 1840.

Fox, Dixon Ryan, ed. *Minutes of the Court of Sessions, 1657-1696, Westchester County.* White Plains, N.Y.: Published for Westchester County by the Westchester Historical Society, Knickerbocker Press, 1924.

Francis, John. *Old New York, or, Reminiscences of the Past Sixty Years.* New York: C. Roe, 1858. Extra-illustrated volume at New-York Historical Society.

Gardiner, Barent. *The New York Reporter Containing Reports of Trials & Decisions in the Different Courts of Judicature.* 2 vols. New York: Published and for sale by the Editor and also by Stephen Gould, 1820.

Garnet, Henry Highland. *A Memorial Discourse.* Introduction by James McCune Smith. Philadelphia: J. M. Wilson, 1865.

———. *Past and Present Condition and the Destiny of the Colored Race: A Discourse Delivered at the Fiftieth Benevolent Society of Troy, New York, February 14, 1848.* Troy, N.Y: Steam Press of J. C. Kneeland, 1848.

———. *Walker's Appeal . . . and Garnet's Address to the Slaves of the United States.* New York: J. H. Tobitt, 1848.

Garrison, William Lloyd. *Thoughts on African Colonization, or an Impartial Exhibition of the Doctrines, Principles, and Purposes of the American Colonization Society Together with the Resolutions, Addresses, and Remonstraces of the Free People of Color.* Boston: Garrison and Knapp, 1832.

Gehring, Charles T., ed. *New York Historical Manuscripts: Dutch Land Papers.* Baltimore: Genealogical Publishing, 1980.

A Genuine Narrative of the Intended Conspiracy of the Negroes at Antigua. Dublin: R. Reilly, 1737.

Gerlach, Larry, ed. *New Jersey in the American Revolution, 1763–1783: A Documentary History.* Trenton, N.J.: New Jersey Historical Commission, 1975.

Gilbert, Olive, ed. *Narrative of Sojourner Truth.* Battle Creek, Mich: Author, 1878.

Godwyn, Morgan. *The Negro's & Indians Advocate, Suing for Their Admission into the Church: Or a Persuasive to the Instructing and Baptizing of the "Negro's" and Indians in Our Plantations. Shewing, That as Compliance Therewith Can Prejudice No Mans Just Interest: So the Wilful Neglecting and Opposing It Is No Less a Manifest Apostasy from the Christian Faith. . . .* London: Printed for the Author by J. D., 1680.

Gooch, Richard. *America and the Americans—in 1833–4.* Edited by Richard Toby Widdicombe. New York: Fordham University Press, 1994.

Graydon, Alexander. *Manners of a Life, Chiefly Passed in Pennsylvania.* Edinburgh: W. Blackwood, 1883.

Greenleaf, Jonathan. *A History of the Churches of All Denominations in the City of New York from the First Settlement to the Year 1846.* New York: E. French, 1846.

Gregoire, Henri. *An Essay Concerning the Intellectual and Moral Faculties and Literature of Negroes Followed with an Account of the Life and Works of Fifteen Negroes and Mullatoes Distinguished in Science, Literature, and the Arts.* Edited by Graham Russell Hodges. Armonk, N.Y.: M. E. Sharpe, 1997.

Griscom, John. *The Sanitary Conditions of the Laboring Population of New York. . . .* New York: Harper and Brothers, 1845.

Gronniosaw, James Albert Ukawsaw. *A Narrative of the Most Remarkable Particulars in the Life of James Albert Ukawsaw Gronniosaw, an African Prince.* Bath, U.K.: Printed for W. Gye, 1770.

Hall, Basil. *Travels in North America, in the Years 1827 and 1828.* Philadelphia: Carey, Lee and Carey, 1829.

[Hamilton, Alexander]. *Papers on Public Credit, Commerce, and Finance by Alexander Hamilton.* Edited by Samuel B. McKee Jr. New York: Columbia University Press, 1934.

Hamilton, Captain Thomas. *Men and Manners in America.* 2 vols. Edinburgh: W. Blackwood, 1834.

Hamilton, William. *Address to the Fourth Annual Convention of the Free People* of Color Delivered on the Opening of Their Session in the City of New-York, June 2, 1834 by William Hamilton, Sr. of the Conventional Board. New York: S. W. Benedict, 1834.

————. An Address to the New York African Society for Mutual Relief Delivered in the Universalist Church, January 2, 1809. New York: N.p., 1809.

————. An Oration at the African Zion Church, on the Occasion of the Emancipation of Coloured People, in the State of New York, July 4, 1827. New York: Gray and Bunce, 1827.

————. A Oration on the Abolition of the Slave Trade Delivered in the Episcopal Asbury Church in Elizabeth Street, January 2, 1815. New York: New York African Society, C. W. Bunce, 1815.

————. A Word to the African: A Sermon for the Benefit of the American Colonization Society, Delivered in the Second Presbyterian Church. Newark, July 24, 1825. Newark, N.J.: W. Tuttle, 1825.

[Hamlet, James]. The Fugitive-Slave Bill: The History and Constitutionality with an Account of the Seizure and Enslavement of James Hamlet and the Subsequent Restoration of Liberty. New York: William Harred, 1850.

Hammond, Harold Earl, ed. The Diary of a Union Lady, 1861–1865. New York: Funk and Wagnalls, 1965.

Hart, Simon, ed. The Prehistory of the New Netherlands Company: Amsterdam Notarial Records of the First Dutch Voyages of the Hudson. Amsterdam: City of Amsterdam Press, 1959.

Hawkins, Christopher. The Adventures of Christopher Hawkins: Containing Details of His Captivity, a First and Second Time on the High Seas, in the Revolutionary War, by the British, and the Consequent Sufferings, and Escape from the Jersey Prison Ship. New York: Privately Printed, 1864.

Horsmanden, Daniel. Journal of the Proceedings in the Detection of the Conspiracy Formed by Some White People in Conjunction with Negro and Other Slaves for Burning the City of New-York and Murdering the Inhabitants. Edited by Thomas J. Davis. Boston: Beacon Press, 1971.

Hough, Charles M., ed. Reports of the Cases of the Vice Admiralty of the Province of New York and Court of Admiralty of the State of New York. New Haven: Yale University Press, 1925.

How, Samuel B. Slaveholding Not Sinful, Slavery, the Punishment of Man's Sin Its Remedy the Gospel of Christ, an Argument before the General Synod of the Reformed Dutch Church, October, 1855. New York: J. B. Gray, 1855.

Howe, Sir William. The Narrative of Lieutenant Sir William Howe. 2d ed. London: H. Baldwin, 1781.

Humphreys, David. An Account of the Endeavours Used by the Society for the Propagation of the Gospel in Foreign Parts to Instruct the Negro Slaves of New York Together with Two of Bishop Gibson's Letters on that Subject. Being an Extract from Dr. Humphrey's Historical Account of the Society for the Propagation of the Gospel in Foreign Parts. London: N.p., 1730.

Jameson, J. Franklin, ed. Narratives of New Netherland, 1609–1664. New York: Charles Scribner's Sons, 1909.

Jameson, J. Franklin, and Bartlett James, eds. *The Journal of Jasper Danckaerts, 1678–1680.* New York: Charles Scribner's Sons, 1913.

Janson, Charles W. *The Stranger in America, 1796–1806.* Edited by Carl S. Driver. New York: Press of the Pioneers, 1935.

[Jay, John II]. *Caste and Slavery in the American Church by a Churchman.* New York: Wiley and Putnam, 1843.

Jeremy, David John, ed. *Henry Wansey and His American Journal, 1794.* Philadelphia: American Philosophical Society, 1970.

Johnson, Amandus, ed. *The Journal and Biography of Nicholas Collin, 1746–1831.* Philadelphia: New Jersey Society of Pennsylvania, 1936.

Jones, Thomas A. *History of New York during the American Revolution.* 2 vols. New York: Printed for the New-York Historical Society, 1879–80.

"Journal of an Officer Who Travelled in America and the West Indies in 1764 and 1765." In *Travels in the American Colonies,* edited by Newton D. Mereness. New York: Macmillan, 1916.

Journal of Lieutenant Isaac Bangs, April 1–July 29, 1776. Cambridge, Mass.: J. W. Wilson & Son, 1890.

The Journal of Madam Knight. Including an Introductory Note by Malcolm Freiberg. Boston: David R. Godine, 1972. Reprint of 1825 edition.

Journal of the Commissioners for Trade and Plantations. 14 vols. London: His Majesty's Stationery Office, 1920–28.

Journal of the Legislative Council of the Colony of New-York, 1691–1775. 2 vols. Albany: Weed, Parsons, 1861.

A Journal of the Life of Thomas Story. . . . Newcastle-on-Tyne, U.K.: Isaac Thompson, 1747.

Judd, Jacob, ed. *Correspondence of the Van Cortlandt Family of Cortlandt Manor.* 4 vols. Tarrytown, N.Y.: Sleepy Hollow Restorations, 1977–84.

Judgement of the Synode Holden at Dort, Concerning the Five Articles: As Also Their Sentence Touching Conradus Vorstivs. London: John Bill, 1619.

Karlsen, Carol F., and Laurie Crumpacker, eds. *The Journal of Esther Edwards Burr, 1754–1757.* New Haven: Yale University Press, 1984.

Kelby, William, ed. "Orderly Book of Three Battalions of Loyalists." In *Collections of the New-York Historical Society,* 49. New York: Printed for the Society, 1916.

"Kemble Papers." In *Collections of the New-York Historical Society,* 15–16. New York: Printed for the Society, 1884.

Klepp, Susan, and Billy G. Smith, eds. *The Infortunate: The Voyage and Adventure of William Moraley, an Indentured Servant.* College Park, Pa.: Pennsylvania State University Press, 1992.

Lambert, John. *Travels through Canada and the United States in the Years 1806, 1807, and 1808.* 2 vols. London: C. Cradeck and W. Joy, 1814.

Larison, C. W., ed. *Sylvia Du Bois (Now 116 Years Old) A Biografy of the Slav Who Whipt Her Mistress and Gand Her Freedom.* Ringoes, N.J.: C. W. Larison, 1883.

Lawrence, George. *An Oration on the Abolition of the Slave Trade, Delivered on the First Day of January, 1813, in the African Methodist Episcopal Church.* New York: Hardcastle and Van Pelt, 1813.

Laws Relative to Slaves and Servants by the Legislature of New-York, March 31, 1817, Together with Extracts from the Laws of the United States Respecting Slaves. New York: Samuel Wood and Son, 1817.

Laws Relative to Slaves and the Slave-Trade. New York: Hardcastle and Van Pelt, 1806.

Laycock [Leacock], John. *The Fall of British Tyranny or American Liberty Triumphant, the First Campaign a Tragi-Comedy of Five Parts as Lately Planned at the Royal Theater Panadamonium at St. James.* Philadelphia: J. Gillis and Powers and Willis, 1776.

Leaming, Aaron, and Jacob Spicer. *The Grants, Concessions, and Original Constitutions of the Province of New Jersey.* Philadelphia: W. Bradford, 1881.

"Ledger Book of Doctor Elias Cornelius." *New York Genealogical and Biographical Record* 111–12 (1980–81): 111:79–89, 134–41, 230–32; 112:25–32, 101–6, 171–76.

Leonard, Ellen. *Three Days' Reign of Terror, or the July Riots in 1863 in New York.* New York: From *Harper's Magazine*, January 1867.

"Letter Book of John Watts." In *Collections of the New-York Historical Society*, 61. New York: Printed for the Society, 1928.

The Letters and Papers of Cadwallader Colden. In *Collections of the New-York Historical Society*, 2d ser., vols. 50–56, 67–68. New York: Printed for the Society, 1917–23, 1934–35.

Letters of Isaac Bobin, Esq., Private Secretary of Honorable George Clarke, Secretary of the Province of New York, 1718–1730. Albany: J. Munsell, 1872.

Life and Adventures of James Williams, a Fugitive Slave, with a Full Description of the Underground Railroad. Sacramento, Calif.: N.p., 1873.

Life of William Grimes, Written by Himself. New York: N.p., 1875.

Life, Trial and Confessions of Thomas Jones, A Colored Man. . . . New York: Sold Wholesale and Retail at no. 208 Water-Street, 1824.

Ligon, Richard. *A True and Exact History of the Island of Barbadoes.* 2d printing. London: P. Parker and T. Guy, 1673.

Lincoln, Charles Z., ed. *The Colonial Laws of New York from the Year 1664 to the Revolution.* 5 vols. Albany: J. B. Lyon, 1894.

———. *New York State: Messages from the Governors, Comprising Executive Communications to the Legislature and Other Papers.* 11 vols. Albany: State Printers, 1909.

Longworth's American Almanac, New York Register and City Directory for the Forty-sixth Year of American Independence. New York: David Longworth, 1821.

Lundie, Grey [Duncan, Mary]. *America as I Saw It by the Mother of Mary Lundie Duncan.* New York: R. Carter & Bros., 1852.

McMurray, William. *A Sermon Preached in Behalf of the American Colonization Society in the Reformed Dutch Church.* New York: J. Seymour, 1825.

"Marriages from 1801–1866 in the Dutch Reformed Church, New York City."

New York Genealogical and Biographical Record 70–72 (1939–41): 35–40, 171–72, 277–79.

Marryat, Frederick. *A Diary in America, with Remarks on Its Institutions.* Edited by Sydney Jackson. New York: Knopf, 1962.

Mars, James. *Life of James Mars, a Slave Born and Sold in Connecticut.* Hartford: Case, Lockwood, 1869.

Martin, Joseph Plumb. *Private Yankee Doodle Dandy, Being a Narrative of Some of the Adventures, Damages, and Sufferings of a Revolutionary Soldier.* Edited by George Brown. Boston: Little, Brown, 1962.

Maser, Frederick E., and Howard T. Maag, eds. *The Journal of Joseph Pilmore, Methodist Itinerant.* Philadelphia: Printed for the Historical Society of the Philadelphia Annual Conference of the United Methodist Church, 1969.

Mellick, Andrew C. Jr. *The Story of an Old Farm, or Life in New Jersey in the Eighteenth Century.* Somerville, N.J.: Unionist-Gazette, 1889.

"Memoirs of Mr. Boston King." In *Methodist Magazine*, March 1798.

Memoirs and Theatrical Career of Ira Aldridge, the African Roscius. London: Ohwhyn, 1849.

Memorial of Semi-Centennial of the American Colonization Society at Washington, January 15, 1867. Washington, D.C.: The Society, 1867.

Miller, Robert B., ed. "Inhabitants of Fordham and Adjacent Places, 1698." *New York Genealogical and Biographical Record* 38 (1907): 218–19.

[Miller, William]. *A Sermon on the Abolition of the Slave Trade Delivered in the African Church on the First of January, 1810, by the Reverend William Miller, Minister of the African Methodist Episcopal Church.* New York: J. C. Totten, 1810.

Miner, John F. *A Tour around New York City and My Summer Acre, Being the Reminiscences of Mr. Felix Oldboy.* New York: Harper and Bros., 1893.

"Minutes of the Committee and of the First Commission for Detecting and Defeating Conspiracies in the State of New York." In *Collections of the New-York Historical Society,* 57–58. New York: Printed for the Society, 1924–25.

Minutes of the Common Council of New York City, 1783–1831. 22 vols. New York: M. B. Brown, 1917–31.

Minutes of the Common Council of the City of New York, 1675–1776. 8 vols. New York: Dodd, Mead, 1930.

Minutes of the Council of Safety of the State of New Jersey. Jersey City: J. H. Lyon, 1872.

Minutes of the Fourth Annual Convention for the Improvement of the Free People of Color in the United States Held by Adjournments in the Asbury Church New-York from the 2nd to the 12th of June, 1834. New York: Printed by Order of the Convention, 1834.

Minutes of the General and Annual Conference of the A.M.E. Zion Church Comprising Four Districts for 1839–1840. Brooklyn: George Hogarth, 1843.

Minutes of the Justices and Freeholders of Bergen County, New Jersey, 1715–1795. Hackensack, N.J.: Bergen County Historical Society, 1924.

Mott, Abigail. *Biographical Sketches and Interesting Anecdotes of Persons of Color. To Which Is Added a Selection of Pieces of Poetry.* New York: Mahlon Day, 1825.

Moulton, Philips, ed. *The Journal and Major Essays of John Woolman.* New York: Oxford University Press, 1971.

M'Robert, Patrick. "A Tour through Part of the North Provinces of America, 1774, 1775." Edited by Carl Bridenbaugh. *Pennsylvania Magazine of Biography and History* 59 (1935): 134–80.

Munsell, Joel. *Annals of Albany.* 12 vols. Albany: J. Munsell, 1850–59.

"Muster Roll of Butler's Rangers." *New York Genealogical and Biographical Record* 31 (1900): 13–18.

"Muster Rolls of the New York Provincial Troops, 1755–1764." *Collections of the Neew York Historical Society* 24. New York: For the Society, 1892.

A Narrative of the Adventures and Escape of Moses Roper from American Slavery. New York: Merrihew and Gunn, 1838.

A Narrative of the Life of Reverend Noah Davis, a Colored Man, Written by Himself, at the Age of Fifty-Four. Baltimore: John F. Weisshampel Jr., 1853.

A Narrative of the Uncommon Sufferings and Surprising Deliverance of Briton Hammond, a Negro Man . . . and Servant of General Winslow of Marshfield, in New England, Who Returned to Boston after Having Been Absent Almost Thirteen Years. . . . Boston: Green and Russell, 1760.

"Nathaniel Holmes Day Book, 1805–1808." *Genealogical Magazine of New Jersey* 54 (1979): 35–40.

Nell, William C. *Colored Patriots of the American Revolution.* Boston: R. F. Wallcut, 1855.

Neville, Samuel. *The Acts of the General Assembly of the Province of New Jersey.* New York: W. Bradford, 1752.

Nevins, Allen, and Milton Halsey Thomas, eds. *The Diary of George Templeton Strong.* 4 vols. New York: Macmillan, 1953.

Newcomb, Harvey. *The "Negro Pew," Being an Inquiry Concerning the Propriety of Distinctions in the Houses of the Lord, on Account of Color.* Boston: I. Knapp, 1837.

The New York African Society for Mutual Relief, An Address. . . . New York: Printed for the Society by Hardcastle and Pelsue, 1815.

"Nineteenth Century Apprenticeship Register, New York City." *New York Genealogical and Biographical Record* 115 (1984): 1–8.

O'Callaghan, E. B., ed. *Calendar of Historical Manuscripts in the Office of the Secretary of State.* 2 vols. Albany: Weed, Parsons, 1865.

———. *Calendar of New York Colonial Manuscripts Indorsed Land Papers . . . 1643–1803.* Albany: Weed, Parsons, 1864.

———. *The Documentary History of the State of New York.* 4 vols. Albany: Weed, Parsons, 1849–51.

———. *Laws and Ordinances of New Netherland, 1638–1674.* Albany: Weed, Parsons, 1868.

———. *Voyages of the Slavers St. John and Arms of Amsterdam.* Albany: J. Munsell, 1867.

O'Callaghan, E. B., and Bertold Fernow, eds. and trans. *Documents Relative to the Colonial History of the State of New York*. 15 vols. Albany: Weed, Parsons, 1865–87.

O'Conor, Norreys Jephson, ed. *A Servant of the Crown in England and North America, 1756–1761, Based upon the Papers of John Appy, Secretary and Judge Advocate of His Majesty's Forces*. New York: D. Appleton-Century, 1938.

"Official Records of Bergen County, New Jersey, in the Clerk's Office." *Proceedings of New Jersey Historical Society*, vol. 1, ser. 2 (1867–74): 79–86.

Ogilby, John. *Africa, Being an Accurate Description of the Regions of . . . the Land of Negroes, Guinea. . . .* London: T. Johnson for the Author, 1670.

An Oration Delivered at the Fifteenth Annual Celebration of the New-York African Society for Mutual Relief at the African Zion Church, the 24th of March, 1823, by a Member. Brooklyn, n.p., 1823.

Palsits, Victor Hugo, ed. *Minutes of the Commissioners for Detecting and Defeating Conspiracies in the State of New York*. 3 vols. Albany: State of New York, 1909.

Pennington, James W. C. *The Fugitive Blacksmith*. London: Gilpin, 1849.

———. *A Text Book of the Origin and History of the Coloured People*. Hartford, Conn.: L. Skinner, 1841.

Peterson, Daniel H. *The Looking-Glass: Being a True Report and Narrative of the Life, Travels and Labors of the Rev. Daniel H. Peterson, a Colored Clergyman; Embracing a Period of Time from the Year 1812 to 1854, and Including His Visit to Eastern Africa*. New York: Wright, 1854.

Pettengill, Ray W., ed. *Letters from America, 1776–1779: Being Letters of Brunswick, Hessian, and Waldeck Officers with the British Armies during the Revolution*. Boston: Houghton Mifflin, 1924.

Prince, Carl, et al., eds. *The Papers of William Livingston*. 5 vols. Trenton, N.J.: New Jersey Historical Commission, 1978–90.

"Proceedings of a Board of General Officers of the British Army at New-York, 1781." *Collections of the New-York Historical Society*. New York: Printed for the Society, 1917.

Proceedings of a Meeting Held at Princeton, New Jersey, July 14, 1824, to Form a Society in the State of New Jersey to Cooperate with the American Colonization Society. Princeton: Printed for the Society by D. A. Borrenstein, 1824.

Public Papers of Daniel D. Tompkins, Governor of New York, 1807–1817. 3 vols. New York: Wynkoop, Hallenbeck, Crawford, 1898.

Ravenstein, E. G., ed. *The Strange Adventures of Andrew Battel of Leigh, in Angola and the Adjoining Regions*. London: Hakluyt Society, 1901.

"Records of St. Mark's in the Bowery, 1799–1865." *New York Genealogical and Biographical Record* 71–72 (1941–42): 71:337; 72:85, 164–66.

"Records of St. Peter's Episcopal Church, Spotswood (New Brunswick, N.J.)." *Genealogical Magazine of New Jersey* 41 (1966): 31–41.

"Records of the First and Second Presbyterian Churches in the City of New York." *New York Genealogical and Biographical Record* 18–19 (1887–89), 18:170; 19:177, 179, 181.

"Records of the First Presbyterian Church of Cranbury." *Genealogical Magazine of New Jersey* 23 (1952): 49–60.

"Records of the Marriages and Baptisms as Contained in the First Book of Records of Christ Church, 71st and Boulevard, New York City." *New York Genealogical and Biographical Record* 42 (1911): 322–28.

"Records of the Presbyterian Church, Newtown (Elmhurst), Queens County, Long Island, 1731–1793." *New York Genealogical and Biographical Record* 55 (1924): 291, 393–98.

"Records of the Reformed Dutch Church in the City of New York." *New York Genealogical and Biographical Record* 61–62 (1928–31): 61:277–79, 373–80; 62:41–45.

"Records of the Reformed Dutch Church of Harlem." *New York Genealogical and Biographical Record* 117–18 (1986–87): 117:223–28; 118:31–32.

"Records of Trinity Church: Baptisms." *New York Genealogical and Biographical Record* 68 (1937): 77–79.

Reflections on Slavery, with Recent Evidence of Its Inhumanity, Occasioned by the Melancholy Death of Romain, a Free Negro, by Humanitas. Philadelphia: For the Author, 1803.

Reflections on the Inconsistency of Man Particularly Exemplified in the Practice of Slavery in the United States. New York: Printed and Sold by John Buel, 1796.

"Reformed Dutch Church, New York, Baptisms, 1639–1800," In *Collections of the New York Genealogical and Biographical Society.* 2 vols. New York: New York Genealogical and Biographical Society, 1901.

Report of the Committee of Merchants for the Relief of Colored People Suffering from the Late Riots in the City of New York. New York: George A. Whitehorn, 1863.

Report of the Resident Physician of the Colored Home from January 1851 to January 1852. New York: Charles Vinton, 1852.

"Reverend John Sharpe's Proposals for Creating a School, Library, and Chapel at New York, 1712–1713." *Collections of the New-York Historical Society* 13: 348–59. New York: Printed for the Society, 1880.

Richmond, Reverend Leigh. *The African Servant, an Authentic Narrative, Communicated by a Clergyman of the Church of England.* Andover, Mass.: Printed for the New England Tract Society, 1824.

Ripley, C. Peter, ed. *The Black Abolitionist Papers.* 5 vols. Chapel Hill: University of North Carolina Press, 1985–92.

Roberts, Robert. *The House Servant's Directory, or a Monitor for Private Families: Hints on the Arrangement and Performance of Servants' Work with General Rules for Setting Out Tables and Sideboards.* Edited by Graham Russell Hodges. Armonk, N.Y.: M. E. Sharpe, 1998.

Robinson, Solon. *Hot Corn: Life Scenes in New York Illustrated: Including the Story of Little Katy, Madaline, the Rag-Picker's Daughter, Wild Maggie, &c.* New York: De Witt and Davenport, 1854.

Rochefoucauld-Liancourt, Duc de la. *Travels through the United States of North America the Country of the Iroquois and Upper Canada in the Years 1795, 1796 and 1797.* 2 vols. London: R. Philips, 1799.

Ruggles, David. *An Antidote for a Poisonous Combination Recently Prepared by a "Citizen of New York" Alias Dr. Reese, Entitled An Appeal to Reason and Religion of American Christians Etc. Also David Meredith Reese's Humbugs Dissected by David Ruggles, Author of the Extinguisher Extinguished, Etc.* New York: William Stuart, 1838.

———. *The First Annual Report of the New York Committee of Vigilance.* New York: David Ruggles, 1837.

[Rush, Christopher]. *A Short Account of the A.M.E. Zion Church, Written by Christopher Rush, Superintendant of the Connection. . . .* New York: Author, 1843.

Sabine, W. H. W., ed. *The New York Diary of Lieutenant Jabez Fitch.* New York: Colberg and Tegg, 1954.

Sainsbury, W. O., et al., eds. *Calendar of State Papers: Colonial Series, America and the West Indies.* 42 vols. London: Public Record Office, 1860–1953.

Sampson, William. *Murders! Report of the Trial of James Johnson, a Black Man, for the Murder of Lewis Robinson, a Black Man, on the 23rd of October Last, Also the Trial of John Sinclair, a German, Aged Seventy-seven Years for the Murder of David Hill on the Eighth Day of April Last. . . . Held on Wednesday the Ninth and Tenth of December, 1810.* New York: Southwick and Pelsue, 1811.

Sanger, William. *History of Prostitution.* New York: Harper and Brothers, 1859.

Schaukirk, Ewald Gustav. *Occupation of New York City by the British.* New York: New York Times, 1969.

Scot, George. *A Model of Government in the Province of East-New-Jersey in America.* Edinburgh: J. Reid, 1685.

Scott, Kenneth, ed. "John Evert Van Allen's Account Book, 1771–1774." *New York Genealogical and Biographical Record* 108 (1977): 10–16.

———. "Records of St. George's Episcopal Church, Flushing, Long Island, 1782–1830." *New York Genealogical and Biographical Record* 110 (1979): 3–6; 112 (1981): 41–4.

Scott, Kenneth, and Kenn Stryker-Rodda, eds. *Denizations, Naturalizations and Oaths of Allegiance in Colonial New York.* Baltimore: Genealogical Publishing, 1975.

———. *New York Historical Manuscripts.* 4 vols. Baltimore: Genealogical Publishing, 1974.

Sidney, Joseph. *An Oration of the Abolition of the Slave Trade in the United States; Delivered before the Wilberforce Philanthropic Association in the City of New York on the Second of January, 1809.* New York: J. Seymour, 1809.

Simmons, R. C., and P. D. G. Thomas, eds. *Proceedings and Debates of the British Parliament Respecting North America, 1754–1783.* 6 vols. Milwood, N.Y.: Krauss International Publications, 1982.

[Sipkins, Henry]. *An Oration on the Abolition of the Slave-Trade Delivered in the African Church in the City of New-York, January 1, 1809, by Henry Sipkins, a Descendant of Africa.* New York: J. C. Totten, 1809.

[Smith, E. H.] *A Discourse Delivered April 11, 1798, at the Request and before the Benefit of the Society for Promoting the Manumission of Slaves and the*

Protecting of Them as Have Been or May Be Liberated. New York: T. and J. Swords, 1798.

Smith, James McCune. *A Lecture on the Haytian Revolutions with a Sketch of the Character of Toussaint L'Overture, February 26, 1841.* New York: D. Fanshaw, 1841.

Smith, William. *The History of the Province of New York.* 2 vols. Edited by 'Michael Kammen. Cambridge, Mass.: Harvard University Press, 1975.

Snelgrove, Captain William. *A New Account of Some Parties of Guinea and the Slave Trade....* London: Printed for J. J. and P. Knapton, 1734.

Stafford, Ward. *New Missionary Field: A Report to the Female Missionary Society for the Poor of New York City and Its Vicinity.* New York: J. Seymour, 1817.

Stanton, Daniel. *A Journal of the Life, Travels, and Gospel Labours of a Faithful Minister of Jesus Christ.* Philadelphia: Joseph Crukshank, 1772.

A Statement of Facts Relative to the Late Fever Which Appeared in Bancker Street and Its Vicinity. New York: Bliss, 1821.

Stewart, Alvan. *A Legal Argument before the Supreme Court of the State of New Jersey at the May Term, 1845, at Trenton for the Deliverance of 4,000 Persons in Bondage.* New York: Finch and Weed, 1845.

Stokes, I. N. P. *Iconography of Manhattan Island.* 6 vols. New York: R. H. Dodd, 1915–28.

Strickland, William. *Journal of a Tour in the United States of America, 1794–1795.* Edited by the Reverend J. E. Strickland. New York: New-York Historical Society, 1971.

Stryker, William S., ed. *Minutes of the Provincial Congress and Council of Safety of the State of New Jersey.* Trenton, N.J.: Naar, Day, and Naar, 1879.

Stryker-Rodda, Kenn, comp. "Baptisms in the Lutheran Church, New York City, from 1725." *New York Genealogical and Biographical Record,* 97–103 (1966–72).

———, ed. "The Janeway Account Books, 1735–1746." *Genealogical Magazine of New Jersey* 33 (1958): 1–10, 73–81.

Stuart, John Ferdinand Smythe. *A Tour of the United States of America.* London: Printed for G. Robinson, J. Robson and J. Sewell, 1786.

Sutcliff, Robert. *Travels in Some Parts of North America in the Years, 1804, 1805 and 1806.* Philadelphia: B. and T. Kite, 1812.

Syrett, Harold C. et al., eds. *Papers of Alexander Hamilton.* 28 vols. New York: Columbia University Press, 1961–75.

Tappert, Theodore G., and Doberstein, John W. *The Journals of Henry Melchior Muhlenberg.* 3 vols. Philadelphia: Evangelical Lutheran Ministerium of Pennsylvania and Adjacent States, 1942–58.

Thompson, Mary W. *Sketches of the History, Character, and Dying Testimony of Beneficiaries of the Colored Home, in the City of New York.* New York: J. F. Trow, 1851.

Through the Looking Glass: Being a True Report and Narrative of the Life, Travels, and Labours of the Reverend Daniel S. Peterson, a Colored Clergyman.... New York: Wright, 1854.

The Trial of Amos Broad and His Wife on Several Indictments for Assaulting and Beating Betty a Slave and Her Little Female Child, Sarah, Aged Three Years. New York: Henry C. Southwick, 1809.

The Trial of Captain James Dunn for an Assault, with Intent to Seduce Sylvia Patterson, a Black Woman, the Wife of James Patterson Held at Martling's Long Room, before Referees, Appointed by Consent of the Parties, December 15, 1808. New York: Printed for the *Reporter,* 1809.

Trott, Nicholas, comp. *The Laws of the British Plantations in America, Relating to the Church and the Clergy, Religion and Learning.* London: B. Cowse, 1725.

Trumbull, Henry. *Life and Adventures of Robert, the Hermit of Massachusetts, Who Has Lived 14 Years in a Cave.* Providence, R.I.: Printed for H. Trumbull, 1829.

Udemans, Godefridus Corneliszoon. *'T geestelyck roer van 't coopmans schip, dat is: Trouw baricht hor dat een coopman, en coopvaerder, helmselven dragan moet in syne handelinge, in pays, ende in oorlooghe.* Dordrecht: F. Boels, 1638.

Uring, Captain Nathaniel. *A History of the Voyages and Travels. . . .* 2d ed. London: J. Peele, 1726.

Valentine, David. *Manual of the Corporation of the City of New York for 1853.* New York: The Council, 1853.

Van Laer, Arnold, J. F., ed. *Correspondence of Jeremias van Rensselaer, 1651-1674.* Albany: University of the State of New York, 1932.

———. *Documents Relating to New Netherland in the Henry E. Huntington Library.* San Marino, Calif.: Huntington Library and Art Gallery, 1924.

———. *New Netherland Council Minutes, 1638-1649.* Albany: University of the State of New York, 1939.

———, trans. and ed. *Van Rensselaer Bowier Manuscripts, Being the Letters of Kiliaen Van Rensselaer, 1630-1643, and Other Documents Relating to the Colony of Rensselaerswyck.* Albany: University of the State of New York, 1908.

Voorhees, David, ed. *Leister Papers.* Forthcoming.

Vosburgh, Royden, ed. *Christ Protestant Episcopal Church, New York City (Baptisms, 1793-1848, Marriages, 1794-1848).* N.p.: New York Genealogical and Biographical Society, 1919.

[Walker, David]. *Walker's Appeal, in Four Articles: Together with a Preamble, to the Colored Citizens of the World, but in Particular, and Very Expressly to Those of the United States of America, Written in Boston, State of Massachusetts, September 28, 1829.* 3d ed. Boston: N.p., 1830.

The War of the Rebellion: A Compilation of the Official Records of the Union and Confederate Armies. Ser. 1, Vol. 37, pt. 2. Washington, D.C.: U.S. Government Printing Office, 1889.

Ward, T. M. D. *A Momento to the Departed Worth.* New Bedford, Mass.: Press of Benjamin Lindsey, 1854.

Warville, Brissot de. *New Travels in the United States of America.* Cambridge, Mass.: Belknap Press of Harvard University Press, 1964.

Washburn, Margaret Floy, ed. *The Diary of Michael Floy, Jr., Bowery Village, 1833-1836.* New Haven: Yale University Press, 1841.

Washington, Margaret, ed. *Narrative of Sojourner Truth.* New York: Vintage, 1993.

Watson, John F. *Annals and Occurrences of New York City and State, in the Olden Time Being a Collection of Memoirs, Anecdotes, and Incidents Concerning the City, County, and Inhabitants, from the Days of the Founders Embellished with Pictorial Illustrations.* Philadelphia: H. F. Anners, 1846.

———. *Methodist Error, Or, Friendly Christian Advice to Those Methodists Who Indulge in Extravagant Religious Emotions and Bodily Exercises.* Trenton, N.J.: D. and E. Fenton, 1819.

Wheeler, Peter. *Chains and Freedom, or, the Life and Adventures of Peter Wheeler, a Coloured Man Yet Living; a Slave in Chains, a Sailor on the Deep and a Sinner at the Cross.* Edited by C. Edwards Lester. New York: E. S. Arnold, 1839.

Wiggins, Rosalind Cobb, ed. *Captain Paul Cuffe's Logs and Letters, 1808–1817: A Black Quaker's "Voice from within the Veil."* Washington, D.C.: Howard University Press, 1996.

Williams, Peter Jr. *A Descendant of Africa: An Oration on the Abolition of the Slave-Trade Delivered at the African Church in the City of New York, January 1, 1808.* New York: Samuel Wood, 1808.

———. *A Discourse Delivered in St. Philip's Church for the Benefit of the Coloured Community of Wilberforce in Upper Canada, on the Fourth of July, 1830.* New York: G. F. Bunce, 1830.

———. *Discourse Delivered on the Death of Captain Paul Cuffe before the New York African Institution in the African Methodist Episcopal Church, October 21, 1817.* New York: B. Young, 1817.

Yates, William. *Rights of Colored Men to Suffrage, Citizenship and Trial by Jury, Being a Book of Facts, Arguments an Authorities, Historical Notices and Sketches of Debates—with Notes.* Philadelphia: Merihew and Gunn, 1838.

Year Book of the Holland Society of New York, 1901, 1902, 1903, 1915. New York: Knickerbocker Press, 1897, 1901, 1902, 1903, 1915.

Young, Robert A. *Ethiopian Manifesto Issued in Defense of the Black Man's Rights in the Scale of Universal Freedom.* New York: For the Author, 1830.

NEWSPAPERS

African Repository (Washington, D.C.), 1825–92
Alarm Bell (Paterson, New Jersey), 1851–52
American Weekly Mercury (Philadelphia), 1719–49
Boston Evening Post, 1735–75
Boston Weekly News-Letter, 1704–76
Colored American (New York), 1837–39
Eastern Argus (Portland, Maine), 1824–44
Elizabeth-Town Federal Republican, 1803
Freedom's Journal (New York), 1827–29
Liberator (Boston), 1831–65
Loudon's New York Packet, 1784–85

New England Chronicle (Boston), 1776
New-Jersey Gazette (Trenton), 1778–86
New-Jersey Journal (Chatham and Elizabeth Town), 1779–83, 1786–1820
New-York City Hall Recorder
New York Commercial Advertiser, 1797–1820
New York Daily Advertiser, 1785–1806
New York Daily Express, 1813
New York Evening Post, 1801–
New-York Gazette (later *New-York Weekly Gazette*), 1725–44
New-York Gazette (Weyman's), 1759–67
New York Gazette and Weekly Mercury, 1768–83
New-York Gazette and Weekly Post-Boy (*New-York Gazette* revived in *Weekly Post-Boy*), 1747–73
New-York Gazetteer, 1783–87
New-York Journal or General Advertiser, 1766–76
New-York Mercury, 1752–68
New-York Minerva, 1796–97
New York National Advocate, 1812–29
New York Packet, 1788–92
New York Times, 1851–
New York Transcript, 1838
New-York Weekly Journal, 1733–51
New-York Weekly Post-Boy, 1743–47
Niles' Register (Washington, D.C.), 1811–49
Pennsylvania Chronicle (Philadelphia), 1767–74
Pennsylvania Evening Post (Philadelphia), 1804
Pennsylvania Gazette (Philadelphia), 1728–1815
Pennsylvania Journal (Philadelphia), 1742–93
Philanthropist (New York), 1817–18
Ram's Horn (New York), 1847
Rivington's New-York Gazetteer, 1773–75
Royal Gazette (New York), 1777–83
Trenton True American, 1801–29
Weekly Anglo-African (New York), 1859–61
Weekly Rehearsal (Boston), 1731–35

GOVERNMENT PUBLICATIONS

Abstract of the Returns of the Fifth Census, Showing the Number of Free People, the Number of Slaves. . . . Washington, D.C.: Duff Green, 1832.
Acts of Assembly Passed in the Province of New York; from 1691 to 1725. Examined and Compared with the Originals in the Secretary's Office. New York: William Bradford, 1726.
Acts of the General Assembly of the Province of New-Jersey, from the Surrender of the Government to Queen Anne, on the 17th Day of April, in the Year of Our

Lord 1702, to the 14th Day of January 1776. Burlington, N.J.: Isaac Collins, 1776.

A Century of Population Growth from the First Census of the United States to the Twelfth, 1790–1900. Washington, D.C.: U.S. Government Printing Office, 1908.

Compendium of the Enumeration of the Inhabitants and Statistics of the United States . . . for 1840. Washington, D.C.: Thomas Allen, 1841.

Compendium of the Ninth Census. Washington, D.C.: U.S. Government Printing Office, 1872.

Department of Commerce, Bureau of the Census. *Negro Population in the United States, 1790–1915.* Washington, D.C.: U.S. Government Printing Office, 1918.

De Bow, J. D. B., comp. *Mortality Statistics of the Seventh Census of the United States, 1850.* Washington, D.C.: A. O. P. Nicholson, 1855.

———. *The Seventh Census, an Appendix.* Washington, D.C.: N.p., 1853.

———. *Statistical View of the United States. . . .* Washington, D.C.: A. O. F. Nicholson, 1854.

Heads of Families, First Census of the United States: 1790, State of New York. Washington, D.C.: U.S. Government Printing Office, 1908.

New York Court of Appeals. *Report of the Lemmon Slave Case Containing Points and Arguments of Council on Both Sides, and Opinions of All the Judges.* New York: W. H. Tinson, 1860.

New York State Census for 1835. Albany: Croswell, Van Benthuysen and Burt, 1836.

New York State Census for 1845. Albany: Carroll and Clari, 1846.

Return of the Number of Whole Persons within the Several Districts of the United States . . . for the Year 1790. Washington, D.C.: William Duane, 1802.

Return of the Whole Numbers of People within the Several Districts of the United States . . . for the Year 1800. Washington, D.C.: Duane and Son, 1802.

U.S. Census Office. *Fifth Census or Enumeration of the Inhabitants of the United States, 1830. . . .* Washington, D.C.: Duff Green, 1832.

———. *Population of the United States in 1860: Compiled from the Original Returns of the Eighth Census under the Direction of the Secretary of the Interior.* Washington, D.C.: U.S. Government Printing Office, 1864.

U.S. Census Office. *Sixth Census of Enumeration of the Inhabitants of the United States . . . 1840.* Washington, D.C.: N. Ross, 1841.

U.S. Department of Census. *Historical Statistics of the United States, Colonial Times to 1970.* 2 vols. Washington. D.C.: U.S. Government Printing Office, 1975.

BOOKS, ARTICLES, AND DISSERTATIONS

Abrahams, Roger. *Singing the Master: The Emergence of African American Culture in the Plantation South.* New York: Pantheon Books, 1992.

Agnew, Jean-Christophe. *Worlds Apart: The Market and Theater in Anglo-American Thought.* New York: Cambridge University Press, 1986.

Alampi, Gary, ed. *Gale State Rankings Reporter.* Detroit, Mich.: Gale, 1996.

Alexander, Arthur J. "Federal Officeholders in New York State as Slaveholders, 1789–1805." *Journal of Negro History* 28 (1943): 326–50.

Allen, Robert S., ed. *The Loyal Americans: The Military Role of the Loyalist Provincial Corps and Their Settlement in British North America, 1775–1784.* Ottawa: Museum of Man, National Museum of Canada, 1983.

Anderson, John R. "Negro Education in the Public Schools of Newark, New Jersey, during the Nineteenth Century." Ph.D. diss., Rutgers University, 1972.

Andrews, William L., ed. *Sisters of the Spirit: Three Black Women's Autobiographies of the Nineteenth Century.* Bloomington: Indiana University Press, 1986.

Anstice, Reverend Henry. *Old Sand Street Methodist Episcopal Church of Brooklyn.* New York: James Pott, 1885.

Aptheker, Herbert. *American Negro Slave Revolts.* New York: Columbia University Press, 1944.

———. "The Negro in the Union Navy." *Journal of Negro History* 32 (1947): 169–200.

———. "The Quakers and Negro Slavery." *Journal of Negro History* 25 (1940): 331–62.

———, ed. *A Documentary History of the Negro People in the United States.* New York: Citadel Press, 1951.

Archdeacon, Thomas J. *New York City, 1664–1710: Conquest and Change.* Ithaca, N.Y.: Cornell University Press, 1976.

Asbury, Herbert. *The Gangs of New York.* New York: Knopf, 1928.

Atkinson, Joseph. *The History of Newark.* Newark, N.J.: William B. Guild, 1878.

Atwood, Rodney. *The Hessians: Mercenaries from Hessen-Kassel in the American Revolution.* New York: Cambridge University Press, 1980.

Austin, Allen D. *African Muslims in Antebellum America: A Sourcebook.* New York: Garland, 1984.

———. *African Muslims in Antebellum America: Transatlantic Stories and Spiritual Struggles.* New York: Routledge, 1997.

Axtell, James. *The Invasion Within: The Contest of Cultures in Colonial North America.* New York: Oxford University Press, 1985.

Bachman, Van Cleaf. *Peltries or Plantations: The Economic Policies of the Dutch West India Company in New Netherlands, 1623–1639.* Baltimore: Johns Hopkins University Press, 1969.

Bailey, Rosalie Fellows. *Pre-Revolutionary Dutch Houses and Families in Northern New Jersey and Southern New York.* New York: William Morrow, 1936.

Bakker, Peter. "First African into New Netherland, 1613–14." *De Halve Maen* 68 (1995): 50–53.

Balandier, Georges. *Daily Life in the Kingdom of the Kongo from the Sixteenth to the Eighteenth Century.* New York: Pantheon Books, 1968.

Balmer, Randall H. *A Perfect Babel of Confusion: Dutch Religion and English Culture in the Middle Colonies.* New York: Oxford University Press, 1989.

Bank, Rosemarie K. *Theater Culture in America, 1825–1860.* New York: Cambridge University Press, 1997.

Barnett, Enid Vivian. "Educational Activities by and in Behalf of the Negroes in New York, 1800–1830." *Negro History Bulletin* 14 (1951): 99–102, 113–14.

Bartels, F. L. "Jacobus Eliza Capetein, 1717–1747." *Transactions of the Historical Society of Ghana* 4 (1973): 3–13.

Baseler, Marilyn C. *"Asylum for Mankind": America, 1607–1800.* Ithaca, N.Y.: Cornell University Press, 1998.

Beckles, Hilary. *Black Rebellion in Barbadoes: The Struggle against Slavery, 1627–1838.* Bridgetown, Barbadoes: Antilles Publications, 1984.

———. *White Servitude and Black Slavery in Barbadoes, 1627–1715.* Baton Rouge: Louisiana State University Press, 1989.

Belasco, Bernard I. *The Entrepreneur as Culture Hero: Preadaptations in Nigerian Economic Development.* New York: Praeger, 1980.

Bell, Howard Holman. *A Survey of the Negro Convention Movement, 1830–1861.* New York: Arno Press, 1969.

Bennett, Robert A. "Black Episcopalians: A History from the Colonial Period to the Present." *Historical Magazine of the Protestant Episcopal Church* 43 (1974): 231–46.

Benson, Lee. *The Concept of Jacksonian Democracy: New York as a Test Case.* Princeton: Princeton University Press, 1961.

Bergen, Teunis. *Register in Alphabetical Order of the Early Settlers of Kings County, Long Island.* New York: S. W. Green's Son, 1881.

Berkeley, Francis L., ed. *Dunmore's Proclamation of Emancipation.* Charlottesville: University Press of Virginia, 1941.

Berlin, Ira, et al. *Freedom: A Documentary History of Emancipation, 1861–1867.* Ser. 2: *The Black Military Experience.* New York: Cambridge University Press, 1982.

———. "From Creole to African: Atlantic Creoles and the Origins of African-American Society in Mainland North America." *William and Mary Quarterly* 3d ser., 53 (1996): 251–88.

———. *Many Thousands Gone: The First Two Centuries of African American Slavery.* Cambridge, Mass.: Harvard University Press, 1998.

———. *Slaves without Masters: The Free Negro in the Antebellum South.* New York: Pantheon Books, 1974.

———. "Time, Space, and the Evolution of Afro-American Society on British Mainland North America." *American Historical Review* 85 (1980): 44–78.

Berlin, Ira, and Ronald Hoffman, eds. *Slavery and Freedom in the Age of the American Revolution.* Charlottesville: University Press of Virginia, 1983.

Bernard, A. C. "Die Pinksterfees in Die Kerklike Jaar." Ph.D. diss., University of Amsterdam, 1954.

Bernstein, Iver. *The New York City Draft Riots: Their Significance for American Society and Politics in the Age of the Civil War.* New York: Oxford University Press, 1990.

Birmingham, David. *Trade and Conflict in Angola: The Mbundu and Their Neighbors under the Influence of the Portuguese, 1483–1790.* Oxford: Clarendon Press, 1966.

Blackburn, Robin, *The Making of New World Slavery from the Baroque to the Modern, 1492–1800.* New York: Verso Books, 1997.

———. *The Overthrow of Colonial Slavery, 1776–1848.* New York: Verso Books, 1988.

Blackett, R. J. M. *Beating against the Barriers: The Lives of Six Nineteenth-Century Afro-Americans.* Baton Rouge: Lousiana State University Press, 1986.

Blackmar, Elizabeth. *Manhattan for Rent, 1785–1850.* Ithaca, N.Y.: Cornell University Press, 1989.

Blackmar, Elizabeth, and Roy Rosenzweig. *The Park and the People: A History of Central Park.* Ithaca, N.Y.: Cornell University Press, 1992.

Blakely, Allison. *Blacks in the Dutch World: The Evolution of Racial Imagery in a Modern Society.* Bloomington: Indiana University Press, 1993.

Blight, David W. *Frederick Douglass' Civil War: Keeping Faith in Jubilee.* Baton Rouge: Louisiana State University Press, 1989.

Bodle, Wayne. "Themes and Directions in Middle Colonies Historiography, 1980–1994." *William and Mary Quarterly* 3d ser., 51 (1994): 355–89.

Boeseken, A. J. *Slaves and Free Blacks at the Cape, 1658–1700.* Capetown, South Africa: Tafelberg, 1977.

Bogin, Ruth, and Bert James Loewenberg. *Black Women in Nineteenth Century American Life.* University Park: Pennsylvania State University Press, 1976.

Bolster, W. Jeffrey. *Black Jacks: African American Seamen in the Age of Sail.* Cambridge, Mass.: Harvard University Press, 1997.

———. " 'To Feel Like a Man' ": Black Seamen in the Northern States, 1800–1860." *Journal of American History* 76 (1990): 1173–99.

Bolton, Robert. *History of the Protestant Episcopal Church in the County of Westchester.* New York: Stanford and Swords, 1855.

Bonomi, Patricia. *A Factious People: Politics and Society in Colonial New York.* New York: Columbia University Press, 1971.

———. *Under the Cope of Heaven: Religion, Society, and Politics in Colonial America.* New York: Oxford University Press, 1986.

Boxer, C. R. *The Dutch in Brazil, 1624–1654.* Oxford: Clarendon Press, 1957.

Boylan, Anne. "Benevolence and Antislavery Activity among African American Women in New York and Boston, 1820–1840." In *Abolitionist Sisterhood: Women's Political Culture in Antebellum America*, edited by Jean Fagan Yellin and John C. Van Horne. Ithaca, N.Y.: Cornell University Press, 1994.

———. *Sunday School: The Formation of an American Institution, 1790–1880.* New Haven: Yale University Press, 1988.

Breen, T. H., and Stephen Innes. *"Myne Owne Ground": Race and Freedom on Virginia's Eastern Shore, 1640–1676.* New York: Oxford University Press, 1980.

Brekus, Catherine A. *Strangers and Pilgrims: Female Preaching in America, 1740–1845.* Chapel Hill: University of North Carolina Press, 1998.

Brewer, Clifton Hartwell. *A History of Religious Education in the Episcopal Church to 1835.* New Haven: Yale University Press, 1924.

Bridenbaugh, Carl. *Mitre and Sceptre: Transatlantic Faiths, Ideas, Personalities and Politics.* New York: Oxford University Press, 1962.

Bruce, Dwight H., ed. *The Empire State in Three Centuries.* 3 vols. New York: Century History Company, 1898.

Buckley, Peter George. "To the Opera House: Culture and Society in New York City, 1820–1860." Ph.D. diss., State University of New York at Stony Brook, 1984.

Bullock, Penelope L. *The Afro-American Periodical Press, 1838–1909.* Baton Rouge: Louisiana State University Press, 1981.

Burr, Nelson. *The Anglican Church in New Jersey.* Philadelphia: Church Historical Society, 1954.

Burrows, Edwin G., and Mike Wallace. *Gotham: A History of New York City to 1898.* New York: Oxford University Press, 1999.

Butler, Jon. *Awash in a Sea of Faith: Christianizing the American People.* Cambridge, Mass.: Harvard University Press, 1990.

———. *The Huguenots in America: A Refugee People in New World Society.* Cambridge, Mass.: Harvard University Press, 1983.

Cadbury, Henry J. "Negro Membership in the Society of Friends." *Journal of Negro History* 21 (1936): 151–213.

Calhoon, Robert M. *The Loyalist Perception and Other Essays.* Columbia: University of South Carolina Press, 1989.

Campbell, Penelope. *Maryland in Africa: The Maryland State Colonization Society, 1831–1857.* Urbana: University of Illinois Press, 1971.

Caro, Edythe Quinn. *"The Hills" in the Mid-Nineteenth Century: The History of a Rural Afro-American Community in Westchester County, New York.* Valhalla, N.Y.: Westchester Historical Society, 1988.

Carretta, Vincent, ed. *Unchained Voices: An Anthology of Black Authors in the English-Speaking World of the 18th Century.* Lexington: University Press of Kentucky, 1996.

Carwardine, Richard J. *Evangelicals and Politics in Antebellum America.* New Haven: Yale University Press, 1993.

Clayton, W. W. *History of Bergen and Passaic Counties, New Jersey: with Biographical Sketches of Many of Its Pioneers and Prominent Men.* Philadelphia: Everts & Peck, 1882.

Clute, J. J. *Annals of Staten Island, from Its Discovery to the Present Time.* New York: C. Vogt, 1877.

Cohen, David Steven. *The Dutch-American Farm.* New York: New York University Press, 1992.

———. "In Search of Carolus Africanus Rex." *Journal of the Afro-American Historical and Genealogical Society* 5 (1984): 149–63.

———. *The Ramapo Mountain People.* New Brunswick, N.J.: Rutgers University Press, 1974.

Collegio, Lee. "The Negro's Legal Status in Pre-Civil War New Jersey." *New Jersey History* 70 (1967): 167–80.

Conroy, David W. *The Public Houses: Drink and the Revolution of Authority in Colonial Massachusetts.* Chapel Hill: University of North Carolina Press for the Institute of Early American History and Culture, 1995.

Cook, Adrian. *The Armies of the Street: The New York City Draft Riots of 1863.* Lexington: University Press of Kentucky, 1974.

Cooley, Henry S. *A Study of Slavery in New Jersey.* Baltimore: Johns Hopkins University Press, 1896.

Cornish, Dudley T. *The Sable Arm: Negro Troops in the Union Army, 1861–1865.* New York: Longmans, Green, 1956.

Corwin, Edwin. "The Church and the Negroes in Colonial Days." In *Tercentenary Studies of the Reformed Church in America.* New York: The Church, 1928.

Countryman, Edward. *A People in Revolution: The American Revolution and Political Society in New York, 1760–1790.* Baltimore: Johns Hopkins University Press, 1981.

Cox, John R. *Quakerism in the City of New York, 1657–1930.* New York: Privately printed, 1930.

Craton, Michael. *Testing the Chains: Resistance to Slavery in the West Indies.* Ithaca, N.Y.: Cornell University Press, 1982.

Cressy, David. *Birth, Marriage and Death: Ritual, Religion, and the Life-Cycle in Tudor and Stuart England.* New York: Oxford University Press, 1997.

———. *Bonfires and Bells: National Memory and the Protestant Calendar in Elizabethan and Stuart England.* Berkeley: University of California Press, 1989.

Crummey, Donald. *Banditry, Rebellion, and Social Protest in Africa.* Portsmouth, N.H.: Heinemann, 1986.

Curry, Leonard P. *The Free Black in Urban America, 1800–1850: The Shadow of a Dream.* Chicago: University of Chicago Press, 1981.

Curtin, Philip. *The Atlantic Slave Trade: A Census.* Madison: University of Wisconsin Press, 1969.

Dann, Jon C. *Memories of the War for Independence: Textual Selections of Veterans' Memories for the Revolution, Eyewitness Accounts of the War for Independence.* Chicago: University of Chicago Press, 1980.

Dann, Martin, ed. *The Black Press, 1827–1890: The Quest for National Identity.* New York: Putnam, 1971.

Davies, K. G. *The Royal African Company.* London: Longmans, Green, 1957.

Davis, David Brion. "American Equality and Foreign Revolutions." *Journal of American History* 76 (1989): 729–52.

———. *The Problem of Slavery in the Age of Revolution, 1770–1823.* Ithaca, N.Y.: Cornell University Press, 1975.

———. *The Problem of Slavery in Western Culture,* Ithaca, N.Y.: Cornell University Press, 1966.

Davis, Thomas J. "Emancipation Rhetoric, Natural Rights and

Revolutionary New England: A Note on Four Black Petitions in Massachusetts, 1773–1777." *New England Quarterly* 57 (1989): 248–64.

———. "New York's Long Black Line: A Note on the Growing Slave Population, 1626–1790." *Afro-Americans in New York Life and History* 2 (1978): 41–59.

———. *Rumor of Revolt: The "Great Negro Plot" in Colonial New York.* New York: Free Press, 1985.

———. "These Enemies of Their Own Household." *Journal of the Afro-American Historical and Genealogical Society* 5 (1984): 133–49.

Davis, William T., et al. *The Church of St. Andrew, Richmond, Staten Island: Its History, Vital Records, and Gravestone Inscriptions.* Lancaster, Pa.: Science Press Printing, 1925.

Day, Lynda R. *Making a Way to Freedom: A History of African Americans on Long Island.* Interlaken, N.Y.: Empire State Books, 1997.

DeJong, Gerald F. "The Dutch Reformed Church and Negro Slavery in Colonial America." *Church History* 40 (1971): 423–36.

———. *The Dutch Reformed Church in the American Colonies.* Grand Rapids, Mich.: Eerdmans, 1978.

Demarest, Mary Arthur. *The Demarest Family: David Demarest of the French Patent on the Hackensack and His Descendants.* New Brunswick, N.J.: N.p., 1938.

Dickenson, Richard B. *Census Occupations of Afro-American Families on Staten Island, 1840–1875.* Staten Island, N.Y.: Staten Island Institute of Arts and Sciences, 1981.

Dolan, Jay P. *The Immigrant Church: New York's Irish and German Catholics, 1815–1865.* Baltimore: Johns Hopkins University Press, 1975.

Drescher, Seymour. "The Long Goodbye: Dutch Capitalism and Antislavery." *American Historical Review* 99 (1994): 44–69.

Du Bois, W. E. B. *The Black North in 1901: A Sociological Study.* New York: Arno Press, 1969.

———. *Economic Co-Operation among Negro Americans.* Atlanta, Ga.: Atlanta University Press, 1907.

———. *The Souls of Black Folk.* New York: A. C. McClurg, 1903.

———. *The Suppression of the African Slave Trade.* Cambridge, Mass.: Harvard University Press, 1896.

Duffy, John. "An Account of the Epidemical Fevers That Prevailed in the City of New York from 1791–1822." *New-York Historical Society Quarterly* 50 (1966): 333–64.

———. *A History of Public Health in New York City, 1625–1966.* 2 vols. New York: Russell Sage Foundation, 1968–74.

Dunlap, William. *A History of the Rise and Progress of the Arts of Design in the United States.* 2 vols. Boston: C. E. Goodspeed, 1918.

Dunn, Richard. "Servants and Slaves: The Recruitment and Employment of Labor." In *Colonial British America: Essays in the New History of the Early Modern Era,* edited by J. R. Pole and Jack Greene. Baltimore: Johns Hopkins University Press, 1983.

Durey, Michael. *Transatlantic Radicals and the Early American Republic.* Lawrence: University Press of Kansas, 1997.

Durie, Howard I. *The Kakiat Patent in Bergen County New Jersey.* Pearl River, N.J.: Star Press, 1970.

Egerton, Douglas R. " 'Its Origin Is Not a Little Curious': A New Look at the American Colonization Society." *Journal of the Early Republic* 5 (1985): 463–80.

Egerton, Hugh Edward. *The Royal Commission on the Losses and Services of American Loyalists.* Oxford: Printed for Presentation to the Members of the Roxburghe Club, 1915.

Ekechin, Felix R. "African Polygamy and Western Christian Ethnocentrism." *Journal of African Studies* 3 (1976): 329–51.

Ekirch, A. Roger. *Bound for America: The Transportation of British Convicts to the Colonies, 1718–1775.* Oxford: Clarendon Press, 1987.

Eltis, David, and David Richardson, eds. *Economic Growth and the Ending of the Transatlantic Slave Trade.* New York: Oxford University Press, 1987.

———. *Routes to Slavery: Direction, Ethnicity and Mortality in the Atlantic Slave Trade.* London: Frank Cass, 1997.

Emmer, Pieter. "The History of the Dutch Slave Trade: A Bibliographic Survey." *Journal of Economic History* 32 (1972): 728–47.

Ernst, Robert. *Immigrant Life in New York City, 1825–1863.* New York: King's Crown Press, 1949.

———. "A Long Island Black Tory." *Long Island Forum* 41 (1978): 18–19.

Essah, Patience. *A House Divided: Slavery and Emancipation in Delaware, 1638–1865.* Charlottesville: University Press of Virginia, 1996.

Fabel, Robin F. A. "Self-Help in Dartmoor: Black and White Prisoners in the War of 1812." *Journal of the Early Republic* 9 (1989): 165–90.

Fabend, Firth Haring. "The Synod of Dort and the Persistence of Dutchness in Nineteenth-Century New York and New Jersey." *New York History* 77 (July 1976): 273–300.

Faber, Eli. *Jews, Slaves, and the Slave Trade: Setting the Record Straight.* New York: New York University Press, 1998.

Field, Phyllis F. *The Politics of Race in New York: The Struggle for Black Suffrage in the Civil War Era.* Ithaca, N.Y.: Cornell University Press, 1982.

Fields, Barbara Jeanne. *Slavery and Freedom on the Middle Ground: Maryland during the Nineteenth Century.* New Haven: Yale University Press, 1985.

Finkelman, Paul. *An Imperfect Union: Slavery. Federalism, and Comity.* Chapel Hill: University of North Carolina Press, 1981.

———. "The Kidnapping of John Davis and the Adoption of the Fugitive Slave Law of 1793." *Journal of Southern History* 56 (1990): 397–422.

———. "The Protection of Black Rights in Seward's New York." *Civil War History* 34 (1988): 211–34.

Fishman, George. *The Struggle for Freedom and Equality: African Americans in New Jersey, 1624–1850.* New York: Garland, 1997.

Fladeland, Betty. *Men and Brothers: Anglo-American Antislavery Cooperation.* Urbana: University of Illinois Press, 1972.

Fleischer, Nat. *Black Dynamite*. 5 vols. New York: C. J. O'Brien, 1938–47.

Flynn, J. K. *Asante and Its Neighbors, 1700–1807*. Chicago: University of Chicago Press, 1971.

Foner, Eric. "Racial Attitudes of the New York Free Soilers." *New York History* 46 (1965): 311–29.

Foote, Thelma Wills. "Black Life in Colonial Manhattan, 1664–1786." Ph.D. diss., Harvard University, 1991.

———. "Crossroads or Settlement? The Black Freedman's Community in Historic Greenwich Village, 1644–1855." In *Greenwich Village: Culture and Counterculture*, edited by Rick Beard and Leslie Cohen Berlowitz. New Brunswick, N.J.: Rutgers University Press for the Museum of the City of New York, 1993.

Fordham, Monroe. *Major Themes in Northern Black Religious Thought, 1800–1860*. Hicksville, N.Y.: Exposition Press, 1975.

Fouchard, Jean. *The Haitian Maroons: Liberty or Death*. New York: E. W. Blyden Press, 1981.

Fox, Dixon Ryan. "The Negro Vote in Old New York." *Political Science Quarterly* 32 (1917): 252–75.

Fredrickson, George. *The Black Image in the White Mind: The Debate on Afro-American Character and Destiny*. New York: Harper and Brothers, 1969.

Freeman, Rhoda Golden. *The Free Negro in New York City in the Era before the Civil War*. New York: Garland, 1994.

Frey, Sylvia R. *Water from the Rock: Black Resistance in a Revolutionary Age*. Princeton: Princeton University Press, 1991.

Furman, Gabriel. *Antiquities of Long Island*. New York: J. W. Bouton, 1874.

Garrett, Clarke. *Spirit Possession and Popular Religion from the Camisards to the Shakers*. Baltimore: Johns Hopkins University Press, 1987.

Gaspar, David Barry. *Bondsmen and Rebels: A Study of Master-Slave Relations from Antigua with Implications for Colonial British America*. Baltimore: Johns Hopkins University Press, 1985.

Gates, Henry Louis Jr. *The Signifying Monkey: A Theory of Afro-American Art and Philosophy*. New York: Oxford University Press, 1988.

Gatewood, Willard B. *Aristocrats of Color: The Black Elite, 1880–1920*. Bloomington: Indiana University Press, 1990.

———, ed. *Free Man of Color: The Autobiography of Willis Augustus Hodges*. Knoxville: University of Tennessee Press, 1982.

Geismar, Joan H. *The Archaeology of Social Disintegration in Skunk Hollow: A Nineteenth-Century Rural Black Community*. New York: Academic Press, 1982.

Gemery, Henry A., and Jan Hogendorn, eds. *The Uncommon Market: Essays in the Economic History of the Atlantic Slave Trade*. New York: Academic Press, 1979.

Genovese, Eugene D. *Roll, Jordan, Roll: The World the Slaves Made*. New York: Pantheon Books, 1974.

George, Carol V. "Widening the Circle: The Black Church and the Abolitionist

Crusade, 1830–1860." In *Antislavery Reconsidered: New Perspectives on the Abolitionist,* edited by Lewis Perry and Michael Fellman. Baton Rouge: Louisiana State University Press, 1979.

Gerlach, Larry R. *Prologue to Independence: New Jersey in the Coming of the American Revolution.* New Brunswick, N.J.: Rutgers University Press, 1976.

Geyl, Pieter. *The Revolt of the Netherlands, 1555–1609.* London: Ernst Benn, 1932.

Gilfoyle, Timothy. *City of Eros: New York City Prostitution and the Commercialization of Sex, 1790–1920.* New York: Norton, 1992.

Gilje, Paul. *The Road to Mobocracy: Popular Disorder in New York City, 1763–1834.* Chapel Hill: University of North Carolina Press for the Institute of Early American History and Culture, 1987.

Gilje, Paul A., and Howard B. Rock, eds. *Keepers of the Revolution: New Yorkers at Work in the Early Republic.* Ithaca, N.Y.: Cornell University Press, 1992.

———. " 'Sweep O! Sweep O!': African-American Chimney Sweeps and Citizenship in the New Nation." *William and Mary Quarterly* 3d ser., 51 (1996): 507–38.

Gilroy, Paul. *The Black Atlantic: Modernity and Double Consciousness.* Cambridge, Mass.: Harvard University Press, 1993.

Ginsberg, Lori D. *Women and the Work of Benevolence.* New Haven: Yale University Press, 1990.

Glassman, Jonathan. "The Bondsman's New Clothes: The Contradictory Consciousness of Slave Resistance on the Swahili Coast." *Journal of African History* 32 (1991): 277–312.

Glatthaar, Joseph T. *Forged in Battle: The Civil War Alliance of Black Soldiers and White Officers.* New York: Free Press, 1990.

Glickstein, Jonathan. *Concepts of Free Labor in Antebellum America.* New Haven: Yale University Press, 1991.

Goebel, Julius, and T. Raymond Naughton. *Law Enforcment in Colonial New York (1664–1776): A Study in Criminal Procedure.* New York: Commonwealth Press, 1944.

Gomez, Michael A. *Exchanging Our Country Marks: The Transformation of African Identities in the Colonial and Antebellum South.* Chapel Hill: University of North Carolina Press, 1998.

Goodfriend, Joyce. *Before the Melting Pot: Society and Culture in Colonial New York City, 1664–1730.* Princeton: Princeton University Press, 1992.

———. "Black Families in New Netherland." *Journal of the Afro-American Historical and Genealogical Society* 5 (1984): 95–108.

———. "Burghers and Blacks: The Evolution of a Slave Society at New Amsterdam." *New York History* 59 (1978): 125–44.

———. "The Social Dimensions of Congregational Life in Colonial New York City." *William and Mary Quarterly* 3d. ser., 46 (1989): 252–78.

Goslinga, Cornelius Ch. "Curacao as a Slave-Trading Center during the War of Spanish Succession." *Nieuwe West-Indische* 52 (1977): 1–51.

———. *The Dutch in the Caribbean and the Wild Coast, 1580–1680.* Assen, Netherlands: Van Gorcum, 1971.

Graveley, William B. "The Dialectic of Double-Consciousness in Black Freedom Celebrations, 1808–1863." *Journal of Negro History* 67 (1982): 302–18.

———. "The Rise of African Churches in America (1776–1822): Re-examining the Contexts." *Journal of Religious Thought* 14 (1984): 58–73.

Gray, Richard. *Black Christians and White Missionaries.* New Haven: Yale University Press, 1990.

Greenberg, Douglas. *Crime and Law Enforcement in the Colony of New York, 1691–1776.* Ithaca, N.Y.: Cornell University Press, 1976.

———. "Crime, Law Enforcement and Social Control in Colonial America." *American Journal of Legal History* 26 (1982): 293–325.

Greene, Evarts B., and Virginia Harrington. *American Population before the Federal Census of 1790.* New York: Columbia University Press, 1932.

Groneman, Carol. "The Bloudy Ould Sixth: A Social Analysis of a Mid-Nineteenth-Century Working-Class Community." Ph.D. diss., University of Rochester, 1974.

Gronowicz, Anthony. *Race and Class Politics in New York City before the Civil War.* Boston: Northeastern University Press, 1998.

Groth, Michael Edward. "Forging Freedom in the Mid-Hudson Valley: The End of Slavery and the Formation of a Free African-American Community in Dutchess County, New York, 1770–1850." Ph.D. diss., Binghamton University, 1994.

Guernsey, R. S. *New York City and Vicinity during the War of 1812–15. . . .* 2 vols. New York: C. L. Woodward, 1889–95.

Hagood, Reverend L. M. *The Colored Man in the Methodist Episcopal Church.* Cincinnati: Cranston and Stowe, 1890.

Hale, Thomas A. *Scribe, Griot, and Novelist: Narrative Interpreters of the Songhay Empire.* Gainesville: University of Florda Press, 1990.

Hansen, Joyce, and Gary McGowan. *Breaking Ground, Breaking Silence: The Story of New York's African Burial Ground.* New York: Henry Holt, 1998.

Hargrove, Hondon B. *Black Union Soldiers in the Civil War.* Jefferson, N.C.: McFarland, 1988.

Harrington, Virginia, and Evarts B. Greene. *American Population before the Federal Census of 1790.* New York: Columbia University Press, 1932.

Harris, Leslie Maria. "Creating the African American Working Class: Black and White Workers, Abolitionists, and Reformers in New York City, 1785–1863." Ph.D. diss., Stanford University, 1995.

Hatch, Nathan O. *The Democratization of American Christianity.* New Haven: Yale University Press, 1989.

Hatfield, Edwin J. *History of Elizabeth, New Jersey, Including the Early History of Union County.* New York: Carleton and Lanahan, 1868.

Hay, Samuel A. *African American Theater: A Historical and Critical Analysis.* New York: Cambridge University Press, 1994.

Headley, Joel T. *The Great Riots of New York, 1712–1873.* New York: E. B. Treat, 1873.

Hefner, Robert W. "The Rationality of Conversion." In *Conversion to Christianity: Historical and Anthropological Perspectives on a Great Transformation,* edited by Robert W. Hefner. Berkeley: University of California Press, 1993.

Hershkowitz, Leo. "The Troublesome Turk: An Illustration of Judicial Process in New Amsterdam." *New York History* 46 (1965): 300–306.

———. *Wills of Early New York Jews (1704–1799).* New York: American Jewish Historical Society, 1967.

Hewitt, John H. "Peter Williams, Jr.: New York's First African-American Priest." *New York History* 79 (April 1998): 101–29.

———. "The Sacking of St. Philip's Church, New York, 1834." *Historical Magazine of the Protestant Episcopal Church* 48 (1980): 7–20.

———. "Unresting the Waters: The Fight against Racism in New York's Episcopal Establishment, 1845–1853." *Afro-Americans in New York Life and History* 18 (1994): 7–31.

Higgenbotham, A. Leon. *In the Matter of Color: Race and the American Legal Process; the Colonial Period.* New York: Oxford University Press, 1978.

Hill, Bridget. *Servants: English Domestics in the Eighteenth Century.* Oxford: Clarendon Press, 1996.

Hilton, Anne. *The Kingdom of Kongo.* New York: Oxford University Press, 1985.

Hinks, Peter P. *To Awaken My Afflicted Brethren: David Walker and the Problem of Antebellum Slave Resistance.* University Park: Pennsylvania State University Press, 1997.

Hirsch, Leo D. "The Negro and New York, 1783–1865." *Journal of Negro History* 16 (1931): 382–473.

Hobsbawm, Eric, and Terence Ranger. *The Invention of Tradition.* New York: Cambridge University Press, 1983.

Hodges, Graham Russell. "Black Revolt in New York and the Neutral Zone." In *New York in the Age of the Constitution, 1775–1800,* edited by Paul A. Gilje and William Pencak. Cranbury, N.J.: Associated University Presses, 1993.

———. "Black Society in Antebellum New York." *Seaport Magazine* 23 (1989): 20–28.

———. " 'Desirable Companions and Lovers': Irish and African Americans in the Sixth Ward, 1830–1870." In *The New York Irish,* edited by Ronald H. Bayor and Timothy J. Meagher. Baltimore: Johns Hopkins University Press, 1996.

———. "Muscle and Pluck . . . Whitman's Working-Class Ties." *Seaport Magazine* 25 (1992): 32–38.

———. *New York City Cartmen, 1667–1850.* New York: New York University Press, 1986.

———. "The Pastor and the Prostitute: Sexual Power among African Americans and Germans in Colonial New York." In *Sex, Love, Race: Essays* on *Crossing Boundaries*, edited by Martha Hodes. New York: New York University Press, 1999.

———. *Slavery and Freedom in the Rural North: African Americans in Monmouth County, New Jersey, 1665–1865*. Madison, Wisc.: Madison House Books, 1997.

———. *Slavery, Freedom, and Culture among Early American Workers*. Armonk, N.Y.: M. E. Sharpe, 1998.

———, ed. *Black Itinerants of the Gospel: The Narratives of John Jea and George White*. Madison, Wisc.: Madison House Books, 1993.

———. *The Black Loyalist Directory: African Americans in Exile after the American Revolution*. New York: Garland, 1996.

Hodges, Graham Russell, and Alan Edward Brown, eds. *"Pretends to Be Free": Runaway Slave Advertisements from Colonial and Revolutionary New York and New Jersey*. New York: Garland, 1994.

Hoff, Henry B. "A Colonial Black Family in New York and New Jersey: Pieter Santomee and His Descendants." *Journal of the Afro-American Historical and Genealogical Society* 9 (1988): 101–35.

———. "The de Vries Family of Tappan, New York: A Study in Assimilation." *American Genealogist* (1997): 345–52.

———. "Frans Abramse Van Salee and His Descendants: A Colonial Black Family in New York and New Jersey." *New York Genealogical and Biographical Record* 121 (1990): 65–71.

———. "Swan Janse Van Luane: A Free Black in 17th Century Kings County." *New York Genealogical and Biographical Record* 125 (1994): 74–77.

Hoffman, Ronald, Mechal Sobel, and Frederika J. Teute, eds. *Through a Glass Darkly: Reflections on Personal Identity in Early America*. Chapel Hill: University of North Carolina Press for the Institute of Early American History and Culture, 1997.

Holden, Edith. *Blyden of Liberia: An Account of the Life and Labors of Edward Wilmot Blyden as Recorded in Letters and in Print*. New York: Vantage Press, 1966.

Holmes, David D. "The Episcopal Church and the American Revolution." *Historical Magazine of the Protestant Episcopal Church* 47 (1978): 261–91.

Hood, James Walker. *One Hundred Years of the African Methodist Church*. New York: A.M.E. Zion Book Concern, 1895.

Horton, James Oliver. *Free People of Color: Inside the African American Community*. Washington, D.C.: Smithsonian Institution Press, 1993.

Horton, James Oliver, and Lois E. Horton. *In Hope of Liberty: Culture, Community, and Protest among Northern Free Blacks, 1700–1860*. New York: Oxford University Press, 1997.

Horton, Robin. "African Conversion." *Africa: A Journal of the International African Institute* 41 (1971): 85–108.

———. *Patterns of Thought in Africa and the West: Essays on Magic, Religion, and Science*. New York: Cambridge University Press, 1993.

Howard, Victor B. *Conscience and Slavery: The Evangelistic Calvinist Domestic Missions, 1837–1861*. Kent, Ohio: Kent State University Press, 1990.

Howard, Warren S. *American Slavers and the Federal Law, 1837–1862*. Berkeley: University of California Press, 1963.

Howe, Stephen. *Afrocentrism: Mythical Pasts and Imagined Homes*. New York: Verso, 1998.

Hunt, Alfred N. *Haiti's Influence on Antebellum America: Slumbering Volcano in the Caribbean*. Baton Rouge: Louisiana State University Press, 1988.

Ignatiev, Noel. *How the Irish Became White*. New York: Verso, 1995.

Iliffe, John. *The African Poor, a History*. New York: Cambridge University Press, 1987.

Inikori, Joseph, ed. *Forced Migration: The Impact of the Export Slave Trade on African Societies*. New York: Africana Press, 1980.

Innes, Stephen, ed. *Work and Labor in Early America*. Chapel Hill: University of North Carolina Press for the Institute of Early American History and Culture, 1988.

Irvis, K. Leroy. "Negro Tales from Eastern New York." *New York Folklore Quarterly* 11 (1955): 165–77.

Israel, Jonathan. *Dutch Primacy in the Seventeenth Century*. New York: Oxford University Press, 1989.

Janvier, Thomas A. "New York Slave-Traders." *Harper's New Monthly Magazine* 40 (1895): 293–305.

Jeffrey, Julie Roy. *The Great Silent Army of Abolitionism: Ordinary Women in the Antislavery Movement*. Chapel Hill: University of North Carolina Press, 1998.

Jentz, John B. "The Antislavery Constituency in Jacksonian New York City." *Civil War History* 27 (1981): 101–22.

Jones, E. Alfred. "A Letter Regarding the Queen's Rangers." *Virginia Magazine of History and Biography* 30 (1922): 369–70.

———. *The Loyalists of New Jersey: Their Memorials, Petitions, Claims, Etc, from English Records*. Newark, N.J.: New-Jersey Historical Society, 1927.

Jones, George Fenwick. "The Black Hessians: Negroes Recruited by the Hessians in South Carolina and Other Colonies." *South Carolina Historical Magazine* 83 (1982): 287–302.

Jordan, Winthrop D. *White over Black: American Attitudes toward the Negro, 1550–1812*. Chapel Hill: University of North Carolina Press for the Institute of Early American History and Culture, 1968.

Joyner, Charles. *Down by the Riverside: A South Carolina Slave Community*. Urbana: University of Illinois Press, 1984.

Judd, Jacob. "Frederick Philipse and the Madagascar Trade." *New-York Historical Society Quarterly* 47 (1963): 66–74.

Juster, Susan, and Lisa McFarlane, eds. *A Mighty Baptism: Race, Gender, and the Creation of American Protestantism*. Ithaca, N.Y.: Cornell University Press, 1996.

Kaestle, Carl. *Pillars of the Republic: Common Schools and American Society, 1780–1860*. New York: Hill and Wang, 1983.

Kallich, Martin. *British Poetry and the American Revolution: A Bibliographic*

Survey of Books and Pamplets, Journals and Magazines. Troy, N.Y.: Whitston, 1988.

Kammen, Michael. *Colonial New York: A History.* Millwood, N.Y.: KTO Press, 1975.

Kaplan, Michael. "The World of the B'hoys: Urban Violence and the Political Culture of Antebellum New York City." Ph.D. diss., New York University, 1995.

Kea, Ray B. " 'I am Here to Plunder on the General Road': Bandits and Banditry in the Pre-Nineteenth-Century Gold Coast." In *Banditry, Rebellion and Social Protest in Africa,* edited by Donald Crummy. London: Currey, 1986.

———. *Settlements, Trade, and Politics in the Seventeenth-Century Gold Coast.* Baltimore: Johns Hopkins University Press, 1982.

Kenney, Alice P. *Stubborn for Liberty: The Dutch in New York.* Syracuse, N.Y.: Syracuse University Press, 1975.

Kent, Raymond R. *Early Kingdoms in Madagascar, 1500–1700.* New York: Holt, Rinehart and Winston, 1970.

Kerber, Linda K. "Abolitionists and Amalgamators: The New York City Race Riots of 1834." *New York History* 58 (1967): 28–41.

Kierner, Cynthia A. *Traders and Gentlefolk: The Livingstons of New York, 1675–1790.* Ithaca, N.Y.: Cornell University Press, 1992.

Kilpatrick, William H. *Dutch Schools of New Netherland and Colonial New York.* Washington, D.C.: U.S. Government Printing Office, 1912.

Kim, Sun Bok. *Landlord and Tenant in Colonial New York: Manorial Society, 1664–1775.* Chapel Hill: University of North Carolina Press for the Institute of Early American History and Culture, 1978.

Kinshasa, Kwando M. *Emigration vs. Assimilation: The Debate in the African American Press, 1827–1861.* Jefferson, N.C.: McFarland, 1988.

Klein, Herbert S. "Anglicanism, Catholicism, and the Negro Slave." In *The Debate over Slavery: Stanley Elkins and His Critics,* edited by Ann J. Lane. Urbana: University of Illinois Press, 1971.

Klingberg, Frank. *Anglican Humanitarism in Colonial New York.* Philadelphia: Church Historical Society, 1940.

Klips, Stephen A. "Institutionalizing the Poor: The New York City Almshouse, 1825–1860." Ph.D. diss., CUNY Graduate Center, 1980.

Kolchin, Peter. *American Slavery, 1619–1877.* New York: Hill and Wang, 1993.

Kruger, Vivienne L. " 'Born to Run': The Slave Family in Early New York, 1626–1827." Ph.D. diss., Columbia University, 1985.

Kulikoff, Alan. "The Origins of Afro-American Society in Tidewater Maryland and Virginia, 1700–1790." *William and Mary Quarterly* 3d ser., 35 (1978): 226–59.

———. *Tobacco and Slaves: The Development of Southern Cultures in the Chesapeake.* Chapel Hill: University of North Carolina Press for the Institute of Early American History and Culture, 1986.

Kull, Irving S. "Presbyterian Attitudes toward Slavery." *Church History* 7 (1938): 101–15.

Landsman, Ned C. *Scotland and Its First American Colony, 1683–1765.* Princeton: Princeton University Press, 1985.

Langley, Harold D. "The Negro in the Navy and the Merchant Service, 1789–1860." *Journal of Negro History* 52 (1967): 273–86.

Lauber, Almon Wheeler. *Indian Slavery in Colonial Times within the Present Limits of the United States.* New York: Columbia University Press, 1911.

Launitz-Shurer, Leopold S. Jr. "Slave Resistance in Colonial New York: An Interpretation of Daniel Horsmanden's New York Conspiracy." *Phylon* 16 (1979): 137–53.

Law, Robin. *The Slave Coast of West Africa: The Impact of the Atlantic Slave Trade on an African Society.* Oxford: Clarendon, 1991.

Leaming, Hugo Prosper. *Hidden Americans: Maroons of Virginia and the Carolinas.* New York: Garland, 1995.

Lee, Brother Basil Leon. *Discontent in New York City, 1861–1865.* Washington, D.C.: Catholic University Press, 1943.

Lee, Everett S., and Michael Lalli. "Population." In *The Growth of Seaport Cities, 1790–1825,* edited by David T. Gilchrist et al. Charlottesville: University Press of Virginia.

Leiby, Adrian C. *The Revolutionary War in the Hackensack Valley.* New Brunswick, N.J.: Rutgers University Press, 1960.

———. *The United Churches of Hackensack and Schraalenburgh, New Jersey, 1686–1822.* River Edge, N.J.: Bergen County Historical Society, 1976.

Levine, Lawrence W. *Black Culture and Black Consciousness: Afro-American Folk Thought from Slavery to Freedom.* New York: Oxford University Press, 1977.

Levitt, James H. *For Want of Trade: Shipping and the New Jersey Ports, 1680–1783.* Newark, N.J.: New-Jersey Historical Society, 1981.

Lewis, W. David. *From Newgate to Dannemora: The Rise of the Penitentiary Movement in New York.* Ithaca, N.Y.: Cornell University Press, 1965.

Lhamon, W. T. Jr. *Raising Cain: Blackface Performance from Jim Crow to Hip Hop.* Cambridge, Mass.: Harvard University Press, 1998.

Lindsay, Arnot G. "Diplomatic Relations between the United States and Great Britain Bearing on the Return of Negro Slaves, 1783–1828." *Journal of Negro History* 5 (1920): 391–419.

Linebaugh, Peter. "All the Atlantic Mountains Shook." *Labour/Le Travailleur* 21 (1981): 87–121.

Link, Eugene. *Democratic-Republican Societies, 1790–1800.* New York: Columbia University Press, 1942.

Litwack, Leon F. *North of Slavery: The Negro in the Free States, 1790–1860.* Chicago: University of Chicago Press, 1961.

Long, John H., ed. *New York: Atlas of Historical County Boundaries.* New York: Simon and Schuster, 1993.

Lorini, Allesandra. "Public Rituals, Race Ideology and the Transformation of Urban Culture: The Making of the New York African-American Community, 1825–1918." Ph.D. diss., Columbia University, 1991.

Lott, Eric. *Love and Theft: Blackface Minstrelsy and the American Working Class.* New York: Oxford University Press, 1993.

Lovejoy, Paul E. "The Volume of the Atlantic Slave Trade: A Synthesis." *Journal of African History* 23 (1982): 473–501.

Luckett, Judith Ann Blodgett. "Protest, Advancement and Identity: Organizational Strategies of Northern Free Blacks, 1830 to 1860." Ph.D. diss., Johns Hopkins University, 1993.

Luidens, John Pershing. "The Americanization of the Dutch Reformed Church." Ph.D. diss., University of Oklahoma, 1969.

Lundlin, Charles. *Cockpit of the Revolution: The War for Independence in New Jersey.* Princeton: Princeton University Press, 1940.

Lustig, Mary Lou. *Privilege and Prerogative: New York's Provincial Elite, 1710–1776.* Madison, N.J.: Associated University Presses, 1995.

———. *Robert Hunter, 1666–1734: New York's Augustan Statesman.* Syracuse, N.Y.: Syracuse University Press, 1983.

Lydecker, John Woolfe. *The Life and Letters of Charles Inglis.* London: Published for the Church Historical Society, 1936.

Lydon, James A. "New York and the Slave Trade, 1700–1774." *William and Mary Quarterly* 3d ser., 35 (1978): 375–94.

Mabee, Carleton. *Black Education in New York State.* Syracuse, N.Y.: Syracuse University Press, 1979.

———. *Black Freedom: The Nonviolent Abolitionists from 1830 through the Civil War.* New York: Macmillan, 1970.

———. *Sojourner Truth: Slave, Prophet, Legend.* New York: New York University Press, 1993.

MacFayden, Robert J. "The Schuyler Copper Mines and the First Steam Engine in America." *Bergen County History Annual* (1974): 7–38.

MacGaffey, Wyatt. *Religion and Society in Central Africa: The BaKongo of Lower Zaire.* Chicago: University of Chicago Press, 1986.

McKay, Ernest A. *The Civil War and New York City.* Syracuse, N.Y.: Syracuse University Press, 1990.

McKee, Samuel B. *Labor in Colonial New York, 1664–1776.* New York: Columbia University Press, 1935.

McKendrick, Neil, John Brewer, and J. R. Plumb, eds. *The Birth of a Consumer Society: The Commercialization of Eighteenth-Century England.* Bloomington: Indiana University Press, 1982.

McKivigan, John R. *The War against Proslavery Religion: Abolitionism and the Northern Churches, 1830–1865.* Ithaca, N.Y.: Cornell University Press, 1984.

McMahon, Reginald. *Jack Was Earnest.* Hackensack, N.J.: Bergen County Historical Society, 1984.

McManus, Edgar J. *Black Bondage in the North.* Syracuse, N.Y.: Syracuse University Press, 1973.

———. *A History of Negro Slavery in New York.* Syracuse, N.Y.: Syracuse University Press, 1966.

McPherson, James. *The Struggle for Equality: Abolitionists and the Negro in the Civil War and Reconstruction.* Princeton: Princeton University Press, 1964.

Main, Jackson Turner. *Political Parties before the Constitution.* Chapel Hill: University of North Carolina Press, 1973.

————. *The Social Structure of Revolutionary America.* Princeton: Princeton University Press, 1965.

Malone, Ann Patton. *Sweet Chariot: Slave Family and Household Structure in Nineteenth-Century Louisiana.* Chapel Hill: University of North Carolina Press, 1992.

Mandeville, Reverend G. Henry. *Golden Memories: A Historical Discourse on the Reformed Dutch Church of Harlem, New York.* New York: Graff, 1875.

Manning, Patrick. *Slavery, Colonialism, and Economic Growth in Dahomey, 1640–1960.* Cambridge: Cambridge University Press, 1982.

Martin, David. *Tongues of Fire: The Explosion of Protestantism in Latin America.* Oxford: Cambridge University Press, 1990.

Martin, Phyllis. *The External Trade of the Loango Coast, 1576–1870: The Effect of Changing Commercial Relations on the Vili Kingdom of Loango.* Oxford: Clarendon Press, 1972.

Mathews, Donald G. *Slavery and Methodism: A Chapter in American Morality, 1780–1845.* Princeton: Princeton University Press, 1965.

Matson, Cathy. *Merchants and Empire: Trading in Colonial New York.* Baltimore: Johns Hopkins University Press, 1997.

Mbiti, John S. *African Religions and Philosophies.* New York: Doubleday, 1969.

Meinig, Donald. *The Shaping of America: A Geographical Perspective on 500 Years of History.* Vol. 1. *Atlantic America, 1492–1800.* New Haven: Yale University Press, 1986.

Melish, Joanne Pope. *Disowning Slavery: Gradual Emancipation and Race in New England, 1780–1860.* Ithaca, N.Y.: Cornell University Press, 1998.

Menard, Russell. "The Africanization of the Lowcountry Labor Force, 1670–1730." In *Race and Family in the Colonial South,* edited by Winthrop Jordan and Sheila L. Skemp. Jackson: University Press of Mississippi, 1987.

Merwick, Donna. *Possessing Albany, 1630–1710: The Dutch and English Experiences.* New York: Cambridge University Press, 1990.

Messler, Abraham. *Forty Years at Raritan: Eight Memorial Sermons with Notes for a History of the Reformed Dutch Churches in Somerset County, New Jersey.* New York: A. Lloyd, 1873.

Midwinter, Sir Edward. "The S.P.G. and the Church in the American Colonies." *Historical Magazine of the Protestant Episcopal Church* 4 (1935).

Miller, Floyd J. *The Search for Black Nationality: Black Emigration and Colonization, 1787–1863.* Urbana: University of Illinois Press, 1975.

Miller, Joseph C. "The Congo-Angolan Slave Trade." In *The African Disapora: Interpretive Essays,* edited by Martin Kilson and Robert Rotberg. Cambridge, Mass.: Harvard University Press, 1976.

————. *Kings and Kingsmen: Early Mbundu States in Angola.* Oxford: Clarendon Press, 1966.

————. *Way of Death: Merchant Capitalism and the Angolan Slave Trade, 1730–1830.* Madison: University of Wisconsin Press, 1989.

Minchton, W. E. "The Slave Trade of Bristol with the British Mainland

Colonies in North America, 1699–1770." In *Liverpool, the Atlantic Slave Trade and Abolition,* edited by Roger Anstey and P. E. H. Hair. Occasional Papers, Vol. 2. Bristol, U.K.: Historic Society of Lancashire and Chester, 1976.

Mintz, Sidney, and Richard Price. *An Anthropological Approach to the Afro-American Past: A Caribbean Perspective.* Philadelphia: Institute for the Study of Human Issues, 1973.

Mohl, Raymond A. "Education as Social Control in New York City, 1784–1825." *New York History* 51 (1970): 219–38.

———. *Poverty in New York, 1783–1825.* New York: Oxford University Press, 1971.

Monnette, Orra Eugene. *First Settlers of ye Plantations of Piscataway and Woodbridge, Olde East New Jersey, 1664–1714.* Los Angeles: Leroy Carman Press, 1930.

Montgomery, David. *Beyond Equality: Labor and the Radical Republicans, 1862–1872.* New York: Knopf, 1967.

Moore, Reverend William. *History of St. George's Church, Hempstead, Long Island.* New York: E. P. Dutton, 1881.

Morgan, Edmund. *American Slavery American Freedom: The Ordeal of Colonial Virginia.* New York: Norton, 1975.

Morgan, Edwin V. *Slavery in New York.* New York: G. P. Putnam's & Sons, 1898.

Morgan, Joseph H. *History of the the Knights of Pythias (Negro), New Jersey.* N.p., n.d. ca. 1913.

———. *Morgan's History of the New Jersey Conference of the A.M.E. Church from 1872–1887 and of Several Churches, as Far as Possible from the Date of Organization with Biographical Sketches of Members of the Conference.* Camden, N.J.: S. Chew, 1887.

Morgan, Philip D. *Slave Counterpoint: Black Culture in the Eighteenth-Century Chesapeake and Lowcountry.* Chapel Hill: University of North Carolina Press for the Institute of Early American History and Culture, 1998.

Morris, Christopher. "The Articulation of Two Worlds: The Master-Slave Relationship Reconsidered." *Journal of American History* 85 (1998): 982–1007.

Morris, Richard B. "Class Struggle and the American Revolution." *William and Mary Quarterly* 3d. ser., 29 (1962): 3–29.

———. *Government and Labor in Early America.* New York: Columbia University Press, 1946.

———. *Select Cases of the Mayor's Court of New York City, 1674–1784.* Washington, D.C.: American Historical Association, 1935.

Moseley, Thomas. "A History of the New-York Manumission Society." Ph.D. diss., New York University, 1963.

Moses, Wilson J. *Afrotopia: The Roots of African American Popular History.* New York: Cambridge University Press, 1998.

———. *Alexander Crummell: A Study of Civilization and Discontent.* New York: Oxford University Press, 1989.

———. *The Golden Age of Black Nationalism, 1850–1925.* Hamden, Conn.: Shoe String Press, 1978.

———. *The Wings of Ethiopia: Studies in African-American Life and Letters.* Ames: Iowa State University Press, 1990.

Moss, Richard Shannon. *Slavery on Long Island.* New York: Garland, 1994.

Mullin, Gerald W. *Flight and Rebellion: Slave Resistance in Eighteenth-Century Virginia.* New York: Oxford University Press, 1972.

Narrett, David E. *Inheritance and Family Life in Colonial New York City.* Ithaca, N.Y.: Cornell University Press, 1992.

Nash, Gary B. "Forging Freedom: The Emancipation Experience in Northern Seaport Cities." In Nash, *Race, Class and Politics: Essays in American Colonial and Revolutionary Society.* Urbana: University of Illinois Press, 1986.

———. *Forging Freedom: The Formation of Philadelphia's Black Community, 1720–1840.* Cambridge, Mass.: Harvard University Press, 1987.

———. *Race and Revolution.* Madison, Wisc.: Madison House Books, 1990.

———. *Race, Class and Politics: Essays on American Colonial and Revolutionary Society.* Urbana: University of Illinois Press, 1986.

———. *The Urban Crucible: Social Change, Political Consciousness, and the Origins of the American Revolution.* Cambridge, Mass.: Harvard University Press, 1979.

Nash, Gary B., and Jean R. Soderlund. *Freedom by Degrees: Emancipation in Pennsylvania and Its Aftermath.* New York: Oxford University Press, 1991.

Nelson, William H. *The American Tory.* Oxford: Oxford University Press, 1961.

Nordstrom, Carl. "Slavery in a New York County: Rockland County, 1686–1827." *Afro-Americans in New York Life and History* 1 (1977): 145–66.

Norton, Mary Beth. "The Fate of Some Black Loyalists of the American Revolution." *Journal of Negro History* 58 (1973): 402–26.

———. *Founding Mothers and Fathers: Gendered Power and the Forming of American Society.* New York: Knopf, 1996.

O'Dell, George. *Annals of the New York Stage.* 15 vols. New York: Columbia University Press, 1928.

Okoye, F. Nwabueze. "Chattel Slavery as the Nightmare of the American Revolutionaries." *William and Mary Quarterly* 3d ser., 37 (1980): 3–28.

Old, Hughes Oliphant. *The Shaping of the Reformed Baptismal Rite in the Sixteenth Century.* Grand Rapids: Eerdmans, 1992.

O'Reilly, Henry. *First Organization of Colored Troops in the State of New York to Aid in Suppressing the Slaveholders' Rebellion.* New York: Baker and Godwin, 1864.

Osborn, John Hosey. *Life in the Old Dutch Homesteads: Saddle River, N.J., from 1708.*

Painter, Nell Irvin. *Sojourner Truth: A Life, a Symbol.* New York: Norton, 1996.

Ottley, Roi. *The Negro in New York.* New York: Oceana Publications, 1967.

Parish, Peter J. *Slavery: History and Historians.* New York: Harper & Row, 1989.

Patterson, Orlando. *Slavery and Social Death: A Comparative Study.* Cambridge, Mass.: Harvard University Press, 1982.

————. *The Sociology of Slavery: An Analysis of the Origins, Development, and Structure of Negro Slave Society in Jamaica.* Rutherford, N.J.: Fairleigh Dickinson University Press, 1967.

Pawley, James A. *The Negro Church in New Jersey.* Hackensack, N.J.: Works Progress Administration, 1939.

Payne, Daniel A. *The Semi-Centenary and Retrospection of the African Methodist Church in the United States.* Baltimore: Sherwood, 1866.

Pease, William, and Jane Pease. *They Who Would Be Free: Blacks' Search for Freedom.* New York: Atheneum, 1974.

Pelton, Robert D. *The Trickster in West Africa: A Study of Mythic Irony and Sacred Delight.* Berkeley: University of California Press, 1980.

Perlman, Daniel. "Organizations of the Free Negro in New York City, 1800–1860." *Journal of Negro History* 56 (1971): 181–98.

Peterson, Arthur Everett, and George William Edwards. *New York as an Eighteenth Century Municipality.* New York: Longmans, Green, 1917.

Peterson, Carla L. *"Doers of the Word": African American Women Speakers and Writers in the North (1830–1880).* New York: Oxford University Press, 1995.

Pierson, William D. *Black Yankees: The Development of an Afro-American Subculture in Eighteenth-Century New England.* Amherst: University of Massachusetts Press, 1988.

Platt, Virginia Bever. "The East India Company and the Madagascar Trade." *William and Mary Quarterly* 3d ser., 26 (1969): 548–77.

Pleat, Geraldine R., and Agnes M. Underwood. "Pinkster Ode Albany, 1803." *New York Folklore Quarterly* 8 (1952): 31–45.

Pointer, Richard. *Protestant Pluralism and the New York Experience: A Study of Eighteenth-Century Diversity.* Bloomington: Indiana University Press, 1988.

————. "Religious Life in New York during the Revolutionary War." *New York History* 66 (1985): 357–75.

Pomerantz, Sidney J. *New York City: An American City, 1783–1803.* New York: Columbia University Press, 1938.

Pomfret, John C. *Colonial New Jersey: A History.* New York: Scribner, 1973.

Porter, Dorothy B. "David Ruggles, an Apostle of Human Rights." *Journal of Negro History* 28 (1943): 23–50.

————. "The Organized Educational Activities of Negro Literary Societies, 1828–1846." *Journal of Negro Education* 5 (1936): 555–76.

Postma, Johannes. *The Dutch in the Atlantic Slave Trade.* New York: Cambridge University Press, 1990.

Potter, Jim. "The Growth of Population in America, 1700–1860." In *Population in History: Essays in Historical Demography,* edited by D. V. Glass and D. E. C. Eversley. London: E. Arnold, 1965.

Pratt, John Webb. *Religion, Politics, and Diversity: The Church-State Theme in New York History.* Ithaca, N.Y.: Cornell University Press, 1967.

Price, Clement Alexander. *Freedom Not Far Distant: A Documentary History of*

Afro-Americans in New Jersey. Newark, N.J.: New-Jersey Historical Society, 1980.

Price, J. L. *Culture and Society in the Dutch Republic during the Seventeenth Century.* London: Batsford, 1974.

Price, Richard. *First-Time: The Historical Vision of an Afro-American People.* Baltimore: Johns Hopkins University Press, 1983.

Prude, Jonathan. "To Look Upon the 'Lower Sort': Runaway Ads and the Appearance of Unfree Laborers in America." *Journal of American History* 78 (1991): 124–60.

Pullis, John, ed. *Moving On: Black Loyalists in the Afro-Atlantic World.* New York: Garland, 1999.

Quarles, Benjamin. *Black Abolitionists.* New York: Oxford University Press, 1969.

———. *Frederick Douglass.* Washington, D.C.: Associated Publishers, 1948.

———. *The Negro in the American Revolution.* Chapel Hill: University of North Carolina Press for the Institute of Early American History and Culture, 1961.

———. *The Negro in the Civil War.* Boston: Little, Brown, 1953.

Raboteau, Albert J. *Slave Religion: The Invisible Institution in the Antebellum South.* New York: Oxford University Press, 1978.

Rael, Patrick Joseph. "The Lion's Painting: African-American Thought in the Antebellum North." Ph.D. diss., University of California at Berkeley, 1995.

Raesly, Ellis R. *Portrait of New Netherland.* New York: Columbia University Press, 1945.

Randall, Thomas H. "Tarleton's Legion." *Collections of the Nova Scotia Historical Society* 28 (1949): 3–5.

Ranger, Terrence. *The Invention of Tradition.* New York: Cambridge University Press, 1983.

Rawley, James A. *The Transatlantic Slave Trade: A History.* New York: Norton, 1981.

Raymond, W. O. "Muster Roll of the Queen's Rangers, 1775–1783." *Collections of the New Brunswick Historical Society* 5 (1905): 243–50.

Rediker, Marcus. *Between the Devil and the Deep Blue Sea: Merchant Seamen, Pirates, and the Anglo-American Maritime World, 1700–1750.* New York: Cambridge University Press, 1987.

Rediker, Marcus, and Peter Linebaugh. " 'The Many-Headed Hydra': Sailors, Slaves, and the Atlantic Working Class in the Eighteenth Century." *Journal of Historical Sociology* 3 (1990): 225–82.

Reed, Harry. *Platform for Change: The Foundations of Northern Free Black Community.* East Lansing: Michigan State University Press, 1994.

Reimers, David M. "Negro Bishops and Diocesean Segregation in the Protestant Episcopal Church." *Historical Magazine of the Protestant Episcopal Church* 31 (1962): 231–42.

Reynolds, Helen Wilkenson. *Dutch Houses in the Hudson Valley before 1776.* New York: Payson and Clarke, 1929.

Rice, Kym. *Early American Taverns: For the Entertainment of Friends and Strangers.* Chicago: Regnery Gateway for the Fraunces Tavern Museum, 1983.

Richards, Leonard L. *"Gentlemen of Property and Standing": Anti-Abolition Mobs in Jacksonian America.* New York: Oxford University Press, 1970.

Richardson, James F. *The New York Police: Colonial Times to 1901.* New York: Oxford University Press, 1970.

Riddell, William Renwick. "Observations on Slavery and Privateering." *Journal of Negro History* 15 (1930): 337-71.

Rink, Oliver. *Holland on the Hudson: An Economic and Social History of Dutch New York.* Ithaca, N.Y.: Cornell University Press, 1986.

Ritchie, Robert C. *Captain Kidd and the War against the Pirates.* Cambridge, Mass.: Harvard University Press, 1986.

———. *The Duke's Province: A Study of New York Politics and Society, 1664-1691.* Chapel Hill: University of North Carolina Press, 1977.

Roberts, John W. *From Trickster to Badman: The Black Folk Hero in Slavery and Freedom.* Philadelphia: University of Pennsylvania Press, 1989.

Robinson, Donald L. *Slavery in the Structure of American Politics, 1765-1820.* New York: Harcourt Brace Jovanovich, 1975.

Robinson, Reverend John. *The Testimony and Practice of the Presbyterian Church in Relation to American Slavery.* Cincinnati: J. D. Thorpe, 1852.

Rock, Howard B. *Artisans of the New Republic: The Tradesmen of New York City in the Age of Jefferson.* New York: New York University Press, 1979.

———, ed. *The New York City Artisan, 1789-1825: A Documentary History.* Albany: State University of New York Press, 1989.

Roediger, David R. *The Wages of Whiteness: Race and the Making of the American Working Class.* New York: Verso Books, 1991.

Rosenberg, Carroll Smith. *Religion and the Rise of the American City: The New York City Mission Movement, 1812-1870.* Ithaca, N.Y.: Cornell University Press, 1971.

Rosenwaike, Ira. *Population History of New York City.* Syracuse, N.Y.: Syracuse University Press, 1972.

Ross, Robert. *Cape of Torments: Slavery and Resistance in South Africa.* London: Routledge & Kegan Paul, 1983.

Rothschild, Nan A. *New York City Neighborhoods: The Eighteenth Century.* San Diego: Academic Press, 1990.

Rury, John L. "The New York African Free School, 1827-1836: Conflict over Community Control of Black Education." *Phylon* 44 (1983): 187-98.

Russell, Elmer B. *The Review of American Colonial Legislation by the King in Council.* New York: Columbia University Press, 1915.

Ryan, Dennis. "Six Towns: Continuity and Change in Revolutionary New Jersey." Ph.D. diss., New York University, 1974.

Ryan, Leo. *Old St. Peter's, the Mother Church of Catholic New York (1785-1931).* New York: United States Catholic Historical Society, 1935.

Ryan, Mary P. *Civic Wars: Democracy and Public Life in the American City during the Nineteenth Century.* Berkeley: University of California Press, 1997.

Sale, Maggie Montesinos. *The Slumbering Volcano: American Slave Ship Revolts and the Production of Rebellious Masculinity.* Durham, N.C.: Duke University Press, 1997.

Salinger, Sharon V. *"To Serve Well and Faithfully": Labor and Indentured Servitude in Pennsylvania, 1682-1800.* New York: Cambridge University Press, 1987.

Salzman, Jack, ed. *Encyclopedia of African-American Culture and History.* 5 vols. New York: Macmillan Library Reference USA, 1996.

Sanbom, Melinda Lutz. "Angela and Elizabeth: An African Family in the Massachusetts Bay Colony." *New England Quarterly* 72 (1999).

Saxton, Alexander. "Blackface Minstrelsy and Jacksonian Ideology." *American Quarterly* 27 (1975): 3-27.

Schama, Simon. *The Embarrassment of Riches: An Interpretation of Dutch Culture in the Golden Age.* New York: HarperCollins, 1987.

Scheiner, Seth. *Negro Mecca: A History of the Negro in New York City, 1865-1920.* New York: New York University Press, 1965.

Schell, Robert C.-H. *Children of Bondage: A Social History of the Slave Society at the Cape of Good Hope, 1652-1838.* Middletown, Conn.: Wesleyan University Press, 1994.

Schmidt, Leigh Eric. *Holy Fairs: Scottish Communions and American Revivals in the Early Modern Period.* Princeton: Princeton University Press, 1989.

Schneider, David M. *The History of Public Welfare in New York State, 1609-1866.* Chicago: University of Chicago Press, 1938.

Schwarz, Philip J. *The Jarring Interest: New York's Boundary Makers, 1664-1776.* Albany: State University of New York Press, 1979.

———. *Twice Condemned: Slaves and Criminal Laws of Virginia, 1705-1865.* Baton Rouge: Lousiana State University Press, 1988.

Scott, Kenneth. "The Church Wardens and the Poor in New York City: 1693-1747." *New York Genealogical and Biographical Record* 99-101 (1968-70): 99:157-65; 100:18-26, 141-67; 101:33-40, 144-51.

———, comp. "Coroner's Reports for New York City, 1823-1842." *Collections of the New York Genealogical and Biographical Society* 12 (1989): 18-21, 88-91.

———. "Prisoners of the Provost Marshall, 1783." *New York Genealogical and Biographical Record* 104 (1973): 1-15.

———. "The Slave Insurrection in New York in 1712." *New-York Historical Society Quarterly* 45 (1961): 43-74.

Scottron, Samuel L. "New York African Society for Mutual Relief—Ninety-Seventh Anniversary." *Colored American Magazine* 14 (1905): 685-90.

Searing, James F. *West African Slavery and Atlantic Commerce: The Senegal Valley, 1700-1860.* New York: Cambridge University Press, 1993.

Seaton, Douglas P. "Colonies and Reluctant Colonists: The New Jersey Colonization Society and the Black Community." *New Jersey History* 96 (1978): 7-22.

Sensbach, Jon F. "Interracial Sects: Religion, Race, and Gender among Early North Carolina Moravians." In *The Devil's Lane: Sex and Race in the Early South*, edited by Catherine Clinton and Michele Gillespie. New York: Oxford University Press, 1997.

———. *A Separate Canaan: The Making of an Afro-Moravian World in North Carolina, 1763–1840*. Chapel Hill: University of North Carolina Press for the Institute of Early American History and Culture, 1998.

Sewall, Richard. *Ballots for Freedom: Antislavery Politics in the United States, 1837–1860*. New York: Oxford University Press, 1976.

Shaw, Douglas V. *The Making of an Immigrant City: Ethnic and Cultural Conflict in Jersey City, New Jersey, 1850–1877*. New York: Arno Press, 1977.

Sheehan, Arthur, and Elizabeth O'Dell. *Pierre Toussaint, a Citizen of Old New York*. New York: P. J. Kenedy, 1955.

Sheridan, Richard. *Sugar and Slavery: An Economic History of the British West Indies, 1623–1775*. Baltimore: Johns Hopkins University Press, 1973.

Sherman, Joan R. *Invisible Poets: Afro-Americans of the Nineteenth Century*. 2d ed. Urbana: University of Illinois Press, 1989.

Shyllon, Folarin. *Black People in Britain, 1555–1833*. Oxford: Oxford University Press, 1977.

Siebert, Wilbur H. *The Underground Railroad from Slavery to Freedom*. New York: Macmillan, 1899.

Silverman, Kenneth. *A Cultural History of the American Revolution*. New York. T. V. Crowell, 1976.

Slater, Courtenay, and George E. Hall, eds. *1994 County and City Extra: Annual Metro, City, and County Data Book*. 3d ed. Lanham, Md.: Bernan Press, 1994.

Smith, Billy G. *The "Lower Sort": Philadelphia's Laboring People, 1750–1800*. Ithaca, N.Y.: Cornell University Press, 1990.

Smith, Billy G., and Richard Wojtowicz, eds. *Blacks Who Stole Themselves: Advertisements for Runaways in the Pennsylvania Gazette, 1728–1790*. Philadelphia: University of Pennsylvania Press, 1989.

Smith, Edward D. *Climbing Jacob's Ladder: The Rise of Black Churches in Eastern American Cities, 1740–1877*. Washington, D.C.: Smithsonian Institution Press, 1988.

Smith, George L. *Religion and Trade in New Netherland: Dutch Origins and American Development*. Ithaca, N.Y.: Cornell University Press, 1973.

Smith, James Wesley. *Sojourners in Search of Freedom: The Settlement of Liberia by Black Americans*. Lanham, Md.: University Press of America, 1987.

Smith, Timothy L. "Slavery and Theology: The Emergence of Black Christian Consciousness in Nineteenth-Century America." *Church History* 41 (1972): 497–512.

Sobel, Mechal. *Trabelin' On: The Slave Journey to an Afro-Baptist Faith*. Westport, Conn.: Greenwood Press, 1979.

———. *The World They Made Together: Black and White Values in Eighteenth-Century Virginia*. Princeton: Princeton University Press, 1987.

Soderlund, Jean R. *Quakers and Slavery: A Divided Spirit.* Princeton: Princeton University Press, 1985.

Solberg, Winton U. *Redeem the Time: The Puritan Sabbath in Early America.* Cambridge, Mass.: Harvard University Press, 1977.

Sommers, Charles G. *Memoir of the Reverend John Stanford, D.D.* New York: Swords, Stanton, 1835.

Southern, Eileen. *The Music of Black Americans: A History.* New York: Norton, 1971.

Spierenburg, Pieter. "Knife-Fighting and Popular Codes of Honor in Early Modern Amsterdam." In *Men and Violence: Gender, Honor, and Rituals in Modern Europe and America,* edited by Pieter Spierenburg. Columbus: Ohio State University Press, 1998.

———. *The Spectacle of Suffering: Executions and the Evolution of Repression from a Preindustrial Metropolis to the European Experience.* New York: Cambridge University Press, 1984.

Sprunger, Keith. *Dutch Puritanism: A History of English and Scottish Churches of the Netherlands in the Sixteenth and Seventeenth Centuries.* Leiden: E. J. Brill, 1982.

Stansell, Christine. *City of Women: Sex and Class in New York, 1789–1860.* New York: Knopf, 1986.

Starobin, Robert, ed. *Blacks in Bondage: Letters of American Slaves.* New York: New Viewpoints, 1974.

Steele, Ian K. *The English Atlantic, 1675–1740: An Exploration of Communication and Community.* New York: Oxford University Press, 1986.

Steinfeld, Robert J. *The Invention of Free Labor: The Employment Relation in English and American Law and Culture, 1350–1870.* Chapel Hill: University of North Carolina Press, 1991.

Sterling, Dorothy. *Speak Out in Thunder Tones: Letters and Other Writings by Black Northerners, 1787–1865.* Garden City, N.Y.: Doubleday, 1973.

———. *We Are Your Sisters: Black Women in the Nineteenth Century.* New York: Norton, 1984.

Stevenson, Brenda E. *Life in Black and White: Family and Community in the Slave South.* New York: Oxford University Press, 1996.

Stewart, James Brewer. "The Emergence of Racial Modernity and the Rise of the White North, 1790–1840." *Journal of the Early Republic* 18 (1998): 181–217.

Still, Bayrd. *Mirror for Gotham: New York as Seen by Contemporaries from the Dutch Days to the Present.* New York: New York University Press, 1956.

———. "New York City in 1824: A Newly Discovered Description." *New-York Historical Society Quarterly* 46 (1962): 137–69.

Stoddard, William O. *The Volcano under the City, by a Volunteer Special.* New York: Fords, Howard and Hulbert, 1887.

Stoeffler, F. Ernest. *The Rise of Evangelical Pietism.* Leiden: E. J. Brill, 1965.

———, ed. *Continental Pietism and Early American Chritianity.* Grand Rapids, Mich.: Eerdmans, 1976.

Stone, William L. *History of New York City from Discovery to the Present Day.* New York: Virtue and Vorston, Anderson and Ramsay, 1872.

Stott, Richard B. *Workers in the Metropolis: Class, Ethnicity, and Youth in Antebellum New York City.* Ithaca, N.Y.: Cornell University Press, 1990.

Stowe, Walter H. "The Reverend Abraham Beach, D.D." *Historical Magazine of the Protestant Episcopal Church* 3 (1934): 81–86, 89–95.

Strassburger, John Robert. "The Origins and Establishment of the Morris Family in the Society and Politics of New York and New Jersey, 1630–1746." Ph.D. diss., Princeton University, 1976.

Stuckey, Sterling. *Going through the Storm: The Influence of African American Art in History.* New York: Oxford University Press, 1994.

———. *Slave Culture: Nationalist Theory and the Foundations of Black America.* New York: Oxford University Press, 1987.

Swan, Robert J. "Did Brooklyn Blacks Have Unusual Control over Their Schools? Period 1: 1815–1845." *Afro-Americans in New York Life and History* 7 (1983): 25–46.

———. "First Africans into New Netherland, 1625 or 1626," *de Halve Maen* 66 (1993): 75–82.

———. "The Other Fort Amsterdam: New Light on Aspects of Slavery in New Netherland." *Afro-Americans in New York Life and History* 22 (1998): 19–42.

Swift, David. *Black Prophets of Justice: Activist Clergy before the Civil War.* Baton Rouge: Louisiana State University Press, 1989.

Syrett, David. *Shipping and the American War, 1775–1783.* Hants, U.K.: Aldershot, 1970.

Tanis, James. *Dutch Calvinistic Pietism in the Middle Colonies: A Study in the Life and Theology of Theodorus Jacobus Frelinghuysen.* The Hague: Martinus Nijhoff, 1968.

Taylor, Clarence. *The Black Churches of Brooklyn.* New York: Columbia University Press, 1994.

Taylor, Mildred K. *The History of Teaneck.* Teaneck, N.J.: Teaneck American Revolution Bicentennial Committee, 1977.

Thayer, Theodore. *Colonial and Revolutionary Morris County.* Morristown, N.J.: Morris County Heritage Commission, 1975.

Thelen, David P., and Leslie H. Fishel. "Reconstruction in the North: The *World* Looks at New York's Negroes, March 16, 1867." *New York History* 44 (1968): 405–40.

Thomas, Lamont D. *Rise to Be a People: A Biography of Paul Cuffe.* Urbana: University of Illinois Press, 1986.

Thompson, Earl. "Slavery and Presbyterianism in the Revolutionary Era." *Journal of Presbyterian History* 54 (1976): 121–41.

Thompson, H. P. *Thomas Bray.* London: S.P.C.K., 1954.

Thompson, Robert Farris. *Flash of the Spirit: African and Afro-American Art and Philosophy.* New York: Random House, 1983.

Thompson, Robert Farris, and Joseph C. Cornet. *The Four Moments of the Sun: Kongo Art in Two Worlds.* Washington, D.C.: National Gallery of Art, 1981.

Thornton, John. *Africa and Africans in the Making of the Atlantic World, 1400–1680.* New York: Cambridge University Press, 1992.

———. "The African Background to American Colonization." In *The Cambridge Economic History of the United States,* Vol. 1: *The Colonial Era,* edited by Stanley Engerman and Robert E. Gallman. New York: Cambridge University Press, 1996.

———. "The African Experience of the '20 and Odd Negroes' Arriving in Virginia in 1619." *William and Mary Quarterly* 3d ser., 55 (1998): 421–34.

———. "Central African Names and African American Naming Patterns." *William and Mary Quarterly* 3d ser., 50 (1993): 727–42.

———. "The Development of an African Catholic Church in the Kingdom of the Kongo, 1491–1750." *Journal of African History* 25 (1984): 147–67.

———. *The Kingdom of Kongo, Civil War, and Transition, 1641–1718.* Madison: University of Wisconsin Press, 1983.

———. *The Kongolese Saint Anthony: Dona Beatriz Kimpa Vita and the Antonian Movement, 1684–1706.* New York: Cambridge University Press, 1998.

———. "On the Trail of Voodoo: African Christianity in Africa and the Americas." *Americas* 44 (1988): 261–79.

Thorpe, Daniel B. "Chattel with a Soul: The Autobiography of a Moravian Slave." *Pennsylvania Magazine of History and Biography* 112 (1988): 433–51.

Tiedemann, Joseph S. *Reluctant Revolutionaries: New York City and the Road to Independence, 1763–1776.* Ithaca, N.Y.: Cornell University Press, 1997.

Toll, Robert C. *Blacking Up: The Minstrel Show in Nineteenth-Century America.* New York: Oxford University Press, 1974.

Towner, Lawrence William. *A Good Master Well Served: Masters and Servants in Colonial Massachusetts, 1620–1750.* New York: Garland, 1998.

Trelease, Allen W. *Indian Affairs in New York: The Seventeenth Century.* Ithaca, N.Y.: Cornell University Press, 1960.

Trendell, Robert. "John Jay II: Antislavery Conscience of the Episcopal Church." *Historical Magazine of the Protestant Episcopal Church* 45 (1976): 237–52.

Tricentenary Studies, 1928, of the Reformed Church in America: A Record of Beginnings. New York: Reformed Church, 1928.

Valuska, David Lawrence. *The Afro-American in the Union Navy, 1861–1865.* New York: Garland, 1993.

Van Den Boogaart, Ernst. "The Servant Migration to New Netherland, 1624–1664." In *Colonization and Migration: Indentured Labour before and after Slavery,* edited by P. C. Emmer. Dordrecht: M. Nijhoff, 1986.

Van Horne, John C., ed. *Religious Philanthropy and Colonial Slavery: The American Correspondence of the Associates of Dr. Bray, 1717–1777.* Urbana: University of Illinois Press, 1986.

Van Winkle, Dan. *Old Bergen: History and Reminscenses.* Jersey City, N.J.: John W. Harrison, 1902.

Vaughan, Alden T. *Roots of American Racism: Essays on the Colonial Experience.* New York: Oxford University Press, 1995.

Vibert, Faith. "The S.P.G.: Its Work for the Negroes in North America before 1783." *Journal of Negro History* 18 (1933): 171–212.

Vlach, John. *The Afro-American Tradition in Decorative Arts*. Athens: University of Georgia Press, 1990.

Vogt, John. *Portuguese Rule on the Gold Coast, 1469–1682*. Athens: University of Georgia Press, 1979.

Wacker, Peter O. *Land and People: A Cultural Geography of Preindustrial New Jersey, Origins and Settlement Patterns*. New Brunswick, N.J.: Rutgers University Press, 1975.

———. "The New Jersey Tax-Ratable List of 1751." *New Jersey History* 107 (1989): 32–34.

———. "Patterns and Problems in the Historical Geography of the Afro-American Population of New Jersey, 1726-1860." In *Pattern and Process in Historical Geography*, edited by Ralph Ehrenberg. Washington, D.C.: Howard University Press, 1978.

Wacker, Peter O., and Paul G. E. Clemens. *Land Use in Early New Jersey: A Historical Geography*. Newark, N.J.: New-Jersey Historical Society, 1995.

Wade, Richard. *Slavery in the Cities: The South, 1820–1860*. New York: Oxford University Press, 1964.

Wageman, Morton. "Corporate Slavery in New Netherland." *Journal of Negro History* 65 (1980): 34–42.

Wakeley, Reverend J. B. *Lost Chapters Recovered from the Early History of American Methodism*. New York: For the Author, 1858.

Waldstreicher, David. *In the Midst of Perpetual Fetes: The Making of American Nationalism, 1776–1820*. Chapel Hill: University of North Carolina Press for the Institute of Early American History and Culture, 1997.

Walker, James W. St. G. *The Black Loyalists: The Search for a Promised Land in Nova Scotia and Sierra Leone, 1783–1870*. New York: Africana Publishing House, 1976.

Walker, Juliet E. K. *The History of Black Business in America: Capitalism, Race, Enterpreneurship*. New York: Macmillan Library Reference, 1998.

Walls, William J. *The African Methodist Episcopal Zion Church: Reality of the Black Church*. Charlotte, N.C.: A.M.E. Zion Publishing House, 1974.

Walvin, James. *Questioning Slavery*. New York: Routledge, 1996.

Ward, W. E. F. *The Royal Navy and the Slavers: The Suppression of the Atlantic Slave Trade*. New York: Schocken Books, 1969.

Warriner, Edwin. *Old Sands Street Methodist Episcopal Church, of Brooklyn, New York*. New York: Phillips and Hunt, 1885.

Washington, Margaret. *"A Peculiar People": Slave Religion and Community-Culture among the Gullahs*. New York: New York University Press, 1988.

Watson, Alan. *Slave Law in the Americas*. Athens: University of Georgia Press, 1989.

Wax, Darold D. "Preferences for Slaves in Colonial America." *Journal of Negro History* 58 (1973): 371–401.

Weiser, Francis X. *Handbook of Christian Feasts and Customs: The Year of the Lord in Liturgy and Folklore.* New York: Harcourt, Brace, 1958.

Wells, Robert V. *The Population of the British Colonies in America before 1776: A Study of Census Data.* Princeton: Princeton University Press, 1975.

Weslager, Clinton Alfred. *The English on the Delaware, 1610–1682.* New Brunswick, N.J.: Rutgers University Press, 1967.

Weston, Rob. "Alexander Hamilton and the Abolition of Slavery in New York," *Afro-Americans in New York Life and History* 18 (1994): 31–45.

White, E. Francis. *Sierra Leone's Settler Women Traders: Women on the Afro-European Frontier.* Ann Arbor: University of Michigan Press, 1987.

White, Shane. "It Was a Proud Day: African American Festivals and Parades in the North, 1741–1834," *Journal of American History* 81 (1994): 13–50.

———. "A Question of Style: Blacks in and around New York City in the Late 18th Century." *Journal of American Folklore* 102 (1989): 23–44.

———. *Somewhat More Independent: The End of Slavery in New York City, 1770–1810.* Athens: University of Georgia Press, 1991.

———. " 'We Dwell in Safety and Pursue Our Honest Callings': Free Blacks in New York City, 1783–1810." *Journal of American History* 75 (1988): 445–70.

White, Shane, and Graham White. *Stylin': African American Expressive Culture from Its Beginnings to the Zoot Suit.* Ithaca, N.Y.: Cornell University Press, 1998.

Wiecek, William. *The Sources of Anti-Slavery Constitutionalism in America, 1760–1848.* Ithaca, N.Y.: Cornell University Press, 1977.

Wilder, Craig. "The Rise and Influence of the New York African Society for Mutual Relief." *Afro-Americans in New York Life and History* 22 (1998): 7–18.

Wilentz, Sean. *Chants Democratic: New York City and the Rise of the American Working Class, 1788–1850.* New York: Oxford University Press, 1984.

Williams, Robert J. "Blacks, Colonization, and Antislavery: The Views of Methodists in New Jersey, 1816–1860." *New Jersey History* 102 (1984): 50–67.

Wilson, Ellen Gibson. *The Loyal Blacks.* New York: G. P. Putnam's Sons, 1976.

Wilson, William Julius. *When Work Disappears: The World of the New Urban Poor.* New York: Knopf, 1996.

Wood, Betty. *The Origins of American Slavery: Freedom and Bondage in the English Colonies.* New York: Hill and Wang, 1997.

———. *Women's Work, Men's Work: The Informal Slave Economies of Lowcountry Georgia.* Athens: University of Georgia Press, 1995.

Wood, Peter. *Black Majority: Negroes in Colonial South America from 1670 through the Stono Rebellion.* New York: Knopf, 1974.

———. " 'Liberty Is Sweet': African-American Freedom Struggles in the Years before White Independence." In *Beyond the American Revolution: Explorations in the History of American Radicalism,* edited by Alfred F. Young. DeKalb: Northern Illinois University Press, 1993.

Woodson, Carter G. *Free Negro Owners of Slaves in the United States in 1830.* Washington, D.C.: Association for the Study of Negro Life and History, 1924.

————. *The History of the Negro Church.* Washington, D.C.: Associated Publishers, 1921.

————. *Mind of the Negro as Reflected in Letters Written during the Crisis, 1800–1860.* Washington, D.C.: Association for the Study of Negro Life and History, 1926.

————. *Negro Orators and Their Orations.* Washington, D.C.: Associated Publishers, 1925.

Woody, Thomas. *Quaker Education in the Colony and State of New Jersey.* Philadelphia: Published for the Author by the University of Pennsylvania Press, 1923.

Worden, Nigel. *Slavery in Dutch South Africa.* New York: Cambridge University Press, 1985.

Wright, Giles R. *Afro-Americans in New Jersey: A Short History.* Trenton, N.J.: New Jersey Historical Commission, 1988.

Wright, Landon G. "Local Government in Colonial New York." Ph.D. diss., Cornell University, 1974.

Wright, Marion Thompson. "New Jersey Laws and the Negro." *Journal of Negro History* 28 (1943): 156–99.

Wright, William C. *The Secession Movement in the Middle Atlantic States.* Cranbury, N.J.: Associated University Press, 1973.

Yoshpe, Harry. *The Disposition of Loyalist Estates in the Southern District of the State of New York.* New York: Columbia University Press, 1939.

————. "Records of Slave Manumissions in New York during the Colonial and Early National Period." *Journal of Negro History* 26 (1941): 78–107.

Young, Alfred F. "English Plebeian Society and Eighteenth-Century American Radicalism." In *The Origins of Anglo-American Radicalism,* edited by Margaret Jacob and James Jacob. London: George Allen & Unwin, 1984.

Zahan, Dominique. *The Religion, Spirituality, and Thought of Traditional Africa.* Chicago: University of Chicago Press, 1979.

Zelinsky, Wilbur. "The Population Geography of the Free Negro in Antebellum America." *Population Studies* 3 (1950): 386–401.

Zilversmit, Arthur. *The First Emancipation: The Abolition of Slavery in the North.* Chicago: University of Chicago Press, 1967.

Zuille, John T. *Historical Sketch of the New York African Society for Mutual Relief.* New York: N.p., 1892.

Index

blacks, 140; American attitudes toward black participation in, 141–44, 150; military operations of, 144–45; "Negro forts," 152–53; and confiscation of Loyalist property, 154; and peace negotiations, 155–58; British boards of inquiry, 156–57; black veterans of, 208. *See also* Black Loyalists

Andrews, Charles C., 207, 215, 242

Andros, Edmund, 37

Anglo-African (magazine), 261

Angola, Ascento, 13

Angola, Domingo, 17, 48

Angola, Dorothy, 17

Angola, Manuel, 48

Angola, 10, 26, 38, 109

Anthony, Domingo, 13

Anthony, Marrije, 35

Antigua, 29

Anton, 35

Antonian movement, 38

Antony, Jochem, 35

Arch, 132

Arfwedson, C. F., 203, 218

Arientsen, John, 72

Arminianism, 20

Articles of Capitulation, 34

Asbury, Francis, 126, 214

Asbury African Church, 190

Assento, 14

Association for the Improvement of the Conditions of the Poor, 266

Auchmuty, Samuel, 119

Aurelia, 83

Auyboyneau, John, 97

Baker, John, 171–72

Baldwin, Nathan, 145

Bancker, Christopher, 94

Bangs, Isaac, 113

Baptism, 16–17, 19–22, 33, 54, 93, 119–20; black perceptions of, 17, 20, 123, 181–82; theological disputes over, 21–23, 54, 122–23; laws regarding, 58–59, 181–82; and slave conspiracy, 93–95

Baquaqua, Mahommah Gardo, 247

Barbados, 28, 36, 38, 49; migrants from, 44

Barber, Jannetje, 50

Barker, George, 245

Bartow, John, 76

Bastienz, Francisco, 35

Bates, Barnabas, 254

Battel, Andrew, 15

Baxter, John, 221

Bayard, Nicholas, 94

Bayles, Augustine, 167

Beach, Abraham, 147

Beck, Mathias, 29

Beeckman, Gerrard, 157

Beekman, William, 78

Bell, Philip, 248

Bellomont, Lord Governor (Richard Coote), 50

Ben, 118

Benezet, Anthony, 125, 188, 252

Benson, Robert, 132

Bergen, Anne, 114

Bergen, Jacob, 114

Bergen County, N.J., 1–2, 23, 31, 34, 44, 52, 70, 74, 77, 79, 107, 109, 112, 118, 133, 172, 175; black population of, 106, 228–29; American Revolution in, 144–45, 151–53; after American Revolution, 164–65, 179–80, 220, 270; size of farms in, 165, 220, 237; opposition to abolition in, 192; drop in black population of, 229, 238; cemeteries in, 258

Berger, Caspar, 141

Berry, Thomas, 44

Betty, 157

Beyerlandt, Gysbert Cornelissen, 12

Bias, David, 183

Bickley, May, 66

Big Manuel, 9, 13–14, 16

Bill, 131

Billy, 219

Birch, Samuel, 157, 159

Bishop, Josiah, 184

Black abolitionists, 188–90, 246–48. *See also* Slave resistance: legal

Black Hans, 35

Black Loyalists, 144–54 passim; Aetheopian Regiment, 144; Black Pioneers, 147–48, 150–51, 153, 155, 158; responsibilities, 147–50; Black Shot, 148; Followers of the Flag, 148; Black Corps, 148–49; black sailors, 149; pay, 149, 155; Royal African Regiment, 151; Black Brigade, 151, 157–58, 162; Armed Boat Company, 153; numbers of, 156. *See also* American Revolution

Blair, Joan, 173

Blauveldt, Johannes, 119

Bleucke, Margaret, 147

Bleucke, Stephen, 147, 159

Bloomfield, Moses, 167

Blyden, Edward Wilmot, 260–61

Boarding, 193–94

Bobin, Isaac, 78

Bobolink Bob, 212–13

Boe, Benjamin, 194

Bogardus, Everardus, 22

Bood, 133

Bowery Road, 13–14, 270

Brassier, Henry, 66, 110

Braveboy, 96, 98

Bray, Thomas, 120

Bridewell (prison), 179

Briel, Fonteyn, 13

Bristol, 133

Brock, 174

Brockholles, Anthony, 37

Brooklyn, N.Y., 23, 230, 241, 263. *See also* Kings County, N.Y.

Brotherhoods, African, 17–18. *See also* Nations, African

Brower, Cornelius, 94

Brown, Leonard, 71

Brown, Robert, 245

Brown, William Henry, 197–98

Brown, William Wells, 253, 264

Bryant, William Cullen, 269

Buckingham, James, 224

Burgess, Samuel, 39

Burke, Samuel, 149–50

Burnet, William, 78

Burr, Esther Edwards, 111

Burton, Mary, 93

Butler, William, 208

Caesar, 98, 118, 132–33, 156

Cajoe, 95

Campbell, Aldred Gibbs, 255. See also *Alarm Bell*

Canada, 242, 247–48, 256

Capetein, Jacobus Eliza, 122

Cappoens, Christiana, 36

Carleton, Guy, 155–56

Carrey, Mary, 133

Cartagena, Francisco, 14

Cartmen, 43, 110, 200, 206, 224, 232–33. *See also* Occupations, African American—colonial: cartmen; Occupations, African American—postrevolutionary: cartmen

Cathy, 219

Cato, 117, 173, 232; tavern owned by, 232

Celes, Jan, 13

Charity, 128

Charles, 117

Charles II (king of England), 55

Charleton, Richard, 85

Chatham Street Chapel, 227

Christiansen, Hendrick, 6

Church of England (Anglicans), 53–63, 84–86, 99, 111, 119–22; schools for blacks, 54–63, 120, 147; black attitudes toward, 121–23, 146; effect on manumission, 165–66

Civil rights, 191–92, 232–33, 253, 270; and suffrage, 191–92, 200, 253, 256–57

Civil War, 263–70; black volunteers in, 266, 269; and blacks in navy, 268

Clarke, Aaron, 233

Clarke, George, 78, 83, 91, 94–96, 100

CPSIA information can be obtained
at www.ICGtesting.com
Printed in the USA
LVHW03s1029180618
580698LV00001B/7/P